Microsoft Project 2010

THE MISSING MANUAL

*The book that
should have been
in the box*®

Microsoft Project 2010

Bonnie Biafore

POGUE PRESS™
O'REILLY®

Beijing • Cambridge • Farnham • Köln • Sebastopol • Tokyo

Microsoft Project 2010: The Missing Manual

by Bonnie Biafore

Published by O'Reilly Media, Inc., 1005 Gravenstein Highway North, Sebastopol, CA 95472.

O'Reilly Media books may be purchased for educational, business, or sales promotional use. Online editions are also available for most titles: *safari.oreilly.com*. For more information, contact our corporate/institutional sales department: 800-998-9938 or *corporate@oreilly.com*.

Printing History:

June 2010:   First Edition.

ISBN: 978-1-449-38195-0

[LSI]   [2011-01-28]

Table of Contents

Part Two:
Project Planning: More Than Creating a Schedule

TABLE OF CONTENTS

Part Three: Projects in Action

Part Four: Project Power Tools

Chapter 24: Defining Your Own Fields 639

Chapter 25: Customizing the Ribbon and Quick Access Toolbar 657

Chapter 26: Reusable Project: Templates 667

Part Six: Appendixes

The Missing Credits

About the Author

 Bonnie Biafore has always been a zealous organizer of everything from software demos to gourmet meals, with the occasional vacation trip to test the waters of spontaneity. Ironically, fate, not planning, turned this obsession into a career as a project manager. When Bonnie realized she was managing projects, her penchant for planning and follow-through kicked in and she earned a Project Management Professional certification from the Project Management Institute.

When she isn't managing projects for clients, Bonnie writes about project management, personal finance and investing, and technology. As an engineer, she's fascinated by how things work and how to make things work better. She has a knack for mincing these dry subjects into easy-to-understand morsels and then spices them to perfection with her warped sense of humor.

Bonnie is also the author of *On Time! On Track! On Target!*, *QuickBooks 2010: The Missing Manual*, and several other award-winning books. Project Certification Insider, her monthly column for the Microsoft Project Users Group, explains the ins and outs of topics on Microsoft's Project desktop certification exam. When unshackled from her computer, she hikes in the mountains with her dogs, cycles, cooks ethnic food, and writes fiction. You can learn more at her Web site, *http://www.bonniebiafore.com* or email Bonnie at *bonnie.biafore@gmail.com*.

About the Creative Team

Brian Sawyer (editor) is an editor for O'Reilly Media's Head First division. He's also served as lead editor for the company's popular Hacks series, editor for Missing Manuals and Make: Books, and contributing editor to *Craft* magazine. When not writing or editing about technology, he uses it to help train for marathons (see Chapter 4 of *Best Android Apps*).

Kristen Borg (production editor) is a recent graduate of the publishing program at Emerson College. Now living in Boston, she originally hails from sunny Arizona, and considers New England winters an adequate trade for no longer finding scorpions in her hairdryer.

Sean Earp (technical reviewer), CISSP, MCITP is Program Manager at a large software company in Redmond, specializing in Project, Project Server, and SharePoint technologies. Trained in the school of hard knocks, Sean has experienced nearly every project management pitfall outlined in Project 2010: The Missing Manual. When not in front of his computer, Sean likes spending time with his wife and three wonderful kids, being a Cub Scout leader, and is training for a marathon.

Michael Wharton (technical reviewer), MBA, PMP, MCT, MCSD, MCSE+I, MCDBA, MCITP, MCTS is the President of Wharton Computer Consulting, Inc. He has been a software developer and project manager for the past 10 years. He is active in the PMI and MPUG community and many technical user groups such as PASS and the .NET User Group. He is happily married to his wife Gwen and loves spending time with his family when not working on his computer.

Acknowledgments

The credit for the publication of this book goes to an awesome project team. My thanks go to Brian Sawyer, Nellie McKesson, and the rest of the O'Reilly folks for shepherding my book through the publication process. I am grateful for the eagle eye of Julie Van Keuren, the copyeditor, for wrangling punctuation, capitalization, and ungainly sentences into submission. The technical reviewers, Michael Wharton and Sean Earp, caught my mistakes and shared their knowledge of the finer points of Microsoft Project and SharePoint.

I am fortunate to have more good friends than my prickly personality deserves. Special thanks go to all of them—who still speak to me after an extraordinarily trying winter of book writing.

The Missing Manual Series

Missing Manuals are witty, superbly written guides to computer products that don't come with printed manuals (which is just about all of them). Each book features a handcrafted index and cross-references to specific pages (not just chapters).

Recent and upcoming titles include:

Access 2007: The Missing Manual by Matthew MacDonald

Access 2010: The Missing Manual by Matthew MacDonald

Buying a Home: The Missing Manual by Nancy Conner

CSS: The Missing Manual, Second Edition, by David Sawyer McFarland

Creating a Web Site: The Missing Manual, Second Edition, by Matthew MacDonald

David Pogue's Digital Photography: The Missing Manual by David Pogue

Dreamweaver CS4: The Missing Manual by David Sawyer McFarland

Dreamweaver CS5: The Missing Manual by David Sawyer McFarland

Excel 2007: The Missing Manual by Matthew MacDonald

Excel 2010: The Missing Manual by Matthew MacDonald

Facebook: The Missing Manual, Second Edition by E.A. Vander Veer

FileMaker Pro 10: The Missing Manual by Susan Prosser and Geoff Coffey

Flash CS4: The Missing Manual by Chris Grover with E.A. Vander Veer

Flash CS5: The Missing Manual by Chris Grover

Google Apps: The Missing Manual by Nancy Conner

The Internet: The Missing Manual by David Pogue and J.D. Biersdorfer

iMovie '08 & iDVD: The Missing Manual by David Pogue

iMovie '09 & iDVD: The Missing Manual by David Pogue and Aaron Miller

iPad: The Missing Manual by J.D. Biersdorfer and David Pogue

iPhone: The Missing Manual, Second Edition by David Pogue

iPhone App Development: The Missing Manual by Craig Hockenberry

iPhoto '08: The Missing Manual by David Pogue

iPhoto '09: The Missing Manual by David Pogue and J.D. Biersdorfer

iPod: The Missing Manual, Eigth Edition by J.D. Biersdorfer and David Pogue

JavaScript: The Missing Manual by David Sawyer McFarland

Living Green: The Missing Manual by Nancy Conner

Mac OS X: The Missing Manual, Leopard Edition by David Pogue

Mac OS X Snow Leopard: The Missing Manual by David Pogue

Microsoft Project 2007: The Missing Manual by Bonnie Biafore

Microsoft Project 2010: The Missing Manual by Bonnie Biafore

Netbooks: The Missing Manual by J.D. Biersdorfer

Office 2007: The Missing Manual by Chris Grover, Matthew MacDonald, and E.A. Vander Veer

Office 2010: The Missing Manual by Nancy Connor, Chris Grover, and Matthew MacDonald

Office 2008 for Macintosh: The Missing Manual by Jim Elferdink

Palm Pre: The Missing Manual by Ed Baig

PCs: The Missing Manual by Andy Rathbone

Personal Investing: The Missing Manual by Bonnie Biafore

Photoshop CS4: The Missing Manual by Lesa Snider

Photoshop CS5: The Missing Manual by Lesa Snider

Photoshop Elements 7: The Missing Manual by Barbara Brundage

Photoshop Elements 8 for Mac: The Missing Manual by Barbara Brundage

Photoshop Elements 8 for Windows: The Missing Manual by Barbara Brundage

PowerPoint 2007: The Missing Manual by E.A. Vander Veer

Premiere Elements 8: The Missing Manual by Chris Grover

QuickBase: The Missing Manual by Nancy Conner

QuickBooks 2010: The Missing Manual by Bonnie Biafore

QuickBooks 2011: The Missing Manual by Bonnie Biafore

Quicken 2009: The Missing Manual by Bonnie Biafore

Switching to the Mac: The Missing Manual, Leopard Edition by David Pogue

Switching to the Mac: The Missing Manual, Snow Leopard Edition by David Pogue

Wikipedia: The Missing Manual by John Broughton

Windows XP Home Edition: The Missing Manual, Second Edition by David Pogue

Windows XP Pro: The Missing Manual, Second Edition by David Pogue, Craig Zacker, and Linda Zacker

Windows Vista: The Missing Manual by David Pogue

Windows 7: The Missing Manual by David Pogue

Word 2007: The Missing Manual by Chris Grover

Your Body: The Missing Manual by Matthew MacDonald

Your Brain: The Missing Manual by Matthew MacDonald

Your Money: The Missing Manual by J.D. Roth

Introduction

People have been managing projects for centuries. The construction of the mountaintop city of Machu Picchu was a project—although no one's really sure whether the ancient Inca had a word for "project manager." In fact, you may not have realized you were a project manager when you were assigned your first project to manage. Sure, you're organized and you can make sure people get things done, but successfully managing a project requires specific skills and know-how. Whether you're building a shining city on a hill or aiming for something more mundane, Microsoft Project helps you document project tasks, build a schedule, assign resources, track progress, and make changes until your project is complete.

Perhaps you're staring at the screen, wondering about the meaning of the Gantt Chart and Resource Usage in the list of Project views. Or maybe you already have dozens of Project schedules under your belt. Either way, some Project features can be mystifying. You know what you want to do, but you can't find the magic combination that makes Project do it.

This book addresses the double whammy of learning your way around project management and Microsoft Project at the same time. It provides an introduction to managing projects and shows you how to use Project to do so. For more experienced project managers, this book can help you take your Project prowess to a new level with tips, timesaving tricks, and mastery of features that never quite behaved the way you wanted.

What's New in Project 2010

Since its introduction, Project Server often gets most of Microsoft's attention and cool new features. This time around, Project 2010 Standard and Professional have a bunch of new and improved features that could quickly grow on you. The big change, of course, is that Project now uses the Microsoft fluent interface (a.k.a. the *ribbon*). It takes some getting used to, but many commands that took a cartload of clicks in the past, like turning summary tasks on and off, are now at your mousing fingertip. But wait, there's more. For example, manually scheduled tasks let you control when tasks occur, but you can use them to plan from the top down or fill in only the information you have available, as you'll learn shortly. Here's an overview of the new Project 2010 features and where to find them in this book:

- **The ribbon user interface.** If you knew the old menu bar inside and out, you might approach the ribbon with some trepidation. It isn't as intuitive as Microsoft would like you to believe, and some exploring is in order before it starts to make sense. But once it does, you'll find that many commands you use frequently—turning the project summary task and summary tasks on and off; inserting summary tasks, subtasks, and milestones; showing critical tasks, late tasks, and baselines in a Gantt Chart; formatting task bars; filtering, grouping, and sorting; and much more—are within easy reach on the ribbon. With project management's focus on tasks and resources, Project's ribbon tabs are even easier to learn than their Office counterparts. Instructions for using the ribbon, tabs, and commands start on page 8 and also are scattered throughout this book wherever their corresponding features are discussed. To learn how to customize the ribbon, see page 657.

- **Working with summary and subtasks.** The Insert Summary command (page 149) creates a new summary command with one subtask below it, ready for you to type its task name. You can also select several subtasks and use the Insert Summary command to make them all subtasks of the new summary task.

- **Easier formatting.** When you right-click a selection—such as a single cell, a row, or several cells—a mini-toolbar (page 619) appears with formatting commands for the font, font color, background color, bold, italic, and more. The mini-toolbar also has other frequently used commands related to what you right-click. For example, if you right-click a task, the toolbar includes buttons for setting the percent complete on the task. The Gantt Chart style gallery on the Format tab lets you choose colors for your task bars.

Note: You can now copy and paste between Project and other programs without losing formatting (page 509). For example, if you paste an indented task list from Word or an email message into Project, the program can keep the formatting from the original document and automatically use the indenting to create tasks at the appropriate outline level.

- **Timesaving features.** Dragging the Zoom slider on the status bar to the left or right adjusts the timescale in a view. The status bar also has icons for displaying the most common views, like the Gantt Chart, Task Usage, Team Planner, and Resource Sheet. Project makes it easier to find your place in a table by highlighting the row ID and column heading for the selected cell, like Excel has always done.

- **Wrapping long names.** The Task Name column automatically wraps text to show the full task name in the current width of the column. You can edit any column's settings to wrap its contents (page 612).

- **Fast and easy column changes.** To insert a column, right-click the table heading and choose Insert Column (page 611). Then, in the drop-down list that appears, choose the field you want to add. Alternatively, you can add a column by clicking the Add New Column heading on the far right of a table. If you begin to type values in Add New Column cells, Project interprets what you've typed to choose the correct type of custom field (page 612). Edit a column by right-clicking its column heading and then choosing Field Settings. Or edit a custom field from within the table by right-clicking the custom field column heading and then, on the shortcut menu, choosing Custom Fields.

- **Faster filtering, grouping, and sorting.** AutoFilter is automatically turned on, so you can filter a table by clicking the down arrow in any column. A drop-down menu appears with choices for sorting, grouping, or filtering by values in the column (page 629).

- **Saving views and tables.** When a view is just the way you want it, you can save the view and its components by clicking a view button on the View tab and then choosing Save View (page 579). A new option tells Project to either automatically copy your customizations to the global template or to keep them in your local file unless you specifically copy them using the Organizer (page 668).

- **User-controlled scheduling.** In Project 2010, the Manually Scheduled mode puts you in total control over when a task is scheduled. You can still set date constraints as you could in earlier versions, but date constraints apply to either the start date or the finish date, not both. With a manually scheduled task, you can pin the start or finish date, or both, to the calendar dates you want (page 116), which is perfect for plunking a training class onto the specific days it occurs. The scheduling that you know and love from earlier versions of Project is now called Auto Scheduled mode.

- **Filling in placeholder information.** Early in planning, you might be missing some task information. For example, you might know that a task must start on June 6, but you don't know how long it will take. Perhaps the only thing you know is that Becky in engineering is the one who will give you the duration and dependencies for a task. Now you can create a manually scheduled task and fill in what you know (page 119). Leave cells like Start, Finish, and Duration blank, or type in placeholder text like *See Becky in Engr.* When you get the full story about a task, you can fill in the information and change it to an auto-scheduled task if you want.

- **Top-down planning.** With Manually Scheduled mode, you can create summary tasks and specify the duration you've been given by management—for example, 12 weeks for design, 18 weeks for development, and 6 weeks for testing. As you create subtasks under summary tasks, Project can keep track of the duration you specified for the summary task and tell you whether the total duration of the subtasks fits within the summary task duration or runs past the allotted time (page 120).

- **Viewing the project timeline.** The Timeline view is aptly named. It starts out showing the date range for your project as a simple horizontal bar—the timeline. You can use the timeline to pan and zoom around the dates in a view timescale—for example, in a Gantt Chart. Drag the current date range (page 600) to move forward or backward in time or drag an end of the timeline bar to change the start or end date you see. You can also add tasks to the timeline to see or communicate a high-level view of your project. Display tasks in the timeline as bars to keep your attention on key tasks. Adding tasks to the timeline as callouts is perfect for showing summary tasks like phases. You can paste the timeline into an email message or a presentation to share with others.

- **Work with resource assignments with Team Planner.** Project 2010 Professional includes the Team Planner view (page 213), which uses swimlanes to show tasks assigned to resources. It's easy to spot unassigned or unscheduled tasks. The unassigned swimlane stockpiles all the tasks you haven't assigned yet, whether they're scheduled or not. Unscheduled tasks sit in the Unscheduled Tasks column of the view, ready for you to drag onto the timescale. Assigning, scheduling, and reassigning tasks is as easy as dragging task assignments to the dates and/or resources you want. Team Planner helps you spot unassigned tasks or overallocated resources. You can drag a task to a resource who doesn't have anything to do or move a task in the timeline to even out workloads. The view even has a setting to automatically prevent overallocations.

- **Leveling overallocations.** The ribbon's Resource tab puts leveling commands within easy reach. In addition, you can choose to level selected tasks or resources, a specific resource, or an entire project.

- **Synching Project tasks with a SharePoint task list.** With Project 2010 Professional, you can share simple projects with team members through SharePoint 2010 (page 534) without using Project Server. Whether you create a task list in SharePoint or in Project, you can synchronize the two. Team members can update task status in SharePoint, which you then see in Project. Or you can make changes in Project that automatically pass back to SharePoint for your team.

- **View scheduling issues and fix them.** Project indicates potential scheduling problems by underlining task values with red squiggles, similar to the ones you see for misspellings in Word. Right-clicking a cell with a red squiggle displays a shortcut menu of commands to help you fix the issue, such as rescheduling the task or simply ignoring it. In addition, you can open the *task inspector* (page 251), a beefier version of task drivers from Project 2007. The Task Inspector pane shows the factors that influence a task schedule, such as a predecessor, calendar, date constraint, resource assignments, overallocations, or all of the above. The Project 2010 Task Inspector pane also offers commands for fixing issues. Then it's up to you to decide which one to change and how.

- **Playing what-if games.** In Project 2007, multilevel Undo provided an easy way to try small experiments or to recover from a mistake you didn't see until six changes later. New in Project 2010, inactivating tasks takes what-if games to a higher level and longer time period for decisions. Add tasks to your Project schedule to document alternatives for a portion of your project and evaluate each one's results. Or create tasks for proposed change requests. Then you can inactivate those tasks. You can still see them and edit their values, but they don't affect your project schedule or the availability of the resources assigned to them. Once you've chosen the alternative you want—or the change review board approves the change request—you can reactivate the tasks, retaining all the information you entered.

Note: Although this book is about the desktop versions of Project 2010, Project Server 2010 now combines both enterprise project management and portfolio management in the same product. In the past, you needed Project Server 2007 and Project Portfolio Server 2007 to accomplish the same capabilities. The enterprise side has lots of new and improved features in areas like time status and reporting, customizable workflows, and resource capacity planning.

Where Microsoft Project Fits In

Any project manager who's calculated task start and finish dates by hand knows how helpful Project is. Simply calculating dates, costs, and total assigned work eliminates a mountain of grunt work and carpal tunnel syndrome, so you'll have time and stamina left over to actually manage your projects.

In the planning stage, Project helps you develop a project schedule. You add the tasks and people to a Project file, link the tasks together in sequence, assign workers and other resources to those tasks, and poof!—you have a schedule. Project calculates when tasks start and finish, how much they cost, and how many hours each person works each day. Project helps you develop *better* project plans, because you can revise the schedule quickly to try other strategies until the plan really works. Views and reports help you spot problems, like too many tasks assigned to the same overworked person.

Once a project is under way, you can add actual hours and costs to the Project file. With actual values, you can use Project to track progress to see how dates, cost, and work compare to the project plan. If problems arise, like tasks running late or over budget, you can use Project tools, views, and reports to look for solutions, once again quickly making changes until you find a way to get the project back on track.

At the same time, plenty of project management work goes on outside Project. Touchy-feely tasks like identifying project objectives, negotiating with vendors, or building stakeholder buy-in are pure people skill (although Project's reports can certainly help you communicate with these folks). Projects produce a lot of documents besides the project schedule. For example, a project plan may include financial analysis spreadsheets, requirements and specifications documents, change requests

---

databases, and diagrams to show how the change management process works. In addition, thousands of email messages, memos, and other correspondence could change hands before a project finishes.

Communication, change management, and risk management are essential to successful project management, but they don't occur in Project Standard or Professional. For example, you may have a risk management plan that identifies the risks your project faces, and what you plan to do if they occur. You may also develop a spreadsheet to track those risks and your response if they become reality. In Project, you may link the risk tracking spreadsheet or risk response document to the corresponding tasks, but that's about it.

Note: The enterprise features in Project Server combined with SharePoint help you track risks, issues, changes, and more.

Choosing the Right Edition

In one respect, choosing between Project Standard and Project Professional is easy. Both editions of Project have about the same capabilities if you manage projects independently and aren't trying to work closely with other project managers, teams, and projects.

Project Standard works for most one-person shows, even if you manage several projects at the same time. You can communicate with your team via email and share documents on a network drive, or using a SharePoint website (page 541). However, Project Professional adds the Team Planner and the ability to inactivate tasks and synchronize Project tasks to a task list in SharePoint 2010.

However, if you manage project teams with hundreds of resources, share a pool of resources with other project managers, or manage your project as one of many in your organization's project portfolio, then you'll need Project Professional, along with Project Server and Project Web App. The difference between Project Standard and Project Professional is that you can turn on the enterprise features in Project Professional and connect it to Project Server and Project Web App to collaborate, communicate, and share across hundreds of projects and people.

Setting up an enterprise-wide project management system takes some planning and effort, depending on the size and complexity of your organization. Whether your company is small, medium, or large, you must weigh the benefits of managing projects company-wide against the effort and expense of defining project management policies, setting up the system, and bringing everyone up to speed. Here are some of the advantages that Project Professional and the enterprise project management software offer:

- **Track all projects in one place.** You build Project schedules with Project Professional. When a project is ready for prime time, you publish it to Project Server to add it to the overall project portfolio. Then the status for all projects appears in a single view.

- **Share resources enterprise-wide.** Instead of playing phone tag with other project managers about when resources are available, Project Server keeps track of all resources and when they work on which project. You can look for the right kind of resources using multilevel resource skill characteristics, and then see who's available for your projects.

- **Communicate with resources.** Project Web App makes it easy for you to communicate with your team, requesting status, sending messages, and so on. It also makes it easy for your team to communicate with you, replying with status, accepting assignments, or providing time worked.

- **Timesheets.** Team members can fill out timesheets for project work. The time they submit shoots straight into the Project Server database to update progress on your projects.

- **Track issues, risks, and documents.** Projects are more than schedules. Issues crop up that must be resolved; risks lurk that you must watch and manage; and there's no end to the additional documents produced, like specifications, plans, work packages, and so on. Using SharePoint websites and Project Web App, team members can collaborate on all these elements online.

Note: Project Standard and Project Professional are both available for purchase in retail stores like OfficeMax or Amazon.com. However, you must purchase Project Server (which includes Project Web App) through Microsoft or Microsoft partners and solution providers.

Complementary Software

Managing a project requires other programs in addition to Project. Word and Excel are eager participants for the documents and financial analysis you produce. PowerPoint is ideal for project presentations and status meetings. And Outlook keeps project communication flowing. This book includes instructions for using these programs in some of your project management duties.

Office 2010 Home and Business includes Word, Excel, PowerPoint, OneNote, and Outlook. The list price is $279, although lower prices are readily available. You can purchase Office at stores like Staples or websites like *www.bestbuy.com*. Office 2010 Professional adds Office Web Apps, Publisher, and Access to the Office Standard suite for a total list price of $499. Here are some of the ways you might use these products in project management:

- **Word.** Producing documents like the overall project plan, work package descriptions, requirements, specifications, status reports, and so on.

- **Excel.** Creating spreadsheets for financial analysis or tracking change requests, risks, issues, and defects reported.

- **PowerPoint.** Putting together presentations for project proposals, project kick-off, status, change control board meetings, and so on.

- **Outlook.** Emailing everyone who's anyone on the project team and setting up a shared address book for everyone to use.

- **Publisher.** Publishing newsletters, fliers, invitations to meetings, and so on.

- **Access.** A more robust alternative to Excel for tracking change requests, requirements, risks, and issues.

Visio 2010 Professional is another program that comes in handy, whether you want to document project processes in flowcharts or generate Visio-based visual reports. Visio Professional's list price (which is required for PivotDiagrams and Data Graphics) is $559.95.

Getting Around Project

Project 2010 has caught up with its Office counterparts by now using the ribbon instead of the menu bar. If you haven't met the ribbon yet, this section provides a brief introduction. The Project window is chockablock with panes and other parts that either show the information you want or help you work faster. Some features, like the ribbon and the main Project view, are always available, while others, like the Task Inspector pane, can hide until you need them. This section shows you the basics of the Project interface. Chapter 3 takes you on a full tour of the Project ribbon and all the components within the Project window.

Using the Ribbon

To provide easy access to an ever-increasing number of commands, Microsoft came up with the *ribbon*. Programs like Word and Excel had the ribbon in Office 2007. Now Project 2010 joins their ranks. The ribbon takes up more space than the old-style menu bar (see page 9 to learn how to hide it), but it can hold oodles of commands. Many procedures that required dozens of clicks in earlier versions of Project (like displaying the project summary task) are now a click or two away on a ribbon tab.

The ribbon groups features onto logically (most of the time) organized tabs. Finding your way around the Project ribbon is easy. For instance, to create tasks, rearrange their outline levels, update their progress, or view their details, go to the Task tab. The Resource tab has commands for creating, assigning, and leveling resources. The Project tab is home base for viewing project information, defining work calendars, setting project baselines, and so on. Project opens initially with six tabs: File, Task, Resource, Project, View, and Format. When you select one of these tabs, the corresponding collection of buttons appears, as shown in Figure I-1.

Tip: Chapter 25 explains how you can customize the ribbon to add tabs, sections (called custom groups), and commands.

Quick Access toolbar   Ribbon tabs   Commands on tab

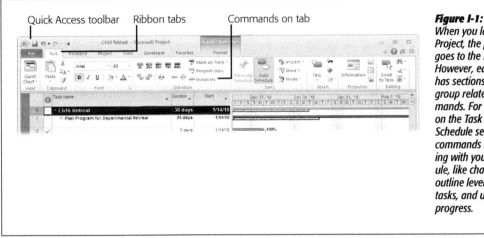

Figure I-1:
When you launch Project, the program goes to the File tab. However, each tab has sections that group related commands. For example, on the Task tab, the Schedule section has commands for working with your schedule, like changing outline levels, linking tasks, and updating progress.

ScreenTips provide a lot more guidance in Project 2010. For example, when you hover over a button on the ribbon, a ScreenTip appears with a description of the command and a keyboard shortcut for triggering the command. If your mouse has a scroll wheel, you can move through the tabs faster than grain through a goose by positioning the pointer over the ribbon and rolling the wheel.

Tip: If the ribbon takes up too much screen for your taste, you can collapse it to a trimmer shape much like the old menu bar by double-clicking any tab. To use features on a tab, click the tab name, and the tab appears. When you choose a command, the tab disappears.

The ribbon contorts itself to fit as you resize the Project window (see Figure I-2). If you narrow your window, the ribbon makes some buttons smaller by shrinking icons or leaving out the icon text. If you narrow the window dramatically, an entire section may be replaced by a single button. However, when you click the button, a drop-down panel displays all the hidden commands.

Tip: If you prefer to keep your fingers on the keyboard, you can trigger ribbon commands without the mouse. To unlock these nifty shortcuts, press the Alt key. Letters appear below each tab on the ribbon. Press a key to pick a tab, which then displays letters under every button on the tab. Continue pressing the corresponding keys until you trigger the command you want. For example, to insert a task with the Insert Task command, press Alt. Press *H* to open the Task tab. You see the letters "TA" below the Task button in the Insert section. Press *T* followed by *A* to display the drop-down menu. To insert a task, press *T* again. See page 716 to get the full scoop on keyboard accelerators.

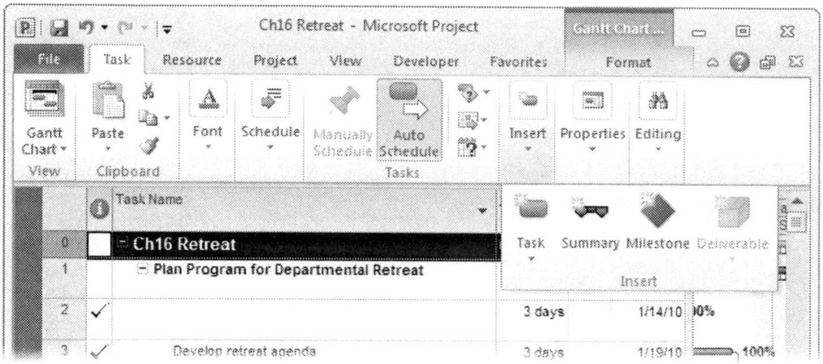

Figure I-2:
When you shrink the Project window, the ribbon rearranges sections and buttons to fit. Some buttons just get smaller. If the window is very narrow, a section turns into a single button (like Insert in this example). Click this button and the hidden commands appear in a drop-down panel.

The Quick Access Toolbar

The Quick Access toolbar is so small that you might not notice it above the File and Task tabs (see Figure I-1). It looks like one of the toolbars from earlier versions of Project. Out of the box, it has icons for Save, Undo, and Redo, because people use them so often. But you can customize the Quick Access toolbar with your top commands. (Chapter 25 tells you how.)

Parts of the Project Window

Managing projects means looking at project information in many different ways, which explains all the built-in views Project provides out of the box. Even so, you'll find that you create quite a few views of your own. As you'll learn in Chapter 23, views come in single-pane and combination variations. The combination view has a top pane and bottom pane (called the Details pane) like the one shown in Figure I-3, which has the Tracking Gantt view (a single-pane view) on top and the Task Form (another single-pane view) on the bottom.

In addition to the top and bottom view panes, some views have two pane-like parts of their own that appear side by side. For views like the Gantt Chart and Task Usage views, the left side of the view is a table with columns of Project fields and rows for tasks, resources, or assignments. You can add or edit values directly in the table or use it simply for reviewing. The timescale and time-phased data on the right side show data apportioned over time. In a Gantt Chart view, taskbars show when tasks begin and end. The Task Usage view uses a time-phased table instead, in which the columns represent time periods, and rows are tasks and assignments.

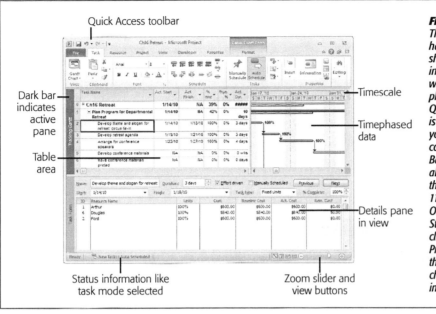

Quick Access toolbar

Dark bar indicates active pane

Table area

Timescale

Timephased data

Details pane in view

Status information like task mode selected

Zoom slider and view buttons

Figure I-3:
The Project window has convenient shortcuts tucked away in every corner of the window and most places in between. The Quick Access toolbar is a handy place for your top-favorite commands. The Status Bar shows information about your project, like the task mode (page 116) you've selected. On the right side of the Status Bar, you can click icons for popular Project views or drag the Zoom Slider to change the timescale in the current view.

Note: The actions you can perform depend on which view pane is active. If you select a new view, then Project replaces the active pane. Project identifies the active pane by darkening the narrow vertical bar to the left of the pane and lightening the vertical bar in the other pane.

Just to keep life interesting, Project also has task panes (no relation to view panes) for different Project-related activities. For example, when you choose Task→Tasks→Inspect, the Task Inspector pane appears to the left of your views (see page 251).

ScreenTips and Smart Tags

ScreenTips and Smart Tags are two other Project features that make temporary appearances. Project's ScreenTips blossom into view when you position the mouse pointer over an item with a ScreenTip, like the icons in the Indicators column in a table. The ScreenTip for a date constraint icon tells you the type of constraint and the date. A Task Note icon displays a ScreenTip with part of the task note. To learn about the purpose of a Project field or how it's calculated, position the cursor over a column header in a view and read the ScreenTip that appears.

Smart Tags, on the other hand, appear when you perform certain Project actions that are renowned for their ability to confuse beginners. For example, if you select the Task Name cell in a table and then press Delete, then Project asks if you want to delete just the task name or the entire task, as illustrated in Figure I-4.

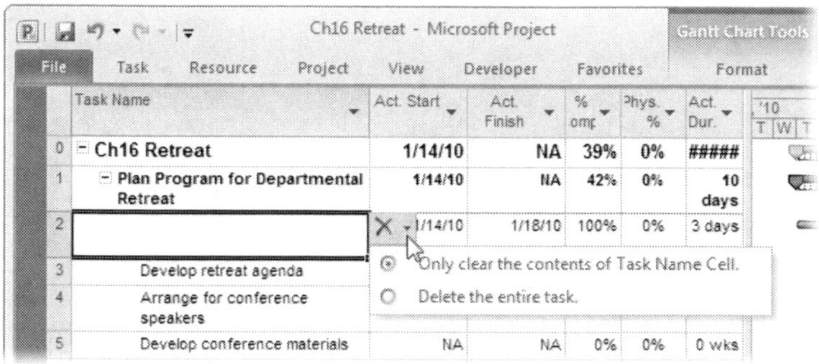

Figure I-4:
SmartTags also appear when you edit a task start or finish date, asking if you want to set a date constraint on the task. Similarly, if you change the duration, work, units, or resources assigned, SmartTags help you tell Project the results you want.

About This Book

Over the years and versions, Project has collected improvements the way sailboat keels attract barnacles. To use Project successfully, you need to understand something about project management, but that's an exercise Microsoft leaves to its customers. The program's Help feature is at least organized around the activities that project managers perform, but Help stills focuses on what Project does rather than what you're trying to do.

Project Help is optimistically named, because it typically lacks troubleshooting tips or meaningful examples. In some cases, the topic you want simply isn't there. Help rarely tells you what you *really* need to know, like *when* and *why* to use a certain feature. And highlighting key points, jotting notes in the margins, or reading about Project after your laptop's battery is dead are all out of the question.

The purpose of this book, then, is to serve as the manual that should have come with Project 2010. It focuses on managing projects with Project Standard or Project Professional, with the aid of a few other Microsoft programs like Word and Excel. The book points out some of the power tools that come with Microsoft's enterprise project management software, but it doesn't explain how to set up or use Project Server and Project Web App. (To learn how to work with Project Server, check out *Microsoft Office Project 2010 Inside Out* by Teresa Stover [Microsoft Press] and *Ultimate Learning Guide to Microsoft Office Project 2010* by Dale Howard and Gary Chefetz [EPM Learning]).

Note: Although each version of Project adds new features and enhancements, you can still use this book if you're managing projects with earlier versions of Project. Of course, the older your version of the program, the more discrepancies you'll run across.

In this book's pages, you'll find step-by-step instructions for using Project Standard and Professional features (minus the ones that require Project Server), including those you might not have quite understood, let alone mastered: choosing the right type of task dependency, assigning overtime, leveling resources, producing reports, and so on. This book helps you be productive by explaining which features are useful and when to use them.

From time to time, this book also includes instructions for using other programs, like Word and Excel, in your project management duties. Because several of these programs got a radical new look in Office 2007, you'll find instructions for both the current and pre-ribbon versions of Word, Excel, and so on.

Although this book is primarily a guide to Project 2010, it comes with a healthy dose of project management guidance. The chapters walk you through managing a project from start to finish: getting a project off the ground (initiating), planning, doing the project work (executing), keeping the project on track (controlling), and tying up loose ends (closing). You'll find practical advice about what project managers do and how those activities help make projects a success.

Microsoft Project 2010: The Missing Manual is designed to accommodate readers at every level of technical and project management expertise. The primary discussions are written for advanced-beginner or intermediate Project users. First-time Project users can look for special boxes with the label "Up To Speed" to get introductory information on the topic at hand. On the other hand, advanced users should watch for similar shaded boxes called "Power Users' Clinic." These boxes offer more technical tips, tricks, and shortcuts for the experienced Project fan. Boxes called "Tools of the Trade" provide more background on project management tools and techniques (Gantt Charts, for example). And, if you've ever wondered how to extract yourself from a gnarly project management situation, look for boxes called "Reality Check" for techniques you can try when project management textbooks fail you.

About the Outline

Microsoft Project 2010: The Missing Manual is divided into six parts, each containing several chapters:

- **Part One: Project Management: The Missing Manual** is like a mini-manual on project management. It explains what projects are, and why managing them is such a good idea. These chapters explain how to pick the right projects to perform, obtain support for them, and start them off on the right foot. You also get a whirlwind tour of planning a project, which Part Two tackles in detail.

- **Part Two: Project Planning: More Than Creating a Schedule** starts with a quick test drive of Project 2010 to whet your appetite. These chapters then take you through each aspect of planning a project, including breaking work down into manageable pieces, estimating work and duration, building a schedule, assembling a team, assigning resources to tasks, and setting up a budget. The remaining chapters explain how to refine your plan until everyone (mostly) is happy with it, and then how to prepare it for the execution phase of the project.

- **Part Three: Projects in Action** takes you from an approved project plan to the end of a project. These chapters explain how to track progress once work gets under way, evaluate that progress, correct course, and manage changes. Other chapters explain how to use Project's reports and complete important steps at the end of a project.

- **Part Four: Project Power Tools** helps you get the most out of Project. These chapters talk about how to work on more than one project at a time and how to share data with programs and colleagues.

- **Part Five: Customizing Project** explains how to customize every aspect of Project to fit your needs—even the ribbon. After all, every organization is unique, and so is every project. Other chapters show you how to save time by reusing Project elements (in templates) and boost productivity by recording macros.

- **Part Six: Appendixes.** At the end of the book, three appendixes provide a guide to installing and upgrading Project, a reference to help resources for Project, and a quick review of the most helpful keyboard shortcuts.

The Very Basics

To use this book—and Project—you need to know a few computer basics. Like other Microsoft programs, Project responds to several types of clicking mouse buttons, choosing commands from menus, and pressing combinations of keys for keyboard shortcuts. Here's a quick overview of a few terms and concepts this book uses:

- **Clicking**. This book gives you three kinds of instructions that require you to use your computer's mouse or track pad. To *click* means to point the arrow pointer at something on the screen, and then—without moving the pointer at all—press and release the left button on the mouse (or laptop trackpad). To *right-click* means the same thing, but using the right mouse button. To *double-click* means to click the left mouse button twice in rapid succession, again without moving the pointer at all. And to *drag* means to move the pointer while holding down the left button the entire time.

  When you're told to *Shift-click* something, you click while pressing the Shift key. Related procedures, such as *Ctrl-clicking*, work the same way—just click while pressing the corresponding key.

- **Keyboard shortcuts.** Nothing is faster than keeping your fingers on your keyboard—entering data, choosing names, and triggering commands, all without losing time by reaching for the mouse. That's why many experienced Project fans prefer to trigger commands by pressing combinations of keys on the keyboard. For example, in most word processors, pressing Ctrl+B produces a **boldface** word. When you read an instruction like "Press Ctrl+C to copy the selection to the Clipboard," start by pressing the Ctrl key; while it's down, type the letter *C*, and then release both keys.

About→These→Arrows

Throughout this book, and throughout the Missing Manual series, you'll find sentences like this one: "Choose Task→Editing→Scroll to Task." That's shorthand for selecting the Task tab on the ribbon, navigating to the Editing section, and then clicking Scroll to Task. Figure I-5 shows what this looks like.

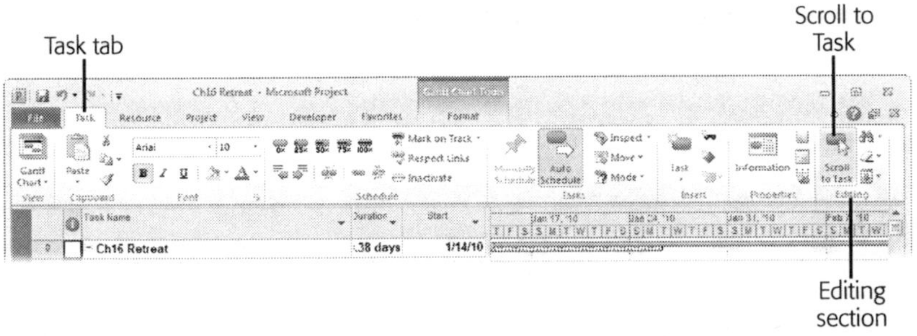

Figure I-5:
Instead of filling pages with long and hard-to-follow instructions for navigating through nested menus and nested folders, the arrow notations are concise, but just as informative. For example, here's how you execute the "Scroll to Task" command.

If you see an instruction that includes arrows but starts with the word File, it's telling you to go to Project's Backstage view. For example, the sentence "Choose File→New" means to select the File tab to switch to Backstage view, then click the New command (which appears in the narrow list on the left).

Similarly, this arrow shorthand also simplifies the instructions for opening nested folders, such as Program Files→Microsoft Office→Office14→1033.

About MissingManuals.com

At *www.missingmanuals.com*, you'll find news, articles, and updates to the books in this series.

But the website also offers corrections and updates to this book (to see them, click the book's title, and then click Errata). In fact, you're invited and encouraged to submit such corrections and updates yourself. In an effort to keep the book as up-to-date and accurate as possible, each time we print more copies of this book, we'll make any confirmed corrections you suggest. We'll also note such changes on the website so that you can mark important corrections into your own copy of the book, if you like.

In the meantime, we'd love to hear your suggestions for new books in the Missing Manual line. There's a place for that on the website, too, as well as a place to sign up for free email notification of new titles in the series.

About the Missing CD

This book helps you use Project. As you read through it, you'll find references to files that you can use to help you manage your projects and websites that offer additional resources. Each reference includes the site's URL, but you can save yourself some typing by going to this book's Missing CD page—it gives you clickable links to all the sites mentioned here. To get to the Missing CD page, go to the Missing Manuals home page (*www.missingmanuals.com*), click the Missing CD link, scroll down to *Microsoft Project 2010: The Missing Manual*, and then click the link labeled "Missing CD."

Safari® Books Online

Safari. Safari® Books Online is an on-demand digital library that lets you easily search over 7,500 technology and creative reference books and videos to find the answers you need quickly.

With a subscription, you can read any page and watch any video from our library online. Read books on your cellphone and mobile devices. Access new titles before they're available for print, and get exclusive access to manuscripts in development and post feedback for the authors. Copy and paste code samples, organize your favorites, download chapters, bookmark key sections, create notes, print out pages, and benefit from tons of other timesaving features.

O'Reilly Media has uploaded this book to the Safari Books Online service. To have full digital access to this book and others on similar topics from O'Reilly and other publishers, sign up for free at *http://my.safaribooksonline.com*.

Note: This Missing Manual includes all the Microsoft Project information you need to pass the Microsoft Project MCTS Exam, including the upcoming exam for Project 2010. An exam study guide will be available in ebook format (for a small additional cost) after Microsoft releases the Project 2010 certification exam. The guide will outline the exam objectives, reference the relevant content in this book, provide test-taking tips, and cover important best practices for using Project to manage projects. After the Project 2010 certification exam is released, check the Missing Manuals website for more information about the guide (missingmanuals.com).

Part One:
Project Management: The Missing Manual

I

Projects: In the Beginning

Microsoft Project is brimming with features to help you manage any kind of project, but you have to know something about project management to make those features sing. If your boss hands you a project to manage and you ask what she means by "project" and "manage," this chapter is for you.

A project is different from day-to-day work, and this chapter explains how. You'll learn what project management is at a high level—and why it's worth the effort. Project management helps you deliver the right results on time, within budget, and without going into crisis mode. When a project falters, project management techniques also help you get it headed back in the right direction.

But before it even begins, a project has to make it through a selection process. Just like a major-league baseball player waiting for a good pitch before he swings, you'll learn what to look for in potential projects. (Even if your boss currently mandates which projects you manage, learning to prioritize and select projects may increase your influence in the future.)

The chapter concludes by covering the one skill that no project manager can afford to ignore: gaining and maintaining the support of project *stakeholders*—the folks who care about the project's success. You'll learn how to identify stakeholders and their expectations, and how to keep them on board so they're ready and willing to pitch in when the project needs their help.

What's So Special About Projects?

Projects come in all shapes and sizes, from learning how to set the date and time on a digital watch to designing and building a timepiece so powerful that you need a PhD to operate it. Likewise, your child's birthday party is a project, although the scale is smaller than coordinating the inauguration of a new President of the United States.

What's the common thread that unites all projects and makes them different from other kinds of work? Here's one definition: *A project is a unique endeavor with clear-cut objectives, a starting point, an ending point, and, usually, a budget.*

- **Unique** is the most important word in that definition because every project is different in some way. Assembling reinforcing steel on site for different buildings, built on different topography, during different weather conditions, constitute different projects. The building designs, site conditions, and weather make every construction job unique, even if the buildings are cookie-cutter copies. On the other hand, a crew that cuts and bends concrete reinforcing bars performs the same work every day, typically called *operations*, even if the dimensions of the rebars vary.

- **Clear-cut objectives** are necessary if you want any hope of reaching the end, staying within budget, and making customers happy. Whether you call them specific, quantifiable, or unambiguous, objectives define what the project is supposed to accomplish so everyone knows when it's done. "Keep the cat off the kitchen counter" is work that never ends. On the other hand, an objective that you *can* complete, albeit with some physical risk, is "Remove the cat from the Thanksgiving turkey carcass."

- Although some projects *seem* interminable, a project **begins** at one point in time and **ends** when it achieves its objectives. When the construction crew wires the last rebar into place and the inspector approves the work, the crew is ready to move on to the next project. However, if the end always seems just out of reach, poorly defined objectives are usually to blame. You'll learn how to define objectives in Chapter 2.

- **Budgets** play a role in most projects, because few people consider money irrelevant. In addition to achieving the objectives within the desired timeframe, you also have to keep the price tag within an acceptable range.

Note: Dr. Joseph M. Juran, best known for his work on quality management, was the impetus for today's Six Sigma methodology; he described a project as a *problem scheduled for solution*. The concept is the same: Working with stakeholders to identify and agree upon the problem that needs solving helps identify the project's objectives. When you schedule the problem for solution, you determine the project's start and end dates.

What Is Project Management?

Project management is the art of balancing project objectives against the constraints of time, budget, and quality. Achieving that balance requires skill, experience, and a boatload of techniques. This section gives you a glimpse of what happens from a project's infancy to its old age.

The Big Book of Project Management

The Project Management Institute (PMI) is a nonprofit organization with its hooks in all aspects of project management. It provides project management education and offers certifications to validate that project managers know what they're doing. PMI also supports research into new project management methods.

PMI publishes the Project Management Body of Knowledge, also known as the PMBOK Guide. This document represents the collective knowledge of a slew of experienced project managers, boiled down into an overview of project management steps, why you perform them, and the results they produce. A word of warning: The PMBOK is dry, formal, and doesn't tell you exactly how to perform project management tasks. It's great as a reference, but (unlike the book you're holding now) useless as a how-to book.

Novices sometimes think of project management as building a sequence of tasks, but those in the know recognize that project management starts *before* a project officially begins, and doesn't end for a while after the project's objectives are achieved. There's no one way to manage projects, but most methodologies cover the following five phases (illustrated in Figure 1-1):

- **Getting started**. Often called *initiating*, the first phase of project management is short but important. It's your only opportunity to get the project off to a good start. In this phase, you answer questions like "Why are we doing this project?" and "Do we really want to do it?" The initial attempts to describe the purpose of a project may produce vague results like "Launch a website to improve customer service." But as you identify the stakeholders (page 32), you learn what the project is about and what the stakeholders hope to achieve. The more specific you are when you describe a project's objectives, the greater your chances for success.

   Neglecting to line up support for a project (page 31) is all too common, and it's *always* a big mistake. A project needs buy-in from an executive sponsor (page 33) and the stakeholders to survive challenges like contradictory objectives, resource shortages, funding issues, and so on. What's more, *you*, the project manager, need official support, too, so everyone knows the extent of your authority.

- **Planning**. This phase, which Chapter 2 covers in greater detail, is where you draw your road map: the objectives to achieve, the work to perform, who's going to do that work when, and how much the whole thing will cost. Moreover, you set out the rules of the game, including how people will communicate with each other, who has to approve what, how you manage changes and risks, and so on.

- **Performing the project**. Also referred to as *executing*, this part of project management lasts a long time, but it boils down to following the plan. As the project manager, you keep the project team working on the right things at the right times.

- **Keeping things under control**. In a perfect world, performing the project would be enough, because things would always run according to plan. But because the world isn't perfect, project managers have to monitor projects to see whether they're on schedule, within budget, and achieving their objectives. Whether someone gets sick, manufacturing asks for design changes, or your data center is plagued with locusts, something's bound to push your project off course. In the *controlling* phase, you measure project performance against the plan, decide what to do if the project is off track, make the necessary adjustments, and then measure again. Chapter 14 and Chapter 15 explain how to use Project to control things.

- **Gaining closure**. Like personal relationships, projects need closure. Before you can call a project complete, you have to tie up loose ends like closing out contracts, transitioning resources to their new assignments, and documenting the overall project performance (page 482). The *closing* phase is when you ask for official acceptance that the project is complete—your sign that your job is done. Chapter 18 describes the information to collect, and different ways to archive a project.

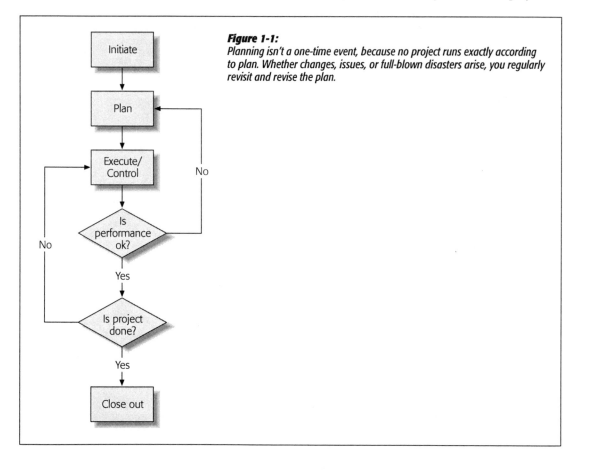

Figure 1-1:
Planning isn't a one-time event, because no project runs exactly according to plan. Whether changes, issues, or full-blown disasters arise, you regularly revisit and revise the plan.

TOOLS OF THE TRADE

Picking a Project Management Methodology

Companies that perform project after project usually pick a project management methodology, such as Six Sigma or Agile Development, and stick with it. That way, all their projects follow approximately the same project management process. Teams learn what works and what doesn't, and everyone learns what to do and expect.

The approach you choose depends a lot on the environment in which you work. Complex environments with large projects, widely distributed teams, or multiple vendors usually need a robust project management methodology with formal, well-documented procedures, standardized forms and documents, and software like Project Server to keep track of everything. Simpler, smaller projects would bog down with that kind of overhead, but run just fine with a more informal approach.

This book introduces the basic steps of project management, which you can use as a starting point. If you want a ready-made methodology to adopt, check out the following resources:

- *Project Planning, Scheduling & Control* by James P. Lewis (McGraw-Hill) bucks the trend in project management books by providing an easy-to-read, and even amusing, description of one way to manage projects.

- *A Management Framework for Project, Program, and Portfolio Integration* by R. Max Wideman (Trafford Publishing) tries to simplify project management—and for the most part succeeds.

- **TenStep, Inc.** (*www.tenstep.com*) offers a project management approach that predictably takes 10 steps from start to finish. This approach can be adapted to projects large and small. If you register with the website (for free), you can mine a mother lode of additional project management wisdom.

Why Manage Projects?

The five phases of an *unmanaged* project go something like this: wild enthusiasm, dejected disillusionment, search for the guilty, punishment of the innocent, and promotion of those not involved. An unmanaged project is like a black hole that sucks up every person, machine, and dollar—and still doesn't deliver what it's supposed to. Despite the unpleasant alternatives, many organizations fear that project management requires bureaucratic and inflexible procedures, and may even make projects take longer. On the contrary, planning projects and managing the plan provide many benefits, including:

- **Happy customers**. Whether a project is for outside customers or groups within your organization, customers like to get *what* they want *when* they want it. Because the first step in project management is finding out what your stakeholders and customers want to accomplish with the project, your customers are more likely to get the results they expect. And by keeping the project under control, you're also more likely to deliver those results on time and at the right price.

- **Objectives achieved**. Without a plan, projects tend to cultivate their own agendas and people forget the point of their work. A project plan ties a project to specific objectives, so everyone stays focused on those goals. Documented objectives also help you rein in the renegades who try to expand the scope of the project.

- **Timely completion**. Finishing a project on time is important for more than just morale. As work goes on for a longer duration, costs increase and budgets blow to bits. In addition, you may lose the resources you need or prevent other projects from starting. Sometimes time is the ultimate objective, like when you're trying to get a product to market before the competition.

- **Flexibility**. Contrary to many people's beliefs, project management makes teams *more* flexible. Project management doesn't prevent every problem, but it makes the problems that occur easier to resolve. When something goes wrong, you can evaluate your plan to quickly develop alternatives—now that's flexibility! More importantly, keeping track of progress means you learn about bad news when you still have time to recover.

- **Better financial performance**. Most executives are obsessed with financial performance, so many projects have financial objectives—increasing sales, lowering costs, reducing expensive recalls, and so on. Project management is an executive crowd-pleaser because it can produce more satisfying financial results.

- **More productive, happier workers**. Skilled workers are hard to come by and usually cost a bundle. People get more done when they can work without drama, stress, and painfully long hours. Moreover, they don't abandon ship, so you spend less on recruiting and training replacements.

Picking the Right Projects

There's never a shortage of projects, but there's not enough time, money, and staff in the world to complete them all. Before you begin managing a project, make sure it earns its place in the project portfolio. Throwing darts or pulling petals off daisies isn't the answer; you're better off knowing what's important to your organization and picking projects that support those objectives.

Project selection criteria are just as helpful once projects are underway, because projects don't always deliver what they promise. If a project isn't meeting expectations, you can decide whether to give it time to recover or cut it loose. Similarly, if a juicy new project appears, you can compare its potential results to those of projects already in progress to see if it makes sense to swap it for a project that's partially complete.

Note: Selection criteria can save time and effort *before* the selection process even starts. People thinking about proposing a project can evaluate potential results before facing the selection committee. If the results don't pass the test, there's little point in presenting the project to management.

To make good decisions, you need some kind of consistent selection process, whether you're a small business owner allocating limited resources or a committee setting up a multiproject portfolio. You can evaluate the candidates and choose the projects with the most compelling results. When you run out of money and resources, you can put any remaining projects that meet your selection criteria on the waiting list.

The Importance of Business Objectives

Some projects are no-brainers, like the ones needed to satisfy government regulations. For example, companies that want to stay in business have to conform to the accounting requirements of the Sarbanes-Oxley Act. On the other hand, you can cull projects from your list by picking only the ones that support the organization's mission and business objectives. If your company dabbles in widgetry, the goal might be getting your tools to market before the competition. In the healthcare industry, safety trumps speed, because recalling devices already implanted in people is going to hurt the patients and the company's pocketbook. Any time you begin to describe a project by saying, "It would be nice…" you may as well stop right there—unless you can link the project to quantifiable business objectives as well.

UP TO SPEED

Picking by Committee

Management by consensus has a bad reputation, but a *project review board* is a good way to make sure your organization selects the right projects. An effective project review board includes decision-makers from every area of your organization with a variety of skill sets, and it applies selection criteria to choose projects as objectively as possible. Without an impartial jury, project sponsors and their project managers may choose projects for less compelling reasons: They find the project intriguing, the work is relatively risk-free, or they simply grow attached to the projects they propose.

A project review board doesn't doom you to a bureaucratic selection process. With documented selection criteria, the steps are pretty simple:

1. **Someone proposes a project**. Project sponsors or project managers usually prepare a proposal to sell the project to the review board—why the project is worthwhile, what benefits it provides, and how it fares against the selection criteria.

2. **The project review board evaluates proposals**. The board meets on a regular schedule to evaluate proposed projects. People who propose projects get a chance to make their pitches, which usually include rigorous Q&A sessions with the board members to clarify ambiguous points. After the presentations, the board discusses the merits of the projects, how they fit with the organization's objectives, as well as any conflicts or issues they see.

3. **The board approves or rejects project proposals**. The board decides which projects get to move forward and notifies proposers of the fate of their projects, and preferably explains the reasons for the decisions.

Here are some common business objectives that trigger projects:

- Increase revenue
- Improve profitability
- Increase market share
- Reduce price to stay competitive
- Reduce costs
- Reduce time to market
- Increase customer satisfaction

CHAPTER 1: PROJECTS: IN THE BEGINNING

- Increase product quality or safety
- Reduce waste
- Satisfy regulations
- Increase productivity

REALITY CHECK

Surviving Without Selection Criteria

Why should you care about project selection criteria if you typically learn about projects only when you're assigned to manage them? What if the selection process is non-existent, and obtaining resources and support is always a battle? If you know what makes a good project (and have some time and patience), you can turn these trials and tribulations to your advantage.

When executives seem to want everything with equal desperation, it's up to you to learn what's really important. Ask managers what their priorities are, and find out what the CEO always inquires about. Listen closely to executives in company meetings.

Once you've identified the key business objectives, manage your projects to deliver the results that count. The more you deliver, the easier it'll be to get the resources and help you need. You can't give everyone everything they want, so focus on the most important objectives.

After you've made an impression with a few successful projects, you can pitch a project selection process to the executive team.

Common Selection Criteria

Although some projects get a free pass due to regulatory requirements or because the CEO says so, most have to earn their spot in the project line-up. Because business objectives vary, you need some sort of common denominator for measuring results—which often comes down to money. This section describes the most common financial measures that executives use, and the pros and cons of each.

Whether you're trying to increase revenue, reduce costs, or improve product quality, you can usually present project benefits in dollars. The winner is the project that makes the most of the money spent on it. Of course, to calculate financial results, you need numbers; and to get numbers, you have to do some prep work and estimating (page 102). You don't need a full-blown project plan (page 40) to propose a project, but you do need a rough idea of the project's potential benefits and costs. That's why many organizations start with *feasibility studies*—small efforts specifically for determining whether it makes sense to pursue a project further.

Note: If some business objectives are way more important than others, you may want to evaluate the projects that support those killer objectives first. Then, if you have money and resources left over, you can look at projects in other areas of the business. Risk is another consideration in selecting projects. Suppose a project has mouth-watering financial prospects *and* heart-stopping risks. Project proposals should include a high-level analysis of risks (page 52) so the selection committee can make informed decisions.

Payback period

Payback period is the time a project takes to earn back what it cost. Consider a project that reduces warranty repairs by $10,000 each month and costs $200,000 to implement. The payback period is the cost of the project divided by the money earned or saved each month:

```
Payback period = $200,000 / $10,000 per month = 20 months
```

Payback period has simplicity on its side: The data you need is relatively easy to obtain and nonfinancial types can follow the math. But if you get really finicky about it, payback period has several limitations:

- **It assumes enough earnings to pay back the cost**. If your company stops selling the product that the warranty repair project supports, the monthly savings may not continue for the calculated payback period, which ends up costing money.

- **It ignores cash flows after the payback period ends**. Projects that generate money early beat out projects that generate more money over a longer period. Consider two projects, each costing $100,000. Project #1 saves $20,000 each month for only 5 months. Project #2 saves $10,000 each month for 24 months. Project #1's payback period is 5 months compared to Project #2's 10 months. However, Project #2 saves $240,000, whereas Project #1 saves only $100,000.

- **It ignores the time value of money**. There's a price to pay for using money over a period of time, just like the interest you pay on the mortgage on your house. Payback period doesn't account for the time value of money, because it uses the project cost as a lump sum, regardless how long the project takes and when you spend the money. The measures explained in the next sections are more accurate when a project spends and receives money over time.

Net present value

Net present value (NPV) takes the time value of money into account, so it provides a more accurate picture of financial performance than payback period does. The *time value* of money is another way to say that money isn't always worth the same amount—money you earn in the future isn't as valuable as money you earn today. For example, the value of your salary goes down as inflation reduces what each dollar of your paycheck can buy each year. Conversely, you pay a price for using money, which is exactly like the interest you pay on a house mortgage.

NPV starts by combining a project's income (earnings or savings) and costs into *cash flows*. If you earn $4,000 a month and spend $3,000 on living expenses, your net cash flow is $1,000. Then, NPV uses a rate of return to translate the cash flows into a single value in today's dollars. If NPV is greater than zero, the project earns more than that rate of return. If NPV is less than zero, the project's return is lower. Where does this magical return come from? In most cases, you use the rate of return that your company requires on money it invests. For example, if your company demands a 10 percent return to invest in a project, you use 10 percent in the NPV calculation. If the NPV is greater than zero, the project passes the company's investment test.

NPV has two drawbacks. First, it doesn't tell you the return that the project provides, only whether the project exceeds the rate of return you use. You can compare NPV for several projects and pick the one with the highest value, but executives like to see an annual return. One way to overcome this issue is with a *profitability index*, which is NPV divided by the initial investment. This ratio basically tells you what bang for your buck you get from each project. The higher the profitability index, the better. The second drawback is that NPV is hard to explain to non-financial folks. (Luckily, however, most people picking projects are well-versed in financial measures.)

Figure 1-2 uses the purchase of a machine as a simple example of net present value. The machine costs $100,000 and saves $10,000 in production costs each month it operates. The machine is obsolete at the end of the first year, at which point its value as a chic boat anchor is $5,000.

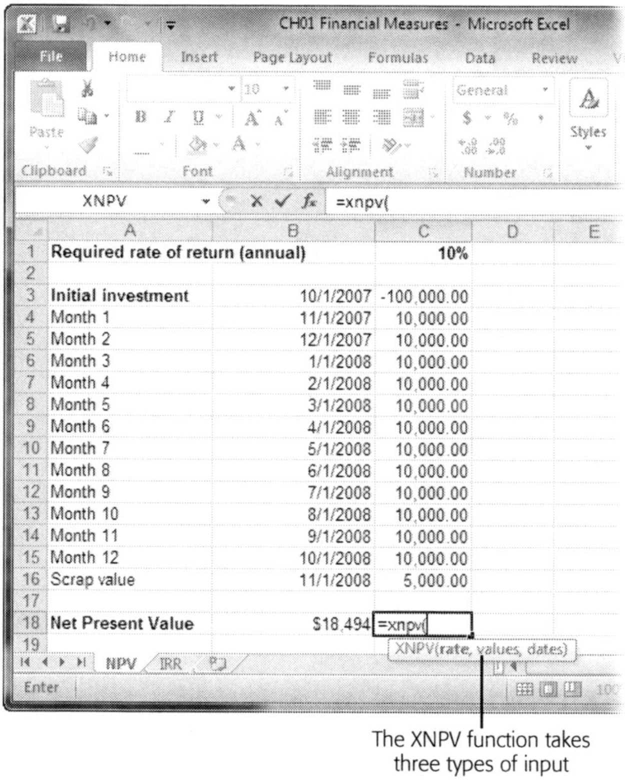

Figure 1-2:
The XNPV function interprets negative numbers as money spent—like $100,000 for a new packaging machine. Positive numbers represent money coming in (as a result of the improved equipment). If you spend and earn money on the same date, simply enter the net amount (the income minus the expense). Because NPV in this example is greater than zero, the machine provides a return greater than the required annual 10 percent return.

The XNPV function takes three types of input

To avoid frenetic finger-work calculating NPV on a handheld calculator, try Microsoft Excel's XNPV function. You provide the required rate of return, the cash flows the investment delivers, and the dates on which they occur (remember the value of money changes over time), and Excel does the rest.

Note: If cash flows occur on a regular schedule like once a month, you can use the Excel NPV function, which doesn't require dates. The function assumes a regular schedule, and you simply input the rate of return between each cash flow. If the annual rate is 10 percent and you have monthly cash flows, you enter the rate as 10 percent divided by 12, or .833 percent. The biggest drawback to the NPV function is that it accepts no more than 29 values, which isn't enough for monthly cash flows for several years.

Here's how to use the XNPV function:

1. **In an Excel workbook, fill in one cell with the rate of return you want to use, and then enter the cash flows and dates in two of the workbook columns, as shown in Figure 1-2.**

   The dates and cash flows don't have to be side by side, but you can read the workbook more easily if they are.

2. **In Excel 2007 or 2010, select the cell where you want to insert the function, and then click the Formulas tab. On the left side of the ribbon, click Insert Function.**

   In Excel 2003, choose Insert→Function instead. In these three versions of Excel, the Insert Function dialog box opens with the "Search for a function" box selected.

3. **In the "Search for a function" box, type *XNPV* and then click Go.**

   In the "Select a function" list, Excel displays and chooses the XNPV function. It also lists related financial functions.

Tip: You can also locate the XNPV function and its siblings in the "Or select a category" box by choosing Financial, and then picking the financial function you want.

---

4. **Click OK to insert the function into the cell, and then fill in the boxes for the function arguments.**

   In addition to adding the function to the cell, Excel opens the Function Arguments dialog box, shown in Figure 1-3, which presents the three arguments for the function with hints and feedback.

5. **Click OK to complete the function and close the dialog box.**

Tip: If you're an old hand at Excel functions, you can just type the entire function into a cell. For example, select the cell and then type =*XNPV(*. Excel shows you the arguments it requires. You can select a cell for the first argument, type a comma, and then select the cells for the next argument.

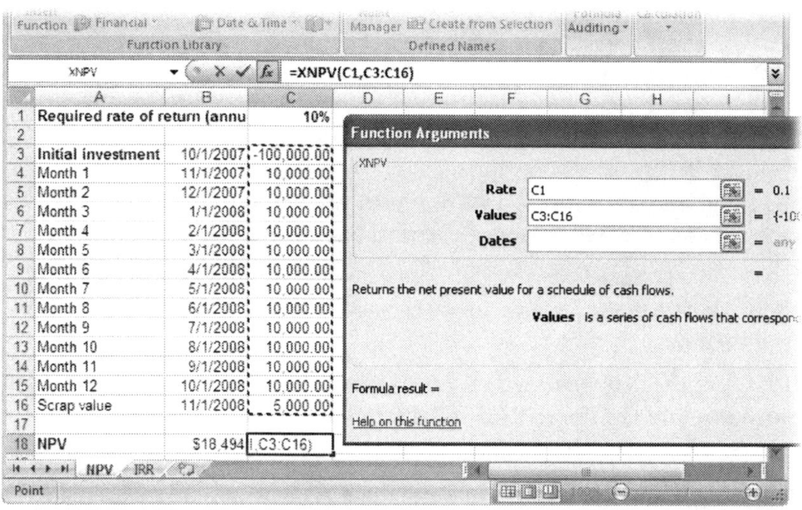

Figure 1-3:
*To fill in an argument,
click the box, such
as Rate. Then, in the
worksheet, click the
cell (or cells) that
contain the input. For
example, for Values,
you can drag over all
the cells that contain
the cash flows.*

Internal rate of return

A project's *internal rate of return* (IRR) tells you the *annual* return that it delivers, taking into account the time value of money. IRR is like the annual percentage yield (APY) you earn on a savings account, which includes the compounded interest you earn during the year. If your project delivers an IRR greater than the return your company requires, you're golden.

Just like NPV, IRR depends on *when* cash flows in or out. For example, money you spend up front drags the IRR down more than money you spend later on. Likewise, if a project brings money in early, the IRR is higher than if the income arrives later.

Like payback period and net present value, internal rate of return has its drawbacks. The big one is that it can give the wrong answer in some situations! It works like a charm when you have one initial cash outlay (a negative number) and then the rest of the cash flows are money coming in. However, if the series of cash flows switches between positive and negative numbers, several rates of return can produce a zero net present value, so mathematically, there are several correct answers. If you calculate IRR in Excel, the program stops as soon as it gets an answer. But if you run the function again, you might get a different result.

Another issue arises if you borrow money for your project. In that situation, the first cash flow is positive (money coming in) and the rest are negative (money flowing out to pay project costs). Because of that, you have to switch the way you evaluate IRR: In such situations, you want to reject a project if its IRR is greater than your company's required rate of return, and accept a project if its IRR is *less than* the required rate of return.

Excel's XIRR function calculates IRR given cash flows and the dates on which they occur, as shown in Figure 1-4. For the mathematicians in the audience, IRR doesn't have a formula of its own. The way you calculate IRR by hand is by running the NPV calculation with different rates of return until the answer is zero—that return is the IRR. The steps for inserting the XIRR function into a worksheet are similar to those for XNPV in the previous section.

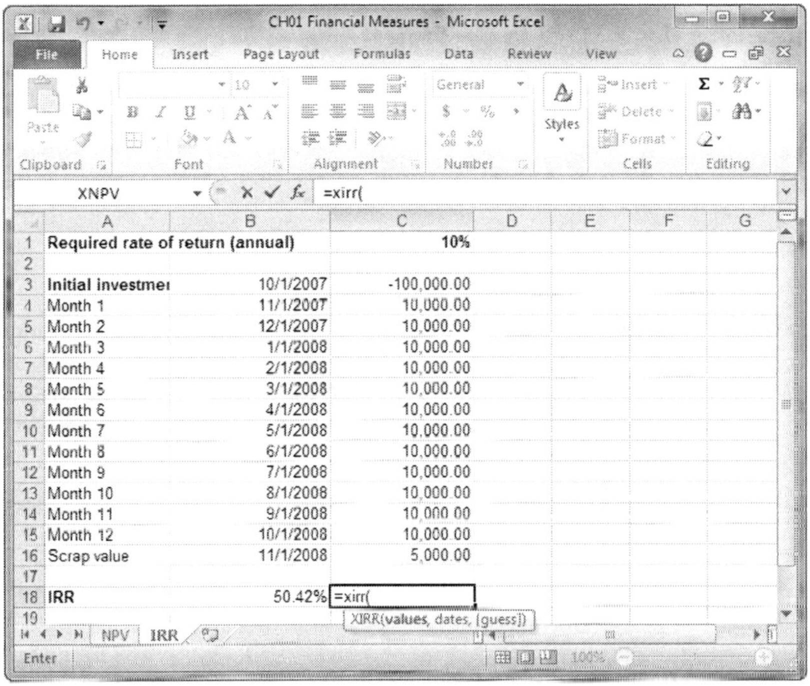

Figure 1-4:
XIRR includes a third argument called "guess," which is the first return you use in the search for the IRR. If you leave the guess argument blank, Excel uses 10%. Depending on whether the resulting NPV is positive or negative, the XIRR function tries a different value until NPV equals zero.

Note: If the XIRR function doesn't find an answer after 100 tries, it displays the #NUM error in the cell. You also see the #NUM error if your series of cash flows doesn't include at least one positive and one negative cash flow.

Gaining Support for a Project

Sponsorship is important during the selection process, but support becomes crucial once projects start up. Projects rarely finish without running into some kind of trouble, and you often need help digging them out. Alas, many people lend a hand only if there's something in it for them, which is why identifying the people who care about a project (the *stakeholders*) is so important.

Stakeholders can play a part in projects from proposal to the final closeout. During the planning phase, stakeholders help define the project and evaluate the project plan. A few lucky stakeholders cough up the money to fund the project. During the execution phase, stakeholders help resolve problems, make decisions about changes, risk strategies, and (if necessary) whether to fork over more money. At the end of a project, some of the stakeholders get to decree the project complete, so everyone can move on to another project.

Identify Who Has a Stake in the Project

Commitment comes from all levels of an organization, from the executive-level project sponsor to the people who work on the project every day. Project stakeholders get their name because they have a *stake* in the project's outcome. They either give something to your project—like the managers who provide the resources you use—or they want something from it, like the customer who implements the software system a project delivers.

Identifying stakeholders can be tough. Some don't realize they're stakeholders, like the development team that learns about a project when they receive the list of impossible requirements from sales. Other people pretend to be stakeholders, but aren't, like an engineering department that gets chummy because they see your project as an inexpensive way to get their new database. If you're not careful, your project can gain extraneous requirements, but of course, no additional money.

Here are the main types of stakeholders, how you identify them, and some hints on keeping them happy:

- **Project customers** are easy to spot, because they're the ones with the checkbooks. Pleasing the stakeholders who fund your project is a matter of delivering the financial results they expect (page 27). Stay on top of financial performance (page 450) so you can explain financial shortfalls and your plan to get back on track. The people who control the pocketbook can be formidable allies if other groups are trying to expand the project.

   Because customers foot the bill, they usually have a lot to say about the project's objectives, requirements, and deliverables. Of course, the person who cuts the check isn't often the person who defines requirements, but they both represent the project's customer. (For instance, if the project is a college search, your teenager may pick a university even if you pay the tuition and board.) Customers also approve documents, intermediate results, and the final outcome. Approvals are much easier to come by if you work closely with customers during planning to identify their objectives and what they consider success.

Note: When a project produces a product to sell, you don't interact with the *final* customers—the ones who buy the product. Instead, you work with intermediaries like sales reps, marketing departments, and focus groups.

- **Project sponsors** are the folks who want the project to succeed and have the authority to make things happen, like the vice president of manufacturing who's backing a project to upgrade an assembly line. If you, as a project manager, don't have that kind of authority, you may depend on sponsors to confer some of their authority to you. A sponsor's role is to support the project manager and the project team to make the project a success. After guiding a project through the selection process, the sponsor's next task is to sign and distribute a project charter (page 35), which publicizes the new project and your authority as the project manager.

A sponsor can help you prioritize objectives, tell you which performance measures are critical, and guide you through the rapids of organizational politics. The sponsor can also recommend ways to build commitment or fix problems. Sometimes, project sponsors are also project customers, whether for internal projects or for those that deliver products to external customers.

If your authority isn't enough or the project hits serious obstacles, the sponsor can step in. While sponsors want their projects to succeed, they expect you to manage the project. Dropping problems at their doorstep every few minutes won't win their hearts, but neither will hiding problems until it's too late. If you need help, don't be afraid to get your sponsor involved.

- **Functional managers** (also called *line managers*) run departments like engineering, marketing, and IT. They have quotas and performance measures to meet in addition to supervising the resources in their departments. Project resources almost always come from these departments, so you have to learn to work with these folks.

REALITY CHECK

When Stakeholders Aren't Supportive

Some projects are good for the organization as a whole, but cause problems for a few stakeholders. For example, a process improvement project may save your company tons of money, but spell layoffs for one group. Unsupportive stakeholders can actively undermine your project, perhaps by withholding resources or raising issue after issue.

Sun-Tzu, a 4th century BC Chinese general, had sound advice for winning over stakeholders: "Keep your friends close, and your enemies closer." Find out what stakeholders' issues are, and you may find ways to appease them.

Sometimes, the project sponsor or other stakeholders can help you bring reluctant stakeholders on board. But politics and relationships that outlast your project often leave you to muddle through on your own. If winning people over is out of the question, be sure to identify the risks that this logjam raises. Then, you can communicate those risks and potential workarounds to the entire stakeholder group and let them decide what to do. Still, the outcome isn't always a success, and the conflicts may permanently damage your project.

The easiest way to win over functional managers is to let them do their jobs. Don't tell them who you need (unless you already have a great working relationship). Instead, specify the skills you need and the constraints you face, like cost, availability, or experience. Then, after the managers provide you with resources, do your best to stick to the assignment dates you requested. When schedules slip, notify functional managers quickly so you can work out an alternative.

Tip: Functional managers spend time listening to employees complain about being overworked, overwhelmed, or bored. If you can demonstrate why you need the resources you request, when you need them, and that the schedule is feasible, managers are more likely to commit their people.

- **Team members** who do project work are stakeholders, too, because they perform the tasks that make up the project. Other types of stakeholders often do double duty as team members, like when a customer defines requirements.

  Keeping team members happy is a combination of reasonable workload, meaningful work, and a pleasant work environment. Communication is as important with team members as it is with every other type of stakeholder. Team members want to know how their tasks support the big picture, what their tasks represent, and when they're scheduled to perform them.

- You already know that **project managers** are stakeholders, because your reputation and livelihood depend on the success of your projects. The project manager is easy to identify when it's you. How to make *yourself* happy is something you have to figure out on your own.

The process of building a project plan (page 40) helps you identify many stakeholders. For instance, the purpose of the project and who benefits from it tell you who the customer is as well as the project's sponsor. Project objectives help you identify which groups participate in achieving those objectives. The responsibility matrix (page 176) identifies the groups involved in a project and their level of involvement, so it acts as a checklist of stakeholder groups. Of course, you still have to identify the specific people to work with within those groups. When you start to build your project team, the list of functional managers and team members falls into place.

Documenting Stakeholders

As projects pick up momentum, your ability to remember details quickly falls away. Stakeholders are so important to projects that you can't afford to forget them. As you identify stakeholders during planning, create a stakeholder analysis table. Listing names and types of stakeholders isn't enough. Also include information about people's roles, which objectives matter to them the most, and whom they listen to.

Figure 1-5 shows a sample stakeholder analysis table, which you can download from *www.missingmanuals.com/cds*. Look for the Word file Ch01_Stakeholder_Analysis.doc.

Here's some info that's helpful to collect about each person who acts as a stakeholder:

- **Organization or department**. Knowing where a stakeholder works helps you remember the objectives they care about, and whether they should participate in different activities. For instance, if your company wants to keep strategy sessions confidential, you don't want to invite external stakeholders to them.

- **Objectives**. List the objectives that each stakeholder cares about—from their hottest button to coolest. If you need help rallying stakeholders around an objective, this info helps you find your allies.

- **Contributions**. List what the stakeholder does for the project. Contributions you list here are different than the responsibilities you put in a responsibility matrix (page 176). In the stakeholder table, you specify the contributions that individuals make to the project in their roles as stakeholders.

- **Advisors**. The people to whom stakeholders listen are great sources for tips on presenting information effectively, or which options a stakeholder might prefer.

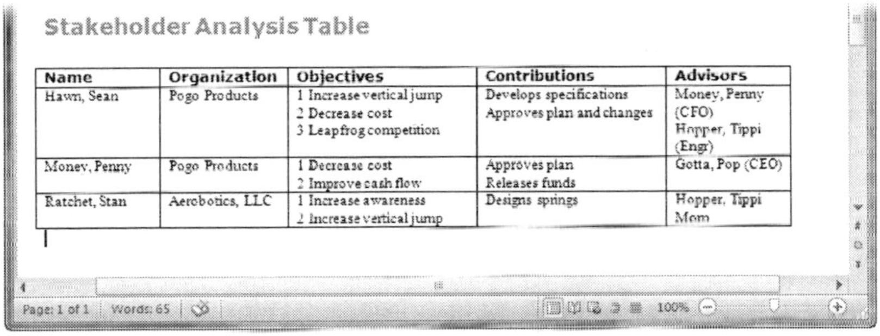

Stakeholder Analysis Table

Name	Organization	Objectives	Contributions	Advisors
Hawn, Sean	Pogo Products	1 Increase vertical jump 2 Decrease cost 3 Leapfrog competition	Develops specifications Approves plan and changes	Money, Penny (CFO) Hopper, Tippi (Engr)
Money, Penny	Pogo Products	1 Decrease cost 2 Improve cash flow	Approves plan Releases funds	Gotta, Pop (CEO)
Ratchet, Stan	Aerobotics, LLC	1 Increase awareness 2 Increase vertical jump	Designs springs	Hopper, Tippi Mom

Page: 1 of 1   Words: 65   100%

Figure 1-5:
When you use a table in a Word document, you can add a new row to the table by pressing Tab when you're done typing in the last cell of a row. To add an additional objective or contribution to a table cell, with the insertion point at the end of the cell text, press Enter.

Publicizing a Project and Its Manager

A project that gets the go-ahead needs publicity just like movies do. You want people to know the project is starting and why it's vital. Most important, you want the entire team to get fired up over their new assignments. The project manager needs some publicity, too. Your authority comes from your project and project sponsor, not your position in the organization, so people need to know how far your authority goes. The *project charter* is like a project's press release—it announces the project and your responsibilities and authority as its manager.

A project charter doesn't impress anyone unless it comes from someone powerful enough to grant you authority, like the project's sponsor or its customer. On the other hand, don't have the biggest kahuna distribute the charter unless that person actually knows something about the project—you need authority, but credibility is important, too.

You may have to tactfully suggest that the project's customer or sponsor develop and distribute the charter. You can often get the charter out more quickly by writing it yourself so the sponsor has only to sign and send it.

A project charter is pretty simple, as Figure 1-6 shows. (You can download a sample charter, Ch01_Project_Charter.doc, from *www.missingmanuals.com/cds.*)

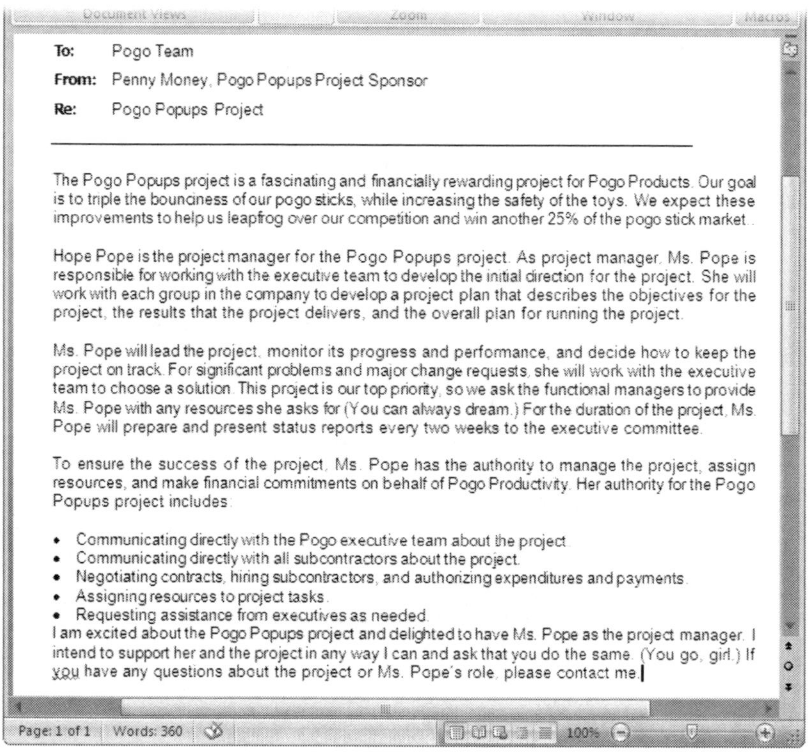

To: Pogo Team

From: Penny Money, Pogo Popups Project Sponsor

Re: Pogo Popups Project

The Pogo Popups project is a fascinating and financially rewarding project for Pogo Products. Our goal is to triple the bounciness of our pogo sticks, while increasing the safety of the toys. We expect these improvements to help us leapfrog over our competition and win another 25% of the pogo stick market.

Hope Pope is the project manager for the Pogo Popups project. As project manager, Ms. Pope is responsible for working with the executive team to develop the initial direction for the project. She will work with each group in the company to develop a project plan that describes the objectives for the project, the results that the project delivers, and the overall plan for running the project.

Ms. Pope will lead the project, monitor its progress and performance, and decide how to keep the project on track. For significant problems and major change requests, she will work with the executive team to choose a solution. This project is our top priority, so we ask the functional managers to provide Ms. Pope with any resources she asks for (You can always dream.) For the duration of the project, Ms. Pope will prepare and present status reports every two weeks to the executive committee.

To ensure the success of the project, Ms. Pope has the authority to manage the project, assign resources, and make financial commitments on behalf of Pogo Productivity. Her authority for the Pogo Popups project includes:

- Communicating directly with the Pogo executive team about the project.
- Communicating directly with all subcontractors about the project.
- Negotiating contracts, hiring subcontractors, and authorizing expenditures and payments.
- Assigning resources to project tasks.
- Requesting assistance from executives as needed.

I am excited about the Pogo Popups project and delighted to have Ms. Pope as the project manager. I intend to support her and the project in any way I can and ask that you do the same. (You go, girl.) If you have any questions about the project or Ms. Pope's role, please contact me.

Page: 1 of 1 Words: 360 100%

Figure 1-6: *Don't skimp on the distribution list for a project charter. Send a copy to anyone who participates in the project or may be affected by it. Whether you email the charter or distribute it on company letterhead depends on your corporate culture.*

Here are typical elements of a charter:

- **Project name**. A catchy name that rolls off everyone's tongue is wonderful, but a brief name that identifies the project will do.
- **Purpose**. The mission statement works well as the purpose, because it's a high-level overview of the reason for the project. If you haven't crafted a mission statement yet, simply summarize what the project is supposed to achieve.
- **Project manager**. Announce who will manage the project. If you're writing the project charter for a sponsor to sign, don't be afraid to blow your own horn. Stakeholders need to know who you are and why you're the person who's going to make sure this project is a success.

- **Project manager's duties**. Summarize the manager's responsibilities. This brief introduction to the project manager's tasks can warn people about what the project manager may expect from them—and educate people about the mysterious activities that project managers perform.

- **Project manager's authority**. Here's where the sponsor or customer sprinkles authoritative fairy dust on you. Much like a power of attorney, this section tells everyone that the sponsor or customer authorizes you to perform certain activities, like hiring contractors or dipping into the project's emergency fund.

- **The official commitment to the project**. Don't forget to include a brief bullet point that confirms in writing that the sponsor or customer supports the project and the project manager.

Now that the introductions are out of the way, it's time to start planning your project. The next chapter provides the big picture of a project plan—all the pieces that go into one and why they're important. After that, you'll learn the finer points of using Project and other programs to build and manage a project schedule.

Planning a Project

I f you're out for a leisurely drive, you can take any road and see where it takes you. But when you're heading to scary Aunt Edith's house for Sunday lunch, you'd better know where you're going. Drive as fast as you like; if you're on the wrong road, you're not going to get there on time. If you want to make Aunt Edith happy, you need to plan how and when you're going to get to her house.

You've probably worked at a few places where people think they don't have time to plan, as the box on page 43 explains. Managers breathe down your neck asking how much you've finished, while you're still wondering what you're supposed to do. You may have to do work over because no one agreed on how to do it right in the first place. Critical deadlines slip by, and the pressure to finish is even greater this time.

There's a better way. Planning ahead helps you do the right things the right way the first time around. A project plan acts as the road map to your destination. The less time, money, or resources you have, the more you need to plan. Think, for example, about those time-share presentations where a company rambles on for a few hours about the benefits of "owning the dream." Then, think about the 30-second commercial selling the same dream. Squeezing the message into a brief commercial actually requires far more planning than putting together a 2-hour sales pitch.

This chapter provides a quick introduction to project planning. You'll see what goes into a project plan. You'll also learn how to create a document for stakeholders to approve before you begin executing the project, along with tips and tricks for getting the information you need.

Project Planning in a Nutshell

Project planning is like other types of planning—you figure out what you're going to do before you do it. And like other types of plans, project plans are destined to change, because the projects they guide never happen exactly as planned. The inevitability of change shouldn't scare you off planning. What you learn during the planning process can help you keep a project on course even when changes occur.

Project planning involves two main elements: *why* you're doing the project, and *how* you're going to do it. You begin by identifying what the project is supposed to accomplish. Only then can you start planning how to achieve the project's goals.

Veteran project managers have official names for each part of a project plan, but any plan boils down to a series of questions. The rest of this chapter describes the components of a project plan in more detail, but here are the basics:

- **Why are we going to perform this project?** The answer to this question describes the point of the project. Project plans present this information in two forms. First, you identify the problem that the project is supposed to solve, which you describe in the *problem statement* (page 44). The *project mission statement* explains the importance and purpose of the project in a short but compelling sound bite, perfect for keeping people inspired and focused.

- **What are we going to achieve?** By definition, a project eventually ends. You have to know what the project is supposed to achieve so you can tell when it's done. The first step is to spell out all the goals, or *project objectives* (page 47). Projects usually have several goals, which can fall into different categories. A media campaign may have a business objective to increase a product's market share, a financial objective to stay within budget, and a performance objective to finish in time for the crucial summer sales season.

  The project plan document states these achievements in a few other forms, each of which plays a specific role. The *project scope statement* (page 50) lists what is and isn't part of the project. It delineates the boundaries of a project so stakeholders know what to expect. The scope statement also helps you rein in pressures to expand the project (*scope creep*).

  Intimately linked to project scope are *deliverables*—the tangible results the project needs to produce (page 49), and the *success criteria* you use to judge whether the deliverables are acceptable. Every section listed in the project scope statement has corresponding deliverables and success criteria, and vice versa.

- **What approach are we going to take?** The problems that projects solve usually have more than one solution. Part of project planning is figuring out which solution—or *project strategy*—is best. Then, the project plan documents the strategy you're going to use to address the problem and how you chose it.

- **What are we going to do?** Starting with this question, you describe how you're planning to perform the project. As its name implies, a *work breakdown structure* or *WBS* breaks down the work that people do on a project into manageable pieces. (This major part of the plan is the sole topic of Chapter 4.)

In addition to the work specific to achieving project objectives, projects need a few administrative processes (like managing risk, controlling changes, communicating, and managing quality, which are explained on page 52) to keep the project under control. A project plan outlines how these processes will work.

- **When will the project start and finish?** Projects have starting and ending points, so the plan documents these dates. In addition, the *project schedule* (page 156) actually shows the sequence of tasks and when each one starts and finishes.

- **Who will work on the project?** People and other resources actually do the work, so the project plan includes a *responsibility assignment matrix* and a *project organization chart* (page 176) to identify the team.

- **How much will it cost?** Blank checks are rare in any environment, so the project plan includes a budget (page 286) showing where all the money goes.

- **How good do the results need to be?** Given constraints on time, money, and resources, you usually don't have the luxury of doing a spectacularly better job than required. The project plan outlines how you intend to achieve the level of quality the project requires, and how you'll measure that quality.

Project planning is a process, not a one-time deal. You may run through the planning steps several times just to get a plan that the stakeholders approve. Then, once you begin to execute the plan, you have to rework it to accommodate the changes and glitches that appear. Figure 2-1 shows the project planning steps and the path you take the first time through.

Tip: Not every project plan requires detailed write-ups for every component described in this chapter. For example, a small project may need only a sentence or two about how you're going to communicate with your two other team members. Use your judgment to decide how much detail to include.

A project plan is the road map you use to guide a project toward completion. But it helps you in many other ways, too, from the very beginning to the end of the project. Here are some of the other benefits such a plan provides:

- **Getting buy-in.** When a project passes the selection process, you've got a commitment from the customer or project sponsor. But you need buy-in from all the other stakeholders and team members, too. Parts of the project plan, like the mission and objectives, help people understand *why* the project deserves their commitment and what's in it for them.

  Having stakeholders and team members help you develop the plan is invaluable. People tend to back away from efforts they didn't help spec out, and rightly so. In addition, without input from the trenches, your estimates of time and money could be way off, and the expectations of results impossibly high. Asking for feedback during planning makes people more willing to pull together when they're working on the project.

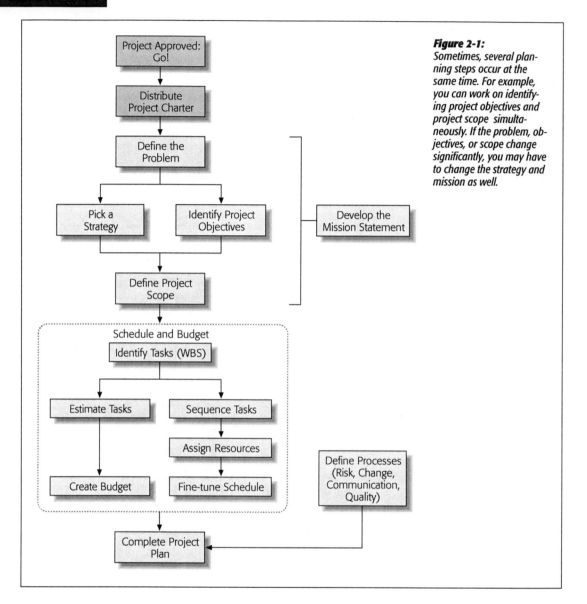

Figure 2-1:
Sometimes, several planning steps occur at the same time. For example, you can work on identifying project objectives and project scope simultaneously. If the problem, objectives, or scope change significantly, you may have to change the strategy and mission as well.

- **Focusing on the goal.** A project plan tells team members what they're supposed to do and where they're headed. In addition to communicating assignments, the plan gives people the background they need to make the right decisions as they work. This focus is good for the project, the team members, *and* the project manager—you can spend less time on day-to-day supervision, and more time proactively managing the project.

- **Tracking progress**. You can't tell how close you are to your destination if you don't know where you are or even where you're going. A project plan tells you where you're supposed to be at every point in a project so you can compare your actual progress (explained in Chapter 14) to what you estimated. If the road gets bumpy, these comparisons can help you figure out how to get back on track.

- **Improving performance**. The project plan is the baseline you compare to your actual performance (you'll learn how in Chapter 15). It helps you see where you went wrong and what went right. If you communicate how things went to everyone involved in the project, they can do better the next time. Then, archive the final performance so other project managers can benefit as well.

Note: For a project plan template, download CH02_Project_Plan.dot from *www.missingmanuals.com/cds*.

Get Enough Planning Time

A well-known cartoon shows a manager telling programmers to start coding while he finds out what the customers want. You can see disaster coming: The ill-fated programmers are about to do hundreds of hours of work that the customer will reject as useless.

With everyone on the go these days, the temptation to *do* something is hard to resist, especially when customers or executives are watching impatiently over your shoulder. But if you cave in to the pressure to skip planning, the failed project ends up on your résumé, not theirs.

To persuade customers and other stakeholders to give you time to plan, you have to speak their language. You can compare project planning to the planning activities that executives perform—preparing a strategic business plan, setting up a product launch, or planning the company's IPO.

After you wrangle planning time into the schedule, don't forget to document project performance and lessons learned when the project is complete (page 484). Publicize the reports showing how planning contributed to success and you'll have an easier time getting the planning time you need in the future.

Defining the Project

As Yogi Berra once said, "You've got to be very careful if you don't know where you're going, because you might not get there." Projects usually get the go-ahead for good reasons, but the motivation for a project may be barely sketched out when the project begins. Before you can work out the details of how you'll perform the project, you need to identify what the project is supposed to achieve.

Dr. Joseph M. Juran's definition of a project is a problem scheduled for solution, so identifying the problem to solve is usually the first step. A project mission presents the problem in a way that makes people care. Because most problems have more than one possible solution, the project strategy outlines the solution you've picked. From there, you identify all the project's goals, the results it'll deliver, and the assumptions you've made in preparing the plan.

What's the Problem?

When you start to identify the problem that needs solving, your colleagues turn into hypochondriacs, overwhelmed with symptoms and making wild guesses at the underlying problem. Just like antibiotics don't help when you have a virus, the right solution to the wrong problem is still wrong. As project manager, your job is to tease out the real problem from the project's sponsor, customer, and other stakeholders.

Most people offer solutions instead of describing the actual problem. For example, suppose your CEO says the problem is that the company doesn't have a TV commercial. You could start planning to make a TV commercial, but does that project have a point? To get to the problem, start asking "Why?" For example, why do we need a TV commercial? If the CEO says that sales are in the toilet or the competition is eating your lunch, a commercial may not be the best answer. Asking "why?" a few more times may uncover that product quality is abominable or product features are behind the times—and no amount of TV advertising will correct those problems. On the other hand, if the CEO's ego needs stroking, a TV commercial could be the perfect, albeit expensive, solution.

In a project plan, a problem statement outlines the problem to solve or the business objective to achieve—not the symptoms or a solution. Here's an example of the right way and wrong way to state the problem:

- **Right way:** Sales have dropped 40 percent in the last year, and a customer survey identifies poor quality as the primary reason. Our investors are getting nervous.
- **Wrong way:** We need a TV commercial to advertise our projects.

A problem statement shouldn't include solutions, but sometimes you have to bend the rules. Maybe your organization bet big money on a database, so your project had better use it. For situations like these, include those constraints in the problem statement, and add them to the assumptions section (page 51) for good measure. That way, when you choose a project strategy, you can be sure to take those constraints into account.

Tip: Different stakeholders often see different problems and want different results. Your job as project manager is to guide the stakeholders to agreement, however tenuous, on what the project will achieve. When you work on the problem statement, you're bound to hear a combination of solutions, objectives, and expectations. Write everything down. You may not need this info at the moment, but you will soon enough for the sections on objectives, strategies, and success criteria.

Giving Meaning to a Project

Project mission statements usually aren't as dramatic as the ones that come on self-destructing tape, but the good ones are just as likely to get your team's attention. Whereas the problem statement documents where you're starting from, a project's mission statement spells out where you want to end up—in a way that makes people want to get there. Other parts of a project plan describe the purpose and goals, but the mission statement helps obtain people's commitment and keeps them focused on the target.

The best mission statements are brief, but still motivate people. Unless you've been a speechwriter, they aren't easy to write. You have to distill the project's purpose and goals, and present them in an inspirational way. If inspiration is out of your reach, a good synopsis is the next best thing. One way to gather the critical information for a project's mission statement is by answering the following questions:

- **Who is the customer?** Mission statements identify the project's customers because they're the final arbiters of project success.

- **What is the project supposed to accomplish?** Although projects have many goals and objectives, the mission statement focuses on the project's overarching purpose, like increasing client satisfaction.

- **Why is the project important?** Here's where you describe the project's significance in the most compelling way you can. Inspiration often involves higher goals—being the best, improving people's lives, or simply turning a profit. Sometimes, projects are important because the future of the business depends on them.

- **What's the approach?** Describe the overall strategy or approach. Share an overview of how the project will look if viewed from 50,000 feet above.

Here's an example of a project mission statement:

The Servers R Us project's mission is to design a new infrastructure for the company's server farm to make it scalable and flexible, and to implement the new design so that the server farm is operational by August 2010 to support the new development work planned for the fall.

Because it has to encompass the problem, strategy, *and* objectives in a nutshell, crafting a mission statement usually takes a while. You can add bits and pieces to the statement or simply keep notes about what you want to include. Once you have the strategy and objectives defined, it's time to draft the statement. Some project managers prepare a rough draft and then invite the stakeholders to a meeting to fine-tune it. Braver project managers hold brainstorming meetings with stakeholders to answer the key mission statement questions, and then retire to a quiet place to craft the message.

Tip: Publicize the mission statement by printing it on small cards, certificates, or posters that you can hang around the office. If you have a fabulously concise mission statement, include it in document headers, footers, or cover pages.

How Will You Solve the Problem?

Every project solves a problem, but most problems have more than one right answer. Part of planning a project is like taking a multiple-choice test that asks you to choose the best possible answer from all your options. You want the solution that does the best job of achieving the project's mission and satisfying its objectives. You can work on identifying objectives and study strategies at the same time. When the objectives gel, the stakeholders can evaluate the strategies and make their choice.

Remember those solutions people tried to pass off as the project's problem? Now that you know the *actual* problem the project is supposed to solve, you can ask stakeholders about potential solutions or review the solutions they gave you earlier. Brainstorming with stakeholders is a good way to start evaluating strategies. The back and forth between different stakeholders can also help you distinguish between must-have and nice-to-have objectives.

These discussions can also give you insight into which strategies are likely to work for your stakeholders (or not). A winning strategy satisfies the must-have objectives and most of the nice-to-have objectives (page 47). A strategy also has to pass a few additional tests to be a success. Here are a few questions to ask while evaluating project strategies:

- **Is it feasible?** If the strategy won't work, the project won't either. If you're considering an untested or rarely used solution, a feasibility study looks at whether the solution will work before you commit the entire project to it.

- **Are the risks acceptable?** Part of a project plan is risk analysis (page 54). Project *risk management* analyzes the hazards in the selected strategy and the plan that goes with it to minimize the chance of failure. Before you choose a strategy, you need to perform a mini risk analysis to eliminate the "We'd be crazy to do that" solutions.

- **Does the strategy fit the culture?** Cultural factors are touchy-feely, but they're also almost impossible to overcome. For example, if your company emphasizes its connection with its customers, an outsourcing solution isn't likely to work. Strategies that run counter to the corporate culture aren't completely out of the question, but if you pick one, you'll need to spend extra time getting—and keeping—commitment from the stakeholders.

Choosing a project strategy isn't an exact process because you have to estimate the potential results for each option. Besides, some project objectives are simply hard to quantify. A *decision matrix* pits project objectives against project strategies. As you can see in Figure 2-2, you can evaluate strategies as quantitatively or qualitatively as you like.

Tip: Consider placing the must-have project objectives at the top of the decision matrix and nice-to-have objectives below. If a strategy doesn't satisfy the must-have objectives, then don't bother rating the other objectives. Or, you can begin evaluating strategies by their must-have performance. Then, when you've shortened the list, you can evaluate the full list of objectives.

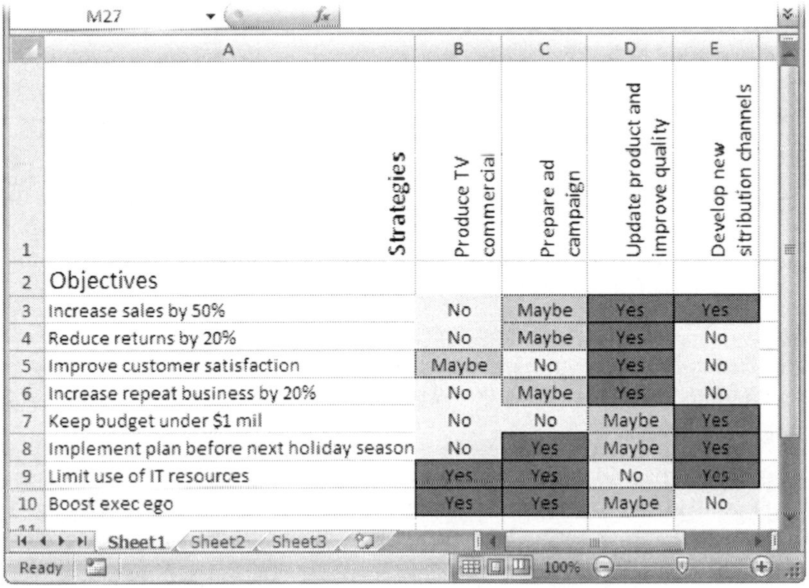

	Strategies	Produce TV commercial	Prepare ad campaign	Update product and improve quality	Develop new distribution channels
2	Objectives				
3	Increase sales by 50%	No	Maybe	Yes	Yes
4	Reduce returns by 20%	No	Maybe	Yes	No
5	Improve customer satisfaction	Maybe	No	Yes	No
6	Increase repeat business by 20%	No	Maybe	Yes	No
7	Keep budget under $1 mil	No	No	Maybe	Yes
8	Implement plan before next holiday season	No	Yes	Maybe	Yes
9	Limit use of IT resources	Yes	Yes	No	Yes
10	Boost exec ego	Yes	Yes	Maybe	No

Figure 2-2: *One way to highlight passing or failing grades in Excel is with conditional formatting, which applies different formatting depending on which condition a cell meets. For example, if you rate strategies with values like Yes, No, and Maybe, you can shade cells based on their values. Download the Excel 2007 workbook, "Ch02_DecisionMatrix.xlsx," complete with sample conditional formatting, from* http://www.missingmanuals.com/cds.

Defining Project Objectives

People often don't know what they want, have trouble putting what they want into words, or simply want everything they see (after all, everyone was once a 3-year-old at an ice cream shop). To make matters worse, different people want different things. Identifying project objectives and getting everyone to agree on them is hard work, as the box on page 48 explains. Regrettably, if you try to shortcut this step, your stakeholders will be quick to tell you if they get something they *don't* want.

Even if its purpose fits in a few short sentences, a project can have all kinds of objectives. The main objective might be to increase market share, but Sales wants the project completed by the end of summer so they can get holiday orders. Project objectives fall into one (or more) of the following categories:

- **Business.** These objectives relate to business strategies and tactics. Whether your executives fixate on increasing sales or extending product life, business objectives are usually the initial impetus for a project.
- **Financial.** These are usually distinct from business objectives but closely related. Financial objectives can apply to the entire business or just the project. A project's business objective may be achieving a 10 percent profit margin on sales, while its financial objective might be delivering an 8 percent return on investment.

- **Regulatory.** Many projects have to conform to regulations, and they all have to obey the law. For example, a project to automate electronic distribution of investment info has to follow SEC guidelines.

- **Performance.** Schedule and budget quickly come to mind when you think of performance objectives—finishing before a crucial deadline or keeping costs low to earn a performance bonus, for example. Meeting requirements and matching specifications are other types of performance objectives.

- **Technical.** These objectives may be the type and amount of technology that a solution uses. For example, an emergency broadcast system requires equipment with highly dependable and redundant systems. Or a project may have internal technical requirements like using software that the company already owns.

- **Quality.** When you talk about decreasing the number of errors or increasing customer survey ratings, you're identifying quality objectives—how good results must be. These objectives also give the project quality plan (page 54) targets to shoot for.

You also have to prioritize objectives because a project is a balance between scope, time, cost, and quality. You're almost guaranteed to find that you can't achieve all the objectives with the time and budget you're given. By prioritizing objectives, you can figure out the best ones to eliminate—or at least scale back. Suppose you're helping plan your daughter and future son-in-law's wedding. You all set objectives for the flowers, the caterer, and the number of people you'd like to invite. Then, when you come to after seeing the price tag, you may see that orchids on every table aren't as important as inviting your loving relatives. An overabundance of objectives dooms projects to failure. If you can't reduce the number of objectives on your own, work with stakeholders to choose the ones to eliminate.

FREQUENTLY ASKED QUESTION

Well-Defined Objectives

How can I tell whether objectives will help me successfully complete a project?

Vague objectives are the main source of difficulty obtaining approval when a project plan is complete. You need solid objectives to build a project plan and complete a project to everyone's satisfaction. Here are the characteristics of well-defined objectives:

- **Realistic**. What's the point of setting an objective that no one can reach? Set attainable goals. Challenging objectives are OK, but people stop trying when goals are too far out of reach.

- **Clear**. If you've ever worked with someone who does exactly what you say, you know how hard it is to clearly specify what you want. For example, saying

you want "an attention-grabbing TV commercial that'll increase market share" could translate into a guy with a loud voice (and plaid jacket to match) selling your product at half the price of your competitors. It'll increase market share...and decimate your profits.

- **Measurable or verifiable**. Make objectives as measurable or provable as you can. For example, how do you measure whether a training class is effective? When you use subjective goals, be sure to define how you'll know whether you've succeeded. For example, you may decide that an average evaluation score of 8 means the class will improve productivity when the trainees get back to the office.

Identifying Project Results

Deliverables are the tangible results that a project produces—like a software program you can install, a bridge you can drive across, or the incriminating pictures you were hired to shoot. Projects churn out a major deliverable at the end, but smaller deliverables surface throughout the projects' lifetimes—like blueprints for a bridge, the fabricated steel girders that support it, and even the project plan itself.

Each major deliverable represents a component of the project, which, in turn, appears as a bullet point in the project scope (page 50). If you find an item in the project scope that doesn't correspond to a deliverable, you've either missed a deliverable or you need to move that item to the "Out of scope" column.

Because deliverables don't appear out of thin air, you need tasks to produce them. You can use the list of deliverables you develop to double-check that you've identified all the tasks in the work breakdown structure (page 77). Although documentation is a deliverable that people tend to overlook, government projects (to name one example) are known for significant documentation deliverables that are also contractual requirements. If documentation is a deliverable, be sure to include tasks to produce it.

Note: The purpose of a project, its scope, and its deliverables provide a high-level view of what the project is supposed to accomplish. These components of the project plan often come packaged as a document called the *statement of work*, a project synopsis that's perfect for including in legal contracts.

Interim deliverables that appear during the course of a project don't always go to the project's customer. For instance, an engineering company may produce a list of building code requirements that apply to the building, but the building owner doesn't need to see them. However, the owner probably wants copies of the permits and county inspection reports.

Interim deliverables are great for keeping everyone on course. Team members use them as short-term targets to shoot for. And you can use deliverables as milestones in your project schedule to gauge the project's progress.

Gauging Success

There's nothing quite as disheartening as reaching the end of a project only to find out that some people think you aren't done yet. The best way to prevent such disappointment is to clearly define what constitutes success during project planning. As you document objectives and deliverables, be sure to specify how you're going to determine whether they've been achieved. For example, software acceptance could hinge on successfully completing several test transactions, eliminating all critical and serious bugs, or completing test transactions in a timed test.

Figure 2-3 shows a worksheet that compares objectives, deliverables, and success criteria to ensure that you can obtain acceptance of each deliverable and the entire project.

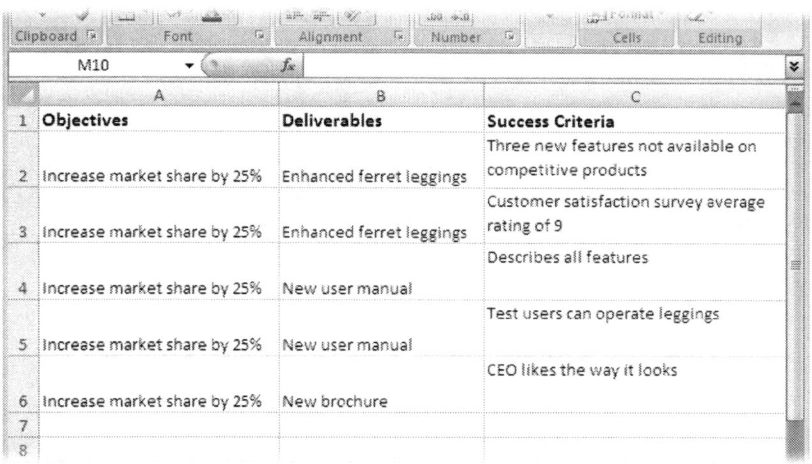

	A	B	C
1	Objectives	Deliverables	Success Criteria
2	Increase market share by 25%	Enhanced ferret leggings	Three new features not available on competitive products
3	Increase market share by 25%	Enhanced ferret leggings	Customer satisfaction survey average rating of 9
4	Increase market share by 25%	New user manual	Describes all features
5	Increase market share by 25%	New user manual	Test users can operate leggings
6	Increase market share by 25%	New brochure	CEO likes the way it looks
7			
8			

Figure 2-3: *This Excel workbook duplicates some entries, because one objective may require several deliverables, whereas one deliverable can apply to more than one objective. In the project plan, you identify objectives, deliverables, and success criteria separately.*

Being specific about success criteria is crucial and requires persistence. You have to make sure that you clearly define every aspect of your criteria. For instance, if acceptance depends on eliminating critical bugs, you also need to carefully define what you mean by "critical bug."

Defining Project Boundaries

Project scope is the delineation of what a project includes and what it doesn't. For example, a remodeling contractor may include all the construction tasks in scope, but declare out of scope the task of picking up your kids' clothes so he can lay carpet. A *scope statement* describes a project's boundaries.

Project scope can derive from the project objectives, deliverables, requirements, and specifications. And, you can play these components off each other to ensure that you've clearly defined the scope.

Like an inexorably spreading waistline, *scope creep* is a dreaded scourge for projects. Without a well-defined scope statement, you're likely to find requests nibbling away at your project's limited budget and time. When you document project scope clearly, you can identify items that are out of scope and fire up your change management process (page 434) to estimate the effects of adding changes to the budget and schedule. Then, the customer can decide whether the request is worth the price or should be added to a follow-up project.

Documenting Project Assumptions

You've probably heard that the word "assume" makes an *ass* out of *u* and *me*. While all clichés have a grain of truth, assumptions are dangerous only when people make them without telling anyone else. A customer might assume that some work is part of the project's scope even though it doesn't appear in the scope statement. Or, you may assume that people from the customer team will turn their reviews around in one week. As you plan a project, you can uncover hidden assumptions by continually asking about what people expect. Then, add the assumptions you find to the project plan.

Assumptions can affect every part of your project plan. Sometimes, they clarify the meaning of project's objectives or end up as items in the scope statement. They can also crop up as expectations about resources, how processes run, or who's responsible for what.

Documenting How You'll Run the Project

Scheduling and budgeting a project takes a lot of time and effort, but the results of that work take up little space in the project plan. You don't have to document *all* the planning that goes into building a schedule and budget, just the end results. This section gives you an overview of project documentation. Other chapters in this book explain in detail how to develop the work breakdown structure, project team, schedule, and budget.

Here's a quick introduction to the sections of a project plan that make up the *project implementation plan*, which maps out how you expect to perform the project:

- **Identifying the work to do**. A *work breakdown structure* or WBS (page 77) breaks up work into small tasks that you then put into sequence and assign resources to when you build your schedule. The lowest level tasks are called *work packages* because they contain the work that people have to perform. All the higher-level tasks merely summarize groups of lower-level tasks. Chapter 4 focuses on building a WBS and getting it into Microsoft Project.

- **Laying out the project's schedule**. With the WBS complete, you can estimate the effort and duration for each task, and then put them into the sequence in which they need to happen. The result is a schedule that approximates how long the project will take and when tasks should start and finish. Chapter 5 talks about estimating task effort and duration; Chapter 6 explains how to turn a WBS into a schedule.

  As you manage the project, its schedule tells you how far you've come and whether the project is still on track to finish on time. In Project, you can compare your original schedule with what's actually happening (page 409) to see where you may have to make adjustments.

- **Building a project team**. You can estimate work hours and duration all you want, but you won't really know what the schedule looks like until you know how many resources work on tasks, and when those resources are available. Building a project team begins with identifying the skill sets you need for tasks and other resources such as equipment and materials. You can assign these generic resources to tasks to get an idea of the schedule. Once you know who's working on your project, you can replace the generic resources with people's names, and finally identify when tasks start and finish. Chapter 8 explains how to put a project team together and add the team to your Project file; Chapter 9 shows how you assign resources to tasks.

- **Setting the project's budget**. Whether the customer has a set amount of money to spend or your company executives require a minimum return on investment (page 30), money matters. The cost of a project is a combination of labor costs, equipment and material costs, and other expenses like travel or training. As you assign resources to tasks in Project, you can see how all these costs add up. (Chapter 8 explains how to assign costs to different types of resources.) Then, you can use these costs to calculate the project's budget and cash flow. Chapter 1 explains some of the financial measures used to evaluate projects, and Chapter 11 describes how to use Project's budgeting features and Excel workbooks to build budgets.

Laying Out Project Processes

As you manage a project, some activities keep running for as long as the project does. For example, you have to keep an eye on changes that people ask for, and run them through a change management process to prevent scope creep. A change management process includes steps for requesting changes, deciding whether to include changes in the project, and tracking the changes. Similarly, risk management, communication, and quality management run until the project is complete. Defining these processes has to occur while you're still planning the project or your team will mill about like sheep without a border collie. This section introduces the four processes you define and document in the project plan.

Tip: How you approach change management, risk management, and other processes depends on your project. Small projects can survive with relatively informal procedures, whereas large, global projects require more rigor. Moreover, corporate culture has an effect on how team members view the processes you define.

Communicating

As a project manager, you already know that most of your job is communicating with people. But everyone else working on a project communicates, too. A *communication plan* describes the rules for sharing information on a project, like whether people should email status updates, post them on a website, or scratch them into banana leaves. Chapter 27 talks about ways to communicate, but you can document the options you choose in the communication plan section of the project plan. A communication plan answers the following questions:

- **Who needs to know?** For instance, who should receive the list of pending change requests?

- **What do they need to know?** The change control board may receive the full documentation of change requests, whereas a team leader receives only info about the associated work tasks and when the work is due.

- **When do they need to know it?** Do status reports come out every week, every other week, or once a month? And do they come out on Friday or a different weekday?

- **How should they receive it?** The methods for distributing information depend on what your organization has available, as well as how people like to communicate. Some organizations place more weight on paper documents, while others prefer the convenience of email or collaboration websites.

Managing Change

When you plan a project, you define its scope, the deliverables it'll produce, and the objectives it will achieve. Inevitably, when the project starts, someone remembers something they need, and someone else finds a better way to tackle a problem. These changes can dramatically affect the plan you so carefully prepared, so you need to evaluate requested changes to decide whether they belong in the project. If they do, then you adjust the project plan accordingly.

A *change management plan* describes how you handle change requests: how people submit them, who reviews them, the steps for approving them, and how you incorporate them into your plan. (It doesn't describe how you manage the extra work that those change requests entail.) For modest projects, an Excel workbook and email may be enough to handle change management activities. But most projects need a *change control board*—a group of people who decide the fate of change requests. Chapter 16 gets into the nitty-gritty of managing changes, but here are the basic activities involved in managing change:

- Submit change requests
- Receive and record change requests
- Evaluate the effects of change requests on cost, schedule, and quality
- Decide whether change requests become part of the project
- Update project documents to incorporate accepted changes
- Track changes as you do other project task work

Managing Quality

Most projects have objectives that relate to quality, whether you need to reduce bugs in software to a specific level, attain satisfaction ratings from customers, or hit a particular decibel level of audience applause. A *quality management plan* starts with a project's quality objectives. Then, for each objective, you define how you plan to achieve those quality levels, which is called quality assurance. Finally, you describe how you plan to monitor and measure quality performance, which is called quality control.

Managing Risk

Things can and will go wrong on your projects. It's easier and faster to recover from troublesome events if you anticipate them and have a plan for how to respond. Risk management starts with identifying what could go wrong. Then, you analyze those risks and decide what you'll do if they actually happen. As the project progresses, you monitor risks to see whether they're getting more threatening or going away. Finally, if a risk does become reality, you launch your counter-attack and monitor the results. This section introduces the different aspects of risk management.

Note: This section is merely an introduction to the robust field of risk management. If you want to learn more, consider reading *Project and Program Risk Management: A Guide to Managing Project Risks and Opportunities* by R. Max Wideman (PMI) or *Risk Management, Tricks of the Trade for Project Managers* by Rita Mulcahy (RMC Publications).

Identifying risks

A *risk management plan* begins with what could go wrong. For example, materials could get lost in transit, a key resource might be unavailable, or price hikes could put the project's budget in jeopardy. For the hopelessly optimistic, identifying risks can be difficult. Here are some questions that can help you uncover potential problems:

- **Are there uncertainties in the plan?** If you don't know whether you'll get a key resource or what time the last bus leaves for home, you have more risk of things going awry. Similarly, the risk to success is high if you don't have a good idea of what the project is supposed to do or have little contact with key stakeholders. Scrutinize your project for anything that isn't clearly spelled out.

- **Are your choices limited?** A single person with critical skills or a single vendor for key ingredients increases the risk of something going wrong. When you don't have many options, it's more difficult to find alternatives to recover from a problem.

- **Are constraints significant?** Tight budgets, fixed finish dates, or limited resources give you little leeway when things go wrong.

- **What level of experience do people have?** Whether one or two resources are new to what you're doing or the project is breaking new ground, lack of experience spells risk.

- **Does the project depend on factors out of your control?** Weather and politics are just a couple of factors that can affect projects. Because you can't control them, you have to work harder to plan for a workaround.

Assessing risks

Projects can face an overwhelming number of risks. If you try to manage them all, you may not have time for anything else. The good news is you can put aside risks that have little impact on your project or are highly unlikely. You make this distinction by drawing an imaginary line based on a combination of impact and probability called *risk value*.

For example, low probability and minimal impact probably means you can ignore the risk and accept the consequences. Why spend time planning a response to something that isn't likely to happen and won't hurt much even if it does? On the other hand, high probability and high impact is a combination you can't afford to ignore. You can decide what other combinations of probability and impact to include in your risk assessments.

You don't have to quantify impact as dollars or time, nor do you have to calculate probabilities to one tenth of one percent. For risk assessment, *high, medium*, and *low* are often enough. However, estimates of dollars and time can help you figure out how much to spend responding to a risk. The workbook in Figure 2-4 places risks on a graph to visually show the risks you want to manage.

Planning risk response

For each risk you intend to manage, you need to decide what you're going to do if it happens. The best responses prevent a risk from occurring in the first place. However, that's not always possible, so here are other ways to respond to risks:

- **Accept**. If the risk won't cause noticeable damage, you can just accept the consequences. For example, you can forego putting money in a parking meter if you don't mind paying $20 if you get caught.

- **Avoid**. Avoidance is one way to handle a risk if the risk doesn't affect the project's ability to achieve its objectives. For instance, if you have two ways to get home and one of them is a narrow, windy road with no guardrails, take the highway.

- **Control the pain**. The formal name for this approach is *risk mitigation*: You take action to reduce the consequences if you can't completely eliminate them. For example, insurance companies share humongous risks with each other. They all accept some of the cost if a big claim comes in, but none of them go bankrupt.

- **Give the risk to someone else.** Transferring risk means that you let someone else take on the risk—but you pay a price. For example, you pay homeowners and auto insurance premiums so that the insurance company covers the cost if something happens. Fixed-price bids are another example of risk transfer; you pay a bit more than you would for time and materials, but the vendor handles the risk if the task takes longer or costs more.

- **Give yourself options.** Contingency plans are another option. They typically make use of funds set aside (called *contingency funds*) to handle the additional cost, as described in the box on page 57.

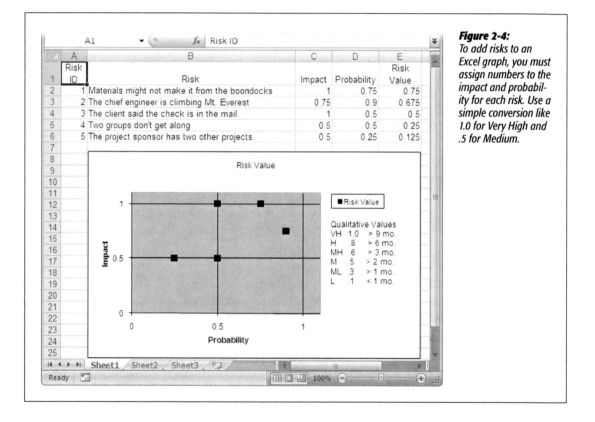

Figure 2-4:
To add risks to an Excel graph, you must assign numbers to the impact and probability for each risk. Use a simple conversion like 1.0 for Very High and .5 for Medium.

Tip: Specify how you plan to measure the success of a response. For instance, the cost or the schedule variance can show you whether the response is keeping the project's schedule and budget where they should be.

Tracking risks

Risk is at its highest in the beginning of a project when you have the least certainty about what will happen and the most time for things to go wrong. Fortunately, the amount of risk you face decreases as the project progresses. Risk management includes tracking risks that have occurred and keeping an eye on those that are still potential problems.

A *risk log* documents the status of each risk you've decided to manage. For risks you monitor, include a summary of the risk and your planned response. Also identify the person who's monitoring each risk. You have to stay on top of risks and update the log regularly. For example, when you monitor the success of your response, update the risk log with the results.

TOOLS OF THE TRADE

Saved by Contingency Funds

Risks you identify are called *known unknowns* because you know they may occur but you don't know if they will. For example, bad weather is a given during the winter, but you don't know when the snowstorms are going to hit. Unfortunately, there are also *unknown unknowns*—risks you don't even know you should worry about. For example, if you don't buy into extraterrestrial intelligence, you won't anticipate the resource crisis when people-eating aliens arrive.

Organizations often set aside contingency funds to spend if known risks occur. One problem is figuring out how much money you need. People often use a percentage of the project's budget to choose the level of contingency funds. You can start with 15 percent. Then, as you gain experience with projects, you can use the performance of past projects to set a level. If the project uses only internal resources, you can set aside time that you can allocate to deal with any unknown unknowns that arise.

Project managers usually have the authority to spend some amount of the contingency fund without asking permission. However, when you exceed that limit, you need to go to management or other stakeholders with hat in hand to ask for more money.

Management reserve is another bucket of money that stakeholders set aside to deal with risks they don't expect. It's usually a fixed percentage of the project's budget. Besides using it to deal with risks, management can apply reserve money, at its discretion, to a project to cover change requests.

CHAPTER 3

Taking Microsoft Project for a Test Drive

Learning how to manage projects while learning to use Project at the same time is too much for most mortals. So this chapter lets you take Project out for a test drive, with a simple map to guide you on your trip. Because Project 2010 has switched from the menu bar to the ribbon, the journey begins with an exploration of Project's ribbon tabs. Then you'll wander through the panes that appear in the Project window. At that point, you're ready to start working on a project.

If this were a real project, you'd start by defining project objectives, listing assumptions, choosing strategies, identifying risks, building project teams, carving out budgets, and so on, as described in the first two chapters. This chapter uses a fictitious project, called the "It's About Time Graduation Party" for the 40-year-old college graduate in your family, to take you through Project's main features and give you the satisfaction of creating a working schedule.

Navigating the Project Ribbon

The Project ribbon is like a cyber-border collie, herding related features onto tabs to make them easier to find. As you plan and manage a project, you shift your focus from tasks to the resources who work on them to the big picture of the entire project, so the Task tab, Resource tab, and Project tab make perfect sense. As it turns out, a few other tabs come in handy for working with your Project files and looking at your project in different ways. This section steps through the six tabs that appear when you launch Project 2010 for the first time. (See page 660 to learn how to add other tabs to the ribbon or to create your own custom tabs.)

Managing Files in the Backstage View

The File menu from earlier Project versions is now the File tab on the ribbon. You can call it the File tab, but Microsoft refers to the page that the File tab opens as the *Backstage view*. When you click a command on the left side of the Backstage view, it takes over the entire Project window, as you can see in Figure 3-1. For example, when you click New, the Backstage view presents a plethora of ways to create a new file (page 123).

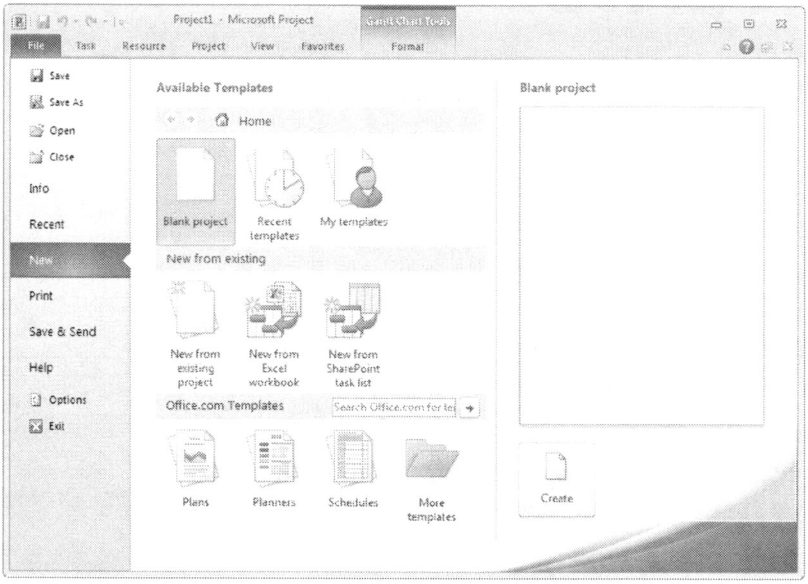

Figure 3-1:
The ribbon tabs appear near the top of the Project window. Select the File tab and the Backstage view takes over. Select any other tab and you see the ribbon across the top of the window while a Project view fills in the rest. If you want to see only the ribbon tabs until you need a command, right-click the ribbon and then choose "Minimize the Ribbon". The tabs remain visible at all times. When you select a tab, the ribbon reappears until you choose a command.

A few commands in the Backstage view need no explanation: Save, Save As, Open, Close, and Exit. Their familiar icons tell you they do what they've always done. When you click Save, Project saves the active Project file. Click Save As, and the Save As dialog box appears. You get the idea.

The other entries on the Backstage menu do more. You'll learn about them in other chapters of the book, but here's a quick intro:

- **Info.** Information about the active Project file, such as its start and finish date, appears on the right side of this page. Click Project Information and choose Project Statistics to see scheduled, baseline, and actual values. This page also includes an Organizer button, so you can copy project elements between files (page 668). If you use Project Server, you can access Project Server accounts from this page.

- **Recent.** The Recent page is a list of all the projects you've opened recently. If you open a lot of Project files—say, as you write a book about Project—this is the quickest way to reopen a file. On the other hand, if you work on one or two projects for months at a time, you can pin a project to the top of the Recent Projects list by clicking the pushpin icon to the right of the filename.

Tip: For even easier access, you can display one or more projects on the Backstage menu itself. At the bottom of the Recent Projects list, turn on the "Quickly access this number of Recent Projects" checkbox and type the number you want. Project displays that number of recent projects above the Info command, starting with any projects pinned to the Recent Projects list. Click the filename to open the Project file.

- **New.** This page offers several ways to create a new file (page 124), including starting from scratch with a blank project, using a template, or creating a file from an existing project, an Excel workbook, or a SharePoint task list.

- **Print.** The Print page looks like a spiffed-up version of the familiar Print dialog box. This one page lets you select a printer, specify print settings like paper orientation, and choose page setup settings like margins (page 477). If you rarely touch any of those settings, you can simply choose the number of copies and click the big Print button at the top of the page. If you don't have one of those widescreen monitors, the Print page leaves little room for a preview of what you're printing (page 456) and you can't shrink the print options area. See page 456 to learn how to work around this limitation.

- **Save & Send.** As its name implies, this page offers features for saving and sending Project files. The Save & Send section helps you send your Project file as an email attachment (page 568), synchronize your file with a SharePoint Task List (page 534), or save the Project file to a SharePoint site (page 541). If you subscribe to Project Online (an online service that works with Project Server and SharePoint), you can also share your file to Project Online.

Note: Choosing Save Project as File is an alternative to choosing Save As on the menu in the Backstage view. The page displays several common file formats, such as Project, Project 2007, Project 2000-2003, Project Template, Microsoft Excel Workbooks, and XML Format.

- **Help.** It's no surprise that the first command on this page opens Project's Help window, but you can also find other help resources, contact information for Microsoft, and other links.

- **Options.** Choose Options to open the Project Options dialog box and specify options to tell the program how you'd like it to behave.

Tip: The Quick Access toolbar sits above the File and Task tabs and looks like one of the toolbars from earlier versions of Project. Out of the box, it has icons for all-time favorite commands: Save, Undo, and Redo. But you can customize the Quick Access toolbar with your favorites. (See page 665 to learn how.)

A Tour of the Other Ribbon Tabs

Project management's focus on projects, tasks, and resources is a natural fit for tabs on the ribbon. This section introduces you to the rest of the tabs on the Project ribbon. You'll learn about each one in detail throughout this book.

- The **Task tab** is home to commands for creating tasks (subtasks, summary tasks, and milestones), rearranging them in the outline, and linking tasks to one another. The first section on this tab lets you choose popular task-oriented views like the Gantt Chart. You can also use this tab to format tasks, copy and paste them, or look at their details. This tab also has the incredibly useful Scroll to Task command, which scrolls the view timescale (page 63) until the selected task's task bar is visible. During project execution, you can use commands on this tab to move tasks to new dates, update task progress, or investigate scheduling issues.

- The **Resource tab** has a section for choosing popular resource-oriented views, like the Resource Sheet or the Team Planner (page 213). Whether you're adding resources to a project, assigning them to tasks, or leveling them to remove overallocations, this is the tab you want. This tab also contains commands for setting up, refreshing, and updating a resource pool (page 500). If you use Project Server, this tab has the commands for accessing the Enterprise Resource Pool and substituting resources.

- The **Project tab** is a catch-all for project-oriented commands. It contains commands for viewing project information, defining work calendars, setting project baselines, inserting subprojects, creating links between projects, running reports, and so on. This is also the tab to select if you want to work on custom fields or your WBS code. In addition, you can also find commands to recalculate your project schedule, update project-wide status, or compare two Project files.

- The **View tab** starts with buttons for the most popular task and resource views, but you can also access the More Views dialog box to choose any view you want. This tab has commands for controlling what information you see in a view: how many levels in the outline; the table applied; highlighting; how the list is filtered, grouped, or sorted; and the time periods used in the timescale. You can turn the Timeline view and the Details pane on and off and choose the view that appears in the Details pane (page 64). You can also switch between windows and arrange windows from this tab. The only command that doesn't seem to fit is in the last section: You choose Macros to run macros.

- The **Format tab** is a chameleon that offers different formatting commands depending on the view that's active. For example, when the Gantt Chart view is applied, the Format tab lets you insert columns in the table, format task bars and text styles, display elements like summary tasks or critical tasks, and so on. When you switch to the Timeline view, the Format tab lets you add tasks to the timeline and format them. For the Resource Usage view, the Format tab has checkboxes for which fields you want to see in the time-phased data grid.

The Project Window

Below the ribbon, most of the Project window is taken up with a view like the Gantt Chart, the Timeline, or the Resource Sheet. Some views, like the Resource Sheet, are like a giant table, but most views have a left and right side. For views like the Gantt Chart and Task Usage, the left side of the view is a table with field values in the columns, as shown in Figure 3-2. The rows show tasks, resources, or assignments. The right side is called the *timescale* and shows values by time period. In a Gantt Chart view, task bars in the timescale show when tasks begin and end. The Task Usage view uses a time-phased table instead, in which the columns represent time periods.

All Cells box

Quick Access toolbar

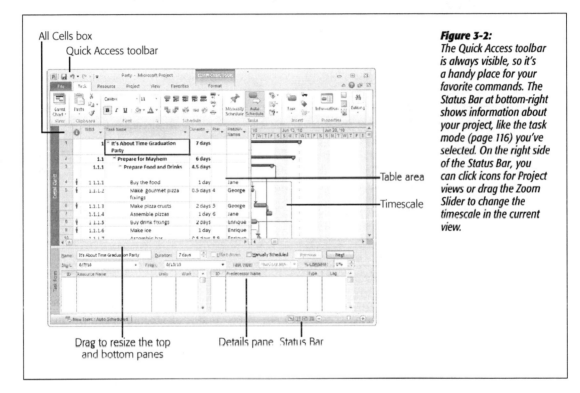

Table area

Timescale

Drag to resize the top and bottom panes

Details pane Status Bar

Figure 3-2:
The Quick Access toolbar is always visible, so it's a handy place for your favorite commands. The Status Bar at bottom-right shows information about your project, like the task mode (page 116) you've selected. On the right side of the Status Bar, you can click icons for Project views or drag the Zoom Slider to change the timescale in the current view.

If you look closely at Figure 3-2, you'll notice another pane at the bottom of the window, which is called the Details pane. In Project, combination views actually contain two single-pane views: one on top and one in the Details pane. For example, the Task Entry view displays the Tracking Gantt view on top and the Task Form on the bottom. The box on page 64 explains how to apply views and switch between one and two panes.

In many cases, the view is fine, but you want to see a different table. You can quickly apply another table using the All Cells box (to the left of the table's column headings and immediately above the first ID cell). If you *click* the All Cells box, Project selects all the cells in the table (hence the cell's name). However, if you right-click it, you can choose a table from the shortcut menu that appears. If the table you want isn't on the menu, choose More Tables. Then, in the More Tables dialog box, double-click the table.

Note: The actions you can perform depend on which view pane is active. If you select a new view, Project replaces the active pane. Project identifies the active pane by darkening the narrow vertical bar to the left of the pane and lightening the vertical bar in the other pane.

One Pane or Two?

While views are set up to include one or two panes, you can change the number of visible panes at any time. For example, if a combination view like Task Entry is in place (Gantt Chart on top and Task Form on the bottom), you can hide the second pane to concentrate on task dependencies in the Gantt Chart or restore the second pane to edit tasks. When two panes are visible and you apply a single-pane view, Project applies the view to the active pane and keeps the other pane as it is.

In Project 2010, you can hide or show the Details pane (the bottom pane) by choosing View→Split View and then turning the Details checkbox on or off. When you turn the checkbox on, in the drop-down list, choose the view you want to see in the Details pane. Less obvious controls are available to hide and show panes. If two panes are visible, you can hide the second pane by double-clicking the horizontal divider between the two panes, shown in Figure 3-2. On the other hand, to bring the second pane back, you can double-click the box immediately below the vertical scroll bar.

Creating a Project Schedule

Building a project schedule might seem as intimidating and interminable as constructing the Great Wall of China. But if you build your schedule stone by stone (or task by task), you'll be done before you know it.

Tip: If you're already a Project maven, you may have a favorite approach to building a schedule. In that case, consider following this test drive anyway—you may just learn some new Project tips and tricks.

For just about any kind of project, you can start constructing a schedule by asking yourself the following questions:

- What work must be done to achieve the project's objectives?
- What tangible results must your project produce—and when?
- How does each task depend upon the completion of other tasks?
- Who's going to do the work?
- How long do they have to get it done?

The first two chapters of this book talk about how to ask and answer these questions as you build a plan for your project. You'll use the answers to these questions as you wend your way through the process of creating a schedule in Project.

What Work Must Be Done?

The foundation for any schedule is the work that will achieve the project's objectives and deliver the desired results. Before you can do anything else, you need a list of the tasks to perform, from beginning the project to sweeping up the confetti at the end. This section describes how to build a list of individual tasks.

Note: If you're not ready to jump in and create a schedule on your own, you can download the sample project (GraduationParty_CompleteProject.mpp) from *www.missingmanuals.com/cds*. As you follow along in the chapter, you can add new tasks to this schedule and modify its tasks and resources.

Listing project tasks

In this test drive, you'll create the steps for part of the project schedule—preparing the food and drinks for the party. For extra practice, you can try filling out the rest of the schedule on your own.

1. **Start Project by choosing Start→All Programs→Microsoft Office→Microsoft Project 2010.**

   Project opens a blank project, called something like Project1.

2. **To change your project's start date, choose Project→Properties→Project Information.**

   Remember, the shorthand in the instructions means you select the Project tab, go to the Properties section on that tab, and then click the Project Information button.

3. **In the Start Date box, select the starting date, and then click OK to close the dialog box.**

   Chances are your project doesn't start the same day you build your project schedule, so change the project's start date to when you expect work to begin. Setting an accurate start date is important, since Project schedules new tasks to start as soon as possible—initially, the project start date.

   The Project Information dialog box, shown in Figure 3-3, also provides opportunities for specifying your project calendar, working time, and so on. For this test project, as for many other projects, the settings are fine as is. (You'll learn all about the Project Information dialog box in Chapter 6.)

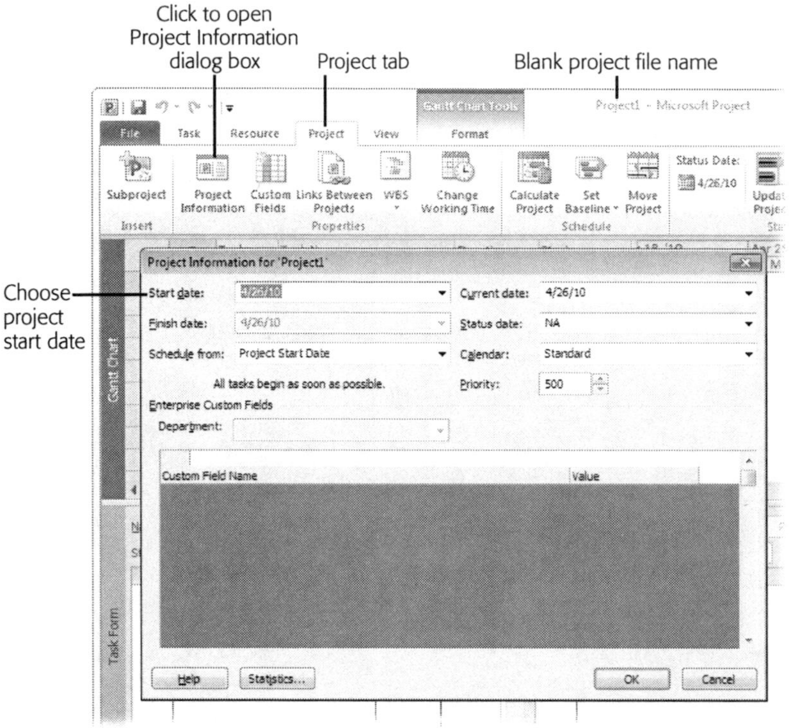

Figure 3-3:
As you can see, you don't step through the ribbon tabs in sequence. When Project launches, it opens to the Task tab. If you're ready to start a new project, you select the Project tab so you can specify the project start date before you create any tasks. However, if you want to open an existing project, choose the File tab.

4. **Add your project's first task: In the first row of the Task Name column, type** *Buy the food* **and then press Enter.**

   For the moment, the task name is the only cell you must fill in. Because Project initially creates new tasks as manually scheduled, it leaves the duration for your first task blank. The icon in the Task Mode cell (a pushpin with a question mark) indicates that more information is needed. (You'll fill in that information later.)

Tip: If you want Project to calculate your schedule for you, create tasks as Auto Scheduled. In the status bar at the bottom of the window, click New Tasks: Manually Scheduled, and then choose Auto Scheduled.

---

5. **Repeat step 4 to add the following tasks:**

   - Make gourmet pizza fixings
   - Make pizza crusts
   - Assemble pizzas

   Figure 3-4 shows what the task list looks like when you're done.

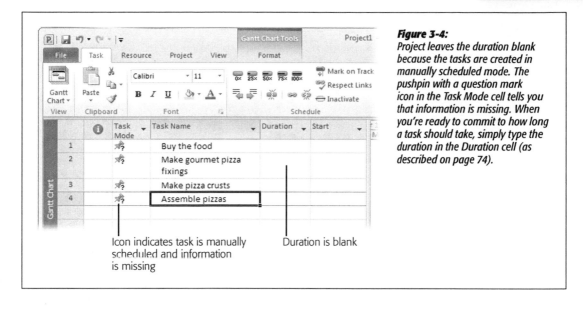

Figure 3-4:
Project leaves the duration blank because the tasks are created in manually scheduled mode. The pushpin with a question mark icon in the Task Mode cell tells you that information is missing. When you're ready to commit to how long a task should take, simply type the duration in the Duration cell (as described on page 74).

Icon indicates task is manually scheduled and information is missing

Duration is blank

Tip: In Project 2010, squiggly red lines indicate scheduling issues, as discussed on page 251, not spelling errors.

As your task list grows, so does the urge to group tasks. People have a hard time focusing on more than half a dozen things at a time, so gathering related tasks into groups makes the project schedule easier to grasp. Chapter 4 provides a detailed description of how to break work down and group it into related chunks. The next step shows how to group a few related tasks under one *summary task*.

6. **Drag over the task rows to select all the tasks. Then choose Task→Insert→Insert Summary Task.**

    Project inserts a new summary task above the selected tasks, named <New Summary Task>. The program indents the selected tasks to make them sub-tasks, as shown in Figure 3-5. You can see that the summary task is set to Auto Scheduled, which means Project calculates the values for the task. For example, the program sets the Duration to "1 day?" The question mark indicates that the duration is an estimate. It also sets the start date to the project start date.

7. **Type the name for the summary task, *Prepare food and drinks*, and press Enter.**

    When Project inserts the new summary task, it selects the Task Name cell, so you can immediately type the name of the summary task.

8. **To create a summary task and subtasks at the same time, select a blank row in the task list and then choose Task→Insert→Summary.**

    Project inserts a new summary task and one subtask, named <New Summary Task> and <New Task>.

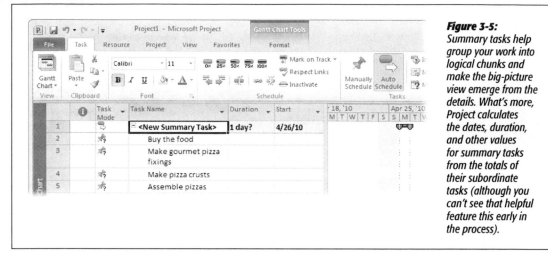

Figure 3-5:
Summary tasks help group your work into logical chunks and make the big-picture view emerge from the details. What's more, Project calculates the dates, duration, and other values for summary tasks from the totals of their subordinate tasks (although you can't see that helpful feature this early in the process).

9. Type *Prepare drinks* in the new summary Task Name cell and press Enter. In the Task Name cell that contains <New Task>, type *Buy drink fixings* and press Enter.

   Project selects the next cell in the Task Name column. As you'll see in the next step, the next tasks you add are subtasks to the summary task you just created.

10. Repeat step 4 to add the following tasks:

    • Make ice

    • Assemble bar

Tip: To move tasks inward or outward at any time, select the tasks and then choose Task→Schedule→ Indent Task or Task→Schedule→Outdent Task. Indent Task is a green arrow pointing to the right. The green arrow for Outdent Task points to the left. (*Outdent* is Microsoftese for the opposite of indent. That is, outdenting moves a task out to the next higher level in the outline.) You can also move selected tasks inward or outward by positioning the pointer at the magic spot in a Task Name cell (over the text of the task name) where the mouse pointer turns into a double arrow. When you see the double arrow, drag the tasks to the left or right.

If you wish, experiment with adding additional tasks and summary tasks to your schedule. (Use the completed schedule in Figure 3-11 at the end of this chapter as a guide.)

What Results Must Your Project Produce—and When?

Waiting until the end to see whether a project meets its deadline isn't just stressful; it also doesn't give you enough time to go back and fix what went wrong. What's more, managers, clients, or other stakeholders expect regular status updates, so you need up-to-date information to keep them happy. Setting up regular checkpoints, appropriately called *milestones,* gives you a chance to gauge your progress frequently. The earlier you discover that the project is falling behind, the more easily you can take corrective action before it's too late—or too costly.

Milestones are perfect for identifying *deliverables*—the tangible products or results required to complete a project—and when they're due. Every project has a major deliverable at the end: a building ready to occupy, a book ready to read, or a design ready to construct. But most projects include additional deliverables along the way, like an approved blueprint or proof copy.

Adding milestones to a project schedule

A milestone typically appears at the end of the tasks that produce the deliverable or achieve a key point in progress. Completing a milestone is like crossing off an item on your To Do list. Project makes it easy to add milestones to your schedule:

1. **Click anywhere in the blank row below the last task ("Assemble bar" in the current example) and then choose Task→Insert→Milestone.**

   The Task Name cell is set to *<New Milestone>* and the Duration is *0 days.* Project switches the Gantt Chart task bar symbol to a diamond. (Don't worry about the date on the milestone just yet.) If you select a row containing a task, Project would automatically insert a new row above the selected row.

Tip: Because milestones have zero duration, you can add as many as you want without increasing the duration of the project.

---

2. **In the Task Name cell, type *Food and drinks ready.***

   Task naming is an art in itself, which you'll learn more about in Chapter 4. One way to differentiate milestones from work tasks is to name the milestone based on what was accomplished: "Documentation printed" or "Design complete," for example.

3. **To move the milestone to the same level as its summary task, make sure the milestone task is selected, and choose Task→Schedule→Outdent Task (the green arrow pointing to the left). (Keyboard mavens can press Alt+Shift+left arrow.)**

   Project places the milestone at the same level in the outline as the summary task, as shown in Figure 3-6.

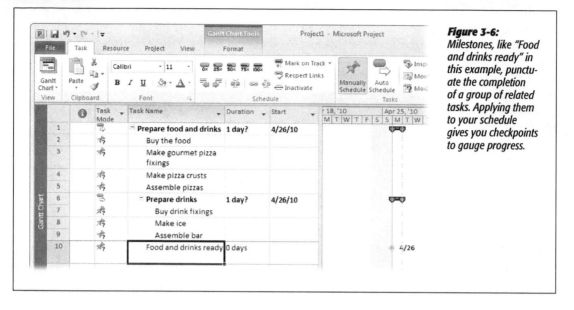

Figure 3-6:
Milestones, like "Food and drinks ready" in this example, punctuate the completion of a group of related tasks. Applying them to your schedule gives you checkpoints to gauge progress.

There are actually two schools of thought regarding where milestones sit in an outline. One is to place milestones at the same level as the summary tasks that produce them (as in this example), so you can collapse an outline to hide subordinate tasks, but still see summary tasks *and* their corresponding deliverables or milestones. Other folks prefer to keep milestones as subtasks, so that the higher-level views show only summary tasks. Try it both ways to see which works for you.

Now's a good time to practice by adding milestones for other checkpoints in your schedule.

How Does Each Task Depend on Other Tasks?

Most likely, the people who work on your project would revolt if you asked them to do all the tasks at the same time. More importantly, some work simply has to be completed before other work can start. Trying to mix a drink before the ice is frozen is a messy and diluted affair. In Project, a relationship between two tasks is known as a *task dependency* or *task link*. Defining the dependencies between tasks helps you determine which tasks start when, as well as when the project might finish.

Creating task dependencies

To link the tasks in the graduation party example, do the following:

1. **Select the tasks related to making the pizzas (from "Buy the food" to "Assemble pizzas").**

   You can select tasks in any number of ways. You can drag your mouse over the ID cells in several rows to select the tasks. To select individual tasks, Ctrl-click each individual task's ID cell. To select adjacent tasks, click the first task, and then Shift-click the last task.

Project highlights the selected tasks.

2. **To create links between the selected tasks, choose Task→Schedule→Link Tasks, which looks like links of chain (shown in Figure 3-7).**

The tasks automatically cascade with Finish-to-Start dependencies (page 156) so one occurs after the other. If you want to remove the dependencies, simply click Unlink Tasks, which looks like a broken link.

Note: When you link the tasks, you might notice that the summary task has two bars. If a summary task is manually scheduled, Project keeps track of the duration you specify for the summary task, as well as the duration of all the subtasks (page 120). That way, you can see whether your estimate for the summary task duration is long enough for all the subtasks.

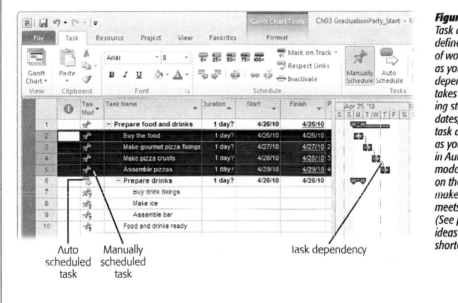

Figure 3-7:
Task dependencies define the sequence of work. Moreover, as you establish dependencies, Project takes care of changing start dates, finish dates, and summary task duration as long as you create tasks in Auto Scheduled mode. Keep an eye on these values to make sure the project meets its deadline. (See page 327 for ideas on how to shorten a schedule.)

3. **Repeat steps 1 and 2 to link the tasks for preparing the drinks.**

The two workflows for food and drinks can occur at the same time, so in the next step, you'll show that you've reached the food and drinks milestone when the pizzas and the bar are assembled.

4. **Click "Assemble pizzas," Ctrl-click the "Food and drinks ready" milestone, and then choose Task→Schedule→Link Tasks.**

A task link appears between the two task bars in the Gantt Chart timescale.

---

5. To link the last drink task to the milestone, click "Assemble bar," Ctrl-click "Food and drinks ready," and then choose Task→Schedule→Link Tasks once more.

Tasks 5 and 9 are the last steps for assembling the food and drinks, respectively, so linking these two tasks to the milestone moves the milestone to occur after both tasks are complete.

Note: Relationships between tasks come in several flavors, with the most common being Finish to Start, as illustrated in the previous steps. See page 157 to learn about the other types of task dependencies.

Who's Going to Do the Work?

People are any project's greatest resource. It's the people and their availability (when folks are assigned to work, and when they're scheduled to take vacation) that ultimately controls when tasks get done and how long the project takes. In Project, *resources* are any people, equipment, or materials needed to complete tasks in your project. Chapter 8 and Chapter 9 provide the full scoop on how to create and manage all types of project resources. In this section, you'll see how to add people as resources to your project, and hook them up with tasks.

List the people on your project

Work could still be up for grabs when you create your schedule. Even if you don't know resource names, you probably know what skills are required to do the work. You can use a person's name if you have a lucky team member lined up, or fill in generic names when all you know is the type of work or skill required.

Project provides a view—the Resource Sheet—specifically for listing your resources. Here's how to fill it in:

1. Choose Resource→View→Resource Sheet.

   A new spreadsheet-like view appears with fields for recording information about your resources, as shown in Figure 3-8.

2. To create the first resource in Project for the best friend you've corralled into helping, in the first Resource Name cell, type *Enrique*, and then press Enter.

   Repeat this step for your other friends.

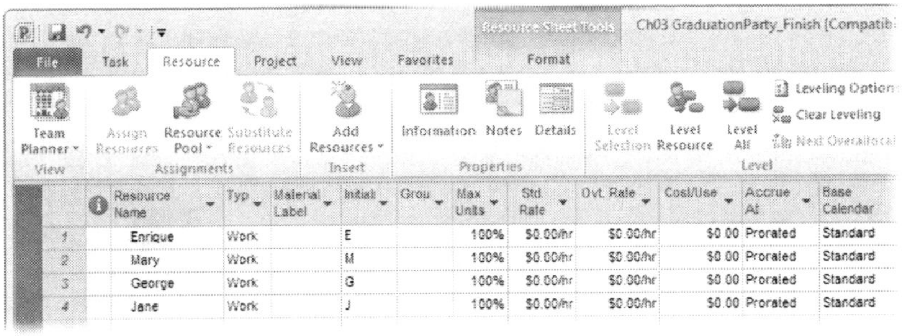

Figure 3-8:
The Resource Sheet captures information about the people, equipment, or materials required for your project, including costs and work schedules. For a start, just enter the names of the resources. (Chapter 8 covers resource creation in intricate detail.)

Assign resources to tasks

At this point, you have a list of all of the people who are pitching in. If you handed them your schedule now and told them to get to work, you'd have a free-for-all. To get the work done on time with a minimum of chaos, all team members need to know which tasks are theirs to do.

Here's how to connect your project's resources to tasks:

1. **Choose Task→View→Gantt Chart.**

   The left side of the Gantt Chart view lists project tasks with fields for details, such as Duration, Start, Finish, Predecessors, and Resource Names. The right side is the Gantt Chart timescale.

   Make sure you see the Resource Names column. If necessary, adjust the Gantt Chart's two panes to display it. Position the mouse pointer over the vertical bar between the panes. When the pointer changes to double arrows, drag the divider bar to the right until the Resource Names column is visible.

2. **To assign Enrique to a task, click the Resource Names field for the "Buy drink fixings" task.**

   Project displays a box around the cell and displays a down arrow for the resource drop-down list.

Note: Summary tasks don't get resource assignments, because the resources are already assigned to the individual tasks that belong to the summary tasks. Likewise, don't assign resources to milestones, because the zero duration means there's no work to perform.

---

3. **To select a name, click the down arrow, turn on the checkbox for a name in the list, and then press Enter.**

   Your selected victim appears in the Resource Names cell next to the task. It also shows up in the Gantt Chart above the task's task bar (Figure 3-9). For other ways to assign resources to tasks, see page 202.

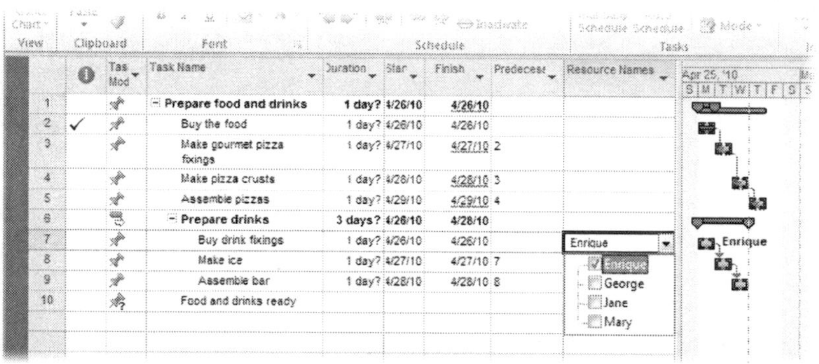

Figure 3-9:
In addition to adding the name to the Resource Names cell, Project places the person's name (Jane, George) next to the task bar in the Gantt Chart timescale.

4. **Repeat steps 2 and 3 until your friends are all appointed to tasks.**

   Or not. If you don't know who to assign and can't determine a generic resource, then leave the resource name blank. You can come back and assign resources later.

You're ready to proceed to the last step of the test drive.

How Long Will All These Tasks Take?

The next step can be the most difficult part of scheduling. You need to look into your crystal ball and give your best guess—er, informed estimate—of how long each project step should take. You can find entire books on this subject alone, but Chapter 5 provides a brief introduction to estimating. For now, you'll revise the task durations in the sample project to see how the schedule changes accordingly.

Here are the steps for defining the duration of tasks:

1. **Click the Duration cell for the first pizza work task ("Buy the food").**

   You can enter durations for summary tasks only if you've set their task mode to Manually Scheduled (page 116). For auto-scheduled summary tasks, Project calculates the duration for you from the duration of the subtasks. Milestones, by definition, have zero duration.

2. **Enter the length of time (duration) you or your buddies think it will take to
do that step (Figure 3-10).**

You can enter durations in minutes (m), hours (h), days (d), weeks (w), or
months (mo). Type the number followed by the abbreviation for the unit you
want to use. For example, type *3d* for 3 days or *6h* for 6 hours.

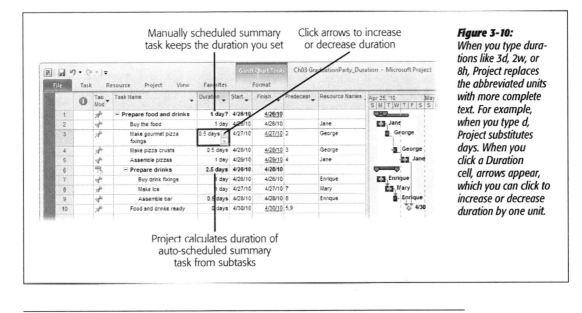

Manually scheduled summary
task keeps the duration you set

Click arrows to increase
or decrease duration

Project calculates duration of
auto-scheduled summary
task from subtasks

Figure 3-10:
When you type dura-
tions like 3d, 2w, or
8h, Project replaces
the abbreviated units
with more complete
text. For example,
when you type d,
Project substitutes
days. When you
click a Duration
cell, arrows appear,
which you can click to
increase or decrease
duration by one unit.

Note: If you don't type a unit, then Project uses the unit specified in the "Duration entered in" Project option. Choose File→Options, select the Schedule tab, and then choose the units in the "Duration is entered
in" drop-down list.

3. **Repeat step 2 for each task in the project.**

When you're done, the schedule shows how long it should take to prepare for
your party, as Figure 3-11 illustrates.

For most projects, you have to tweak your schedule to meet project objectives, such
as finish date, budget, or scope. Chapter 10 explains different methods for evaluating whether a project schedule is accurate. Chapter 12 discusses ways to fine-tune
schedules, for instance, to shorten them, to reduce costs, or simply to bring them
more in touch with reality.

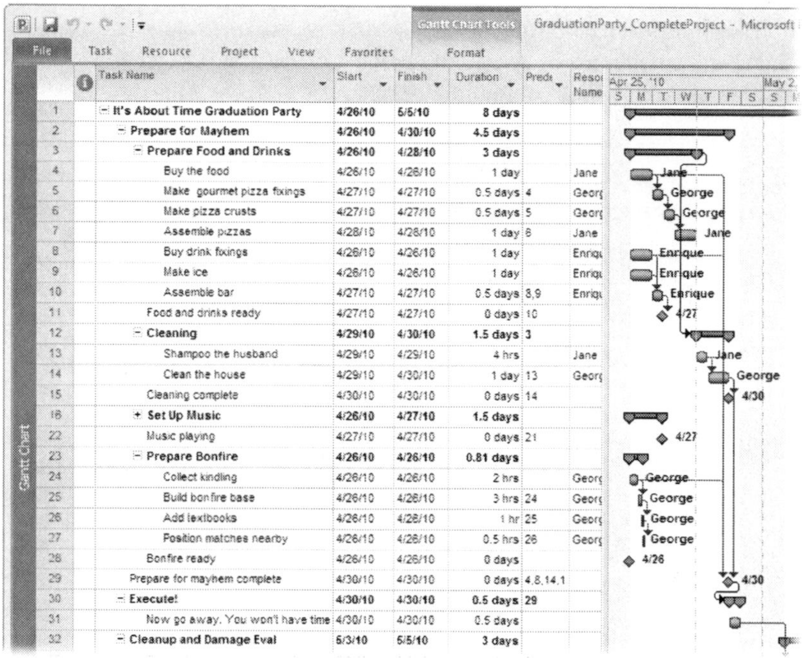

Figure 3-11:
A complete schedule has many tasks with resources assigned to them, and links between the tasks. There's no guarantee that your first pass at a schedule will meet your objectives, but you have to reach this point to find out. (To compare your schedule to this example, you can download a completed version, as described in the tip on page 65.)

Saving Your Project

Now, save your hard work so you can come back to it later. You must save Project files, just like any document or spreadsheet.

1. **Choose File→Save.**

   The Save As dialog box appears. If you've saved the project file before, then the Save dialog box appears.

2. **In the "File name" field, type a name, and then click Save.**

   Project saves the file in the location you specified.

As you work on your project, remember to save early and save often. Pressing Ctrl+S to save a Project file is so fast that you can make it a habit in no time. Chapter 6 explains other ways to save projects (page 76).

Congratulations! You've created your first project.

CHAPTER 4

Breaking Work into Task-Sized Chunks

When you organize a simple activity like seeing a movie with friends, you probably don't bother writing out the steps. You just call your friends, pick a movie, get tickets, and buy popcorn without a formal plan. But for more complex projects—like doing your taxes or launching a new product line—identifying the work involved is key to planning how and when to get it done. For example, missing the April 15 tax deadline can cost you hundreds of dollars in penalties. And that new product may make a profit only if you keep costs below $100,000 and get it on store shelves before Thanksgiving. In cases like these, cost, delivery dates, and other objectives are important.

That's where a WBS (*work breakdown structure*) comes in. Carving up the project's work into a hierarchy of progressively smaller chunks until you get to bite-sized pieces is the first step toward figuring out how and when everything will get done. If you're new to managing projects, don't panic—you've built a WBS before. The movie example in the previous paragraph is actually a simple WBS.

The structure of a WBS is much like the system of blood vessels in your body, with the aorta representing the entire project and the smaller blood vessels as progressively smaller chunks of the overall work at each level (*summary tasks*). The hordes of tiny capillaries that deliver blood to every part of your body correspond to the individual tasks (called *work packages*) at the bottom of the WBS, which are the smallest chunks of work that you assign to people to complete the project.

In this chapter, you'll learn how to create a WBS that successfully communicates the work within a project. Equally important, you'll learn how to tell when the WBS is broken down enough. The rest of the chapter helps you get your WBS into Microsoft Project so you can move on to constructing a project schedule as described in Chapter 6.

The fastest way to create a WBS is to construct it directly in Project, and this chapter shows you several ways to do just that. If you're working alone, you can empty your brain into Project, or you can just as easily transcribe the results of collaborative WBS sessions. If you love working in Microsoft Word, or if teams submit individual Word documents for their portions of the project, you can also build a WBS in Word and transfer the results into Project. (When you copy an indented list of tasks from Word or Outlook, Project 2010 automatically transforms them into a hierarchy of summary tasks and subtasks.) Finally, you'll learn how to create documents that describe and support your project's work packages.

Identifying the Work to Be Done

Knowing the high-level tasks that make up your project is important, but big chunks like Build Bridge, Hire New Staff, and Plan Grand Opening Party don't help when you're trying to estimate costs, line up resources, schedule work, or track progress. You need to get much more specific about the work all this is going to take. The point of a WBS is to break down the work into small enough pieces that you can:

- **Improve estimates**. Smaller tasks are not only less intimidating, they make it much easier to figure out how many people you need to perform each portion of work, how long it'll take, and how much it'll cost.

- **Keep the team focused**. Because the WBS spells out exactly what's needed to achieve the project's objectives, it acts as a checklist for the work on the project team's plate. It also gently guides team members *away* from doing things outside the project's scope.

- **Assign work to resources**. When work is broken down into discrete tasks, it's easier to identify the skills needed to complete the assignment. The project manager can clearly determine who's responsible for what. Also, team members are more likely to understand their individual assignments, which makes them happy and helps keep the project on track.

  On the other hand, don't go overboard by dissecting work into miniscule assignments. Productivity drops when team members keep switching to new assignments, and your temptation to micromanage increases. (You'll learn how to determine the appropriate size for a work package in the next section.)

- **Keep the project on track**. Shorter tasks give you frequent checkpoints for tracking costs, effort, and completion dates. Moreover, if tasks have strayed off course, you can take corrective action before things get out of hand.

Note: In the PMI project management methodology, introduced briefly in Chapter 1, a WBS is the result of the scope definition process. The starting point is a scope statement (page 50) in which you define what's within the scope of the project and, just as important, what isn't. For example, knowing whether the cleaning service you hire takes on teenagers' rooms could be essential to success. For many projects, especially those performed for government agencies, the WBS is a contractually binding document, making the correct inclusion and exclusion of work essential.

Breaking Down Work

Like Goldilocks, you have to find the right size for the work packages—not too big, not too small, but just right. Large work packages can be so vague that team members aren't sure what they're supposed to do. Moreover, your team could reassure you for weeks that a large chunk of work is running smoothly, only to beg for a schedule-busting extension just when you thought they'd be done. Too-small work packages, on the other hand, carry all the disadvantages of micromanagement: excessive communication, unending status reporting, lost productivity, and so on. So how do you build a WBS with work packages that are just right?

Each project is unique, so don't expect the same approach to work for every project you manage. Identifying work can run the gamut from invigoratingly informal to scrupulously methodical, depending on whether you're planning a small project for a close-knit group or wrestling with a multi-year, multi-vendor project. (Whatever the project, a sure-fire shortcut is to borrow from existing sources, as described in the box on page 79.)

Borrowing a WBS

Even with input from all the project's stakeholders, a blank WBS can be as daunting as the first blank page of the novel you want to write. Fortunately, several methods of developing a WBS let you learn—or even borrow outright—from the ideas and work of project managers who've walked this path before:

- **Similar projects**. If you know of a project that's similar to the one you're working on, the fastest way to create a WBS is to use one that's already finished, whether it's stored in Project or another program. Be sure to check that project's final schedule and its closeout documents (page 479) to identify work that was added during that project's execution.

- **Experienced resources**. If people in your organization (or outside consultants and contractors, for that

matter) have experience with your kind of project, they can help flesh out a WBS or identify work you've missed. You can write up the WBS as best you can, and then ask those folks to look it over.

- **Microsoft Project templates**. When you install Project, you automatically get a set of built-in templates for different types of projects, from technology deployments to residential construction (page 125). If these templates don't meet your needs, Microsoft Office Online (*http://office.microsoft.com*) and other websites offer hundreds of specialized Project templates. Start with one of these templates to launch your WBS, and tweak it until it fits your project like a glove.

A WBS has only two types of elements: summary tasks and work packages. As you learned in Chapter 3, the lowest level tasks in a WBS are work package tasks—hunks of actual work that you assign to team members. Anything else in a WBS is simply some level of summary of that work, which can nest to as many levels as you need, as shown in Figure 4-1. As it turns out, you can build a WBS from whichever direction you prefer—top down, bottom up, or side to side—as described in the following sections.

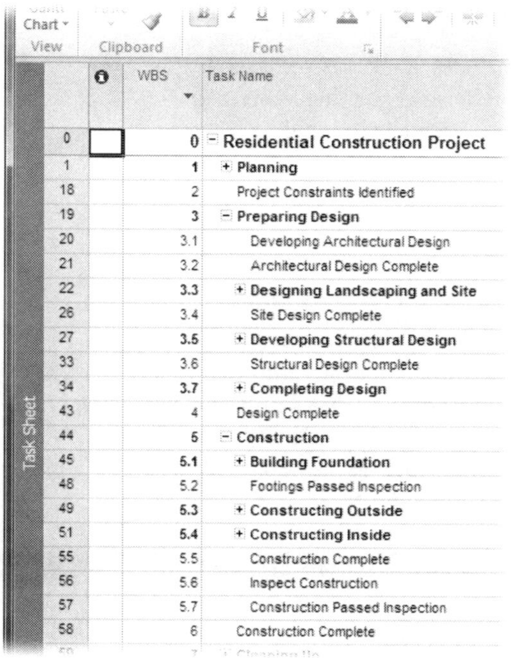

Figure 4-1:
The organization of a WBS can vary, but the work packages remain the same. For example, you might track a project by phases (planning, design, and construction) or by completed components (from condo unit to floor to building). As you build a WBS, you can change summary tasks and move work packages around.

Building a WBS from the top down

As the name "work breakdown structure" implies, the most common way to build a WBS is to start with the entire project and break it down until you reach assignable work packages at the bottom. (The box on page 88 describes how to show a top-down view of a WBS.) The most common way to *decompose* (that is, break down) a project is by the deliverables that you want the project to produce and the milestones you want it to attain. (See page 49 for detailed definitions of *deliverables* and *milestones*.)

A project scope statement (page 50) usually lists a set of deliverables that the project's customer and other stakeholders expect to receive. One of the best ways to identify project work is to create high-level tasks for every deliverable. For example, if you're planning the party of the century, you'd create summary tasks for food, drinks, music, and the video you need to blackmail your friends after the fact.

Once you have these top-level tasks, you take another pass at decomposition by identifying intermediate deliverables and critical milestones, like completing the celebratory rum cake or finalizing the reservations for all the party vendors. For each intermediate deliverable and milestone, ask yourself what work it entails. For instance, the music requires an audio system as well as a song list, so you add one task for renting the audio equipment and another for building a playlist of songs on your computer. Then, you simply repeat this process for each deliverable until you have work packages that you can assign to your spouse, your kids, the caterer, and other folks you hire. (See the box on page 81 for advice on naming tasks effectively.)

Once you complete your WBS, take some time to verify it. Make sure all the items in the scope statement have corresponding work in the WBS, and look out for work packages that don't support the scope. Add missing summary tasks and work packages. If you think of a deliverable that isn't in the scope statement, add the work to the WBS and revise the scope statement. Keep in mind, though, that if you're doing projects for customers, you probably need their approval to change the scope statement.

GEM IN THE ROUGH

Good Task Names

The better a task name conveys the work it represents, the less you have to worry about whether team members are doing what they're supposed to. Effective task names include a verb and noun—the action you want people to take and the result you expect.

Using the present tense of a verb presents the task as a command or directive. For example, "Write How-to Manual" clearly identifies the type of work and which deliverable the work applies to. "How-to Manual" alone doesn't tell the assigned resources whether they are reading, writing, editing, or printing the manual. Unambiguous verbs help clarify work.

You can help your audience interpret tasks by differentiating summary tasks, work packages, and milestones with different grammatical forms:

- Because summary tasks represent a series of activities that span time, change the verbs for summary tasks to a gerund (a verb with "ing" at the end), like "Moving Household Goods."

- Milestones (which represent goals or states) typically have names that include the deliverable and its state, such as "Steel Columns Fabricated" or "Steel Columns Erected."

Developing a WBS from start to finish

Another way to slice and dice a project is to identify what you have to do from the beginning of the project until the end. This approach isn't all that different from the top-down decomposition described in the previous section, except that you decompose each branch of the tree until you reach its work packages. Then, you go back to the top and work your way to the bottom of the next branch.

This variation on the top-down method is ideal when different teams or groups work on a project. Once you identify top-level tasks, you can assign their decomposition to the groups that do the work. See page 90 for instructions on assembling WBSs from several groups.

CHAPTER 4: BREAKING WORK INTO TASK-SIZED CHUNKS

Tip: Don't forget to include project initiation and management tasks in your WBS. Sure, some of your work goes on behind the scenes without obvious deliverables, but project management is essential to keeping projects within budget and on schedule. Besides, project management *does* have deliverables, since most customers and stakeholders sign off on project plans and want to see status reports, documents, and expenditures.

Constructing a WBS from the bottom up

Identifying work packages and then organizing them into summary tasks usually works only for small projects, but small projects occur often enough to make this a popular approach. Whether you write tasks on sticky notes or type them into Project, you and your team can identify every iota of work you can think of. Then, you can head to a quiet spot to organize it into higher-level tasks.

WORD TO THE WISE

Too Many Cooks Can Spoil the WBS

If you're a team of one but tend to argue with yourself, asking another person to act as a tiebreaker can save time and frustration. In most cases, however, the problem is too many people with their own unquestionably correct ideas about how to break down the project. You'll end up changing your WBS's organization, rearranging summary tasks, and revising work packages with little progress toward a completed WBS.

Start with a small group of renaissance folks—people knowledgeable in one or more sections of the project and

familiar with the overall goal. For example, you could work with the managers of each department involved in the project to craft the top two or three levels of the WBS. Then, you can assign the decomposition of the lowest summary tasks of this initial WBS to work teams that have experience with the type of work involved. The party caterer can identify the food tasks, say, and your brother-in-law can write up the tent-wrangling tasks.

When Is Enough Enough?

Most people can keep track of up to five things at once, although stress and age increase forgetfulness. If you're a juggler extraordinaire, you might be able to absorb eight items, but, beyond that, all bets are off. Between three and seven levels of summary tasks is ideal for a WBS that audiences can digest. For example, you can divide the entire project at the top level into phases like defining requirements, designing systems, and developing components. Then, within each phase, you can create lower levels to identify work in more detail.

For monster projects, though, you can exceed the level limit without losing focus by breaking the behemoth into subprojects. If the overall project is building a new jet, you can have a few levels of decomposition to reach a set of subprojects, each of which contributes major deliverables (engines, fuselage, electronics, and so on). Then, separate WBSs for each subproject can include their own three to seven levels. When vendors or subcontractors perform subprojects, ask them to develop the WBSs for their subprojects.

Tip: If you have a bunch of folks helping you create the WBS, see the box on page 82 for advice on working together effectively.

As with almost any endeavor, the last 20 percent is the most difficult. The first several levels of the WBS might appear almost effortlessly, but then the decomposition can slow to a crawl as you try to decide whether something represents a work package or not. Here are some ideas for how to decide what constitutes a work package:

- **To estimate work.** When you break tasks down into work packages based on the work you know how to estimate, figuring out the overall project is as easy as adding up estimates for all the chunks. For example, you may not have a clue how long it will take to deploy Windows 7 throughout your organization, but you know that it takes 3 hours to install and reconfigure one computer.

- **To track progress.** One rule of thumb for defining work packages is to keep task duration between 8 and 80 hours (in other words, anywhere from one workday up to two work weeks). These durations also give you early warning when tasks overrun their estimates. In addition, if you break work down into durations no longer than the time between status reports, you're likely to have concrete progress to report. The downside is that you need a clear idea of how long various tasks take, but this approach works well for projects similar to those you've performed in the past.

- **To maintain focus.** Guidelines aside, simply decompose work to the level of detail that you can handle. If you're a keep-things-simple type, you can keep your WBS at a high level and let team leaders manage details. On the other hand, if you can remember details the way a Starbucks barista remembers coffee orders, you can break down the work to your heart's content. Just remember that dividing work into portions that take less than a day can reduce productivity and morale (with certain exceptions, as discussed in the box on page 84).

When Short Is Sweet

Most of the time, you don't want to break down your WBS into tasks that take less than a day. Most people can handle a task like sending out invitations without reporting back to their boss after they buy the postage stamps. But suppose your project's goal is replacing a mission-critical software system. When it's time to flip the switch to the new system, you probably have only a few hours or even minutes to make the change. That's when you need a detailed plan with short work packages for the crucial period.

Fortunately, situations like this are few and far between. But here's an example: You spend months preparing for

the changeover with work broken into day-or week-long chunks. However, for the work that has to be done over a single night before the staff starts coming back to work in the morning, you can create a subproject that breaks work down into minute-by-minute packages. These miniature work packages help you line up the people you need (because you won't have time to call them in at the last minute) and spot potential delays.

Building a WBS in Microsoft Project

Your WBS may not have started out in Project. Maybe you scribbled it on a whiteboard, scrawled it on sticky notes pasted to flip charts, or it's just rattling around noisily in your head. Regardless of where your ideas are, you can make short work of getting them into Project. Once you get familiar with the techniques for outlining tasks described on the next few pages, you'll develop a rhythm to your data entry. If you already have an outline, you can quickly type or copy it into Project from the top down. Or if work packages are bubbling up in your brain, you can enter them without worrying about the order of the tasks or the overall structure. You can rearrange and add summary tasks and work packages later.

Creating a WBS in Project from the Top Down

One of the more efficient data entry methods is to start at the top of a WBS and complete each level of tasks before dropping to the next level. Because Project creates a new task at the same outline level as the previous task, this approach keeps indenting and outdenting to a minimum.

For maximum efficiency, when you flesh out a lowest-level summary task, insert as many rows as there are work packages for that summary task, and then type the names of the work packages in the Task Name cells. The following steps show you exactly how to work your way down a WBS one level at a time:

1. **Click the File tab, and then choose New.**

   Project selects "Blank project" in the Available Templates pane.

2. **On the right side of the window, click Create to create a new blank project file.**

   The Gantt Chart view appears with the Entry table on the left and the Gantt Chart timescale on the right. If you don't see the Gantt Chart view, click the Task tab, and then choose Gantt Chart in the View section.

3. **If the WBS column doesn't appear in the Entry table, right-click the Task Name heading and, from the shortcut menu, choose Insert Column.**

   Project inserts a new column to the left of the Task Name column with "[Type Column Name]" in the heading cell.

4. **Type *WBS*, and then press Enter.**

   You could also scroll in the drop-down list, as shown in Figure 4-2, and then click WBS, but, in this case, typing is quicker.

Note: The WBS code format that Project uses out of the box is a number at each level, with levels separated by periods. If your organization has a custom WBS format, you can set up your own WBS code (see page 93).

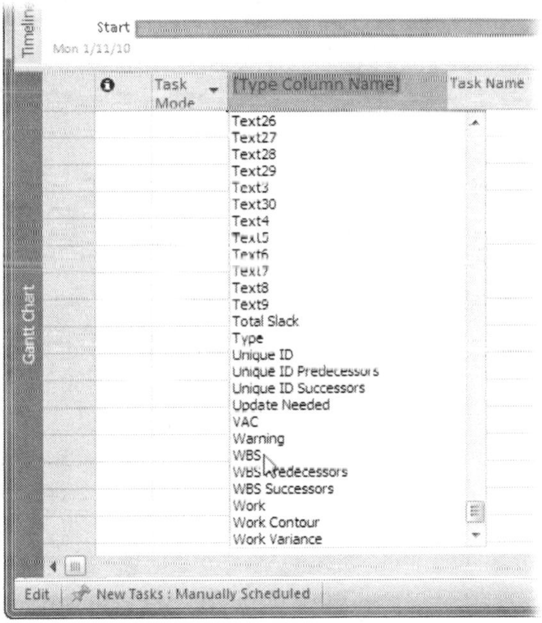

Figure 4-2:
Project keeps track of WBS numbers for tasks whether the WBS column is visible or not. You can label the column with a different name, align the text in the column, and specify the column width. After you add the column, right-click the heading cell and then choose Field Settings on the shortcut menu. Type the column heading you want in the Title box. Choose the alignment you want, the width, and then click OK.

5. **In the Entry table, click the first Task Name cell, and then type the name of the first top-level summary task.**

   Press Enter to save this task, and then move down to the Task Name cell in the next row, as shown in Figure 4-3.

Note: You don't have to create a top-level task for the overall project. Project has a *project summary task*, which sits in an exalted position of Row 0 and rolls up the values for all the other tasks in the schedule. If you want to see the Project Summary task, choose Format Show/Hide Project Summary Task. To always show the project summary tasks, click the File tab and choose Options. In the Project Options dialog box, click Advanced. Finally, scroll to the "Display options for this project" section, and then turn on the "Show project summary task" checkbox.

---

6. **Repeat step 5 for each top-level task in the WBS.**

   Creating the tasks at the top-level is as easy as it gets: You type a task's name, press Enter, and repeat until all your top-level tasks are there. Now you're ready to add tasks at the next level of the WBS.

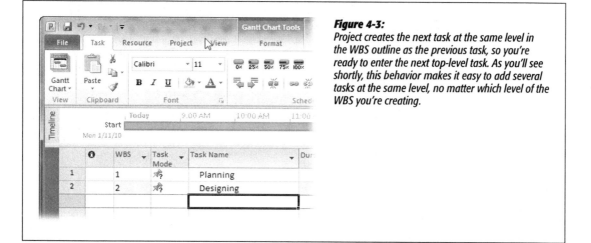

Figure 4-3:
Project creates the next task at the same level in the WBS outline as the previous task, so you're ready to enter the next top-level task. As you'll see shortly, this behavior makes it easy to add several tasks at the same level, no matter which level of the WBS you're creating.

7. **To add subtasks to a summary task, click the Task Name cell immediately below the summary task you're fleshing out, and then press Insert as many times as there are subtasks, as demonstrated in Figure 4-4.**

   This step is the secret to speedy outlining because it works in the same way at every level of the WBS: second-level, third-level, or lowest-level summary task. When you insert rows for the lowest-level summary task, insert as many rows as there are work packages for that summary task. Then you can type away and fill them all in quickly.

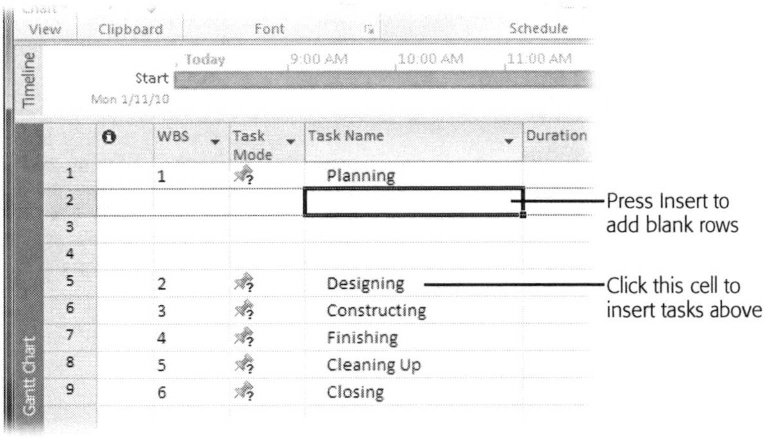

Figure 4-4:
You can insert blank task rows by clicking anywhere in the row below the summary task and pressing Insert. But if you click the Task Name cell, when you press Insert, the blank task's Task Name cell becomes the active cell—ready for you to type the name of the first subtask.

8. With the blinking insertion point in the blank Task Name cell beckoning you, type the name of the subtask, and then press Enter to create the task.

   Pressing Enter moves the active cell to the next Task Name cell. However, the first subtask isn't at the right level—it's still at the same level as the summary task.

9. To indent the task, press the up arrow key, and then press Alt+Shift+right arrow. Or, on the Task tab, click Indent Task (the green, right-pointing arrow in the Schedule section).

   Project indents the subtask and indicates its subordinate position in two ways: with the WBS number and the outline box—both shown in Figure 4-5.

10. Press the down arrow key to move to the next Task Name cell, type the name, and then press Enter.

   Because the first subtask is at the correct level, the remaining subtasks come to life at the right level for their summary task.

11. Repeat steps 7 through 10 for every summary task in the WBS, ultimately filling in each level of the WBS.

   Your initial draft of the WBS is complete.

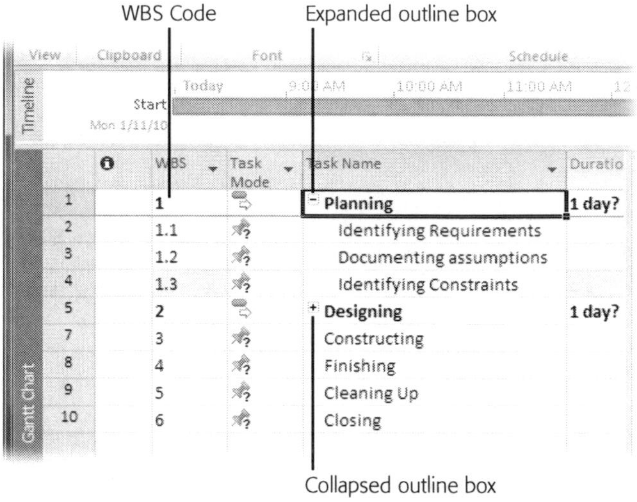

WBS Code   Expanded outline box

Figure 4-5:
The WBS code for the subtask includes an additional level of numbers. If the summary task WBS number is 2.4, its first outline box subtask has the number 2.4.1. Summary task names are preceded by an outline box—a square with a minus sign inside that indicates that the summary task is expanded. If you click the box, the summary task collapses and hides its subtasks, and the outline box changes to a square with a + sign.

Collapsed outline box

Displaying a WBS in a Hierarchy

The outline in Project shows the levels of the WBS hierarchy, but you might prefer to view the WBS as a hierarchy similar to an organization chart, for example, when you're presenting the WBS to audiences unfamiliar with Project. In Microsoft Project 2003, the Visio WBS Chart Wizard transformed a task list in Project into a tree diagram in Visio, but that tool went the way of the dodo bird in Project 2007.

If you use Visio Professional (2007 or 2010), you can download the Visio WBS Modeler to generate a hierarchical work breakdown structure from an existing Project file. Search the Microsoft Download Center (*www.microsoft. com/downloads*) for "WBS Modeler." In addition, many companies offer add-on products that generate WBS diagrams from Project files. To find them, search the web for "Project WBS diagram".

You can also use a visual report (page 464) to turn a task list into a tree, but the process and result aren't nearly as satisfying as the Visio WBS Chart Wizard. Project doesn't include a built-in visual report for displaying a WBS. But you can head to *www.missingmanuals.com/cds* and download a visual report template for a WBS. When you work with visual reports, you can specify which folders to search for customized templates, as described on page 473. Project then displays the templates in that folder in the visual report list. This template uses only the task name, WBS, Work, and Duration fields and sets up a tree structure. (See page 474 to learn how to generate a visual report from a template.)

Creating and Modifying a WBS on the Fly

If you're in high gear churning out project tasks, you can gleefully insert, delete, and rearrange the WBS outline as you go. The resulting WBS looks exactly the same as one methodically typed from the top down. Also, the methods for adding, moving, and changing outline levels for tasks are the same whether you're creating or modifying a WBS. You can use the following techniques to develop a WBS in any order:

- **Insert a new summary task without subtasks.** In the row below the new summary task, click the Task Name cell, and then press Insert. Type the task name and press Enter. Select the new summary task, and then either press Alt+Shift+left arrow or, on the Task tab, click Outdent Task (the green, left-pointing arrow in the Schedule section) until the summary task is at the level you want.

- **Insert a new summary task for selected subtasks.** If you want to summarize several existing tasks, you can use the Insert Summary Task command (new in Project 2010). First, select the subtasks. Then, on the Task tab, click Insert Summary Task in the Insert section. (The icon looks like a summary task bar with a yellow asterisk.) Project selects the Task Name cell, which contains the text "<New Summary Task>", so you can simply start typing to name the new summary task.

- **Insert a new subtask.** In the row below an existing subtask, click the Task Name cell, and then press Insert. The task appears at the same outline level as the task you clicked.

- **Make a summary task into a subtask.** Select the first subtask for the summary task, and then either press Alt+Shift+left arrow or, on the Task tab, click Outdent Task (the green, left-pointing arrow). When you outdent the subtask, the summary task's outline box disappears.

- **Move a subtask to the next lower level.** Select the task, and then press Alt+Shift+right arrow or, on the Task tab, click Indent Task (the green, right-pointing arrow). The task drops to the next lower level while the task above it turns into a summary task.

Tip: If you want to move, indent, outdent, or delete several tasks at once, select them all, and then use the techniques in this section. To select adjoining tasks in the outline, drag across the adjacent tasks. To select several separate tasks, Ctrl-click each task.

- **Elevate a subtask to the next higher level.** Click the task. Then, on the Task tab, click Outdent Task (the green, left-pointing arrow) or press Alt+Shift+left arrow.

- **Move a subtask to another summary task.** Click the ID cell (the first column of the view table) for the task you want to move. After the pointer turns into a four-headed arrow, drag the task to its new home in the outline. Then change its outline level, if necessary.

- **Delete a subtask.** Select the subtask, and then press Delete.

- **Delete a summary task.** To delete a summary task and all of its subtasks, select the summary task, and then press Delete, or right-click the summary task and choose Delete Task from the shortcut menu. (And if you want to delete a summary task and *keep* all its subtasks, see the box on page 90.)

Note: To use the Delete key to get rid of a task, you have to select the entire task row by clicking the row's ID number. If you select only the Task Name cell and then press Delete, Project deletes the text in the cell. Alternatively, if you click the Smart Tag with an X, which appears to the left of the Task Name cell, you can choose "Only clear the contents of the Task Name Cell" or "Delete the entire task".

FREQUENTLY ASKED QUESTION

Sparing the Subtasks

How do I delete a summary task without deleting its subtasks?

It depends on what you want to do with the subtasks. If you want to shift the subtasks to a different summary task, it's easiest to first relocate the subtasks to their new home. Then you can delete the empty summary task by selecting it and pressing Delete.

But if you're not sure where you want the orphaned subtasks to end up, simply change them to the same outline level as the summary task before deleting the summary task.

Here's how:

1. Select the subtasks by dragging across their Task Name cells.

2. Press Alt+Shift+left arrow to change the tasks to the same outline level as their summary task. You can tell that the summary task is devoid of subtasks because the outline box with the + or – sign disappears.

3. Select the summary task demoted to a regular task, and then press Delete.

Documenting a WBS in Another Program

You can also whip up a list of indented tasks in Microsoft Word or Outlook, and then copy and paste them into Project 2010. More of your team members are likely to be familiar with Word or Outlook than with Project, so you're likely to get project info from them in Word documents or emails. In Word and Outlook, it's easy to indent, outdent, insert, move, and delete tasks. Then, all you have to do is copy the text in either of those programs and paste it into Project.

Note: In Project 2007 and earlier versions, you could build an outline in Word and import it into a Project file. Project 2010 reduces that unwieldy process to a few simple steps.

Here are techniques you can use to build a task list in Word or Outlook:

- **Promote a task.** Position the cursor to the left of the task text and then press Backspace.

- **Demote a task.** Position the cursor to the left of the task text and then press Tab.

- **Move tasks.** Select the task(s) you want to move, and then drag them to a new position. Or, use Ctrl+X and Ctrl+V to cut and paste the tasks from one position to another. If need be, demote or promote the tasks to the correct level.

- **Delete tasks.** Select the task(s) you want to delete, and then press Delete or Ctrl+X.

Pasting a WBS into Project

If you paste a list of tasks from Word or Outlook into Project 2010, the program is smart enough to transform the indents in Word documents or Outlook emails into WBS levels in Project. Suppose different teams use Word documents to define the tasks they plan to perform. They can send them to you and all you have to do is open the Word documents, copy the text, and paste it into Project. Here's how:

1. **Open the document in Word or, if the tasks are in an email in Outlook, open the email.**

2. **Select the tasks you want to paste into Project, as shown in Figure 4-6 (top), and then press Ctrl+C.**

3. **Switch over to Project and click the first blank Task Name cell where you want to paste the tasks; then press Ctrl+V.**

   Project inserts the task names into the Task Name cells and indents the tasks to the same level that they were at in the Word document or Outlook email, as shown in Figure 4-6 (bottom).

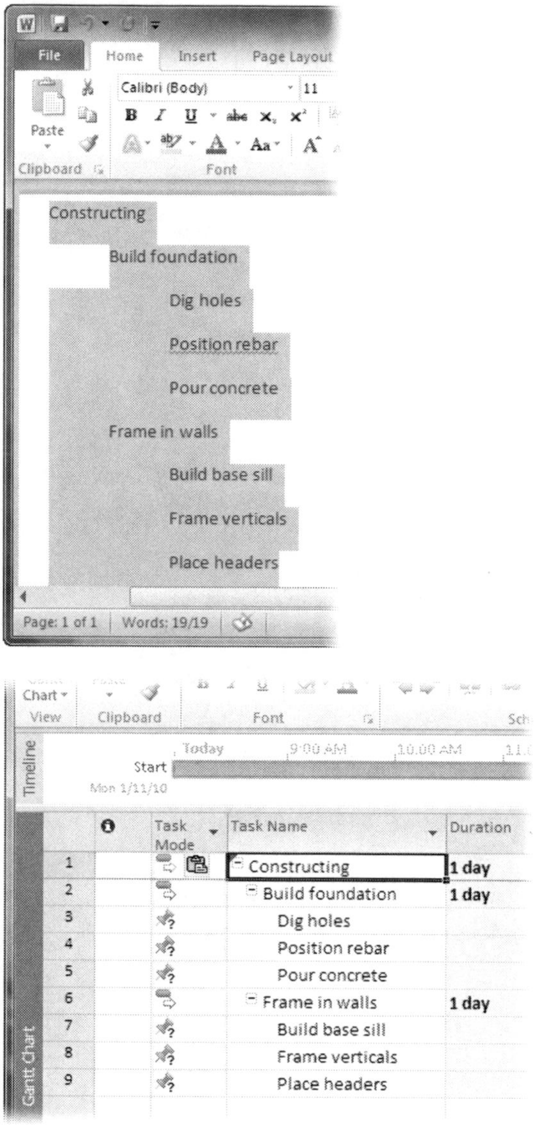

Figure 4-6:
Top: Type each task name on a separate line in a Microsoft Word document. To make a line a subtask, select it and then press Tab. To promote an item to a higher level, position the cursor to the left of the text, and press Backspace.

Bottom: When you paste tasks into Project, it figures out the correct outline level.

Assembling a WBS Without a Computer

Sticky notes and an empty wall or whiteboard might be the best solution for capturing tasks when a team is tossing around ideas. In fact, sticky notes offer enough advantages that you might use them even when WBS sessions proceed at a more leisurely pace.

Sticky notes are a democratic way to collect tasks when several people collaborate on a WBS. Team members can have their own pens and pads of sticky notes so no one is stuck being the sole scribe. Moreover, anyone can walk up to the WBS and move summary tasks and work packages around. The hardest part of the sticky note approach could be too much enthusiasm. If disagreements begin to break out over added or relocated tasks, then it's time to jump in and take over sticky note maintenance until things calm down.

Sticky notes are slick when you're searching for the ideal project organization. You can peel such a note off the wall and move it to wherever you want without mouse clicks or keyboard shortcuts. And if you buy sticky flip charts, you can use them for summary tasks and attach sticky notes representing work packages to them.

One drawback to sticky notes is that they lose their stickiness over time. The safest approach is to record the contents of a sticky note WBS in Project or another program before you leave the meeting room. If your room reservation has expired, fold the pages carefully and transport them to your office. For sticky notes stuck directly to the wall or whiteboard, post a polite note asking others to leave your masterpiece alone until you can come back and transcribe it.

Setting Up Custom WBS Codes

The WBS codes built into Project are simple outline codes with a number for each level in the outline hierarchy. For instance, a WBS code of 2.1.3 might represent the second phase of the project, the first summary task in that phase, and the third work package for that summary task. If your organization uses custom codes, you can build a tailored numbering system—called a *code mask*—to specify each level of your WBS code. If you use abbreviations for phases, numbers for summary tasks, and letters for work packages, say, a customized WBS for the design phase of a project might look like this: Dsn 1.a.

To define a custom WBS code, follow these steps:

1. **On the Project tab, click WBS, and then choose Define Code.**

   The WBS Code Definition dialog box appears. Although any existing WBS codes show numbers for each level with a period as a separator, the boxes in the WBS Code Definition dialog box are empty until you specify a custom scheme for your WBS codes.

Note: If you assemble several projects into a single master project (page 491), you can make WBS codes unique for each project, even if they use the same code mask. If you work with multiple projects, set up the code mask for a new project before you get too deep into defining the project's tasks. That way you don't have to renumber all your tasks later. In the Project Code Prefix box, type a prefix for the current project, like "PRJ01." Project then inserts this prefix at the beginning of the WBS codes for the tasks in the project; for instance, PRJ01.1.4.1.

---

2. **In the "Code mask" section's first Sequence cell, choose the type of characters you want to use for the top level of the hierarchy, as shown in Figure 4-7, top.**

   You can choose from Numbers (ordered), Uppercase Letters (ordered), Lowercase Letters (ordered), and, for the most flexible coding, Characters (unordered). With ordered numbers and letters, Project automatically increments the numbers or letters as you add tasks to the WBS, proceeding, for example, from 1.1 to 1.2. to 1.3.

3. **In the first Length cell, choose a number (from 1 to 10) for the length of the top level's mask.**

   Project initially selects Any, which means the entry for the level can be of any length. If the level uses a number, Project increments the number beginning at 1 and continuing to 10, 100, or 1000, if necessary. If the level uses letters, then you can type a code of any number of characters at that level.

   Choosing a number limits the entry to between one character and the length you specify. If you limit a numeric entry to one character, Project cycles through the numbers 1 through 9, moves to 0, and then repeats.

4. **In the Separator cell, choose the character that separates the top level from the next level.**

   Your only choices for separators are periods (.), minus signs (−), plus signs (+), or slashes (/).

5. **Repeat steps 2–4 for each additional level of the code mask.**

   You can specify dozens of levels in a code mask (in fact, a WBS code can be as long as 255 characters), but being miserly with levels makes the schedule easier to comprehend.

6. **After you've defined all the levels in the code mask, be sure that the "Generate WBS code for new task" checkbox is turned on if you want Project to automatically assign a WBS code to new tasks you create.**

   The only time you might want to turn this checkbox off is when you plan to renumber all the WBS codes after you've organized your tasks and don't want to be distracted by the interim codes that Project assigns.

   To ensure that your WBS codes are unique, keep the "Verify uniqueness of new WBS codes" checkbox turned on. Click OK, and then review the refreshed WBS codes in the task list, as shown in Figure 4-8. Although Project adds WBS codes to tasks when the "Generate WBS code for new task" checkbox is turned on, sometimes you want to type WBS codes manually, and that can lead to duplicate WBS codes. The only time you might turn off the "Verify uniqueness of new WBS codes" checkbox is if you're planning to renumber tasks later and you get tired of the warnings Project displays. As the box on page 96 explains, you can renumber the WBS codes for tasks to correct or reorder your project.

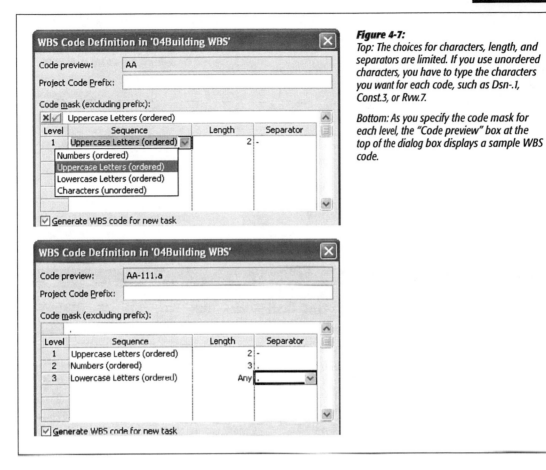

Figure 4-7:
Top: The choices for characters, length, and separators are limited. If you use unordered characters, you have to type the characters you want for each code, such as Dsn-.1, Const.3, or Rvw.7.

Bottom: As you specify the code mask for each level, the "Code preview" box at the top of the dialog box displays a sample WBS code.

7. If the WBS column isn't visible in the current view, add it so you can verify that the code is set up the way you want.

   Right-click the Task Name heading and, from the shortcut menu, choose Insert Column. In the new column, type *WBS* and then press Enter.

Congratulations! You've customized your WBS codes.

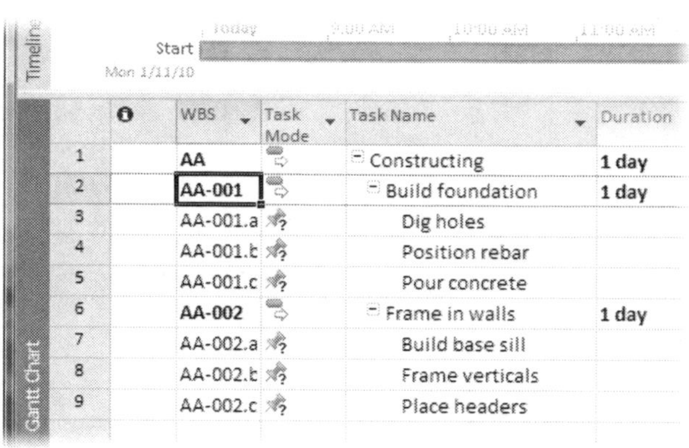

Figure 4-8:
When you click OK, Project automatically applies the code mask to all the tasks in the schedule.

Renumbering Task WBS Codes

When you customize WBS codes, the "Generate WBS code for new task" checkbox tells Project to automatically assign WBS codes to new tasks you create, whether you insert tasks within the outline or add new tasks at the end. With this setting, as soon as you press Enter to save a new task, the WBS code pops into the WBS cell, maintaining the sequence you've defined. Moving tasks around also adjusts WBS codes and, before you know it, your WBS sequence can be a mess.

The alternative is to turn *off* this checkbox, and then, after a heated session of adding or modifying the task order, renumber the WBS codes all at once. Fortunately, that's pretty easy to do. When the WBS is the way you want it, do the following:

1. If you want to renumber only some of the tasks in the Project file, select them.

2. On the Project tab, click WBS, and then choose Renumber.

3. In the WBS Renumber dialog box, select the "Entire project" option to renumber all your tasks. If you want to renumber only the selected tasks, choose the "Selected tasks" option instead.

4. Click OK. Project reapplies the WBS code scheme to the tasks, alphabetizing ordered letters and incrementing ordered numbers.

When you start to build other documents that reference your WBS codes (like work package Word files), you don't want Project to change the existing codes. That's another time to turn off the "Generate WBS code for new task" checkbox. As you type in new WBS codes manually, leave the "Verify uniqueness of new WBS codes" checkbox turned on so Project will warn you if you've duplicated an existing WBS code.

Documenting Work Package Details

If you've ever asked a teenager to do a chore, you know the importance of clearly specifying the work to perform and the results you expect. Otherwise, the dishes in the dishwasher might be placed in the cupboards—before they've been washed.

Providing project team members with clear guidance is equally important, but the task names in Project are too short to get into detail. For that reason, separate documents that describe work packages are a great way to tell team members how to do their assignments completely and correctly. And you don't even have to worry about keeping track of lots of loose documents: You can link them to the Project schedule, as described on page 551.

Ideally, a work package document describes the work to perform, how to know when it's done, and how to tell whether it's done right. A work package for baking a loaf of bread might include the steps for mixing, kneading, forming, and baking the bread. The document could specify that the bread is done when tapping it delivers a hollow thump. Similarly, the work package might state that a successful loaf is an attractive brown color, twice as tall as the unbaked dough, and full of evenly sized holes.

Building Work Package Documents in Word

Even small projects require dozens of work package documents. You can speed up your work by creating a Word template for work packages that's as basic or as fancy as your knowledge of Word. That way, you can open the template and have a document all labeled and ready for you to fill in. For example, you might set up a basic work package template with the following information:

- **WBS number**. The WBS number that Project assigned to the task in your project schedule.

- **Work package name**. The task name from the project schedule.

- **Description of work**. You can use paragraphs or bullet points and provide as much detail as you need to ensure success. If you know an experienced resource is going to do the work, the document can be brief. For trainees, on the other hand, you can provide detailed checklists of steps or the name of the person who can mentor the assigned resource.

- **Result**. Describe the final state when the work is done as well as how to verify that the work was done correctly. In a work package for setting up a computer, for example, you might include the list of programs that should launch when the installation is complete.

- **Reference materials**. Projects use many types of documents to specify deliverables: requirements, specifications, blueprints, and so on. If other detailed documentation exists, list where to find those documents, like the folder on the network drive or the project notebook.

Making a Word template

Creating a Word template is no harder than creating a Word document. However, finding and using a template takes some setup. Here's how to create a Word template and save it for reuse:

1. **Create a Word document with the labels you want to include.**

   If you want to get fancy, you can insert a logo, add instructions to help others fill in work packages, and so on.

2. **In Word 2010, on the File tab, click Save. In Word 2007, choose Office button→ Save.**

   The Save As dialog box appears.

3. **Navigate to the folder you use for your custom templates.**

   For example, create a folder called Templates in the My Documents folder.

4. **In Word 2010, in the "File name" box, type the name of the template. In the "Save as type" box, choose Word Template, and then click Save.**

   In Word 2007, in the navigation bar on the left side of the dialog box, click Trusted Templates before you click Save.

5. **To set up faster access to your template, on the File tab, click Options.**

   Telling Word where to find your custom templates makes it easier to locate and open this template later. That way, you can see these templates right in the New Document dialog box every time you start a new project, as described in the next section.

Tip: If you don't specify a folder for templates, then you can always use Windows Explorer to navigate to the folder that contains your template files. When you double-click a Word template file, Word launches and creates a new document based on that template.

---

6. **In the Word Options dialog box, click Advanced. Then scroll to the General section at the bottom of the dialog box and select File Locations.**

   You want to tell Word where to find your templates.

7. **Select "User templates" or "Workgroup templates", and then click Modify. In the Modify Location dialog box, navigate to your template folder, and then click OK.**

   Choose the folder you created in step 3.

8. **Click OK again to close the Options dialog box.**

Tip: The box on page 99 explains how to find the File Locations feature in Word 2003.

Opening a Word template

In Word 2010, on the File tab, click New. (In Word 2007, choose Office button→New.) Under the Available Templates heading, click "My templates". The New dialog box appears showing the templates in your user templates folder. Select the template you want, and then click OK.

To use a template in Word 2003, choose File→New. In the New Document task pane, under the Templates heading, click "On my computer". The Templates dialog box appears open to the General tab, which displays the templates in your User templates or Workgroup template folders (whichever you chose in the previous steps). Select the template, and then click OK.

Setting File Locations in Word 2003

If you're still using Word 2003—and plenty of folks are—you'll find File Locations in a different spot than in Word 2010. To specify where you store your custom templates, do the following:

1. Choose Tools→Options, and then click the File Locations tab.

2. Select "User templates" or "Workgroup templates", and then click Modify.

3. Navigate to and select the folder you created in step 3 on page 98, exactly as for Word 2010.

Linking Work Packages to the Project Schedule

After you create work package documents (as described in the previous section) that spell out the details of tasks, you're likely to refer to those documents as you work on your Project schedule. There's no need to open them by hand or try to remember where they are. Instead, you can insert a hyperlink from a task in the Project schedule to the corresponding work package document. With a hyperlink in place, opening the work package document is a quick click in Project.

To create a hyperlink in a Project task, do the following:

1. **In Project, right-click the task you want to link to a work package document, and then choose Hyperlink from the shortcut menu.**

   The Insert Hyperlink dialog box appears.

2. **In the "Link to" bar, click Existing File Or Web Page.**

   Navigate to the folder that contains the work package document, and then double-click the name of the work package file. The "Look in" box shows the folder while the Address box displays the filename.

3. **Click OK.**

   In the Indicators column, a hyperlink icon appears, as shown in Figure 4-9.

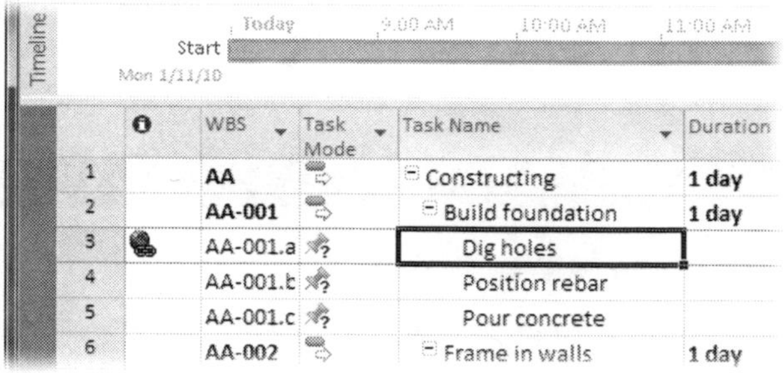

Figure 4-9:
The Hyperlink icon looks like a globe with a link of chain, a not-so-subtle commentary that hyperlinks connect the world. If the Indicators column isn't visible, then right-click the Entry table and choose Insert Column on the shortcut menu. In the Field Name drop-down list, choose Indicators.

4. To access a hyperlinked file, simply right-click the hyperlink icon in the Indicator cell and then choose Hyperlink→Open Hyperlink.

The program associated with the file launches, and the file opens.

CHAPTER 5

Estimating Task Work and Duration

Once you've identified the tasks that comprise a project, the next step is figuring out how many hours or days of work those tasks entail—and the time to allow for that work. For example, you need to know how long it takes to repair and paint the front of a '67 Mustang Fastback to figure out whether you can hide the evidence before your parents get home from vacation.

You'll never predict project duration with total accuracy. However, estimating work time as closely as you can is the goal, because both high and low estimates can cause problems. Overestimate how long your project will take, and the project might get squelched before it begins. Underestimate, and you might run into disappointment, extensions, and financial consequences.

In this chapter, you'll learn different ways to estimate time and duration, how to improve estimates, and how to avoid estimation land mines. You'll also learn how to create spreadsheets for collecting estimated numbers from team members, and then import the numbers into Microsoft Project.

One challenge early in project planning is trying to define tasks and build a schedule when you don't have all the information you need. You may not know when some tasks must occur or how long other tasks may take. In Project 2010, you can fill in the information you do know and leave the rest blank without hearing a peep from the program. In fact, you can type notes in date or duration fields to jog your memory when you fill in the missing information later. Project 2010 uses colors and end caps on task bars to indicate what information a task includes. In addition, you can plan your project from the top down by setting durations for summary tasks. Then, as you add subtasks to a summary task, you can see how much of the summary task duration the subtasks consume. This chapter shows you how to use all these nifty planning features.

Once your Project file includes tasks with estimated values, you can start transforming the file into a true schedule, which is the topic of the next several chapters.

Understanding Work and Duration

In Project, *work* and *duration* are both ways of measuring project time, but each term has a specific meaning:

- **Work.** The number of person-hours (or equipment-hours) a task requires. For example, packing all your belongings may take you (that is, one person) 20 hours. (Hey, you have a lot of sentimental keepsakes.)

- **Duration.** How long a task lasts. Duration varies according to how many resources (people or equipment) you use, and when those resources are available. You may need 5 days for the 20-hour packing task, because you have other things to do and can't spend more than 4 hours each day on packing. If you convince four other friends to help, the duration decreases to half a day, but the five of you still devote 20 hours of work to boxing up gewgaws.

Whether you estimate work, duration, or both depends on whether you know how many people are available to work on tasks. Start by estimating work. If you don't know how many resources are available, you can use the work estimate as the duration estimate. When only one person works full-time on a task, the number of hours of work initially equals the hours of duration. However, if you have resources in mind, you can estimate a duration that differs from hours of work. Up to a point, you can shorten task duration by adding additional resources, as in the previous packing example. Either way, when you assign resources, Project adjusts the task work and duration accordingly (page 222).

Note: After you estimate work and task duration, you're ready for the chapters on building a schedule (page 156) and assigning resources (page 202).

Getting Good Estimates

Guesswork is the more candid name for estimating, but important project decisions hinge on guesses being good. Project stakeholders care deeply about financial measures like return on investment, cash flow, payback period, and so on. Because time *is* money, the time you estimate for project work translates into the financial measures that make or break your project. Too-high and too-low estimates of time—and therefore costs—can both jeopardize a project, albeit for different reasons, as the box on page 103 explains.

Why Not to Over- or Underestimate

The temptation to tell people what they want to hear is almost irresistible. Lowering your initial estimates to more optimistic numbers might make stakeholders happy for a while. Invariably, though, underestimated projects come in late and over budget. The projects don't meet their targets, but worse than that, the money would have been better spent on other projects.

On the other hand, being too pessimistic can be just as bad. Ironically, high estimates tend to come true, even though their low-ball relatives hardly ever do. Lavish estimates sometimes lead stakeholders to expect—or demand—more features or higher quality. Moreover, team members feel flush with time and might embellish their assignments beyond what is required or work at a more leisurely pace. The result could be an unacceptable return on the money invested, which may persuade the stakeholders to can the project—or worse, pass over a good project.

Overly padded estimates can also limit an organization's productivity. When bloated projects commandeer the budget and resources, other worthy projects and their benefits get squeezed out.

Estimating is part science, part sorcery, so it takes some time to master. You're trying to forecast the future as accurately as possible. To make your estimates more precise, you can choose an appropriate estimating method, obtain estimates from experienced people, ask for a range instead of a single number, and avoid the estimate padding game. To improve future estimates, be sure to tell estimators how their estimates compared to the actual project numbers.

How Accurate Do You Need to Be?

Before you launch into estimating, find out how good your estimates have to be. If your clients for a custom-built home tell you their budget is $5 million, give or take a million, you have some room to maneuver. On the other hand, the harried parents who are building an addition to house their triplets probably have a tight budget and want the estimate right on the nose.

Objectives, requirements, specifications, and other project planning details affect the estimates you develop, so accurate estimates require research and planning—and those take time and effort. No one wants to spend a lot of time or money estimating a project that's going to cost too much or finish too late, so sometimes a quick-and-dirty estimate can help determine whether the project should proceed at all. There are a couple of ways to trade off up-front effort for accuracy:

- **Estimate based on the required level of accuracy.** If a rough estimate is fine—for example, plus or minus 50 to 75 percent—you can produce a high-level estimate in almost no time. This type of estimate is called a *rough order of magnitude estimate* (also known as SWAG, which stands for scientific wild-assed guess) and works well for selecting projects. Typically, a second round of estimates for organization-wide budgeting strives for plus or minus 25 percent.

For the final project budget, you have to spend time up front clarifying project details in order to produce a more accurate estimate (for instance, plus or minus 10 percent).

- **Estimate more accurately as you progress.** Big projects often use *feasibility studies,* small projects whose sole purpose is to determine whether it makes sense to pursue the full-blown project any further. For example, a small team could develop a prototype system to see whether the time savings are sufficient. The time and money spent early on can save the organization from spending orders of magnitude more on a dead-end project. You can use order-of-magnitude estimates to make go/no-go decisions for projects. If a project gets approval to proceed, you perform another round of estimating with more detail. Then, at the end of each project phase, you can review performance and refine your estimate for the next phase to see if the project should continue.

Finally, give yourself enough time to come up with an estimate you feel confident in, even if you have to stall a little while, as the box on page 104 explains. After you admire your initial estimate, look at it with a more critical eye. Does the estimate seem ridiculously high or optimistically low? Either way, dive back in and tweak the estimate until you think it's realistic. Because stakeholders usually hope for good news and balk at higher estimates, document your reasoning and assumptions. Not only will you be able to defend your results, but you'll also know to rework your estimates if any of your assumptions change.

REALITY CHECK

Know When to Hold 'Em

Managing stakeholders' expectations would be a breeze if they patiently waited for your thoroughly analyzed estimates. But stakeholders and management are an impatient bunch, so the pressure is on for estimates before you're ready. Don't cave in to that pressure, or you may end up making promises you can't keep. Innocent questions like, "What's the finish date looking like?" don't call for a specific, set-in-stone answer on the spot. Indeed, the people asking don't expect you to answer right away (but they are sure to remember your answer if you give them one). And if you provide a date prematurely, your answer may come back to haunt you. (If you're like most people, your off-the-cuff estimates are almost always overly optimistic.)

Without the project plan in hand, it's easy to forget details or even major components. Instead of caving, you're better off saying something like, "I'll have the analysis done by tomorrow (or next week, or next month) and can give you a better answer then."

Of course, if a bigwig is asking for an answer, you might feel queasy about stonewalling. If you feel compelled to give an answer, then deliver a document called a *basis of estimate* (BOE), which documents the elements that go into your current estimate: assumptions, risks, risk mitigation, constraints, and so on.

Ways to Estimate Work

Estimating is an art form because there are so many ways to approach it. And identifying the best method for a specific project is a matter of experience. Here are a few of the approaches you're most likely to use:

- **Estimating from the bottom up.** With this approach, you estimate each work package for a project; the estimates for work packages total up to produce the estimated numbers for their summary tasks. In turn, the estimates for summary tasks roll up until you have an estimate for the entire project. Microsoft Project is the perfect tool for bottom-up estimating, because summary tasks automatically calculate totals from the values for lower level-tasks.

- **Estimating from the top down.** This approach works best if you have experience with similar projects, because you estimate the project at higher levels, like phases, and progressively allocate the estimated time to lower levels of work.

Tip: Whether you estimate from the bottom up or the top down, don't forget to include time for rework. Deliverables aren't always right the first time around, but most people estimate how long it takes for the first delivery. Be sure to add time to your estimates for correcting first-round shortcomings.

- **Parametric estimating.** This method of using historical data along with project variables to estimate a job is common in construction, for example, when your contractor tells you that your addition will cost $200 per square foot and take 4 months. This approach is helpful only when you have a significant history of documented performance (page 486), so you know what the duration and cost should be, for example by the square feet of construction, modules in software development, or pages of documentation. In the construction industry, estimating programs use typical construction costs and times to develop estimates, but you can use Microsoft Excel to develop estimating formulas as well. For an example of a parametric estimating tool, check out the software development tool at *www.costxpert.com.*

Tip: Groups of people almost always produce better estimates than any one person. Learn why at the following websites:

http://en.wikipedia.org/wiki/The_Wisdom_of_Crowds

http://en.wikipedia.org/wiki/Delphi_method

http://en.wikipedia.org/wiki/Wideband_delphi

Getting Estimates from the Right People

You want someone experienced in the work involved to estimate its effort. You wouldn't ask your auto mechanic to estimate the time for building an addition to your house. Regardless of the type of project you manage, you have to track down experts to help you estimate what the work is going to take.

If you know who's likely to work on your project, those resources can produce even better estimates, because they know their strengths and limitations. Besides, when people set targets for themselves, they are often more motivated to meet those targets.

Tip: When several people provide estimates, you must make sure you know what the numbers represent. Suppose someone tells you that developing a brochure takes 2 weeks. Is that 80 hours of work, or is it a 2-week duration for a writer, a copy editor, and a graphic artist? Spelling out tasks in work package documents is one way to obtain clarity. The next section explains another technique for clarifying estimates.

Don't Ask for Only One Number

In project management circles, the Program Evaluation and Review Technique (PERT) uses *best, worst,* and *most probable* estimates to get a better idea of how projects might play out. Packing the contents of a house might usually (that is, most probably) take 3 days. If the owners live with Zen simplicity or reminisce over every tchotchke, then packing could take only a day (best) or weeks (worst). You can borrow the concept of PERT to get better estimates from your team members, even if you don't use PERT to manage your project.

Tip: Project 2010 doesn't include the PERT add-in that was available in previous versions. That's OK. Project's PERT features weren't really worth the effort. PERT is a statistical approach that uses Monte Carlo simulations to show possible project outcomes. The result is a probability of a project finishing on time given combinations of optimistic, pessimistic, and expected values. If you want to use PERT, consider a third-party program that integrates with Project, such as @Risk for Project (*www.palisade.com*) or Risk+ (*www.deltek.net/products/riskplus/default.asp*).

Simply by asking for best, worst, and most probable estimates, as shown in Figure 5-1, you start your estimators thinking about what could go wrong, what could go right, and what's happened most often on similar efforts. You still use the most probable estimate in Project, but PERT can increase your confidence in that number.

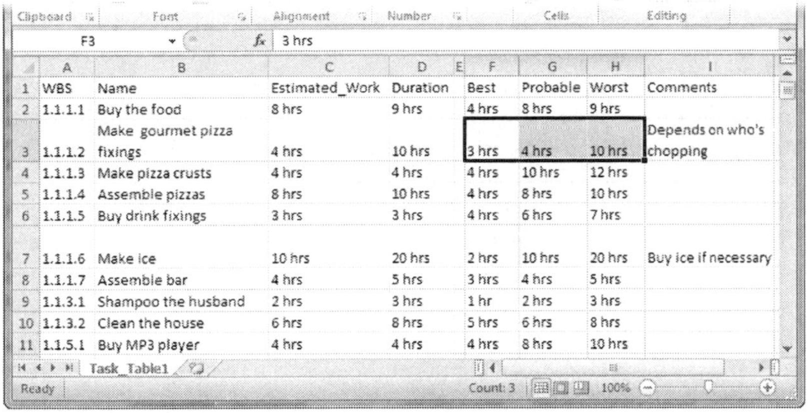

	A	B	C	D	E	F	G	H	I
1	WBS	Name	Estimated_Work	Duration		Best	Probable	Worst	Comments
2	1.1.1.1	Buy the food	8 hrs	9 hrs		4 hrs	8 hrs	9 hrs	
3	1.1.1.2	Make gourmet pizza fixings	4 hrs	10 hrs		3 hrs	4 hrs	10 hrs	Depends on who's chopping
4	1.1.1.3	Make pizza crusts	4 hrs	4 hrs		4 hrs	10 hrs	12 hrs	
5	1.1.1.4	Assemble pizzas	8 hrs	10 hrs		4 hrs	8 hrs	10 hrs	
6	1.1.1.5	Buy drink fixings	3 hrs	3 hrs		4 hrs	6 hrs	7 hrs	
7	1.1.1.6	Make ice	10 hrs	20 hrs		2 hrs	10 hrs	20 hrs	Buy ice if necessary
8	1.1.1.7	Assemble bar	4 hrs	5 hrs		3 hrs	4 hrs	5 hrs	
9	1.1.3.1	Shampoo the husband	2 hrs	3 hrs		1 hr	2 hrs	3 hrs	
10	1.1.3.2	Clean the house	6 hrs	8 hrs		5 hrs	6 hrs	8 hrs	
11	1.1.5.1	Buy MP3 player	4 hrs	4 hrs		4 hrs	8 hrs	10 hrs	

Figure 5-1: *Giving people a chance to explain their estimates helps you understand the project better. Pessimistic numbers could be red flags for risks you need to manage. Or estimators might give optimistic estimates because they've found shortcuts that work in some situations.*

Don't Pad Estimates

Padding estimates dooms projects to failure. At the same time, you need some kind of insurance to protect your project's finish date and cost. Increasing estimates for all to see is good—you create a safety margin that the entire team can share, using some of it if something goes seriously wrong. On the contrary, padding that's hidden in estimates is a self-centered approach that leads to any number of problems.

The disadvantages of padding

People want to look good and deliver to their estimates, so they decide to build in extra time to cover problems that might arise with *their* work. This hidden padding happens all too often and is tough to get rid of because it's hard to see. But padding can lead to some problems:

- **Bloated estimates.** If everyone slips in some padding, estimates get bigger as they move up the food chain. By the time the top-level management gets the estimates, they're as engorged as well-fed ticks and so inaccurate that no one knows how long the project will really take.
- **Padding games.** Some project managers try to eliminate hidden padding by trimming each of the estimates they get. If team members see their estimates cut, they simply plump their padding more the next time. With games like these, no one knows whether they can trust each other's estimates, and the relationship between the project manager and the team members worsens each time around.
- **Lack of feedback.** Without feedback, the estimators never get to find out whether their estimates were high, low, or somewhere in between. As you'll learn on page 108, estimators need feedback if you want them to improve.

Using safety margins to increase success

Contingency funds and management reserve are two types of safety margins that produce a more honest and cooperative scenario. Instead of pockets of personal padding throughout the project, everyone shares one pot of time and money and receives some only if they need it. This way, the project is likely to contain less padding and the leeway is more likely to go to the people who need it most. Because the safety margins are public, people must ask permission to draw on them.

Savvy project managers and management teams use two types of safety margins:

- **Contingency funds and hours.** Project contingency funds and hours are set aside to cover problems and risks that might crop up (page 57). You can dip into the pot if something goes wrong. If it's smooth sailing, then the project might come in early or under budget. For example, banks make builders set aside money for problems so that the building doesn't end up half-built because the builder ran out of money.

  The amount of contingency padding is based on the risks involved. If you're estimating a project that isn't well defined or represents unfamiliar work, then the contingency could be 50 to 75 percent or more. For projects you can perform with your eyes closed, the contingency might be only 5 to 10 percent. Contingency funds and hours are part of the project plan, so you, as project manager, can hand them out as you see fit.

- **Management reserve.** A second level of public padding is management reserve. As its name implies, this safety margin isn't at the project manager's discretion. It's a pool of time and money that management can distribute if unexpected events occur—risks that aren't in the risk management plan (page 54). While you have to ask management for a piece of management reserve, the benefit is that you don't have to beg the project's sponsor or customer for time or money.

Give Feedback on Estimates

In a common scenario, you ask people for estimates. You use those estimates, perform the project, and then discover that the tasks take longer or (occasionally) shorter. If you don't tell the estimators how their estimates compared to what actually happened, then you'll get the same incorrect estimate the next time you ask. If you want estimates that keep getting better, you have to track actual results (page 388) *and* share the comparisons of estimated to actual performance (page 409) with the people who estimate. In addition, these results go into a project archive (page 48) so project managers on future projects can learn from previous projects and achieve more accurate estimates. As the box on page 109 describes, accounting systems don't always track a project's actual performance the way you need to see it. In those cases, you need a tracking system within your project environment.

The Problem with Accounting Numbers

Some companies juggle numbers in corporate accounting systems—sometimes to keep costs for different parts of a project within the limits set by a customer or to satisfy some esoteric financial need. Moving numbers between parts of a project means you have no idea what the actual performance was. To make matters worse, timesheet categories might not gather the project data you need. If you want to obtain project management history and feedback, you might have to ask team members to fill out a second timesheet.

No one likes filling out timesheets, so it's best to minimize your imposition on team members. For instance, you can request time at a summary task level instead of individual work packages, or request weekly totals instead of daily ones. When you ask for team members' time, collect not only the hours worked, but also the hours that the people estimate are remaining. If their numbers don't match your plan, you can act on that early warning sign to figure out how to bring the tasks back on track (page 327).

Getting Estimates into Project

Although you can type estimates directly into task fields in Project, an Excel spreadsheet has several advantages. First of all, many people who estimate tasks are familiar with Excel but not Project. (In addition, estimators may not have a copy of Project, but they almost certainly have Excel.) Excel makes it easier to adjust estimates than Project, for instance, recalculating hour estimates into days or choosing worst-case estimates for high-risk tasks.

You can export work package tasks from Project to build a simple estimating spreadsheet in Excel. You can divvy up the tasks for each estimator into a separate Excel workbook, and then reassemble the results in one master spreadsheet that you import back into Project. If you ask for three estimates (page 106), you can use Excel functions to set your estimated values.

To get estimates into a Project file, you first export the task names and WBS codes for work package tasks to an Excel workbook. Because WBS codes are unique, you can use them as a link between tasks in the spreadsheet with the corresponding tasks in Project. Then, after you complete your spreadsheet of estimate numbers, you import those values into the existing tasks in your Project file.

Exporting Work Packages to Excel

If you're estimating from the bottom up, the only tasks you estimate are the work packages—the lowest-level tasks in the Project outline. You don't have to export summary tasks because Project calculates their values from the tasks below them. In Project, you use a *filter* (page 620) to display only the tasks that pass the tests you specify—in this case, work package tasks for a project. Then you load those tasks into an Excel spreadsheet, using a set of instructions called an *export map* to set up the column names. This section shows you how to export tasks to an Excel estimating spreadsheet. Then, in the next section, you'll learn how to import the estimates back into Project.

Tip: If you're finding the terms *filter* and *export map* hard to grasp, fear not. These tools will make much more sense when you see them in action in the following steps. In fact, there's a ready-made filter and export map you can download from *www.missingmanuals.com/cds*. The ProjectMM_Customizations. mpp file contains a filter called "Work packages," which shows only work package tasks (Figure 5-2). The export map called "Estimate worksheet" exports the Name, Work, and Scheduled Duration fields to Excel—just the ones you need for estimates. After you download the file, use the Project Organizer to copy the maps into your Project global.mpt file, as described on page 669. For maps to appear in the Export Wizard or Import Wizard, they must be in your Project global template, not your Project file.

Here are the steps for exporting work package tasks to Excel, assuming that you've copied the export map from ProjectMM_Customizations.mpp into your Project global template (the steps also explain how to use a new map):

1. **Open a Project file of your own, and then choose File→Save As.**

   The Save As dialog box opens.

2. **In the "Save as type" drop-down list, choose Excel Workbook. In the "File name" box, type the name for the file, and then click Save.**

   Project launches the Export Wizard.

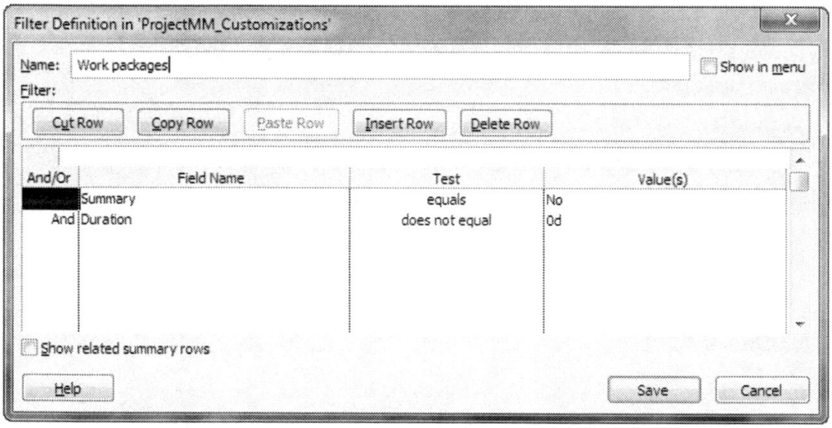

Figure 5-2:
The "Work packages" filter hides both summary tasks (whose Summary field values equal No) and milestones (Duration equals 0d). Summary tasks obtain their values by rolling up the values of their subtasks, so you don't have to estimate them. Tasks that represent milestones have a duration of zero, so they too require no estimating.

3. **Click Next to start the wizard.**

   On the Export Wizard's Data page, the wizard automatically selects the Selected Data option, which means you can define the export map you want to use, so simply click Next to continue.

4. **On the Export Wizard's Map page, select the "Use existing map" option, and then click Next.**

   If you haven't copied the map from the ProjectMM_Customizations.mpp file into your global template, select the "New map" option, click Next, and then proceed to step 6 to define the export mapping.

5. **On the Export Wizard's Map Selection page, select the "Estimate worksheet" map, and then click Next.**

   Stepping through the next few screens lets you review or change the map settings before you export.

6. **On the Export Wizard's Map Options page, review the checkboxes that specify the data you're exporting. Click Next.**

   Because your Project file is still in its infancy, the only checkbox that should be turned on is Tasks. In this example (like most of the time), you want the Project field names to become column names in Excel, so turn on the "Export includes headers" checkbox.

7. **On the Export Wizard's Task Mapping page, review the export filter and the field mappings, as shown in Figure 5-3.**

   The "Destination worksheet name" box automatically sets the name for the Excel worksheet to Task_Table1. You can stick with that or change the name to something more meaningful.

   The fields you export include WBS (which uniquely identifies each task), Name (so you know which task you're estimating), Work, and Scheduled Duration. Because WBS codes are unique, exporting the WBS field to the estimate spreadsheet simplifies importing your estimates, as you learn on page 113.

   As you can see in this example, you can name the columns in Excel whatever you want. For example, to clearly show that the workbook is for estimating, change the field name in the To: Excel Field column corresponding to Work to *Estimated_Work*. For extra credit, you can export a text field, such as *Text1*, which you can use to capture estimating comments in your Excel workbook. When you import estimates back into Project, your assumptions and reasoning will be readily accessible in the Text1 field in your Project file.

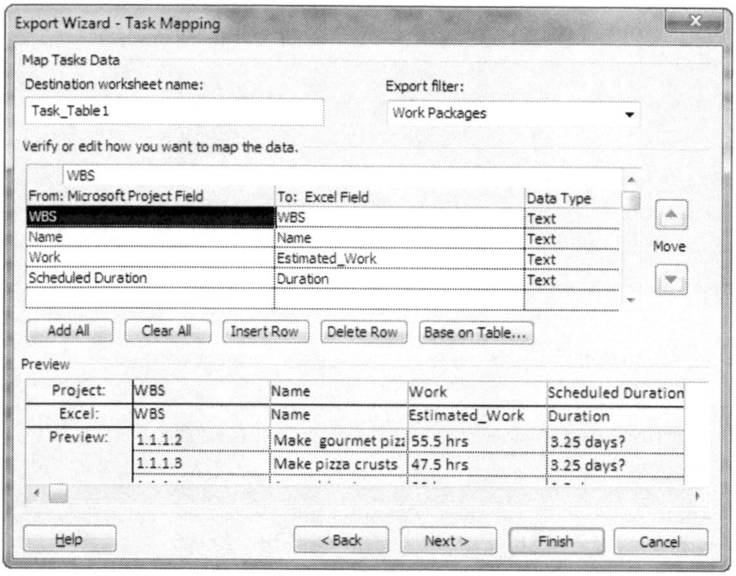

Figure 5-3:
If you use the "Estimate worksheet" map, the "Export filter" box is set to Work Packages, which means that you export only low-level tasks with no summary tasks or milestones. (In Project 2010, the Preview area shows the filtered list of tasks.)

8. Click Finish.

    Project exports the tasks into a new workbook, shown in Figure 5-4, but you must launch Excel and then open the file to see it.

    If clicking Finish displays a message about trying to save a file in an older file format, then you haven't set up Project to work with older Microsoft file formats. To instruct Project to play nicely with older Microsoft file formats (as well as other file formats Project doesn't initially recognize), choose File→Options. In the Project Options dialog box, click Trust Center and then click Trust Center Settings. Under Legacy Formats, select the "Allow loading files with legacy or non default file formats" option, and then click OK.

WORKAROUND WORKSHOP

Copying Estimates from Excel to Project

If you're estimating a small project and tasks employ only one resource, then you can copy estimate cells in an Excel spreadsheet directly into cells in the Work or Duration column in the Project table area. To copy cells from a spreadsheet into cells in a Project file, follow these steps:

1. Open the Excel spreadsheet and select the cells that contain your work estimates (work or duration).

2. Press Ctrl+C to copy the cells to the Clipboard.

3. Switch to Project, and click the first blank cell in the Work or Duration column in the table area. (If the Work column isn't visible, then right-click the table heading area, and then choose Insert Column. In the drop-down menu, choose Work, and then click OK.)

4. Press Ctrl+V to paste the estimated values. Project copies each cell from the spreadsheet into the selected cells and the ones below it.

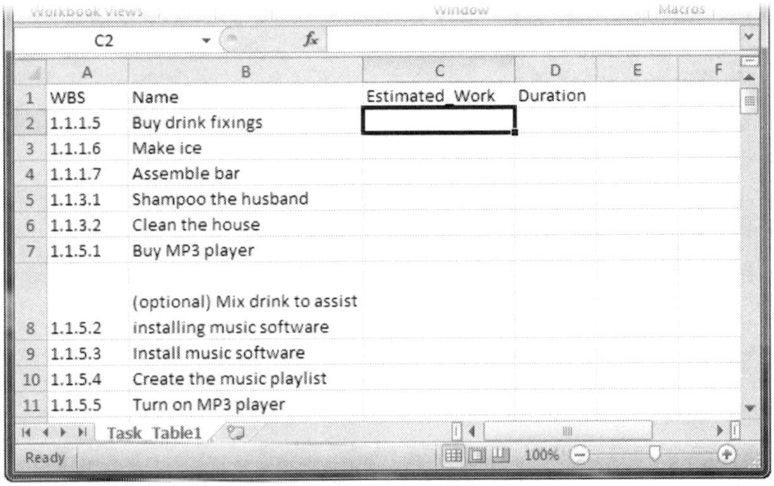

Figure 5-4:
You can add additional columns in the Excel workbook for best and worst case estimates, or a column for the name of the person responsible for estimating the task. Add whatever columns you need to make your work in Excel easier: You don't have to import those columns back into your Project file.

Importing Estimates into Project

Unlike importing a WBS (page 516), when you import estimates into a Project file, the tasks already exist. Instead of adding new tasks to the project, you want your estimated values to sidle into the fields for the appropriate tasks. The Import Wizard includes an option to do just that.

The following steps show you how to create a map to import estimates into Project. However, these steps also tell you where to find the instructions for using the existing map from the ProjectMM_Customizations.mpp file. Here's how you import estimated effort into the tasks already in your Project file:

1. **If you want to use an existing import map, download the ProjectMM_Customizations.mpp file at** *www.missingmanuals.com/cds.*

    This Project file contains a map called "Import estimates" that maps fields in an Excel workbook to Project fields. You can use the Organizer to copy that map into your Project global.mpt template (page 669).

2. **With the Project file that you want to import into open, choose File→Open.**

    The Open dialog box opens set to open Microsoft Project Files (the button to the right of the "File name" box), but you want to choose Excel Workbook instead.

3. **Navigate to the folder that contains your estimating workbook (the one you created in the previous section, for example), and then, in the file list, double-click its name. Alternatively, select the file name, and then click Open.**

    Project launches the Import Wizard. Click Next to start the wizard.

4. On the Import Wizard's Map page, the wizard automatically selects the New Map option, which is what you want if you don't have a map defined. Click Next.

If you've saved a map to import estimates into Project, select the "Use existing map" option, as described on page 522.

5. On the Import Wizard's Import Mode page, select the "Merge the data into the active project" option, and then click Next.

The "Merge the data into the active project" option stuffs the values from your Excel workbook into fields in existing tasks in Project.

6. On the Import Wizard's Map Options page, select the Tasks option, and then click Next.

If the first row of the workbook includes column names, as the Excel spreadsheet exported in the previous section does, then turn on the "Import includes headers" checkbox.

7. On the Import Wizard's Task Mapping page, in the "Source worksheet name" drop-down list, choose the worksheet that contains the information you want to import.

If the Excel file contains only one worksheet, Project selects it automatically. You can choose a worksheet if Project doesn't select the one you want.

8. On the same page, match the values in the workbook to Project fields, as shown in Figure 5-5.

In addition to WBS and Name, this map matches the columns for work and duration in the workbook to the Work and Duration fields in Project.

9. When all the fields are mapped, and the Preview area shows values coming into the correct Project fields, click Next.

A message box might appear telling you that Project needs a primary key before it can merge the data. In English, this means you have to tell Project which fields in the Excel workbook and the Project file contain unique identifiers for tasks. A WBS code makes a perfect primary key, since each task has a WBS code and no two WBS codes are alike. Click OK to close the message box.

10. On the Import Wizard's Task Mapping page, in the table of matched fields, select the first WBS cell, and then click Set Merge Key.

In the table, both cell values change to MERGE KEY:WBS to indicate that the import process uses the WBS values to match up tasks. If you didn't export the WBS field with the tasks when you created the estimate worksheet, you may be able to use the Name field, which contains task names. (The one caveat for using the Name field as a merge key is that your task names must be unique.)

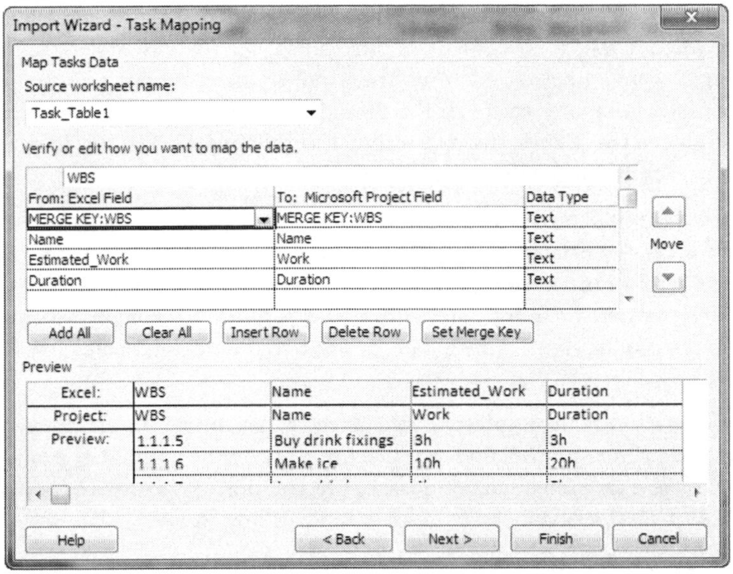

Figure 5-5:
After you open an exported spreadsheet in Excel, you can add additional columns for best and worst case estimates. If you added other columns to your Excel workbook, such as Best and Worst, you might see the words "(not mapped)" in the To: Microsoft Office Project Field column. That information remains in the workbook instead of transferring over to Project (which may be exactly what you want).

11. **Click Next, and finally click Finish to merge the estimates into your Project file.**

    The estimated values appear in the Work and Duration cells in Project. (The Entry table that comes with the Gantt Chart view doesn't include the Work column. To see the imported Work values in the Gantt Chart table area, insert the Work column by right-clicking the table heading and then choosing Insert Column. In the drop-down list, choose Work, and then click OK.)

Note: Sharp eyed readers may notice that Project converts work estimates to hours, regardless of whether you create estimates in days, weeks, hours, or minutes. Remember, the "Work is entered in" option (File→Project Options→Schedule) tells Project the units you want to use for work.

If you want to save the map, then click Save Map before you click Finish. In the Save Map dialog box, name the map in the "Map name" box, and then click Save.

Planning with Manually Scheduled Tasks

Project 2010 has a new scheduling mode, Manually Scheduled, which gives you total control over when a task is scheduled. At first blush, manual scheduling sounds like project management heresy. After all, the point of using project management software is to let a computer calculate the project schedule and adjust the schedule automatically as you change tasks, resource assignments, and so on. In reality, though, manual scheduling comes in handy in several ways:

- **Control over task dates.** Every so often, you run into a task that must occur on a specific date—for example, a training class for team members or a company-wide meeting. In earlier versions of Project, you could set a date constraint for either the start date or finish date, but not both. With a manually scheduled task, you can pin the start or finish date, or both, to the calendar dates you want (page 166).

- **Task information is incomplete.** In the early stages of project planning, you may not have all the information you need to fully define a task. For example, you know that a task must start on June 6, but you don't know how long it will take. Project 2010 lets you create tasks without filling in every field, as you'll soon learn.

- **Planning from the top down.** Executive management and project customers have a habit of telling you how long you have to complete a project long before you know whether that length of time is sufficient. With manually scheduled tasks, you can create summary tasks with the duration you've been given. Then, as you create tasks for all the project work, you can see whether they fit within the summary task duration or run over the allotted time (page 121).

Setting the Scheduling Mode

Out of the box, Project comes with Manually Scheduled mode turned on for all new tasks. If you're new to project management, you can leave that option alone and merrily set the dates for the tasks in your project. If you're a project management veteran, you can change this option to Auto Scheduled, so Project calculates the dates for new tasks you create. But you can also mix and match manually scheduled tasks and auto-scheduled tasks to your heart's content, as you'll soon see. This section tells you how to set the scheduling mode you want to use.

Setting the scheduling mode for new tasks

Project 2010 comes with a scheduling mode option for new tasks, set to Manually Scheduled by default. Here's how you change the mode Project uses for new tasks:

1. Choose File→Options, and then choose Schedule.

   The Project Options dialog box opens.

2. **Below the "Scheduling options for this project" heading, in the "New tasks created" drop-down list, choose how you want Project to assign dates to new tasks.**

   Initially, this box is set to Manually Scheduled. If you want new tasks to be automatically scheduled, then in the "New tasks created" drop-down list, choose Auto Scheduled. Then you have two choices. In the "Auto scheduled tasks scheduled on" drop-down list, choose Project Start Date if you want Project to set new tasks to be auto-scheduled with their start dates at the project's start date (page 135). Choose Current Date to create auto-scheduled tasks starting on today's date.

3. **Click OK.**

   The Project Options dialog box closes, and the scheduling mode appears at the bottom of the Project window, as shown in Figure 5-6.

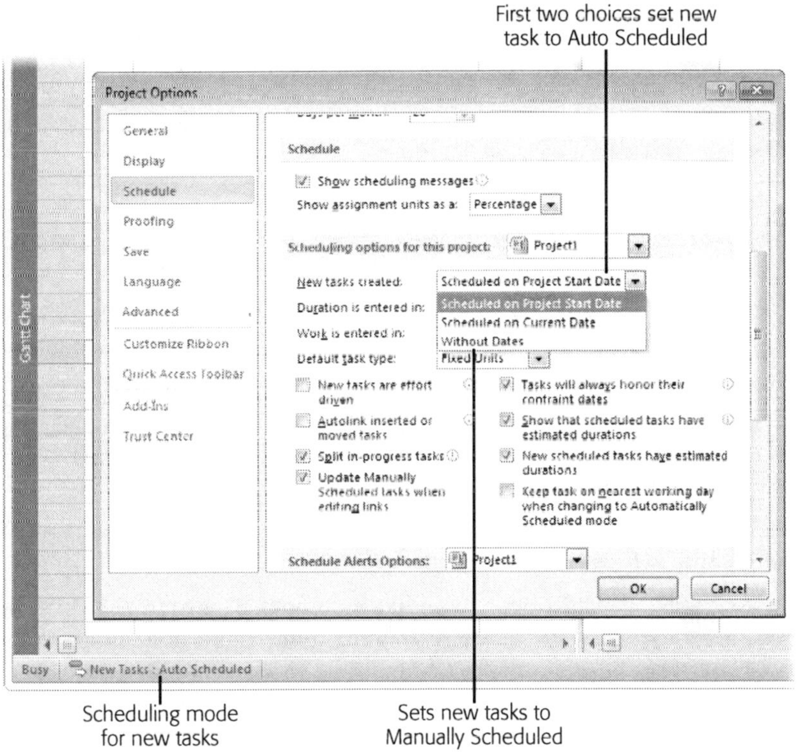

First two choices set new
task to Auto Scheduled

Scheduling mode
for new tasks

Sets new tasks to
Manually Scheduled

Figure 5-6:
The "Scheduling options for this project" drop-down list contains all the project files currently open in Project. Before you change any options, choose the project whose options you want to change. If you want your future projects to use a specific scheduling mode, create a template (page 675) with Project options set the way you want.

Switching the scheduling mode as you work

You don't have to open the Project Options dialog box every time you switch between Manually Scheduled and Auto Scheduled mode. You can change the mode as you work. In the Status panel at the bottom of the Project window (see Figure 5-6), click New Tasks, and then choose either Auto Scheduled or Manually Scheduled. Project sets new tasks to the mode you choose, until you change the mode again.

Changing the scheduling mode for an existing task

If you're in the early planning stages of a project, you may want tasks set to Manually Scheduled because you don't have all the info you need. As the project picture becomes clearer, many of those manually scheduled tasks fall into place in your overall schedule, and you'll likely want them to be auto-scheduled. On the other hand, if you usually work with auto-scheduled tasks but have one task that occurs on a specific date, then you can switch it to manually scheduled. Either way, you can change the scheduling mode for a task anytime you want.

Note: Changing the scheduling mode works only in Project files saved in the Project 2010 file format. If you open a file from an earlier version in Compatibility Mode, you can click the task mode cell but not change it. In addition, if you save a Project file containing manually scheduled tasks to an earlier file format, those tasks revert to being automatically scheduled.

The Entry, Schedule, and Summary tables automatically include the Task Mode column. To change a task's scheduling mode, follow these steps:

1. **Right-click the selection cell at the intersection of the column heading row and the task ID column, and then choose Entry, Schedule, or Summary to display the corresponding table.**

    To show the Task Mode field in another table, right-click the column heading to the right of where you want to insert the field, and then choose Insert Column. In the drop-down list, choose Task Mode.

2. **Click the task's Task Mode cell, click the down arrow that appears, and then choose Auto Scheduled or Manually Scheduled.**

    The Manually Scheduled icon looks like a pushpin. The Auto Scheduled icon looks like a task bar with an arrow pointing to the right. In addition, the task bar style in the timescale changes to indicate whether the task is manually or automatically scheduled, as described on page 119.

Creating Tasks with Incomplete Information

In previous versions of Project, you had to make your best guess for values like duration, start date, and finish date. But early in project planning, you may not have all the information you need. With manually scheduled tasks, you can fill in the information you have and worry about other fields later. For manually scheduled tasks, Project accepts the values you type in without complaint and changes the task bar style to show what information is available, as you can see in Figure 5-7.

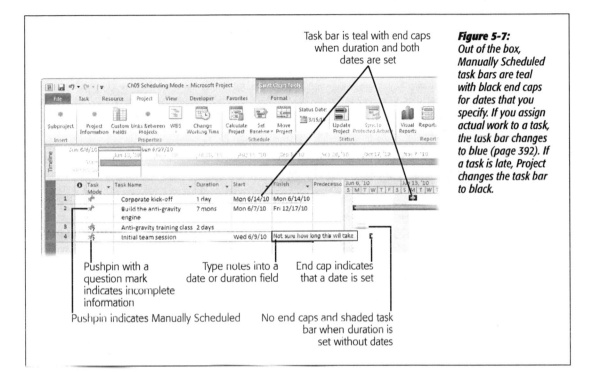

Figure 5-7:
Out of the box, Manually Scheduled task bars are teal with black end caps for dates that you specify. If you assign actual work to a task, the task bar changes to blue (page 392). If a task is late, Project changes the task bar to black.

Here's what happens when you create manually scheduled tasks with different types of information:

- **Setting task duration.** If you set the duration for a manually scheduled task without setting either date (task ID 3 in Figure 5-7), Project draws a task bar starting at the project start date with the duration you specify. The task bar doesn't have end caps, because you haven't defined either date. In addition, the task bar is only partially shaded.

- **Setting one date.** When you specify a date (Start or Finish) for a manually scheduled task, Project draws an end cap at that end of the task bar, as you can see with task ID 4 in Figure 5-7.

- **Typing notes in a date or duration field.** If you don't know the value for a date or duration field but you have some information about the value, you can type placeholder notes in the field. For example, in task ID 4 in Figure 5-7, the start date is set, but the duration is uncertain. When you determine the duration or the date, simply fill in the value, and Project adds end caps or colors to the task bar to indicate that the value is now present.

- **Setting two of three values.** If you specify two of the three values Project needs to schedule a task, it calculates the third value. For example, if you set the Start and Finish dates, Project calculates the duration. Or, you can set one date and the duration and let Project calculate the other date.

Tip: As you find out more about project tasks, you can filter your task list to display only the tasks without dates. To filter the list for tasks without a start or finish date, click the View tab. In the Data section, click the Filter down arrow and then choose More Filters. In the More Filters dialog box, double-click the Tasks Without Dates filter (or select the Tasks Without Dates filter and then click Apply).

Planning from the Top Down

If you're planning a project based on timeframes you've been given by the project customer or your management team, you can use manually scheduled tasks to schedule from the top down. To do this, you create manually scheduled summary tasks with the duration and dates you're trying to meet. Then you create subtasks within your summary tasks. Project keeps track of both the duration you specify for the summary task and the total duration of all the subtasks, so you can see whether the summary task is long enough.

Here's how you plan from the top down:

1. **Set the scheduling mode to Manually Scheduled by clicking New Tasks in the status bar at the bottom of the Project window and then choosing Manually Scheduled.**

    Project creates all new tasks as manually scheduled until you change the scheduling mode.

2. **Insert a new summary task by choosing Task→Insert→Insert Summary Task.**

    Project inserts two new rows, one for the summary task (task name <New summary task>) and one for a subtask (task name <New Task>). The program selects the Task Name cell for the new summary task. Type the name of the summary task, and then press Enter. Project selects the Task Name cell for the new subtask. Type the name of the subtask.

3. **Type the duration of the summary task in the summary task's Duration cell.**

Project draws a summary task bar the length of the duration. If you haven't set a start date, the task bar starts at the Project start date. If you type a date in the Start field, the task bar moves to start at that date.

4. **Add subtasks to the summary task.**

You can create subtasks as manually scheduled or auto-scheduled and create task dependencies between them. Project keeps track of the duration you specified for the summary task and the total duration of all the subtasks, as you can see in Figure 5-8. Project draws the summary task bar between the dates you specify in the summary task's Start and Finish fields. The task bar immediately below the summary task bar shows the rolled-up duration of all the subtasks, which is drawn between the Scheduled Start and Scheduled Finish dates.

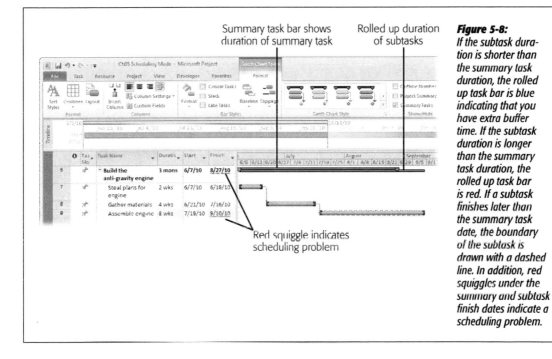

Summary task bar shows
duration of summary task

Rolled up duration
of subtasks

Red squiggle indicates
scheduling problem

Figure 5-8:
If the subtask duration is shorter than the summary task duration, the rolled up task bar is blue indicating that you have extra buffer time. If the subtask duration is longer than the summary task duration, the rolled up task bar is red. If a subtask finishes later than the summary task date, the boundary of the subtask is drawn with a dashed line. In addition, red squiggles under the summary and subtask finish dates indicate a scheduling problem.

Setting Up a Project Schedule

For days, weeks, sometimes months, you build the foundation of your project plan—the project mission statement, objectives, scope, requirements, and so on. At long last, you're ready to build the project schedule, the framework that defines the entire project. It tells everyone what work is required, who's supposed to do it, when it should be done, and how much it should cost. Something this fundamental to project management takes some preparation—and the next several chapters of this book—to construct.

The project schedule is where Microsoft Project becomes indispensable. In Project, you build a list of project tasks, link them to define their sequence, and assign resources and costs. The resulting schedule acts as your road map for getting the project done.

This chapter is the first leg of this schedule-building marathon. It begins with creating and saving a new Project file, whether you make one from scratch or start from an existing project or template. You'll learn how to set up basic options, such as the project's start date. The rest of the chapter describes adding the meat to the project file—entering the tasks and milestones that represent work and progress points. As you proceed to the remaining chapters in this section, you'll learn the rest of the process for building a project schedule.

Creating a New Project File

Before you can create that schedule you're itching to get started on, you must start a new Project file. This file is like a container that holds the project tasks, its resources, and the relationships between them. You can create a new Microsoft Project file in a few ways: from scratch, from a template, or from an existing Project file.

Tip: A template or existing file is usually a faster path to a new file, because they contain elements that are common to many other projects. Just edit the tasks, names, dates, and so on to match your current project. Furthermore, using existing elements as inspiration is much less intimidating than facing blank pages. (To learn how to create a new project based on a project you've done before, see the box on page 128.)

Creating a Blank Project File

A blank project file gives you a clean slate. If you're starting an unconventional project or just want to unleash your maximum creativity, you can use a new blank Project file like an empty canvas. Here are two ways to create a blank Project file:

- **When Project isn't running.** All you have to do is launch Project (for standard Microsoft Office installations, choose Start→All Programs→Microsoft Office→Microsoft Project 2010). The program immediately displays a blank project named *Project 1*. When you save the file for the first time (page 76), which you should do before you get too far, you can give it a meaningful name.

- **When Project is running.** Simply press Ctrl+N or, choose File→New and double-click "Blank project", and voilá—Project creates a new file with nothing in it.

Note: In Project 2010 (and other Office 2010 programs), the File tab contains many of the same commands that appeared on the File menu in earlier versions of Project. But it goes by a new name—Backstage. The Options command is now in the Backstage, instead of its old home on the Tools menu. (The Tools menu and the rest of the menus on the Project menu bar have been replaced by the ribbon in Project 2010.)

Creating a Project File from an Excel Workbook

If you define tasks in an Excel workbook, you can import those tasks into Project. The tried-and-true way to create a Project file from an Excel workbook is with the Open command (page 516). In the Open dialog box, choose Excel Workbook for the file type and then click Open, which launches the Import Wizard.

In Project 2010, there's a more obvious way to accomplish the same task:

1. **On the File tab, choose New.**

   The Backstage displays the Available Templates screen with commands for creating a new project in several ways.

2. **Click New from Excel Workbook.**

   The Open dialog box appears with the file type already set to Excel Workbook. If the Excel workbook you want to use was created in Excel 2003 or earlier, then in the file type drop-down list, choose Excel 97-2003 Workbook.

3. **Double-click the name of the workbook.**

The Project Import Wizard opens. See page 516 to learn how to use the Import Wizard to bring tasks into Project from Excel.

Note: Project 2010 can also create a new project from a SharePoint task list, if you happen to define tasks with that program. On the Available Templates screen, click "New from SharePoint task list".

Using a Template to Create a Project File

Projects, by definition, are unique endeavors, so you might think that a template won't be much help for creating a new Project file. But it turns out that the basic tasks for similar projects are often pretty much the same, even if the dates, team members, and results might be different.

Microsoft Project templates can contain a little project information or a lot. Templates commonly include typical tasks linked to one another in a logical sequence. You can add durations if the work almost always takes the same length of time. You can even include resources and resource assignments if you always use the same team.

Microsoft Project comes with several built-in templates for personal endeavors, such as moving your home, and business projects, such as helping your company comply with Sarbanes-Oxley regulations. Microsoft Office Online offers additional templates, as page 679 explains.

Tip: If your projects tend to follow a regular approach, you can also customize your own templates. See page 675 for instructions.

No matter where you get the template you're starting from, the steps for creating a new project file from a template are similar:

1. **On the File tab, choose New.**

The Backstage displays the Available Templates screen with commands for creating a blank project or choosing a template, as shown in Figure 6-1.

2. **To use a template you created, click "My templates" (near the top of the page). To use a template from Office.com, go down near the bottom of the page, and navigate under Office.com Templates to the category you want.**

For example, when you click Plans, you see subcategories for Business, Community, and Home. The Business category contains templates for launching new products, commercial construction, and so on. To find a particular type of template without bothering to browse through categories, type keywords in the "Search Office.com for templates" box and then click the right arrow.

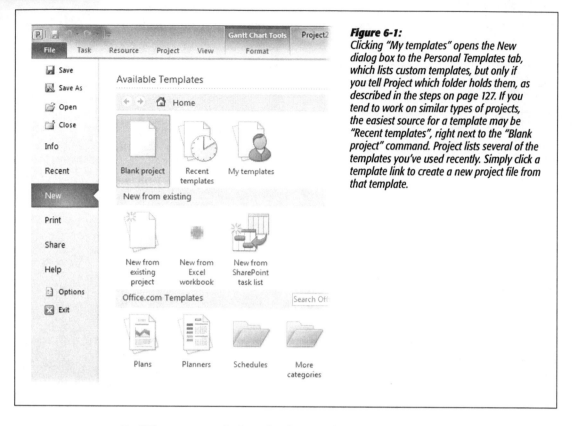

Figure 6-1:
Clicking "My templates" opens the New dialog box to the Personal Templates tab, which lists custom templates, but only if you tell Project which folder holds them, as described in the steps on page 127. If you tend to work on similar types of projects, the easiest source for a template may be "Recent templates", right next to the "Blank project" command. Project lists several of the templates you've used recently. Simply click a template link to create a new project file from that template.

3. **When you see the icon for the template you want to use, double-click it.**

   Project creates a new file based on the template.

   Presto! You're ready to work on or save your new file (page 76).

Note: If you choose a template from Office.com, double-clicking the icon downloads the template to your computer and creates a new Project file based on the template. To download the template to use later, click the icon. Then, on the right side of the Backstage, click Download.

Specifying a Template Folder

If you've invested time and effort in customizing templates, you want those templates to be easy to find. One way to keep your templates close by is to pin them to the Recent Projects page (page 134). It's a good idea to store the templates you create in a folder that your backup procedure saves along with your other data. If you share templates with other project managers, then keep your Project templates where all the project managers in your organization can reach them, so everyone can take advantage of the work others have done. Then, to create a new Project file, in Windows Explorer, double-click the template you want to use.

Project has an option for specifying your user template folder, but it's fussy about your template folder location—so fussy that the option is helpful only for templates you don't share with others. The templates you store in this folder appear when you click "My templates" on the Available Templates screen.

Tip: You can trick Project into showing your template by specify a template folder in another Office program like Word. To specify a template folder in Word, choose File→Options. In the Word Options dialog box, choose Advanced. Below the General heading, click File Locations. In the File Locations dialog box, click "Workgroup templates" and then click Modify. In the Modify Location dialog box, select the folder where you store your templates (which can be anywhere on your computer or network), and then click OK.

Here's how to specify your user template folder:

1. **On the File tab, click Options.**

   The Project Options dialog box opens.

2. **Click Save. Under "Save templates" to the right of the "Default user template location" box, click Browse.**

   The Modify Location dialog box appears, as shown in Figure 6-2.

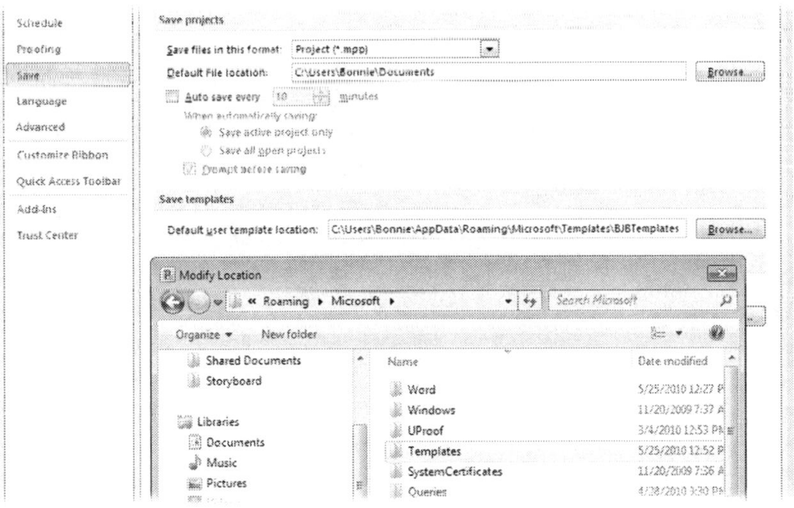

Figure 6-2:
The Modify Location dialog box lets you show Project where you keep your templates. If you want to see your templates in the "My templates" section of the Backstage view, you have to store your templates in Project's default template folder, a subfolder within it, or set the template folder in another Office program like Word."

3. **In the Modify Location dialog box, choose the folder that holds your templates** (*C:\User\<username>\AppData\Roaming\Microsoft\Templates* **or a subfolder below it) and then click OK.**

When you click OK, the Modify Location dialog box closes and the path to the template folder appears to the right of the "Default user template location" label.

4. **To tell Project which folder to open for your Project schedule files, under "Save projects", click Browse to the right of the "Default file location" box, and then navigate to the folder with your schedules.**

Project will point the Open dialog box to this folder whenever you choose File→Open.

5. **Click OK to close the Project Options dialog box.**

The next time you click "My templates" in the Available Templates screen, you'll see the templates in your user templates folder. If you store your template in subfolders within *C:\User\<username>\AppData\Roaming\Microsoft\Templates*, then the "My templates" dialog box includes a tab for each subfolder.

GEM IN THE ROUGH

Creating a New Project from an Existing Project

If you're planning a project similar to one you've done in the past, you may long to borrow those ready-made tasks and dependencies. But you probably won't use the same people, monetary values, and other details of that old project. You could clear the values from all those fields, but that would take just as long as creating the new project from scratch. Although the Available Templates screen contains a "New from existing project" command, it simply opens the file you select. It doesn't remove any of the old values you want to leave behind. The best way to turn an existing project into a *clean* new project is to create a template from the existing project.

Here's what you do:

1. Open the existing project, and then immediately choose File→Save As.

2. In the Save As dialog box, navigate to the folder for the new file. If you plan to use the file as a new project *and* a template for future projects, then choose your user templates folder (page 126).

3. In the "File name" box, type a new name or append additional text, such as *_temp*, to the filename.

4. In the "Save as type" drop-down list, choose Project Template, and then click Save. Project creates a template file, which uses an .mpt file extension.

5. In the Save As Template dialog box that opens, turn on the checkboxes for the data you want to *remove* from the project (not the data you want to keep). You can remove baseline values, actual values, resource rates, and fixed costs—typically, you want to remove all of those.

6. Click Save to close the dialog box.

7. On the File tab, click Recent, and then double-click the template you just saved. Project opens a new file based on the template.

8. To save your squeaky-clean project file, on the File, tab, click Save As. In the Save As dialog box, make sure that the "Save as type" box is set to Project, and then save the file in the folder you want, with the name you want.

Saving a New Project

Whether you start with a blank project or use a template, the first time you choose File→Save, the Save As dialog box opens so you're sure to create a brand-new file. That's Project's way of protecting you from saving blank projects named Project1. Project, like other Microsoft programs, automatically opens the Save As dialog box whenever you use a template, so you can name the new file whatever you want. Most of the time, you choose a folder, choose a filename, and you're done. But Project mavens know that there are other handy tools hidden within the Save and Save As dialog boxes for saving files in special ways. Here are the steps for saving a new project with options you might want to use:

1. **On the File tab, click Save.**

   The Save As dialog box opens.

Tip: If you started from an existing project and want to save it as a new one, then on the File tab, choose Save As. Otherwise, you'll write over the existing project and lose that information forever.

---

2. **Navigate to the folder in which you want to save the project.**

   In the left pane, click Documents, Computer, or Network to navigate to potential storage sites. To store a file you plan to use temporarily, click Desktop to store the file right on the desktop. (You might save a file temporarily if you're creating a template from an existing project, as described in the box on page 128.)

3. **In the "File name" box, type a name for the project.**

   Short but meaningful filenames—for example, *SupportWebSiteOverhaul*— help you and your colleagues find the right files.

Tip: To automatically associate your name and initials with files you create, choose File→Options. In the Project Options dialog box, choose General. Under "Personalize your copy of Microsoft Office", type your name and initials in the "User name" box and Initials box.

---

4. **Leave the "Save as type" drop-down list set to Project to create a regular Project .mpp file, and then click Save.**

   See page 130 to learn about the different file formats to which you can save Project files, and when to use them.

5. **If you want to set options to specify how Project both saves and opens this file, click Tools (to the left of the Save button at bottom right of the Save As dialog box), and then choose General Options.**

   The Save Options dialog box opens, as shown in Figure 6-3.

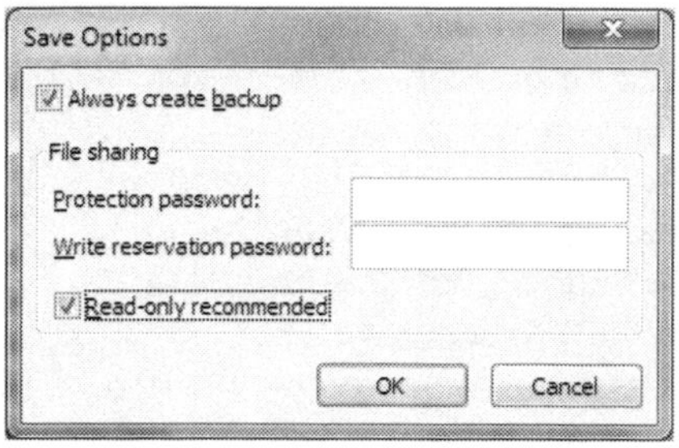

Figure 6-3:
To open this dialog box with options for saving and opening files, click the Tools button in the Save dialog box, and then select General Options.

6. **In the Save Options dialog box, turn on checkboxes for the options that interest you.**

For example, you can create a safe way to test what-if scenarios by turning on the "Always create backup" checkbox. That way, Project saves a backup copy of the original file before saving the file with changes.

In the "File sharing" section, you can set passwords that you must enter to either open or type into the file. Turn on the "Read-only recommended" checkbox if you want the file to open with a message that asks whether you want to open the file as read-only or for editing.

After you save a file for the first time, you can prevent untold grief by getting into the habit of frequently pressing Ctrl+S to save your file as you work. The old adage "save early, save often" applies just as much to Project as it does to old favorites like Word and Excel. The box on page 131 describes another way to make sure you save your work.

Tip: You can set options to control how Project saves your projects. Choose File→Options, and then in the Project Options dialog box, choose Save. To specify the file format that Project automatically selects when you save a file, in the "Save files in this format" drop-down list, choose the format you want, such as Project (*.mpp) or Microsoft Project 2007 (*.mpp). If you specify a folder in the "Default File location" box, Project automatically opens the Save As dialog box to that folder. If you've lost work in the past because you forgot to save your file often enough, Project can automatically save your work every few minutes. To do that, turn on the "Auto save every __ minutes" checkbox, and type the number of minutes in the box. You can specify whether to save only the active project or all open projects.

Saving Projects to Other File Formats

The most common file format for a Project file is the Microsoft Project Plan, identified by a .mpp file extension. Project 2010 can open .mpp files created in Project 2007, 2003, 2002, 2000, and 1998. However, people with earlier versions of Project can't open Project 2010 .mpp files, so you have to save your files in these *legacy formats,* Microsoft's term for earlier file formats. In addition, you can save Project files in other formats to do things like use Excel to analyze costs, or to publish project information to the web. Chapter 20 covers exporting from and importing to Project using different file formats.

Save Early, Save Automatically

Project has another option that's useful if you don't remember to save often enough. The Auto Save option regularly saves your files at an interval you can specify. Auto Save isn't the same as Auto Recover; Auto Save saves your Project files with any changes you've made. That means that if you're playing what-if with a schedule, Auto Save could make the current scenario permanent. However, Auto Save is indispensable if you get lost in schedule work and forget to save for hours.

You can tell Project to ask you whether you want to save. On the File tab, click Options, and then click Save. Turn on the "Auto save every" checkbox, and then type the number of minutes between saves in the box. For example, 45 minutes is a good trade-off between security and interruption. Project selects the option to save only the active file. If you work on several files simultaneously, select the "Save all open projects" option. Keep the "Prompt before saving" checkbox turned on so Project doesn't save files without your knowledge.

To save a Project file in another format, choose File→Save As. Then, in the Save As dialog box, from the "Save as type" drop-down list, choose the format you want.

Here are some occasions when you might choose other formats:

- **Working with earlier versions of Project.** If a colleague uses an earlier version of Project, you can save a Project 2010 file that opens in those versions by choosing Microsoft Project 2007 or Microsoft Project 2000-2003. Project warns that you may lose data from Project 2010's new enhanced features. In the warning dialog box, click Help to see the changes or omissions that come with saving to the earlier format. In Project 2010, if you open files created in Project 2007 or earlier, you can edit them, although with reduced functionality.

Note: You can open Microsoft Project 98 files in Project 2010, but you can't save to the Project 98 format.

- **Exporting data to Excel.** If you want to export data from Project fields to a spreadsheet, say to create a budget from estimated costs, then choose Excel Workbook, Excel Binary Workbook, or Excel 97-2003 Workbook. When you save to these formats, Project launches the Export Wizard (page 520), which steps you through selecting and exporting the data you want in the way you want. You can also import Excel spreadsheets into Project.

- **Exporting Project data to use in other programs.** As you manage projects, other programs like Word and Excel sometimes are better tools for working with data—creating a WBS, estimating, or managing risk, for example. Depending on the format that the other program reads, choose "Text (Tab delimited)" or "CSV (Comma delimited)" to create a more generic text format (page 520). With these formats, Project saves the active table (the table area in the left pane of the view), not the entire project, to the file.

- **Publishing to the web or interchanging data.** If you want to publish a project to the web or use extensible markup language (XML) to exchange structured data, choose "XML format".

Project 2007 can open but not save to some other older file formats, including the following:

- **Project Databases (.mpd).** Earlier versions of Project used this format to store one or more projects.

- **Microsoft Access Databases (.mdb).** Project 2010 can open Microsoft Access databases that contain Project information, but it doesn't save to this file format.

- **Open Database Connectivity (ODBC).** Earlier versions of Project could open and save projects to an ODBC-compliant SQL Server database. Project 2010 can open this format (in the Open dialog box, click ODBC below the file list), but not save to it.

Project 2010's factory settings don't let you open or save files to older (legacy) Project file formats or to other formats like database file formats (called *non-default formats*). If your and your compatriots' files are in older formats, one of the first actions to take after installing Project 2010 is to tell it to work with these older files.

To save and open legacy and non-default formats, do the following:

1. **On the File tab, click Options, and then click Trust Center.**

   The Trust Center opens, containing several links related to privacy and security.

2. **Click Trust Center Settings.**

   The Trust Center lets you sprinkle your trust onto publishers, add-ins, macros, legacy formats, and more. In addition to the options for working with file formats, you can clear a few file properties when you save a file. Click Privacy Options and then turn on the "Remove personal information from file properties on save" checkbox. This checkbox removes Author, Manager, Company, and Last Save By, presumably to cover your tracks when distributing a project to others.

3. **Click Legacy Formats, and then select the Legacy Format option you want, as shown in Figure 6-4. Then click OK.**

   Project selects "Do not open/save file with legacy or non-default file formats in Project" automatically, but this option means that you can't work with existing files in older formats.

If you have lots of files in legacy or non-default formats, then the most sensible option is "Allow loading files with legacy or non default file formats", although this choice lowers the security level and increases the chance of your computer becoming infected by a virus embedded in a file. However, you can open and save legacy and non-default file formats without any interruptions.

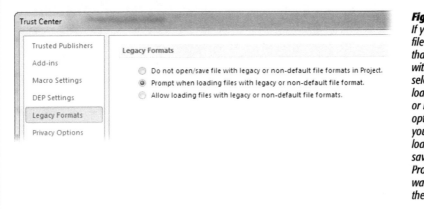

Figure 6-4:
If you try to open an older file format or a file format that Project doesn't work with directly when you've selected the "Prompt when loading files with legacy or non-default file format" option, a dialog box asks you whether you want to load the file. When you save these types of files, Project asks whether you want to save these files to the Project 2010 format.

Protecting Your Project Files

Your investment of time and brainpower grows as you build your project schedule. At some point, you've probably been devastated by the disappearance of an important file. You can protect the work in your Project files from inadvertent changes by creating backup copies. Moreover, passwords can protect files from unauthorized editing by a desperate team member trying to obtain more time for a task.

Some security options don't appear in the Project Options dialog box. Instead, they're tucked away in the Save and Save As dialog boxes. On the File tab, choosing Save with a Project file that you've already saved immediately saves the file without opening a dialog box. If you want to add security options to an existing file, choose File→Save As. In the Save As dialog box, click Tools (to the left of the Save button), and then choose General Options. After you choose the security options you want (from the ones described below), click Save.

Tip: Even if you open the Save As dialog box, you can save the file with the same name.

Here's what Project's security options can do for you:

- **Always create backup.** Creates a backup copy of a file when you first open it, so you can quickly eliminate all the changes from the current session. The file extension for a backup is .bak. To open a backup file, choose File→Open. In the Open dialog box, in the "Files of type" box, choose All Files. Select the backup file, which looks like FileName.BAK, and then click Open.

- **Protection password.** Sets a password that you must type before Project will open the file. Without the password, the file can't be opened for editing or even viewed as read-only. In the "Protection password" box, type the password for the file. When you click OK to close the Security Options dialog box, a Confirm Password dialog box opens, so you don't end up with a file you can't open due to a typo in the password. Retype the password, and then click OK.

   When you open a file with a protection password, a Password dialog box opens. In the Password box, type the password, and then click OK. Project opens the file.

Note: In Project 2003, you could remove a password by opening the file and using the General Options in the Save As dialog box a second time. In this case, you would delete the passwords in the password boxes, and then save the file to the same name. However, in Project 2007 and 2010, there's no way to remove passwords once you add them.

- **Write reservation password.** Sets a password on a file that you must type if you want to edit the file. You can open the file as read-only without a password. In the "Write reservation password" box, type the password. When you click OK to close the Security Options dialog box, a Confirm Password dialog box opens so you can retype the password.

   When you open a file with a write reservation password, a Password dialog box opens that asks for a password if you want to edit the file. To open the file for editing, in the Password box, type the password, and then click OK. If you want to open the file as read-only, click Read Only.

- **Read-only recommended.** Tells Project to ask if you want to open the file for editing or read-only before it opens the file. When you open a file with this checkbox turned on, a message box appears that tells you to open the file as read-only unless you must write to it. To take Project's suggestion, click Yes to open the file as read-only. To write to the file, click No.

Opening a Project File

Although File→Open is the tried and true method for opening Project files, the program offers several shortcuts to open a file:

- **Use the Recent page.** Choose File→Recent to see a list of all the projects you've opened recently. Simply click the filename to reopen that file. If you work on a few projects for months at a time, you can pin projects to the top of the Recent Projects list so they won't be replaced by other files. Simply click the pushpin icon to the right of the filename, and the project name leaps to the top of the list.

- **Display projects on the Backstage menu itself.** When you click the File tab, the Backstage view opens with a menu on the left side. You can display projects on that menu so you don't have to choose Recent. To set this shortcut up, choose

File→Recent. At the bottom of the Recent Projects list, turn on the "Quickly access this number of Recent Projects" checkbox and type the number you want. Project displays that number of recent projects above the Info command, starting with projects pinned to the Recent Projects list. Click the filename to open the Project file.

- **Open the last file you worked on when Project launches.** If you work on one project, a slick shortcut is to have Project open the last file you worked on automatically. That way, each time you launch Project, your latest project is waiting for you. Choose File→Options. In the Project Options dialog box, choose Advanced. In the General section, turn on the "Open last file on startup" checkbox.

Setting Up Options For a Project

The second step for any new Project file is tweaking a few Project options to fit the file to your project—the date the project starts and the days available for work, for example. This section describes how to set up the details that make each project unique.

Tip: To ensure that you set the project start date and other file options, you can tell Project to ask you for that information when you create a new file. Choose File→Options, and then, in the Project Options dialog box, choose Advanced. In the General section, turn on the "Prompt for project info for new projects" checkbox. Click OK to close the dialog box. After that, as soon as you create a new project, the Project Information dialog box appears.

Setting the Project Start Date

Projects rarely start on the day you create your Microsoft Project file. You usually have some business to take care of before the work begins, like obtaining project plan approvals or lining up funding. The date on which you plan to start the project is the option you're most likely to change.

Here are the steps:

1. **On the File tab, click Open. In the Open dialog box, select the project, and then click Open.**

   If you're reopening a project you've worked on recently, a shortcut is to choose Recent on the File tab, and then choose the project name from the entries of recently opened projects.

2. **On the Project tab, choose Project Information.**

   The Project Information dialog box opens. If you created the file from scratch, Project sets the date in the "Start date" box to today's date, as shown in Figure 6-5. For templates or existing projects, the project starts on the existing date set in the "Start date" box.

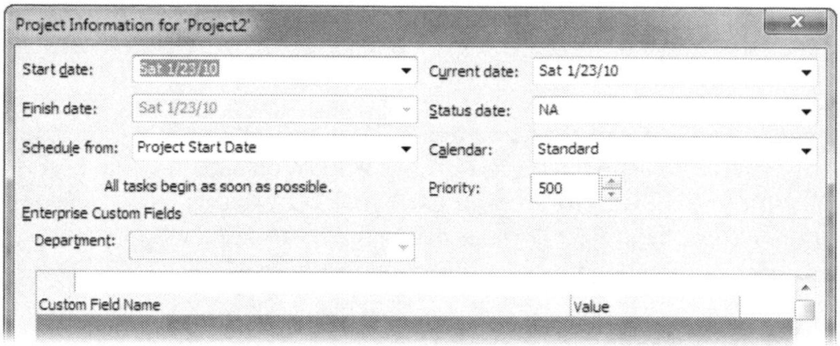

Figure 6-5:
Out of the box, the Schedule From box is set to Project Start Date, which is almost always what you want. When you set the start date, Project calculates the finish date for you. Even if you know the end date you want, you're better off scheduling from the start date as the box below explains.

3. **In the "Start date" box, type or choose the date on which you plan to start the project, and then click OK.**

   Project adjusts the start date you enter to the next business day if you choose a weekend day or other non-workday for the project start. The "Finish date" box shows the date Project calculates for when the project will finish. If the Project file doesn't have any tasks yet, then the "Finish date" value is the same as the "Start date" value. The date in the "Finish date" box isn't meaningful until you've completely defined your project schedule.

UP TO SPEED

Scheduling from the Start or Finish Date

You can schedule a project in two ways: by entering a start date and working forward, or by entering an end date and working backward. Although customers and executives always seem to have a finish date in mind, scheduling projects from the start date is usually the best approach. Entering a specific end date cripples one of Project's most powerful features—the ability to calculate a realistic end date based on tasks, resources, and work time.

If you know when the project can start and how long it should take, Project spits out when the project should finish. With a calculated finish date, the first advantage is that you can show the stakeholders when the project can realistically finish. Armed with this information, you may be able to negotiate for a different deadline.

If the finish date can't move, in cases like the Y2K software projects of yore, schedule from the start date anyway. If the project deadline is scheduled before the finish date that Project calculates, you can evaluate whether techniques like crashing or fast-tracking (both of which are described in Chapter 12) can shorten the schedule sufficiently.

Another reason to avoid scheduling from a finish date is how Project behaves. When you schedule from a finish date in Project, all the task constraint types are set to As Late As Possible. As the name implies, this constraint type means that tasks are scheduled to start as late as possible, which removes any wiggle room that you might need to respond to problems.

Setting the Standard Workdays

The working time available is a big part of how quickly a project finishes. An urgent project to beat the competition to market might opt for longer workdays during the week with some weekend overtime as well. On the other hand, if you're building a vacation house on a tropical isle, you might have to adjust the working time for the more relaxed work schedules that hot sun and siestas induce. You need a calendar to indicate which days and times are available for work.

In Microsoft Project, *calendars* have working and nonworking days and times blocked out. You can use one of the built-in calendars, modify existing calendars, or build brand new ones for unusual work schedules. Then, you can apply a calendar to an entire project to set the standard working times, which is perfect for specifying the holidays for your organization or telling Project that Fridays are half-days for your company. You can also define and apply calendars to individual people—for instance, to specify luxuriously long scheduled vacations—or to tasks—for example, to schedule a task to run around the clock until it's done. (See the box on page 139 for more detail.) Regardless of which type of calendar you want to work with, on the Project tab, choose Change Working Time to open the dialog box with calendar tools.

If you plan for 10-hour workdays but your resources skip out after putting in 8 hours, projects quickly fall behind. Project's calendar options control how Project converts durations (page 139) into hours of work. To keep Project's work and duration calculations accurate, it's important that the number of hours Project assumes for duration matches the hours those durations represent in your organization's typical work schedules.

Choosing a project calendar

Project uses the project calendar to schedule tasks and resources that don't have their own special calendars. For most projects, the project calendar looks a lot like your organization's work schedule—its standard workdays, the official start and end of the workday, the time off for lunch, and official holidays. But some projects follow a different drummer. For instance, construction work on a busy highway might take place from 9 p.m. to 5 a.m. to minimize agonizing gridlock during rush hour.

Project comes with three built-in *base calendars,* which are calendar templates, that you can use as-is or modify to represent your organization's work schedule:

- **Standard.** Sets working time to Monday through Friday from 8 a.m. to 5 p.m. with an hour for lunch from 12 p.m. to 1 p.m., shown in Figure 6-6.

- **Night shift.** Sets working times from Monday through Friday from 11 p.m. to 8 a.m. with lunch from 3 a.m. to 4 a.m.

- **24 Hours.** Schedules work 24 hours a day, 7 days a week. Although many high-pressure projects *feel* like they run on 24-hour schedules, this calendar is suitable for projects that *actually* run three shifts or tasks that run 24 hours a day.

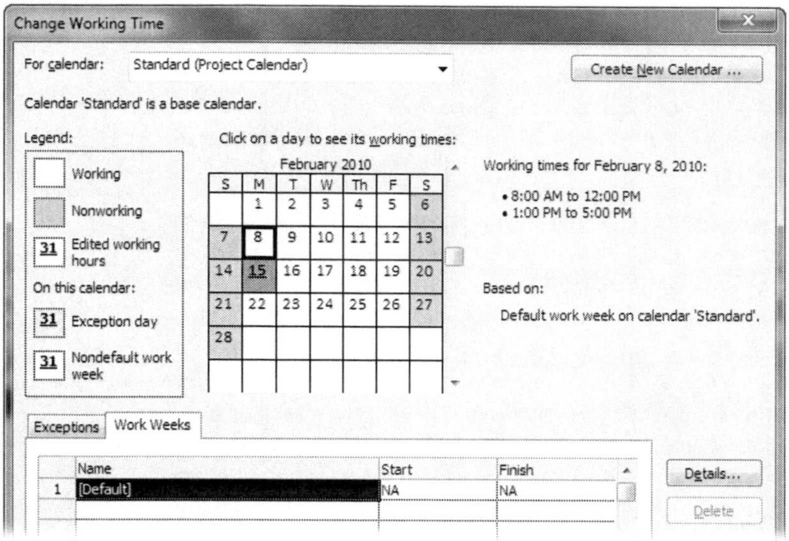

Figure 6-6:
The Standard calendar comes without any days off for holidays, but you can—and should— change this calendar to add holidays or tweak working times. Project automatically assigns this calendar to new projects.

Tip: Whether you modify the Standard calendar to mirror your organization's work schedule or create a brand new calendar for that purpose, you can tell Project to use that calendar for every new project you create. To do so, use the Organizer to copy that calendar to the Global.mpt template, as described on page 669.

Once the Standard calendar reflects your working and nonworking times, you're all set. When you create a new project, Project automatically assigns the Standard calendar as the project calendar. If you want to choose a different project calendar, follow these simple steps:

1. **With the project open, on the Project tab, click Project Information.**

    The Project Information dialog box opens.

2. **In the Calendar box, shown in Figure 6-5, choose the calendar you want, whether it's a built-in calendar or one you've customized (page 238), and then click OK.**

    If you open the Change Working Time dialog box described on page 240, then in the "For calendar" box, you see "(Project Calendar)" to the right of the name of the calendar that the entire project uses. The working and nonworking time for all tasks and resources without special calendars conform to the project calendar work schedule.

How Calendars Control Schedules

Calendars can affect different aspects of a Project file with dramatically different scheduling results. Calendars can apply to any of these three uses. Here are the three kinds of calendars and how to apply them.

- **Project calendar.** Assigning a calendar to an entire project sets the standard working days and times. If none of your tasks or resources use special calendars, then your calendar work is done. The smart way to set up a project calendar is to modify the built-in Standard calendar with your company's standard workdays, work times, and holidays (page 240). Microsoft Project automatically assigns the Standard calendar from your Global.mpt file as a project's calendar, and your working times are set. On the other hand, if you work with other companies and subcontractors who don't have the same work schedules and holidays, you can use the Standard calendar as a foundation for your company calendar, which you then apply to your projects.

- **Resource calendar.** A resource calendar (page 192) is ideal when an individual or a group of resources

work specialized schedules. If your project spans multiple shifts, then you can define a calendar for each shift and then apply the shift calendar to the folks lucky enough to work that shift. For the ultimate in schedule accuracy, you can set up a resource calendar for each person to reserve dates for scheduled vacations. Individual resource calendars help you see whether your schedule needs tweaking to deliver a deadline before a key resource heads off on a Tahitian honeymoon. A lower-maintenance but less accurate solution is to use shorter workdays throughout the schedule. See page 250 for how to assign a calendar to a resource.

- **Task calendar.** Most tasks run according to the project calendar and any resource calendars applied to the assigned resources. Occasionally, tasks follow their own schedules, in cases like installing new security cameras only when the bank vault is open. Applying a calendar to a resource is ideal to specify offbeat work times that apply only to that task.

Setting calendar options

Calendars, like the project calendar you assigned in the previous section, specify the working days and times. But calendar options, stored in the Project Options dialog box, tell Project how to translate durations for those working times into hours of work. For example, if the "Hours per week" option is set to 40, a task with a 2-week duration represents 80 work hours. With "Hours per week" set to 35, a 2-week task represents 70 hours of work. Because calendar options and calendar work times must match, calendar options can be different for each project, as Figure 6-7 shows.

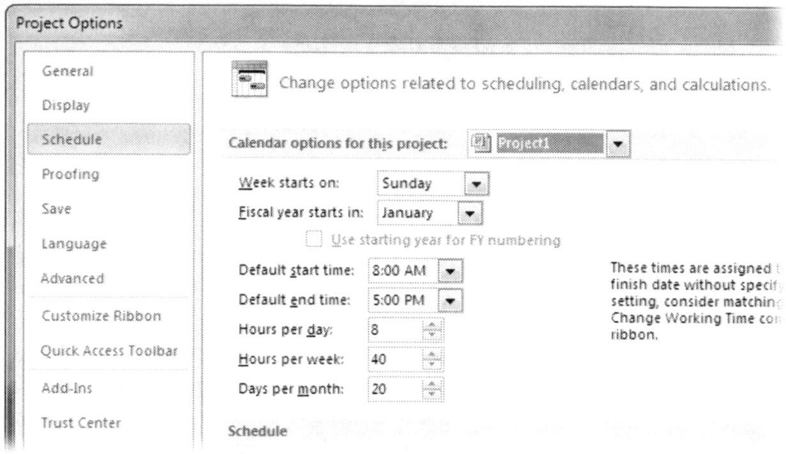

Figure 6-7:
The label "Calendar options for this project" means that the option settings on the Calendar tab apply to the project whose name appears in the box. You can modify these options without affecting the calendar options in other projects. When more than one project is open, you can choose a different project name to assign calendar options to that project.

Tip: If your organization uses an unusual work schedule and you adjust the calendar options to follow suit, then in the drop-down list to the right of the "Calendar Options for this project" label, choose All New Projects to apply the current calendar options to all new (not existing) projects.

Project's out-of-the-box calendar options are perfect for your typical 8-to-5 operation. Usually, a quick glance at these options confirms that they fit your organization's schedule, and you can move on to other project management duties.

To view calendar options, on the File tab, click Options. In the Project Options dialog box, click Schedule. Here are the options you can set and what each one does:

- **Week starts on.** This option specifies the first day of the week in your schedule and is set initially to Sunday, which is usually fine. You might change this option when you exchange actual project values with your corporate time-tracking system, for example, so both programs start workweeks on the same day of the week.

- **Fiscal year starts in.** You need to change this option only when your corporate fiscal year starts in a month other than January *and* you want to produce fiscal period reports in Project.

   When you set the month for the fiscal year, the Gantt Chart timescale displays the fiscal year. For example, if the fiscal year begins in July, then September 30, 2010, appears under the 2011 fiscal year. If the fiscal year starts in a month other than January, the "Use starting year for FY numbering" checkbox springs to life. Turning on this checkbox sets the fiscal year to the calendar year in which the fiscal year begins. With this checkbox turned on, September 30, 2010 is in fiscal year 2010.

Calendars and Calendar Options

Project doesn't warn you when your calendar options and project calendar don't jibe, so it's a good idea to make sure they do. For example, if you set the Hours Per Day to 8 hours, the number of hours of working time for a day in the project calendar should also equal 8 hours (such as 8 a.m. to 5 p.m. with an hour for lunch).

Project uses the calendar options to convert one time period into another—for instance, to calculate the work hours that correspond to a duration you enter in weeks. If the calendar options and the calendar disagree, then duration and work estimates don't agree, and resource assignments may not make sense.

Suppose the Hours Per Day option is set to 6 hours. For a task with a 5-day duration, Project multiplies the 5 days by 6 hours per day to get task work of 30 hours. Someone assigned to the task at 100 percent may work 8-hour days according to the project calendar. But when Project converts workdays into work hours, it thinks he's working only 6 hours a day because of the Hours Per Day option. The solution to this brainteaser is to set the same number of work hours per day in your calendar options *and* the calendar.

- **Default start time.** For most tasks, the start time depends on when predecessor tasks finish. The time in this box affects the start time for tasks only when you create and specify a start date without a start time. This option is set to 8:00 a.m. initially. If your workday starts earlier or later, adjust the value of this box accordingly.

- **Default end time.** The finish time for most tasks depends on when the task begins and how long it takes. The time in this box becomes the finish time for a task only when you specify a task's finish date without specifying a finish time. It's set to 5:00 p.m. initially. If your workday ends earlier or later, adjust the value of this option accordingly.

- **Hours per day.** Sets the number of working hours for a single workday. For example, with the standard setting of 8.00, one workday represents 8 hours of work.

- **Hours per week.** Defines the number of working hours in one week and is set to 40.00 initially.

- **Days per month.** This option is the conversion between days and months and is set to 20 workdays (4 weeks each with 5 workdays) per month initially.

Adding Tasks to a Project

With calendars and calendar options in place, you're ready to add tasks to your Project file. If you already have a work breakdown structure (WBS), flip to Chapter 4 to learn how to enter (page 84) or import (page 90) those tasks into Project. Or see page 124 to learn how to create a Project file from an Excel workbook. Then you can add additional tasks as they arise.

Linking to More Information

If you have files with additional information about tasks, such as work package Word documents, you can keep them near at hand by connecting them to your Project tasks. By creating a hyperlink between a task and a document (page 560), one click is all you need to open up a file of information. Hyperlinks are fast, and they keep your Project file from ballooning with documentation fat.

Alternatively, you can include these supplementary files right in your Project file. For instance, when you plan to distribute the file to people who can't access your computers, you can copy files into the Notes field of tasks. You can find instructions for pulling external files into Project fields on page 551.

Adding Tasks

Whether you add newly identified tasks or insert tasks that don't appear on the WBS (milestones, meetings, and so on), the table on the left side of the Gantt Chart view is the place for fast input of basic task information. You don't have to worry about the order in which you enter tasks. You can rearrange tasks anytime after you create them, as described on page 149.

Here's how you add tasks in a table in the Gantt Chart view:

1. **If the Gantt Chart view is not the current view, on the Task tab, click the down arrow on the Gantt Chart icon (Figure 6-8), and then click Gantt Chart.**

   Project displays the Gantt Chart with a tabular view of tasks on the left side and the timescale on the right.

2. **In the tabular area, click a blank Task Name cell, and then type the name for the task. Press Enter or the down arrow to save the task, and move to the Task Name cell in the next row.**

   After you name your task but before you press Enter or the down arrow, the insertion point remains in the Task Name cell, which renders most commands on menus inactive. If Project menus are awash with grayed-out commands, press Enter to save the current task. (See the box on page 145 for task-naming tips.)

   If you're wondering where the Entry bar from previous versions is hiding, the answer is Project Options. The Entry bar is hidden initially. To display it in Project, choose File→Options. In the Project Options dialog box, choose Display, and then turn on the "Entry bar" checkbox.

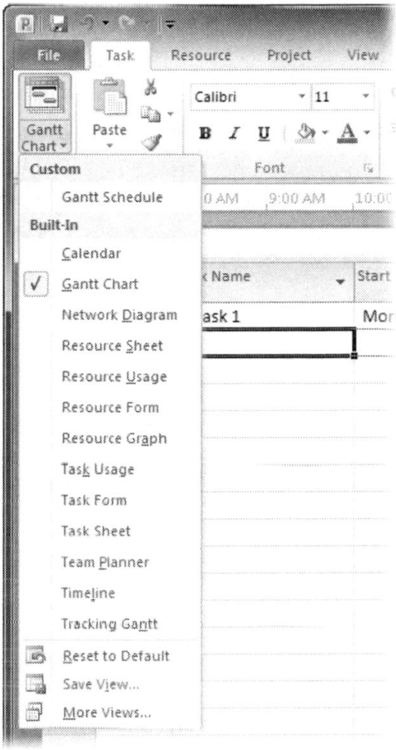

Figure 6-8:
The name of the current view appears along the left side of the Project window (hidden here by the drop-down menu). Commonly used views also appear on the drop-down menu, where you can choose the view you want. If the view doesn't appear on the drop-down menu, choose More Views. In the More Views dialog box, select the view, and then click Apply.

Tip: If you press Delete when a Task Name cell (or a Resource Name cell) is selected, Project displays an indicator (a box containing an X) to the left of the Task Name cell. You can click the indicator down arrow and select the "Only clear the contents of Task Name Cell" options to delete the name or the "Delete the entire task" option to delete the whole task. To hide the delete indicator, choose File ▸ Options. In the Project Options dialog box, choose Display, and then turn off the "Deletions in the Name columns" checkbox. The "Edits to start and finish dates" checkbox specifies whether Project displays an indicator when you choose a date in a Start or Finish cell. Project warns you that choosing dates isn't the way to schedule your project. You can select options to keep or remove the date constraint or to schedule the task a different way.

3. If the Task Mode cell isn't set the way you want, click the down arrow and choose Manually Scheduled or Auto Scheduled.

If you want to change the schedule mode for all new tasks, click New Tasks (at bottom left of the Project window). Then choose Manually Scheduled if you want to tell Project when the tasks occur or Auto Scheduled if you want Project to calculate task dates. You can switch this setting as often as you like.

You can also tell Project to automatically set the task mode. Choose File→Options. In the Project Options dialog box, choose Schedule. In the "Scheduling options for this project" section, in the "New tasks created" box, choose Auto Scheduled or Manually Scheduled.

That's all you have to do for the moment.

Other task values

If estimated durations are burning a hole in your project dossier, you can enter them in the Duration cells of project tasks. If you create an auto-scheduled task, Project automatically fills in the Duration field with "1 day?", which means the duration is estimated to be 1 day (the question mark indicates an estimated value).

Note: You can tell Project to fill in regular durations. Choose File→Options. In the Project Options dialog box, choose Schedule. In the "Scheduling options for this project" section, turn off the "New scheduled tasks have estimated durations" checkbox. With this setting, Project sets the duration to 1 day. The "Show that scheduled tasks have estimated durations" checkbox is turned on initially, and you want to keep it that way so you can see which tasks have estimated durations and fill in the confirmed durations later.

Project automatically sets an auto-scheduled task's start date to the project start date. You can specify whether auto-scheduled tasks start on the project start date or the date on which you create the task. In the Project Options dialog box, choose Schedule. In the "Auto scheduled tasks scheduled on" drop-down list, choose Project Start Date or Current Date.

Tip: If you use Project's automatic scheduling, resist the temptation to specify start and finish dates for tasks, or you'll lose one of the advantages of using Project in the first place. Project calculates dates for you based on the sequence and duration of tasks. If you enter dates for tasks, the resulting constraints (page 166) make your project schedule inflexible and difficult to maintain. On the other hand, early on in project planning, you can set tasks to manual scheduling and type rough dates. You can even type notes about potential dates in the date fields, as page 119 explains.

Creating Milestones

In bygone days, a milestone was literally a stone that marked a distance of one mile from the last stone. With projects, milestones typically measure work progress, not distance. However, milestones can represent all kinds of progress: events, deliveries, or achievements—the completion of a phase, the delivery of the requirements document, or a payment. Because milestones have zero duration, you can add as many as you want without extending the project finish date.

Making Task Names Unique

Like poetry, the best task names communicate the work they represent in a few well-chosen words. As you learned in Chapter 4 (page 81), task naming conventions can differentiate milestones, work tasks, and summary tasks. Moreover, unambiguous verbs help everyone understand what must be done. But what if you have the same type of work in different phases of a project?

Effective task names are easy to identify, whether you see them alone or in the WBS hierarchy in Project. The problems with duplicate task names aren't always obvious. The issue arises when you generate reports, group tasks with similar characteristics using the Group command, or hide summary tasks. In those cases, duplicate task names can appear side by side with no indication of which is which. The simple fix is to add a few words to make task names unique: "Heat water for potatoes" and "Heat water for sterilizing utensils," for example.

Creating tasks for milestones couldn't be easier. To create a milestone, you create a new task, and then set its duration to zero (by typing *0d* in the Duration cell). The Gantt Chart timescale indicates the task's milestone status by changing its shape from a bar to a black diamond. Even better, because the milestone duration is zero, you don't have to assign any resources to it.

Tip: Even tasks with durations can be milestones. To appoint any task to milestone-hood, double-click the task in the task table to open the Task Information dialog box. (Or select the task and then, on the Task tab, click Information.) Select the Advanced tab and turn on the "Mark task as milestone" checkbox.

Here are several ways to put milestones to use:

- **Project start or project phase.** Using a milestone as the first task in a project makes it easy to reschedule an entire project or a portion of one. For example, if your customer doesn't send in the deposit payment you require to begin work, you can delay the entire schedule by changing the date for the deposit payment milestone. Once a project is under way, you can delay a section of the project by modifying the date of the section's starting milestone.

- **Project completion.** By adding a milestone as the last task in a project schedule and linking the final project tasks to it, you make it easy to see the current estimated finish date.

- **Decisions and approvals.** High-risk, big-budget projects often use feasibility studies to determine whether the project and funding continue. Milestone tasks are perfect for representing go/no-go decisions, approvals required before work can continue, or other decisions that affect the tasks that follow. For example, a go/no-go milestone might be the end milestone if the project is canceled, but it controls when successor tasks begin if the project gets the OK to continue. Milestones can also delay work that hinges on other types of decisions. For instance, the choice of programming language determines the people you hire, the software design, and the code written.

- **Progress.** Progress is hidden within the status of the tasks that represent work packages, but you can gauge progress by adding milestones at significant points during a project, such as the completion of project deliverables, be they documents, programs, or buildings. However, you can add a milestone at the end of any summary task, for example, to show that it's complete.

- **Handoffs and deliveries.** A milestone can document the change when the responsibility for work transfers to a new group (for instance, when materials loaded on a truck become the responsibility of the recipient). Milestones also work for deliveries you expect from subcontractors or vendors. When you place an order for building materials, you don't manage the supply company employees who assemble the order. You simply plan for the materials to arrive on the day they're promised. Thus, all you need is a milestone for that delivery date.

Tip: Unlike the names for work tasks and summary tasks, don't include action verbs in milestone names. Nouns and adjectives (or verbs in past tense) are all you need to identify the deliverable and the state it's in: "Marshmallows toasted."

Creating Repeating Tasks

Some tasks occur on a regular schedule—for example, monthly meetings of the change control board, biweekly status meetings, or nightly backups of project management files. Fortunately, you don't have to create each occurrence separately. Instead, you can create a *recurring task* in Project, which creates individual tasks for each occurrence and a *summary task* for all the occurrences.

To create a recurring task, do the following:

1. **Click anywhere in the row below where you want the new recurring task. On the Task tab (in the Insert section), click the Task down arrow, and then choose Recurring Task.**

   The Recurring Task Information dialog box appears.

2. **In the Task Name box, type the name for the recurring task, such as *Stakeholder Status Meeting*.**

   Project automatically sets the value in the Duration box to 1 day (abbreviated as 1d). The Duration box sets the duration for one occurrence, that is, one status meeting. If the occurrence takes less than a day, then in the Duration box, type the new duration, such as *2h* to set a meeting to 2 hours.

3. In the "Recurrence pattern" section, first choose an option to specify the frequency of the task.

Choose from Daily, Weekly, Monthly, or Yearly. For each option, you see additional settings that let you add more detail about the timing, as illustrated in Figure 6-9. To schedule occurrences for more than 1 day a week, you can turn on the checkbox for each day of the week on which occurrences are scheduled. So if you run status meetings on Mondays and Thursdays, turn on the Monday and Thursday checkboxes.

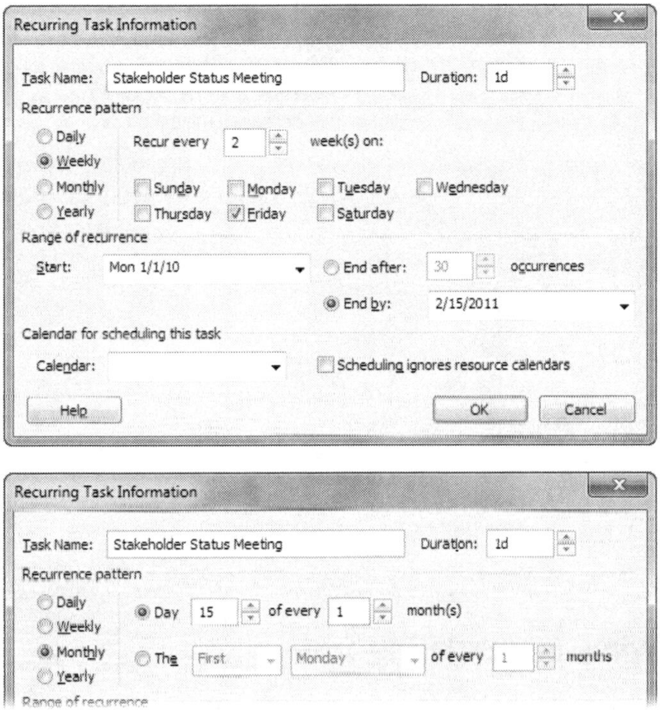

Figure 6-9:
Top: If the occurrences don't happen every single period, choose the number of periods, like 2 to schedule a meeting every 2 weeks.

Bottom: Occurrences for other periods have different frequency settings. For example, when you select the Monthly option, you can specify when the tasks occur each month, such as on the 15th of the month or on the first Monday of each month.

4. In the "Range of recurrence" section, in the Start box, choose the date you want the occurrences to begin.

Project initially sets the start date to the start date of the project.

5. To specify when the occurrences end, select the "End after" option, and then specify a number of occurrences. Alternatively, select the "End by" option if you want to specify the end date.

Project initially selects the "End by" option and sets the date to the end date for the project. With either option, you'll have to edit your recurring task later if the project runs longer than you anticipated. Project doesn't automatically extend recurring tasks to conform to a new finish date.

6. Click **OK** to close the dialog box and add the recurring task to the project, as shown in Figure 6-10.

In the Indicator column, a circular icon with arrows indicates that the task has multiple occurrences.

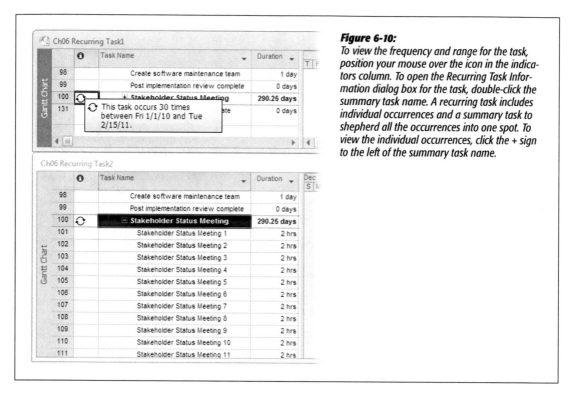

Figure 6-10:
To view the frequency and range for the task, position your mouse over the icon in the indicators column. To open the Recurring Task Information dialog box for the task, double-click the summary task name. A recurring task includes individual occurrences and a summary task to shepherd all the occurrences into one spot. To view the individual occurrences, click the + sign to the left of the summary task name.

Inserting, Moving, and Deleting Tasks

You can organize tasks as you create them, or come back later to change your tasks' order and indent them to the correct outline level. Summary tasks, work package tasks, milestones, and repeating tasks all respond to Project's organizational techniques. The following sections describe the techniques you can use to arrange tasks in your Project file.

Inserting Tasks

Sometimes you realize that your project entails more work than you thought, and want to add tasks to your existing task list. At other times, you might decide to change the way you summarize work or break down work further, which means creating new summary tasks.

Here's how to insert tasks in an existing list:

- **Insert a summary task.** Project 2010 has made it a lot easier to insert summary tasks—at any level of a project. Click the row below the new summary task and then, on the Task tab, click the Insert Summary Task icon (it's in the Insert section and looks like a summary taskbar). Project inserts the new summary task at the same outline level as the task above it, fills in the Task Name cell with the text "<New Summary Task>", and turns the task below it into a subtask. Type the task name, and then press Enter to save the task.

Tip: To add a new summary task for several existing tasks, first select the subtask wannabes. Then, on the Task tab, click Insert Summary Task. Project inserts the new summary task as usual but transforms all the selected tasks into subtasks.

- **Insert a task at any level**. To insert a task between two existing tasks, click the lower of the two task rows, and then press Insert. In the Task Name cell of the blank task row that appears, type the task name, and then press Enter. If the task isn't at the correct outline level, press Alt+Shift+left arrow or Alt+Shift+right arrow to indent or outdent the task.

Tip: In Project 2010, it's easier to toggle summary tasks and outline levels on and off. For example, if you want to focus on work package tasks, then on the Format tab, turn off the Summary Tasks checkbox. If you want to see the outline level for each task, then on the same tab, turn on the "Outline Number" checkbox.

Moving Tasks

If you decide that tasks belong in another section of your WBS, you can move them in the Project task list. For example, you might move a subtask to a different summary task to change how you break down work. Or you can move a subtask to a position before or after another subtask to show tasks in the sequence they occur.

To move one or more tasks, do the following:

1. **In the Gantt Chart view's table area, select the entire task row by clicking the task's ID cell, as shown in Figure 6-11.**

   When it's in the ID column, the pointer turns into a four-headed arrow, indicating that you can move the task.

   If you want to select more than one task, then drag the pointer across adjacent task ID cells. If you want to select nonadjacent tasks, then Ctrl-click each task's ID cell.

2. **Drag the task or tasks to the new location.**

   As you drag, a gray line moves in the border between rows, showing where the task or tasks will end up when you release the mouse button.

Tip: Project used to scroll like lightning, which made dragging tasks accurately beyond the visible rows all but impossible. Although Project 2010's scrolling has slowed down to a manageable pace, cutting and pasting tasks is still a convenient way to move tasks when their new location is several pages away. To cut and paste tasks, select the tasks, and then press Ctrl+X. Then select the row below where you want to paste the tasks, and then press Ctrl+V.

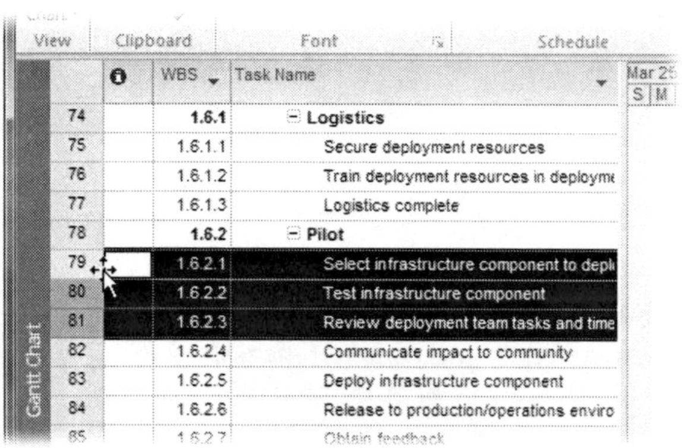

Figure 6-11:
The ID cell does not have any text in its column heading, and it's the first column in the table area. The ID number is a single sequence of integers, unlike the WBS code, which can have levels to correspond to the outline levels of your tasks.

3. **If the task isn't at the correct outline level, press Alt+Shift+left arrow or Alt+Shift+right arrow to indent or outdent the task.**

   You can also click Indent or Outdent on the Task tab (in the Schedule section, the icons with the green left and right arrows) to change the outline level.

Copying Tasks

If your project plan uses similar tasks in several phases, it's often easier to create a set of tasks and copy them to each phase. Or, if you have a task that shares many characteristics of another task, you can copy it so that the new task includes the same field values, such as resources, notes, and deadlines. (You should, of course, rename the new, copied task to avoid confusion. There's a shortcut for renaming tasks in the box on page 151.)

To copy one or more tasks, do the following:

1. **In the Gantt Chart view's table area, select the entire task row by clicking the task's ID cell.**

   The pointer turns into a four-headed arrow.

   If you want to select more than one task, then drag the pointer across adjacent task ID cells. To select nonadjacent tasks, Ctrl-click each task's ID cell.

2. **Press Ctrl+C or, on the Task tab (in the Clipboard section), choose Copy.**

   What the command does depends on how you select your task. If you click the ID cell, then the command copies the entire task row. If you click anywhere else in the task row, then the Copy command copies only the value in the cell you clicked.

Tip: If you want to copy tasks without copying any field values other than task names, you can copy task names into blank rows in the list. Select the Task Name cells for the task names you want to copy (click a single cell, drag across the cells for adjacent tasks you want to copy, or Ctrl-click each Task Name cell). Press Ctrl+C or, on the Task tab, click the Copy icon. Click the first Task Name cell in the blank rows corresponding to the new tasks, and then press Ctrl+V or, on the Task tab, click Paste.

---

3. **To insert the task or tasks, click the task row below where you want to copy the task, and then press Ctrl+V.**

   To add the copied task to an empty row, select the row, and then press Ctrl+V. You can also paste the tasks on the Task tab by clicking Paste.

4. **If the task isn't at the correct outline level, press Alt+Shift+left arrow or Alt+Shift+right arrow to indent or outdent the task.**

   You can also click Indent or Outdent on the Task tab to change the outline level.

Tip: If you copy tasks after you've entered actual values, be sure to delete the actual values in the copied tasks.

WORKAROUND WORKSHOP

Renaming Copied Task Names

If you work hard to keep task names unique, copying tasks raises an issue. The copied tasks have the same names as the originals. Don't despair: The Replace command can come to the rescue and replace the adjectives for each phase or deliverable. Here's how it works:

1. Select the tasks you want to rename that use the same adjectives or qualifiers. Say you've copied tasks called "Write requirements document," "Edit requirements document," and "Review requirements document," and you want to change the word "requirements" to "design."

2. To open the Replace dialog box, press Ctrl+H (or on the Task tab, click the Editing down arrow, then click the Find down arrow, and finally choose Replace).

3. Be sure that the Search box is set to Down, indicating that Project will begin at the first selected task and search in *all* subsequent tasks in the list.

4. In the "Find what" box, type the word or words that you want to replace—*requirements* in this example.

5. In the "Replace with" box, type the new term for the copied tasks, for instance, *design* to change the name from "Write requirements document" to "Write design document."

6. Click Replace to replace the first occurrence of the term. Continue to click Replace once for each selected task.

It's tempting, but don't click Replace All, because it replaces that word in all tasks in the schedule.

Deleting Tasks

Although work rarely disappears in real life, you may sometimes need to delete tasks in Project. Perhaps you've decided to break down work differently, or the customer has decided to reduce the project scope to fit the budget. (See page 353 to learn how to inactivate tasks instead of deleting them.)

To delete a task, select its ID cell and then press Delete. For a subtask, Project deletes only the task. If you delete a summary task, Project deletes the summary task and all its subtasks. To delete a summary task without deleting its subtasks, you must first move the subtasks to another summary task or outdent them to the same level as the summary task.

Modifying a Task's Level in the Outline

As detailed in Chapter 4, getting the work breakdown structure to be just so is a ballet of moving tasks to different locations or different levels in the outline. You can easily change a task's level in the outline, although the results depend on what type of task you modify, and whether you move it lower or higher in the outline. First, select the tasks you want to change, and then use the following techniques to change the outline level:

- **Indent a task to the next lower level.** If you type several task names for summary tasks and their subtasks in a row, the tasks all start out at the same level. To turn the tasks into summary tasks and subtasks, you indent the subtasks.

  To indent them, select the task or tasks, and then press Alt+Shift+right arrow or, on the Task tab, click Indent. If the task is at the same level as the task above it, then the task indents to the next-lower level in the outline, while the task above it turns into a summary task. If the task you indent is at a higher level than the task above it, the task above doesn't become a summary task.

- **Elevate a task to the next higher level.** Moving a task higher in the outline comes in handy when you want to disconnect a task from its summary task (for example, when you want to delete the summary task without deleting the subtasks) or you're changing how you break down work. Select the task or tasks, and then press Alt+Shift+left arrow or, on the Task tab, click Outdent.

  If the outdented task was one of several at the same level, it turns into a summary task. In addition, a summary task immediately above the outdented task turns into a regular task.

The table in the Gantt Chart view indicates outline level in several ways, as shown in Figure 6-12.

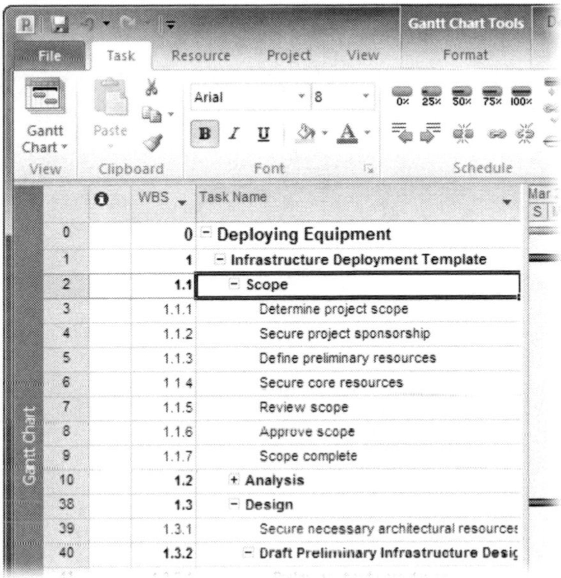

Figure 6-12:
A + sign or - sign precedes summary task names. If you click a + sign, the summary task expands to show its subtasks, and the + sign changes to a - sign. Clicking a - sign hides the subtasks, and changes the - sign to a + sign. The WBS codes also change to represent the level of the outline.

CHAPTER 7

Making a Schedule That's Easy to Maintain

I n Project, as in life, building good relationships is a key to success. When you define relationships between tasks in a Project file—*task dependencies*—the program calculates task start and finish dates based on how tasks affect one another. Some tasks have to finish before others can start. For example, the law of gravity requires that you finish a building's foundation before you start pouring the concrete for the first floor's walls.

With all the task dependencies in place, tasks cheerfully nestle into sequence, and you can finally see the schedule for the entire project from the start date for the first task to the finish date of the last task. Placing your tasks in sequence is what turns a task list into a project schedule.

This chapter describes the different types of task dependencies, how to create and modify them, and the pros and cons of each one. Also, although task dependencies let Project adjust task start and finish dates automatically, some situations call for specific dates for tasks. In this chapter, you'll learn two ways to specify when tasks can start or finish. Project 2010's new manual scheduling feature makes it easy to fix start and finish dates. But you can also apply date constraints with different levels of flexibility. More importantly, you'll find out how to use date constraints and deadlines to handle specific dates *without* limiting Project's ability to calculate the schedule.

Note: Before you dig into defining the relationships between tasks, you should have completed a work breakdown structure and built a list of all project tasks and milestones, as described in the previous chapters. Otherwise, you won't have all the information you need to put tasks into a logical sequence.

How Tasks Affect One Another

Clearly defined task dependencies are essential to creating an easy-to-maintain schedule. Project tasks can relate to one another like parents, children, and siblings do. Like DNA passing from parent to child, the start or finish date of one task (the *predecessor*) determines when the second task (the *successor*) starts or finishes. These connections are called *task dependencies,* but you might also hear them called by less needy terms, like *relationships* or *links.*

When you get your task dependencies in place (and use Project's automatic scheduling), project tasks snuggle cozily into sequence, and the program can automatically calculate task start and finish dates—and from those, the beginning and end of the entire project.

As Figure 7-1 illustrates, Project indicates task dependencies with small arrows showing how the start or end point of each task relates to the start or end of another.

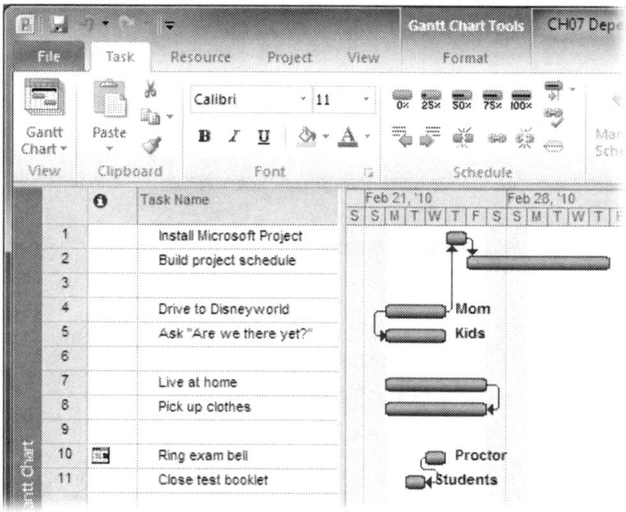

Figure 7-1:
Although the tasks in a relationship are called successor and predecessor, a dependency isn't about which task starts first—it's about which task controls the timing of the other. For example, in a start-to-start dependency, both tasks start at the same time, but the start of the predecessor controls when the successor starts.

Task dependencies come in four flavors, listed here from the most to least common:

- **Finish-to-start (FS)** dependencies are the most common by far. In this relationship, the predecessor task *does* come first. When it finishes, the successor task begins—for example, when you finish installing a program on your computer, you can start using the program to do your real work.

- **Start-to-start (SS)** dependencies come in handy when the start of one task triggers the start of another. For instance, as soon as you start driving to your vacation destination, your kids start asking, "Are we there yet?"

Start-to-start dependencies often come with a delay (called a *lag*) between the predecessor and successor tasks (page 162). On that vacation drive, if your son starts poking his sister, she might not start crying until 2 minutes have passed.

- **Finish-to-finish (FF)** dependencies are the mirror image of start-to-start relationships. The successor task continues only as long as the predecessor does. For instance, as long as your teenagers live at home, you pick up their clothes from the bathroom floor.

  These dependencies also tend to come with lag between the tasks. When a road crew inches along painting the lines on a highway, the folks who pick up the traffic cones finish a little while after the paint has dried.

- **Start-to-finish (SF)** dependencies are rare, which is for the best, since this relationship can be confusing. To better grasp the relationship, avoid the terms "predecessor" and "successor," and simply remember that the start of one task controls the finish of another. When an exam proctor rings the bell to indicate that time is up, the students have to close their test booklets, whether or not they've answered all the questions.

All of these examples are pretty straightforward. In real life, it may not always be so clear what kind of dependency you're dealing with. See the box on page 157 for advice.

UP TO SPEED

Choosing the Right Relationship

For your project schedule to be accurate, you must use the right type of dependency to link tasks. Simply put, if you don't connect tasks in the right way, the project won't proceed according to plan. Fortunately, the relationships between tasks are usually easy to identify. Most of the time, you're dealing with finish-to-start dependencies. But if you have trouble figuring out which relationship to use, ask yourself the following questions:

1. **Does the start or finish of one task control the other task?** When you answer this question, you know which task is the predecessor and which is the successor. You also know whether the dependency begins with "finish-to" or "start-to," in the list on page 156.

2. **Does the predecessor control the start or finish of the successor?** The answer to this question settles the type of dependency. Simply add the answer to

this question to the answer from question 1. For example, if the predecessor determines when the successor task starts, then "finish-to" becomes "finish-to-start."

Another way to sort out the relationship is to complete the following sentence: This task must (start/finish) before I can (start/finish) that task.

In addition to choosing the right type of dependency, it's important to identify *all* the dependencies between tasks. Find relationships you missed by reviewing each task and asking yourself which other tasks affect it. Once you've identified those predecessor tasks, you can identify the relationship between those tasks and the current task.

Building Relationships Between Tasks

It's dependencies that transform a ragtag group of tasks into a well-mannered project schedule, so Project offers several ways to create and modify all types of task dependencies. This section describes your task dependency options and the pros and cons of each one, starting with the most common type—finish-to-start.

Creating Finish-to-Start Task Dependencies

Finish-to-start dependencies are so common that the Link Tasks command on the ribbon's Task tab is dedicated to creating them. When your tasks follow one another like elephants, with one's trunk connecting to the next one's tail, the Link Tasks command is the fastest way to create those finish-to-start dependencies. It's also the easiest way to link two tasks when you can't see both task bars in the Gantt Chart simultaneously.

Here's how to create a finish-to-start task dependency:

1. **Select the predecessor task and the successor task you want to link.**

   If the predecessor and successor aren't adjacent, then click the predecessor first, and then Ctrl-click the successor.

   If the predecessor and successor appear one after the other in the table area of the Gantt Chart, simply drag across the two tasks to select both. When you link the tasks, the one higher in the list becomes the predecessor to the one immediately following it.

2. **On the ribbon Task tab, click Link Tasks (which looks like links of chain) to create the connection.**

   Project creates finish-to-start dependencies between the selected tasks. The timescale of the Gantt Chart shows the link lines of these dependencies, as illustrated in the bottom window of Figure 7-2, but you can also see predecessors and successors in task forms, the table area of the Gantt Chart, and the Task Information dialog box, as you'll learn shortly.

Tip: The Task tab's Unlink Tasks command (which looks like a broken link of chain) does different things depending on the tasks you select. If you select a single task and then click Unlink Tasks, then Project removes *all* the links to that task, not just the task dependency you probably had in mind. If you select two linked tasks, then clicking Unlink Tasks removes the dependency between them. See page 162 for other ways to remove dependencies.

When the task bars for two related tasks are visible in the Gantt Chart timescale, you can also create a finish-to-start link by dragging from the predecessor task bar to the successor task bar. This approach can be a perilous path and is advisable only if you pay attention to what you're doing. If you don't select the first task correctly, you can move the task instead of linking it, which creates an unintended date constraint (page 166) as well.

When you position the pointer over the first task, make sure you see a four-headed arrow. Then, as you drag the pointer to the second task, make sure the pointer changes to a link of a chain, as illustrated in Figure 7-3.

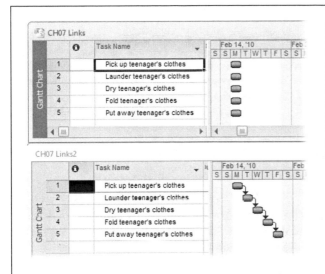

Figure 7-2:
You can link more than two tasks. If several adjacent tasks link with finish-to-start dependencies, drag from the first to the last, as shown in the top Gantt Chart window. Unlike earlier versions in which you could link only 10 tasks, Project 2007 can simultaneously link as many tasks as you want. If the order of the tasks in the table doesn't match their sequence, click the very first predecessor, and then Ctrl-click each task in the order that you want Project to link them.

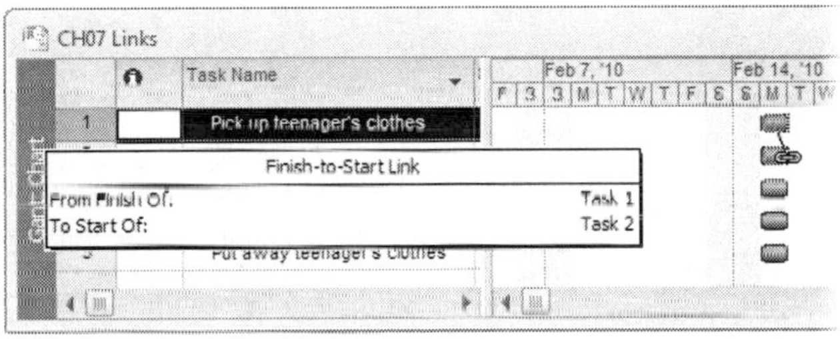

Figure 7-3:
In addition to the chain link pointer, a pop-up box identifies the link that Project will create when you release the mouse button. If the pointer turns into a one-headed or two-headed arrow as you drag, you're about to add a split into the middle of the task, or move it, instead of linking it to its successor.

Creating and Modifying All Types of Task Dependencies

When you want to create, modify, or delete any kind of task dependency, you can take your pick from several locations in Project. This section is your guide to where you can define task dependencies in Project, and the advantages or drawbacks of each.

Filling in task forms in the Gantt Chart view

The bottom pane of the Gantt Chart view typically displays the Task Form, which includes fields for specifying predecessors, successors, types of links, and lag (page 162). When you select a task in the top pane of the Gantt Chart view, the Task Form in the bottom pane shows the values for that task, so you can define, modify, or delete a task dependency. If the bottom pane doesn't appear at all, it might be temporarily hidden. To display it, double-click the small rectangle just under the vertical scrollbar.

Note: Out of the box, Project turns on the "Update Manually Scheduled tasks when editing links" option, which tells Project to change the dates for manually scheduled tasks if you link auto-scheduled tasks to them as predecessors. (If you link manually scheduled tasks, Project creates the task link but doesn't change the task dates.) If you want manually scheduled tasks to stay put, regardless how you link them to other tasks, turn this checkbox off. To access this checkbox, choose File→Options. In the Project Options dialog box, choose Schedule. The option is below the "Scheduling options for this project" heading.

To link the selected task to its predecessor, do the following:

1. **In the Task Form, click a Predecessor Name cell and then, from the drop-down list, choose the predecessor task, demonstrated in Figure 7-4.**

   If the bottom pane contains a different view, you can switch to a task form by clicking the View tab and then, in the Split View section, choosing Task Form or Task Details Form in the Details drop-down list.

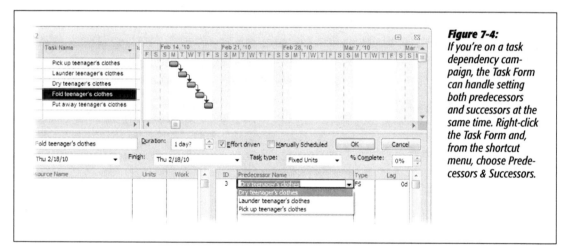

Figure 7-4:
If you're on a task dependency campaign, the Task Form can handle setting both predecessors and successors at the same time. Right-click the Task Form and, from the shortcut menu, choose Predecessors & Successors.

2. **In the Type cell drop-down list, choose the task dependency.**

   The names are abbreviated to initials, like FS for finish-to-start, SS for start-to-start, FF for finish-to-finish, and SF for start-to-finish.

Tip: If you want to introduce a delay or to overlap the tasks, enter a time value or a percentage in the Lag box. For more details on how lag time works, see page 162.

---

3. **Click OK to create the link.**

 The values appear in the Task Form, as do the link lines between the task bars in the Gantt Chart timescale.

The Task Form method is a great timesaver, because you can add, modify, or remove links with equal ease:

- **Add a dependency.** In a blank predecessor row, specify the values for the ID (or Predecessor Name), Type, and Lag for the link. Click OK.

- **Modify a dependency.** Click the cell you want to change, and then choose a different value. If you created a task as start-to-start and you meant finish-to-finish, then click the dependency's Type cell and choose FF. You can modify the predecessor task and the lag as well. Click OK.

- **Delete a dependency.** Click anywhere in the dependency's row, and then press Delete. Click OK.

Note: If you decide you don't want the changes you've made, press Esc (or click Cancel) instead of clicking OK.

Working on task dependencies in the Task Information dialog box

The Task Information dialog box is abuzz with information about the currently selected task. To open the dialog box, press Shift+F2, or on the Task tab, click Information. In the dialog box, select the Predecessors tab to define links from the selected task to its predecessors, shown in Figure 7-5.

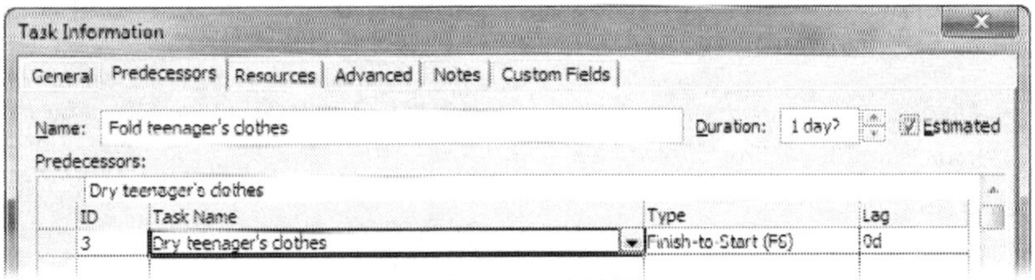

Figure 7-5:
Double clicking a task opens the Task Information dialog box, displaying the values for that task.

Although the Task Information dialog box is great when you want to see or edit everything about a task, it has a few limitations compared with setting dependencies in a task form:

- To work on links, you must open the dialog box, as opposed to seeing the fields at all times in a task form.

- The Task Information dialog box lets you define only predecessors to the selected task, not successors.

- To work on links for another task, you must close the dialog box, select the other task, and then reopen the Task Information dialog box.

Defining task dependencies in the table area

The Entry table, which the Gantt Chart view displays out of the box, includes the Predecessors column, which is great if you prefer typing to mousing. You can specify everything about a link in a task's Predecessor cell—as long as you know the code:

- **Create straightforward finish-to-start links.** All you do is type the ID number (the first column in the table area) for the predecessor.

- **Create several finish-to-start links to the selected task.** Separate each ID number with a comma, like this: *1,2,5,10*.

- **Create a dependency other than finish-to-start.** Type the dependency abbreviation immediately after the ID number. For instance, to create a start-to-start link with task number 3, type *3SS*. (The abbreviations for the dependency types are the first letters of each half of the relationship: FS, SS, FF, SF.)

- **Designate the lag or lead time (page 162).** Type a plus sign (+) followed by the length of the delay or a minus sign (–) followed by the length of the lead, such as *3SS+5days*.

Double-clicking existing links

Double-clicking a link in the Gantt Chart timescale opens a small dialog box, shown in Figure 7-6, for modifying or deleting the link. Needless to say, you can't use the double-click method to *create* a task dependency, because you need a link to double-click. Double-clicking a link is easy, unless you've got link lines splattered all over the Gantt Chart timescale, making finding the right link line a challenge.

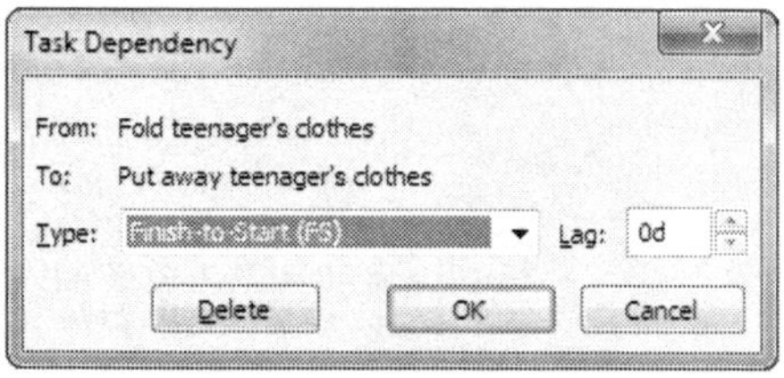

Figure 7-6:
Before you change any values, make sure that the From and To tasks represent the link you want to modify. Then, in the Type drop-down list, choose the new dependency. The Lag box is where you specify the lag or lead time. If you want to delete the link, click Delete.

Delaying or Overlapping Tasks

Tasks don't always occur in rapid-fire succession. When a company submits an invoice, it usually has to wait 30 days to receive payment. In the real world, delay between linked tasks is called *lag time,* because the second task lags for a while before it starts (or finishes). When tasks overlap, the overlap is called *lead time*—like giving someone a 30-minute head start because you're faster than they are. In Project, lag is the name for both delays and overlaps. Typing a positive number creates a delay between the tasks, while a negative number overlaps the two tasks.

Automated Dependencies

How can I prevent Project from automatically creating links between tasks?

Sometimes, Project can be helpful to the point of annoyance. One way it tries to help is by automatically modifying task dependencies as you add, move, and delete tasks. For example, if you insert a new task (page 148) between two existing tasks, Project removes the existing link, and then creates finish-to-start dependencies between all three tasks. Likewise, if you delete a task, Project links the tasks above and below the deleted task. And if you move a task, Project cleans up the links at the old spot and then creates new links in the task's new location.

If none of this is what you want, taking linking into your own hands is as simple as turning off one checkbox in the Project Options dialog box.

3. On the File tab, click Options, and then, in the Project Options dialog box, click Schedule.

4. If more than one project is open, to the right of the "Scheduling options for this project" label, choose the project for which you want to change the setting.

5. Turn off the "Autolink inserted or moved tasks" checkbox. (Because this checkbox sits underneath the label that specifies settings for a specific project file, you can rest assured that this setting applies only to the project you chose.)

These automated dependencies can save time when you're building your initial schedule. Turn on this checkbox, and you can insert, rearrange, or remove tasks, while Project manages the dependencies. Once the task dependencies are arranged the way you want, go back and turn off the checkbox, so the links are completely under your control.

Note: Lag is a delay between tasks that comes about no matter what happens. Project also includes a field called Assignment Delay (page 271), which delays a task until an assigned resource is available to work on it.

In Project, you use the Lag box to specify lag or lead, which can be a duration or a percentage:

- **Add a time delay.** If you have to wait 30 minutes after eating to get in the pool, you enter *30min* in the Lag box.

- **Add lead time.** Enter a negative value, such as *–30min* for your friend's head start in the race.

- **Add a percentage delay or lead.** Using a percentage tells Project to adjust the length of the lag or lead if the duration of the predecessor changes; for instance, to increase the length of the lead for a longer foot race. To define lag or lead as a percentage, simply type a percentage like *75%* in the Lag box.

Whether you use lag or lead depends on the type of task dependency. If you link tasks with a start-to-start link, a value of 50 percent tells Project to start the second task when 50 percent of the first one is complete. If you link the tasks as finish-to-start, you can obtain the same results by entering *-50%* in the Lag box. For example, consider a task for raking leaves and another for mowing the lawn. You can create a start-to-start link from raking leaves to mowing with a 50 percent lag, so your spouse doesn't start mowing until you've raked half the yard. If you create a finish-to-start link between these two tasks with a *-50%* in the Lag box, the yard-mowing task still starts halfway through raking leaves.

All methods for creating and modifying task dependencies, except for the Link Tasks command, include a place to specify the lag or lead. When you use the Link Tasks command, you can edit those links later to add lag or lead.

Here's how you set lag or lead for each method of defining task dependencies:

- **Task Form.** When you display predecessors or successors in a task form, each dependency includes four fields: ID, Predecessor Name, Type, and Lag. In the Lag cell, enter the lag (a positive number) or lead (a negative number).

- **Task Information dialog box.** When you display the Predecessors tab in the Task Information dialog box, the last column is Lag. As in the task form, type the duration or percentage you want in the Lag cell.

- **Table area.** In the table area's Predecessor cells, you append the lag or lead to the link information. If the successor task (for instance, with task ID 7) starts 3 days after the end of the predecessor task (whose task ID is 6), the Predecessor cell would be 6FS+3day.

- **Double-clicking a link line.** The Task Dependency dialog box includes a Lag box for the lag or lead value.

Scheduling Task Work Time with Calendars

Sometimes tasks must run at specific times of the day or days of the week. For example, scheduling computer maintenance during off-hours keeps complaints from information workers to a minimum. Microsoft Project calendars help you specify working and nonworking time to schedule tasks on the days and times you want. By applying a calendar to a task, you can specify the hours when work should occur for that task.

You can easily assign a calendar to a task. Here are the steps:

1. **In a view's table area, select the task or tasks to which you want to assign a calendar, and then, on the Task tab, click Information.**

   If you select only one task, the Task Information dialog box opens. If you select more than one task, you see the Multiple Task Information dialog box, which is identical to the Task Information dialog box, except that fields unique to individual tasks are disabled.

2. **Click the Advanced tab and, in the Calendar drop-down list, choose the calendar you want to apply, as illustrated in Figure 7-7.**

   Project comes with three built-in calendars: Standard for an 8-to-5 work schedule, Night Shift for the 11 p.m. to 8 a.m. grind, and 24 Hours for the gerbils on treadmills in your organization. If you want a different calendar, you must create it (page 238) before opening the Task Information dialog box.

3. **Click OK to close the dialog box and apply the task calendar to the task.**

Setting Specific Task Dates

Anyone who's taken a project management course knows the monumental tedium of manually calculating start dates, finish dates, slack time, and other schedule values. Letting Project calculate a schedule is much more satisfying, so normally you don't want to place limits on the program's scheduling capabilities. (See Chapter 5 to learn when it makes sense to take control of scheduling and how to do so with Project 2010's manual scheduling feature.) From time to time, though, you need more control over task dates. Suppose the backhoe you need isn't available to dig the foundation until after June 1. A new database guru who starts work on October 12 probably won't start her tasks before that date. Or the trade show your company is attending takes place from July 8–12 whether your booth is ready or not.

To keep your schedule low-maintenance, let Project calculate it as much as possible. That way, the program recalculates dates automatically when predecessors get delayed or take longer (or shorter) than planned. However, when you want tasks to occur on or around specific dates, you can make that happen in two ways:

- **Set a task's schedule mode to Manually Scheduled.** When tasks are set to Auto Scheduled mode, Project does what you expect project management software to do. It calculates when tasks start and finish based on predecessors, resource availability, and so on. But there are times when you want complete control over when tasks occur. Setting a task to Manually Scheduled means Project quietly steps aside as you change the task dates to your heart's content. Manually scheduling tasks is perfect when you want to pick specific start and finish dates.

- **Add a date constraint to a task.** A *date constraint* (or simply *constraint*) limits when a Project task either starts or finishes. Every task has a constraint, even if it's the completely flexible As Soon As Possible constraint. On the other hand, completely inflexible constraints like Must Start On make tasks behave a lot like manually scheduled tasks, except that you can specify a date constraint on only one of a task's dates. One reason to use a date constraint instead of manual scheduling is when you want a constraint that's partially flexible—for example, when you want a task to start before a specific date, but you don't care how much before.

This section explains how to use manual scheduling and date constraints to set task dates. You'll learn about the types of date constraints at your disposal and how to use them without forfeiting schedule flexibility. In addition, you'll learn how to use deadlines to spotlight key dates without applying inflexible date constraints.

Manually Scheduling Task Dates

If a task occurs on specific dates—for example, a safety training course scheduled for October 10 and 11—Project 2010's new manual scheduling mode is the way to set task dates in a jiffy. When a task is set to Manually Scheduled, you're in the driver's seat date-wise. (To learn everything you can do with manual scheduling, see page 116.)

If you usually let Project automatically schedule tasks, here's how to set task dates with manual scheduling:

1. **Select the task whose dates you want to control. On the Task tab, click Manually Schedule.**

   You can also right-click the task and choose Manually Schedule from the shortcut menu.

2. **In the task table, type the dates you want in the task's Start and Finish cells.**

   Project places brackets on each end of the task bar, as shown in Figure 7-8, and changes the bar color to teal to show that the task is manually scheduled. If the manually scheduled task's predecessors are delayed, then Project draws a red squiggle below the task's dates to indicate that there's a problem. See page 251 to learn your options when that happens.

Types of Constraints

Date constraints run the gamut from totally flexible to totally controlled, and each type has its place. Unless a task is associated with a specific date, stick to the most flexible constraints—As Soon As Possible or As Late As Possible. Here are the constraint types in Project and when to use them:

- **As Soon As Possible.** When you schedule a project from its start date (page 135), Project automatically assigns the As Soon As Possible date constraint to tasks, because this constraint makes no demands on when a task occurs. The start and finish date for the task are scheduled as soon as possible given its task dependencies, duration, resources, and work times.

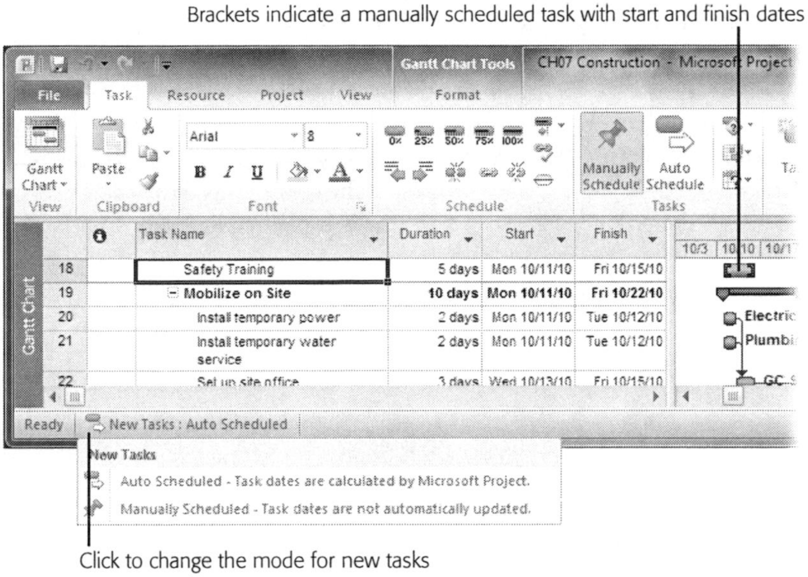

Brackets indicate a manually scheduled task with start and finish dates

Figure 7-8:
You can change the Schedule Mode for all new tasks by clicking New Tasks at the bottom right of the Project status bar and then choosing either Auto Scheduled or Manually Scheduled.

Click to change the mode for new tasks

- **As Late As Possible.** This date constraint automatically applies to every task when you schedule a project from the finish date. It's just as flexible as As Soon As Possible. The one problem with As Late As Possible tasks is that they don't leave any wiggle room for delays if something goes wrong. If you have to delay a task with this type of constraint, its successors and in many cases the project finish date are delayed as well.

- **Start No Earlier Than.** You use this partly flexible date constraint for tasks that can start only after a certain date. For example, you can't buy concert tickets until they go on sale, but you might buy them at any time after that date (until the tickets sell out). If you type a date in a task Start field in projects scheduled from the start date, then Project changes the constraint type to Start No Earlier Than.

- **Finish No Earlier Than.** Another date constraint with some built-in flexibility, Finish No Earlier Than is ideal for tasks that must continue until a specific date, for instance, processing conference registrations until the cutoff date. If you type a date in a task Finish field for projects scheduled from the start date, Project changes the constraint type to Finish No Earlier Than.

- **Start No Later Than.** This date constraint sets the latest date that a task can begin. If you schedule a project from the finish date, Project uses this constraint type when you type a date in a task Start field. You might use this constraint to make sure that construction begins early enough to enclose a house before winter hits. However, if everything goes smoothly, you're happy to begin construction earlier.

- **Finish No Later Than.** You can apply this date constraint to control the latest date for a task to finish. For example, if a customer requires that proposals be submitted before a specific date, then you can schedule your proposal task to finish several days earlier to leave time for mailing. If you schedule a project from the finish date, then Project uses this constraint type when you type a date in a task Finish field.

- **Must Start On.** This date constraint is completely inflexible. It specifies when a task starts, no ifs, ands, or buts. Moreover, the inflexibility of this date constraint overrides the task dependencies you set, as explained in the box on page 170. Avoid using this type of constraint unless it's absolutely necessary.

- **Must Finish On.** The control freak on the finish date, this date constraint specifies the exact date when a task ends. It also overrides task dependencies and is best left unused unless you absolutely must.

Note: If you change a task's mode to Manually Scheduled, you set the start and finish date for the task, so it's like applying Must Start On and Must Finish On date constraints.

Setting and Changing Constraints

Microsoft has been called a lot of things: *Minimalist* is not one of them. As with most of its features, Project gives you several locations where you can work with constraints:

- **Task Details Form.** The Task Details Form (*not* the Task Form) includes the Constraint box and Date box. To set or change the constraint for a single task, select the task in the table area of a view like the Gantt Chart. Then in the bottom pane of the view, in the Constraint drop-down list, choose the type of constraint you want. If you're setting a constraint other than As Soon As Possible or As Late As Possible, choose the date in the Date box.

- **Task Information dialog box.** In the Task Information dialog box, click the Advanced tab. In the "Constraint type" and "Constraint date" boxes, choose the type and date for the constraint.

- **Table area.** The table area is ideal when you want to change the constraints for many tasks at once. If you've just learned about the evils of inflexible constraints, you may want to change all tasks back to As Soon As Possible. To do so, right-click a column heading, and then choose Insert Column on the shortcut menu. In the drop-down list that appears for the new column, choose Constraint Type. In a Constraint Type cell, choose the new constraint type (As Soon As Possible, in this case). To copy that type to additional tasks, position the pointer over the small square in the bottom-right corner of the cell (called the Autofill handle) until the pointer changes to a crosshairs. Then drag down through the Constraint Type cells you want to change.

Preventing Unwanted Date Constraints

Because Project assigns the most flexible constraint automatically to auto-scheduled tasks (As Soon As Possible if you schedule from the start date, or As Late As Possible if you schedule from the finish date), the golden rule is to leave the constraint alone, unless you have a very good reason to change it. But date constraints have an exasperating way of appearing when you're sure you didn't set them. It turns out that a few seemingly innocent actions on your part can create date constraints in Project.

To make sure your schedule doesn't gain date constraints you didn't intend, heed the following guidelines:

- **Don't type a specific date in a Start or Finish cell.** When you do this, Project changes the date constraint to Start No Earlier Than in a project scheduled from the start date or Start No Later Than in a project scheduled from the finish date.

- **Don't set the finish date for a task just because that's the deadline.** The whole point of using Project is to find out ahead of time that a task won't finish on time, so you can adjust your plan to bring the finish date back in line.

Tip: For a better way to indicate deadlines without adding inappropriate date constraints, read on to the next section.

- **Don't drag a task bar horizontally in the Gantt Chart timeline.** This action tells Project to change the constraint to Start No Earlier Than or Start No Later Than, depending on whether you've scheduled the project from the start date or finish date. Dragging task bars incorrectly can also link tasks you don't want connected, or split a task into two pieces. Avoid editing tasks in the timescale unless you're completely fastidious, and a maestro with the mouse.

Note: If you set a task's mode to Manually Scheduled, you can drag the task bar horizontally to change when it occurs. Project doesn't change the Constraint Type field when tasks are set to Manually Scheduled.

Setting Deadline Reminders

As their name implies, deadlines are dates that usually have ghastly consequences if you miss them. Yet Project's date constraints don't guarantee that you'll meet your deadlines and, as explained in the previous section, setting too many constraints can have serious drawbacks. The best way to stay on top of deadlines in Project is to define the deadline date in a task's Deadline field. Meanwhile, schedule the project as you would normally. Then, with the deadlines set on tasks, you keep on the lookout for Project indicators that a deadline is in jeopardy. If you spot a missed deadline indicator, you can investigate the issue and develop a plan to pull the task dates in earlier.

When Constraints and Dependencies Clash

Setting a Must Finish On constraint sounds definite, but the constraint doesn't guarantee on-time completion. Moreover, inflexible constraints, such as Finish No Later Than or Must Start On, can generate subtle and dangerous behavior on Project's part. Suppose a predecessor task runs late and pushes a successor past its must-finish-on date. Project can't keep both the Must Finish On constraint and the finish-to-start task dependency. Out of the box, Project honors the date constraint, which seems fine until you notice that the two tasks now overlap instead of following each other, as shown in the top project window in Figure 7-9. When you execute the project, those tasks aren't likely to overlap, pushing the task dates beyond the constraint you see in the Project schedule.

Most of the time, you want Project to warn you when your schedule might miss an important date. To obtain this type

of warning, you have to tell Project to honor task dependencies, not date constraints. That way, predecessors and successors interact in the way they should, but a task that blows past its constraint date displays a Missed Constraint indicator (shown in the bottom project window in Figure 7-9).

To honor task dependencies over date constraints, on the File tab, click Options. In the Project Options dialog box, click Schedule, and then turn off the "Tasks will always honor their constraint dates" checkbox. If you want this setting to apply to all future projects, then in the "Scheduling options for this project" drop-down list, choose All New Projects, and then turn off the checkbox.

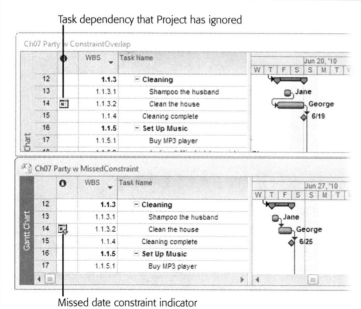

Task dependency that Project has ignored

Missed date constraint indicator

Figure 7-9:
Tasks that should follow each other can end up overlapping when Project ignores a task dependency in order to honor a date constraint. Project doesn't warn you about these overlaps, so you might not notice them unless you're really paying attention. If you turn off the "Tasks will always honor their constraint dates" option, Project keeps things in the correct sequence, and warns you about missed date constraints with an icon in the Indicator column.

Tip: As you execute your project plan, remember to check regularly for missed date constraints and missed deadlines, as described in Chapter 15.

Here are the steps for setting and tracking a deadline for a task:

1. **Double-click the task to open the Task Information dialog box.**

   You can also select the task, and then, on the Task tab, click Information.

2. **In the Task Information dialog box, select the Advanced tab. In the Deadline box, click the arrow to display a calendar, and then choose the deadline date. Click OK.**

   In the Gantt Chart view, Project displays a downward-pointing arrow with a black border at the task's deadline date. If the task bar ends before or at the black arrow, the task is ahead of its deadline. The task is late if the bar ends to the right of the arrow, as shown in Figure 7-10.

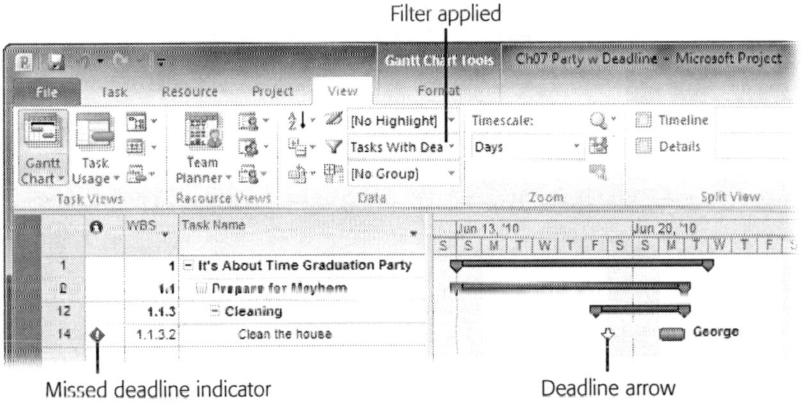

Figure 7-10:
To display tasks with deadlines, on the View tab's Filter drop-down list, choose More Filters. In the More Filters dialog box, double-click Tasks With Deadlines.

3. **To see whether any tasks have missed their deadlines, review the Indicators column for red diamonds with exclamation points inside.**

   To make missed deadlines easier to see, you can filter the task list to show only tasks with Deadline dates assigned. On the View tab's Filter drop-down list (the icon looks like a funnel), choose More Filters. In the More Filters dialog box, double-click Tasks With Deadlines. Project displays tasks with deadlines assigned along with the summary tasks to which those tasks belong.

   If you want to hide the summary tasks, on the Format tab, in the Show/Hide section, turn off the Summary Tasks checkbox.

Part Two: Project Planning: More Than Creating a Schedule

II

Building a Team for Your Project

Without people, projects wouldn't start and certainly wouldn't finish. To keep projects running smoothly in between the start and finish, you need the right people, and *they* need to know the parts they play. Otherwise, collaboration and communication is like a rousing rendition of Abbott and Costello's "Who's On First?"

You can start building your project team once you've identified the project tasks. You analyze the work, identify the skills and other resources required, and then look for resources that are both suitable and available. After you've added your resources to Project, you can assign them to tasks to calculate the schedule and cost, and then track progress.

In this chapter, you'll learn the difference between Project's work, material, and cost resources, and when to use each one. You'll learn how to identify and organize your resources (which may involve help from another program), enter resources in Project, and fill in fields for availability, costs, and so on.

Note: People are every project's most important resource, and when this book says "resource," that usually means "person." However, projects also rely on help from nonhuman team members, such as equipment, materials, and training. In Project, work resources represent anything you assign by time—people, a conference room you reserve by the hour, or a paper shredder you rent by the day. Material resources come in other units, like gallons of gas or reams of paper. Cost resources (introduced in Project 2007) cover expenses that aren't work or material, like travel or fees.

Identifying Project Resources

For small projects and tight-knit organizations, a list of skills might be enough to identify Bob and Jan as the people you need. In most cases, planning a project and building its project team means working with numerous groups and managers. Before you start working in Project, it's important to have a clear idea of what resources you have and what they can do for you. A *responsibility matrix* is a high-level view of resource groups and how much responsibility each has for each part of the project. Create a responsibility matrix, and you have a tool for settling those "I thought somebody else was doing that" arguments. Although Project doesn't have a built-in responsibility matrix, Microsoft Excel makes an ideal tool, since an Excel worksheet is nothing more than a matrix of cells.

Another helpful document for defining who's involved in a project is a *project organization chart*. This type of chart shows the reporting structure for team members, similar to an organization chart for a company. Especially important for projects with all sorts of partners—internal, external, third-party, outsourcing, and so on—the project organization chart identifies the go-to person when a decision is needed. Does the project sponsor have the final say, or is it an external customer who's picking up the check? If you'd like to clarify these relationships in a chart, Microsoft Visio is the perfect tool for creating one. The Visio Organization Chart template works for companies and projects alike, and you'll see how to use it on page 179. You can also create organization charts in Microsoft Word.

Who's Responsible for What

Just as too many cooks spoil the broth, too many groups claiming responsibility for the same work is a recipe for disaster. Turf wars waste time and money. Tasks get weighed down with extraneous requirements from fringe groups. Far more dangerous is when *no one* takes responsibility for work, because the work doesn't get done, or isn't done on time and within budget. The responsibility matrix (sometimes called the *responsibility assignment matrix*) prevents these project gaffes by spelling out who's in charge, who's responsible for performing work, who can offer opinions, and who simply needs to know.

The responsibility matrix is a compact document that identifies groups and their responsibilities. The list of project stakeholders is a great place to start identifying groups involved in a project, such as departments or business units like engineering, or even external groups like subcontractors. What those stakeholders want out of the project can provide hints about their level of involvement—do they have to approve decisions, do they do the work, or do they just need to be told what's going on?

Note: Because the responsibility matrix comes early in project planning, it doesn't identify every person assigned to a project.

You review the responsibility matrix with stakeholders to sort out the following items:

- **Who's in charge?** You've probably seen those cop movies where the local police and the FBI eye each other warily and grouse about the other group doing everything wrong. The responsibility matrix helps you dispel ownership disagreements *before* you need urgent and crucial decisions.

- **Is any work orphaned?** Like the pop fly ball that drops to the ground as the third baseman and shortstop stare at each other, project work can fall between the cracks. If you notice work without an owner in the responsibility matrix, you can track down stakeholders until someone accepts responsibility.

- **How do groups interact?** Most of the time, groups have to work together to get things done. The responsibility matrix identifies the level of involvement each group has for each part of a project, so groups know what they have to do, and what they can expect from others. Clarifying involvement is important when groups all belong to the same organization, but it's essential when a project uses contractors, partners, and outsourcing vendors. No doubt you've experienced a technical support horror story. You call in and get bounced from group to group, retelling your plight each time. A responsibility matrix can show who's on the hook until the issue is resolved.

TOOLS OF THE TRADE

Levels of Responsibility

A responsibility matrix shows levels of responsibility, from the group that's in charge to those who just need to know what's going on. If your project is a bacon-and-eggs breakfast, the chicken is involved, but the pig is committed. Here are the levels you'll find in most responsibility matrixes:

- **Accountable** means a group can make decisions, delegate work, and approve deliverables or other groups' decisions. For example, the general contractor for a construction project is accountable for the project. The general contractor decides whom to hire, delegates work to subcontractors, and supervises and approves work. Moreover, the general contractor earns more or less profit depending on whether the project is under or over budget.

- **Responsible** represents ownership of performing the work for a section of the project. The plumbing subcontractor is responsible for installing the piping and plumbing fixtures in a building.

- **Consulted** indicates that the group participates in discussions about a topic or decision but isn't accountable for the outcome. The general contractor might consult with a subcontractor about different solutions to a problem, but the general contractor is still accountable for the results of the chosen solution.

- **Informed** means the group receives information. The property management company needs to know about building amenities to prepare a brochure to attract tenants.

Creating a responsibility matrix in Excel

A responsibility matrix links groups to major sections of a project. Typically, you put the groups in the columns and the project sections in the rows, as shown in Figure 8-1. Because an Excel worksheet comes with a matrix of columns and rows, you can enter headings for each group in the cells in the first row, and then, in the cells in the first column, adding headings for the project sections. In the cell at the intersection of a group column and project section row, fill in all the levels of responsibility (described in the box on page 177) that the group has for that part of the project.

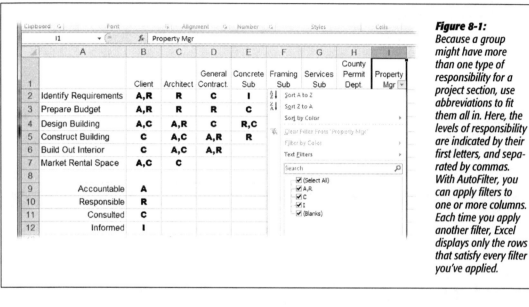

Figure 8-1:
Because a group might have more than one type of responsibility for a project section, use abbreviations to fit them all in. Here, the levels of responsibility are indicated by their first letters, and separated by commas. With AutoFilter, you can apply filters to one or more columns. Each time you apply another filter, Excel displays only the rows that satisfy every filter you've applied.

Note: Remember, a responsibility matrix is a high-level view—it documents major sections of a project, not each individual task; and groups involved, not individuals. Later on, as you build your project team in Project, you can use the Group resource field to categorize resources (page 191).

Groups can have more than one type of responsibility, so some cells might contain more than one entry. You may be both *accountable* for the family vacation (paying the bill, for instance) and *responsible* for making the reservations. Your teenagers are *consulted* on the destination (to reduce complaining), and also *responsible* for packing their gear.

Don't worry if your Excel skills are rusty. A responsibility matrix relies mainly on plain old spreadsheet columns and rows. However, for huge projects, you can filter an Excel worksheet to see only the sections that a particular group works on. Suppose you've decided to ditch a subpar subcontractor, and you want to know how that subcontractor is involved in the project so you can get the replacement up to speed ASAP. Here's how to filter an Excel responsibility matrix to find a group's involvement:

1. With the responsibility matrix file open in Excel 2010, click the column heading cell for the group in question, such as Property Mgr in Figure 8-1.

   If you plan to filter the responsibility matrix group by group, then select all groups by dragging across the cells that contain the group headings. You can also drag across Excel's letter headings to select columns.

2. To apply AutoFilter to selected columns, in the ribbon, choose Data→Sort & Filter→Filter or choose Home→Editing→Sort & Filter→Filter. In Excel 2003, from the menu bar, choose Data→Filter→AutoFilter.

   A small down-pointing arrow appears in the selected columns.

3. To display the drop-down list of filters you can apply, shown in Figure 8-1, click the arrow that's in the heading cell for the group you want to look at first.

   The drop-down menu suggests several filters based on the data in the column. However, you can create a custom filter by choosing Text Filters→Custom Filter and, in the Custom AutoFilter dialog box, specifying the filter tests.

4. To display all the rows that contain any level of responsibility for the group, at the bottom of the menu, turn off the Blanks checkbox.

   The worksheet hides any rows that have an empty cell for the group. The rows that appear contain at least one responsibility level for the group.

5. To remove the filter, click the down arrow in the group's heading cell, and then turn on the "(Select All)" checkbox.

   All the rows in the worksheet reappear. Repeat steps 3 through 5 to look at a different group.

   To turn off AutoFilter completely, choose Data→Sort & Filter→Filter.

Who Reports to Whom

As you identify the people who work on your project, you can start building a *project organization chart*, which shows the chain of command within your project, not the organization as a whole. Just like a regular organization chart, a project organization chart helps people figure out whom to ask if an issue needs escalating, a decision needs deciding, or any other situation requires higher authority.

In Microsoft Project, you can associate resources to groups with the Group resource field (page 191), and you can use outline codes (page 652) to link resources to an organizational structure. However, creating a project organization chart is best left to Microsoft Visio—or whatever tool your organization uses to document the companywide hierarchy.

Creating a project organization chart in Microsoft Visio

With Visio, you can build a project organization chart using the Organization Chart template. (In Visio 2010, on the File tab, click New. Under Template Categories, click Business, and then double-click Organization Chart. In Visio 2003, choose

File→New→Organization Chart→Organization Chart.) This template contains shapes that create reporting relationships when you drop them onto manager shapes on a drawing. Even better, the Organization Chart tab that appears when you create a diagram from this template includes the Organization Data Import command for importing resource information from Excel, and other sources like databases.

REALITY CHECK

Getting and Holding onto Resources

In this downsized, competitive world, there are never enough resources to go around. Asking for resources with the right skills or characteristics just increases the challenge. Some resources are scarce due to their unusual combination of skills—like a C# programmer with a health insurance background who also speaks Japanese. Other resources are scarce because everyone needs them—like a bulldozer after a seven-foot snowstorm.

Plus, projects don't have resources to call their own. People assigned to projects usually work for other departments, outside vendors, the customer, and so on. The perfect person for the job might sit across from you, but the approach that works more consistently is to give work package and assignment information to the people who have the resources you covet, and let them pick the right ones

based on skills and availability. Providing thorough descriptions and showing a realistic schedule help you build good relationships with these resource managers. The time that relationship-building takes is worth it, especially if you need favors later on.

Resourcing efforts aren't complete when you've finished assigning resources. You have to keep the resources on the project, and that means keeping workloads as consistent as you can (page 259). If resources sit idle, you're likely to lose them to other projects; or worse, the resources may get laid off. On the other end of the scale, pushing people to work long hours incurs overtime costs, increases errors, and generates rework. With a reputation as a bad project manager, you'll have trouble finding people for future projects.

Note: In most organizations, people report to functional managers. Then, when these people work on projects, they end up with two bosses—the functional manager, and their supervisor within the project. A project organization chart isn't the place to track both sets of bosses. Rely on the companywide organization chart or the corporate human resources system to track functional managers.

Understanding Project's Resource Types

Microsoft Project 2010 offers three types of resources for projects—two old standbys and one particularly handy addition introduced in Project 2007. Each resource type has its purpose and idiosyncrasies, so it's important to understand what each resource type represents and how it can affect your project. Here are the resource types in Project, and what each one represents:

- **Work.** Time is what separates work resources from other resource types in Project. For example, people and equipment are work resources, because you track their participation by the amount of time they spend. Whether you're assigning a cinematographer or an IMAX camera array, your project tasks depend on when those work resources are available, and how much time they have. Of course, work resources cost something, but those costs are usually based on the amount of time you use the resource; like whether you pay someone by the hour or the month, as shown in Figure 8-2.

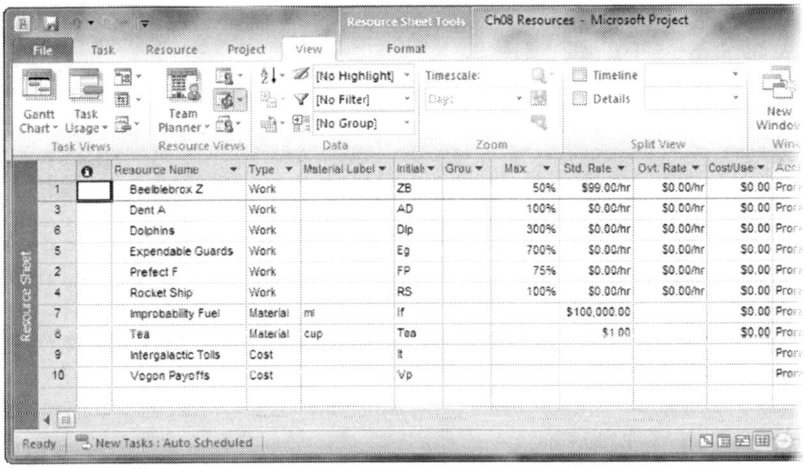

Figure 8-2:
Fields in the Resource Sheet may be blank or contain different types of information depending on the type of resource. For example, a work resource doesn't have a Material label, and costs are calculated initially as dollars per hour. Material resources have a cost per unit–per pound, gallon, or piece–and the Material label field defines the units. Cost resources receive a cost value only when you assign them to tasks.

- **Material.** You assign material resources by the quantity you need: two tons of gravel or 300 gallons of diesel fuel, for instance. Because materials aren't measured by time, quantities usually affect only the cost of your project. Materials affect dates or duration only when you have to wait for those materials to become available. For example, you can't begin steel erection until the building girders arrive from the fabricator.

- **Cost.** Cost resources came on the scene in Project 2007, and they're strictly cost; no time, no quantities—just dollars or dinero. Cost resources are perfect for ancillary costs that aren't directly associated with the people, equipment, and materials you assign to tasks. Expenses, such as travel or fees, increase the project price tag, but they aren't associated with work or material resources.

The advantage of the cost resource type is that you can track different types of costs separately. You might set up cost resources for travel, building permits, and blackmail payoffs, as illustrated in Figure 8-2. You can assign each cost resource that applies to a task (page 289), and then total what you spend on different types of costs for the entire project (page 299). A kickoff meeting might have $20,000 in travel costs and $5,000 in communications costs for the people who attend in person and via videoconference. The change control board might have $1,000 in travel costs and $2,000 for videoconferencing. When you see the $21,000 for travel vs. $7,000 for videoconferencing, you might consider changing your approach to meetings.

Note: Whether required skills are the only thing you know about tasks or you have real names for warm bodies, you can create resources in Project to assign to tasks. Generic resources act as placeholders to help you flesh out the schedule and identify how many resources you need. Then, as you identify the real resources you've obtained, you can add them to Project as well.

UP TO SPEED

How Resources Affect Project Schedules

For a quick-and-dirty project schedule, all you need are tasks, estimated task durations, and links between the tasks. Project shows a start date and finish date for the project, but how do you know whether these dates are any good without resources assigned to do the work? Then, as you begin to execute the project, how can you tell whether the project is proceeding according to plan? Assigning resources to tasks in Project provides the information you need to answer these questions. Resource assignments help you manage your project in several ways:

- **Defining the project schedule.** Because you can specify work schedules for resources, and when resources are available (page 192), your project schedule is more accurate, since it calculates task durations based on when resources work.

- **Managing resources.** Resource assignments tell you whether resources have too much work or too little. As you plan the project, you can balance people's workloads to make the schedule more realistic (and make your team members happier). In addition,

you can play what-if games with time versus money. For example, you might decide to use less expensive resources when the budget is more important than the finish date.

- **Preventing ownership problems.** Resource assignments also ensure that someone is working on every project task. At the same time, assignments can prevent overly enthusiastic team members from sticking their noses into someone else's work.

- **Tracking progress.** By updating your schedule with the actual progress people make, you can see whether or not the project is on track. This information is indispensable later on when you want to evaluate your estimating prowess and do better the next time (page 108).

- **Tracking spending.** With costs for work, material, and cost resources, you can not only estimate the budget for the project (page 297), but also track actual costs as the project progresses.

Adding Resources in Microsoft Project

Before you can play matchmaker between project tasks and resources, you must tell Project about the resources you're using. You can get started with a few basic fields, such as the resource name and resource type. As you identify detailed information, such as work schedules, availability, and costs, you can add that information to Project, as described in the box on page 182. In turn, Project uses that information to more accurately calculate your project schedule and price tag.

Project offers two methods for entering resource data directly. The Resource Sheet is ideal for specifying values for every resource—you can either copy and paste values, or simply drag values (even into several cells at once). To tell Project everything about a resource, the Resource Information dialog box presents every resource field in one place. If you have resource information stored in a company directory or other database, you can make short work of data entry by importing information into Project. This section explains each approach.

Tip: If you type a resource name or initials that don't exist in your project, the program is happy to add a new resource with default values for you automatically. At times, this behavior is a tremendous time-saver, because you can simply type a resource name in the Task Form or in a Resource Names cell without having to detour to the Resource Sheet to create the resource. However, if a typo sneaks in, your project can acquire resources that don't actually exist. To tell Project to notify you when it creates a new resource as it assigns the resource to a task, choose File→Options. In the Project Options dialog box, click Advanced. In the "General options for this project" drop-down list, choose the project you want to work on, and then turn off the "Automatically add new resources and tasks" checkbox. Turning off this checkbox also tells the program to notify you when it creates a task if you type a task name that doesn't exist while assigning a resource to a task, for example, in a new row in the Resource Usage view.

TOOLS OF THE TRADE

When to Tell Microsoft Project About the Team

Some project managers identify skills and material resources required as they define project work packages. Others focus on completing the work breakdown structure, and then go back to identify the required resources. Either way, resources typically start out as skill sets (crane operator, financial analyst with tax expertise, or JavaScript web developer) and major equipment (crane, supercomputer, or printing press) You can't identify specific resources until you know the skills and task dates.

Microsoft Project can handle this iterative approach. *Generic resources* (page 192) act as placeholders for the skill sets and people you need. Of course, if you have only a few employees, you can add all their names to Project, so they're fair game for task assignments.

Maybe you know the number of people you need for a task, and maybe you don't. You can assign generic resources to tasks in Project to get an estimate of task durations. If the schedule is too long or too costly, you can make changes, perhaps adding resources to shorten duration, or using different resources to reduce cost. When you're satisfied with the schedule and resource requirements, you have the information you need to hit up the management team for specific resources.

Then, as you obtain specific people or equipment, you can replace the generic resources with the resources that represent the warm bodies you're allocated (page 254). You can filter your project for tasks with generic resources assigned to see where you have holes in your team.

Note: If you use Project Professional in conjunction with Project Server, the Resource Substitution Wizard can search the enterprise resource pool for resources with the right skills and availability for your assignments. Without Project Server, though, you can still use the Assign Resources dialog box to look for qualified resources (page 343).

Adding Resources Manually

The Resource Sheet view is a quick way to get resources' names, ranks, and serial numbers into Project. In fact, you can specify most information about resources by adding columns to the table (page 611). For the resources that require more detail, like complicated cost rates or availability, the Resource Information dialog box is your only option.

Adding resources in the Resource Sheet view is similar to adding task information in the Gantt Chart's table area. Here's how to enter basic information for resources:

1. **Choose View→Resource Views→Resource Sheet (the icon that looks like two people in front of a tabular chart).**

   If a view with a top and bottom pane is open (like the Gantt Chart), the Resource Sheet replaces the view in the top pane and lists all existing resources.

   The Entry table that appears initially contains fields for both work and material resources.

2. **In the first Resource Name cell, type the name of the resource.**

   The Resource Name field is the only one you need to create a resource. To make resources easy to find later on, follow a standard naming convention. Commas and brackets are verboten in resource names, so consider something like "Smith J" for people. For generic resources, the job description, like Database Administrator, works well. Similarly, a brief description is fine for equipment and materials.

Tip: If you want to add several resources of the same type, you can apply a specialized resource table with the fields for that resource type, as shown in Figure 8-3.

---

3. **If you want to specify values for other fields for the resource, press Tab to move one column to the right.**

4. **To save the resource and move to the next resource row, press Enter.**

   Project saves the resource and moves to the Resource Name cell in the next row, so you can immediately type the next resource name. The fastest way to create lots of resources is to repeat this step until you've created and named all your resources. Then you can specify other values only if necessary. New resources are initially set as a Work resource type, because that's the most common type.

5. **For each material and cost resource in the list, click its Type cell. Click the down arrow that appears, and then, in the drop-down list, choose Material or Cost.**

   When you choose Material or Cost, Project removes values in columns that don't apply to that type of resource (like the Std. Rate field for a Cost resource).

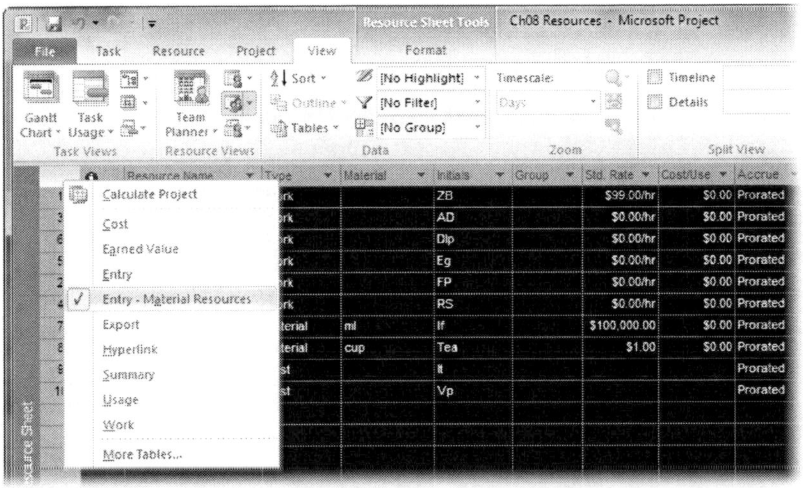

Figure 8-3:
To apply the Entry - Material Resources table to the Resource Sheet, right-click the Select All cell at the intersection of the column headings row and the resource ID column and then choose the table name on the shortcut menu. This table hides the Calendar column, because materials aren't assigned during specific times.

Tip: If all your material or cost resources are grouped together, you can change the Type cell for the first resource in the group. Then, position the pointer over the small square in the cell's lower-right corner, and drag to copy the value to the other cells.

---

6. **Change other values—such as Initials or Max. Units—by clicking a cell and then entering the value.**

    See "Providing Detailed Resource Information" on page 189 for descriptions of the available resource fields.

Importing Resources from Other Programs

Although typing resource information into Project is easy enough, there's no point in duplicating effort. You may have already drawn up a list of your team's names in an Excel spreadsheet, or you may have all the names you need right in your Outlook address book. Either way, you're in luck—Project can pull resource names from either program.

Importing resources from Excel

Getting resource information from an Excel workbook into Project is easy when you use the Microsoft Project Plan Import Export Template, which comes with Excel, and maps columns in an Excel worksheet to Project resource fields. The only catch is that both Excel and Project must be installed on the same computer for the template to appear.

Here are the steps for importing resource information from an Excel spreadsheet into Project:

1. **In Excel, on the File tab, click New.**

   The Available Templates screen appears.

2. **Under Available Templates, click Sample Templates, and then double-click Microsoft Project Plan Import Export Template.**

   Excel creates a new workbook with separate worksheets for tasks, resources, and assignments.

   To create a resource workbook in Excel 2003, choose File→New. In the New Workbook task pane, click "On my computer". When the Templates dialog box opens, select the Spreadsheet Solutions tab, and then double-click Microsoft Project Plan Import Export Template.

3. **At the bottom of the Excel window, select the Resource_Table tab, shown in Figure 8-4.**

   If you're importing only resources, you can ignore the worksheets for tasks and assignments.

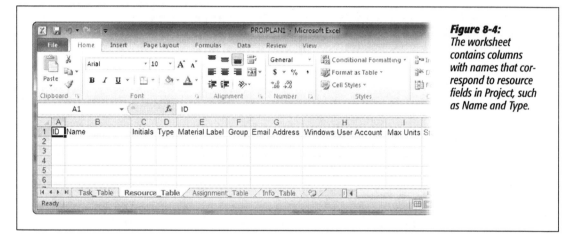

Figure 8-4:
The worksheet contains columns with names that correspond to resource fields in Project, such as Name and Type.

4. **Paste resource information into the appropriate cells, and then save the file when you're done.**

   Type information into cells if you don't have an existing file with resource data. If you have a spreadsheet that contains your resource information, then copy and paste the column headings in the template file to the corresponding column heading cells in your resource workbook. Paste names into the Name column. Project takes in this data based on the column headings in the template, so make sure your information aligns with the correct headings. (Of course, if you haven't done a resource spreadsheet yet and want to, then you can type the information right into this worksheet.)

Sorting Resources by Names and More

After an invigorating session of resource definition, your Resource Sheet might be a hodgepodge of resources in no particular order. An unsorted list not only makes it hard to see what resources you've got, but it also increases the likelihood of duplicating resources by mistake.

Removing duplicate resources before you assign them to tasks prevents confusion and scheduling problems. You may create two or more resources with the same name, but Project considers those resources separate entities. If you assign some tasks to one resource and other tasks to its doppelganger, your schedule will be wrong. Tasks look like they can run simultaneously, and workloads seem reasonable. But in reality, those tasks might have to run in sequence, or you might have double-booked a resource. Sorting the resource list by name places duplicate names next to each other, so you can delete the duplicates and assign the remaining ones to the correct tasks.

Project 2010 makes it easy to sort your resource list by name. Simply click the down arrow to the right of the Resource Name column heading. On the drop-down menu, choose Sort A to Z or Sort Z to A.

If you want to sort the list by more than one field, here's what you do:

1. With the Resource Sheet view active, on the View tab, click Sort, and then, on the drop-down menu, choose Sort By.

2. In the Sort dialog box, in the "Sort by" box, choose the field you want to use to sort the resources, and then select the Ascending or Descending option. For example, choose Generic to separate generic resources from specific resources. (Project selects the Ascending option automatically, which is perfect for alphabetical order.)

3. In the "Then by" box, choose the next field to sort by, such as Type or Group.

4. For the "Then by" sort field, choose the Ascending or Descending option, if necessary.

5. If you want to sort by another field, like Std. Rate, then in the second "Then by" box, choose the final sort field. If you use the first "Then by" field for Type or Group, use the second "Then by" field to sort by name.

6. To make this order permanent, turn on the "Permanently renumber resources" checkbox. When you complete the sort, Project reassigns the ID numbers that uniquely identify the resources.

7. Click Sort to rearrange the resources.

If you chose to renumber the resources permanently, reopen the Sort dialog box, click Reset to turn off the "Permanently renumber resources" checkbox, and then click Cancel to close the dialog box without resorting the list. This tells Project not to permanently renumber resources the next time you sort.

5. To import the resources into Project, launch Project, open the Project file, and then on the File tab, click Open.

   In the Open dialog box, in the "Files of type" drop-down list, choose Excel Workbook.

6. Navigate to the folder that contains the Excel workbook with your resource information, and then double-click the file name.

   The Import Wizard appears. On the first wizard page, click Next.

7. **On the next page, select the "New map" option, and then click Next.**

   The Import Wizard's Import Mode page appears. To import the resources into the active project, select the "Append the data to the active project" option, which adds the resources to the end of the existing resource list. Click Next.

8. **Turn on the Resources checkbox, and then click Next.**

   The Import Wizard's Resource Mapping page appears. Project automatically chooses Resource_Table for the "Source worksheet name" option. The Excel fields and Project fields should match up perfectly. If they don't, simply choose the correct Excel field to go with a Project field, or vice versa.

9. **Click Finish.**

   Project imports the resources to your project file, and they appear in the Resource Sheet.

Importing resources from your address book

Chances are you have resource information (for people resources, anyway) in Outlook or on a Microsoft Exchange Server. If so, you can import that information into a Project file, as long as Project is installed on the same computer as Outlook or the Microsoft Exchange Server.

To import resources from an address book, do the following:

1. **With the Resource Sheet view visible, on the Resource tab, click Add Resources.**

   A drop-down menu appears with commands for creating or importing resources.

   If a view other than the Resource Sheet is active, the Add Resources command is disabled.

2. **Choose Address Book.**

   The Select Resources dialog box appears. If you see the Choose Profile dialog box instead, then choose the profile name for the email system you want to use. For example, if you have a profile for your business email and one for personal, choose the business profile.

Note: If your organization uses Active Directory to store information, choose Active Directory to import resources from that data source. Then search through the Active Directory for resources instead of browsing as you do with an address book.

---

3. **In the Select Resources dialog box, select the resources you want to import, and then click Add.**

   Ctrl-click to select resources when they aren't adjacent. For resources that are adjacent, simply click the first resource, and then Shift-click the last. You can also select resources in batches and then click Add to append each batch to the import list.

4. **When all the resources you want to import appear in the Add box, click OK.**

Project adds the resources to the Resource Sheet. Any information you store in your address book that applies to Project fields transfers over. For example, Project imports email addresses into its own Email Address field.

Deleting Resources

If you've created duplicate resources or lost someone to another project, you may want to delete those resources in Project. In the Resource Sheet, click the row number of the resource, and then press Delete. Or right-click anywhere else in the resource row and choose Delete Resource from the shortcut menu.

Project removes the resource from your project, which means any assignments you've made are gone as well. That's right—when you delete a resource, you run the risk of orphaning tasks. In other words, you may end up with tasks that have no one assigned to do them. One way to prevent this issue is to replace the resource (page 269) on task assignments before you delete it. Filter the task list to show only the tasks to which the resource is assigned. Then you can edit each task to replace the resource. To see the tasks to which the resource is assigned, do the following:

1. **Display a task-oriented view like the Gantt Chart and hide the summary tasks. On the Format tab, turn off the Summary Tasks checkbox.**

The task list shows only work tasks and milestones.

2. **On the View tab, click the Filter arrow, and then choose Using Resource.**

The Using Resource dialog box opens with a "Show tasks using" drop-down list.

3. **In the "Show tasks using" drop-down list, choose the resource you want to delete, and then click OK.**

Project displays any tasks that have used that resource. After you finish editing resource assignments, click the Format tab and turn on the "Show summary tasks" checkbox.

Providing Detailed Resource Information

The resource fields you change most often appear in the table in the Resource Sheet view, so you might never have to give up the convenience and familiarity of entering values in table cells. Besides, if you have other resource fields that you always enter, then you can insert those columns in the resource table (page 611). The Resource Information dialog box contains all the resource fields you can set, and it's the only easy way to add a few of the more intricate resource settings. This section describes all the available resource fields and how to specify them.

To display the Resource Sheet view, on the View tab, click Resource Sheet. To open the Resource Information dialog box, use any of the following methods:

- With the Resource Sheet view active, on the Resource tab, click Information.

- With the Resource Sheet view active, press Shift+F2.

- Double-click a resource in the Resource Sheet view to open the Resource Information dialog box with the information for the resource you clicked.

Filling in General Information

The Resource Sheet view shows the fields most project managers fill in: name, resource type, initials, and workgroup. In the Resource Information dialog box, the General tab, shown in Figure 8-5, includes these fields, along with a few more. This section describes the Project resource fields that define resource basics. Then the remainder of this chapter shows you how to flesh out resources with work schedules and costs.

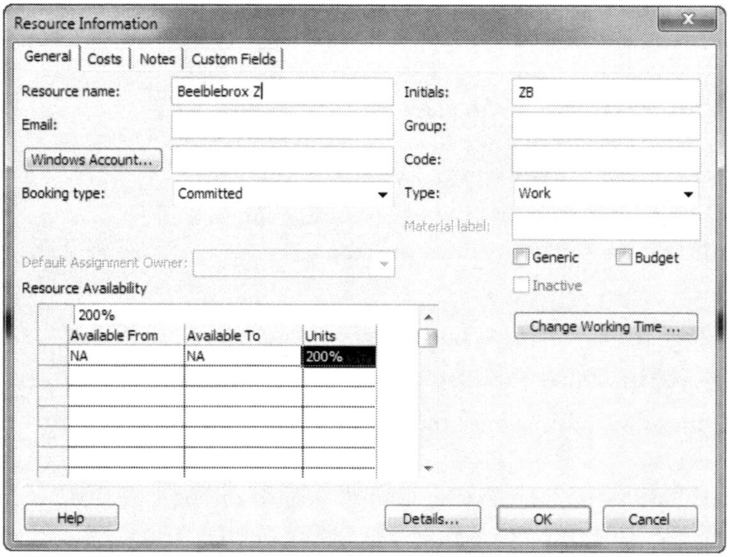

Figure 8-5:
If the tables in the Resource Sheet view don't show all the fields you want, then the General tab of the Resource Information dialog box is the next place to look. If you don't work with costs, you might not have to venture beyond the General tab.

Here are the basic resource fields found on the Resource Information dialog box's General tab, along with their uses:

- **Type.** Project sets the Type field to Work at first, which is often just what you want. For many projects, the only resources you handle in Project are people and equipment, both represented by the Work resource type (page 180). Choose Material if you want to assign quantities of materials, such as bricks, to tasks. Choosing Cost as the resource type defines a category of costs that you can track.

- **Initials.** The benefit of the Initials field might not be obvious at first. When you view a schedule in the Gantt Chart timescale, seeing the resources assigned to tasks on the task bars is a quick way to see who does what, or spot tasks without resources. Full names take up too much room and hide task link lines, especially when several resources work on the same tasks. You can see who's assigned to tasks without the clutter by displaying resource initials instead of names.

Project initially sets the Initials field to the first letter of the resource name. With all but the tiniest teams, that approach doesn't help. You can change it to whatever you want, like a person's first and last initials or an abbreviated job description.

- **Group.** The Group field can represent any type of category you want—departments, subcontractors and vendors, or skill sets. In addition to grouping resources in the Resource Sheet, you can use the Group field to filter the task list to tasks performed by specific work groups, or group tasks by the type of resource required.

- **Code.** The Code field provides another way to categorize resources, which you can then use to sort, filter, or group tasks and resources. If your organization assigns job codes, you can enter them in the Code field and then filter for tasks that require a specific job code. (For more detail on job codes and what you can do with them, see the box on page 191.)

- **Email.** If you use File→Send To to distribute information directly from Project, then be sure to fill in the Email box with the person's email address.

POWER USERS' CLINIC

Categorizing Resources in Detail

For a project with a cast of thousands, the Group and Code fields might not be enough to express all the categories you have. For excruciating detail, *resource outline codes* are a better approach. Similar to WBS codes (page 93), resource outline codes are hierarchical identifiers that can reflect the organizational structure of your company or employee skill sets. You might change a custom outline field like Outline Code1 (page 653) to something that represents the job levels within your organization, like "Eng. Elec. Sr." for a senior level electrical engineer.

To assign a custom outline code to a resource, in the Resource Information dialog box, select the Custom Fields tab. Resource outline codes that you've set up appear in the list. In the Value cell, type the code for the resource.

Whether you use a resource outline code, the Group field, or the Code field to categorize resources, you can filter the list of resources in the Assign Resources dialog box to find resources that match your desired characteristics (page 343).

Note: The Windows Account button applies only if you use Project Server to manage a portfolio of projects. Clicking the Windows Account button looks up the person's Windows account information and then uses that information to log into Project Server.

- **Booking type.** If you don't share resources among different projects, then ignore this field. Project sets it to Committed, which means any resource assignment you make reduces the resource's available hours so you can see the person's workload (page 213). On the other hand, Proposed lets you tentatively assign resources to tasks without locking up their time. Suppose you want to work out a project schedule and a budget based on resources that aren't officially assigned to your project. Creating them as Proposed means you can calculate dates and costs without taking away any of their available time. When a resource becomes yours officially, you can change the booking type to Committed.

Note: When you set a resource that's stored in a resource pool to Proposed, the resource shows up as Proposed in every project attached to the resource pool. If you're using a resource pool, you can assign a generic resource instead, and then assign the real resource later.

- **Generic.** Creating resources with job descriptions as names is one way to create generic resources. By turning on the General tab's Generic checkbox, you can filter your project (page 619) for assignments that still have generic resources assigned. That way, you can find real people to fill those slots until your entire project is staffed (page 343).

- **Budget.** Budget resources are like a line in the sand to tell you where your project costs stand compared with budget line items for the project. Budget resources can be Work, Material, or Cost. The difference is that you assign budget resources only to the project summary task. In addition to turning on the Budget checkbox, it's a good idea to name the budget resource in a way that indicates its budget status. For example, you can add a prefix like Budget or B-. Chapter 11 (page 285) describes how to use Project's budgeting features.

- **Material Label.** As soon as you choose Material in the Resource Information dialog box's Type field, the "Material label" field springs to life. Because material resources come in units from gallons to tons to cartons, you define a material resource's units in this field. You can enter any value you want, such as "gal" for gallons or "cup" for tea. Then, when you set a dollar value in the Std. Rate cell, Project knows the price per unit and can calculate costs when you assign a quantity of the material resource to tasks.

Defining When Work Resources Work

You may have already assigned a calendar for your project, as described on page 138, to indicate when work usually takes place. Your office may be open from 8:00 a.m. to 5:00 p.m., but not everybody works the same hours. Creating separate calendars for people whose schedules don't follow the norm tells Project when people are available to work on their assigned tasks. The schedule is more accurate when Project schedules around people's vacations, days off, and odd work hours. Project has two ways to specify when resources work, but they approach working time differently:

- **Calendars** spell out the specifics of a resource's work schedule—for example, Monday through Thursday from 8:00 a.m. to 7:00 p.m. with an hour at 12:00 p.m. for lunch.

- **Availability,** specified by resource *units,* tells Project what percentage of time the resource is available. For example, most resources work full time during normal working hours. For the folks who work part time, you can adjust the units to reflect how much they work—for instance, 60 percent for people who work 3 days a week.

Note: Project's terminology is downright confusing. First, resource units are always expressed as percentages, not units you'd expect, like hours or days. Units get more confusing when you assign resources to tasks. Assignments have their own Units field, which is the percentage of time the resource is assigned to the task. (See page 203 for a more detailed description of how units and assignment units work together.)

If everyone on your project works full time during regular work hours, you don't have to worry about resource calendars *or* units of availability. Project automatically sets a resource's maximum units (the Max. Units field) to 100 percent for full time and uses the calendar that applies to the entire project. A resource calendar comes in handy for setting aside days off and spelling out specific hours of the day that a resource works. Resource units are the fastest way to tell Project that someone works part time, or that a resource is really a three-person team and has maximum units of 300 percent. In reality, you can use a calendar and units separately or together to identify how much a resource works, as described in detail on page 256.

Note: Resource calendars and units apply only to resources set to the Work type, because these are the only resources assigned by time.

Specifying a resource's work schedule

If a resource doesn't work according to the overall project's work schedule, then you can specify a special work schedule by applying a calendar to that resource. Resource calendars come in handy for a variety of special situations like the following:

- Your project spans multiple shifts, and you want to assign people to the shifts that they work.

- Your resources work in different time zones, and you want to assign working times according to their local times.

- A resource will be away from work for an extended period of time. For instance, your star programmer is recuperating from carpal-tunnel surgery or taking a sabbatical to study emperor penguins in Antarctica.

- Your company offers the option to work either 4-day or 5-day workweeks, and you want to assign calendars to the people who choose each option.

- Equipment resources require preventative maintenance, such as a helicopter that requires an overhaul after every 100 hours of flying time.

A calendar must exist before you can apply it to a resource (or task or project). To learn how to create and fine-tune calendars, see Chapter 10. Once you've created a calendar, applying it to a resource is easy:

- In the **Resource Sheet**, click the resource's Base Calendar cell (if the column is narrow, then you may see only the word "Base") and then, in the drop-down list, choose the calendar you want to apply, as shown in Figure 8-6.

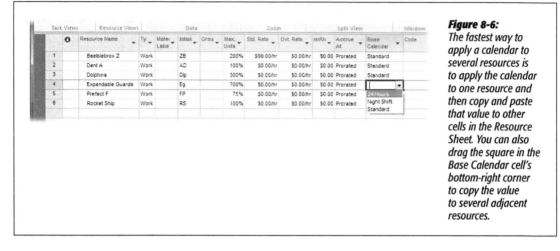

Figure 8-6:
The fastest way to apply a calendar to several resources is to apply the calendar to one resource and then copy and paste that value to other cells in the Resource Sheet. You can also drag the square in the Base Calendar cell's bottom-right corner to copy the value to several adjacent resources.

- In the **Resource Information dialog box**, on the General tab, click Change Working Time, shown in Figure 8-5. In the Change Working Time dialog box, in the "Base calendar" box, choose the calendar you want to apply, and then click OK. With the Resource Information dialog box, you can apply a calendar only to the current resource. However, the Change Working Time dialog box lets you create a calendar if it doesn't already exist.

Specifying how much time resources are available

Availability is the percentage of time a resource is available during the resource's work schedule, whether it's the standard work schedule or a special one. Here's how availability works:

- If the resource doesn't have a special calendar assigned, then Max. Units set to 100 percent represents full time during regular working hours.

- If the resource has a resource calendar with Monday through Thursday as 8-hour workdays, then Max. Units set to 100 percent represents full-time workdays for the four days the resource works—that is, 32 hours a week.

- If the resource has the Monday-through-Thursday 8-hour workday calendar, then Max. Units of 50 percent means the resource is available half of the calendar's working time, or 16 hours a week.

Tip: Units aren't limited to 100 percent or less. In fact, if you have a four-person landscaping team, you can set up one work resource for the entire team and set the maximum units to 400 percent.

The Resource Sheet is the fastest way to specify maximum units. Simply click the Max. Units cell for a work resource, type the number for the maximum units, and then press Enter. Project adds "%" automatically.

Note: Project Server uses an administrative project to account for nonproject work time.

REALITY CHECK

Plan for Downtime

No one is productive every minute of every day. Even workaholics spend some work time on tasks that aren't a part of your project. An alarming amount of time is spent on unrelated meetings and administrative tasks like filling out health insurance forms. Moreover, the workdays just prior to holiday weekends are renowned for their low productivity. (For more about the importance of building slack time into a schedule, read *Slack* (Tom De Marco, Broadway, 2002). You can make your Project schedules reflect this downtime in one of two ways:

- **Set resource Max. Units to less than 100 percent.** For example, if experience tells you that 2 hours of every workday are spent on administrative tasks, you can set the Max. Units for your resources to 75 percent. This approach can also take into account corporate holidays and vacation time, although those days are distributed over the course of a year.

- **Adjust Project's calendar options (page 139) to reflect shorter workdays.** In the Project Options dialog box, you can tell Project that workdays are shorter by changing the values for "Hours per day", "Hours per week", and "Hours per month".

Setting resource Max. Units has a couple of advantages over adjusting calendar options. First, visibility. Management may decide to streamline administrative procedures when they see how much resource time they lose to unproductive hours. Second, Max. Units is also more flexible. For example, you can assign percentages based on the productivity in different groups, like 75 percent for your team and 100 percent for a subcontractor with no overhead time.

What do you do when availability changes over time? Suppose you're working in Kansas duplicating a few of the geoglyphs found in Peru. Carving the giant lizards takes at least a year with everyone working full time, but the local workers are available full time only in the winter, and just 20 percent of the time from spring planting to fall harvest. To help you figure out how long a project like this would take, the Resource Information dialog box's General tab includes a table for setting varying availability levels.

Note: When the work calendar changes over time, set up different workweeks in a resource calendar (page 240).

Here are the steps for setting up different levels of availability for different time periods:

1. **In the Resource Sheet, double-click the resource you want to edit.**

   The Resource Information dialog box opens. In the General tab's lower-left corner, look for the "Resource availability" section (Figure 8-7).

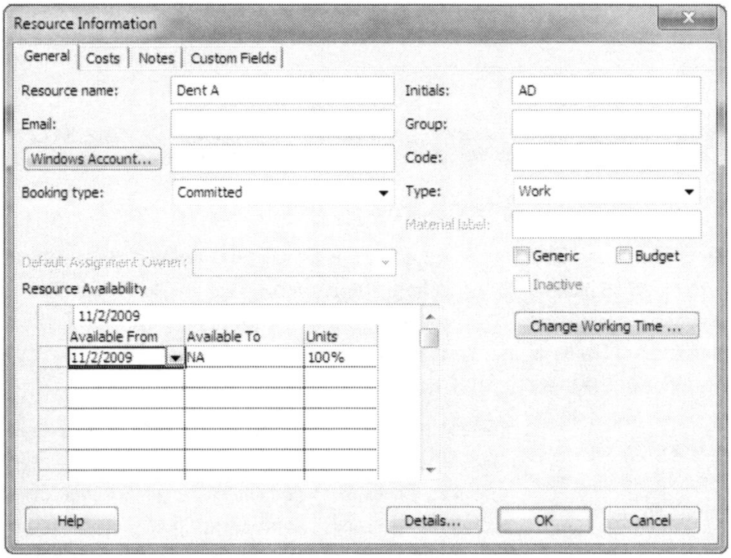

Figure 8-7:
The Available From and Available To cells in the first row are initially set to NA, which indicates that the maximum units apply to all time periods. The NA in the Available From cell represents from the beginning of time. The NA in the Available To cell represents all dates to the end of time. The Units cell is set initially to the percentage that appears in the Resource Sheet's Max. Units cell.

2. **In the Available From column's first cell, choose the date on which the level of availability begins.**

   Any time periods you don't explicitly cover use the value from the Resource Sheet's Max. Units cell.

3. **In the Available To column's first cell, choose the end date.**

   The units you specify apply to all assignments that occur between the beginning and end dates.

4. **In the Units cell, type the number for the maximum units, and then press Enter.**

   Type the percentage value, such as *50* for 50 percent. If you omit the percentage sign, Project adds it.

5. **Repeat steps 2 through 4 in additional rows to specify levels of availability for other time frames.**

   When you assign the resource to tasks, Project uses the availability percentages that apply for the timeframe during which the task occurs.

Defining Costs for Work and Material Resources

Labor and materials usually represent the bulk of cost for a project. Unless money is no object (yeah, right), you need to keep a close eye on project costs. When you assign costs to work and material resources, Project calculates project costs as well as the schedule. The cost fields for work and material resources are available in both the Resource Sheet and the Resource Information dialog box, but the Resource Sheet is usually the quickest option.

Here are the cost fields for resources and what they do:

- **Std. Rate** (Standard Rate) is the typical pay rate for a work resource, the cost per time period for a piece of equipment, or the cost per unit for material. For example, a contractor's pay rate of $50 per hour shows up as $50.00/hr. Because work resources are assigned by time, Project automatically adds "/hr" to the number you type. If you pay a contractor a flat rate per month, you can use a different unit of time, for instance, "$5000/mon."

  Material resources are allocated by units other than time, such as gallons of diesel fuel, board-feet of lumber, or cups of coffee. For material resources, Std. Rate represents the price per unit, where the unit is whatever you type into the Material Label cell. For example, for lumber, the Material Label unit might be board-feet. When you type $1.25 in the Std. Rate cell, Project calculates cost as $1.25 per board foot.

Tip: Project includes options for setting the standard rate and overtime rate for resources. Initially, these options are set to $0.00/hr (that's $0 per hour). However, if most of your resources cost the same amount per hour, you can save a few steps creating resources by setting a default standard or overtime rate. Choose File → Options. In the Project Options dialog box, click Advanced. In the "General options for this project" drop-down list, choose the project for which you want to set default resources rates, and then type values in the "Default standard rate" and "Default overtime rate" boxes.

- **Ovt. Rate** (Overtime Rate) applies only to work resources and is the rate charged if you assign overtime hours to a resource (page 429). People who work for a salary don't cost extra, so their Ovt. Rate is zero. If someone gets the same hourly rate regardless how many hours he works, you don't have to bother with overtime, as you learn on page 429. For anyone who earns a premium for overtime, type that value into the Ovt. Rate cell.

Note: When you assign resources to tasks, Project doesn't automatically use the overtime rate for hours assigned beyond the standard workday. You must modify the resource assignment to designate overtime hours (page 430) to tell Project to apply the overtime rate.

- **Cost/Use** applies only when you pay an amount each time you use the resource. For example, if you pay a flat $50 each time the network technician comes on site, then add $50 in the Cost/Use field. Every time you assign the network technician to a task, the task cost includes the hourly rate for the technician and $50 for the appearance fee.

- **Accrue At** is important only if someone cares when money is spent. For example, if cash flow is tight, knowing whether you pay up front, after the work is done, or spread out over time can make or break a budget. Setting Accrue At to Start means the cost occurs as soon as the task begins—like paying for a package delivered COD. End represents cost that occurs at the end of a task, such as paying your neighbor's kid when he finishes mowing your lawn. Prorated spreads the cost over the duration of the task, such as the wages you pay to employees assigned to long tasks.

Note: Project includes several options for specifying currency. Choose File→Options. In the Project Options dialog box, choose Display. Below the "Currency options for this project" heading, you can choose the currency symbol you want to use, such as $ for dollars. Type the number of decimal digits (for example, 2 for cents) in the "Decimal digits" box. Choose the currency in the Currency drop-down list. The Placement option specifies whether the currency symbol appears before or after the currency value with or without a space between the symbol and the value.

The Resource Information dialog box comes in handy for setting costs when a resource has different pay rates or when rates change over time, like if you hire a hermit who charges $50 per hour for work performed at his cave, and $300 per hour for work performed onsite.

Here's how you define different or variable pay rates:

1. **In the Resource Information dialog box, select the Costs tab.**

   The Costs tab contains a table with five tabs of its own, labeled A through E and shown in Figure 8-8, so you can define up to five different pay rates for a resource. (If only Project let you assign names to each table so you could tell what each one is for…) When you assign a resource to a task, you can specify which pay rate to use (see below).

2. **To set a second pay rate for the resource, select tab B and then, in the first Standard Rate cell, type the second pay rate.**

   To remind yourself what each pay rate is for, select the Notes tab, and then type the kind of work and the pay rate that applies.

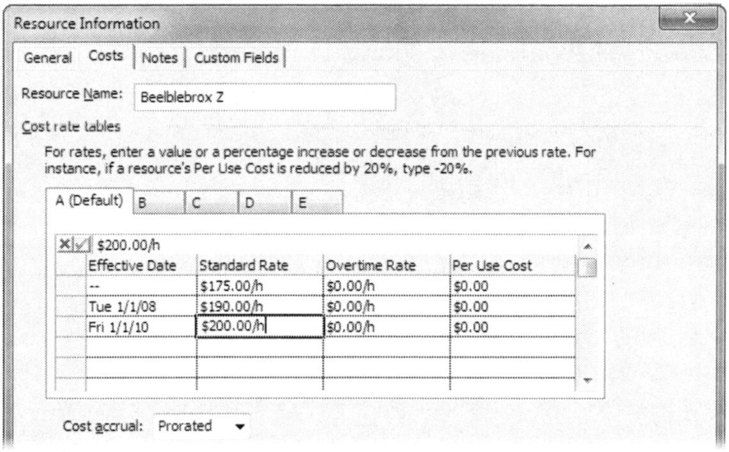

Figure 8-8:
If you know the dollar amount of the future rate, type it in the Standard Rate cell (or Overtime Rate or Per Use Cost cell). You can also specify a rate change with a percentage. If a consultant tells you rates are going up 10 percent, then type 10% in the Standard Rate field. When you press Enter, Project calculates the new rate and replaces the percentage with the new dollar value.

3. If the pay rate changes over time, select the second cell in the Effective Date column, and then choose the starting date for the new rate.

   The pay rate in the first row applies to any assignments that occur before the first effective date. For example, if the hermit is raising rates on January 1 of the next year, choose that date in the second Effective Date cell.

4. Repeat step 3 to define additional pay rate changes and when they take effect.

5. To set additional pay rates, select the less-than-helpfully-named tab C, D, or E, and then repeat steps 2 and 3.

   Project applies the pay rate in effect during the timeframe for a task.

To apply a cost rate table to a resource assignment, display the Task Usage or Resource Usage view (on the Task tab, click Gantt Chart, and then choose Task Usage or Resource Usage). Double-click an assignment (the row containing a resource name) to open the Assignment Information dialog box. On the General tab, in the "Cost rate table" drop-down list, choose the letter that corresponds to the rate table you want to apply.

Tip: If your organization manages lots of projects all the time, even a resource pool is unwieldy. Microsoft Enterprise Project Management (Project Server) software provides the tools for mega-project operations. You can categorize resources by skill sets to locate the right resources, coordinate multiple projects, and view project performance and status for your entire portfolio of projects.

Making Resources Available to Multiple Projects

More often than not, the same resources work on more than one project, whether the projects all occur at once or conveniently follow one after the other. You don't have to recreate the same resources for every project file. More efficiently, you can create a *resource pool* for the resources you use time and again, and then apply that resource pool to as many projects as you want.

When your projects don't occur simultaneously, a Microsoft Project resource pool saves you the drudgery of defining the same resources over and over. However, if you

manage several projects at once (page 491) without the benefit of Project Server, you can create a resource pool in Project to help you see who's available, who's already booked, or who's overloaded and needs some assistance.

Creating a resource pool is almost identical to creating a regular Project file. In Project, create a new blank project, and then add (or import) your resources. The difference is that you save the file after creating the resources but before creating any tasks. To learn how to connect a resource pool to projects and share pooled resources, see page 500.

Setting Up Cost Resources

The Cost resource type introduced in Project 2007 is perfect for costs that aren't based on time or any sort of material. Unlike the Fixed Cost field that you had to use in pre-2007 versions of Project, more than one cost resource can apply to a task, like travel, fees, and communication links. You can also total the costs for each cost resource to see what those categories of costs add up to for the entire project.

A cost resource is the easiest type of resource to create. Here are the steps:

1. **In a blank Resource Name cell, type the name of the cost, such as Travel or Bribes.**

   Project automatically sets the Type cell to Work.

2. **Click the down arrow in the Type cell, and then, from the drop-down list, choose Cost. Press Enter.**

   When you press Enter, the standard values for a work resource disappear. The only other fields with values are Initials and Accrue At. To change either the initials or when the cost occurs, click the appropriate cell and then type the new value.

   That's all there is to it. You might think that you would set a cost for a cost resource, but you don't. You specify the monetary value when you assign the cost resource to a task (page 289), so the cost can vary from task to task.

CHAPTER 9

Connecting Resources to Tasks

So far, you've created tasks in Project (Chapter 6), connected them in the correct sequence (Chapter 7), and told Project about the resources you need (Chapter 8). Now, all that hard work on your Project file is about to pay off. You're ready to turn it into a real schedule that shows when tasks start and finish—and whether they finish on time.

Although you may estimate hours of work or task duration early on (page 102), you don't see the whole timing picture until you assign resources to your Auto Scheduled tasks (page 202). The number of resources you use, how much time those resources devote to their assignments, and when they're available to work all affect how long tasks take and when they occur. And if you've set up your Project resources with costs and labor rates, resource assignments generate a price tag for the project, too.

In Project 2010, you can manually schedule tasks (page 116), which puts you in complete control over when they start and finish. The new Team Planner view shows who's doing what and when, which tasks aren't assigned, or who's overallocated. With manually scheduled tasks, all you have to do in the Team Planner view to change any of these situations is drag tasks to a resource or move the tasks in the timescale.

This chapter clarifies how duration, work, and units interact and explains how to use this information to create and modify resource assignments. Assigning resources isn't just picking a task team. You also specify how much time those lucky folks devote to their tasks. For example, once a giant construction crane is on a building site, it's available 100 percent of the time until you move it to another site. However, when you need an attorney 10 percent of the time to resolve a legal fiasco, you don't want 100 percent of her time—or the monumental invoice that comes with it.

Assigning Work Resources to Tasks

Project lets you assign work resources in most of the usual places that you set up other task information. Once you've created resources as described in the previous chapter, all you have to do is match them up with the tasks they'll work on. The best way to do that depends on how much assignment detail you want to specify.

Here are the methods and when to choose each one:

- **Using the Assign Resources dialog box.** The Assign Resources dialog box is the Swiss Army knife for resource assignments, teeming with indispensable features. Assigning a resource to a task is as simple as clicking a resource name, but you can also search for specific types of resources, or for resources that have enough available time. You can use this dialog box to assign several resources to a task or to several tasks at once. Moreover, you can use it to add, remove, or replace resources already assigned.

- **Using the Team Planner view.** The Team Planner view, new in Project 2010 Professional edition, is a slick way to assign resources, whether you're trying to assign resources to as-yet-unassigned tasks or to reassign resources to get rid of overallocations. Team Planner shows each resource in the project and the tasks they're working on in a timescale. Unassigned tasks appear at the bottom of the view. All you have to do to assign a resource is drag an unassigned task to the resource's row. Or to reassign a resource, drag a task from one resource to another. Page 213 gives you the full scoop.

- **Filling in a task form.** When you already know the resource you want, the Task Form has all the fields you need to craft precise resource assignments. The Task Form is readily available in the bottom pane of the standard Task Entry view. The Task Form also excels when you want to make surgically precise modifications to existing assignments (page 224).

- **Entering names in a Task table.** Choosing a resource in a table like the Entry table is good only for the simplest of resource tasks—assigning one or two full-time resources to a task, for example. On the other hand, the table is ideal for dragging and copying resource assignments to several tasks (page 208).

- **Using the Task Information dialog box.** The Resource tab of the Task Information dialog box is another place you can assign resources. But since you have to open and close the dialog box for each task you want to edit, you may want to use it for assignments only when you've already opened the dialog box to make other changes to a task.

Assigning Resources with the Dialog Box

Whether you're assigning one resource full time, assigning several resources to multiple tasks, or searching for the most qualified resources, the Assign Resources dialog box is the place to be. The Assign Resources dialog box can even remain open while you perform other actions in Project. For example, you can assign a few resources, and then filter the schedule to evaluate what you've done. If you spot a problem, then you can jump right back to the dialog box to make the fix.

What Project Calls a Unit

You'll see the term "units" in a couple of different places in Project: There's a Max. Units (maximum units) field on the Resource Sheet, plus a Units field that pops up whenever you assign a resource to a task in the Assign Resources dialog box. Understand, Project uses the term loosely. These are two types of different, though related, units. Both types of units are percentages of time (or the equivalent decimal). The Max. Units field applies to a resource, while the Units field applies to the assignment. Here's how to keep them straight:

- A resource's **Max. Units** field (page 194), which appears in the Resource Sheet and the Resource Information dialog box, is the highest percentage of time that resource is available to work on your project. For

example, full time is 100 percent; part-time availability can be any value between 1 percent and 99 percent (but 50 percent is pretty common). If you define a team's resource, its Max. Units can even be a value like 300 percent, representing three full-time workers.

- The **Units** field in the Assign Resources dialog box and the Task Form is the percentage of time that the resource works on a specific assignment. For example, a resource working on two concurrent tasks may dedicate 75 percent of his time to one task and the remaining 25 percent to the other.

The Max. Units and Units fields work together to help Project determine whether a resource is overallocated, as you'll see in Chapter 10 (page 260).

To assign resources in the Assign Resources dialog box, follow these steps:

1. **Choose Resource→Assign Resources (the icon looks like the heads and shoulders of two people).**

   When the Assign Resources dialog box opens, drag it out of the way of what you're doing. It stays put, and remains open, until you move it or click its Close button.

2. **In the Gantt Chart view or any other task-oriented view, select the task to which you want to assign resources.**

   If any resources are already assigned to the task, they appear at the top of the list, preceded by a checkmark.

Warning: Project doesn't stop you from assigning resources to summary tasks, but the practice is more confusing than it is helpful. The rolled-up values (like cost and work) on summary tasks won't equal the totals from all the subtasks, because the rolled-up values include values from the summary task resource assignment. Moreover, summary task bars in the timescale area of the Gantt Chart don't show assigned resource names at the right end of the bar, so unless you customize the view, you don't even see the resources assigned to summary tasks. (You can see the names in the Entry table.)

---

3. **In the Resource Name column, click the name of the resource, and then click Assign.**

   Project provides several visual cues for the new resource assignment, as illustrated in Figure 9-1.

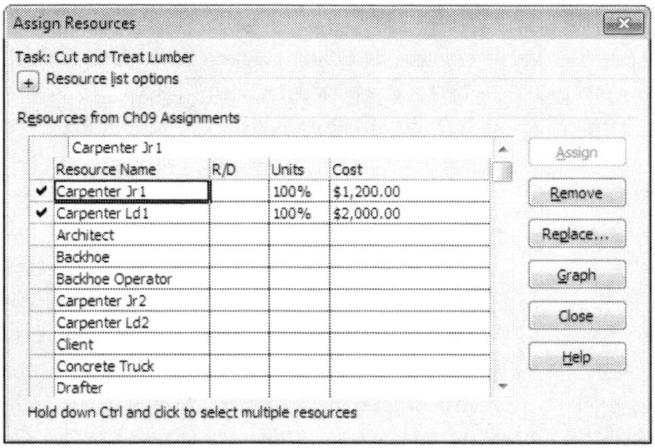

Figure 9-1:
When you click Assign, the selected resource shoots to the top of the list, above the unassigned resources. A checkmark appears to the left of the assigned resource's name, and its Units cell automatically fills in with the resource's Maximum Units (page 195) or 100% if the maximum units are greater than 100% as they are for a team. The cost of using the resource for the time involved appears in the Cost cell.

4. **To change the units for the assignment, type the percentage in the Units cell. Press Enter or click another field to save the change.**

   To allocate half of a full-time resource's time, type *50*. Project adds the percentage sign for you. Or click the up and down arrows that appear when you click the Units cell to jump to commonly used percentages. For example, if the Units value is 100%, clicking the down arrow once changes the Units to 50% and clicking a second time changes the units to 0%.

Note: Units can appear as percentages or decimal values (50% and .5 represent the same allocation), but you have to stick with one format or the other. To switch to decimal units, choose File→Options. In the Project Options dialog box, choose Schedule, and then, under Schedule, in the "Show assignments as a" drop-down list, choose Decimal.

---

5. **To assign another resource to the same task, click the resource's name, and then click Assign.**

   If you want to assign several resources at the same time, click the first resource's name, and then Ctrl-click additional names. If the resources you want are adjacent to one another in the list, click the first resource you want, and then Shift-click the last one. When you click Assign, all the selected resources move to the top of the list and sport the assigned-resource checkmark.

6. To assign resources to another task, select the task, and then repeat steps 3 through 5.

When you're finished assigning resources, click Close to close the dialog box.

You don't have to assign resources to only one task at a time. The Assign Resources dialog box can add assignments to several tasks, as you can see in Figure 9-2. Simply select all the tasks you want to staff, for instance by dragging across the tasks or using Shift-click and Ctrl-click. Then use the Assign Resources dialog box as you would for a single task.

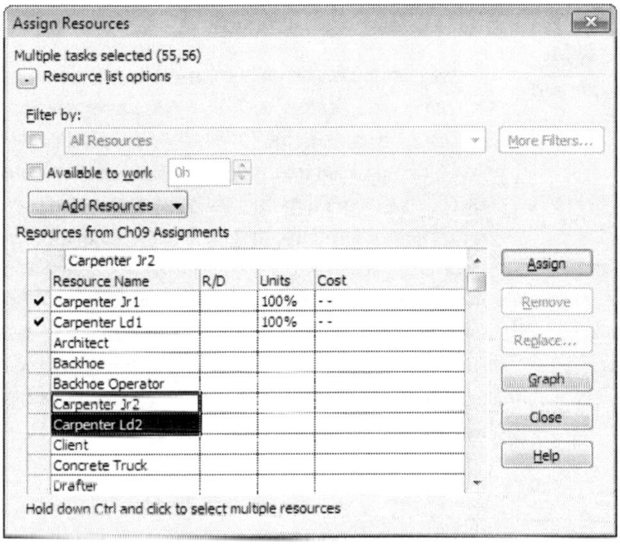

Figure 9-2:
When you select several tasks, the label at the top of the Assign Resources box changes to "Multiple tasks selected (x,y)", where x and y are the ID numbers of the selected tasks. In addition, gray checkmarks identify all resources assigned to at least one of the selected tasks.

Tip: If a nail gun accident puts your lead carpenter out of commission, you can turn to the Replace button in the Assign Resources dialog box. Click the name of the resource you want to replace, and then click Replace. In the Replace Resource dialog box, select the new resource (or resources), and then click OK. Project removes the original resource from the task, and then assigns the replacements.

Assigning Resources in the Task Form

The Assign Resources dialog box may hog too much screen real estate when you're jumping around in Project. The Task Form and its sibling, the Task Details Form, don't have the fancy features of the Assign Resources dialog box, but you can assign resources with them without breaking a sweat. The Task Form's main limitation is that it works with only one task at a time—the one that's currently selected in the Gantt Chart or other task view. (But selecting another task is as easy as clicking it.)

Here's how you assign resources in the Task Form or the Task Details Form:

1. **Choose Task→View→Gantt Chart or another task-related view.**

    The Task Form is the standard form that appears in the Gantt Chart view's bottom pane. If you don't see the Task Form there, choose View→Split View. In the Details drop-down list, choose Task Form.

POWER USERS' CLINIC

Creating and Assigning Resources at the Same Time

Suppose the person you want to assign is absent from the list of resources in the Assign Resources dialog box. This omission means that the person (or equipment) doesn't exist in your Project file. You can create the resource and immediately assign it without leaving the Assign Resources dialog box. Here are the steps:

1. In the Resources table, click the first blank Resource Name cell. Type the resource's name.

2. To confirm the addition and select the new resource, press Tab.

3. Click Assign. Project moves the resource to the top of the list, displays the assigned checkmark, and changes the Units value to 100%.

4. Adjust the Units value if necessary.

After you've completed your assignments, you can add the rest of the information about the resources you added on

the fly. Display the Resource Sheet, and then use any of the techniques described in Chapter 8.

The Assign Resources dialog box can also import resources from your email address book or Active Server directory (for a computer running the Windows Server operating system). Click Add Resources, and then choose either From Active Directory or From Address Book. (If you can't see the Add Resources button, click the + to the left of the "Resource list options" label.) If you use Project Server, you can also import resources from the enterprise resource list. Select the names in the Select Resources dialog box, and then click Add. When all the resources appear in the Add box, click OK. The Select Resources dialog box closes, and the resources appear in the Resources table.

Tip: If the current view seems to have only one pane, the bottom pane may be hidden. To bring the bottom pane into view, double-click the small rectangle immediately below the vertical scroll bar. (If you point to the rectangle, the pointer changes to two horizontal lines. Drag up to display and size the bottom pane.) Hide the bottom pane by double-clicking the horizontal divider between the two panes.

---

2. **In the table in the top pane, select the task to which you want to assign resources.**

    The Task Form displays the information for the selected task.

3. **In the Task Form, click the first blank Resource Name cell, and then, from the drop-down list, choose the name of the resource you want to assign.**

    Clicking the down arrow on the right end of the Resource Name cell displays the drop-down list of resources. For large project teams, scrolling can be tedious. When the drop-down list is open, you can begin typing a resource's name, and Project jumps to the closest matching name in the list. For example, to skip right to "Smith Brian," type an *S*. If Project hasn't located the exact resource, keep typing the letters of the resource's name until it does, and then click the resource name as soon as you see it in the list.

Note: If you turn on the Project option that automatically adds new resources to your file, a typographical error may create a new—and nonexistent—resource in your file. To prevent these inadvertent resources from joining your project team, choose File→Options. In the Project Options dialog box, choose Advanced, and then, in the "General options for this project" section, make sure the project you want appears in the project box, and then turn off the "Automatically add new resources and tasks" checkbox.

4. **To specify the percentage of time the resource devotes to the task, click the Units cell in the same row and type the number—for example,** *50* **for 50 percent, as shown in Figure 9-3.**

   If you want to assign the resource at 100 percent (or the resource's maximum units from the Resource Sheet), simply leave the Units cell blank. Project sets Units to 100% or the resource's maximum units automatically when you click OK. The only exception is group resources. If the group resource's maximum units are more than 100 percent, Project still fills in 100%.

   The percentage in the Units cell is based on the resource's work schedule, whether it's your organization's standard schedule or a special one. For example, for regular work schedules, 50 percent represents half time (20 hours a week for the typical 40-hour week).

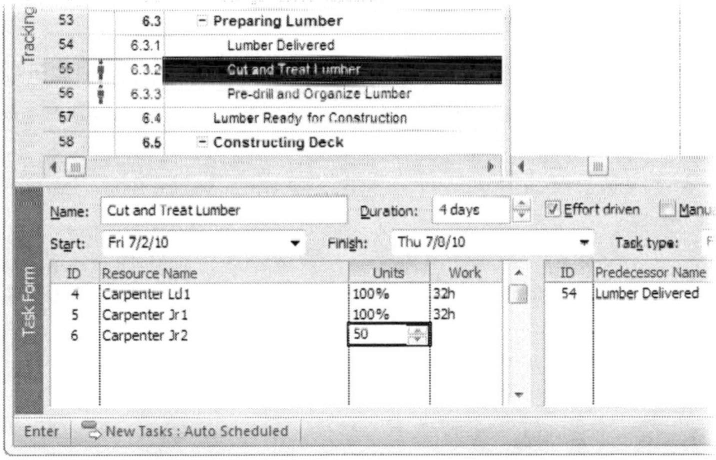

Figure 9-3:
To assign work instead of units, click the Work cell, and then type the hours, days, or other time units. Project calculates the units based on the work and the task's duration. If you set the "Work is entered in" Project option to the time unit you use most often (for example, "h" for hours or "d" for days), then you can type a number without the time unit. To set the standard time unit for work, choose File→Options, and then choose Schedule.

5. **To assign another resource to the task, click the next blank Resource Name cell, and then repeat steps 3 and 4.**

   After you assign all the resources, click OK. Project calculates the work hours for each resource based on the Units percentage and the task duration, as described in the section "Understanding Duration, Work, and Units" on page 219.

Assigning Resources in a Gantt Chart Table

The Assign Resources dialog box and the Task Form described so far give you the power to enter varying percentages in the Max. Units field, create new resources on the fly, and so on. However, if all you need to do is simply assign all of a resource's available time to one task, then nothing is faster than working directly in a table in the Gantt Chart view.

To assign a resource in a Gantt Chart table, follow these steps:

1. **Choose Task→View→Gantt Chart.**

   The standard table for the Gantt Chart view is the Entry table, which includes columns for the task name, duration, start and finish, predecessors, and resource names. If you don't see these columns, right-click the Select All cell (between the column heading row and the ID column) and then choose Entry.

   The Resource Names column is the last column in the Entry table, so it's typically out of sight. Rather than scroll to display the column, making the table area wider shows the columns for both task names and resource names. Position the mouse pointer over the vertical bar between the table and the timescale. When the pointer changes to double arrows, drag the divider bar to the right until the Resource Names column is visible.

2. **In the table, click the Resource Names cell for the task.**

   Project encloses the cell with a heavy black border and displays a down arrow for the resource drop-down list.

3. **To assign a resource, click the down arrow, and then, in the list, click the resource name.**

   The name you choose appears in the Resource Names cell. Project automatically assigns the resource at the resource's maximum units (page 195) or 100% for a team resource. If the resource's Max. Units value is 100%, then the Resource Names cell shows only the resource name. However, if Max. Units is less than 100%, then the assignment value looks something like "Bob[50%]."

Copying a resource to multiple tasks

Suppose your kitchen is big enough for only one person, so you want Enrique to handle all the kitchen tasks for your party: making pizza dough, slicing the pepperoni, and assembling the pizzas. A table makes copying assignments between tasks easy. When you want to apply the same resource and units to several tasks, follow these steps:

1. Click the Resource Names cell that contains the resources and units you want, and then press Ctrl+C.

   Project copies the values from the Resource Names cell to the Clipboard.

2. Select the other Resource Names cells into which you want to copy the assignment, and then press Ctrl+V.

Tip: If several consecutive tasks use the same resources, select the Resource Names cell with the value you want to copy. Then, position the pointer over the lower-right corner of that cell. When the pointer changes to a + symbol, drag over the rows that use the same resources.

Finding the Right Resources

When resources are plentiful, scrolling through the list of names to assign a resource takes forever. The Assign Resources dialog box can reduce scrolling by listing only the resources appropriate for the current assignment. All you have to do is tell it what you're looking for. You can apply a resource filter to find people who possess the right skills, belong to a specific group, or have the job code you're looking for. If you use resource outline codes (page 652) to categorize resources, you can filter by those codes, too. The most qualified resources don't help at all if they aren't available. The Assign Resources dialog box also helps you find resources with enough available time.

These filtering features may not appear when you first open the Assign Resources dialog box. To coax the Resource list options into view, click the + to the left of "Resource list options", shown in Figure 9-4.

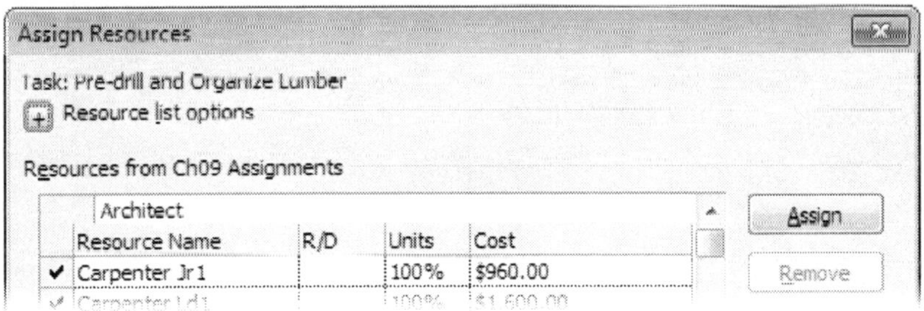

Figure 9-4:
When the filtering options are visible, the + button to the left of the "Resource list options" label changes to -, which you can click when you want to hide the options once more. The Assign Resources dialog box reopens with the filtering options expanded or hidden, depending on their visibility when you last closed the dialog box.

Finding resources by criteria

The Assign Resources dialog box uses resource filters to restrict the resources that appear in the Resources table. For example, you can filter the resource list with a built-in resource filter like Group to see only the resources that belong to a specific group. If you've customized resource filters, for instance to filter by the Code resource field, then you can filter the resource list with those, too. (For the details on customizing filters, see page 620.)

To filter the resource list by criteria, follow these steps:

1. **With the "Resource list options" visible, turn on the top "Filter by" checkbox.**

    Project automatically fills in the "Filter by" box with the All Resources filter, so the list in the Resources table continues to show all available resources. If the filter options are grayed out, make sure the first "Filter by" checkbox is turned on.

2. **In the "Filter by" drop-down list, choose the filter you want to apply.**

    The Resources table displays only the resources that pass the filter, as illustrated in Figure 9-5.

    If a filter name ends with an ellipsis (…), then the filter requires some input from you. For example, if you select the "Group…" filter, a dialog box opens so you can type the name of the group you're interested in. Enter the value, and then click OK.

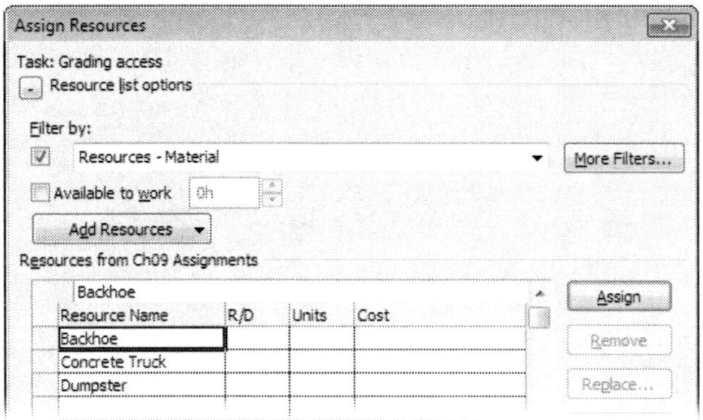

Figure 9-5:
The "Filter by" drop-down list includes all existing resource filters. If none of these filters suit your needs, click More Filters to open the More Filters dialog box. You can create a new filter, edit an existing filter, or copy a filter to obtain exactly the resource filter you want, for example, to search for resources based on their Outline Code values, or to view only Confirmed resources.

3. **Once the resource list is filtered, you assign resources as you would normally (page 203).**

    To view the entire resource list again, in the "Filter by" drop-down list, either choose All Resources or turn off the "Filter by" checkbox.

Finding resources with available time

Resources with the right skills aren't any help if they don't have enough time to complete an assignment. Suppose you've added some customer change requests to your schedule, and you want to find people with the spare time to complete these shorter tasks. The "Available to work" checkbox is just the ticket for finding the folks who are available when the task is scheduled. When you turn it on, Project searches for the resources that have the amount of time you specify available between the task's start and finish dates.

Building Teams with Project Server

If you use Project Server to manage your project portfolio, you can classify resources by skill sets with enterprise resource outline codes and resource breakdown structure codes. Project Server offers multi-value resource outline codes, which means you can assign more than one skill set to extraordinarily talented resources.

The Team Builder tool in Project Server searches the enterprise resource pool for available resources with the skills you need. If you have to replace someone on a task, Project Server's Resource Substitution Wizard looks for resources with the same skills as the resource you're replacing. For more information on these tools, see the recommended books on Microsoft Project Enterprise Software (page 12).

To find people who have enough hours available, do the following:

1. **Select the task to which you want to assign resources.**

   If the Assign Resources dialog box isn't open, then, choose Resources→Assign Resources (the icon that looks like two people).

2. **With the "Resource list options" visible, turn on the "Available to work" checkbox.**

   The box to the right of the "Available to work" label becomes active.

3. **In the "Available to work" box, type the time the assignment requires, such as 4d or 32h, as illustrated in Figure 9-6, and then press Enter.**

   The Resource table shows only the resources who have that amount of time available between the task's start and finish dates.

   When you press Enter or click another field, Project converts the time you enter to the standard units for work, which is one of Project's options. (Choose File→Options, and then choose Schedule. The "Work is entered in" box specifies the standard time units for work.) For example, if work units are hours and you type 5d, Project converts the "Available to work" value to 40h.

4. **Choose resources from the filtered list as you would normally.**

   To view resources regardless of availability, turn off the "Available to work" checkbox.

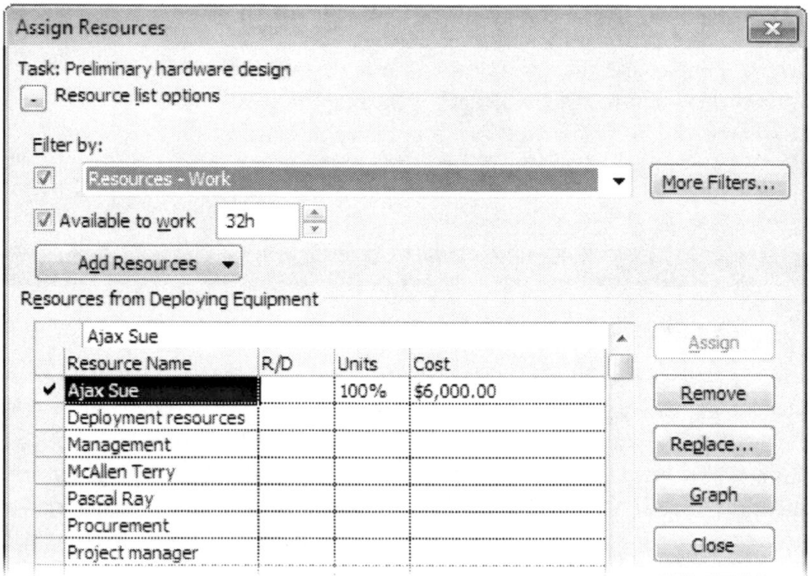

Figure 9-6:
Although you can filter the list of resources by available time alone, filtering by type of resource and available time shows you the resources that are both qualified and available. In the "Resource list options" section, simply turn on both the "Filter by" and "Available to work" checkboxes. Then, choose the resource filter and specify the time required.

Reviewing availability in detail

Project doesn't see shades of gray when it filters resources by availability. Resources either have enough time available or they don't. But you can use the Resource Graph instead, to get a better idea of whom to assign to a task. For example, if one resource is almost completely booked, then someone with more available time would give you more wiggle room if task dates slip. Or you may see that the perfect resource has *almost* enough time available and realize that the assignment may work if you simply delay it by a day or increase its duration.

The Resource Graph, shown in Figure 9-7, shows the number of hours the resource has available during each time period. For instance, if you have a change request that requires 8 hours of work during a week, you can look for 8 available hours on a resource's graph.

You can also evaluate the work assigned to proposed resources to see how many more real resources you have to round up, as described in the box on page 213.

You can display a resource graph in the following ways:

- In the Assign Resources dialog box, select the resource you want to evaluate, and then click Graphs.

- Choose View→Split View and turn on the Details checkbox. Then, in the drop-down list, choose Resource Graph.

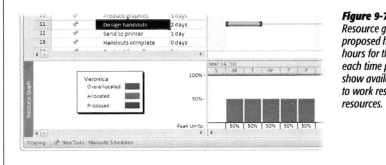

Figure 9-7:
Resource graphs show assigned work hours, proposed hours, and any overallocated hours for the selected resource during each time period. Because resource graphs show availability over time, they apply only to work resources, not material or cost resources.

To see a graph of the resource's *available* time, which is usually what you want when you have an assignment to fill, right-click the background of the timescale and then choose Remaining Availability. See page 602 for other ways to customize the Resource Graph.

GEM IN THE ROUGH

Viewing Proposed Bookings

As described in Chapter 8, when you can add resources to your Project file, you can specify that they're either Committed or Proposed resources (page 191). Committed resources are those you know you have in your roster, whereas Proposed resources represent resources you'd like to get, but don't have for sure. The Resource Graph shows work you've assigned to proposed resources in the graphs. The only difference is that the vertical bars for proposed work are purple. (Be careful about changing the status if you use a resource pool. Changing a resource to "Proposed" in a resource pool changes the resource's status to "Proposed" in every project to which the resource is assigned.)

Quickly Assigning Resources with Team Planner

The Team Planner view (new in Project 2010) is perfect for more informal assignments, when you have several tasks (manually or automatically scheduled) that you want to fling resources at in a jiffy. The anatomy of the Team Planner view makes it easy to see which tasks are currently orphaned without resources. Then you can drag a task onto a resource's row and—poof!—you've got a resource assignment.

In addition to initial assignments, Team Planner helps you spot unassigned tasks or resources who are overallocated. You can drag a task to a resource who doesn't have anything to do or move a task in the timeline to even out workloads—without messing with Project's fancier leveling features (page 277).

> **Warning:** Moving tasks around in Team Planner is easy. Maybe too easy. If you're working with manually scheduled tasks, dragging a task to a new date is often exactly what you want to do—for example, to nudge the task one day later so the assigned resource isn't overallocated. However, if your tasks are auto-scheduled tasks, then dragging tasks in the timeline creates date constraints (page 166), which limit Project's ability to calculate start and finish dates. If you use Team Planner to assign or swap resources on auto-scheduled tasks, take care that you don't drag auto-scheduled tasks to different dates.

Anatomy of the Team Planner view

The Team Planner view is divided into four quadrants, each with its own story to tell, as shown in Figure 9-8:

- **Resources.** The upper left of the Team Planner view contains resources assigned to the project itself, one resource per row. You can scan the timescale on the right side of the view to see when a resource is assigned to tasks. If a resource is assigned to tasks that don't have start or finish dates, then those tasks appear in the Unscheduled Tasks column.

- **Assigned task timescale.** Similar to the timescale in a Gantt Chart view, the upper right of the Team Planner view shows a timescale that positions bars based on task start and finish dates. However, these bars are assignment bars, not task bars. If a task has more than one resource assigned to it, you see a bar for the task in the row for each resource assigned. The tasks in this quadrant are both assigned to resources and scheduled in time.

- **Unassigned but scheduled tasks.** The timescale in the bottom half of the Team Planner view shows scheduled tasks that have no resources assigned. If you're trying to tie up the last loose unassigned tasks, look no further.

- **Unassigned and unscheduled tasks.** The pane in the lower left is reserved for the least defined tasks of all: tasks that don't have start or finish dates, or assigned resources.

> **Tip:** You can format the Team Planner view to change the size of bars or to control the information you see. For example, to display a single row for each resource, choose Format→Show/Hide and then turn off the Expand Resource Rows checkbox. To hide unassigned tasks or unscheduled tasks, choose Format→Show/Hide and then turn off the Unassigned checkbox or Unscheduled checkbox, respectively.

Assigning tasks with Team Planner

If a task sits forlornly unassigned in the bottom half of the Team Planner, you can assign a resource in no time. Just drag the task from its place in the Unassigned Tasks portion of the view to the row for the resource to whom you want to assign it, as Figure 9-9 shows.

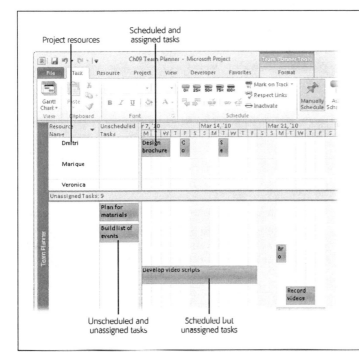

Figure 9-8:
If you create manually scheduled tasks, you don't have to assign dates to them (page 119). You can even type text like TBD for To Be Determined in the tasks' Start and Finish fields, if you want. In effect, you create unscheduled tasks and that's where they appear in the Team Planner view, the Unscheduled Tasks column.

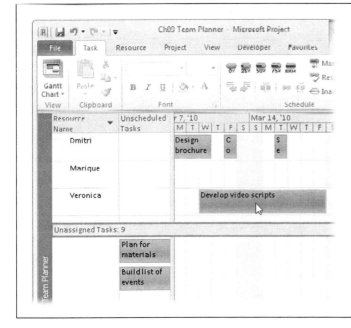

Figure 9-9:
You can reassign tasks just as easily as setting up initial assignments. Just drag a task from one resource's row to another to reassign the task. If you want to add a brand new task, choose Task→Insert→Task. The bar for the new task immediately appears in the Unscheduled Tasks column and a new row in the Unassigned Tasks portion of the view.

When you figure out when you want an unscheduled task to occur (whether or not it's assigned to a resource), you can drag it to the date in the timescale. If it's still unassigned, simply drag it to the date you want in the unassigned portion of the timescale. If you know who will perform the task, drag the bar to the row for the resource and to the date you want in the timescale.

Tip: You can tell Team Planner to prevent overallocations in the first place. Simply choose Format→ Schedule→Prevent Overallocations. If you try to assign a task to a resource when the resource is already allocated, Project pushes the assignment to when the resource is available.

Eliminating overallocations with Team Planner

A resource can work on two tasks at the same without a problem, as long as neither task is full-time. In this case, each task appears in its own row, as Figure 9-10 shows. However, if the concurrent tasks take up more time than the resource has available, red stripes appear at the top and bottom of the overlapping bars.

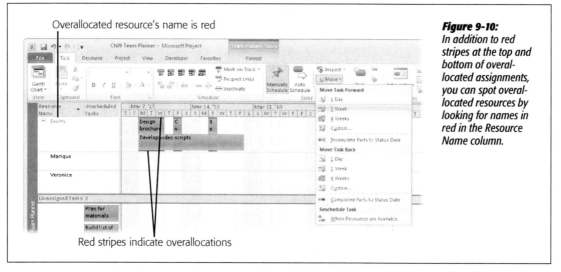

Overallocated resource's name is red

Red stripes indicate overallocations

Figure 9-10:
In addition to red stripes at the top and bottom of overallocated assignments, you can spot overallocated resources by looking for names in red in the Resource Name column.

Resolving overallocations in Team Planner is as simple as assigning resources in the first place. Here are methods you can use:

- **Reassign a task to another resource.** To reassign a task to a resource who has time available, simply drag the bar to the row for the new resource or right-click the taskbar and choose Reassign To on the shortcut menu. Then, on the submenu, choose the resource.

- **Move the task to a different date.** If the resource has a short backlog, you can bump the task into the future or move it earlier. You can reschedule a task by dragging it to a new date in the timescale. Or you can choose a Move Task Forward or Move Task Backward command. For example, to push the task into the future by a week, choose Task→Tasks→Move→1 Week.

- **Reschedule the task to when a resource is available.** If a resource works on a hodgepodge of short assignments, finding adjacent time for a longer assignment is almost impossible. Instead, you can tell Project to chop the assignment up and slide it into a resource's open slots. Select the assignment you want to reschedule. Then choose Task→Tasks→Move→When Resources Are Available.

Assigning Material Resources to Tasks

Assigning material resources is similar to assigning work resources, with one exception: When you assign material resources, you specify the required quantity of material instead of the time the resource spends.

Work resources are always allocated by time, but you can dole out material resources by whatever unit of measurement makes sense: milligrams of medication, cubic yards of concrete, or cartons of eggs. Truth be told, Project couldn't care less about a material resource's unit of measurement. It calculates cost by multiplying the material resource's Standard Rate (page 197) by the quantity you enter in the assignment. It's your responsibility to define the unit of measurement in the resource's Material Label cell and the Standard Rate as the cost of one unit of the material. Figure 9-11 shows how the material resource fields fit together, using the example of making chocolate mousse for a catered party.

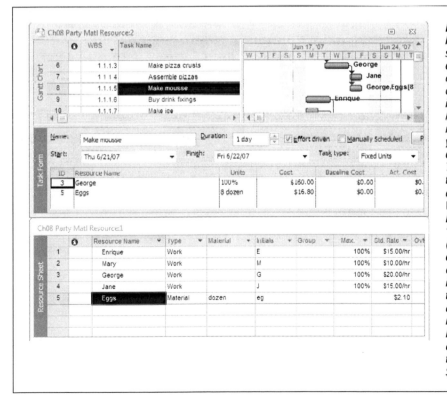

Figure 9-11:
In the Resource Sheet, shown at the bottom of the figure, you create a resource called "Eggs" and, in its Type cell, choose Material. The Material Label cell is where you specify that eggs come in dozens. The Std. Rate cell tells Project that one dozen eggs cost $2.10. When you assign the Eggs resource to the "Make mousse" task (as shown at the top of this figure), you enter the quantity in the Units cell (8 if the recipe calls for 8 dozen eggs). Project multiples the Std. Rate ($2.10) by the quantity to calculate the total egg cost of $16.80.

You can assign material resources using any of the methods described in "Assigning Work Resources to Tasks" starting on page 202. To assign a material resource to a task using the Assign Resources dialog box, do the following:

1. **Choose Resources→Assign Resources.**

   The Assign Resources dialog box opens.

2. **In the Gantt Chart view or any other task-oriented view, select the task to which you want to assign a material resource.**

   Any resources already assigned to the task appear at the top of the list, preceded by a checkmark. (At this point, you can add either work or material resources to the task.)

3. **In the Resource Name column, click the name of the material resource, and then click Assign.**

   The material resource moves to the top of the list (just like assigned work resources do), as shown in Figure 9-12.

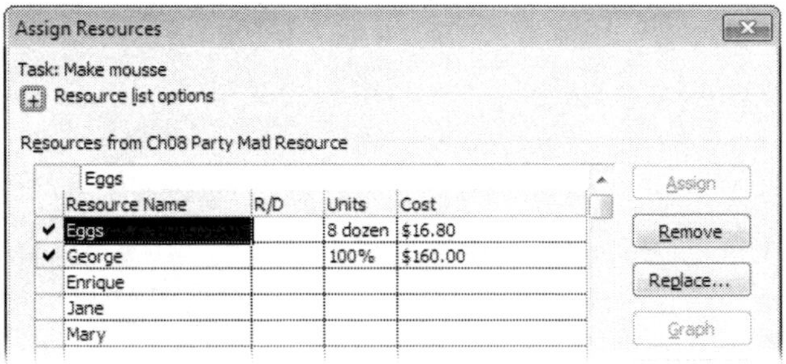

Figure 9-12:
In the Assign Resources dialog box, Project initially fills in the Units cell automatically with the quantity "1" followed by the material label from the Resource Sheet. To specify the quantity, type the number in the Units cell.

4. **In the Units cell, type the correct quantity. Press Enter or click another cell to complete the change.**

   Project automatically recalculates the Cost field by multiplying the quantity by the material's Std. Rate.

5. **To assign another resource, select the resource name, and then click Assign.**

   To assign resources to another task, in the Gantt Chart view, select the next task. Close the Assign Resources dialog box when you're done assigning resources.

When Material Quantity Depends on Time

With some material resources, the quantity assigned to a task is the same regardless of how long the task takes. In other words, that resource has a *fixed consumption rate.* If your task is to tag 50 grizzly bears with radio transmitters, the quantity of radio transmitters is 50, whether the task takes 2 weeks or 12. A *variable consumption rate,* by contrast, means the quantity of material varies based on the duration of the task. Say your Hummer chugs 100 gallons of gas each day you wallow around in the wilderness. If you collar your bears in 2 weeks, you use 1,000 gallons of gas, whereas a 12-week escapade guzzles 6,000 gallons.

You specify the units of measurement for a material resource in the Material Label field, and the cost per unit in the Std. Rate field. But after that, entering variable consumption rates in Project gets a little tricky. Typing *gallons/day* into a Material Label cell *doesn't* tell Project to calculate quantity based on task duration. The solution—and it's a bit obscure—is to type the quantity per unit of time in the Units field when you assign the material resource to a task. For example, assign the Gasoline resource to the "Tag bears" task. Then, in the Units cell, type *100 gallons/d*. Project calculates the total cost of gasoline by multiplying the standard rate (the price per gallon) from the Resource Sheet by the duration in days.

Understanding Duration, Work, and Units

Assigning one resource to a task and obtaining the results you want is relatively easy, but modifying assignments can be a puzzle. For example, if you assign two more people to attend a meeting in Project, the program makes the meeting shorter (as if that would happen) instead of adding those people's time to the total hours. Understanding how duration, work, and units interact is the first step toward getting the right assignments results every time.

Project has built-in rules about which values it changes, as well as features that let you control which variables hold steady and which ones change. Task duration, work (think person-hours), and resource units (the proportion of time resources work on a task) are like three people playing Twister—when one of these variables changes, the others must change to keep things balanced.

Task duration is inextricably connected to the work and units of a resource assignment. The formula is simple no matter which variable you want to calculate. The basic algebra you learned in high school is all you need: If Duration = Work ÷ Units, then Work = Duration × Units. Project calculates one of these three variables when you set the other two:

- **Work = Duration × Units.** If you estimate task duration and specify the units that a resource devotes to a task, then Project calculates the hours of work the resource must perform. For example, a 5-day duration with a resource assigned at 100% (or 1 as a decimal) results in 40 hours of work for a typical workweek: 40 hours = 5 days (× 8 hours/day) × 1.

- **Duration = Work ÷ Units.** If you estimate the amount of work a task requires, Project calculates task duration based on the resource units. For instance, 40 hours of work with a resource assigned at 50% (or .5) produces a 10-day duration based on 8-hour workdays: 10 days = 40 hours ÷ .5.

- **Units = Work ÷ Duration.** If you estimate the work involved and also know how long you want the task to take, Project calculates the units that a resource must spend. 16 hours of work over 4 days is 4 hours a day, or a resource assigned 50 percent.

Tip: Project includes several options for defining the standard number of work hours for different durations (page 139). Choose File→Options, and then choose Schedule. For the typical 40-hour workweek, set "Hours per day" to **8** and "Hours per week" to **40**.

If you leave some of the assignment fields blank, Project plays favorites when it decides whether to calculate duration, work, or units. Unless you tell Project otherwise, the program first tries to change duration, then work, and, as the last resort, units. Table 9-1 shows how this favoritism works depending on the values you enter.

Table 9-1. *The only time Project calculates units is when you specify both task duration and the amount of work.*

Duration	Work	Units
Project calculates	Your input	Your input
Project calculates	Your input	If blank, Project uses 100% or Max. Units.
Your input	*Project calculates*	Your input
Your input	*Project calculates*	If blank, Project uses 100% or Max. Units.
Your input	Your input	*Project calculates*
Your input	*Project calculates*	If blank, Project uses 100% or Max. Units.

Modifying Resource Assignments

Sometimes you want to control how Project calculates resource assignments, because the built-in calculations described in the previous section don't quite fit your situation. For example, if you assign two people to a 3-day task, Project initially assigns each person full-time for all 3 days. Suppose what you really want is the 3-day task collapsed into 1.5 days of 12-hour days. Using the "Task type" field, you can tell Project that you want to adjust the duration, not the work hours or assigned units.

Another factor to consider when modifying resource assignments is Project's *effort-driven scheduling,* which means that the total amount of work for a task drives the changes that Project makes. Effort-driven scheduling keeps a task's total work the same when you add resources to a task by reducing the work each resource performs. But effort-driven scheduling doesn't always hold true, particularly for tasks like diabolical project meetings that refuse to grow shorter no matter how many people attend. This section explains how to integrate task type and effort-driven scheduling with duration, work, and units to modify resource assignments exactly the way you want.

You can modify resource assignment in all manner of ways, as described in the rest of this section: You can add resources to a task or remove them, modify task duration or work time, or modify a resource's allocated units (the percentage of time devoted to a task).

Tip: When you change your project in certain ways, Project may ask you to clarify what you're trying to accomplish. For example, if you change the duration of a task, Project shows indicators (a small triangle in the corner of the task's Task Name cell and a yellow diamond with an exclamation point). Clicking the yellow diamond opens a shortcut menu with options that let you specify that the task will take less time because the work decreased, or because the assigned resources are going to work more each day. If you don't want to see these indicators, choose File→Options. In the Project Options dialog box, choose Display, and then turn off the "Edits to work, units, or duration" checkbox. Similarly, you can turn off messages about schedule inconsistencies, like a successor that starts before the predecessor. In the Project Options dialog box, click Schedule, and then turn off the "Show scheduling messages" checkbox.

Adding and Removing Resources from Tasks

For quick assignment changes, the Assign Resources dialog box is once again your best friend. After you add or remove resources, Project asks you what you're trying to do and then modifies the appropriate values.

Here's how you add and remove resources with the Assign Resources dialog box:

1. **Choose Resource→Assign Resources.**

   The Assign Resources dialog box opens.

2. **In the Gantt Chart view or any other task-oriented view, select the task you want to modify.**

   The resources already assigned to the task appear at the top of the list, preceded by a checkmark.

3. **To assign another resource to the task, in the Resource Name column, click the name of the resource, and then click Assign.**

   To remove an existing resource from the task, do the same thing but click Remove. The assigned checkmark disappears, and the resource takes its place back in the alphabetical list of unassigned resources.

4. **To change the units for the new assignment, in the Units cell, type the percentage.**

   If you remove a resource, Project automatically clears the resource's Units cell.

5. **Repeat steps 3 and 4 to add or remove other resources.**

   You can add or remove several resources before you close the dialog box or select another task.

---

6. **When you're done, either select another task in the Gantt Chart table or close the Assign Resources dialog box.**

   In the Gantt Chart table, a green feedback triangle may appear in the Task Name cell's upper-left corner, advising you that Project needs some help completing your change. If so, move the cursor over the task, and then click the SmartTag indicator that appears, as shown in Figure 9-13. Then you can choose how you want Project to adjust work, duration, or units.

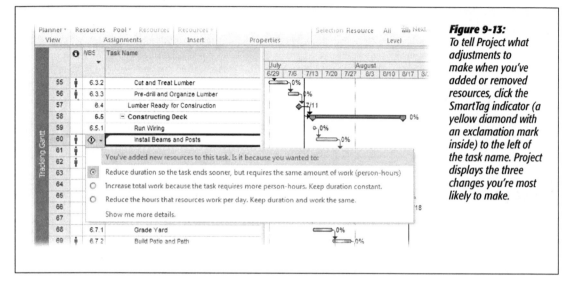

Figure 9-13:
To tell Project what adjustments to make when you've added or removed resources, click the SmartTag indicator (a yellow diamond with an exclamation mark inside) to the left of the task name. Project displays the three changes you're most likely to make.

7. **In the SmartTag menu, select the option for what you want Project to change.**

   If you've added resources, the first option is "Reduce duration so the task ends sooner, but requires the same amount of work (person-hours)". This option keeps the work the same, and recalculates the duration based on the units you specified. (Project selects this option automatically, because shortening duration is the most common reason for adding resources.)

   Selecting "Increase total work because the task requires more person-hours. Keep duration constant." keeps the same duration but recalculates the work based on the units you specified. This option is perfect when you add resources to a task because the client asked for more features.

   The "Reduce the hours that resources work per day. Keep duration and work the same." option calculates the units that resources work based on the duration and work. This choice keeps the same duration and total work, while redistributing work to all assigned resources.

If you remove resources, the three options are similar: The first option increases duration because you have fewer resources; the second option decreases the total work; and the third option increases the units that the remaining resources work each day to compensate for the missing resources.

Tip: Sometimes you don't have to add or take away resources, just replace one assigned resource with another. In the Assign Resources dialog box, select the resource you want to replace, and then click Replace. In the Replace Resource dialog box, select the new resource, and then click OK. To replace a resource in the Task Form, in the Resource Name drop-down list, just click the new resource.

When Effort Drives the Schedule

When does the amount of work control the schedule? Almost always. Project managers typically add resources to finish the same amount of work in less time. If resources disappear, the sad fact is that the work doesn't. Tasks take longer as the remaining resources shoulder the work. Project's term for this conservation of total work is effort-driven scheduling, because the effort (the total amount of work) drives the schedule (how long the task takes). With effort-driven scheduling, adding resources reduces the work each resource performs; removing resources increases the work assigned to each remaining resource.

Because you typically add resources to shorten duration, Project turns on the "Effort driven" checkbox for every new task. But you don't have to leave it turned on. Some tasks take the same amount of time no matter how many people you add. For example, adding attendees to a meeting doesn't shorten the meeting duration. Each attendee has to suffer through the same number of hours. For these uncompressible tasks, the total work grows with each resource you add. (As you watch the alarming increase in cost, you see why keeping meetings focused is so important.) Consider a 2-hour status meeting. If you meet with two other people, the total amount of work is 6 hours—2 hours for each attendee. If you decide to invite the entire 10-person team, the total work expands to 20 hours.

Other reasons total work increases may be change requests or unforeseen problems. For example, if you want to add resources to complete the change requests the client just delivered, turn off the "Effort driven" checkbox. As you add resources, Project adds work based on the units you specify.

Note: Effort-driven scheduling kicks in only when you add or remove resources from a task. Project doesn't apply effort-driven scheduling when you change resources already assigned to a task. If you modify the duration of a task, the task type determines whether the work or units change (page 224).

Table 9-2 shows how Project adds resources with or without effort-driven scheduling:

Table 9-2. *Effort-driven scheduling keeps total work the same*

Task type	Effort-driven scheduling turned on	Effort-driven scheduling turned off
Fixed units	Adding resources shortens duration.	Adding resources increases total work but keeps units and duration the same.
Fixed duration	Adding resources decreases units for each resource.	Adding resources increases total work but keeps the units and duration the same.
Fixed work	Adding resources shortens duration.	Doesn't apply. Fixed work is the same as effort-driven scheduling turned on.

To turn off effort-driven scheduling for a task, do the following:

1. **In the table in the top pane, select the task.**

   The Task Form in the bottom pane displays the values for the selected task. (If the Task Form isn't visible, double-click the small rectangle immediately below the Gantt Chart's vertical scroll bar.)

2. **In the Task Form, turn off the "Effort driven" checkbox.**

   If you edit assignments in the Task Information dialog box, select the Advanced tab, and then turn off the "Effort driven" checkbox.

3. **Click OK.**

   When you add resources to the task, the duration remains the same, and each new resource represents additional person-hours. If you remove resources, the duration remains the same, but the task represents fewer total person-hours.

After you finish adding or removing resources, restore the "Effort driven" checkbox to its original setting.

Controlling Assignment Changes with Task Types

Depending on the assignment change you're trying to make, you may want duration, work, or units to stay the same. Say you want to reduce task duration by adding another resource to take on some of the estimated work hours. Or perhaps you want to keep the units the same as you add more work. The "Task type" field tells Project which variable you want to anchor. You already know that duration, work, and units are inseparable, so you won't be surprised to learn that Project has three task types: Fixed Units, Fixed Work, and Fixed Duration.

Tip: Although the Assign Resources dialog box is a powerful tool for initial resource assignments, the Task Form is better for changing assignments with precision.

Keeping resources assigned with the same units

The Fixed Units task type keeps the same units for each assigned resource regardless of the changes you make to the task duration or work. Out of the box, Project automatically sets the "Task type" field to Fixed Units, because a resource's availability is usually the limiting factor. For example, if you add work to a task, you shouldn't expect a resource assigned at 100 percent to work 200 percent to finish in the same timeframe.

The Fixed Units task type keeps units constant. Here's what Project does, depending on whether you change duration, work, or units:

- **Duration.** If you change the task duration, then Project adjusts the work based on the set units.

- **Work.** If you change the amount of work, then Project adjusts the duration based on the set units.

- **Units.** If you change the units in a Fixed Units task, then Project adjusts the duration and keeps the work the same, because of the program's built-in bias toward changing duration before work.

Maintaining task duration

Suppose you lose a resource assigned to a task. You want the remaining resources to step up to complete the work without increasing the task duration. Fixed Duration helps you do just that.

Here's how a fixed-duration task behaves:

- **Work.** If you change the amount of work, then Project adjusts the units to keep the set duration.

- **Units.** If you change the units, then Project adjusts the work to keep the set duration.

- **Duration.** If you change the duration in a fixed-duration task, then Project adjusts the amount of work, because of Project's bias toward changing work before units.

Here's how you modify assignments without affecting task duration:

1. **In the Gantt Chart view, select the task you want to modify.**

   The values for the selected task appear in the Task Form, in the bottom pane.

2. **In the Task Form, in the "Task type" drop-down list, choose Fixed Duration.**

   Project keeps the duration the same until you change the "Task type" to another value, or type a new value in the Duration field.

3. **To reduce the percentage of time that a resource works on the task, select that resource's Units cell, and then type the new value, for example, changing units from 100% to 50%, as shown in the top window of Figure 9-14.**

   The value in the Work cell doesn't change just yet. The recalculations occur when you click OK.

4. **To add additional resources, in the Task Form, click the first blank Resource Name cell, and then, from the drop-down list, choose the name of the resource you want to assign, illustrated in the top window of Figure 9-14.**

   You can add as many additional resources as you want to the task by clicking blank Resource Name cells and then choosing a resource name.

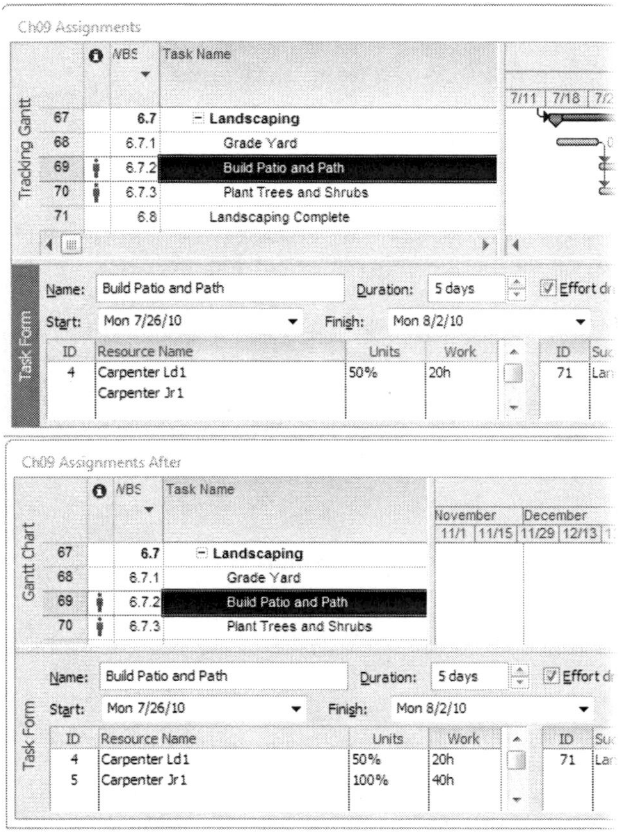

Figure 9-14:
The Duration is 5d (5 days) and the new units for the resource are 50% (top). Although you can add resources to the task, you can't specify their units. Project automatically fills in the cell with 100% or the resource's Maximum Units (bottom). After you add the resources and click OK, you can edit the assignments to modify the units.

5. **After you've made the changes you want, click OK.**

   The duration remains the same, and Project calculates the work assigned to each resource, as shown in the bottom window of Figure 9-14.

6. **To change the units for a new resource, select the resource's Units cell, and then type the new value. After you've adjusted all the unit values, click OK.**

   The duration still remains the same, but Project recalculates the work based on the new unit values.

7. In the "Task type" drop-down list, choose Fixed Units to reset the task to its standard task type, and then click OK.

   Restoring the task type to Fixed Units ensures that every task will behave consistently. Whenever you choose a different task type for a specific assignment change, remember to choose Fixed Units when the modification is complete.

POWER USERS' CLINIC

Combining All the Assignment Features

Suppose a task already has resources assigned, but you want to replace one resource, add an assistant, and yet keep the task duration exactly the same. Doing so means incorporating all of Project's assignment features at the same time, which is like juggling eggs—if you don't keep everything in order, life gets messy. You'll find the duration changing instead of the work hours, or the resources assigned at 300 percent while the duration remains the same. But you can neatly change task type, effort-driven scheduling, and assignments values all at the same time if you proceed in the correct order:

1. In the view in the top pane, select the task you want to modify.

2. In the Task Form in the bottom pane, change the task type. "Task type" is typically set to Fixed Units, which tells Project to change duration or work. To keep the duration, choose Fixed Duration; or, to keep the amount of work, choose Fixed Work.

3. Turn the "Effort driven" checkbox (page 223) on or off, if necessary.

4. In a Resource Name field, choose the resource you want to assign.

5. To specify the assignment units for the resource, type a value in the Units field. To specify the work, type a value in the Work field.

6. To assign more resources to the task, repeat steps 3, 4, and 5.

7. Click OK, and Project calculates the appropriate task and assignment values.

8. If you changed the "Task type" field or the "Effort driven" checkbox, restore them to their original values, and then click OK one more time.

Maintaining the same amount of work

If you've estimated the amount of work that tasks involve, you don't want Project messing with task work values. Using Fixed Work means you can adjust the duration or units without modifying the amount of time a resource spends. For example, if you discover that a resource is available only 50 percent of the time, then Project can keep the work while changing the duration.

Here's how a fixed-work task behaves:

- **Duration.** If you change the task duration, Project adjusts the units to keep the work the same. For example, if a resource is assigned 40 hours of work in a week, the units are 100%. If you change the duration to 6 days, the units drop to 83%.

- **Units.** If you change units, Project adjusts duration. If a resource is assigned to work 40 hours in 5 days and you change the units to 50%, the duration increases to 10 days.

- **Work.** If you change the work in a fixed-work task, Project adjusts the duration, because of its bias against changing units.

Note: You can change the standard task type if you typically keep a different variable steady. Suppose you estimate the work for project tasks, and you don't want Project changing those values as you adjust resource units or change task duration. To change the standard task type, choose File→Options, and then choose Schedule. Below "Scheduling options for this project" in the "Default task type" box, choose Fixed Duration or Fixed Work.

CHAPTER 10

Does the Schedule Work?

After sequencing tasks and assigning resources, you finally have a project schedule (and a feeling of accomplishment). But like a crossword puzzle with some letters out of place, your Microsoft Project schedule can look okay even though mistakes are lurking under the surface. Until you've made sure that all elements of your project are based in reality—like task duration, dependencies, and resource assignments—your project's finish date, cost, and schedule remain in question.

In addition to the inherent inaccuracy of project work and duration estimates, schedules pick up imperfections in several ways. Take tasks, for example. If you forget a link between two tasks, or your mouse snags the wrong task for a dependency, the task sequence doesn't reflect the real relationships between tasks. In turn, these missing or incorrect task dependencies affect when tasks begin and end. Task constraints and tasks you schedule manually go on the calendar where you tell them to—for example, as soon as possible, no earlier than a specific date, or starting and finishing on specific dates. But if those constraints or dates are wrong—or you accidentally create constraints you don't need, the schedule is both incorrect and less flexible. This chapter tells you how to find and correct task dependencies and inadvertent constraints.

While your project is under the microscope, you're bound to find imperfections, like a task that starts before one of its predecessors or tasks that overallocate assigned resources. Project's Task Inspector scans your file for scheduling problems and ways to improve your schedule, flagging scheduling problems with red squiggly lines and opportunities for improvement with green squiggly lines. When you make changes to your schedule, Project highlights all the fields affected by your edits. In this chapter, you'll learn how to use the Task Inspector, change highlighting, and other handy tools for fixing your schedule.

Resource assignments are another weak link. It's crucial to schedule around the availability of people or equipment, but you may have forgotten to tell Project about these schedule idiosyncrasies. In this chapter, you'll learn how to use calendars to identify working and nonworking times for an entire project as well as individual resources. This chapter also describes other techniques for making a schedule more realistic, including how to handle part-time resources and take productivity levels into account.

After all that, you're still not quite finished. Are the workloads assigned to resources reasonable? If you discover that some resources have crushing workloads, you can relieve the pressure by reassigning resources, contouring resource assignments, and leveling assignments to match the time resources have available. This chapter explains how to do all of the above.

Making Sure Tasks Are Set Up Correctly

Project can't read your mind. It can't point out missing task dependencies or dependencies that depend on the wrong things. Similarly, Project adds the task constraints you tell it to add. The problem is, seemingly innocuous actions produce constraints you never intended. Review tasks to make sure you have the dependencies and constraints you want—and only those. What Project *can* do is make it easier to find task dependencies and constraint problems.

WORD TO THE WISE

Leaving Buffers Between Tasks

In reality, nothing ever runs according to plan, so some tasks are going to finish late. If your schedule is tighter than a Hollywood face-lift, the tiniest delay in one task will work its way through the schedule to delay the finish date. A good way to protect your schedule from delays is to add wiggle room at key points during the schedule. For example, you can create a task specifically as a buffer between the end of one phase and the beginning of another. Or you can set up a manually scheduled summary task and add the buffer to it. (With a manually scheduled summary task, Project keeps track of the summary task duration you specify *and* the total duration of all the subtasks, so you can see whether the length of the subtasks remains within

the duration of the summary task, as shown in Figure 10-1.) Project managers often add a buffer equivalent to 15 percent of the duration for each phase of a project. Then, if a few tasks take longer in the earlier phase, they eat into the buffer instead of your due date.

You don't need buffers between every task. Breathing room for phases or key summary tasks is usually good enough. In many projects, tasks that end early may offset the tasks that run late, and you don't need the buffer at all. If a series of tasks adds up to a real delay, you can reduce the buffer by the time that's been lost. The project finish date will hold fast unless a delay completely consumes the buffer.

Duration of summary task

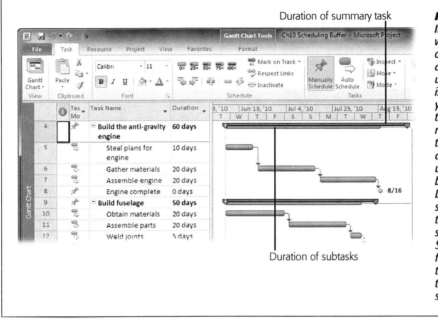

Figure 10-1:
If the subtasks stay within the duration of the summary task duration, the rolled up summary task bar is blue, showing that you have extra buffer time. If the subtasks run longer than the summary task duration, the rolled up summary task bar turns red. The Duration field for the summary task shows the duration you specified, while the Scheduled Duration field shows the duration of the subtasks that belong to the summary task.

Duration of subtasks

Reviewing Task Dependencies

Following the link lines in a Gantt Chart is like trying to untangle a plate of spaghetti. It's hard to trace the lines to see if a task links to the right predecessors or if dependencies are set up correctly. Although there's no shortcut for checking task dependencies, this section describes some techniques to lighten the chore.

Most people find identifying the precursors to a particular task easier than figuring out the downstream effects. However, reviewing both predecessors and successors is the most reliable way to find problems with task dependencies. Here's how you do it:

1. **If the Task Entry view isn't visible, choose Task→View. Click the down arrow and choose More Views. In the More Views dialog box, double-click Task Entry.**

   With the standard Task Entry view, the Gantt Chart table area appears on the left, and the timescale is on the right in the Project window's top pane. The Task Form appears in the bottom pane.

2. **Scroll through the list of tasks, and review the task link lines in the Gantt Chart timescale for any errors.**

   Although link lines can look messy, you may still spot problems with task dependencies by quickly scanning the timescale. You may notice a task dependency connected to the wrong task. More often, you spot tasks with missing predecessors; they're the ones stranded at the project start date. The box on page 234 tells you how to make link lines easier to see.

If you find a task that's missing a predecessor, link it to the appropriate task with your favorite method (page 158).

3. **For a clearer look at task dependencies, first right-click the Task Form and then, from the shortcut menu, choose Predecessors & Successors.**

   Project changes the tables in the Task Form to show predecessors on the left side and successors on the right side, as shown in Figure 10-2. In this view, you can really scrutinize your task dependencies.

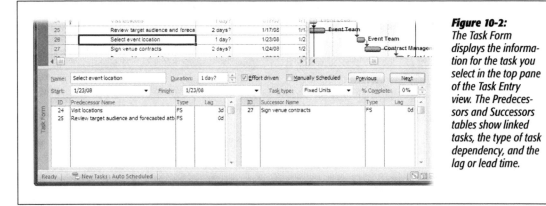

Figure 10-2:
The Task Form displays the information for the task you select in the top pane of the Task Entry view. The Predecessors and Successors tables show linked tasks, the type of task dependency, and the lag or lead time.

4. **To begin reviewing at the very first task, press Ctrl+Home.**

   Project selects the first task in the Gantt Chart table area. Press the down arrow to select the next task.

5. **For each task in the task list, examine the values in the Task Form.**

   Look at the tasks in the Predecessor Name column. Make sure that they're predecessors to the selected task. Are there other predecessor tasks that aren't listed? If so, link the two tasks as you would normally. Review the tasks in the Successor table in the same way.

   Most tasks connect to one another with a Finish-to-Start task dependency (page 156). Make sure the dependency type is correct for each predecessor and successor. Also verify the lag or lead time. Remember, lag time (a delay from one task to the other) is a positive number. If the second task gets an early start, the lag becomes a negative number. (The box on page 230 describes a different kind of buffer—one that many tasks can share in case they require more time.)

6. **As you move through the project dates, use the timeline to quickly scroll to different date ranges in the timescale (page 600).**

   If the timeline doesn't appear above the Gantt Chart view, choose View→Split View, and then turn on the Timeline checkbox. (You can display either the timeline or the Details pane, but not both. Displaying the timeline closes the Details pane if it's visible.) To scroll the timescale, hover the pointer over the blue bar at the top of the timeline. When it changes to a four-headed arrow, drag to the left to move the Gantt Chart timescale back in time or drag to the right to advance forward in time. You can drag either end of the blue bar in the timeline view to adjust the earliest or latest date in the Gantt Chart timescale, as shown in Figure 10-3.

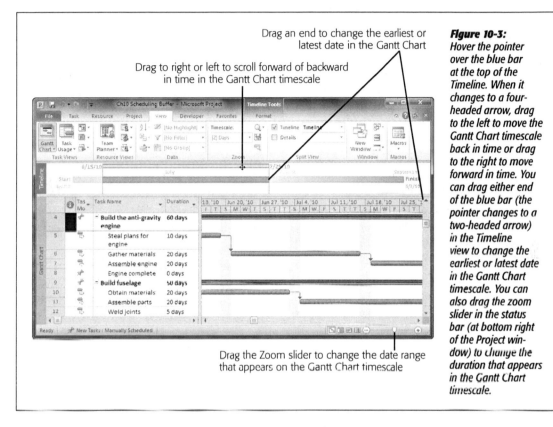

Drag an end to change the earliest or latest date in the Gantt Chart

Drag to right or left to scroll forward of backward in time in the Gantt Chart timescale

Drag the Zoom slider to change the date range that appears on the Gantt Chart timescale

Figure 10-3:
Hover the pointer over the blue bar at the top of the Timeline. When it changes to a four-headed arrow, drag to the left to move the Gantt Chart timescale back in time or drag to the right to move forward in time. You can drag either end of the blue bar (the pointer changes to a two-headed arrow) in the Timeline view to change the earliest or latest date in the Gantt Chart timescale. You can also drag the zoom slider in the status bar (at bottom right of the Project window) to change the duration that appears in the Gantt Chart timescale.

7. **Repeat steps 5 and 6 until you've reviewed all the tasks in the project.**

When you get to the final task or milestone, you're done!

Changing Manually Scheduled Tasks to Auto Scheduled

If some task information was unavailable when you started your project plan, you may have created manually scheduled tasks to record the info you did have. Project changes the task bar's appearance to indicate what information is available or missing (see page 119). As your task information gains shape, you can fill in the missing task fields and turn many of those manually scheduled tasks into auto-scheduled ones. (In some cases, you create manually scheduled tasks so you can pin the tasks' dates to the calendar. Those tasks remain manually scheduled for the duration of the project.) Be sure to review all your manually scheduled tasks to make sure you've filled in missing task information.

Seeing the Trees, Not the Forest

Most of the time, you want to see information like resource names and milestone dates associated with task bars in the Gantt Chart timescale. However, these fields get in the way when you're looking at task dependencies. Project connoisseurs know you can remove task bar text by formatting bar styles (choose Format→Bar Styles, click the Format down arrow, and choose Bar Styles). But you have to repeat this step for each type of task bar. The Gantt Chart Wizard can sweep away all task bar text at once.

Changing the appearance of the Gantt Chart is easy, but you can save more time by using a customized view (page 583) for your Spartan Gantt Chart. The easiest way to obtain a cleaned-up Gantt Chart is to download the Project-MM_ Customizations.mpp file from *www.missingmanuals.com/cds*. It includes a Clean Gantt view that you can copy to your global.mpt file using the Organizer (choose File→Info→Organizer).

If you'd rather build your own, here are the steps for creating a view and cleaning up the timescale with the Gantt Chart Wizard:

1. Choose View→Task Views. Below the current view name, click the down arrow, and then choose More Views.

2. In the More Views dialog box, select Gantt Chart, and then click Copy.

3. In the View Definition dialog box, type a name for the view, like *Clean Gantt*.

4. To display the view on the View drop-down menu for easy clicking, leave the "Show in menu" checkbox turned on. If you turn the checkbox off, then you open the view by choosing View→Task Views, clicking the down arrow, choosing More Views, and, in the More Views dialog box, selecting the view name.

5. To save and display the view, click OK. Back in the More Views dialog box, click Apply.

6. To use the Gantt Chart Wizard, you must first add it to a custom group on the ribbon (see page 661 to learn how).

7. In that custom group, choose Gantt Chart Wizard.

8. On the first screen, click Next.

9. Make sure the Standard option is selected, and then click Next.

10. On the next screen, select the None option to remove all task bar text. Click Next.

11. On the next screen, make sure the Yes option is selected to show link lines, and then click Next.

12. On the last screen, click Format It, and then click Exit Wizard. The wizard's formatting is already in place in the view.

The built-in Tasks Without Dates filter (choose View→Data→Filter→More Filters and then double-click Tasks Without Dates) shows tasks without start and finish dates. However, incomplete task info comes in other forms, like tasks with start dates but no finish dates, so that filter doesn't show all the tasks you need to see. Filtering your task list to show all manually scheduled tasks is a better place to start. Here's how you can filter your task list and switch tasks to auto-scheduled as you fill in their missing info:

1. **Display the Entry table by right-clicking the Select All cell at the intersection of the column heading row and the Task ID column and then choosing Entry.**

   To insert the Task Mode field in the current table, right-click the column heading to the right of where you want to insert the field and then choose Insert Column. In the drop-down list, choose Task Mode.

2. To filter your task list to show only Manually Scheduled tasks, click the down arrow in the Task Mode field, as shown in Figure 10-4; turn off the Auto Scheduled checkbox; and then click OK.

The task list includes all manually scheduled subtasks and the summary tasks to which they belong. A filter icon appears to the right of the Task Mode column name, to indicate that the list is filtered by the column.

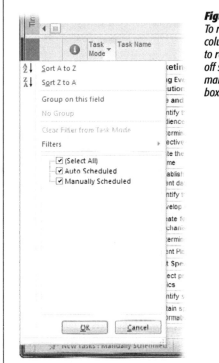

Figure 10-4:
To return to the full task list, you can click the down arrow in the Task Mode column again and turn on the Auto Scheduled checkbox. An even easier way to restore the full task list is by pressing F3, which removes the filter. To turn off summary tasks, choose Format→Show/Hide, and then turn off the Summary Tasks check box. Keep in mind, turning off the Summary Tasks check box hides all summary tasks, including those that are manually scheduled.

3. Review each task in the list, and fill in any missing information.

A partially shaded task bar without end caps means you haven't defined either a start or a finish date. If a task has only one end cap, then the duration or one of the task's dates is missing. To keep the task manually scheduled, fill in the task's Start or Finish fields. You can also switch the task to auto-scheduled, as described in step 4, so Project can use the task's predecessors and successors to calculate its dates.

4. To switch a task to auto-scheduled, click the task's Task Mode cell, click the down arrow that appears, and then choose Auto Scheduled. Or right-click the task and then choose Auto Scheduled from the shortcut menu.

The Auto Scheduled icon looks like a task bar with an arrow pointing to the right. In addition, the task bar style in the timescale changes to show that the task is auto-scheduled. The auto-scheduled task remains in the view. To reapply the Manually Scheduled filter, simply press Shift+F3. Project hides any tasks you've switched to auto-scheduled.

5. **Repeat steps 3 and 4 until you've filled in all the missing information.**

   When the task list shows only the manually scheduled tasks you created to control task dates, you're done!

Freeing Tasks from Date Constraints

Most schedules originate from a start date, and the project's finish date is calculated from there. When you schedule a Project file from the start date (page 135), Project automatically assigns the As Soon As Possible constraint to new auto-scheduled tasks, so every task begins on the earliest possible date. (If you work backward from a finish date, Project assigns the As Late As Possible constraint.) Other date constraints come in handy now and then. For example, you can change the assignments for a key resource to a Start No Earlier Than constraint to schedule assignments for when she returns from sabbatical. Unfortunately, some Project actions create date constraints you don't intend (page 166). For example, typing a specific date in a Start or Finish cell creates a new date constraint for that task.

Tip: In Project 2010, you can go one step further and fix both the Start and Finish dates for a task by changing its Task Mode to Manually Scheduled and then filling in the Start and Finish fields. See page 116 to learn more.

The hunt for unwanted, unintended constraints is a must-do task on every project manager's checklist. Project offers two ways to examine your date constraints: the Constraint Indicator icons, and the Constraint Type field.

Here are the steps for finding and fixing date constraints:

1. **Display the Task Details Form in the Task Entry view's bottom pane by choosing View→Split View. If necessary, turn on the Details checkbox. Then choose More Views in the Details drop-down list.**

   The More Views dialog box appears.

2. **In the More Views dialog box, select Task Details Form, and then click Apply.**

   The Task Details Form includes the Constraint Type and Constraint Date fields. When the Details pane is turned on, you can temporarily hide it by positioning the cursor over the horizontal gray divider between the top and bottom pane. When the cursor changes to a two-headed arrow, double-click the gray bar. To make the bottom pane visible again, double-click the small rectangle immediately below the vertical scroll bar.

3. **To display the Constraint Type column in the view table, right-click in the table heading area. From the shortcut menu, choose Insert Column, and then choose Constraint Type.**

   The Constraint Type column appears in the table.

4. **Filter the task list for constraints other than As Soon As Possible by clicking the down arrow to the right of the Constraint Type column heading, turning off the As Soon As Possible checkbox, and then clicking OK.**

Project filters the task list showing only tasks that have a constraint type other than As Soon As Possible, as you see in Figure 10-5.

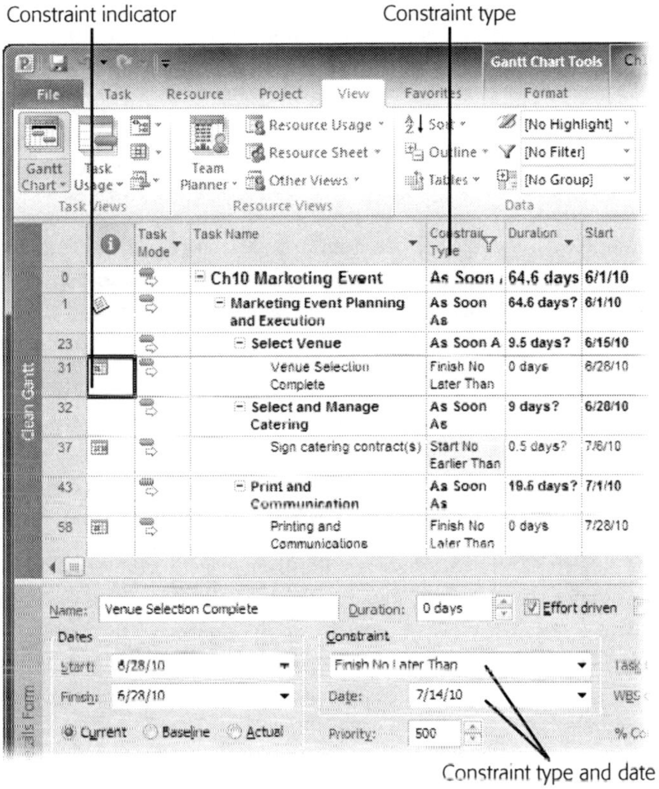

Constraint indicator   *Constraint type*

Constraint type and date

Figure 10-5:
Tasks that have a date constraint other than As Soon As Possible or As Late As Possible sport a date constraint icon in the Indicators column. Project shows tasks that pass the filter along with the summary tasks to which they belong.

Tip: You can obtain the DateConstraints custom filter, which hides As Soon As Possible tasks, by downloading the ProjectMM_Customizations.mpp file from *www.missingmanuals.com/cds*. See page 670 to learn how to copy elements to your global.mpt file.

---

5. **Select a task with a date constraint so its information appears in the Task Details Form in the bottom pane.**

The Task Details Form shows both the constraint type and the date, which can jog your memory about why you set a constraint.

6. If the constraint shouldn't be there, choose As Soon As Possible from the Constraint Type drop-down list, and then click OK.

Project changes the constraint date to NA, and the Constraint icon disappears from the Indicators column. When you're done, the only date constraints you should see are the ones that belong there.

Defining Work Schedules with Calendars

Resources aren't at your beck and call 24/7. Team members take vacations, attend training and conferences, and get sick. In addition, team members may work part time or work 4 long days and take Friday off. Incorporating nonworking time and specialized work arrangements makes a Project schedule more likely to forecast how the project will actually play out. In Project, *calendars* carve out working and nonworking times.

Calendars are multitalented: You can apply a calendar to an entire project, individual resources, or specific tasks, as described in Chapters 6 and 8. For instance, you can set up a calendar to indicate corporate holidays or factory closures, and use that calendar for all your projects. On the other hand, a resource calendar shows a team member's particular work schedule and time off.

Project comes with a few built-in calendars (page 137), and automatically applies the built-in Standard calendar to new projects you create. However, you can modify existing calendars or build completely new ones, and then apply them to custom-fit your resources' work hours.

This section explains creating and customizing calendars in Project. (Working with calendars changed radically beginning in Project 2007, as the box on page 241 explains.) You'll also find a quick review of how to apply calendars to projects, resources, and tasks. See "Building Reality into Assignments" on page 253 to learn how to integrate calendars, resource units, and resource availability to resolve common resource scheduling issues.

Tip: You can copy calendars you create using the Organizer so they're available to other projects. If you modify the Standard calendar in one Project file to include company holidays, copy that calendar into the Project global template to share that calendar with all new projects.

Creating New Calendars

You can create as many calendars as you need. Whether you want to create a calendar for a project, a resource, or task, the steps are the same: Create the new calendar, edit it to reflect your project's actual working and nonworking times, and then apply it. Here are the steps for creating a new calendar:

1. **Choose Project→Properties→Change Working Time.**

   The Change Working Time dialog box opens. The "For calendar" box shows the calendar you've applied to the project. For example, Standard (Project Calendar) indicates that the Standard calendar is set as the project calendar for the current Project file.

2. **Click Create New Calendar.**

   The Create New Base Calendar dialog box appears, as shown in Figure 10-6. *Base calendar* is Project's name for calendars that act as templates for other calendars. The Standard calendar is a base calendar, because you can use it as the foundation for customized project calendars or for resource calendars.

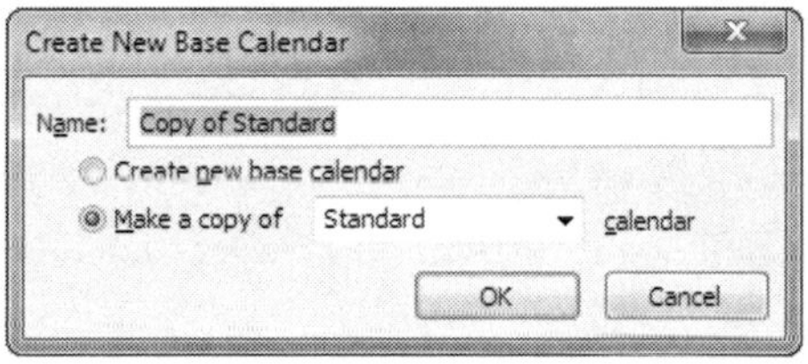

Figure 10-6:
Project suggests that copying an existing calendar is the preferred way to create a new base calendar by automatically selecting the "Make a copy of" option.

3. **To use an existing calendar as your starting point, leave the "Make a copy of" option selected, and then, in the "Make a copy of ___ calendar" drop-down list, choose the calendar you want.**

   For a calendar that's very different from any you have already, you can create one from scratch by selecting the "Create new base calendar" option.

4. **In the Name box, be sure to type a new name for the calendar.**

   If you copy an existing calendar, Project adds "Copy of" in front of the calendar name. If you create a new calendar, Project fills in the box with a name like *Calendar 1*. The best names are short but give you a good idea of the working time they represent, like "Night Shift."

5. **Click OK.**

   The Create New Base Calendar dialog box closes, and the new calendar name appears in the "For calendar" box. Because this new calendar is not the project calendar, only the calendar name appears in the box. (Page 249 shows how to make a calendar the project calendar.) Now you're ready to set the calendar's working times, which the next section describes in detail.

Modifying Calendars

Any calendar in a Project file, built in or one of yours, is fair game for modification. You can most easily define the work and holiday schedule for your organization by modifying the built-in Standard calendar to match your organization's work time and days off. Then, if you store that modified Standard calendar in the Project global template (page 670), every new Project file already knows about your work weeks and time off. (If you're a Project 2003 veteran, the way you specify working time changed in Project 2007 and takes some getting used to, as the box on page 241 explains.)

Setting up work schedules for people and tasks is another reason to modify calendars. You could create a "Night Shift" calendar for the teams that work the graveyard shift and specify the work times as 11 p.m. to 8 a.m. Then you apply that calendar to every resource on the night shift.

Selecting a calendar to modify

If you create a brand new calendar, Project selects it as soon as you create it. However, if you want to modify an existing calendar, you have to select it first by performing the following steps:

1. **Choose Project→Properties→Change Working Time.**

    The Change Working Time dialog box opens, showing the project calendar in the "For calendar" box.

2. **In the "For calendar" drop-down list, choose the calendar you want to modify, as illustrated in Figure 10-7.**

    The "For calendar" drop-down list starts with built-in calendars and any new calendars you've created. Calendars for each resource in the Project file appear at the end of the list.

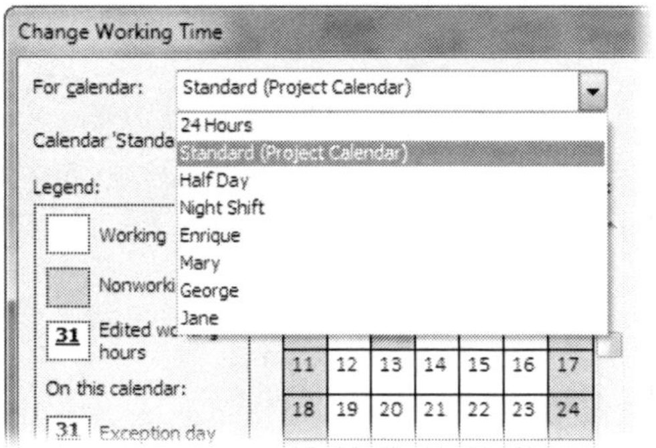

Figure 10-7:
The "For calendar" drop-down list displays the built-in calendars, any new calendars you've created, and calendars for each resource in the Project file.

Defining work weeks for a calendar

Every calendar in a Project file comes with one work week. When you select a calendar and select the Work Weeks tab, the name of the first entry is [Default]. The Start and Finish cells are set to NA, which means that the work week applies to all dates. To define the typical work week, simply modify the [Default] work week. For example, the built-in Night Shift calendar schedules work hours from 11 p.m. to 8 a.m. with a break between 3 and 4 a.m. If your night shift runs from 12 a.m. to 8 a.m., then you'd change the work times in the [Default] work week, as described in the next section.

GEM IN THE ROUGH

Changing Times in Project 2007 and 2010

Setting working time changed in Project 2007, as you'll learn in detail in the following sections. Some calendar tasks are easier, while others take a few more steps.

In Project 2003 and earlier versions, you selected the days you wanted to modify in the calendar area. Initially, Project selected the "Use default" option, which set weekdays as workdays and weekends as non-workdays. However, you could specify any day as working or nonworking and then set work hours if they differed from the standard start and finish times you specified in the Calendar Options (page 139).

In Project 2007 and 2010, *work weeks* identify the work and non-work days in a 7-day week, as well as the work hours for each workday. (These settings are hidden behind the Details button in the Change Working Time dialog box.) In other words, work weeks give you the opportunity to define as many work schedules as you want within the same Project calendar, like a summer-schedule work week, a winter-schedule work week, and the standard work week in force the rest of the year. The work week feature is handy if your work schedules last several weeks or several months, with lots of variation in work times—like a stint of 12-hour days to meet a critical deadline. You define the work week and tell Project the dates when that work week schedule applies. Project modifies the current calendar to use that work week between the start and stop dates you specified.

You can't create a work week and apply it to several different time periods. If you want to schedule a week's worth of 12-hour days in April, and then again in August, you have to define two different work weeks.

The other calendar feature is called *exceptions,* which are like the changes you made to calendars in Project 2003 and earlier versions. Exceptions are primarily for nonworking time, but you can also use them to represent alternate work schedules. For example, for Project 2007 and 2010, you define company holidays as exceptions. Working days with slightly altered schedules, like half-days before holidays, are calendar exceptions as well. You can also set up recurring exceptions—for example, to schedule a non-workday once a quarter for the ever-popular all-hands meeting.

Work weeks and exceptions can do some of the same things. You can, for example, show a resource's vacation time either with a nonworking work week or an exception.

The one disadvantage to exceptions is that you have to name each one and choose a date range. In Project 2003, all you did was select one or more days in the calendar, and then select the "Non working time" (or "Non default working time") option. Now you have to create a separate exception for each company holiday or other special day.

Note: Initially, the [Default] work week considers weekdays as workdays and weekends as non-workdays. In addition, the start and end work times you specify in Project calendar options (page 139) are the basis for the standard start and end times for work hours for all days in all calendars. To set different work times on specific days, you must specify those work times in either calendar work weeks or exceptions.

Because you can define as many work weeks as you want in a calendar, here are some examples of why you might create additional work weeks:

- **Company-wide work schedules.** Create additional work weeks for company-wide nonworking time that lasts one or more weeks—for example, a factory shutdown for the last two weeks of the year or Fridays off during the winter. If your project team has hockey practice every Friday from December 1 until March 31, you can create a Hockey Season work week in the project-wide Standard calendar to define winter work weeks as Monday through Thursday.

- **Resource work schedules.** Work weeks in a resource calendar are great when someone works an altered schedule for a few weeks or months; for example, when someone works half-days for two months while recuperating from an illness. You simply select the resource calendar and then create a work week for the recuperation schedule.

- **Resource vacations.** Resource calendar work weeks are one way to show people's vacation time, although a calendar exception achieves the same result.

A new work week needs a name as well as start and stop dates for the modified work schedule. Then you define the working days and hours as you do for the [Default] work week, as described in the previous section. Here are the steps for creating a new work week:

1. **In the Change Working Time dialog box, in the "For calendar" drop-down list, select the calendar, and then click the Work Weeks tab.**

   [Default] appears in the first row with any other work weeks you've defined in Rows 2 and higher.

2. **On the Work Weeks tab, click the first blank Name cell, and then type a name for the work week schedule.**

   Use a meaningful name, like "*Hockey Season*," for the winter work week. If you create a work week in a resource calendar, you might call the work week "*Spring Vacation*" or "*Medical Leave*."

3. **Click the Start cell in the same row, click the down arrow that appears in the cell, and then choose the first date to which the work week applies, as shown in Figure 10-8. Click the Finish cell in the same row, and then choose the last date to which the work week applies.**

   When you click the down arrow in a Start or Finish cell, a calendar drop-down appears. Click the left arrow or right arrow to move one month into the past or future. To select a date, click the date in the monthly calendar. If the date is several months in the future, typing the date (like *12/1/10*) may be faster.

4. **To specify workdays and times, click Details. Then specify the workdays and times as described in the next section. Click OK when you're done.**

   When you open the Details dialog box for a work week, the title of the dialog box is "Details for" followed by the name of the work week.

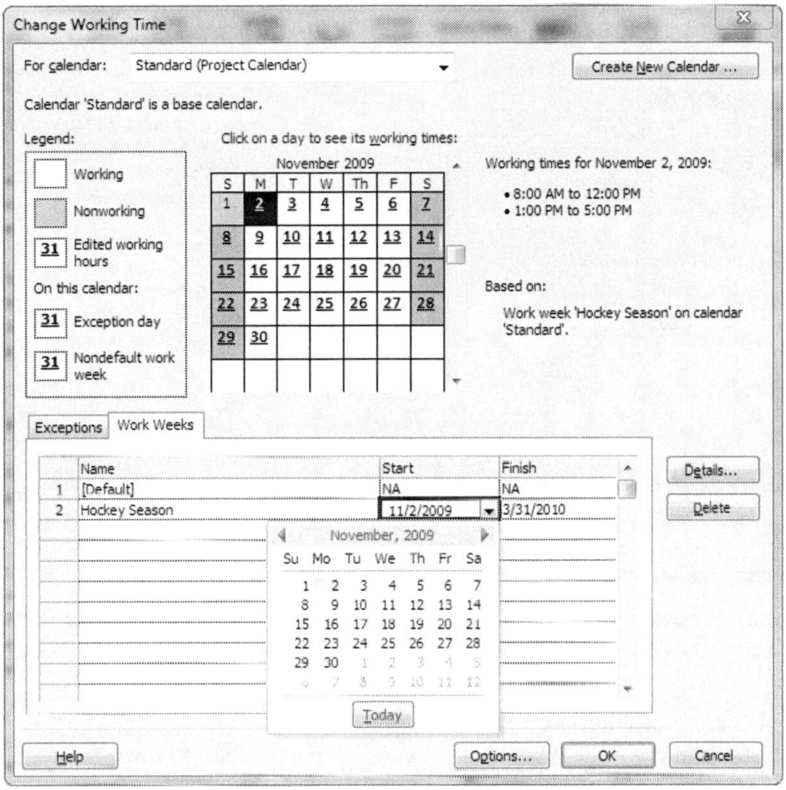

Figure 10-8:
*If you click a day in the
calendar at the top of
the Change Working
Time dialog box, Project
displays the working
times for that day, and
the work week that ap-
plies to that day.*

Defining the working and nonworking days and times for a work week

Whether you want to change the workdays or work hours for a calendar's standard
work week or for a special work week you created, here's how you define workdays
and work hours for a work week:

1. In the Change Working Time dialog box, select the calendar, and then click
   the Work Weeks tab. Select the work week you want to modify.

   If you haven't added any additional work weeks, the only entry you see in the
   Work Weeks tab is [Default] in the Name cell of Row 1.

2. To specify the workdays and times, click Details.

   The Details dialog box appears with the heading "Details for 'work week name' ",
   as shown in Figure 10-9.

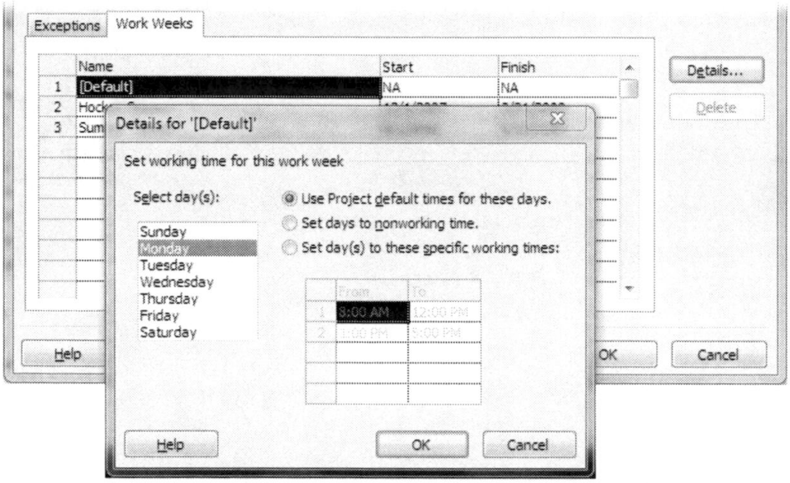

Figure 10-9:
*If you select a workday,
you see the current work
hours in the working
time table. The working
time table is empty
when you select a
nonworking day.*

3. **In the "Select day(s)" list, select the day or days you want to modify.**

   To select a single day, click it. To select several adjacent days, drag over the days (or click the first day and Shift-click the last). To select nonadjacent days, Ctrl-click each day you want to select.

   If you select multiple days that use different settings, none of the options are selected and the work time table is blank. When all selected days use the same settings, Project shows the common work times in the work time table.

4. **Select the appropriate working time option.**

   The initial setting for every day of the week is "Use Project default times for these days", which sets weekdays as workdays and weekends as non-workdays. To change a workday to a nonworking day (for example, to change Friday to a nonworking day), select the "Set days to nonworking time" option.

   To change the work hours for any workday, select the "Set day(s) to these specific working times" option. This option makes the working time table editable, so you can change the work hours for the selected days. In addition to changing work hours, use this option to change a non-workday like a weekend day to a workday.

5. **To change the work hours in an existing entry, click the cell, and then type the new time.**

   When you click a cell in the working time table, Project selects the entire contents, so you simply start typing to change the value.

   Working time text boxes behave like all other text boxes. You can edit times by clicking to position the insertion point, or by dragging to select the text you want to edit. The box on page 245 provides some shortcuts for editing times.

UP TO SPEED

Telling Project Time

Project recognizes a few time shortcuts in the working time table. For example, if you type *8* in a cell, Project fills in 8:00 AM. In fact, Project switches to an a.m. time whenever you type a number from 7 to 11. Project changes the number 12 and the numbers from 1 to 6 to p.m. times; for instance, *12* becomes 12:00 PM. To type a time shortcut including a.m. or p.m., simply type a value like *8 pm*.

Project double-checks the times you enter and tries to be helpful. If you type a time in a From cell that's later than the To time, Project automatically adjusts the To time to be one hour later than the From time. Suppose the first set of work times run from 8:00 a.m. to 12:00 p.m. If you change the From cell to 1:00 PM, then Project changes the To cell to 2:00 PM.

Overlapping times in different rows are a problem. For instance, suppose you enter work times of 1:00 PM to 5:00 PM in the first row and 4:00 to 5:00 PM in the second row. Project doesn't complain until you click OK, when it warns you that the start of one shift must be later than the end of the previous shift. Click OK, and remove the overlap.

6. **To add a new row of working time, click the first blank From cell, and then type the starting time.**

   Suppose you switch to 14-hour days and add a second break a few hours after lunch. You can add a new row for the third set of work hours.

7. **To remove a row of work time, drag across both the From and To cells, and then press Delete.**

   To change a full workday to a half workday, you can delete the after-lunch work hours. (Don't delete the value in only one of the cells. If you try to leave an empty cell, Project tells you the value isn't valid. Press Esc to restore the deleted value, and then drag across the From and To cells and press Delete.)

8. **To specify working times for other days, repeat steps 3–7.**

   Otherwise, click OK to close the dialog box.

Setting aside holidays and other exceptions to the work schedule

Work weeks assign the same schedule of workdays and times over a period of time. As the name implies, calendar exceptions are better for shorter changes to the work schedule. Consider using calendar exceptions for the following situations:

- **Single days with a different schedule.** A company holiday and a half-day for a corporate meeting are perfect examples of single-day exceptions.

- **Multiple days with a different schedule.** For example, you can set a modified schedule for a multiday training class that someone attends, a conference, or a series of short days when the auditors are in town.

- **Recurring changes.** Use exceptions to specify altered work times that occur on a regular schedule, like company meetings or the monthly ice cream social.

- **Altered work schedules longer than a week.** You can use an exception for a schedule change that lasts longer than a week as long as all the days of an exception are either nonworking days or have the same working times. (For that reason, work weeks and exceptions work equally well for factory shutdowns and people's vacations.)

Here are the steps for defining an exception in a calendar:

1. **In the Change Working Time dialog box, in the "For calendar" drop-down list, select the calendar, and then click the Exceptions tab.**

   Project doesn't set up any exceptions automatically, so all the rows on the Exceptions tab start out blank.

2. **On the Exceptions tab, click the first blank Name cell, and then type a name for the exception, like *Quiche Training*.**

   You can create as many exceptions in a calendar as you need—to set each company holiday in the year or to reserve vacation time for someone who frequently flits around the world, for example.

3. **Click the Start cell in the same row, click the down arrow that appears in the cell, and then choose the first date to which the exception applies. Click the Finish cell in the same row, and then choose the last date for the exception.**

   Start and finish dates can be the same day, a few days apart, or any two dates you want.

4. **To define the days and times for the exception, click Details.**

   The "Details for" dialog box opens. Because many exceptions are holidays and other days off, Project automatically selects the Nonworking option. If the exception is for nonworking time, just click OK. However, if you're creating an exception for a few days of altered work times, select the "Working times" option, as shown in Figure 10-10.

   For one or more adjacent days, you can ignore the settings in the "Recurrence pattern" and "Range of recurrence" sections. Project automatically sets them to model your nonworking and working settings for every day between the start and finish dates. The next section explains how to create recurring exceptions.

5. **If the exception specifies modified working times, click OK when you've finished setting the working times in the Working Times table.**

   The Details dialog box closes, and the exception is ready to go on the Exceptions tab.

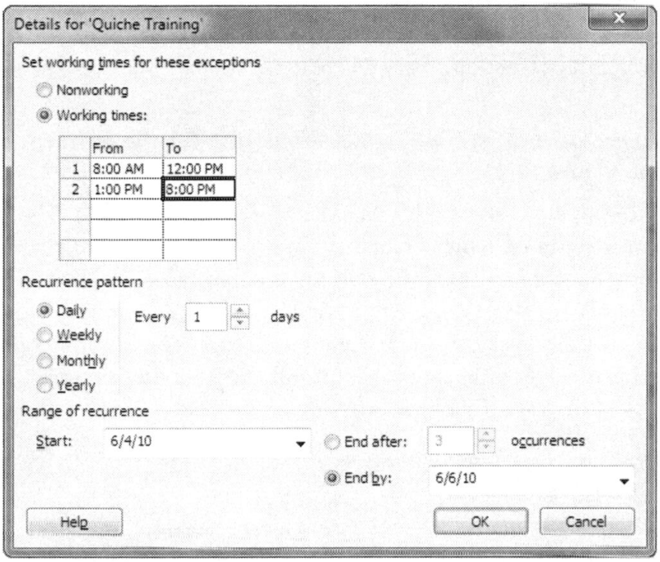

Figure 10-10:
When an exception is for one or more days with working times outside the norm, select the "Working times" option. The working times table springs to life, and fills in the standard working times you set in the Project calendar options (page 139). As you do for work week details, fill in the From and To times that apply to every day of the exception, and then click OK.

Defining recurring exceptions

Sometimes, exceptions to the work week occur on a regular schedule—like the quarterly half-days of nonworking time for all-hands meetings. Recurring tasks and recurring exceptions have the same types of frequency settings, as the box on page 249 explains. However, recurring tasks represent project work that repeats, while recurring exceptions represent repeating special work times.

The details for a calendar exception specify whether exception days are nonworking or working days (along with the work hours). The lower part of the "Details for" dialog box has options to set a frequency for the exception and when it starts or ends. Here are the steps for defining a recurring exception in a calendar:

1. **In the Change Working Time dialog box, select the calendar from the "For calendar" drop-down list, and then click the Exceptions tab.**

    The Exceptions tab appears.

2. **Enter the name, start date, and finish date as you would for a regular exception.**

    Recurring exceptions tend to span longer periods of time than exceptions for holidays or training classes. For example, the start and finish dates for an annual corporate retreat exception could be 3 years apart—if you're scheduling the next three retreats at once.

3. **Click Details and specify the nonworking or working time settings for the days in the recurring exception.**

   Page 243 describes how to specify nonworking and working times for days. With a Project calendar exception, every day of the exception must use the same settings.

4. **In the "Recurrence pattern" section, select the option for the frequency, as demonstrated in Figure 10-11.**

   The frequency options include Daily, Weekly, Monthly, and Yearly. The settings that appear depend on which frequency option you select. For example, the Weekly option has a checkbox for specifying the number of weeks between occurrences (1 represents every week, 2 represents every other week) and checkboxes for the days of the week on which the event occurs. The Monthly option has one option for specifying the day of the month, and another for specifying the week and day of the week (like first Monday).

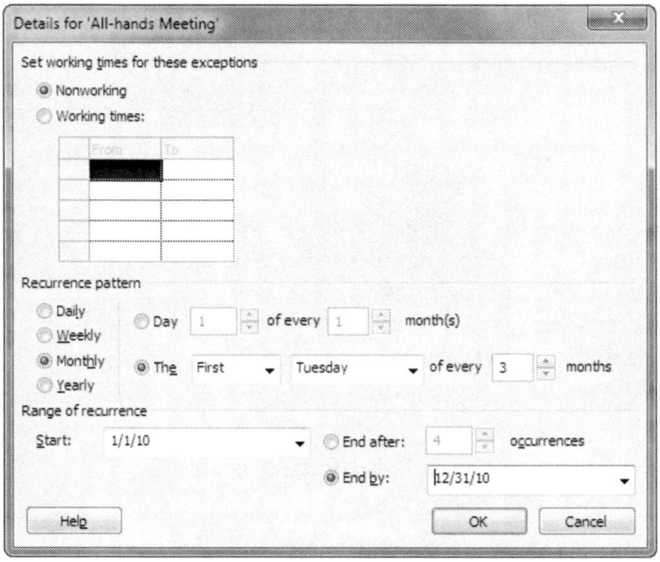

Figure 10-11:
For a recurring exception, you specify the recurring pattern as well as how long the pattern lasts. Project initially sets the pattern to every day by selecting the Daily option and filling in the "Every _ _ days" box with 1. Project also fills in the Start and "End by" dates using the exception start and end dates.

5. **In the "Range of recurrence" section, specify the date range or the number of occurrences.**

   Project fills in the "Range of recurrence" Start box with the start date from the Exceptions tab—basically, the first date of the first exception. It selects the "End by" option and then fills in that box with the finish date from the Exceptions tab, the latest date for the entire recurrence. Suppose you want to carve out time from your project for a quarterly meeting every 3 months during the calendar year. You could set the Start date to *1/1/10* and the "End by" date to *12/31/10*.

If the frequency is set to Monthly on the first Tuesday of every 3 months, then Project automatically sets aside 1/5/10, 4/5/10, 7/6/10, and 10/5/10 for the meetings.

Sometimes you want to specify a number of occurrences instead, which is in fact the easier way to schedule a specific number of meetings. You don't have to change the Start date. However, to set a number of occurrences, select the "End after" option, and then type the number (4 in this example) in the "occurrences" box. If the Finish date you set on the Exceptions tab is too early to schedule all the occurrences, Project automatically changes it. For example, if the Finish date were set to 2/15/10, Project would change it to 10/5/10 to accommodate the four quarterly meetings.

6. **Click OK.**

   Whether you set dates or a number of occurrences, a recurring exception can repeat up to 999 times. If your recurrence pattern results in 1,000 occurrences or more, Project displays a warning when you click OK.

UP TO SPEED

Recurring Tasks vs. Recurring Exceptions

The settings for recurring exceptions look like the ones for recurring tasks (page 147). However, recurring exceptions and recurring tasks do very different things.

A recurring task is project work that occurs on a regular schedule, like a biweekly status meeting. When you add these tasks to your schedule as recurring tasks, you can track the work hours and meeting costs.

A recurring calendar exception specifies a work or non-work schedule that repeats regularly, like a half-day the last Friday of every month (so security consultants can sweep the office for bugs, for example). Project takes the exception days and times into account when it schedules project work for any project that uses that calendar. When you copy a calendar from one file to another (page 670), the exceptions and work weeks for the calendar copy over, too.

Applying Calendars

Sometimes, entire projects follow a different work schedule, like a subproject with a partner who has an enviable holiday schedule. More often, one or more resources need their own work calendars to reflect work shifts, vacations, or unique working hours (like those of the token vampire on your team). The occasional task may have its own calendar, like the highway repaving task that has to run from 9 p.m. to 5 a.m.

To apply a calendar to a project, follow these steps:

1. **With the project open, choose Project→Properties→Project Information.**

   The Project Information dialog box opens.

2. **In the Calendar box, choose the calendar you want, and then click OK.**

   Project uses this calendar for the project's working and nonworking time (except where you've applied a special calendar to any resource or task).

Applying a calendar to a resource is even easier:

1. **In the Resource Sheet, at the very right end of the table, click the resource's Base Calendar cell.**

   The down arrow appears on the right side of the cell.

2. **In the drop-down list, choose the calendar you want to apply.**

   Project uses that calendar whenever you assign that resource to tasks.

Tip: Resources start out using the calendar you apply to the project, unless you tell Project otherwise. If you want to define a resource's vacation time, you make those changes in the resource's calendar: Choose Project→Properties→Change Working Time. In the "For calendar" drop-down list, choose the resource's name. Now you can define the work weeks or exceptions for the resource. (If you double-click a resource's name in the Resource Sheet, the Resource Information dialog box opens. On the General tab, click Change Working Time. The Change Working Time dialog box opens right to that resource's calendar.)

Sometimes tasks must run at specific times, like a planned outage that has to take place in the middle of the night. Although task calendars aren't that common, you can apply a calendar directly to a task.

Note: You must create the task calendar you want to apply *before* you open the Task Information dialog box.

To apply a calendar to a task, do the following:

1. **In the table area of a view, select the task or tasks that require a special calendar, and then choose Task→Properties→Information.**

   If you select only one task, then the Task Information dialog box opens. If you select more than one task, then the Multiple Task Information dialog box opens instead. The fields in these two dialog boxes are identical.

2. **Click the Advanced tab and, in the Calendar drop-down list, choose the calendar you want to apply. Click OK to close the dialog box and apply the task calendar.**

   The "Scheduling ignores resource calendars" checkbox is initially turned off, so Project schedules work only during working hours common to both the assigned resources and the task. If the task calendar and resource calendars don't have any mutual work time, a message box warns you that the calendars don't jibe. You can change either the task calendar or the resource calendar to create some common time. Another approach is to schedule work by the task calendar only—by turning on the "Scheduling ignores resource calendars" checkbox. Project then assumes that the assigned resources work during the task's work time.

Task Inspector: Help with Schedule Problems

In Project 2007, the Task Drivers pane showed you the factors that affect when tasks occur. In Project 2010, the Task Inspector takes a more proactive approach to this responsibility. The Task Inspector scans your project for problems like tasks starting before their predecessors or a subtask's finish date occurring after the summary task's finish date. Because Project doesn't calculate dates for manually scheduled tasks, they're particularly prone to schedule problems. In Project 2010, red squiggly lines indicate potential schedule problems, just like the ones for typos in Microsoft Word. When you right-click a cell with a red squiggly line, you can open the Task Inspector to see what the fuss is about or choose the action you want to perform from the shortcut menu.

Note: The Task Inspector also checks your schedule for ways to improve it. For example, if it sees a task that could start earlier, the program draws a green squiggly line under the Start date value. Make decisions about schedule optimizations in the same way you use Task Inspector to correct problems.

A schedule problem in one task often starts somewhere else in your project—in an element that controls the task's start date, like predecessors, calendars, or date constraints, to name a few. The Task Inspector lists all the factors that affect the task you select, so you can decide what to do. The Task Inspector can also help *after* you've begun project execution. If an important task is delayed, you can look at the factors that affect the task to identify items to change to get back on track. For instance, you might talk to the team leader for the task that's causing the delay, or the manager for a person who's unavailable.

If you see a red or green squiggly line below a task value, right-click the cell to display a shortcut menu, as shown in Figure 10-12. Here are some ways you can fix tasks with the Task Inspector and the commands on the shortcut menu:

- **Respect Links.** Because manually scheduled tasks start and finish when you tell them, those dates may conflict with the task dependencies you've defined. Even with auto-scheduled tasks, date constraints you set can conflict with task dependencies. If you want Project to use task dependencies to determine when to schedule tasks, choose Respect Links on the shortcut menu.

- **Ignore Problems for This Task.** Sometimes a problem that Project finds isn't really a problem. Say you schedule a task to occur over a weekend, and the person you've assigned has agreed to that schedule. Sure, you can change the resource's calendar, but it's easier to simply ignore the problem. In this case, choose Ignore Problems for This Task, and Project turns off the red squiggly line.

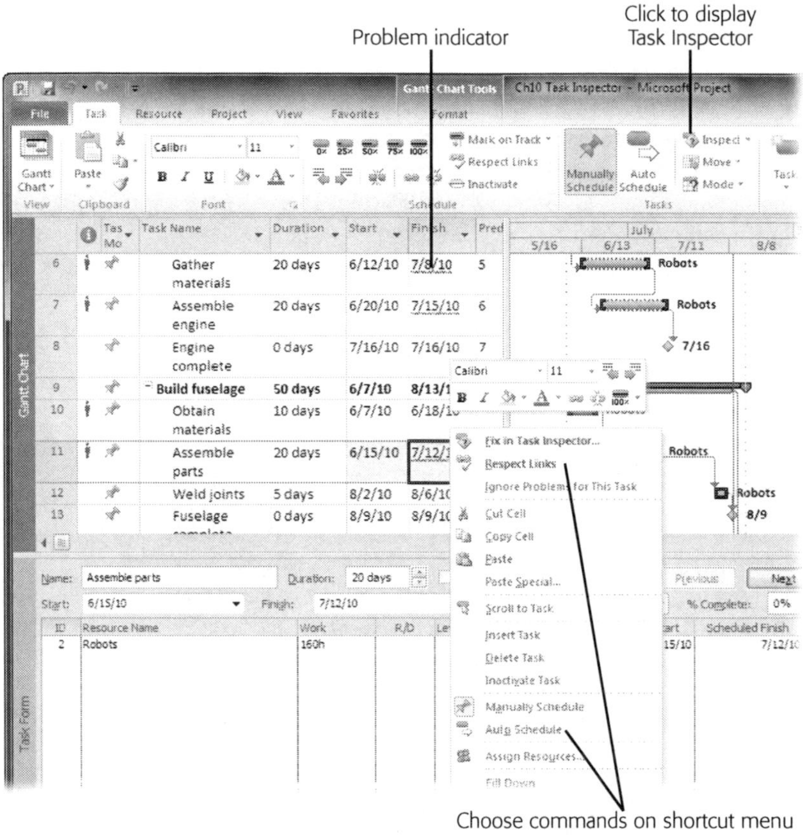

Problem indicator

Click to display
Task Inspector

Choose commands on shortcut menu

Figure 10-12:
*The solution to a
problem may be to
switch a task from
Manually Scheduled
to Auto Scheduled,
so Project can take
over calculating the
task's dates. To switch
the task mode, on
the shortcut menu,
choose Auto Sched-
ule. Other commands
on the shortcut menu
may help resolve a
problem as well, such
as Assign Resources
to shorten the task
or remove over-
allocations.*

- **Fix in Task Inspector.** If you aren't sure how to resolve a problem, choose Fix in Task Inspector to open the Task Inspector pane, shown in Figure 10-13. You can open the Task Inspector pane at any time by choosing Task→Tasks→Inspect. The first section of the Task Inspector displays the name of the selected task and the problems the Inspector identified, such as overallocations, resource calendar issues, predecessor conflicts, and so on. The second section provides commands you can use to correct the problem, like Respect Links and Auto Schedule for task scheduling problems or Increase Duration and Assign Resources for resource overallocations. To dig deeper into the source of the problem, look at the Factors Affecting Task section.

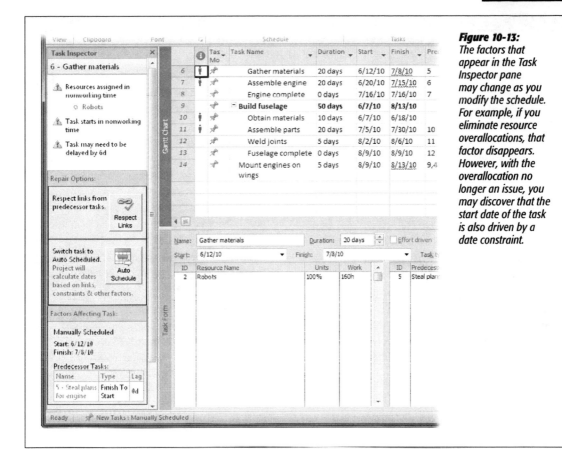

Figure 10-13:
The factors that appear in the Task Inspector pane may change as you modify the schedule. For example, if you eliminate resource overallocations, that factor disappears. However, with the overallocation no longer an issue, you may discover that the start date of the task is also driven by a date constraint.

- **Show ignored problems.** After you've fixed a slew of problems, you may decide to take another look at the problems you ignored. To restore problem indicators to the view, choose Task→Tasks. Click the down arrow to the right of Inspect and then, on the drop-down menu, choose Show Ignored Problems. The red squiggly lines reappear for problems you had previously ignored.

Building Reality into Assignments

A first-draft schedule almost always represents the way projects would go in an ideal world. But you live in the real world, and just as the jeans you buy never look like they do on the catalog model, your real-world project will have a few bumps and wrinkles. Understanding resource units (page 193) and calendars is only half the battle. You also have to figure out how to combine them to handle real-world resourcing situations. This section explains how to make Project's resource features model reality.

Editing Options

When you're busy editing tasks and assignments, you may want Project to behave differently during editing sessions. Choose File→Options. Then, in the Project Options dialog box, click Advanced and scroll to the Edit section. Although the default options are set to the way most people use them, here are the options and how you can change them:

- **Allow cell drag and drop.** This checkbox is turned on initially, so you can drag values from one set of fields or rows to another. If you turn this checkbox off, you can't use your mouse to move or copy values, although you can still use the Cut, Copy, and Paste commands.

- **Move selection after enter.** Project turns this checkbox on by default, so when you press Enter, the program automatically selects the field below the current field. That's handy when you're building a task list by typing one task name after another in the Name column of a task table. If you prefer to type the task name, press Enter, and then press the right arrow to move to the Duration field, turn this checkbox off to tell Project to stay in the same field when you press Enter.

- **Edit directly in cell.** This checkbox is also turned on by default, so you can edit values in the Entry bar or directly in a table cell. However, if you find that you're editing cell values inadvertently, turn this checkbox off. Then you can edit values only in the Entry Bar or in fields within a dialog box like Task Information. (If the Entry bar isn't visible, choose File→Options. In the Project Options dialog box, click Display and, below the "Show these elements" heading, turn on the "Entry bar" check box.)

The Edit section also has the "Ask to update automatic links" option, which is initially turned on and asks if you want to update links to other files (page 546).

Replacing Generic Resources with Real Ones

Sometimes you know the type of resource you need, but you don't know exactly who you'll get. In these situations, you can define a resource based on the role that resource plays, such as database designer, painter, or programmer's muse. Later on, when the powers that be have assigned a real person to your project, you can replace the generic resource with one that represents the flesh-and-blood team member. The Assign Resources dialog box makes it easy:

1. **In a task view like the Gantt Chart, apply the Entry table by right-clicking the cell at the intersection of the column headings and the row ID numbers and then choosing Entry on the drop-down list.**

    The Entry table includes the Resource Names field.

2. **Filter the task list to show only tasks assigned to the generic resource you want to replace.**

    Click the down arrow to the right of the Resource Names column heading and then turn off the Select All checkbox. Turn on the checkbox for the generic resource, such as "Marketing Lead."

3. Turn off summary tasks by choosing Format→Show/Hide and then turning off the Summary Task checkbox.

   Only subtasks appear in the task list.

4. Select the tasks that appear in the table by dragging over their ID cells.

   Project changes the background for the selected tasks to black.

5. Choose Resource→Assignments→Assign Resources.

   The Assign Resources dialog box opens.

6. Select the generic resource you want to replace, and then click Replace.

   The Replace Resource dialog box opens, as shown in Figure 10-14.

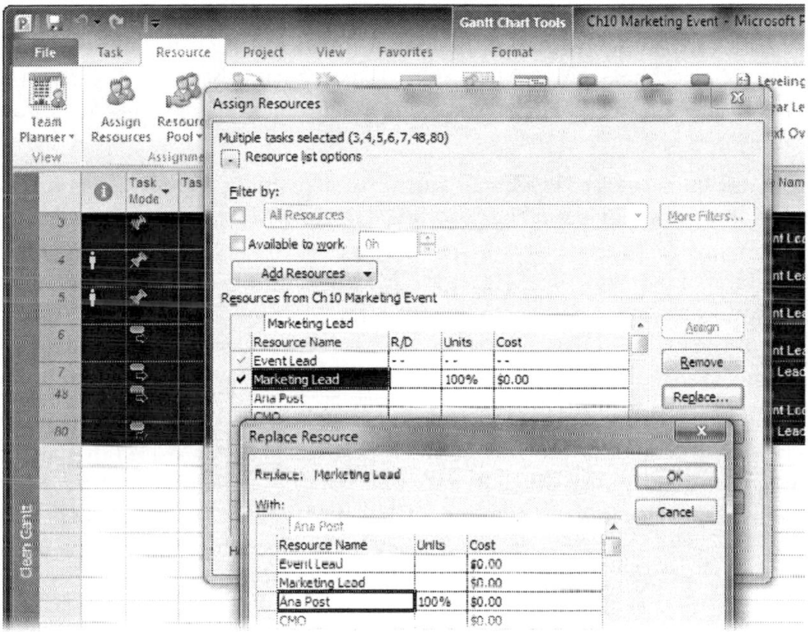

Figure 10-14:
You can select only one resource in the Replace Resource dialog box. Type the Units that you want to use for the assignment. When you click OK, Project replaces the generic resource in all selected tasks with the named resource using the units you specified.

7. In the Resource Name column, select the named resource you want to use. Type the units to assign the resource, and then click OK.

   Project replaces the generic resource with the named resource in every selected task.

8. Repeat steps 2 through 7 for each generic resource in your project.

   To see whether you've reassigned all your generic resources, display the Resource Usage view (choose Resource→View→Resource Usage). The generic resources in the project shouldn't have any tasks listed below their names.

Note: Project Server includes the Build Team from Enterprise feature, which lets you replace a resource in a project with one from the Enterprise Resource list.

Assigning Part-Time Workers

Part-time workers don't work full days, so they take longer to finish tasks. Someone working half-days takes twice as long, because you get only 4 person-hours a day, instead of 8. To make sure you don't overassign part-timers, you must adjust the resources' maximum units and, in some cases, their calendars. Then, when you assign them to tasks, Project automatically doles out time based on their availability.

Here's how you handle part-time workers in Project:

- **Set the resource's maximum units.** When someone works the same amount of time each workday, change the Max. Units field (page 195) in the Resource Sheet. Click the resource's Maximum Units cell, and then type the percentage that the person works. For example, the maximum available units for someone who works half-time is 50%.

- **Change the resource's work schedule.** Project assumes that resources are available every workday up to the percentage in their Maximum Units cells. Some part-time schedules are a combination of a few full days and more days off. For this kind of part-time work, leave the Maximum Units field alone, because the person works 100% of the day on work days. To model a part-time schedule like 3 days on and 4 days off, change the resource's calendar instead (page 249). Simply change the resource's work week to set more days to nonworking time.

- **Assign a part-time worker to a task.** Whether you modify maximum units, the resource calendar, or both, assigning a part-time worker is no different from assigning a full-time person. Project automatically fills in the resource's Maximum Units value in the assignment's Units field, whether the percentage is 20%, 50%, or 100%. To assign the resource at a lower percentage, type the percentage in the assignment's Units field (page 204).

Project calculates the duration of a task based on the resource units assigned to the task and the resource's calendar. If the resource calendar includes a vacation the first week of June, Project assigns the resource at the assignment units, but skips the week that the resource is absent.

Modeling Productivity in Project

People are usually optimistic about how much they can get done in a given amount of time. (Have you ever had a "5-minute" trip to the grocery store turn into 2 hours?) In the project world, a 40-hour work week does *not* mean people spend 40 hours on their project assignments. Filling out paperwork, attending meetings, and keeping up with gossip can eat into productive time by as much as 25 percent a day. Widely distributed teams—whether they're scattered around the world or throughout a skyscraper—often require more time because of time spent communicating, waiting for someone else to complete a task, or even riding elevators. Working on too many simultaneous tasks also hurts productivity, as the box on page 260 explains.

If you assign resources at 100 percent, one of two outcomes is likely:

- **People have to work longer days to stay on schedule.** Some folks work longer to finish their tasks according to the schedule, but this won't last. Eventually, low morale and exhaustion take their toll, and work starts to slip.

- **The project falls behind.** Expecting 100 percent productivity usually leads to late deliveries. People work the normal workday, but their project work gets only a portion of that day, and durations increase beyond what you estimated. For example, a task that requires 24 person-hours takes 3 days when resources work at 100 percent. Reduce the units to 75 percent, and the duration increases to 4 days, 33 percent longer.

You can tackle the productivity problem in a couple of ways in Project. Either approach provides a more realistic estimate of project duration. The one you choose depends on whether or not you want to publicize productivity. Here are the two ways to make a Project schedule reflect your project team's productivity:

- **Shorten the standard Project workday.** If non-project work consumes 25 percent of each day, an 8-hour day contains only 6 productive hours, and a work week is 30 productive hours. The fastest way to come up with realistic task durations is to reset Project's standard 8-hour workday to fewer hours, as shown in Figure 10-15.

  The downside to shortening the Project workday is that the productivity problem is hidden within Project's calculations. Resources look like they're assigned 100%, but Project assigns them only 6 hours of work a day. To make productivity visible in an attempt to correct the problem, use the next method instead.

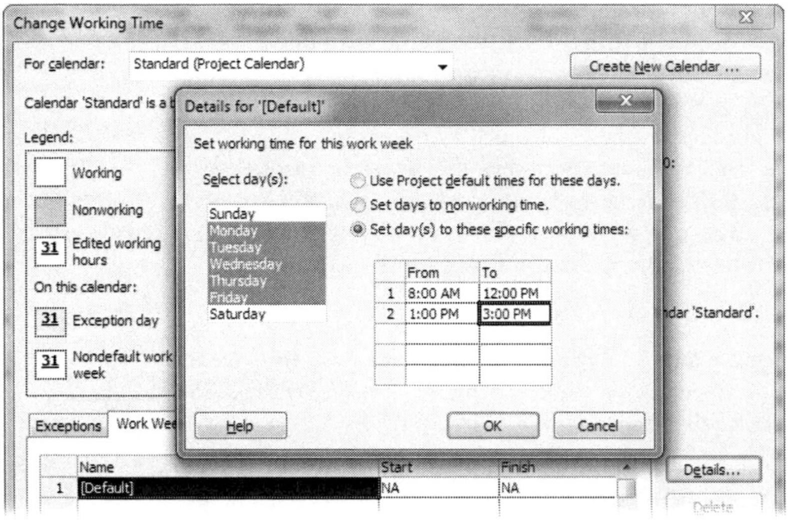

Figure 10-15:
Shortening the workday takes two steps. First, you must change the "Hours per day" and "Hours per week" calendar options (page 139), so Project translates the person-hours into the correct duration in days and weeks. For example, you may change "Hours per day" to 6 and "Hours per week" to 30. You also redefine the standard work week in the project calendar. For example, to snip 2 hours off each day, set each day's end time 2 hours earlier, as shown here.

- **Assign resources at lower units.** To assign resources at their real percentage of productive time, in the Task Form Units field, fill in the lower percentage. For example, to schedule team members for 6 hours of work each day, in the Task Form, set the resource's Units field (page 207) to 75%.

  Tired of changing the units in every assignment? Go to the Resource Sheet (Resource→View→Resource Sheet), and then change the Maximum Units values to 75%. Then Project automatically assigns resources at 75%. Moreover, when you look for resource overallocations (page 260), Project shows resources assigned at more than 75% as overallocated.

Note: If you use lower assignment units, a stakeholder is bound to ask why people aren't working full-time. That's your cue to talk about the drain on productivity and recommend your brilliant plan for increasing productive time. To get some ideas for your plan, read *Slack: Getting Past Burnout, Busywork, and the Myth of Total Efficiency* by Tom DeMarco (Broadway, 2002).

Adjusting Tasks for Resource Capability

Occasionally, you get someone who polishes off work like a dog does an untended plate of hamburgers. Other times, you may use trainees who take longer and need more guidance. Most organizations don't reward fast workers by letting them go home early, and you can't make newbies work around the clock to keep up. The only way to account for people's appetite for work is by changing the person-hours you assign to people. When you change the task work or duration, Project recalculates the other value (page 223).

If you change work or duration due to people's capabilities, keep track of your original estimate, in case you switch resources again.

Consider adding a note to the task to explain the adjustments you made. In a task-oriented view, right-click the task and then, from the shortcut menu, choose Notes. When the Task Information dialog box opens, the Notes tab is visible. Type the note, and then click OK.

Tip: If potential names for an assignment go back and forth faster than an Olympic ping-pong match, consider creating tasks for each potential resource. Activate the task with the current contender and make the other tasks with alternate resources inactive, as described on page 353.

Balancing Workloads

When you overload your resources with work, the project finish date may look good, but it's bogus, because your resources are *overallocated*. In other words, giving people 20 hours' worth of work a day doesn't mean they're going to *do* it. On the other hand, resources who don't have *enough* work cause a whole other set of problems. Besides distracting the people who are working full out, these resources could cost money without delivering results—like the networking consultant who sits idle while your IT staff puts out the fire in the server room. The ideal workload is when you assign your resources at exactly—or as close as possible to—the amount of time they have to give.

Before you can call a schedule done, you must balance workloads so your assigned resources (people and equipment) are busy, but not burning out. The first step is recognizing the problem, and Project makes it easy to find assignment peaks and valleys.

Then you have to correct the workload imbalances you find. Before you look for additional resources, you can try adjusting *work contours* (the pace at which work ramps up and down during an assignment), delaying assignments, or *leveling resources* (rescheduling tasks so that assigned resources aren't overallocated). This section describes how to spot resource allocation issues, and several ways to fix them. If these strategies don't help, you can always look for other available resources, or ask resources to work more.

When Multitasking Is Too Much

In Project, you can assign someone to as many simultaneous tasks as you want. Project doesn't complain until the total assigned units exceed the resource's Maximum Units percentage. In the real world, people need time to find where they left off and reacquaint themselves with the work every time they switch from one task to another. Each delay may be small, but they add up until your most productive resource is as slow as a Los Angeles rush hour.

The only way to prevent this problem is to limit the number of concurrent tasks people work on. Some folks can handle more tasks than others, but no more than three or four tasks at a time at most. Project doesn't have any tools specifically for finding multitasking, but you can get help from the Who Does What When report. It groups all the tasks

that one person works on. You can scan each time period looking for too many tasks with hours assigned to the same resource. Several tasks during the same time period may not be a multitasking problem. For example, if you analyze the project week by week, someone could have six tasks, but only one or two a day. To generate the Who Does What When report, follow these steps:

1. Choose Project→Report→Reports.

2. In the Reports dialog box, double-click Assignments.

3. In the Assignment Reports dialog box, double-click Who Does What When. When the report appears on the Print tab of the Backstage view, look for periods in which the resource has hours assigned to several tasks. See Chapter 17 to learn more about reports.

Finding Resource Over- and Under-Allocations

Assigning resources to tasks is like using a credit card. While you're dealing out time, you don't see the deficit you're running up. The Gantt Chart and other task-oriented views that you use when assigning resources show the assignments for the current task, but not all the other tasks a resource may work on, so you can't see when you've assigned someone too much time overall. Project's resource- and assignment-oriented views provide a better picture of resource allocation. This section identifies the talents of different views and tools for finding overallocations.

Finding overallocated resources in the Resource Sheet

For a sneak peak at the workload balancing ahead, the Resource Sheet (Resource→ View→Resource Sheet) tells you whether or not resources are overallocated—but not when, how much, or on which assignments. If a resource is overallocated at least once during the project, all the text in the resource's row is bold and red, and the Indicators column displays a yellow diamond with an exclamation mark. You can quickly spot the resources whose assignments you need to revise.

Tip: The Overallocated Resources filter is another helpful tool for finding resources with too much work, regardless which resource view you use (Resource Sheet, Resource Usage, and so on). This filter displays only resources that are overallocated at some point during a project. Choose View→Data, click the Filter down arrow, and then choose Overallocated Resources. You can apply this filter to any view, from the Resource Sheet to the Resource Graph to the Resource Allocation view (page 263). To display all resources again, in the Filter drop-down list, choose [No Filter].

Finding overallocations with the Team Planner

The Team Planner view, new in Project 2010, makes it easy to spot overallocated resources. Resource names appear in red in the Resource Name column, and overallocated assignments in the timescale have red stripes at the top and bottom of the assignment bars. Especially for smaller projects, Team Planner offers easy ways to remove overallocations. You can reassign a task by dragging it to a resource who doesn't have anything to do, or right-clicking the taskbar and choosing Reassign To on the shortcut menu. Or you can drag a task to a date when the assigned resource isn't busy. See Figure 9-8 on page 215 to see what overallocations look like in Team Planner.

Tip: Team Planner also has a Prevent Overallocations setting, which won't let you create overallocations in the first place. When the Team Planner view is visible, simply choose Format→Schedule→Prevent Overallocations. Then if you try to assign a task to a resource who's fully allocated, Project flings the task to the next available spot in the resource's calendar.

Finding overallocations with the Resource Graph

For analyzing each resource's overallocations individually, the Resource Graph plots allocation over time, resource by resource. A vertical bar graphically indicates the selected resource's allocation in one time period, while a horizontal line represents the resource's maximum units. When the vertical bar is higher than the horizontal line, as illustrated in Figure 10-16, the resource is overallocated. Project emphasizes the overallocation by coloring the portions above the line bright red.

In the Resource Graph, you don't see the assignments for the allocated time. But you can find the problem time periods and then switch to the Resource Usage or Resource Allocation views (page 265) to correct the issue.

To open the Resource Graph view, choose Resource→View→Resource Graph (or to display the Resource Graph in the bottom pane of a window, choose View→Split View, turn on the Details checkbox, and then choose Resource Graph).

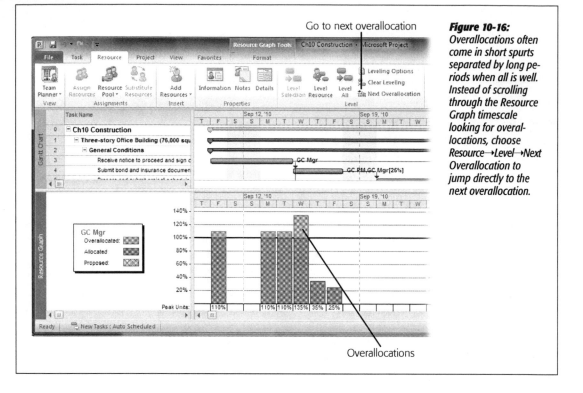

Go to next overallocation

Figure 10-16:
Overallocations often come in short spurts separated by long periods when all is well. Instead of scrolling through the Resource Graph timescale looking for overallocations, choose Resource→Level→Next Overallocation to jump directly to the next overallocation.

Overallocations

Here's how to use the Resource Graph to find overallocations:

- **Choose a resource.** The Resource Graph shows the allocations for just one resource at a time. The current resource appears in the Resource Graph's left pane with a legend for the information that's displayed in the timescale. Press Page Down to display the next resource, or Page Up to view the previous resource. You can also click to the right or left of the horizontal scroll bar.

- **Change the timescale.** Sometimes, resources are overallocated for 1 or 2 days but have enough time for assignments over the course of a week or so. Before you start rearranging short overallocations, increase the Resource Graph time period to see whether the overallocations work themselves out. To lengthen the time period, in the status bar, drag the Zoom slider to the left to switch from days to weeks and so on. To shorten the time period, drag to the right.

- **Graph other values.** Although percentage allocation values make overallocations stand out, the Resource Graph can show other values, such as Work (the hours of assigned work), Overallocation (only the hours beyond the resource's maximum units), Remaining Availability, and so on. For example, after you use the Resource Graph to find an overallocation, you can switch to Remaining Availability to locate someone to take over the extra hours. Right-click the Resource Graph timescale, and then, from the shortcut menu, choose the field you want to display in the graph.

Viewing assignments with the Resource Usage view

To see the assignments that contribute to allocation, turn to the Resource Usage view. For example, the Resource Graph may show that your labor crew is overallocated the week of May 20. The Resource Usage view lists all the labor crew assignments so you can see the hours assigned during that week.

To display this view, choose Resource→View→Resource Usage. The left pane of the Resource Usage view lists each resource in your project and displays the tasks to which the resource is assigned underneath the resource's name. The timescale on the right side of the view shows the assigned hours during each time period, as shown in Figure 10-17.

Like other views, Resource Usage highlights overallocated resources with bolded red text. In the Resource Usage view time-phased data, hours that exceed the resource's maximum available time appear in red, too. For example, if a single task exceeds the resource's available time in one period, the hours in the cell are red. However, if several tasks contribute to the overallocation, the individual task hours may be black, but the total hours in the resource row are red.

Note: The Next Overallocation command starts looking for overallocations from the currently selected date and assignment. If the command doesn't find any overallocations, be sure to search from the beginning by selecting the first cell in the first row. In the Resource Usage view, press Ctrl+Home to move to the first cell in the current row. Then press Ctrl+up arrow to move to the first cell in the first row.

To see overallocations more easily, modify the Resource Usage view in the following ways:

- **Show only overallocated resources.** To the right of the Resource Name column heading, click the Filter down arrow and then choose Filter→Overallocated Resources. Only resources with overallocations appear in the left pane. Alternatively, you can choose View→Data and then, in the Filter drop-down list, choose Overallocated Resources.

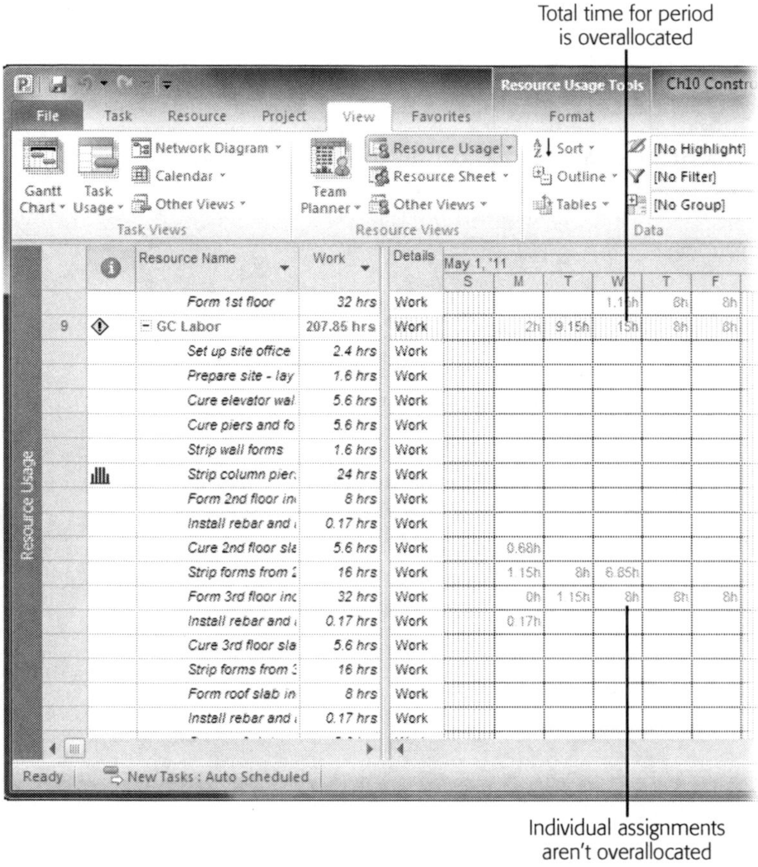

Total time for period
is overallocated

Figure 10-17:
*If you choose Resource→
Level→Next Overalloca-
tion on the ribbon, Project
looks first for additional
overallocations during the
same time period, working
its way down through
additional resources. Only
after searching the time
period does Project move
to the next time period.*

Individual assignments
aren't overallocated

- **Display other fields.** Other fields help you figure out how to correct overallocations. For example, the Overallocation field tells you exactly how many hours
are beyond the resource's availability. The Remaining Availability field helps
you find resources who have enough time to take over the extra hours. In the
time-phased data, right-click anywhere in the Details column. On the shortcut
menu, choose the fields you want. You can turn on as many fields as you want
at the same time. (Remember, the Assign Resources dialog box lets you look for
resources with sufficient time and the right skills, as described on page 343.)

Viewing and leveling assignments in the Resource Allocation view

The Resource Allocation view displays the Resource Usage view in the top pane so you can see the tasks that overallocate a resource. In the bottom pane, the Leveling Gantt view appears, so you can manually add a leveling delay to resolve over-allocations, as shown in Figure 10-18. Choose View→Resource Views→Other Views→More Views. In the More Views dialog box, double-click Resource Allocation.

The table in the Leveling Gantt chart includes the Leveling Delay field. If you want to delay tasks to remove conflicts, type the length of delay in the Leveling Delay cell, for example, type *1* to push the task start out by 1 elapsed day (leveling delay uses elapsed time units, which means it doesn't differentiate between working time and nonworking time).

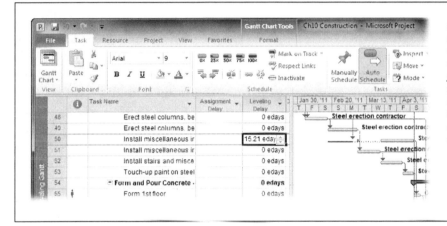

Figure 10-18:
Leveling delay changes the start date for a task, not just the overallocated resource's assignment. See page 271 for instructions on delaying individual assignments.

Getting hard copies of allocation reports

A few built-in Project reports show assigned work, so you can spend a relaxing evening of resource management with paper and a highlighter. Reports are also helpful for hashing out assignments at team meetings.

Tip: If you prefer information the way it looks in the Resource Usage view or any other view, print the *view* instead of a report. To print a view, display it and then choose File ►Print. In the Print page of the Backstage view, choose the printer, page range, and dates, as you would for any printout (page 455).

The Who Does What When report and the Resource Usage report both show tasks assigned to resources and assigned hours by time period. The Who Does What When report initially shows day-by-day assignment hours (for work resources only). The Resource Usage report shows week-by-week assignments (for all resources). However, you can edit the reports to use other time periods and the resources you want.

Here are the steps to create a week-by-week resource usage report for overallocated work resources:

1. **Choose Project→Reports→Reports.**

   The Reports dialog box appears.

2. **In the Reports dialog box, click Workload, and then click Select.**

   The Workload Reports dialog box appears.

3. **Click Resource Usage, and then click Edit.**

   The Crosstab Report dialog box opens. For the full scoop on customizing reports, see Chapter 17.

4. **If you want to save a customized version of the report, in the Name box, type a new name for the report, such as** *Overallocated Usage*.

   If you don't change the name, Project saves your changes to the built-in Resource Usage report definition. If you want the original report definition back, you can copy if from your global template (page 669).

5. **To include only overallocated resources in the report, in the Filter drop-down list, choose Overallocated Resources, as shown in Figure 10-19.**

   To change the time period represented by each column, in the Column boxes, choose Weeks, Months, and so on. The report shows work hours initially. In the Row drop-down list, you can choose another field to display, such as Overallocation.

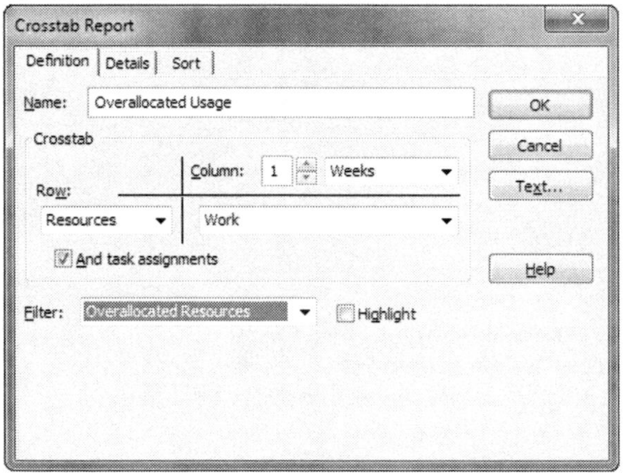

Figure 10-19:
The Crosstab Report dialog box offers additional report settings on the Details and Sort tabs. For example, on the Details tab, you can specify whether to show totals for rows and columns, and where to place gridlines in the report. On the Sort tab, you can specify how the resources are sorted. Initially, the report sorts resources by ID, but you can choose Group to keep related resources together.

6. **Click OK.**

   The Crosstab dialog box closes and nothing else happens. At this point, all you've done is edit the report definition.

7. To run the report, in the Workload Reports dialog box, click Select.

   Project displays the report in the Print page of the Backstage view (page 456).

Adjusting Assignments to Correct Allocations

Project offers several ways to even out workloads. The easiest way to eliminate overallocations is to ask resources if a heavier schedule is OK with them. Pragmatically, you should consider this approach only when overallocations are small and short-lived.

Adding more resources, or replacing a resource with someone who has more time, is the next best thing. Of course, you must have another resource available with the right skills. When longer hours or more resources aren't an option, delaying assignments may do the trick. For example, when a resource has two assignments overlapping by a day, delaying one of those assignments by 1 day solves the problem. In this section, you'll learn all these techniques, as well as how contouring work hours can smooth out assignment conflicts.

Accepting overallocations

When a resource is overallocated by a small percentage for a short period of time (for example, no more than 20 percent and 2 weeks), the simplest solution is to leave the assignment exactly as it is—as long as the person is willing to work a few long days. The schedule shows the assignment as an overallocation, but you can add a note to the task that documents your agreement with the resource, as described in the box on page 267. Be aware that scheduling longer hours during project planning is a risky move. If tasks take more time than you estimated, your resources are already maxed out and you'll have to use other strategies to prevent delays (page 268).

UP TO SPEED

Writing Notes to Yourself

Schedule-tweaking often requires special arrangements with team members and stakeholders. Fine-tuning assignments may involve research like analyzing work peaks and valleys. Task notes are a great way to store this information so you don't forget it. If a question arises later, you can just look at the notes attached to the task to find your answer.

To attach a note to a task, follow these steps:

1. In the Gantt Chart view or another task-oriented view, right-click the task and choose Notes from the shortcut menu. The Task Information dialog box opens to the Notes tab.

2. In the Notes box, type to your heart's content. The toolbar within the Notes box includes buttons for changing the font, setting the justification, creating bulleted lists, and inserting objects from another program (like including an Excel spreadsheet or an email message).

3. Click OK. A notepad icon appears in the task's Indicators cell. Position the pointer over the Note icon, and Project displays the beginning of the note. To see the entire note, double-click the Notes icon, and Project opens the Task Information dialog box to the Notes tab.

Say you want to formally schedule a resource to work longer days, but you don't want assignments to show up as overallocations. Don't change a resource's maximum units in the Resource Sheet. Maximum units redefine the number of hours the resource devotes for the *entire* project. Instead, modify the resource's calendar to lengthen specific workdays. For example, if you ask someone to work a few weeks of longer days, you can create work weeks (page 240) to reflect that. For a few long days, creating a calendar exception is easier.

Tip: If resources cost more when they work beyond the normal workday, you can account for the extra cost by assigning work hours specifically as overtime (in the Overtime Work field). Project calculates the cost of regular work hours by multiplying those hours by the Standard Rate value. The cost of overtime is the overtime hours multiplied by the Overtime Rate value.

Working with overtime is tedious, so you should use it only if resources cost more after hours and if you find during project execution that you need more hours to finish tasks on time.

Eliminating overallocations with Team Planner

In Team Planner, you can easily reassign or reschedule tasks to eliminate overallocations. If two or more concurrent tasks eat up too much of a resource's time, red stripes appear at the top and bottom of the overlapping task bars. Here's how to remove overallocations in Team Planner:

- **Reassign a task to another resource.** To reassign a task to a resource with available time, drag the task bar to the row for the new resource. or right-click the task bar and choose Reassign To on the shortcut menu..

- **Reschedule the task to a different date.** You can reschedule a task by dragging it to a new date in the timescale. To move the task into the past or future by a period of time, choose Task→Tasks→Move. In the drop-down menu, choose a command, as shown in Figure 10-20. In Team Planner, you can drag each assignment independently. However, if more than one resource is assigned to a task, you usually want to reschedule both assignments. To select all the assignments for a task, right-click one of the task's assignment bars and then, from the shortcut menu, choose Select All Assignments on This Task.

Tip: Dragging a task to a new date is often the easiest way to remove an overallocation when tasks are manually scheduled. However, dragging auto-scheduled tasks in the timeline creates date constraints (page 166), which limit Project's ability to calculate start and finish dates. Take care not to drag auto-scheduled tasks to different dates in Team Planner or any other view.

- **Reschedule the task to when a resource is available.** If a resource works on a hodgepodge of short assignments, finding adjacent time for a longer assignment is almost impossible. Instead, you can tell Project to chop the assignment up and slide it into a resource's open slots. Select the assignment you want to reschedule. Then choose Task→Tasks→Move→When Resources Are Available.

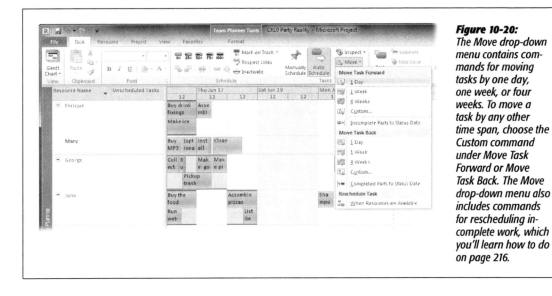

Figure 10-20:
The Move drop-down menu contains commands for moving tasks by one day, one week, or four weeks. To move a task by any other time span, choose the Custom command under Move Task Forward or Move Task Back. The Move drop-down menu also includes commands for rescheduling incomplete work, which you'll learn how to do on page 216.

Replacing resources

If you have resources who can pinch hit, you can reassign only the overallocated hours or an entire assignment—Project doesn't care which. Whichever hours you want to reassign, you use the Assign Resources dialog box. (Chapter 9 includes instructions for adding and removing resources to tasks.)

Here's how you reassign a portion of work with the Assign Resources dialog box:

1. **Choose Resource→Assignments→Assign Resources.**

   The Assign Resources dialog box opens.

2. **In the Gantt Chart view (or any other task-oriented view), select the task you want to modify.**

   The resources already assigned to the task appear at the top of the list, preceded by a checkmark.

3. **To switch a portion of the work to another resource, click the assigned resource's Units cell, and then type the new percentage.**

   For example, if units are 20 percent too high, you can remove that by reducing the units from 80 percent to 60 percent.

4. **Click the Units cell for the resource you want to add to the task, and then type the percentage to assign. Press Enter or click outside the Units cell.**

   Project updates the existing assignment. The newly assigned resource pops up to the top of the list with the other assigned resources and has a checkmark to the left of its name.

You can add as many additional resources as you want. The Assign Resources dialog box includes features to help you find resources with the right characteristics, as well as enough free time to take on the new assignment (page 209).

If you want to replace one resource with another, follow these steps:

1. **With the Assign Resources dialog box open, select the task you want to modify.**

   The assigned resources for the selected task appear at the top of the Resources table, with checkmarks next to them.

2. **Select the assigned resource you want to replace.**

   Click the resource's name—not the checkmarked cell. You can replace only one resource at a time.

3. **Click Replace.**

   The Replace Resource dialog box appears (Figure 10-21). The Replace label at the top of the dialog box shows the resource you want to replace. The With table lists all the resources in your project.

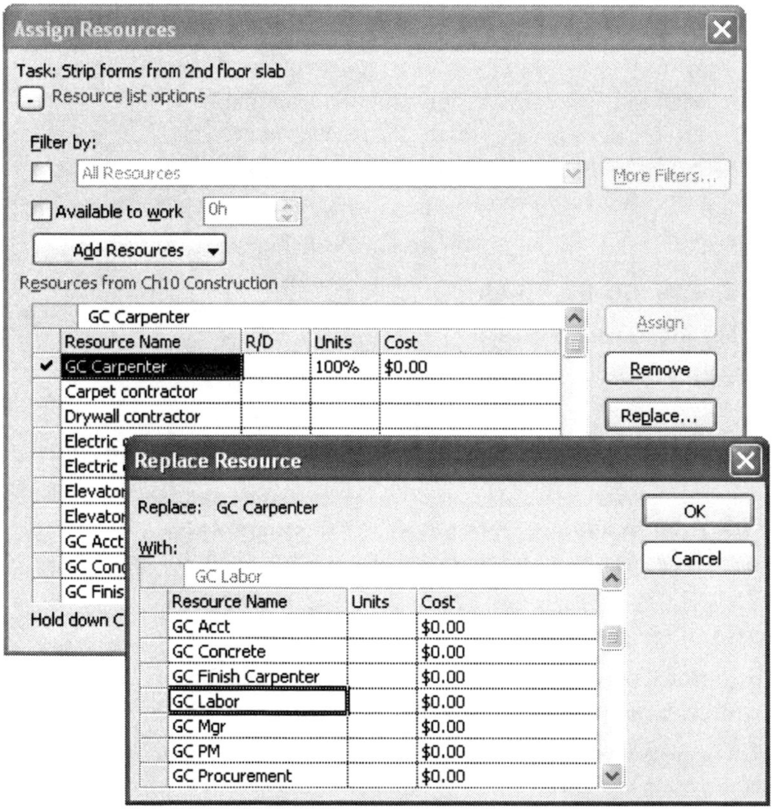

Figure 10-21:
You can assign different units for a replacement resource, for instance, if the replacement isn't as productive as the person you're replacing. Before you click OK, select the replacement's Units cell and then type the percentage you want to assign.

4. **Select the replacement resource, and then click OK.**

    Project swaps the original resource with the replacement, and assigns the units for the original resource (or the units you typed) to the replacement.

Delaying assignments

When tasks overlap, one solution is to delay the second task so the assigned resources can work on the tasks one after the other. You can manually add delays to tasks and assignments with the help of a few Project views.

Note: Project has a leveling feature, which calculates delays and splits for you, but it can be challenging to master, as you'll learn on page 275.

Project offers two types of delays:

*   **Leveling delay.** This type of delay applies to tasks; it pushes out the start date for the task and all its resource assignments. It's meant specifically for removing resource overallocations. With the Leveling Delay field, you can remove all leveling delays by choosing Resource→Level→Clear Leveling.

Note: A leveling delay isn't the same as lag time. Lag time is the delay between the end of one task and the start of another—for example, waiting 5 minutes after starting a game of hide and seek so your playmates have time to hide. Lag time remains in place regardless of resource availability.

---

*   **Assignment delay.** This type of delay applies to a single assignment within a task. Suppose you have a security consultant coming in to help lock down your site. However, your employees have prep work to do before the consultant can get started. You can assign everyone to the same "Try hacking into office" task but delay the consultant's assignment by 5 days.

To delay an entire task using leveling delay, do the following:

1. **Choose View→Resource Views→Other Views→More Views. In the More Views dialog box, double-click Resource Allocation.**

    The Resource Usage view appears in the top pane, with the Leveling Gantt view in the bottom pane.

2. **In the Resource Usage pane, select the task you want to delay.**

    The Resource Usage pane shows assignments, whereas the Leveling Gantt Chart shows tasks. When you select an assignment in the top pane, the task to which that assignment belongs appears in the bottom pane.

3. **In the Leveling Gantt Chart view, in the Leveling Delay cell, type the length of time you want to delay the task.**

To delay the task by 2 days, type *2d*. Project replaces your entry with "2 edays," as shown in Figure 10-22. The "e" at the beginning stands for elapsed time, because the number of resources or the percentage they're assigned doesn't affect the delay. You want the task to start a specific amount of time later, and elapsed time does just that.

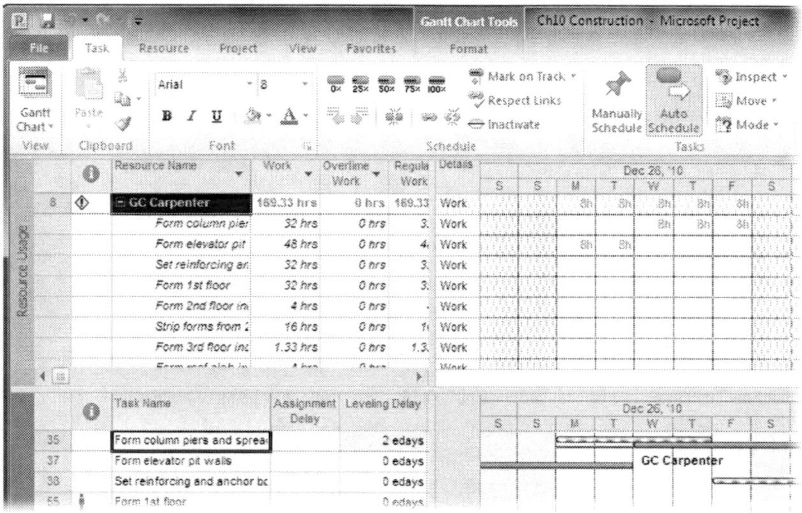

Figure 10-22:
If you type 2d in the Leveling Delay cell, Project replaces your entry with "2 edays." In the Leveling Gantt chart, Project shows leveling delays that you've added by a thin line at the start of a task.

To delay a single assignment within a task, add an assignment delay by doing the following:

1. **Display the Resource Allocation view (see page 265).**

The Resource Usage view appears in the top pane, with the Leveling Gantt view in the bottom pane.

2. **To add the Assignment Delay column to the Resource Usage pane, right-click the column header in the table area, choose Insert Column, and then, in the field name drop-down list, choose Assignment Delay.**

The new column appears to the left of the column you right-clicked.

If you use the Task Details Form to work on assignments, you can see the Assignment Delay field by right-clicking the Task Details Form table area and then choosing Schedule. The Delay column represents the Assignment Delay field.

3. Click the Assignment Delay cell for the assignment you want to delay, and then type the length of delay.

Unlike a leveling delay, you enter an assignment delay in regular days, not elapsed days.

Adjusting work contours

Most people don't leap out of bed in the morning raring to go. Nor do they work full speed up till the moment they close their eyes at night. Yet Project assumes that resources work full speed from the start to the finish of every task—unless you tell it otherwise. To reflect how work *really* gets done, you can apply work contours to reshape assignments. Work contours alter the amount of work assigned over the entire duration of assignments. Like people's energy, tasks tend to start slowly, run at their peak in the middle, and then trail off at the end. Work contours work only for auto-scheduled tasks, not manually scheduled ones.

Because work contours reduce the hours for some time periods (for example, the hours assigned on the first and last days of an assignment), they extend assignment duration and, in turn, task duration. The Flat contour, which is what Project applies automatically, schedules the same hours of work each day during an assignment, like 8 hours if a resource works 100 percent on the task. Every other contour type has high and low points; the highs schedule the same number of hours in a day as a Flat contour. Because the lows are less than a full schedule, the task ends up taking longer. Figure 10-23 shows how the Bell contour reschedules work hours for a task.

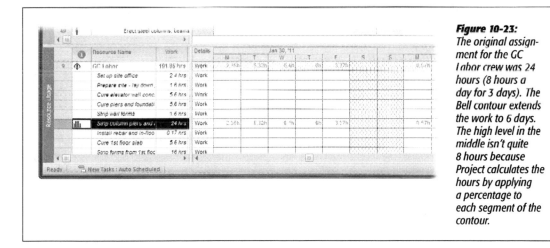

Figure 10-23:
The original assignment for the GC Labor crew was 24 hours (8 hours a day for 3 days). The Bell contour extends the work to 6 days. The high level in the middle isn't quite 8 hours because Project calculates the hours by applying a percentage to each segment of the contour.

The levels of work can take many shapes. Table 10-1 describes Project's work contours and what they're good for. The great thing about work contours is that you can assign resources to work on other tasks when other assignments don't demand their full attention. Work contours may be all you need to eliminate some overallocations.

Table 10-1. *Work contours and their uses.*

Contour name	Purpose
Flat	Project automatically assigns this constant contour to new tasks.
Back Loaded	This contour starts off slow and increases until the task is complete. For example, if your work hours correspond to your adrenaline level, the Back Loaded contour is perfect.
Front Loaded	This contour starts at full effort and decreases, which is like unpacking after a move. The first few days you spend all day unpacking boxes, but as time goes on, you unpack less and get back to your life.
Double Peak	Double Peak looks like the profile of a suspension bridge with a peak near each end and lower hours at the beginning, middle, and end. For example, a debugging task could have an early peak when hundreds of bugs need fixing, and a second peak to fix the bugs that stand between you and project acceptance.
Early Peak	This contour starts slowly but quickly peaks and then drops off. This gives you some time to get oriented to a task before really digging in.
Late Peak	Late Peak ramps up to a peak, but has a drop-off at the end for tying up loose ends.
Bell	The Bell is like a Back Loaded contour followed by a Front Loaded contour. The work continually increases to a peak and then gradually drops off.
Turtle	This contour has low levels at the beginning and the end with fully scheduled resources in the middle. It's probably the closest match to how tasks really proceed.

Here are the steps for applying a work contour to a resource assignment:

1. **Display the Task Usage or Resource Usage view by choosing View→Task Views→Task Usage or View→Resource Views→Resource Usage.**

   Because you must apply contours to assignments, you have to open either the Task Usage or the Resource Usage view to see assignments.

2. **In the view, double-click the assignment you want to contour.**

   In the Task Usage view, double-click the row for the resource assigned to the task. In the Resource Usage view, below the resource name, double-click the task name for the assignment you want to contour. (You can also select the name and then press Shift+F2.) The Assignment Information dialog box appears.

Tip: The time-phased portion of the view doesn't automatically show the time periods in which the assignment occurs, so you can't see the results of the contours you pick. To see them, select the task, and then choose Task→Editing→Scroll to Task. The time-phased portion of the view jumps to the dates that have work for the selected assignment.

---

3. In the General tab, in the Work Contour list, choose the contour, as illustrated in Figure 10-24, and then click OK.

   Project calculates the new work hours for each day and then applies them to the assignment. The Task Usage view shows the newly contoured hours.

Tip: Although you can't define custom contours, you can contour an assignment any way you want by manually changing the hours in the Task Usage time-phased data. For example, click an assignment cell and then type the new hours for that period. Continue changing cells until you've reassigned all the work hours. The drawback to this method is that you have to ensure that the hours you type add up to the original hours. When you manually edit work hours, you see the Edited Work icon (which looks like a bar chart with a pencil), in the Indicators cell.

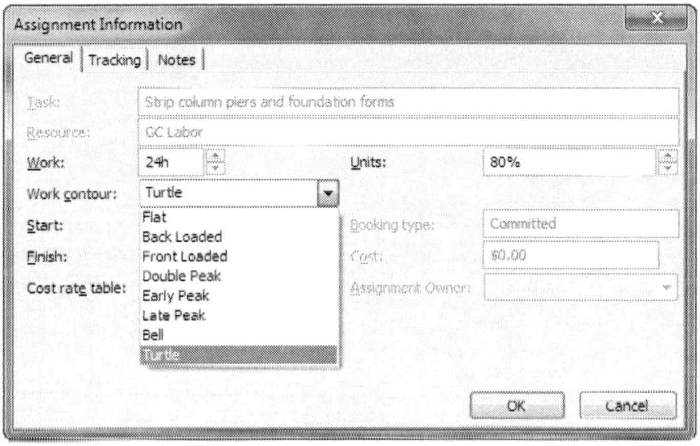

Figure 10-24:
When you apply a contour to an assignment, the Indicators column in a view table displays an icon for the applied contour. For example, if you use a Turtle contour, the Turtle contour icon appears in the Indicators cell for the assignment.

Leveling Assignments

The Level Resources feature can automatically eliminate overallocations by delaying or splitting tasks. If you try to level an entire project, you may set option after option, and prioritize tasks, only to find that leveling rarely does what you'd hoped for. It seems to delay the tasks you want to stay put and ignore tasks you'd like to delay. Moreover, Level Resources often splits tasks into a bazillion short pieces, so resources can multitask, as described in the box below. The good news is that Project 2010 lets you apply leveling to specific tasks or resources, so you don't have to level your entire project.

As you learned in "Delaying Assignments" on page 271, you can delay tasks so a resource can work on them in sequence. Leveling resources can delay tasks in the same way, but it can also split tasks (introduce small gaps in assigned work), so resources can divide their energy among multiple tasks. Either way, tasks finish later.

Using the Leveling Gantt view

Because Project's leveling prowess leaves something to be desired, don't assume that the leveling results are what you want. By displaying the Leveling Gantt view, shown in Figure 10-25, before you level assignments, you can see the results immediately—and undo them if they aren't what you want. To display the Leveling Gantt view, choose View→Task Views→Other Views→More Views, and then, in the More Views dialog box, double-click Leveling Gantt.

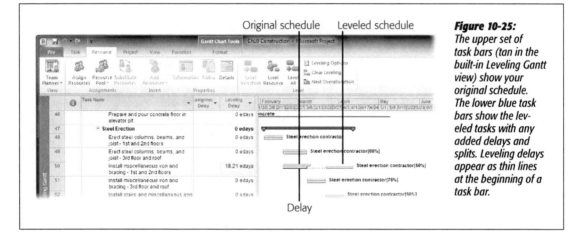

Figure 10-25:
The upper set of task bars (tan in the built-in Leveling Gantt view) show your original schedule. The lower blue task bars show the leveled tasks with any added delays and splits. Leveling delays appear as thin lines at the beginning of a task bar.

During leveling, Project looks for resource overallocations. For each one it finds, Project locates the offending tasks and decides whether to delay or split them to eliminate the overallocation. Unlike the techniques in your bag of tricks (reassigning or replacing resources, adjusting resource units, or contouring work), Level Resources can only delay or split tasks.

Note: Are you wondering how you delay and split tasks in a project scheduled from the finish date? You can't push the finish date later, so Project adds negative delays to tasks and changes the start dates. The result of leveling a from-finish-date project is moving the project start date earlier.

Leveling Multiple Projects

When you share resources among projects, overallocations from other projects can create delays and splits. But you can change task and project priority and relevel the assignments to try for better results. The trick is seeing which tasks are causing the problems.

To solve this problem, create a master project that contains all the projects that share the resources you use. This master project contains all the tasks that compete for your resources' time, so you can see why the delays and splits are there. To view tasks that share resources with tasks in other projects, follow these steps:

1. Choose File→Open, and then open the Project file for your resource pool (page 500).

2. In the Open Resource Pool dialog box, select the "Open resource pool read-write and all other sharer files in a new master project file…" option. Project creates a new master project, which contains the resource pool and all its sharer files.

3. Choose View→Window→Switch Window→Project 1 to view the new master project.

4. Choose View→Task Views→Other Views→More Views and then, in the More Views dialog box, double-click Leveling Gantt.

5. Choose View→Split View and then turn on the Details checkbox if necessary. In the Details drop-down list, choose Resource Usage.

6. Select a task that has a questionable split or delay. In the bottom pane, Project displays the resources assigned to the task and their assignments from all the sharer projects.

7. Choose Task→Editing→Scroll to Task.

8. In the Resource Usage pane, examine the competing assignments to see which split or delay should win.

Leveling resources

In Project 2010, you can level the entire project, tasks you select, or a single resource. By leveling several tasks that are all vying for the resource, or alternatively, leveling only the most in-demand resources, you can focus on the problematic portions of your project. Project automatically chooses popular settings in the Resource Leveling dialog box. In most situations, you might as well run Resource Leveling with these settings. You can undo the leveling if you don't like the results, but you can get some clues from the initial results to help you determine the settings you need. Here's how to level different parts of your project using the leveling settings currently in place:

- **Level an entire project.** Choose Resource→Level→Level All.

- **Level selected tasks.** Select the tasks you want to level, and then choose Resource→Level→Level Selection.

- **Level a resource.** Select the resource you want to level, and then choose Resource→Level→Level Resource.

If the results don't work, the quickest way to remove the leveling is to press Ctrl+Z to undo the leveling command. However, if you've leveled a task here and a resource there, you can remove all delays and splits by choosing Resource→Level→Clear Leveling.

Setting leveling options

Once you've gotten your feet wet with leveling, try other leveling options to fine-tune the results. For example, if you're happy to let overallocations work out over time, you can tell Project to look for overallocations over longer time periods. You can even tell Project which task characteristics to consider when choosing tasks to level, as shown in Figure 10-26.

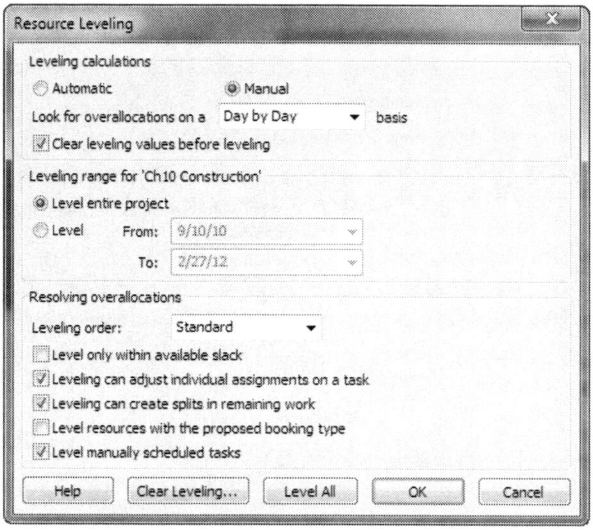

Figure 10-26:
Project remembers the leveling settings you choose until you change them.

Here's a guide to the options and settings in the Resource Leveling dialog box and how to use them:

- **Automatic or manual calculations.** At the top of the Resource Leveling dialog box, the Automatic option sounds like you can select it and sit back while Project does the tough leveling work. The Automatic option does just that, but it also tells Project to recalculate your schedule every time you make a change. Before you know it, the program slows to a crawl for all but the smallest projects. The Manual option is the better choice, because you control when Project relevels the schedule, and Project's performance doesn't deteriorate. Simply choose one of the leveling commands to calculate the schedule. You can review the changes—and undo them if they aren't what you want.

- **The overallocation time period.** To Project, one minute beyond a person's available time is an overallocation. But you know that an overallocation one day often balances out with available time on the next day, so longer time periods generally mean fewer overallocations to resolve. In the "Look for overallocations on a _ _ basis" box, choose the longest time period you're comfortable with. For most projects, Week by Week or Day by Day eliminate overallocations without too much leveling.

- **Remove previous leveling values.** Turn on the "Clear leveling values before leveling" checkbox to tell Project to remove any previous delays (added by you or Project) before starting the next round of leveling. If you level the entire project in one fell swoop, starting fresh each time is the best approach, because you can more clearly see the changes Project makes. If you've added leveling delays manually, turn off the "Clear leveling values before leveling" checkbox. Otherwise, Project removes your leveling delays along with any it's added. To clear leveling delays, you can click Clear Leveling in the Resource Leveling dialog box or choose Resource→Level→Clear Leveling.

- **How much of the project to level.** The "Leveling range" section includes the project name, which means that the option you select applies only to the current project. Project automatically selects the "Level entire project" option, which predictably looks at every task as a leveling candidate. To level only the tasks that occur during a date range, select the Level option, and then, in the From and To boxes, choose the start and end dates to level. If a phase runs from October 1 to March 1, level between those dates. (Of course, after leveling, Phase 1 will finish later than March 1.)

- **How Project decides which tasks to level.** Initially, Project uses predecessor dependencies, slack (how long a task can delay before it affects the end of the project), task dates, task constraints, and task priority to decide which tasks to level. That order is called Standard in the "Leveling order" drop-down list. If you choose Priority, Standard, then Project weights task priorities first and then the other criteria. Setting priorities is almost a necessity if you want Project to level tasks the way you expect. If you take the time to prioritize tasks, put those priorities to use by choosing Priority, Standard.

The reasoning behind Project's order of characteristics is that you can delay tasks that don't have successors without affecting other tasks, so they're the best candidates for leveling. When tasks have successors, the ones with the most slack can delay longer without delaying other tasks. Similarly, the later tasks start, the less they affect the project schedule. Task constraints make tasks less flexible schedule-wise, so Project leaves those tasks alone if possible.

The ID Only leveling order is usually not very helpful, because it levels tasks with higher ID numbers first.

- **Level within slack.** Project initially turns off the "Level only within available slack" checkbox, which is perfect during planning. This setting removes all overallocations and pushes the project finish date out as far as necessary. When you first level the project, you can calculate the finish date based on the resources you currently have. If the project finish date must be earlier, you can use several techniques to shorten the schedule (page 340).

  Once the project is underway, you can turn on this checkbox so Project levels tasks without delaying the overall finish date. However, using only slack typically doesn't resolve many overallocations.

- **Level individual assignments.** Project initially turns on the "Leveling can adjust individual assignments on a task" checkbox, which levels only assignments that overallocate resources. In reality, task duration may still change because of the splits and delays Project adds. If you turn this checkbox off, Project levels entire tasks.

- **Split remaining work.** The "Leveling can create splits in remaining work" checkbox controls whether Project splits tasks that have already started. When this checkbox is turned on, Project levels tasks that haven't started and adds splits to the remaining work for tasks in progress. With this checkbox turned off, Project delays assignments only until the resource can complete the work without stopping, which often pushes tasks out for exceedingly long periods of time.

- **Level proposed resources.** Proposed resources are resources you want to use but don't yet have permission for (page 191). If you turn on the "Level resources with the proposed booking type" checkbox, Project levels both committed and proposed resources to show what the project schedule would look like if you get everyone you ask for.

- **Level manually scheduled tasks.** Project turns this checkbox on automatically, which is exactly what you want, because manually scheduled tasks are more prone to overallocating resources than auto-scheduled ones.

Tip: Deadlines (page 169) in Project aren't carved in stone. Leveling resources can push a task beyond its deadline, because Project's leveling doesn't pay any attention to task deadlines. To prevent Project from leveling a task with a deadline, change its priority to 1,000 (page 282).

Leveling Skips Overallocations

After leveling, oftentimes the overallocations you wanted to remove are still there. Project doesn't level tasks and resources for a number of reasons.

Check for the following circumstances to see if they're preventing leveling:

- Project doesn't delay tasks that have Must Start On or Must Finish On date constraints. To level these tasks, you must first change the date constraint to a more flexible type, like As Soon As Possible (page 166).

- When you've scheduled a project from the start date, As Late As Possible date constraints prevent leveling. For projects scheduled from the finish date, As Soon As Possible date constraints inhibit leveling.

- Tasks with the highest priority of 1,000 (page 282) tell Project to go elsewhere to level resources. To level a task, change its priority to 999 or less. Conversely, if you manually add delays or splits to a task with a priority of 1,000, then the Clear Leveling command doesn't remove your manual changes.

- Project doesn't delay tasks that have already started, although it might split remaining work if the "Leveling can create splits in remaining work" checkbox is turned on.

- Setting a resource's Can Level field to No prevents Project from leveling that resource's overallocations. If leveling isn't working for any obvious reasons, add the Can Level field to the Resource Sheet (page 189), and then change the value to Yes.

- For tasks, the Level Assignments and Leveling Can Split fields control whether Project levels the tasks. If these fields are set to No, then Project doesn't level the tasks no matter which settings you choose in the Resource Leveling dialog box. Change values to Yes to allow leveling.

Prioritizing Projects and Tasks

In the real world, finish dates for some projects and tasks are more important than others—for example, when a big bonus hangs on meeting a key date. But Project has no way of knowing these priorities unless you tell it. The Priority field tells Project which projects and tasks have to stick to their schedules, and which ones it can delay during leveling.

Note: The Priority field affects only leveling. Project doesn't use this field during your regular scheduling activities. However, you can use Priority to focus on key tasks. For example, when you're trying to manage a schedule, you can filter or group the task list by priority to find the tasks to fast-track or *crash* (the project management term for spending more money to shorten duration, described on page 350).

Priority values go from 0 to 1,000. Project automatically assigns 500 (the middle-of-the-road value) to new tasks and projects. 1,000 is the highest priority, which means that Project doesn't delay projects or tasks with that value. If you don't want Project to level a task, just set its priority to 1,000. You can also change a task's Can Level field to No, but that field doesn't appear in any tables automatically (which often produces mystifying leveling behavior, as the box on page 281 explains).

You're not likely to use all 1,000 priorities, no matter how many projects and tasks you want to level. Whether you need three, five, or 20 levels, keep 500 as the standard setting. For example, if you use only three levels, you can use 1,000 for high priority (tasks that don't level), 500 for most tasks, and 0 for low priority. (You can use 499, 500, and 501 as well—or 400, 500, and 600—as long as you don't have to reassign all the tasks with a priority of 500.)

Changing task priority

The Priority field appears on the Task Information dialog box's General tab, which is fine if you plan to change the priority for only the most important tasks. Select a task, and then press Shift+F2. In the Task Information dialog box, select the General tab, and then, in the Priority field, type the number. However, if you prioritize many tasks, add Priority to a Gantt Chart table so you can quickly type, copy, and paste priority values to every task, as shown in Figure 10-27.

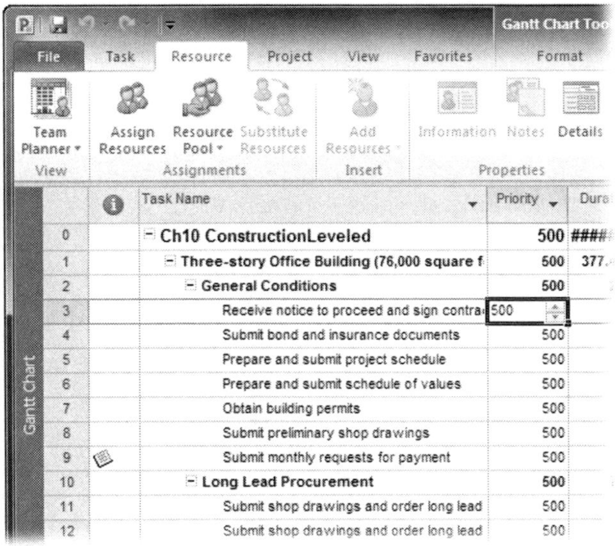

Figure 10-27:
When you click a Priority cell, you can click the up and down arrows to change the value by 20 points; from 500 to 520, for example. Typing is faster if you use values like 0 and 1,000.

To change task priorities, follow these steps:

1. **In the Gantt Chart or other task-oriented view, add the Priority field to the table.**

   Right-click the table heading, and then, on the shortcut menu, choose Insert Column. In the "Field name" drop-down list, choose Priority. Project inserts the Priority column into the table.

2. **Click a Priority cell, and then type the new value.**

   You can copy and paste values from one cell to another using Ctrl+C and Ctrl+V. If several adjacent tasks have the same priority, drag the black square from the bottom-right corner of the cell over the other Priority cells.

Changing project priority

If you have several subprojects in a master project, then entire projects may have a higher priority than the rest, like the presentations for a tradeshow that had better be ready when the show starts. Projects have a Priority field, too. Project priority is powerful, so use it sparingly. Project levels all tasks in lower-priority projects before the lowest-priority tasks in high-priority projects. Suppose a project has a priority of 800. Project avoids leveling a task with Priority 0 in that project before a task with a Priority of 900 in a 500-priority project.

Note: A priority of 1,000 is sacred, so tasks set to Priority 1,000 aren't leveled regardless of any priorities the projects have.

To change the priority for a project, follow these steps:

1. **Open the project, and then choose Project→Properties→Project Information.**

   The Project Information dialog box opens.

2. **In the Priority box, type the new priority, and then click OK.**

   The Project Information dialog box closes.

The next time you level projects, Project's leveling uses the new priority.

CHAPTER 11

Setting Up a Project Budget

Projects cost money. Whether you're planning a small department retreat at the end of next month or building the next space station for a 2020 launch, the project budget will be a key factor in all the planning and tracking decisions you make.

The budget is a controlling benchmark—a line in the sand beyond which project costs should not overstep. Initially, the cost of a project is based on your forecasted costs for scheduled tasks and their assigned resources. Once the project begins and you start tracking progress on tasks, Project adjusts these forecasts to reflect actual work and actual costs. One of your jobs as project manager is to make sure project costs don't exceed your allocated budget.

This chapter starts with a brief introduction to some methods that organizations use to develop project budgets. You'll focus on setting up your project schedule so Project calculates costs appropriately—for example, identifying resource costs as well as any additional costs associated with tasks. Along the way, you'll learn how to use cost resources in addition to work and material resources.

This chapter also explains how to look at project costs from different points of view, depending on the level of detail you want. You'll learn how to compare project costs against your budget using the budget resource feature. If Project gives you bad (but realistic) news that costs are outrunning the budget, this chapter provides specific cost-cutting measures you can pull from your project manager's arsenal. Finally, you'll learn how to set up accounting codes at the task or resource level so that your project costs can work with your organization's financial systems.

With this cost and budget information in place, you can analyze whether your project is within budget or in need of belt-tightening. Moreover, your project is primed for proactive cost monitoring once it gets under way. You can keep a close eye on any wavering from that budget benchmark in order to nimbly make adjustments *before* going over budget.

Tip: This chapter focuses primarily on costs and budgeting during the planning stage, although some of the techniques work just as well during project execution. Other chapters delve into detail on monitoring project costs after your project is under way. For example, Chapter 13 describes setting a baseline, which is the snapshot of the approved project plan. Chapter 14 talks about entering progress information, or *actuals,* into your project. Then Chapter 15 describes how to evaluate project performance and the techniques you can use to bring a project back on track.

Putting a Price Tag on Your Project

It's the old chicken-and-egg scenario—which comes first, the project budget or the project cost estimates? Either way, the organization wants to know how much the project will cost. Or, looking at it from the other direction—what's the maximum this project *should* cost to get the financial benefit the organization requires?

The financial benefit comes down to whether the project is worth the effort. How much money will the project make or how much will it save? What will it cost to get that result? For example, suppose the R&D eggheads have a fabulous idea for a new thingamabob that will revolutionize helium balloon distribution. The bean counters think sales could peak at $200,000 in the first year and then would drop off incrementally, earning $400,000 over the product's life cycle. The company has to decide how much they're willing to spend on the development project and how much profit they need to earn to make the project worthwhile. As the project manager, you're expected to provide cost estimates based on the agreed-upon project scope. The hard part is making the two figures agree with each other.

If you're in the enviable position of proposing the budget, one approach is to develop your schedule, assign resources to tasks, and let Project calculate the resulting costs. You can use that cost figure as you go, hat in hand, to present the budget. The powers that be often reduce that number, although they also set aside contingency funds and management reserve (page 57) as insurance.

A more scientific method for setting the project budget is *capital budgeting,* which is a set of financial calculations that help determine a project's potential rate of return, return on investment, and payback period (page 27). Capital budgeting can also show the impact of not taking on other projects while the organization's resources are busy with the current project. Thus, capital budgeting analysis can help an organization determine whether a project is in line with its financial and other strategic goals—with the result of a go/no-go decision for that project.

For an example, you can download an Excel capital budgeting template from Microsoft Office Online (*http://tinyurl.com/ROIWorksheet*). Enter your data, and the spreadsheet calculates the rate of return on an investment, the net present value of the investment, and the payback period, as shown in Figure 11-1.

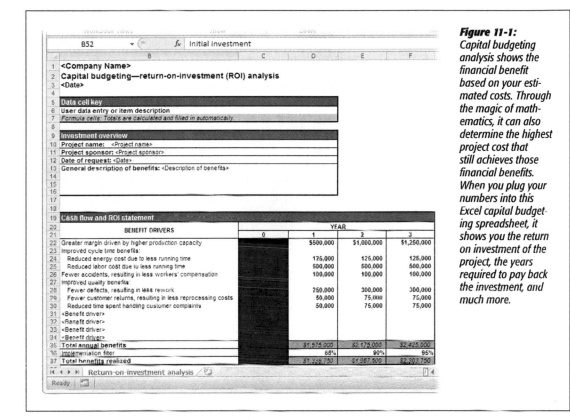

Figure 11-1:
Capital budgeting analysis shows the financial benefit based on your estimated costs. Through the magic of mathematics, it can also determine the highest project cost that still achieves those financial benefits. When you plug your numbers into this Excel capital budgeting spreadsheet, it shows you the return on investment of the project, the years required to pay back the investment, and much more.

If you create a work breakdown structure, assign resources, and specify costs for those resources, Project can give you a total cost estimate for the project. The program also breaks it down into its component parts—total costs for a resource, total costs for a phase, even costs for an individual task.

When you compare the amount determined in the capital budgeting analysis with your project's cost estimates, you can see how far apart they are. This comparison is valuable for deciding whether the project is even feasible. For example, suppose the capital budget analysis shows that the project is worth doing as long as the cost doesn't exceed $50,000. If your project cost estimate perches steadfastly at $200,000, chances are good that the project won't fly, because trimming 75 percent from the estimate isn't likely.

Keep in mind that project budgeting is an iterative process. The project sponsor may have a ballpark number in mind, but you can help hone that number with your project cost estimate and give the budget a basis in reality. Explanations and negotiations may ensue, along with further analysis, until finally you obtain a realistic project budget figure that everyone is willing to accept.

Remember that you need to do everything in your power to not exceed that budget once the project gets under way. If you overshoot the budget, you may have to pay dearly, in unpopular schedule adjustments, reduced scope, cost overruns, not to mention your own reputation. In the end, people say two things about successful projects: "It came in on time and under budget."

Incorporating Resource Costs

Resource costs are often the lion's share of project cost. They include the human resources and equipment that perform project tasks (*work resources*), as well as the consumable materials and supplies used while carrying out a task (*material resources*). To make sure you have accurate costs in your project plan, check that you've entered all resource costs. You enter costs for work and material resources in the Resource Sheet (see Figure 11-2). For the details on assigning costs to resources, see "Defining Costs for Work and Material Resources" on page 197.

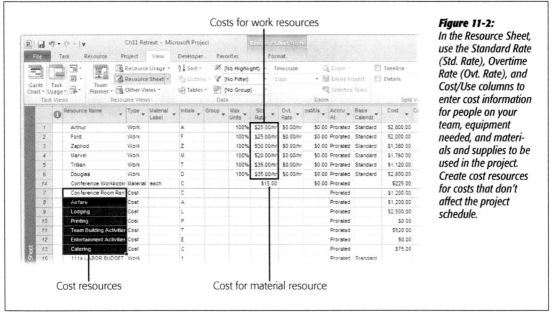

Figure 11-2:
In the Resource Sheet, use the Standard Rate (Std. Rate), Overtime Rate (Ovt. Rate), and Cost/Use columns to enter cost information for people on your team, equipment needed, and materials and supplies to be used in the project. Create cost resources for costs that don't affect the project schedule.

Introduced in Project 2007, *cost resources* represent things that are instrumental to completing a task but don't include work time, duration, or an amount of material consumed. Examples of cost resources are travel costs, room rentals, printing services, training costs, and so on. These costs affect the project price tag, but not the project schedule.

Like work and material resources, you create a cost resource in the Resource Sheet (page 184). Unlike work and material resources, however, you don't enter the cost in the Resource Sheet. Instead, you enter the cost after you assign the cost resource to a task (page 289).

Preparing for Cost Calculations

Suppose you're responsible for planning your departmental retreat, appropriately scheduled to coincide with the circus that's coming to town. It's a great opportunity for team-building and entertainment. You've entered work resource rates and material resource costs. You've also diligently assigned resources to their tasks. Project multiplies task time by resource cost rates, and suddenly something magical happens—reliable cost information about your tasks and the project as a whole appears in your Project file.

Add any necessary cost resources or miscellaneous fixed costs to tasks that need them—and your cost forecasts are now looking pretty accurate.

In this section, you'll learn about the importance of entering accurate costs for labor and materials. You'll also learn how to assign cost resources to tasks and how to specify the costs for those assignments. Finally, you'll learn how to enter a miscellaneous cost for a task if needed.

Note: To see costs, make sure your resources have rates and costs in place (page 197), and then check that tasks have resources assigned.

Assigning Cost Resources to Tasks

Now you're ready to assign your cost resources. Remember those cost items that contribute to tasks but have no bearing on the schedule? Items like lodging, rentals, or printing can't make a task finish any faster, and yet they contribute to the project cost, so you must figure them in. The departmental retreat project is teeming with cost resources.

Assigning cost resources with the Assign Resources dialog box

After you create cost resources in the Resource Sheet, it's time to assign them to the appropriate tasks and enter their cost for that particular assignment. Here are the steps:

1. **Display any task-oriented view.**

   You may gravitate to the all-purpose Gantt Chart view, but you can assign resources to tasks in the Network Diagram, Calendar view, Task Usage view, or any other task-oriented view.

---

2. **Choose Resource→Assignments→Assign Resources.**

   The Assign Resources dialog box opens.

3. **In the task list, select the task to which you want to assign a cost resource.**

   Project aficionados know that the Assign Resources dialog box is one of the few dialog boxes that can stay open while you do something in the active view.

4. **In the Assign Resources dialog box, select the name of the cost resource, and then click Assign.**

   A checkmark appears next to the cost resource's name, which scoots up near the top of the list of resources with other resources already assigned to the selected task.

5. **In the Cost column for the assigned cost resource, type its cost for the task.**

   What makes cost resources so useful is that they don't have a set cost value—you can enter a different cost for each task to which you assign a specific cost resource. But since it's a single cost resource, you can also see how much you're spending on that one cost resource across all the tasks to which it's assigned.

   For example, suppose you need to assign the "Conference Room Rental" cost resource to two different tasks: "Conduct day 1 of retreat" and "Conduct day 2 of retreat." Day 1 is a full 8-hour day, and the cost is $200. Day 2 is just a 5-hour day, so the conference room rental cost for that day is only $125.

   You select the "Conduct day 1 of retreat" task, assign the "Conference Room Rental" resource to it, and then, in the Cost column, enter *$200*. Then you select the "Conduct day 2 of retreat" task, assign the "Conference Room Rental" resource to it as well, and then, in the Cost column, enter *$125*.

6. **If the same task uses a second cost resource, select its name, as shown in Figure 11-3, and then click Assign.**

   For example, you might have a cost resource called "Catering" that goes with the "Conduct Day 1 of Retreat" task in addition to the "Conference Room Rental" cost resource.

7. **To assign cost resources to another task, select the task, and then repeat steps 4–6.**

   When you're finished assigning cost resources, click Close to close the Assign Resources dialog box.

You don't even have to know the cost for a cost resource when you're assigning it to a task. Go ahead and make the assignment, and then add the cost later. Even better, enter a ballpark figure in the Assign Resources dialog box's Cost field, so you have some kind of cost estimate for the task. Enter a task note indicating that you're waiting on cost information, as illustrated in Figure 11-4. That way, you won't lead yourself, or anyone else, astray. (The box on page 292 describes how to document items you're waiting for using task notes.)

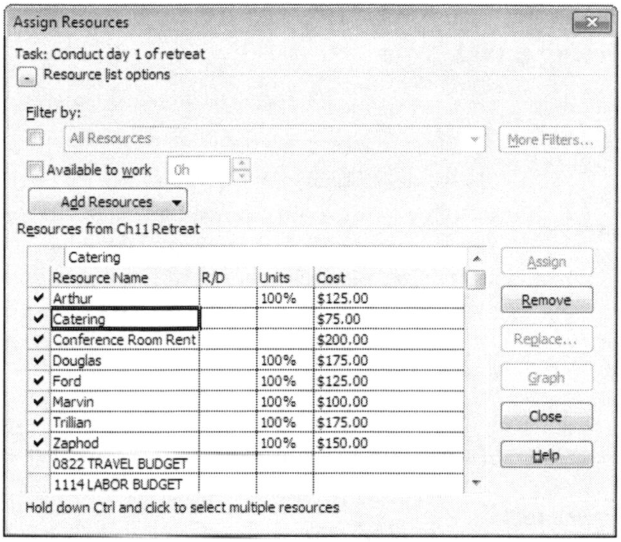

Figure 11-3:
Not only can you assign the same cost resource to different tasks with different cost amounts, you can also assign multiple cost resources to a single task. That trick differentiates cost resources from fixed costs. There's only one Fixed Cost field. If a task has more than one fixed cost, then you must enter the total in the field.

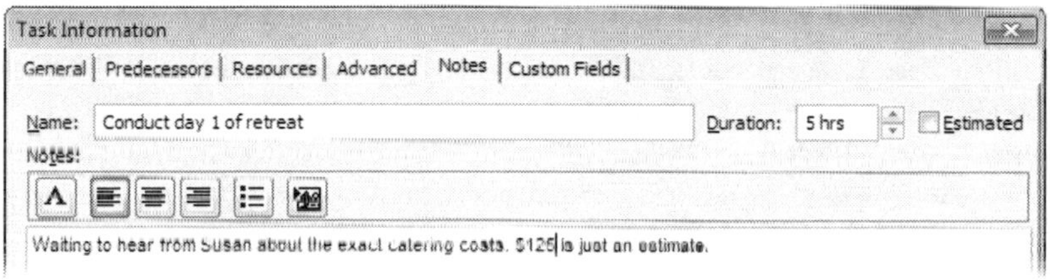

Figure 11-4:
In the Task Information dialog box (double-click a task to open it), select the Notes tab, and then type a note for the current task. You can format your note in a few rudimentary ways, and even insert objects from other programs.

Tip: The Assign Resources dialog box isn't the only game in town for entering or changing cost resource costs. You can also use the Task Information dialog box. The Resources tab lists all resources assigned to the selected task. The Cost column is available for your editing pleasure.

Entering a Task Note

Task notes are the electronic equivalent of a yellow sticky note for tasks. You may find such notes handy for a quick reminder to yourself that you're awaiting some cost information. The note can also be as elaborate as a copy of an email from a supplier providing a full breakdown of their cost estimate to you. Of course, the note can be about anything—not just costs.

Select the task for the note, and then choose Task→ Properties→Task Notes, which incidentally looks like a yellow sticky note. Project opens the Task Information

dialog box's Notes tab. Type or paste your note, and then click OK.

In some views, like the Gantt Chart view with the typical Entry table applied, a little note icon appears in the indicators column to the left of the Task Name column. You can just rest your mouse pointer over that icon to read the note in a pop-up. Otherwise, double-click the task to open the Task Information dialog box. Select the Notes tab, and then read or revise the note as you will.

Assigning cost resources in a table

You can also add cost resource values in a usage view's table area, because these views show assignments. To enter costs in the Task Usage view or Resource Usage view, do the following:

1. **Display the view you want.**

   Choose Task Usage if you want to see the assigned resources under each task. Choose Resource Usage if you want to see the assigned tasks under each resource. With either usage view, you get to see *assignments,* that intersection of tasks with resources, and you can get additional assignment information you can't see anywhere else.

2. **In the table area on the left, right-click the column heading next to where you want to add the Cost column, and then choose Insert Column. In the "Field name" drop-down list, type *cost* to quickly scroll to and choose the Cost field.**

   Project displays the Cost column in the sheet to the left of the selected column. In the Task Usage view, the Cost field for the task and resource assignment are both editable. However, in the Resource Usage view, the Cost field is editable only for the assignment (the task name under the resource name).

3. **Enter or change the cost information for assigned cost resources as necessary.**

   When you change cost information for an assignment in a usage view, the cost at the rolled-up summary level (the task cost) changes to reflect the additional assignment cost. The box on page 293 explains how you can define exactly when costs are incurred.

Specifying When Costs Are Incurred

Ordinarily, when you enter costs for cost resources, they're prorated and distributed equally over the task duration. For example, suppose you assigned a cost resource of "Airfare" at $200 to a 5-day task. Project automatically distributes the $200 across the 5 days for $40 each day. In the Resource Sheet, you can change a resource's Accrue At field to Start or End if you want the cost to be incurred on the task's start date or finish date.

However, if you want to change when one instance of a cost resource is incurred, you can do that in the time-phased portion of the Task Usage or Resource Usage view. In this example, it makes sense for the full $200 to show up on the task's start date.

To do that, follow these steps:

1. Choose View→Task Views→Task Usage or View→Resource Views→Resource Usage.

2. Choose Format→Details and then turn on the Cost checkbox. This adds the Cost row to the time-phased portion of the usage view.

3. Enter or change the time-phased cost information for the cost resource as you wish.

Entering an Oddball Cost for a Task

Every once in a while a miscellaneous cost crops up that may not warrant the creation of a cost resource. For example, the "Clown workshop team-building activity" task requires rubber noses and a couple of pairs of oversized shoes. One option is to set up one catch-all cost resource, for example called Miscellaneous Costs. However, if you know this task is the only one that needs this kind of cost, a *fixed cost* tied to the task is quicker. The box on page 296 explains when to use cost resources or fixed costs. Here's how you enter a fixed cost:

1. **Display any task sheet view.**

   Examples of task sheet views include the good old Gantt Chart view, the Tracking Gantt, and the Task Entry view. All you need is a table area for task information

2. **Display the Cost table by choosing View→Data. Click the down arrow next to Tables and then, on the drop-down list, choose Cost.**

   In the upper-left corner of the table, you can also right-click the Select All cell, at the intersection between the first row and the first column. In the menu that appears, choose Cost. The Cost table appears, as shown in Figure 11-5.

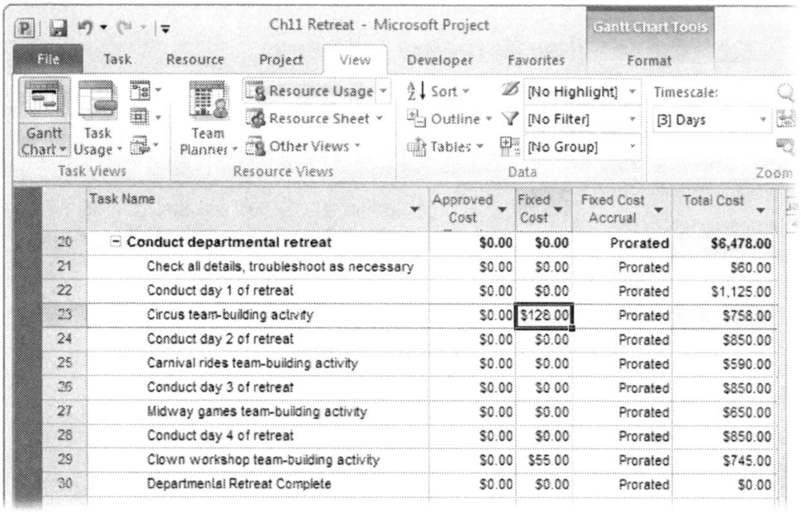

Figure 11-5:
In addition to entering fixed costs, you can use the Cost table to see total scheduled cost for each task. Later on, after you've set a baseline and are tracking progress, you can use this table to see whether you're blasting past your planned cost for the task.

3. **Select the Fixed Cost cell for the task, and then type the cost.**

If necessary, select the Fixed Cost Accrual field for the task, and then select Prorated, Start, or End to indicate when the cost should be incurred during the task duration.

The typical accrual for fixed costs is Prorated, which means the fixed cost is divided into equal portions across the task's duration. For example, if you have a fixed cost of $100 on a 5-day task, the prorated setting incurs $20 each day, which you can see if you add the Cost field to the time-phased portion of the Task Usage or Resource Usage view.

Change the fixed cost accrual to Start if you want the full cost to be incurred on the day the task begins. Change the accrual to End if you want the full cost to be incurred on the day the task ends. Which one you choose can depend on the nature of the cost or your accounting guidelines.

You can change the typical method for fixed-cost accrual for the current project. Choose File→Options. In the Project Options dialog box, choose Schedule. Under "Calculation options for this project", in the "Default fixed cost accrual" box, select Start, End, or Prorated. This setting takes effect for all new tasks you create.

Tip: Although you can enter fixed costs easily enough, there's nothing that makes you explain what the cost is for. Unless it's stunningly obvious, a notation about the cost is always a good idea. A task note, as described on page 292, is one way to describe a fixed cost. If you have multiple fixed costs throughout your project, consider using a custom text field instead. After you create the custom field (page 61), add it to the Cost table next to the Fixed Cost field so the fixed-cost description sits right next to the cost it describes.

Summary tasks can have fixed costs, too. Entering a fixed cost on a summary task is helpful when a cost corresponds to a project phase, rather than just an individual task. Add fixed costs to a summary task in the same way you add them to regular tasks.

You may wonder how you can add a fixed cost to a summary task. The other cost fields, like Total Cost, roll up subtasks' values to calculate the corresponding cost for the summary task. However, as shown in Figure 11-6, Project doesn't roll up the Fixed Cost field, which can be both convenient and perplexing.

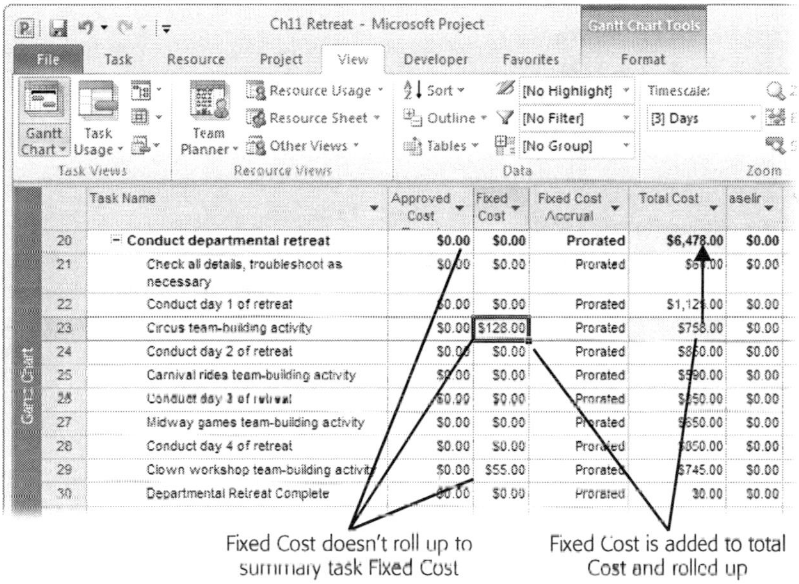

Figure 11-6:
If you expect fixed costs to roll up in the summary task, you'll be disappointed by the summary task Fixed Cost field showing $0.00. The benefit of Fixed Cost not rolling up is that you can add fixed costs to project phases. Fixed costs do become part of the Total Cost field, which also includes any work and material resource costs.

You can also enter a fixed cost for the project as a whole. To do this, you must first show the project summary task. Choose Format→Show/Hide, and then, turn on the Project Summary Task checkbox. Apply the Cost table as usual, and then, in the project summary task, enter the fixed cost.

Reviewing Cost Information

As you planned your circus retreat, the project sponsor made it very clear that the maximum price tag is $15,000, and hinted that less than $12,000 would be even better. Now that you've added tasks, resources, and any associated costs, it's time to see whether the retreat costs $12,000, $15,000, or a value that isn't as funny as the retreat's entertainment. Here's where you really start to see the value of entering costs in Project.

In this section, you'll learn how to review total planned costs for all project tasks. By extension, you get a handy forecast of your overall project costs. You'll also learn how to review planned costs for tasks, resources, and assignments, so you can analyze costs at the level of granularity you need.

Fixed Costs vs. Cost Resources

When should I use a fixed cost instead of a cost resource?

Before Project 2007, when cost resources were but a gleam in Bill Gates's eye, the fixed cost field was the best way to include travel costs, printing costs, and other nonlabor or nonmaterial costs. Now cost resources are the best way to show such costs. Really, fixed costs are now useful only when you're working with a file created in a previous version of Project that doesn't have cost resources. Otherwise, convert those fixed costs to cost resources to take advantage of what cost resources offer.

Unlike fixed costs, you can assign multiple cost resources to a single task, making different types of costs easier to see and track. Moreover, you can assign the same cost resource to multiple tasks, even if they have different cost

amounts. Say you have a cost resource like Lodging that applies to several tasks. You create just the one cost resource and then assign it to the various tasks, entering different cost amounts for each assignment. You can see total cost information for the Lodging cost resource so you can tell how much your team is spending on those posh suites during business trips. Even if you do have an oddball cost on a single task, it's a good practice to handle costs consistently throughout a project.

If you plan to use budget resources to compare budgeted and planned costs, then cost resources are better than fixed costs. Budget resources don't take fixed costs into account; they summarize only costs associated with resources assigned to tasks.

Seeing Overall Project Costs

When you first compare your project plan's performance against the budget, start with a quick bottom-line snapshot. A single number for your project's planned cost tells you whether you need to delve into cost containment or can sit back and relax. This section shows a few ways to come up with that top-level number.

Remember the garbage in/garbage out maxim. Your total project cost forecast is only as reliable as the information you provide. At this stage of the game, many costs and durations are estimates. Still, because these estimates affect your budget, it pays to be as accurate as possible. To forecast total project cost reliably, make sure you have the following information in your project plan:

- Costs, including hourly rates and per-use costs, for all work resources assigned to tasks
- Costs for all material resources assigned to tasks
- Costs for all cost resources assigned to tasks
- Any additional fixed costs for tasks

Viewing the total project cost in the project summary task

The project summary task is a great place to spot the total planned project cost, because it rolls up the totals for all tasks and you can keep it visible in the first row of the project task list. To use the project summary task to see rolled-up cost values, follow these steps:

1. **With a task-oriented view like the Gantt Chart visible, choose Format→Show/ Hide and then turn on the Project Summary Task checkbox.**

    A new row appears at the very top of the table in most views. A project summary node also appears in the Network Diagram view. The project summary task rolls up the column values in the current table. For example, in the Entry table, the typical table shown with the Gantt Chart view, you can see the total duration, the start date, and the finish date for the entire project.

    For columns that aren't supple enough to roll up, like the Predecessor or Resource Names columns, the corresponding project summary cells remain blank.

2. **Apply the Cost table by choosing the View tab. In the Data section, click the down arrow to the right of Tables and then, from the drop-down list, choose Cost.**

    The project summary task shows the total cost for the project in its Total Cost cell. It also shows rolled-up values for Baseline Cost, Cost Variance, Actual Cost, and Remaining Cost in other columns.

    As you learned on page 293, values in the Fixed Cost column don't roll up into outline summary tasks or the project summary task. This behavior has a purpose: It's so you can enter a fixed cost for a project phase or the project as a whole.

Tip: If you spend most of your time in the Gantt Chart view and its sidekick, the Entry table, consider adding the Cost column to the Entry table. Right-click the table, and then, on the shortcut menu, choose Insert Column. In the field name drop-down list that appears, choose Cost.

Viewing the total project cost in Project Statistics

To get to the single number that indicates your total project costs, use the Project Statistics dialog box as follows:

1. **Choose Project→Properties→Project Information.**

    The Project Information dialog box appears.

2. **At the bottom of the dialog box, click the Statistics button.**

    The Project Statistics dialog box appears, as shown in Figure 11-7.

3. **In the Cost column, review the value in the Current field, which is the forecasted cost for the project as currently planned.**

    After you set a baseline (page 365) the Baseline fields are also filled in. When you start tracking progress (page 388), the Actual and Remaining fields have values, too.

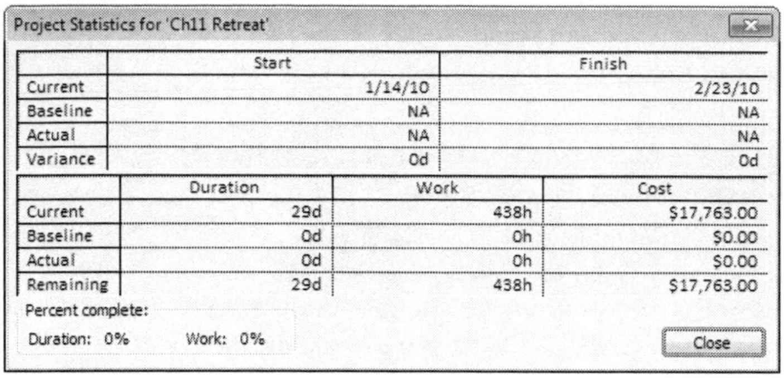

Project Statistics for 'Ch11 Retreat'				
	Start		Finish	
Current		1/14/10		2/23/10
Baseline		NA		NA
Actual		NA		NA
Variance		0d		0d

	Duration	Work	Cost
Current	29d	438h	$17,763.00
Baseline	0d	0h	$0.00
Actual	0d	0h	$0.00
Remaining	29d	438h	$17,763.00

Percent complete:

Duration: 0%   Work: 0%

Close

Figure 11-7:
The Project Statistics dialog box includes bottom-line project information that lets you and others gauge the most important aspects of the project as a whole: when the project starts, when it's scheduled to finish, how much work is involved, and how much it's forecasted to cost.

Viewing total project cost in the Project Summary report

You can get overall project cost information in a printed text report. Choose Project→Reports→Reports, and then double-click Overview. In the Overview Reports dialog box, double-click Project Summary. A preview appears of the Project Summary report, which shows the same information available in the Project Statistics dialog box.

Use the Project Summary report for status reports, especially since you can print this report but you can't print the Project Statistics dialog box. Click Print to get a hard copy. For more information about generating reports, see Chapter 17.

Seeing Costs for Tasks, Resources, and Assignments

Now that you've seen the big picture of forecasted costs, you're probably champing at the bit to learn how to find task costs when all resources are assigned and where to look for the total cost of one resource's assignments. This section shows how to break costs down to individual assignments—that is, how much it costs for one particular resource working on one particular task. Use one of the following methods to drill down into costs:

- **Total cost for a task.** First apply the Cost table (View→Data→Tables→Cost) to a task view, and then, in the Total Cost column, check the value. Or insert the Cost field (right-click the table and choose Insert Column) into any task view, and then check the Cost value for the task. In both cases, the Cost value is the scheduled (planned) cost for the task, including all assigned resources (work, material, and cost) and any fixed costs. See Chapter 15 (page 407) to learn the difference between baseline, scheduled, and actual values.

Note: Depending on the table you display, you may see the Total Cost or the Cost column. However, both columns show the same field: Cost. The Cost table simply uses "Total Cost" as the column title.

- **Total cost for a resource.** Display the Resource Sheet, and then insert the Cost field (right-click the table and choose Insert Column) somewhere in the table. The Cost value for a given resource is the total cost for the resource for all assigned tasks, based on the standard rate, overtime rate, cost/use, or other specified resource cost. This technique is perfect when you want to see how much you're spending for a specific cost resource, such as travel or training.

- **Total cost for an assignment.** Display the Task Usage view or Resource Usage view. As usual, you can either apply the Cost table or insert the Cost field in the Usage table (or whatever table you want to use), as shown in Figure 11-8.

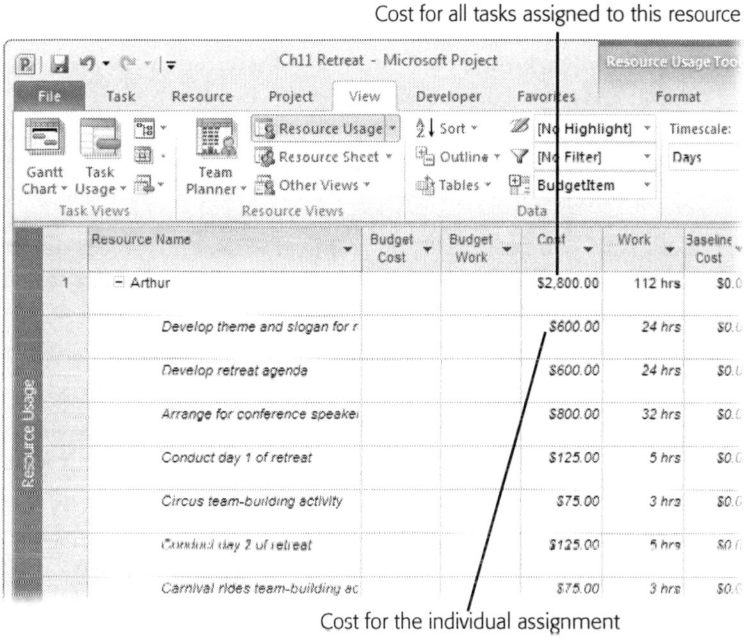

Cost for all tasks assigned to this resource

Cost for the individual assignment

Figure 11-8:
In the Resource Usage view, the Cost field in the task assignment row represents the cost for the individual assignment. The cost in the resource name row represents all assignment costs rolled up to give you a total for all tasks assigned to the resource.

In the Task Usage view, the cost in the resource name row represents the cost for the individual assignment—what it costs to have the resource assigned to the task. The cost in the task name row represents all assignment costs rolled up to give you a total for the task.

Tip: You can transfer cost information from your Project file to an Excel file for further analysis (page 523). Whether you copy and paste fields from Project into Excel or export Project information into an Excel spreadsheet, you can apply formulas, crunch numbers, and create whiz-bang charts and graphs until the cows (or stakeholders) come home.

Adding Custom Budget Information

The Cost field is great while you're in the project planning phase and setting up cost information to compare against your allocated budget. In this section, you'll learn how to create your very own type of cost field. You may have specialized cost or budget information you'd like to see in your project, like budget targets for key tasks and phases. To create a custom cost field for these types of costs, follow these steps:

1. **To create a custom field without adding it to a table, choose Project→ Properties→Custom Fields.**

   The Custom Fields dialog box appears.

   To insert a custom Cost field in a table, right-click the table and choose Insert Column on the shortcut menu. In the field name drop-down list, choose a field, such as Cost2. Right-click the new column and then, on the shortcut menu, choose Custom Fields to open the Custom Fields dialog box.

2. **Select the Task option for a custom cost field to be used in task views. Select the Resource option if the new field is for resource views.**

   A task cost field represents just task costs, while a resource cost field works only with resource costs. If you add a custom cost field to a table, Project automatically selects the custom field in the Field list and selects the Task or Resource option, depending on whether a task or resource view is visible.

3. **In the Type box, select Cost, and then select one of the Cost fields that isn't already in use.**

   The Field box lists all the custom cost fields, Cost1 through Cost10, as shown in Figure 11-9. Project displays custom fields along with their designated names.

   The alias for a renamed custom field appears as the column title when you insert the field into a table. The alias and built-in name both appear together in other places. For example, if you rename the Cost2 field to "Approved Cost Target," then the field appears in the field name listings as "Approved Cost Target (Cost2)" as well as "Cost2 (Approved Cost Target)."

4. **In the Custom Fields dialog box, click OK.**

   The cost field is ready for you to use in tables. If you haven't already added the custom cost field to the table, see step 1. The box on page 301 explains ways you can make cost fields do tricks.

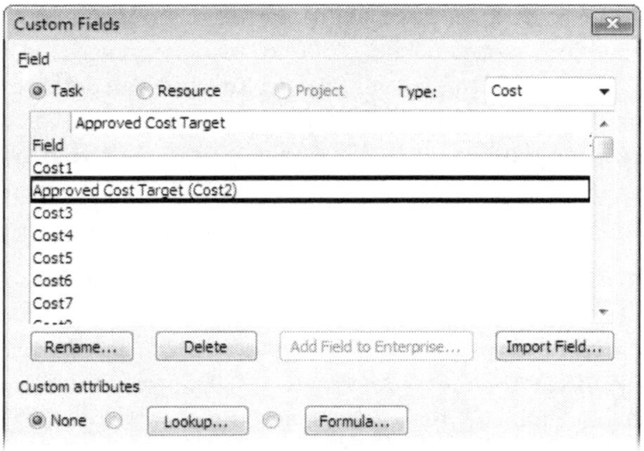

Figure 11-9:
Although Project doesn't force you to rename a custom field, in the Custom Fields dialog box, an alias is your only indication that the field is spoken for. Select the task, and then click Rename to rename the cost to something like Approved Cost Target.

POWER USERS' CLINIC

Programming Your Custom Cost Fields

Custom fields can do more than go by a different name. You can tell them to calculate values in certain ways or provide hints about valid values. The section "Customizing a Field" on page 641 provides the details, but here's a quick overview of what you can do.

- **Calculate values with formulas.** You can create a formula to calculate the contents of other fields and display the result in a custom cost field—for example, the variance between the planned cost and the target cost

- **Provide values with lookup tables.** You can create a lookup table with a list of cost values to choose from when entering values in a custom cost field.

- **Roll up values.** You can tell Project how it should roll up values in a custom cost field into task or group summary rows—for example, by taking the maximum amount of the group, averaging the amounts, or adding all amounts in the group together.

- **Roll down values.** You can specify whether Project should distribute the value in the custom cost field in the time-phased portion of assignment rows in a usage view.

Comparing Costs to Your Budget

In planning your departmental retreat, suppose you have specific budget targets for certain cost categories, $2,500 for travel expenses, $500 for printing, and $1,000 for conference room rentals. Using Project's *budget resource* feature, you can define your budget for different categories of items. You can then group your resources to compare your budgeted costs to your planned costs. This way, you can view your travel budget of $2,500 side by side with your planned costs of, say, $3,700, and immediately see that your next goal is to find a way to trim those travel costs.

Budget resources are great for comparing budgeted costs against the planned costs for cost resources. When it comes to budgeted labor costs, however, it's a different story. For labor and equipment costs (work resources), you can enter only budgeted work amounts, not costs. So instead of a labor budget of $10,000, you have to enter an overall work amount like 200 hours. Knowing what amount of work to enter can be tricky when different work resources all have different cost rates. The box on page 307 provides a workaround to this challenge.

This section describes how to set up budget resources to compare to your planned costs and work. This setup is an involved five-step process, summarized as follows:

1. **Create and designate budget resources.**

2. **Assign your budget resources to the project summary task.**

3. **Enter budgeted cost and work amounts for budget resources.**

4. **Associate other types of resources with their budget type.**

5. **Group resources to compare budget cost and work alongside the planned values.**

The whole process isn't quite as bad as it sounds. If your project is highly cost-driven, then budget resources may give you the budget performance information you need. Take budget resources for a test drive to see if they help.

After you've done the first four steps, everything is in place for you to compare budget and planned values (step 5) as you monitor and adjust your project plan to keep it in line with your budget. To make it even easier, you can create a custom view (page 312) with the columns and grouping you want already in place. Then for step 5, all you have to do is display your custom view.

Step 1: Create and Designate Budget Resources

Creating budget resources is the first step in the budget resource process. Your budget resources should correspond with the budget line items you want to track in your project, for example line items that the accounting department uses. They can be as broad as Labor Budget, Materials Budget, and Travel Budget, or as detailed as Equipment Rental, Lodging, Airfare, Publications, and Meals. It's entirely up to you how much budget detail you want.

Budget resources apply only to a project as a whole. You can't assign them to tasks, as you do regular resources. Create your budget resources as follows:

1. **In the Resource Sheet, in a blank Resource Name cell, type the name of the budget resource.**

   When you enter names that differentiate budget resources from regular resources, as shown in Figure 11-10, you can more easily pick the right fields for your budget comparisons. Such a naming convention also helps when working with regular resources, as shown in Figure 11-10.

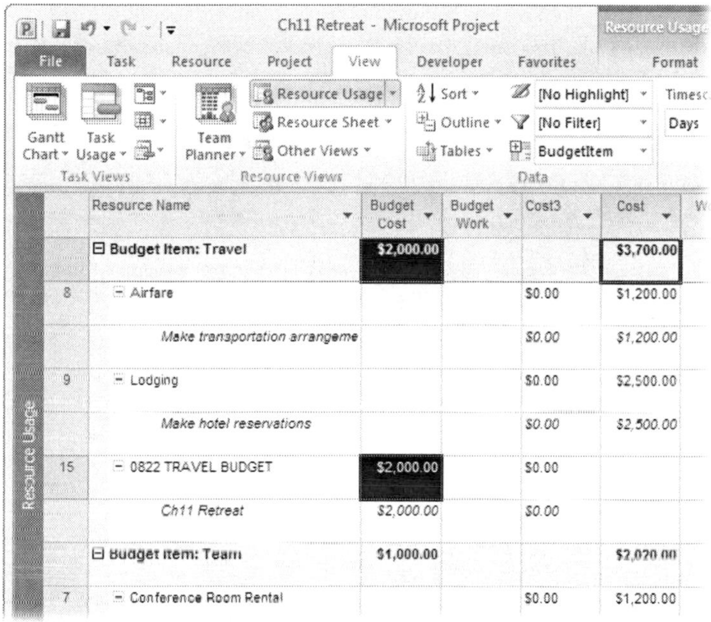

Figure 11-10:
Name budget resources so it's easy to identify them as budget resources, for example, "Budget-Travel", all caps like TRAVEL BUDGET, or starting a budget resource name with the corresponding budget account number. One advantage to starting with a number is that budget resources appear together at the top of a resource list that's sorted alphabetically from A to Z, which is helpful because they're summary numbers.

2. **In the Type field, choose Work, Material, or Cost, depending on the type of cost.**

   For example, a budget resource named *"0822 TRAVEL BUDGET"* would be a cost resource, while a budget resource named *"1114 LABOR BUDGET"* would likely be a work resource.

   For a material budget resource, in the Material Label field, type the unit of measurement, like *cubic yards* or *boxes*.

   Although you can lump different types of labor together under a single labor budget item (regular employees, temporary employees, and so on), create a separate budget resource for each resource category whose budget you want to track, such as employees, contractors, and vendors.

Tip: If you want to express your labor budget in dollars rather than hours, identify the budget resources for it as a cost resource rather than a work resource. See the box on page 307 for instructions.

3. **Double-click the name of the new budget resource to open the Resource Information dialog box.**

   You can also open the dialog box by selecting the budget resource and then choosing Resource→Properties→Information.

4. **On the General tab, turn on the Budget checkbox, as demonstrated in Figure 11-11, and then click OK.**

   Turning on the Budget checkbox means you can assign this resource only to the project summary task, making it, in effect, a kind of project summary resource.

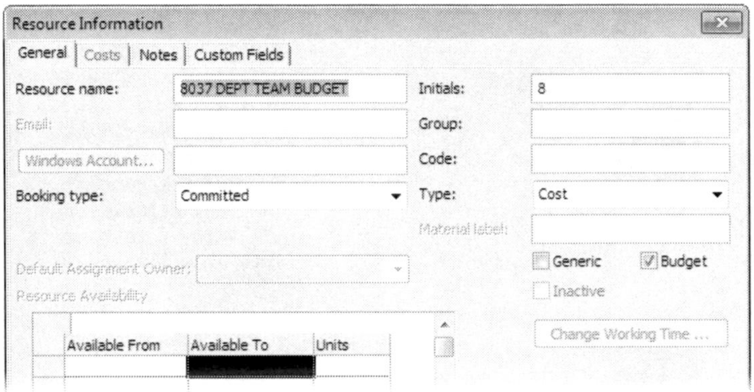

Figure 11-11:
The Budget checkbox lives on the General tab. It's grayed out in the Multiple Resource Information dialog box (which opens when you select several resources and press Shift+F2), so you must set budget resources one at a time. Other fields that relate to work or material resources, like Email and "Material label" are grayed out.

5. **Repeat steps 1–4 to create additional budget resources.**

   The box on page 305 describes a shortcut for creating several budget resources at once.

Step 2: Assign Budget Resources to the Project Summary Task

With your budget resources created, you're now ready to assign them to your project. A budget resource is meant to convey the overall amount allocated to a budget category for an entire project, which is why you assign them to the project summary task, not individual tasks. In fact, a budget resource can't be assigned to anything *except* the project summary task.

If you can't see the project summary task (the one at the top with row number 0), choose Format→Show/Hide and turn on the Project Summary Task checkbox. Now assign budget resources to your project summary task by following these steps:

1. Select the project summary task, and then choose Resource→Assignments→ Assign Resources.

   The Assign Resources dialog box appears.

   If your resource list is long, your job will be easier if you name budget resources so they appear in a group; for example, by starting all the budget resource names with a number, as shown in Figure 11-12.

WORKAROUND WORKSHOP

Creating Several Budget Resources at Once

Most project managers create their budget resources in one fell swoop. Even so, the Multiple Resource Information dialog box doesn't let you turn on the Budget checkbox for all selected resources. Evidently, Project expects you to waste time double-clicking budget resources one at a time, turning on the Budget checkbox, clicking OK, and then doing it again with the next budget resource. Since you have more important things to do, here's a shortcut for designating several budget resources at once: Add the Budget column to the Resource Sheet, and change the Budget value there. Here are the steps:

1. In the Resource Sheet, right-click the column heading next to where you want to add the Budget column, and then choose Insert Column.

2. In the "Field name" drop-down list, choose Budget. Project inserts the Budget column to the left of the selected column and usually shows the value No.

3. Select the cell for the first budget resource and, in the drop-down list, choose Yes. If budget resources are grouped together, you can drag the black square at the cell's bottom-right corner to copy Yes to other Budget cells.

4. When you're done, hide the column by right-clicking the Budget column heading and then choosing Hide Column.

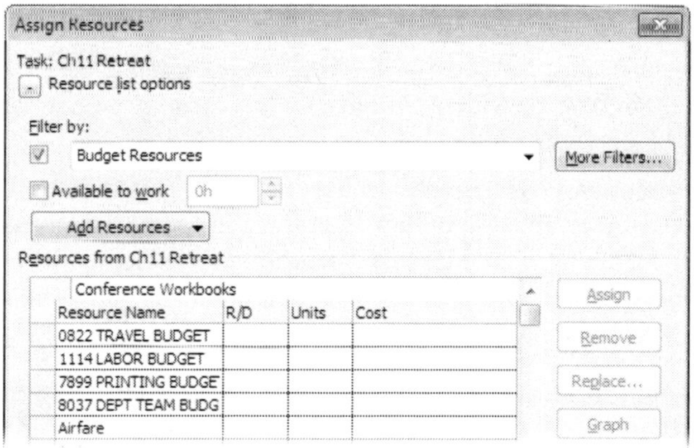

Figure 11-12:
To display only budget resources in the Assign Resources dialog box, expand the "Resource list options" section by clicking the +. Turn on the "Filter by" checkbox, and then, in the drop-down list, choose Budget Resources.

2. **Select the first budget resource you want to assign, and then click Assign.**

   As you can with regular resources, you can select several budget resources and click Assign to assign them all to a task at once.

   Budget resources are the only kind of resource you can assign to the project summary task. So if you select one resource and the Assign button is missing in action, then the resource you selected isn't a budget resource. Perhaps you named the resource as a budget resource but forgot to turn on its Budget checkbox in the Resource Information dialog box (page 192).

3. **Repeat the previous step for any additional budget resources you want to assign to the project summary task.**

   When you're done, you can close the Assign Resource dialog box if you want to see more of the screen.

Step 3: Enter Budget Cost and Work Values

With budget resources assigned to the project summary task, you're finally ready to add budget cost amounts for cost resources, budget work amounts for work resources, and the total number of units for material resources. These budget values are the targets against which you compare project costs and work as you monitor project progress.

You can enter budget cost and work amounts as a project total or as incremental totals by time period. This section explains how to do both.

Entering budget totals for the project

If time isn't a factor in your budget, you can add budget cost and work amounts to the entire project. Here are the steps:

1. **Display the Task Usage or Resource Usage view.**

   The Task Usage view is ideal for entering budget values, because the project summary task sits at the very top with its assigned budget resources below it like fawning admirers, as shown in Figure 11-13.

   If you use the Resource Usage view instead, budget resources appear at the bottom of the list, because they show up in the order you add them to the project. You can assign a budget total in the Resource Usage view by selecting the project summary task under the budget resource and then typing its budget value.

2. **Insert the Budget Cost field into the table. Then insert the Budget Work field.**

   Right-click the column heading next to where you want to insert the Budget Cost column, and then choose Insert Column. In the "Field name" drop-down list, choose Budget Cost. Repeat these steps for the Budget Work field.

3. **Select the Budget Cost cell for an assigned budget resource, and then type the overall project budget value for that resource.**

   For a budget resource that's a cost resource, type the budget value in dollars in the Budget Cost cell.

For a budget resource that's a work resource, type the budget value as work (hours or days) in the Budget Work cell. The Budget Work cell is also where you type the total number of units (cubic yards, tons, packages, each, and so on) for a budget resource that's a material resource.

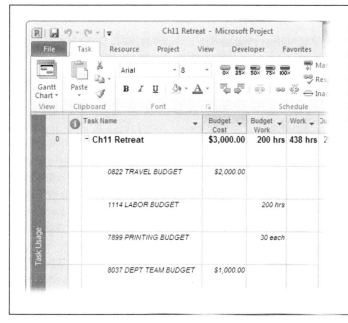

Figure 11-13:
Unlike the Task Usage view shown here, the Resource Usage view displays budget resources appear at the bottom of the list, because they show up in the order you add them to the project. Select the project summary task assignment under the budget resource, and then type its budget value.

WORKAROUND WORKSHOP

Comparing Budgeted Labor Costs

Project calculates labor costs for work resources (people and equipment) by multiplying rates by hours. However, you can't compare these labor costs to the budgeted costs from the budget resource feature. Frustratingly, you can compare only budgeted *work* amounts to the work amounts in tasks—that is, the number of hours, days, and so on.

You can work around this problem by creating a single representative rate for work resources. For example, you could use an average or a weighted average based on how your labor costs are distributed and whether you expect to pay overtime. If you have a labor budget of $25,000, for example, and your average standard rate is $50 per hour, you could divide $25,000 by $50 for a resulting work budget of 500 hours.

On the other hand, if you insist on seeing your budgeted labor costs in dollars, not work, a little sleight-of-hand is in order. Instead of setting up the budget resource that relates to work resources as a work resource itself (like you're supposed to), you can set it up as a cost resource instead. Then you can enter budgeted labor cost and compare it to the rolled-up labor costs from tasks. The same trick works equally well for material cost budgets.

Entering budget totals by time period

The budget amounts you enter for a project summary task are the total project amounts for those budget items. Unless you tell it otherwise, Project spreads that budget amount equally over the duration of the project. To divvy up the overall budget amounts to the time periods when you expect them to be spent, you can edit budget amounts in the time-phased portion of a task or resource usage view.

Follow these steps to add the Budget Cost and Budget Work rows to the time-phased portion of the usage view:

1. **With the Task Usage or Resource Usage view displayed, choose Format→ Details→Add Details.**

   The Detail Styles dialog box appears.

2. **In the "Available fields" box, select Budget Cost, and then click Show. Do the same for the Budget Work field.**

   Project moves the Budget Cost and Budget Work fields to the "Show these fields" box, as illustrated in Figure 11-14. The order of fields in the "Show these fields" box is the sequence in which Project displays the field rows. To change this sequence, select a field name in the "Show these fields" box, and then click the Move buttons until the name is where you want it.

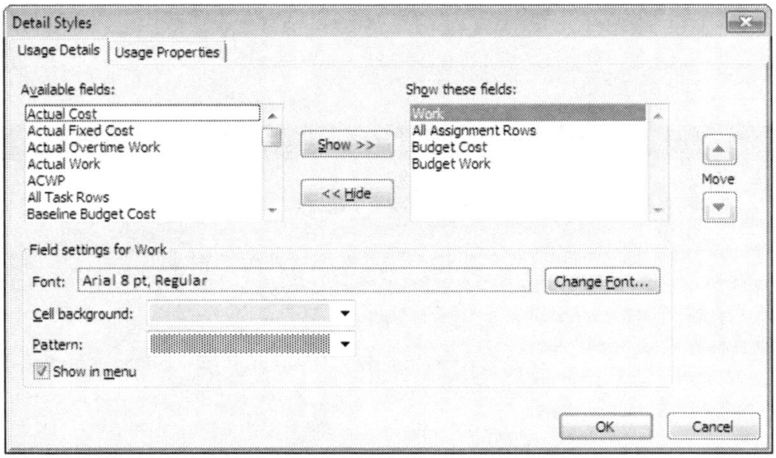

Figure 11-14:
To open this dialog box another way, right-click the time-phased portion of the view, and then, on the shortcut menu, choose Detail Styles.

3. Click OK.

    The two fields appear in the time-phased portion of the view, although you can see only part of their names. To see the full field names, drag the right edge of the Details column heading further to the right. You can also simply double-click the right edge of the column heading to automatically widen the column to display the longest field name.

4. **Drag the Zoom slider on the status bar to display the time period for which you want to enter time-phased budget values. Or adjust the time period in the Timeline view, as described on page 600.**

    For example, you can zoom the timescale to show a week or a month at a time. Then you can enter budget amounts per week or per month for budget resources.

    If you already entered budget amounts in the table, then those amounts are distributed equally across the project's time span. You can edit them to the budget values you expect for each time period.

5. **In the cell at the intersection of the row for a budget resource's Budget Cost or Budget Work field and the column for the time period you want, type the budget cost or work amount, as shown in Figure 11-15.**

    You can't edit the Budget Cost and Budget Work cells for nonbudget resource assignments. The box on page 310 tells you where you can enter budget amounts.

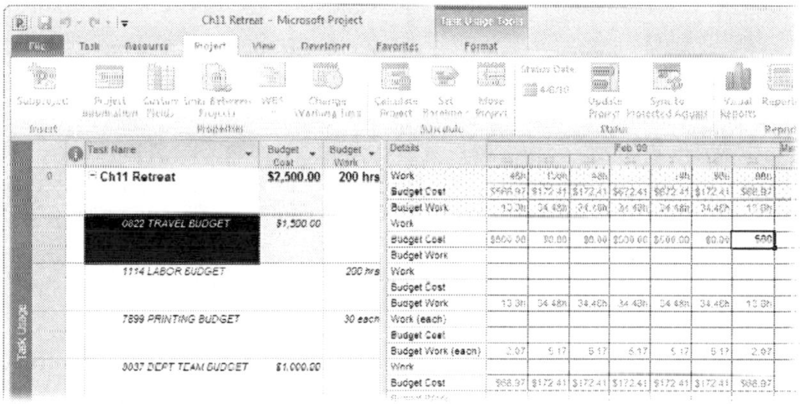

Figure 11-15:
Even if you enter budget values in the time-phased portion of the view, it's good to keep the Budget Cost and Budget Work columns in view in the table. Those fields show you the overall project totals for each budget category you've created.

Entering Values in Budget Fields

Where can I enter budget amounts in a view?

When you add the Budget Cost and Budget Work fields to a usage view's table or time-phased portion, it's not always clear where you can actually enter your budget amounts. No visual cue like shading or hatching indicates areas that are off limits, so the fields seem to be available throughout the entire view. If you try to enter a value and nothing happens, that's your clue that the cell isn't editable.

Project is particular about where you can enter budget amounts. Here are the rules:

- Enter budget amounts in an assignment field (in the Task Usage view, the row with the budget resource name; in the Resource Usage view, the row with the project summary task name).

- In a project summary task's Budget Cost or Budget Work cell, enter project-wide budget totals.

- Enter time-specific amounts in the Budget Cost or Budget work cells, in the time-phased portion.

You can't enter budget amounts in assignments for regular resources to regular tasks.

Step 4: Associate Resources with Their Budget Type

Creating budget resources and entering target budget amounts for them in the project summary task is all well and good, but it's only one side of the equation. You must also set up the other side: the resource costs you want to compare against the budget. This section explains how to hook up work, material, and cost resources to cost categories in the budget, whether you want to track all resources against the budget or only a few.

The trick is to use a text field to specify the budget category for each resource you want to track. If you aren't using the Group or Code fields (on the Resource Sheet) already, they're both great candidates for your budget categories. They're text fields and already included in the Entry table for the Resource Sheet. On the other hand, if Group and Code are in use, you can set up a custom text field to specify budget categories, as described in the next section.

Creating a custom resource text field

If you want to use a custom text field for budget categories, you must first set it up for that purpose and then add it to the Entry table in the Resource Sheet. Here are the steps:

1. **Display the Resource Sheet, right-click in the table, and then choose Insert Column. In the drop-down list, choose the custom text field you want to use, such as Text1 or Text2.**

   Project inserts a new column for the text field to the left of the column you right-click.

2. **Right-click the new column and then, on the shortcut menu, choose Custom Fields.**

   The Custom Fields dialog box opens with the text field and the Resource option already selected.

3. **Click Rename and then, in the Rename Field dialog box, type the name you want for this field. Click OK.**

   If you rename custom fields you use (page 642), a second name in parentheses tells you what fields are already used.

   Because this text field is for budget categories, name it something like *"Budget Type"* or *"Budget Item."*

4. **In the "Calculation for assignment rows" section, select the "Roll down unless manually entered" option. Click OK.**

   When you select this option, you're telling Project to distribute the budget category field values across assignments in usage views unless you manually type a value in a time-phased assignment cell.

Categorizing resources by budget category

Before you begin typing values in the text field, decide on the budget category names you want to use. Have a different budget category for each budget resource you've created, for example, Labor, Consultants, Materials, Travel, and Printing.

With your text field (Group, Code, or custom) prominently displayed in the Resource Sheet, work your way through the resources, typing the appropriate budget category name for each one, as illustrated in Figure 11-16. Be sure to enter a budget category for the budget resources themselves, because that's how you connect resource costs and budget costs.

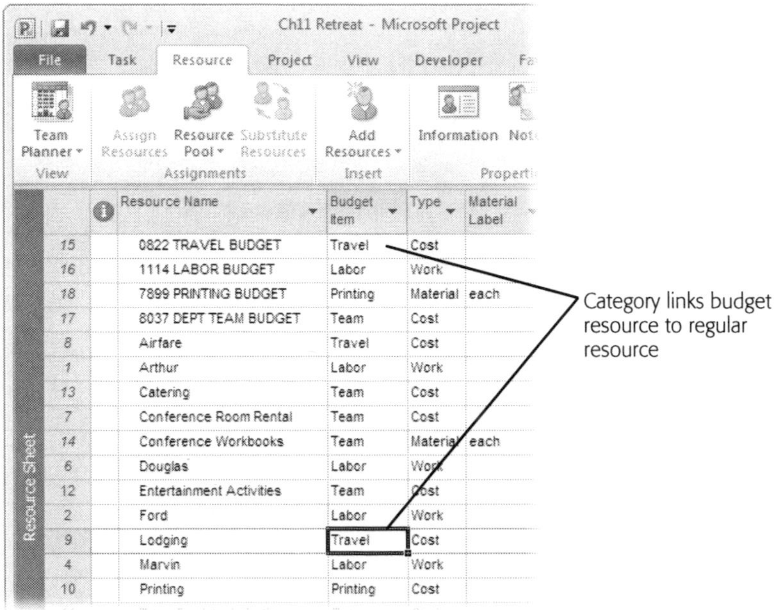

Figure 11-16:
When you type budget categories into the Resource Sheet, be sure to use exactly the same names with the same spelling. To prevent spurious entries due to typos, set up a custom text field with a lookup table of valid budget categories as described on page 311.

Congratulations! You've completed the daunting task of setting up Project to compare resource costs and work values against your budget.

Tip: You can add new resources, create new budget resources, and create and assign additional budget categories at any time throughout your project. If you add a new resource, be sure to assign it a budget category if you plan to compare its cost or work values against your budgeted values. If you create a new budget category, update any resources that belong in this new category.

Step 5: Compare Budget Resource Values

Finally, you're about to reap the harvest of the previous four steps: You're going to compare your project resource cost and work values against the budgeted values from your budget resources. You may find the occasional bad apple if your costs outrun your budgeted values. The good news is that budgeted costs help you see potential problems when it's early enough to find solutions.

To compare budget values to planned values, you need a table that shows both budgeted and planned fields. Then you can group the contents of the view by your budget categories. The result is groups of budgeted and planned values for each budget category, and voilà—your budget situation becomes crystal clear. Follow these steps to set up your budget comparison view:

1. Switch to the Resource Usage view.

   The Task Usage view is better for entering budget cost and work values, because it shows the project summary task at the top, with the assigned budget resources just under it.

   For comparing budget values, the Resource Usage view inherits the throne, because you want to group resources by the custom resource text field you set up on page 311, and resource fields aren't available in the Task Usage view. Moreover, you want to look at budget values in terms of resources and their assignments.

2. If they aren't there already, add the Budget Work, Budget Cost, Work, and Cost columns to the table.

   To add a column, right-click the heading of the column next to where you want to insert the new column and then, on the shortcut menu, choose Insert Column. In the Field Name drop-down list, choose the field you want to add. Project displays the new field to the left of the selected column.

3. To group the resources by the custom resource text field, click the down arrow to the right of the Resource Name column heading and then, on the drop-down menu, choose "Group by"→Custom Group.

   The Customize Group By dialog box appears. See page 634 for the full scoop on creating groups.

4. In the Group By row, click the arrow in the Field Name cell, and then, in the drop-down list of resource fields, choose the name of the custom text field for your budget categories (or Group or Code if you used them), and then click OK.

   Project groups the resources in your project by the budget categories you set up, as demonstrated in Figure 11-17.

5. In the group summary row, compare the Budget Cost or Budget Work values to the Cost or Work values.

   The Budget Cost or Budget Work cells in the group summary rows show the budget values for each budget resource. For each group, you see a value for Budget Cost or Budget Work, depending on whether the budget resource is a cost or work resource.

   The Cost and Work cells in the group summary cells show the rolled-up cost and rolled-up work for the resources in that particular budgetary group. If the value in the Cost cell is higher than the Budget Cost cell, then you've exceeded your budget. If the value in the Work cell is higher than the Budget Work cell, then your work hours are over budget.

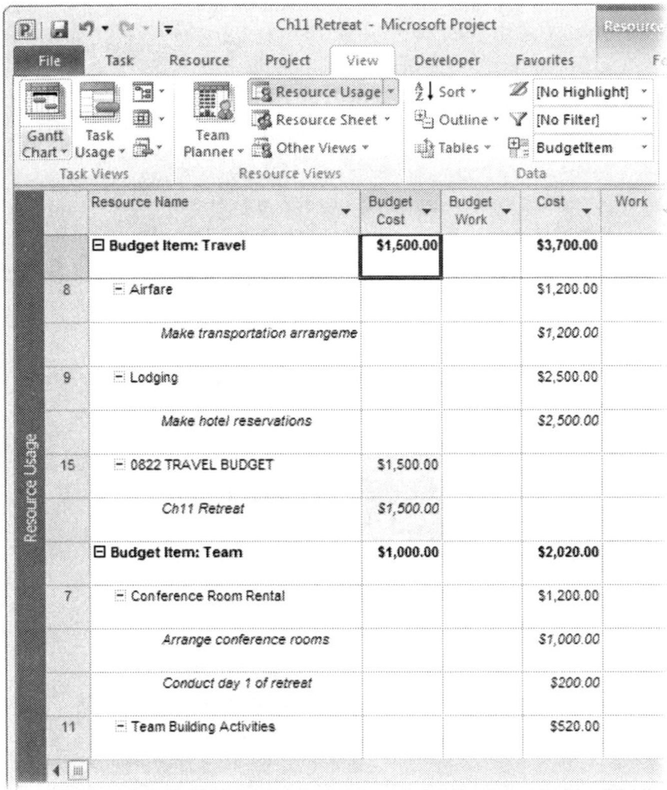

Figure 11-17:
When the Resource Usage view groups resources by budget category, each group includes one budget resource and all the work, material, and cost resources that apply to that budget line item.

Tip: If you want to see resources in alphabetical order, click the down arrow to the right of the Resource Name column heading, and then choose Sort A to Z. Project sorts resources within each group in alphabetical order.

6. **To dismantle the groups, click the down arrow to the right of the Resource Name column heading, and then, on the drop-down menu, choose No Group.**

   The Resource Usage view returns to its ungrouped state.

Tip: Given all the steps needed to fashion a view for comparing budget values, a view with everything already in place can save you time. You want the Budget Cost, Budget Work, Cost, and Work columns side by side, the group by budget category text field applied, and resources sorted by name. See Chapter 23 to learn how to create a custom view, custom table, and custom group. You can also download the BudgetVSPlanned view (with its custom table and group) from ProjectMM_Customizations.mpp at *www. missingmanuals.com/cds*.

With your budget fields and values in place, and a custom budget resource view created, you have everything you need to compare budget values to planned values at any point during the project. See Chapter 15 for more information about monitoring costs during the execution phase.

Reducing Project Costs

You've diligently entered costs into your project plan and either looked at the resulting cost totals as described in "Reviewing Cost Information" on page 295, or compared your planned costs against your budget, as described in "Comparing Costs To Your Budget" on page 302. If your costs are coming out to $110,000 when your maximum is $95,000, you have to figure out how to trim $15,000 from your planned project costs or heads will roll—most likely yours. How does one go about cutting thousands of dollars from a project? Answer: very carefully.

First, look at your cost assumptions to make sure mistakes haven't sent project costs into the stratosphere. If you're lucky, you can correct the misplaced zero you find and everything becomes hunky-dory. The next line of defense is to reschedule tasks to reduce costs. You can also examine resource assignments to look for ways to cut costs.

Note: For more information about viewing costs in your project plan, including running cost reports, see pages 334 and 335.

This section discusses each of these cost-cutting techniques. However, if these methods aren't enough to solve your budget crisis, it's time to take a hard look at the budget itself and propose a change to the project budget, scope, or schedule.

Checking for Cost Errors

When your TV suddenly doesn't turn on, or you can't get the channel that's showing world championship bass fishing, you probably don't schedule a technician service call right away. You poke around, hit buttons on the remote, turn things off and on, and see if the picture comes back. If you're really thinking straight, the very first thing you check is whether your dog unplugged the TV cables or power cord again.

The same troubleshooting principle applies when planned project costs don't jibe with your project budget. Don't assume that the project is really $15,000 over budget just yet. Look for errors, starting with the simple, most obvious things first. In this section, you learn how to systematically scan your project plan for mistakes in cost values or calculations.

Here are cost-related items to check, and where to look for them:

- **Task durations.** Review task durations for any that approach the length of geologic eras. Durations affect cost because Project multiplies duration by rates to calculate cost.

- **Cost per use.** In the Resource Sheet, look for values in the Cost Per Use column (page 198). Remember that a cost per use is levied for each task a resource is assigned to. For example, suppose a crane costs $5,000 to get it on-site. If you apply the $5,000 as cost per use, and then assign the crane to six tasks, your project cost includes $30,000 for crane setup instead of only $5,000. In this situation, a cost resource for getting the crane on-site makes more sense than cost per use. On the other hand, a Dumpster may cost $5 a day to have on-site as well as $450 each time you empty it. If a resource has a standard rate combined with a cost per use, make sure they're both legitimate.

- **Resource rates.** Also in the Resource Sheet, review the rates you've assigned to human, equipment, and material resources. If you have a lot of resources, consider sorting by standard rate so that excessively high or low rates stand out. (For example, if a janitor comes out higher than your information architect, someone's standard rate is off.) Click the down arrow to the right of the Std. Rate column heading and then, on the drop-down menu, choose Sort Descending. To return the view to its normal order, choose View→Data→Sort→"by ID".

- **Planned assignment costs.** Apply the Cost table to the Resource Sheet, and then check your resources' costs on their assignments. The Cost field shows the total planned cost for a resource for all tasks it's assigned to. To see the resources that run the tab up the most, sort the view by the Cost field (click the down arrow to the right of the Cost column heading and then, on the drop-down menu, choose Sort Largest to Smallest). Then you can focus on ways to reduce the costs for those resources.

- **Cost resource amounts.** To easily review cost resource amounts, display the Resource Usage view, apply the Cost table, and then group the view by resource type (click the down arrow to the right of the Resource Name column heading and then, on the drop-down menu, choose "Group by"→Resource Type). Scroll down to the Type: Cost grouping, and the result looks similar to Figure 11-18. To return the view to its normal ungrouped arrangement, choose the down arrow to the right of the Resource Name column heading and then, on the drop-down menu, choose No Group.

- **Fixed costs for tasks.** In the Gantt Chart view, check any fixed costs for tasks to see if they have one or two zeroes too many. Apply the Cost table to the view, and then sort by the Fixed Cost field. (Click the down arrow to the right of the Fixed Cost column heading and then, on the drop-down menu, choose Sort Largest to Smallest to show the highest fixed costs at the top of the view.) Make sure you're not using a fixed cost and a cost resource for the same expense on the same task.

After you've thoroughly reviewed resource cost assumptions, as well as task information that affects cost, be sure to take a closer look at the budget itself. Rather than being carved into stone by lightning bolts from on high, the budget is prepared by a human being like you. Check the assumptions in the budget, and make sure someone hasn't made any outlandish mistakes there.

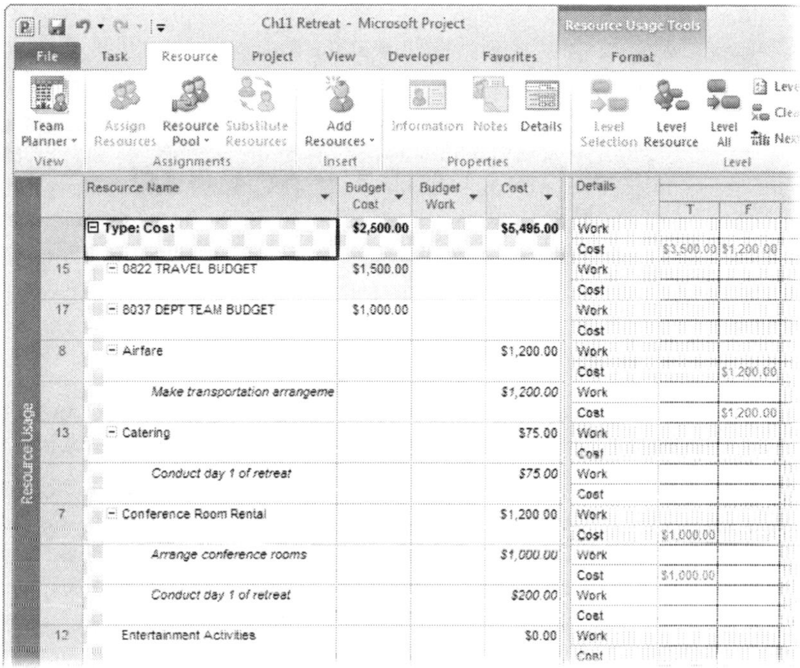

Figure 11-18:
When you apply
the Cost table to the
Resource Usage view,
and then group the
view by resource type,
you see all the cost
resources together,
the tasks they're
assigned to, and the
amounts designated
for each assignment.
If you find an error,
you can change it
right there in the
assignment row.

Adjusting the Schedule

If your planned costs and the budget still don't see eye-to-eye after you've corrected cost mistakes, it's time for Plan B: adjusting the schedule. Here are some ways you can adjust the schedule to reduce costs:

- **Task durations, part deux.** You've already scrutinized task durations looking for possible errors. Now see if there's any way to *realistically* shorten durations and still get the job done. Sometimes shortening tasks actually costs *more,* as described in the section on crashing projects on page 350.

  In the Gantt Chart view, make sure the Entry table is visible. You can run down the tasks in order or sort the schedule by duration to cherry-pick the longest durations for your scrutiny. To show the longest durations at the top of the view, choose View→Data→Sort→Sort By, and then, in the "Sort by" box, choose Duration and select the Descending option. Turn off the "Keep outline structure" checkbox, and then click Sort. To hide summary tasks, choose Format→Show/Hide and turn off the Summary Tasks checkbox.

- **Task relationships.** Sometimes by linking tasks more aggressively (fast-tracking, described on page 347), you can shorten the time you have to pay resources while they wait for their next task to begin. To most easily review task relationships, in a Gantt Chart view, look at the Gantt bars.

- **Date constraints.** Any constraints other than As Soon As Possible (or As Late As Possible for a project scheduled from the finish date) are worth a second look (page 168). If you have a task with a Must Finish On or Start No Earlier Than date constraint applied, resources may be waiting in limbo unnecessarily for the right time to work on tasks. Removing that limbo time can help you cut costs. Add the Constraint Type and Constraint Date fields to a table, and then sort or group by Constraint Type.

Adjusting Assignments

If you've adjusted the schedule to optimize your costs but you still have more belt tightening to do, try adjusting resource assignments. Here are a few strategies to try:

- **Replace expensive resources with cheaper ones.** Consider having your more experienced (and probably more expensive) resources mentor your less costly resources for a short time on tasks, rather than working the entire task. Or use cheaper in-house—perhaps borrowed—resources, rather than more expensive outside consultants. On the other hand, sometimes hiring temporary contract labor is cheaper than using your in-house employees.

- **Do away with overtime.** If your current schedule involves overtime, see if you can adjust assignments to eliminate overtime (on resources that cost more for overtime, of course).

Rethinking Your Project Budget

If your best efforts on project costs still don't line them up with the project budget, then it's time for renegotiation. You've checked and rechecked that your costs reflect the project reality—as you know it so far. The next step is talking to the customer, the project sponsor, or whichever head honcho holds the purse strings. There are two choices in this situation.

- **Get a bigger budget.** The first and usually most difficult option you may consider is trying to get more money appropriated for the project.

- **Cut back on project scope or quality.** Cutting the number of tasks, for example, a particular phase, or reducing quality objectives can cut costs—but only if all the stakeholders agree. See page 353 to learn how to inactivate tasks you cut from the project. If the stakeholders find more money and decide to add the scope back in, you can reactivate those tasks in no time.

Setting the Project Fiscal Year

You can set the fiscal year for a project, whether it's the one your own company uses or that of the project customer's organization. Whether the fiscal year starts in January, July, or October, a project fiscal year can make working with financial accounting departments much simpler.

Note: You may have heard that Project lets you set up fiscal periods in the project, like 28-day periods, 13-week periods, and so on. This timesheet-related feature is available in the enterprise project management features through Project Server.

Project handles fiscal years in a rather limited way, and it may cause more confusion than convenience. While Project can show you the fiscal year in the timescale headings of Gantt Chart views and usage views, Project doesn't change any other dates in the project: The project start and finish dates, working time calendar, resource availability dates, and reports all still use the calendar year. If you want to see fiscal year dates in views, here's what you do:

1. **Choose File→Options, and then, in the Project Options dialog box, choose Schedule.**

   You can choose the project in the "Calendar options for this project" drop-down list to set its fiscal year.

2. **In the "Fiscal year starts in" box, choose the month in which the fiscal year begins.**

   For example, if your fiscal year runs from June 1 through May 31, choose June.

3. **If your fiscal year is named by the calendar year in which the fiscal year begins, turn on the "Use starting year for FY numbering" checkbox.**

   Suppose your fiscal year 2010 runs from calendar dates June 2010 through May 2011. With the "Use starting year for FY numbering" checkbox turned on, Project sets your fiscal year 2010 dates so they start in 2010: that is, from June 2010 through May 2011.

   Turn off the "Use starting year for FY numbering" checkbox if your fiscal year is named by the calendar year in which the fiscal year *ends*. For example, if your 2011 fiscal year runs from June 2010 through May 2011 and you use the calendar year in which the fiscal year ends, Project refers to the months as "June 2011" through "May 2011."

4. **If you want this fiscal year setting to apply to all projects from this point forward, in the "Calendar options for this project" drop-down list, choose All New Projects.**

   Do this only if most of your projects work on this fiscal year. Otherwise it's probably best to set the fiscal year individually for each project.

The fiscal year is reflected in the timescale headings of Gantt Chart views and usage views, as shown in Figure 11-19.

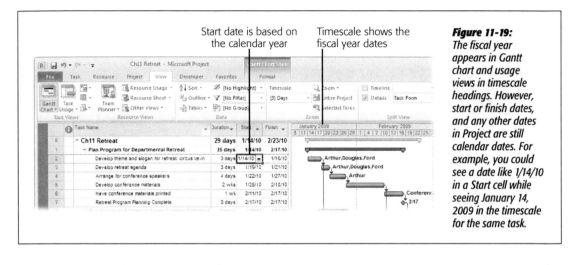

Start date is based on the calendar year

Timescale shows the fiscal year dates

Figure 11-19:
The fiscal year appears in Gantt chart and usage views in timescale headings. However, start or finish dates, and any other dates in Project are still calendar dates. For example, you could see a date like 1/14/10 in a Start cell while seeing January 14, 2009 in the timescale for the same task.

Tip: If you've set your fiscal year but the timescale headings haven't changed, first check the zoom level of your timescale. If it's zoomed way in to an hour-by-hour basis, Project typically doesn't list the year. Drag the Zoom slider on the status bar until you can see days. The major timescale should show the year. If the year still isn't "fiscal," then right-click anywhere in the timescale heading. In the Timescale dialog box, make sure the "Use fiscal year" checkbox is turned on for the tiers (top, middle, bottom) you're using in your project. Also check the label, and make sure the label includes the year.

Assigning Accounting Codes

Sometimes it takes more than a handful of chocolate-covered peanuts to keep the accountants happy. Project data that maps to the organization's accounting codes may be just the ticket. Fortunately, it's easy to include accounting codes in Project, whether it's just a simple account number or a hierarchical structure of multilevel codes. Either way, you can enter accounting codes that map to resources, tasks, or project phases. In this section, you'll learn how to create accounting codes in either a flat listed structure or a multilevel outline structure.

Entering Accounting Codes in a Custom Field

To associate accounting codes with resources or tasks, you must set up a custom field. To create a custom field for accounting codes, choose Project→Properties→Custom Fields. For a refresher on the details of setting up a custom field, refer to "Adding Custom Budget Information" on page 300, and "Coding Tasks and Resources" on page 652. Here are some of the settings accounting codes rely on:

- **Task or Resource field.** Select the Task option if your accounting codes map to tasks or phases. Select the Resource option if your accounting codes map to employees, equipment, materials, or cost resources.

- **Number or Text field type.** If your accounting codes consist strictly of numbers, like "100103" or "4400," select Number as the custom field type. If your accounting codes include numbers with any letters or special characters, like "25-4400" or "BT_052466," then select the Text field, which is more flexible.

Note: If your accounting codes have multiple levels in a hierarchical structure, select the Outline Code field, and refer to "Creating Multilevel Accounting Codes" on page 322.

- **Field name.** Click Rename, and then give the custom field a descriptive name, like "Accounting Code" or "Acct #."

- **Lookup table.** A lookup table makes it easy to pick valid values, which accountants worship. To set up a lookup table that acts as a drop-down list, click Lookup. Type the first accounting code in row 1 under Value, and then, in the Description column, type an explanation of the code, as shown in Figure 11-20.

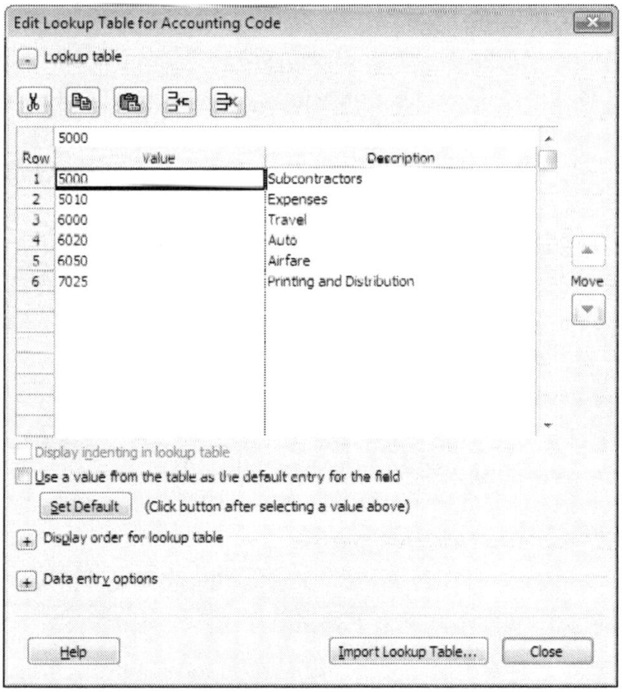

Figure 11-20:
An explanation of codes in the Description column helps you choose the proper codes when you're assigning them to project resources or tasks. In a table in a view, clicking the down arrow in the accounting code cell displays a drop-down list of the values in the lookup table.

Creating Multilevel Accounting Codes

If your organization's accounting codes are a hierarchical structure of levels within levels, create a custom outline code rather than a number or text field. Then, the drop-down list that appears in the custom field cell in a table shows this hierarchy. In a long list of accounting codes, this multilevel outline code can help you find the code you need more quickly. This section describes how to create a new outline code, set up the format for the code, and create the outline code's lookup table.

Selecting and naming your new outline code

Follow these steps to begin to create an outline code to hold your multilevel accounting codes:

1. **Choose Project→Properties→Custom Fields.**

   The Custom Fields dialog box appears.

2. **At the top of the dialog box, select either the Task or Resource option as appropriate.**

   If some accounting codes apply to tasks and others apply to resources, you'll have to create two sets of outline codes—one for tasks and the other for resources. You can't combine them.

3. **In the Type box, choose Outline Code.**

   Although almost all the custom fields let you create a lookup table for them, the outline code is the only custom field for which you can create a multilevel lookup table.

4. **In the list of fields, select the next available outline code, for example, Outline Code1 or Outline Code10.**

   You typically know a custom field is available if it doesn't include a second name in parentheses.

5. **Click Rename, type the name you want for this field, for example, *Code Number* or *Accounting*, and then click OK.**

   The renamed field appears in the list of outline codes.

6. **Keep the Custom Fields dialog box open, and go on to the next section to set the format for your accounting code.**

Setting the format for the multilevel accounting code

Create the format and multilevel structure for your accounting code as follows:

1. **In the "Custom attributes" section, click Lookup.**

   The Edit Lookup Table dialog box appears. It has additional options from the Edit Lookup Table dialog box for other types of custom fields.

2. **At the top of the Edit Lookup Table dialog box, click the + next to "Code mask".**

   Project expands the "Code mask" section.

3. **Click Edit Mask.**

   The Code Mask Definition dialog box appears, as shown in Figure 11-21.

   The *code mask* is the template that specifies the type of characters, the sequence, and the length of the code in each level of the outline code, as well as the character that separates each of the multiple levels. For example, suppose one of your typical accounting codes looks like "B-20.1544." You can specify this format as the code mask.

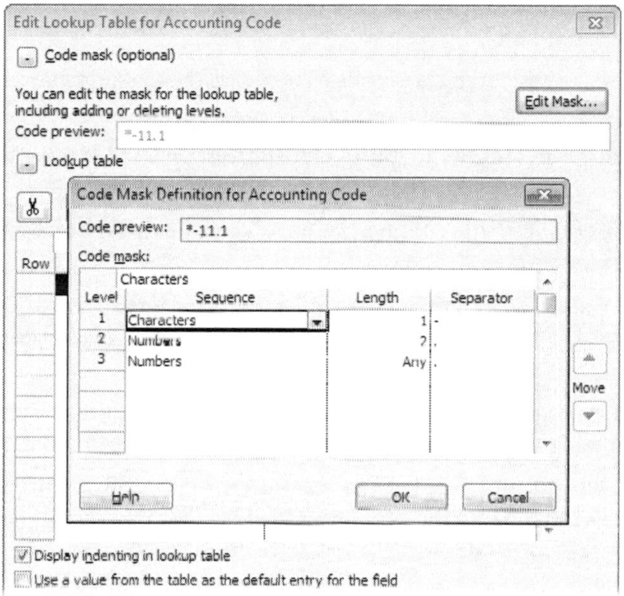

Figure 11-21:
In a code mask, you can set a level of the mask to a specific length or a variable length. If the length is always one digit, for example, select 1. If it could be one to three digits, you must select Any, even though this choice allows any length in that section of the outline. As you define the code mask, the "Code preview" box shows what the mask you're defining looks like.

4. **In the first row of the Sequence column, choose whether the first part of your accounting code is a number, uppercase letters, lowercase letters, or alphanumeric characters.**

   In the B-20.1544 example, the first level is an uppercase letter.

5. **In the Length column for the first row, specify how many characters the first level of the code can have.**

   If it's always one digit, for example, select 1. If it could be one to three digits, select Any.

6. **In the Separator column for the first row, select the character that separates the first and second levels of the code.**

   In the B-20.1544 example, the first-level separator is a hyphen.

7. **In the second row, repeat steps 4–6 to define the second level of the code.**

   As you specify the format for each outline code level, the "Code preview" box shows an example of your code. Repeat this step for each level in the code.

8. **When you're done, click OK to close the Code Mask Definition dialog box.**

   Keep the Edit Lookup Table dialog box open and go on to the next section to create the multilevel lookup table for your accounting code.

Creating a multilevel lookup table for an accounting code

Now enter the actual accounting codes in the multiple levels you need by following these steps:

1. **In the Edit Lookup Table dialog box, be sure the "Display indenting in lookup table" checkbox is turned on.**

   This checkbox shows the hierarchical outline structure in the lookup table while you're setting it up.

2. **Select the first Value cell, and then type a value for the top level of your first accounting code.**

   For the B-20.1544 example, you would type *B* in the Value field. Type a description in the Description field.

3. **Select the second Value cell, and then type a value for the second level of your first accounting code. Then click Indent to show that this level is subordinate to the first level.**

   For the B-20.1544 example, you would type *20* in the Value cell. If you enter a value that doesn't match the code mask, Project displays the value in red.

4. **Select the third Value cell, and then type a value for the third level of your first accounting code. Then click the Indent button to show that this third level is subordinate to the second level.**

   For the B-20.1544 example, you would type *1544* in the Value cell, as shown in Figure 11-22.

5. **Continue entering accounting codes until all the levels in all the codes are done.**

   Click Close. Then click OK to close the Custom Fields dialog box. Your multilevel accounting codes are saved with the project.

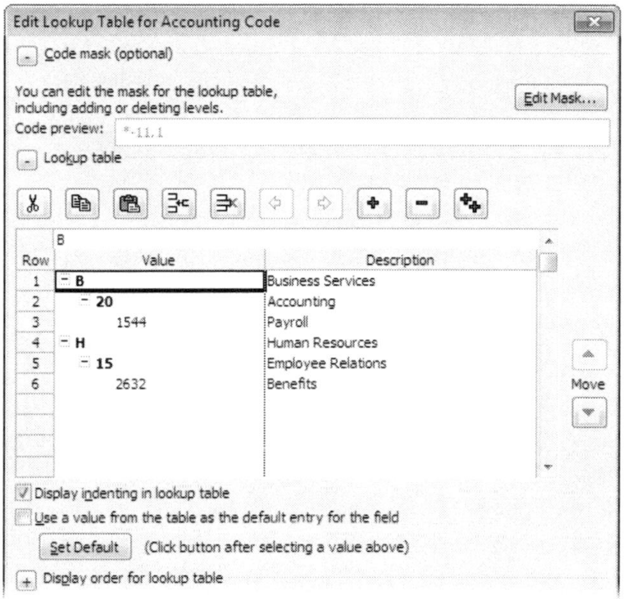

Figure 11-22:
Click Indent or Outdent to move a value to another level. You can also cut, copy, and paste values to other locations in the lookup table. If a value doesn't match the code mask you specified, then the characters appear in red. Click the Insert Row button to add the number of rows necessary for the succeeding level.

Applying Accounting Codes to Your Project

With a custom accounting code field in hand, add it to the table of your choice (right-click the table heading and then choose Insert Column). Remember, you can add only a task field to a task-oriented view and table. Likewise, you can add only a resource field to a resource-oriented view and table. With the new column in place, work through your tasks or resources, and then enter the appropriate accounting codes.

After you've applied your accounting codes, you can sort, group, and filter information by accounting code, as described in Chapter 23. You can also create reports that use the accounting code. For more information about generating reports, see Chapter 17.

CHAPTER 12

Refining a Project Schedule

Balancing a project's scope, schedule, budget, and quality is a bit like juggling eggs. If you don't keep an eye on every element, you'll end up with egg on your face. In the chapters so far, you've built a Project schedule based on scope and quality objectives. Now it's time to see whether the actual timeline and price are right.

Most of the time, a schedule's first draft doesn't satisfy all project objectives. You must make changes until the equation works—for instance, you might shorten task duration, decrease cost, or reduce scope. As you go, you must review the schedule to see if your changes are getting the results you want. Shortening the schedule may increase the cost, but so can lengthening the schedule.

This chapter starts by describing how to use Project to see whether the schedule and costs are what stakeholders want. You'll learn how to find the best tasks to shorten if the schedule is too long. If you need to modify the schedule, you'll learn how to use the Task Inspector to evaluate your options. Change highlighting shows you whether your changes will achieve what you want.

Techniques for shortening a schedule and reining in spending start with the same resource assignment approaches you learned in Chapter 9: finding resources with more availability, assigning more resources, and so on. You'll also find out about a few brawnier (though riskier) techniques like *fast-tracking* (vigorously overlapping tasks) and *crashing* (aggressively adding resources or spending more money to shorten duration).

Evaluating the Project Schedule

The fat lady won't sing until the finish dates in Project meet the project's deadlines *and* the project price is right. Keep fine-tuning the Project schedule until both the schedule and price are in line. This second round of work is also a good time to correct any errors lurking in your schedule, as the box on page 330 describes. In this section, you'll learn how to review dates and costs in your Project file. You'll also learn how to find the best tasks to change.

Comparing Finish Dates to Deadlines

Finish dates are conspicuous in the Gantt Chart timescale, because that's where task bars end. The Finish field also appears in the Entry, Schedule, Summary, Usage, and Variance tables, to name a few. But what you really want is to see whether the finish dates come on or before the project's deadlines.

During planning, you can compare the finish date for the project and key milestones to the deadlines requested by stakeholders. However, as you learned on page 169, the Deadline field helps track important dates during planning and project execution. You can filter the task list to focus on tasks with deadlines, and look for missed deadline indicators to identify problem areas.

Tip: Tasks that finish on time during planning may not stay that way when the work begins. Missed deadline indicators appear as soon as estimated finish dates are later than their corresponding deadline dates, so it's a good idea to check for missed deadline indicators regularly.

When you assign a date in a task's Deadline field, a deadline arrow appears at that date in the Gantt Chart timescale (the arrow may be solid green or outlined in black, depending on the view). The task's finish date is late if the task bar ends to the right of the arrow. However, these deadline arrows aren't especially eye-catching. Filtering the task list to show missed deadlines makes them easier to see. The missed deadline indicator is another hint that the finish date isn't working. Here's how to compare finish dates with deadlines:

1. **To show only tasks with deadlines, choose View→Data, click the down arrow next to the filter box, and then choose More Filters. In the More Filters dialog box, double-click Tasks With Deadlines.**

    Project shows tasks with deadlines but also shows the summary tasks to which they belong, as you can see in Figure 12-1.

2. **To find tasks that miss their deadlines, look in the Indicators column in the Entry table for red diamonds with exclamation points inside.**

    If tasks miss their deadlines by a mile, the deadline arrows in the timescale may be a long way from the end of the task bar, so the two may not be visible in the timescale at the same time, depending on the timescale units. Remember, you can drag the Zoom slider in the status bar to change the time periods that appear in the timescale.

By scanning the Indicators column for missed deadline indicators, you can identify the tasks to focus on. Of course, if you don't see any missed deadline indicators, you can move on to checking whether the project's cost works.

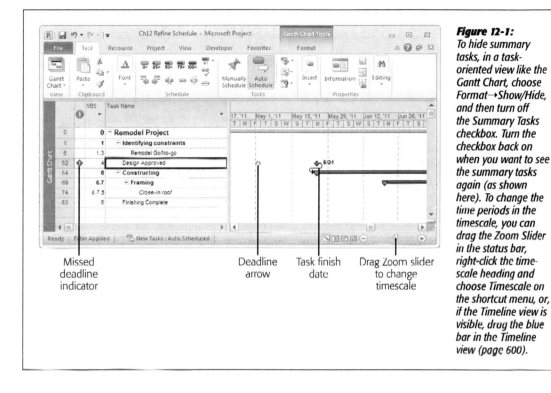

Figure 12-1:
To hide summary tasks, in a task-oriented view like the Gantt Chart, choose Format→Show/Hide, and then turn off the Summary Tasks checkbox. Turn the checkbox back on when you want to see the summary tasks again (as shown here). To change the time periods in the timescale, you can drag the Zoom Slider in the status bar, right-click the timescale heading and choose Timescale on the shortcut menu, or, if the Timeline view is visible, drag the blue bar in the Timeline view (page 600).

Missed deadline indicator

Deadline arrow

Task finish date

Drag Zoom slider to change timescale

Finding the Best Tasks to Shorten

When a project schedule is too long, you want to rein it in with the least amount of disruption to the work you've done so far. The *critical path* controls a project's finish date, because it's the longest sequence of tasks in a project. If the critical path gets delayed, so does the end of the project. (That's why it's called the *critical* path.) Because tasks on the critical path directly affect a project's finish date, they're the best candidates for shortening.

To find the critical path on your own, locate the task with the latest finish date, and then trace back through its predecessors until you reach the beginning of the project. Each task on the critical path is called a *critical task*.

To be precise, the critical path is the longest sequence of tasks without any scheduling leeway (called *slack time*). Slack time is the amount of time a task's finish date can move without affecting another part of the project. Free slack is how much a task can move without affecting its successors. Total slack is the time a task can move without affecting the end of the project. The lack of slack time is the reason critical tasks affect a project's finish. (If you want insurance for your project's finish date, you can add buffers to your schedule. Then, if tasks delay, they eat into the buffers instead of delaying the finish date, as described on page 121.)

REALITY CHECK

Double-Checking the Schedule

Mistakes will always linger in your project schedule, no matter how many times you check it. Moreover, as you refine the schedule, you can introduce mistakes that weren't there before. So as you fine-tune the schedule, stay on the lookout for errors. For example, you may notice a task scheduled when you know the assigned resource is on vacation, or spot the wrong kind of task dependency between two tasks. Watch for the following items:

- Task dependencies that shouldn't be there or should be a different type (page 156).
- Tasks with inflexible date constraints (page 166) that they shouldn't have.
- Manually scheduled tasks that you should have switched to auto-scheduled (page 233).
- Work or duration values that seem too low or too high (page 239).

- Work package tasks without assigned resources (page 214).
- Summary tasks *with* assigned resources.
- Overallocated resources (page 269).
- Resource calendars that don't represent people's actual availability (page 239).

In addition, make sure you've included tasks and time for often-overlooked types of work, like project-related meetings (including status meetings and project management meetings) and work reviews. Because several people attend these powwows, the time and expenses add up fast. Even approvals aren't as simple as signing the sign-off sheet. Be sure to include time for people to review documents or other deliverables before they approve them.

Note: Microsoft didn't come up with the concept of the critical path. Project uses the critical path method (CPM) to calculate the start and finish dates for tasks. To learn about the critical path method and its task date calculations, check out *Project Planning, Scheduling & Control,* by James P. Lewis (McGraw-Hill). (Chapter 5 of that book has the CPM information.)

Driving somewhere is a simple example of a critical path and slack time. Suppose you and your brother are both heading to your elderly Aunt Thelma's for lunch, which starts at noon sharp. You're taking the highway, which takes 65 minutes. Your brother, on the other hand, is driving his sports car over the scenic route, which is 90 minutes of twists and turns. Your brother's drive is the critical path, because it takes the longest. That gives you 25 minutes of slack time before you must start driving (or you can use the time to stop and pick flowers for your dear auntie).

Once you start executing a project, you must keep close watch on the critical path. Delays that occur in critical tasks directly affect the project finish date.

Displaying the critical path in Project

The standard Gantt Chart view doesn't show the critical path or slack time initially. All you see are blue task bars. However, in Project 2010, you can easily format the view to display the critical path and slack time. Choose Format. In the Bar Styles section, turn on the Critical Tasks checkbox and the Slack checkbox. The Gantt Chart displays critical tasks in red and shows slack as narrow black bars at the right end of task bars.

The critical path appears in red in the Tracking Gantt view (choose Task→View, click the down arrow, and then choose Tracking Gantt) and the Detail Gantt view (choose Task→View, click the down arrow, choose→More Views, and then double-click Detail Gantt). The Tracking Gantt view displays gray task bars for the baseline schedule, blue task bars for noncritical tasks, and the Entry table in the table area. The Detail Gantt view shows noncritical path task bars in blue and critical path task bars in red along with the Delay table so you can evaluate leveling delays.

Filtering the task list to show critical tasks

Filtering the task list to show only critical path tasks helps you focus on shortening the tasks with the most bang for the buck. When you use filters, you must reapply them regularly, like sunscreen, as the box on page 333 explains. To filter the task list to show only critical path tasks, do the following:

1. **Choose View→Data. Click the down arrow next to the filter box, and then choose Critical.**

    Project shows critical path tasks and the summary tasks to which they belong.

2. **To hide the summary tasks, choose Format→Show/Hide, and then turn off the Summary Tasks checkbox.**

    The summary tasks disappear, so you see only critical work package tasks.

Tip: Grouping by critical status keeps noncritical tasks visible but out of the way. Click the down arrow to the right of the Task Name column heading. In the drop-down menu, choose "Group by"→Critical. Project lists all the noncritical tasks first (under Critical: No), and then lists critical tasks (under Critical: Yes). Revert to the regular order by right-clicking the down arrow to the right of the Task Name column heading and then choosing No Group.

Showing critical tasks in a Gantt Chart table

Bright red task bars in the timescale make the critical path easy to see. But the tasks in the table area still look exactly the same. Project has formatting features that can highlight the critical path in tables as well. If you want to see the critical path even in the Gantt Chart table area, do the following:

1. **To change the appearance of the table text for critical tasks, choose Format→Format→Text Styles.**

   The Text Styles dialog box opens. The advantage to formatting text styles instead of individual text elements is that Project applies the style whenever it's appropriate. For example, if you modify the appearance of text for critical tasks, then Project applies or removes the formatting as tasks join or drop off the critical path, making it easier for you to spot the changes.

2. **In the Item to Change drop-down list, choose Critical Tasks.**

   Any changes you make to the font or colors apply to all critical path tasks.

3. **Choose the font, font style, and font size.**

   The Font list displays the fonts installed on your computer. The "Font style" list controls whether or not the text is bold or in italics. The Size list includes the standard font sizes. (You can type a number in the box to specify a font size not in the list.) Turn on the Underline checkbox if you want the text underlined as well.

4. **Optionally, to change the font color, in the Color drop-down list, choose the color you want (for example, red to match the task bars).**

   Colors other than black can make text hard to read. If you do change text color, opt for dark colors. In addition, remember that colors may not reproduce well when you print in black and white. Consider yourself warned.

5. **To highlight cells that use a text style, in the Background Color drop-down list, choose the color you want.**

   For example, you can change the background for critical cells to red (shown as light gray highlighting in Figure 12-2). As you select options and settings, the Sample box previews the text appearance.

6. **Click OK.**

   Cells that use the text style immediately show the new formatting. The background color and pattern apply to all critical task cells, except for the Indicators column. These changes appear every time you apply the current table. You can also create a custom table (page 611) to show critical tasks in this way.

Reviewing Project Costs

By assigning work, material, and cost resources to tasks, as you learned about in Chapters 8 and 9, Project can calculate the price tag for your project. You can show costs in many of the standard views by applying a table with cost fields. For example, the Gantt Chart view shows both costs for the entire project and individual tasks. The Cost table applied to a usage view shows the cost of individual assignments.

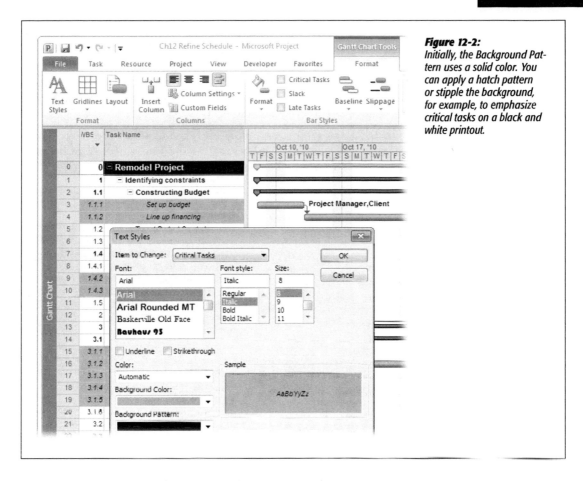

Figure 12-2:
Initially, the Background Pattern uses a solid color. You can apply a hatch pattern or stipple the background, for example, to emphasize critical tasks on a black and white printout.

The Ever-Changing Critical Path

The critical path can be a slippery path, too. Sometimes shortening a critical task adds a different task to the critical path that wasn't there before. Conversely, since the critical path shows the longest path from start to finish, shortening a task may actually turn it into a *noncritical* task. To understand how this works, consider two tasks that start on the same day. The critical task takes 10 days, and the noncritical one takes 9 days. If you shorten the critical task to 8 days, it isn't the longest path anymore, and it becomes

a noncritical task. In the meantime, the 9-day task is now the longest and, thus, is now on the critical path.

Because the critical path changes, make sure you're using the current critical path to choose the tasks you want to work on. Although the Critical filter initially shows only critical tasks, it doesn't update itself as tasks change their critical status. To quickly reapply the current filter, press Ctrl+Shift+F3.

Here are a few ways to review project costs:

- **Reviewing total project cost.** If the total price is the only thing that matters, look at the cost for the entire project. The project summary task is an easy way to see project-wide cost (page 297). Display the project summary task by choosing Format→Show/Hide and then turning on the Project Summary Task checkbox. When you're ready to compare estimated cost to actual cost, the Project Statistics dialog box (page 297) can't be beat.

- **Seeing costs in the table area.** Apply the Cost table by choosing View→Data→Tables→Cost. As shown in Figure 12-3, the Total Cost cell for the project summary task represents the total cost of the project.

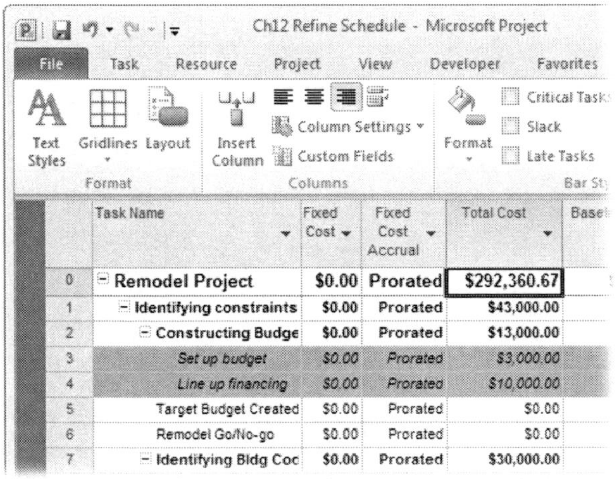

Figure 12-3:
The Total Cost cell for the project summary task is a rolled-up value of cost for every task in the project. Total cost includes labor and material costs, other costs you've assigned with cost resources, and any cost you've added as fixed cost. Project calculates this current estimate of the total cost by adding the actual cost of completed work to the estimated cost for work that hasn't been done.

- **Review project statistics.** The Project Statistics dialog box (page 410) provides an overview of project status. To open it, choose Project→Properties→Project Information, and then click Statistics.

- **Displaying task and assignment costs.** To see task and assignment costs, simply apply the Cost table to the appropriate view (page 611). The Cost table includes columns for planned and actual costs. For example, Baseline shows the cost when you saved the baseline, Actual is the actual cost for work completed so far, and Variance is the difference between the baseline and the current scheduled cost.

The view you apply depends on which costs you want to see. If you apply the Cost table to task-oriented views, the table area shows task costs. In the Task Usage and Resource Usage views, the Cost table shows the total cost by task and assignment, while the timescale shows values for each time period, as shown in Figure 12-4.

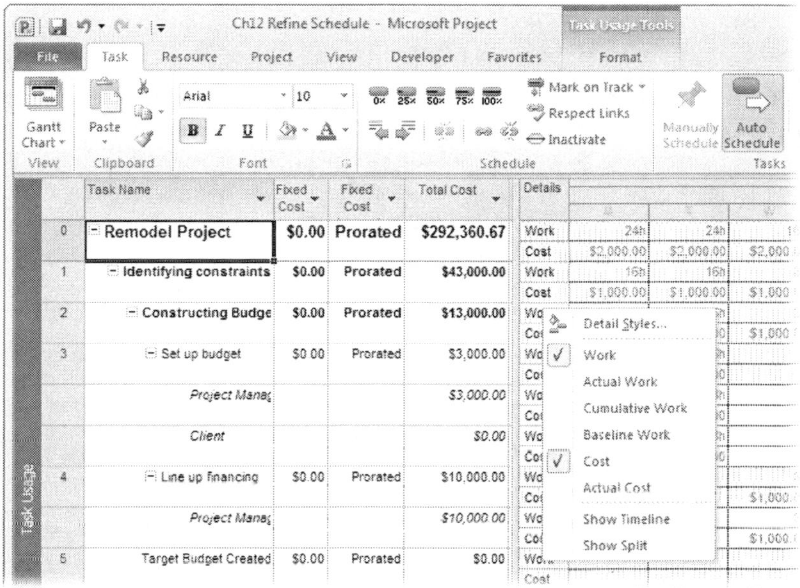

Figure 12-4:
Initially, usage views show only the Work field in the timescale. To see cost for each time period, right-click anywhere within the timescale, and then, on the shortcut menu, choose Cost. Project then adds a second row to each assignment for cost.

Using Project cost reports

Project includes several reports that show you project costs—both text reports and the visual reports. You can use these reports to look at cost for tasks and assignments or to evaluate cash flow over time. Whether text or visual, budget reports show overall cost, while cash flow reports show cost by time period. You can choose from the following reports:

- **Budget report.** The text-based Budget report is like a hard copy of the Cost table. It shows total cost, baseline, and actual costs for each task. One difference is that this report sorts tasks by total cost in descending order, which can be helpful for finding tasks that may be breaking your budget.

- **Cash Flow report.** The text-based Cash Flow report shows Total Cost by week. The last *row* in the report sums the weekly total costs for all tasks. The last *column* in the report shows total cost for each task over the full project duration.

- **Budget Cost Report visual report.** This report displays costs in an Excel pivot table. The Chart1 worksheet contains a Microsoft Excel chart that initially shows cost by quarter. Display the Assignment Usage worksheet to view the data behind the chart and to use pivot table tools to modify the costs you see (page 467).

- **Cash Flow Report visual report.** Project has one Excel-based cash flow visual report and two Microsoft Visio visual reports (one metric and one using US dimensions). Cash Flow Report is an Excel pivot table rendition of project costs initially by quarter, as shown in Figure 12-5.

To open a text-based cost report, choose Project→Reports→Reports. In the Reports dialog box, double-click Costs. In the Cost Reports dialog box, double-click the report you want to see. To open a visual report, choose Project→Reports→Visual Reports. In the Visual Reports dialog box, double-click the name of the visual report you want to generate. Chapter 17 provides the details on generating and customizing text-based and visual reports.

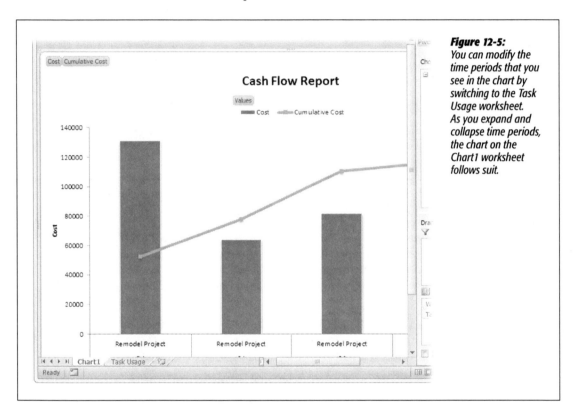

Figure 12-5:
You can modify the time periods that you see in the chart by switching to the Task Usage worksheet. As you expand and collapse time periods, the chart on the Chart1 worksheet follows suit.

Project Tools for Change

As you start changing the schedule in search of shorter duration or lower cost, you can put a triumvirate of Project's change-oriented features through their paces:

- **Task Inspector** is a beefed-up version of Project 2007's Task Drivers feature. It shows the elements that make tasks start when they do or last as long as they do, so you get some hints about how to fix them. In many cases, the task or assignment editing commands you need (Reschedule Task and Team Planner if resources are overallocated) are ready for you, right in the Task Inspector pane.

- **Change highlighting** shades all the cells whose values change in response to an edit you make. You can easily review these highlighted cells to see whether the changes you make produce the results you had in mind.

- **Multilevel Undo** lets you undo as many changes as you want. If you zip through several edits only to find that another strategy is in order, you can undo the changes you made and try a different tack.

See Why Tasks Occur When They Do

Whether you're trying to shorten a schedule during planning or recover from delays during execution, a typical strategy is to make tasks start or end earlier. What you must change to start a task sooner isn't part of the task that should start earlier—it's an element that controls the task's start date, like predecessors and date constraints, to name a few. If an important task takes too long, the factors affecting it help identify what you can change to get back on track. For instance, you may talk to the person whose work calendar is overbooked. In Project 2010, when you select a task and open the Task Inspector, it lists factors that affect the task and any issues like overallocations.

Tip: The Task Inspector is a good start, but it isn't the be-all and end-all for optimizing your schedule. For example, the Task Inspector shows task predecessors. But *you* have to dig deeper to discover that a predecessor's duration is due to a resource who's scheduled for medical leave and that the resolution may be to reassign the predecessor task to someone else. Chapters 9, 10, and 11 show you how to inspect your tasks and assignments from every angle.

To open the Task Inspector pane, choose Task→Tasks→Inspect. Similar to the behavior of the Task Form, the Task Inspector pane shows the factors for the selected task, as shown in Figure 12-6.

If resources are overallocated or task links are a problem, the Task Inspector includes repair options. For example, in Figure 12-6, Task Inspector includes Reschedule Task and Team Planner if you want to remove the overallocation on an overallocated resource. Learn more about Task Inspector on page 251.

Seeing What Changes Do

There's no guarantee your changes will correct the problems you're trying to fix. For example, you could assign more resources to shorten a critical path task only to find out that another task prevents the finish date from changing. Fortunately, Project's *change highlighting* feature shades table cells that have changed due to your last task edit, so you can see whether the results are what you want.

Suppose you assign an additional resource to shorten a task's duration. When the task finishes earlier, its successor tasks start and finish sooner. Change highlighting lights up the task Start and Finish cells with background color, as Figure 12-7 demonstrates. Similarly, if the additional resource increases the cost, the task's Cost field (and its summary task's Cost field) might light up as well.

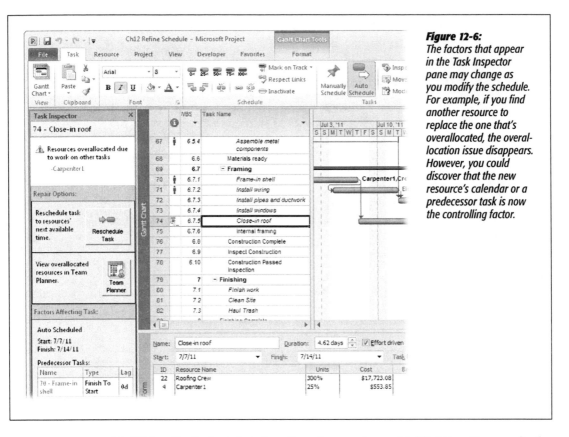

Figure 12-6:
The factors that appear in the Task Inspector pane may change as you modify the schedule. For example, if you find another resource to replace the one that's overallocated, the overallocation issue disappears. However, you could discover that the new resource's calendar or a predecessor task is now the controlling factor.

Modifying the Project view doesn't wash away change highlighting. You can display a new table, filter the schedule, or group tasks, and still see highlighted cells from the last edit. For example, if the Summary table is visible, you can review the changes in dates, duration, and cost. Switching to the Cost table would highlight cost cells affected by the last edit.

When you make another edit, change highlighting shows the effect of this new change. In addition, saving the Project file erases any current change highlighting.

Tip: It's unlikely, but if you want to turn change highlighting off for some reason, you must add the Change Highlighting command to a custom group on the ribbon. See page 661 to learn how to customize the ribbon. The Change Highlighting command is in the All Commands group on the "Customize the Ribbon" screen.

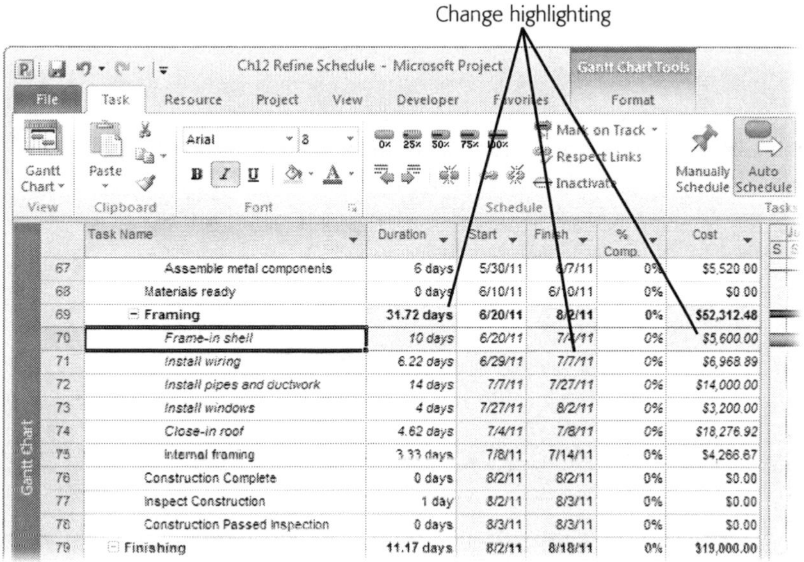

Figure 12-7:
Change highlighting shades cells affected by the last task edit. Project considers all changes you make in a Task Form before you click OK as one edit. So to make the most of change highlighting, make all of your changes in the Task Form at the same time. As soon as you click OK, change highlighting shows the results.

Undoing Changes

Some adverse results are obvious, like a delay in a project finish date after you change the standard work time. Most of the time, though, as in a game of chess, you can't tell whether a strategy will pay off until you're a few moves in. Multilevel Undo, introduced in Project 2007, lets you try short what-if games in your current Project file. You can backtrack through any number of actions if they don't pan out. (See page 355 to learn how to work on more involved what-if scenarios.)

Note: You can specify how many actions Multilevel Undo remembers. Choose File→Options. In the Project Options dialog box, choose Advanced. Under General, in the "Undo levels" box, choose the number of actions to track (up to 99) and then click OK.

Multilevel Undo keeps track of your actions and displays them on a menu so you can select the ones you want to undo. Here's how to put Multilevel Undo to work:

1. **On the Quick Access toolbar, click the down arrow to the right of Undo (which looks like a curved arrow sweeping from right to left).**

   A drop-down menu appears, listing your previous actions with the most recent at the top to the earliest at the bottom. Project clears the Multilevel Undo list when you save your Project file or close and reopen it.

2. **To undo actions, drag down to the earliest one you want to undo.**

   Project highlights the actions from the most recent to the one where the pointer is. The last entry in the drop-down menu says "Undo x Actions", where x is the number of actions you've selected, as in Figure 12-8.

   If you're a prolific editor, you may see a few recent actions and a scroll bar on the drop-down menu. Drag the slider until you reach the earliest command you want to undo, and then click to revert to that point.

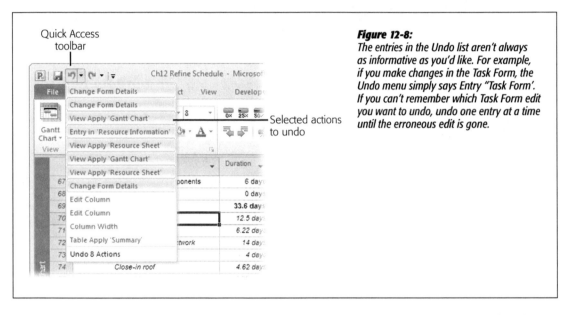

Quick Access toolbar

Selected actions to undo

Figure 12-8:
The entries in the Undo list aren't always as informative as you'd like. For example, if you make changes in the Task Form, the Undo menu simply says Entry "Task Form". If you can't remember which Task Form edit you want to undo, undo one entry at a time until the erroneous edit is gone.

3. **Click the earliest action to undo the recent commands up to and including the action you clicked.**

   Multilevel Undo can unravel everything a macro does, or reverse changes that other applications make to your Project file.

Adjusting Resource Assignments

As you schedule your project, you assign some number of resources to tasks, depending on how much help you need (and how many helpers you can manage). After you complete a draft schedule, you often end up fine-tuning some assignments—and that requires finesse, as discussed in the box on page 341. For example, stakeholders may try to throw resources at a problem, only to have learning curves and chaos delay the task even more. Additional resources can increase costs, which may or may not be OK, as you learn on page 350.

Experienced project managers know that most schedule problems have several solutions. For example, if you find underallocated resources working on critical path tasks, you can increase their assignment units to shorten task durations. Or you can look for a person with the right skills and more available time. If you're trying to cut costs, you can look at replacing expensive resources with people with lower rates.

After you find assignments to change, the editing techniques are the same ones you learned in Chapter 9. This section identifies Project views that help you find the assignments to change, and reviews your assignment editing options.

The Fine Art of Assigning Resources

Experienced project managers assign resources carefully, because they know that resource assignments can affect schedule, cost, risk, and quality. The wrong resources assigned to tasks can increase the risk of delays on the critical path or costs going through the roof. On the other hand, smart assignments can reduce costs or decrease duration—or both. Because critical tasks are so critical, you can't be too choosy with critical task assignments. Here are a few resource assignment strategies to try:

- **Keep resources on critical tasks focused.** When resources have to juggle several tasks at the same time, the risk of delays increases. Although you can tell people to prioritize their critical tasks, one way to prevent delays is to limit the multitasking that resources on critical tasks do. Assign those resources to only one or two tasks at a time.

- **Use less expensive resources.** Some tasks use both experienced and inexperienced people, who typically have different price tags. You can reduce cost by reassigning some or all task work to less expensive, less experienced resources. Offloading work to less expensive resources can be risky, because the people may take longer to do the same work. In addition, newbies on the job may interrupt the experts to the point that no one works productively.

- **Use faster resources.** Sometimes, more expensive resources are *less* expensive in the long run. An inexperienced backhoe operator may cost $50 an hour and take 24 hours to do the job ($1,200 total). If an expert operator costs $100 an hour but finishes the excavation in 8 hours, the cost ($800) *and* duration decrease.

Increasing Units to Decrease Duration

Before you ask people to work extra hours, look for resources on critical path tasks who have time available. You can assign them more work to reduce critical task duration. Project doesn't have a dedicated view for this combination of conditions. However, you can filter a task-oriented view to show the critical path and alter the Resource Graph to show available time, as illustrated in Figure 12-9.

Selecting a task in the table area shows the first resource assigned to that task in the Resource Graph in the bottom pane. To see other resources assigned to the task, click the horizontal scroll bar under the resource legend (on the left).

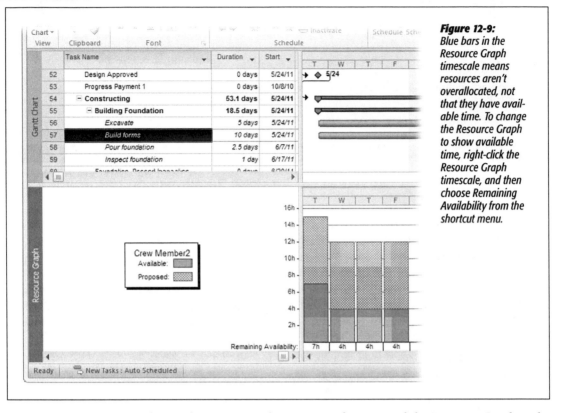

Figure 12-9:
*Blue bars in the
Resource Graph
timescale means
resources aren't
overallocated, not
that they have avail-
able time. To change
the Resource Graph
to show available
time, right-click the
Resource Graph
timescale, and then
choose Remaining
Availability from the
shortcut menu.*

To see the Tracking Gantt in the top pane of a view, and the Resource Graph in the
bottom pane, do the following:

1. **Choose Task→View. Click the down arrow to the right of the view button, and
   then, on the drop-down menu, choose Tracking Gantt.**

   Project displays the Tracking Gantt view. You can use the Detail Gantt or the
   Task Entry view if you've formatted it to show critical tasks.

2. **Choose View→Split View. Turn on the Details checkbox, and then choose
   Resource Graph in the Details drop-down list.**

   The Resource Graph appears in the bottom pane of the view.

3. **Click the bottom pane to make it active.**

   You can tell the bottom pane is active when the narrow vertical bar on the left
   side of the pane is dark, while the vertical bar in the top view is a lighter shade.

Tip: To obtain a ready-made view like this, download ProjectMM_Customizations.mpp from *www.
missingmanuals.com/cds*, and then use the Organizer to copy the "Critical Gantt Resources" view to your
global template (page 669).

Assigning a Different Resource

Suppose a resource works on two simultaneous tasks on the critical path. You can't delay either one without affecting the project finish date. In this situation, the Assign Resources dialog box (choose Resource→Assignments→Assign Resources) can help you find someone with similar skills who has more time available. If money is a bigger problem than time, you can replace the person with someone who costs less (assuming that the replacement can get the work done in the same amount of time).

Note: "Assigning Resources with the Dialog Box" on page 203 describes Assign Resources features in detail. You can also use the Team Planner view to drag an assignment from one resource to another (page 213), although Team Planner doesn't help you find resources with similar skills or identify cost implications.

If you use a custom field like an outline code to identify resources' skills, in the Assign Resources dialog box, turn on the "Filter by" checkbox. Apply a filter to show resources with similar skills, like the Group filter or a custom filter that looks for job description codes. Then, turn on the "Available to work" checkbox, and then type the number of work hours you want from the new resource during the task duration. If the resource you're replacing is assigned 80 hours over 2 weeks, type *80h* to look for someone who can work full time, as Figure 12-10 shows. When you use the "Filter by" features, the Resources table displays the assigned resources, plus any others who have the available time you specified.

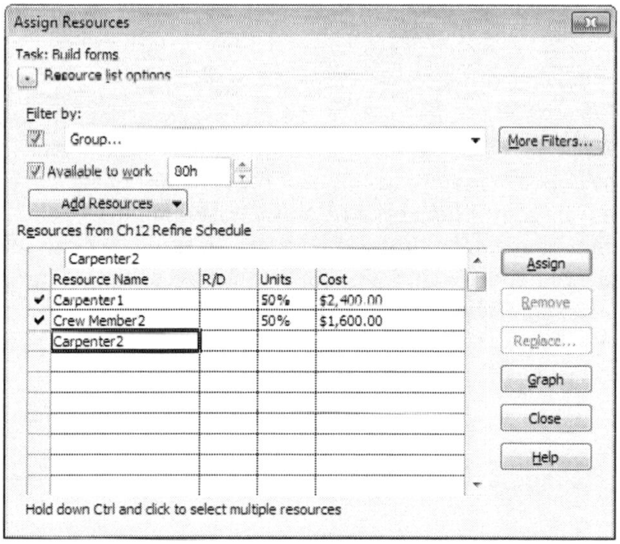

Figure 12-10:
To look for expensive resources to replace, scan the Resources table's Cost cells. For help finding less expensive resources, display the Resource Sheet (choose View→Resource Views→Resource Sheet). You can filter the Resource Sheet to find resources in the same work group (click the down arrow next the Group column heading and then choose "Group on this field") or sort by the resource rate (click the down arrow next to the Standard Rate column heading and then choose Sort Ascending). When you find the resource you want, return to your task-oriented view to replace the resource.

Select the resource you want to replace, and then click Replace. In the Replace Resource dialog box, type a percentage in the replacement's Units field, and then click OK.

Tip: The Assign Resources dialog box doesn't tell you how many hours the current resource is assigned, which makes it difficult to fill in the "Available to work" box. To see how many hours the current resource is assigned, display the Task Form in the view's bottom pane. (Choose View→Split Views, and then, in the Details drop-down list, choose Task Form.) The Work cell shows the number of hours the resource is assigned.

Adding Resources

You can add resources to any task you want. The only special view that may help is the one that shows only the critical path (page 331). However, you must use judgment to decide whether more resources are going to help or hinder.

Using Slack Time to Shorten the Schedule

When a resource works on critical and noncritical tasks at the same time, you can shorten the critical task's duration by assigning more of the resource's time to it. By definition, the noncritical task has slack time, which means you can delay its finish date without delaying the project. Although the noncritical task takes longer, the increase in duration merely consumes some of the task's slack time, as you can see in Figure 12-11.

To see slack time in a Gantt Chart timescale, use the Detail Gantt view. Choose View→Task Views, click the down arrow next to the view button, and then choose Detail Gantt. Task slack time appears as narrow black bars on the right end of task bars. The text at the right end of the slack bar gives you the amount of free slack. (The box on page 346 explains why you may not see any slack in your schedule, and how to fix the problem.)

In Figure 12-11, the critical "Build forms" task in the top window ends on June 7. The "Assemble frame components" task in the top window has 6.5 days of slack. The "Build forms" task in the bottom window uses more of the person's hours, so it ends earlier, on June 2. By moving some of the person's hours to "Build forms," the slack time for "Assemble frame components" drops to zero (which turns this task into a critical task). This juggling of hours was successful, because the critical "Frame-in shell" task went from a start date of June 20 to starting on June 15, 5 days earlier, reducing the critical path by 5 days. The box on page 347 provides another technique for shortening the critical path when other techniques fail.

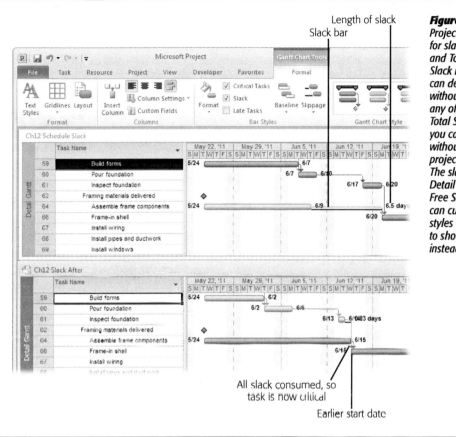

Figure 12-11:
Project has two fields for slack: Free Slack and Total Slack. Free Slack is the time you can delay a task without affecting any of its successors. Total Slack is the time you can delay a task without affecting the project finish date. The slack bars in the Detail Gantt show Free Slack, but you can customize bar styles (page 588) to show Total Slack instead.

Length of slack

Slack bar

All slack consumed, so task is now critical

Earlier start date

My Schedule Has No Slack

If two tasks start at the same time and link to the same successor, the shorter task has slack time (the time between when it ends and its successor begins). Suppose you've applied the Detail Gantt view, and tasks like these show no slack at all. If you've applied deadlines to Project tasks, that's the culprit. Project's Deadline field affects late finish dates, which can go haywire when your tasks don't meet their deadlines. Here's what happens:

In Project, the Late Finish field is the latest date a task can end without affecting the project finish date; the Finish field is a task's currently scheduled finish date. Project's Free Slack field (which the Detail Gantt displays) is the length of time between a task's late finish and finish. For example, if the late finish date is 10/1/2010 and the finish date is 9/1/2010, then the free slack is 30 days.

When you fill in a date in a task's Deadline field, Project sets the late finish to the deadline date—for instance 8/1/2010.

In this example, the late finish date (8/1/2010) is earlier than the finish date (9/1/2010), so the slack is gone.

These missed deadlines can foul up slack in many, if not all, of your tasks. When Project calculates Late Finish dates, it starts at the end of the project and works back toward the beginning. If the successor has a late finish of 9/30/2010 and a duration of 2 weeks, then the late finish of its predecessor is 9/16/2010.

You can see the true slack in your project by removing the deadlines you've set. (You can add the deadlines back in after the schedule is working.) To simplify finding all the tasks with deadlines, choose View→Data, click the filter down arrow, and then choose More Filters. In the More Filters dialog box, double-click Tasks with Deadlines. To remove a deadline from a task, double-click the task name to open the Task Information dialog box. Select the Advanced tab. Clear the value in the Deadline box, and then click OK.

Splitting Tasks into Smaller Pieces

Sometimes splitting a long task into several shorter ones can help you shorten your schedule. For example, instead of asking one person to carry out one big task, you may be able to assign different people to perform some of the work simultaneously. Huge, single-handed tasks are rare, as they should be, if you've created a thorough work breakdown structure. However, if a long task sneaked past your WBS work, you can turn the original task into a summary task and create subtasks underneath it.

Here are the steps to create a subtask:

1. **Select the Task Name cell below the original long task, and then press the Insert key to create a new task.**

   A blank row appears underneath the original long task.

2. **Press the Insert key repeatedly until you have enough blank rows for the subtasks you want to create.**

   When you're done, select the blank Task Name cell immediately below the original task.

3. **Type the name of the subtask, and then press Enter.**

   Project selects the next Task Name cell, so you can repeat this step to fill in the Task Name cells for all the subtasks.

4. Select all the tasks you just created, and then choose Task→Schedule→Indent Task (a green arrow pointing to the right).

   The original task turns into a summary task with the newly created tasks as its subtasks.

5. Edit each subtask to define their durations or work, add the resources you want, and then link them.

   Be sure to remove the resource assigned to the original long task, or you'll have double the work and cost.

UP TO SPEED

Shorten Lag Time Between Tasks

If critical path tasks have lag time between them, shortening that lag time seems like a simple way to shorten the critical path. You don't have to jockey resources around or pay more for faster results. Remember, lag time is there for a reason, like the delay you add while you wait for paint to dry. Sometimes you can streamline processes to cut lag time, like expediting a mortgage approval by having someone carry your paperwork through every step in the process.

In projects, approvals can chew up time, especially if you have to wait until the next meeting of stakeholders or the change control board. When you've shortened the schedule as much as you can with other techniques, you can see whether faster turnaround on approvals is feasible. For example, ask stakeholders if they can meet more often or request that people take 3 days to review documents instead of 5. You can also investigate whether paying extra for faster deliveries from vendors is worthwhile.

Overlapping Tasks

Fast-tracking is about getting where you're going faster than usual. Unfortunately, like applying makeup, drinking coffee, and dialing into conference calls while driving to work, fast-tracking in project management can also increase risk considerably.

Fast-tracking a project means overlapping tasks that usually follow one another. At its best, fast-tracking shortens a project schedule without increasing cost or sacrificing quality. For example, if you're launching products in different markets, the creative advertising folks can work on the ads while the media planners line up advertising outlets and the Accounting Department negotiates the price of advertising spots.

The risk is that work done in a predecessor task doesn't mix with work that's already been done in an overlapping successor task. Backtracking to recover from these wrong turns can negatively affect your project time, money, quality, or scope. For example, say the technical writing team writes help topics before the software is complete. Late-stage software design changes could require rewriting help topics, or worse, reprinting documentation.

Finding Tasks to Fast-Track

Some tasks are more conducive to overlapping than others. For example, tasks earlier in the project are riskier to overlap. Designs tend to change in the early stages, so you wouldn't want to pour concrete based on early sketches. But once the design is finished and approved, you can overlap plumbing and wiring without too much trouble. You may need to tell each contractor where to start working, but the systems shouldn't interfere as long as everything goes where the architectural plans say it should.

Critical tasks are still the best candidates for fast-tracking, because a shorter critical path means shorter project duration. Long tasks on the critical path are the most effective choices because a small percentage of task overlap represents a significant cut in project duration. Moreover, overlapping the longest tasks may shorten the schedule with only a few changes, so you don't have as many risks to monitor. For example, overlapping a 3-month task by 10 percent shortens the critical path by 9 days. Overlapping a 10-day task by 9 days is a 90 percent overlap—the tasks practically run simultaneously, so changes in the first task are more likely to affect the second task.

Filtering the task list for critical tasks is the easiest way to find which tasks to evaluate for fast-tracking. You can work backward from the finish date and look for critical path tasks that you can overlap with acceptable risk. To focus on fast-track candidates in Project, do the following:

1. **Hide the summary tasks in the task list by choosing Format→Show/Hide and then turning off the Summary Tasks checkbox.**

   If your project uses several WBS levels, the summary tasks can outnumber the critical tasks, so hiding summary tasks helps you focus on critical work tasks.

2. **Focus on critical tasks by applying the Critical filter.**

   Click the down arrow to the right of the Task Name column heading, and then choose Filters→Critical.

3. **Jump to the last task in the task list by pressing Ctrl+End, and then work backward, looking at every pair of linked critical tasks for tasks you can overlap.**

   If you want to look at the longest critical path tasks first, sort tasks by duration from longest to shortest. Click the down arrow to the right of the Duration column heading, and then choose Sort Largest to Smallest. You see the critical tasks listed with longest durations at the top, as shown in Figure 12-12.

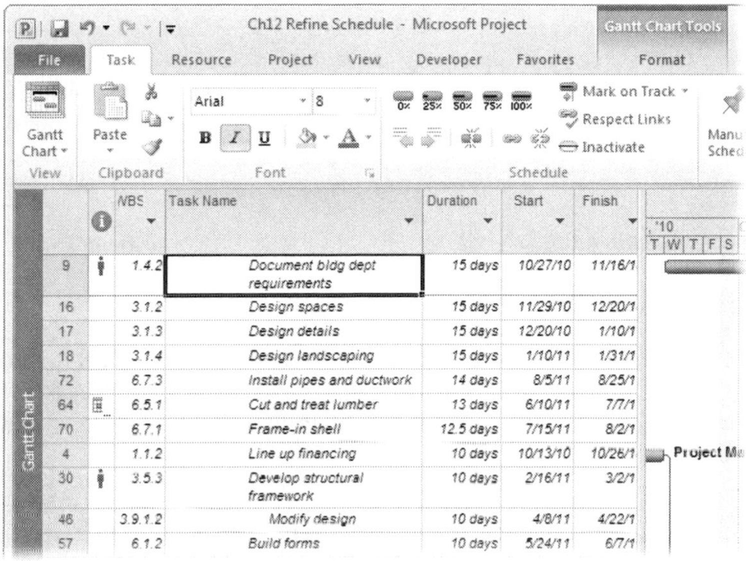

Figure 12-12:
When you sort tasks by duration, the task ID numbers are as jumbled as the task bars in the timeline. After you've located long tasks to overlap, sort the tasks by WBS (click the down arrow to the right of the WBS column heading and then choose "Sort A to Z") or ID (choose View→Data→Sort→"byID") so you can see links in the Gantt Chart timescale.

Modifying Task Dependencies to Overlap Tasks

Fast-tracking means starting the next task before its predecessor is complete. For instance, you could tell your accountants to start counting the chickens before all the eggs have hatched. When you identify partial overlaps, you create them in Project by adding negative lag to the link between the tasks.

When the link lines in your project look like fishing line in a tackle box, finding the right link line in the timescale is impossible, so don't even try. The Task Information dialog box is the easiest place to add lag.

Here are the steps:

1. **In the Gantt Chart table area, double-click the successor task.**

   The Task Information dialog box opens.

2. **Select the Predecessors tab.**

   All the predecessor tasks appear in the list, even those that aren't on the critical path.

3. **Click the Lag cell for the predecessor you want to overlap, and then type a negative number for the overlap.**

   For example, to overlap the two tasks by 2 days, type *-2d*. You can also overlap by a percentage of the predecessor task's duration. For instance, if you type *-25%* on a predecessor that takes 8 days, the overlap is 2 days. Keep in mind that a percentage lag changes the length of the overlap when the predecessor duration changes.

4. **Click OK.**

   The value appears in the Lag cell, and the task bars overlap in the timescale.

Paying More for Faster Delivery

Spending more money to deliver in less time can make financial sense. A high-tech doodad that will be obsolete in 2 years can't afford a delay getting to market. The sales you make could add up to more than the premium you have to pay to finish the project earlier.

Crashing is the term project managers use for shortening a schedule by throwing more resources at tasks. It's not as dire as it sounds, although it sometimes describes what happens when a horde of people try to work on the same task. To the uninitiated, crashing seems like an easy choice. If two people can build your website in 12 weeks, then four web developers should wrap it up in only 6 weeks, but it doesn't always work out that way. (And sometimes crashing doesn't work at all. The box on page 351 explains why.)

It's easy to assume that crashing won't change cost—it looks like you're paying the same rate for the same number of hours. In reality, there's always a trade-off between time and money. When you crash tasks, you must choose the tasks that shorten the schedule for the least amount of money. That's because every task has a magical duration that results in the minimum cost. If the task runs longer, you spend more money on things like office space, people's salaries and benefits, and keeping the freezer stocked with Cherry Garcia ice cream. Ironically, shorter tasks can cost more, too—for items like additional computers, higher-cost contractors, and managing the larger team it takes to expedite the work.

Time vs. Money

Stakeholders might open the checkbook to crash a project, but they don't want to spend more than they have to. Shortening tasks that aren't on the critical path is a waste of money, because the project duration doesn't change a bit. At the same time, crashing doesn't mean shortening *every* task on the critical path. Like cars, some tasks cost more to crash than others. Your job is to shorten the schedule for the least amount of money.

Crash tables help you compare the cost and time you can save by crashing different tasks. For example, one task might cost an additional $50,000 to cut 2 weeks from the schedule, whereas another task cuts 2 weeks for only $25,000. To choose cost-effective tasks, you must compare apples to apples, that is, how much it costs for each week of duration you eliminate. One method is to build a crash table in an Excel spreadsheet. You can enter the duration you can cut and the cost, and create an Excel formula that calculates the cost per week (or month or day). The next section explains how to do that.

Long critical tasks are the best candidates for crashing, since you can eliminate longer durations in fewer tasks. Shortening a few long tasks may cost less—and save more time—than crashing a bunch of shorter tasks.

REALITY CHECK

When Crashing Doesn't Work

Sometimes, crashing simply won't work. Some tasks can't finish in less time, no matter how many resources you assign (much to the dismay of most pregnant women).

In many cases, adding more resources increases duration instead of decreasing it. New people need time to get up to speed, so they run up the cost while they're less productive than the original team. The problem can be compounded because the original resources sacrifice productivity when they have to help the new people. And more bodies mean more costs for supervision and communication. To learn more, read *The Mythical Man-Month* (Addison-Wesley, 1995) by Frederick Brooks.

Using a Spreadsheet to Choose Tasks to Crash

You could create custom fields in Project that hold crash costs and durations, and calculate the crash cost per week with formulas you define for the custom fields. However, it's faster to move task data to an Excel spreadsheet and calculate crash costs there.

Finding the perfect combination of tasks to crash can get complicated. One task might offer several weeks worth of low-cost crashing. However, if shortening that task by 2 weeks takes it off the critical path, there's no point spending money to shorten it any more. The most effective approach is to crash one task at a time (by adding resources to it in Project), and then evaluate the critical path again to see what the next step should be.

Since you start with the longest tasks and usually crash only a few, start by sorting the critical tasks by duration, and then copy the first several tasks from Project to Excel. Here are the steps for finding critical tasks to crash, and then copying them to Excel:

1. **With a task-oriented view displayed, click the down arrow to the right of the Task Name column heading, and then choose Filters→Critical.**

   To hide summary tasks, choose Format→Hide/Show, and then turn off the Summary Tasks checkbox.

2. **To list the longest critical tasks first, click the down arrow to the right of the Duration column heading, and then choose Sort Largest to Smallest.**

   The task IDs and task bars show up out of order, but the longest tasks appear at the top of the task list. In addition to copying task names to Excel, Duration and Cost come in handy if you want to sort tasks in Excel by their original duration or cost.

Tip: The Entry table places the Task Name and Duration columns one after the other. To simplify copying the fields you want, insert the Cost field immediately after Duration. Right-click the Start column heading, and then choose Insert Column. In the field name drop-down list, choose Cost.

---

3. **Drag from the Task Name cell of the first critical task to the Cost cell for the last critical task you want to copy, and then press Ctrl+C.**

   Project copies the cells to the Clipboard.

4. **In Excel, click the top-left cell where you want to copy the values, and then press Ctrl+V.**

   Excel pastes the values into worksheet cells starting at the top-left cell and filling in cells to the right and down, as illustrated in Figure 12-13. (If the values aren't completely visible, widen the columns by dragging the dividers between the column headings.)

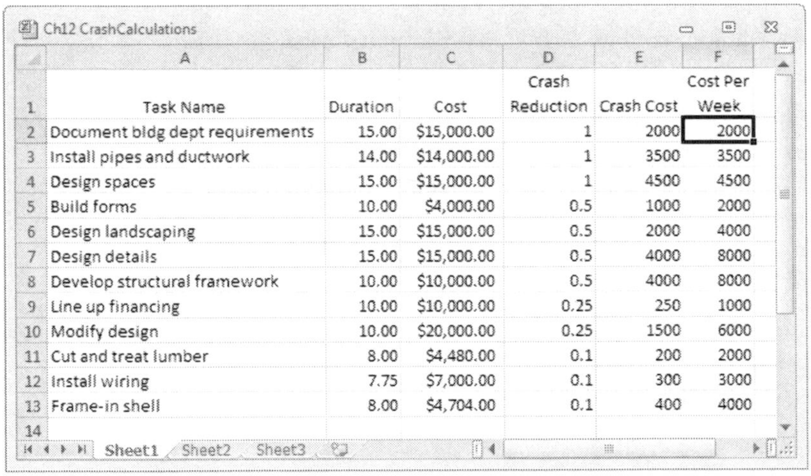

	A	B	C	D	E	F
				Crash		Cost Per
1	Task Name	Duration	Cost	Reduction	Crash Cost	Week
2	Document bldg dept requirements	15.00	$15,000.00	1	2000	2000
3	Install pipes and ductwork	14.00	$14,000.00	1	3500	3500
4	Design spaces	15.00	$15,000.00	1	4500	4500
5	Build forms	10.00	$4,000.00	0.5	1000	2000
6	Design landscaping	15.00	$15,000.00	0.5	2000	4000
7	Design details	15.00	$15,000.00	0.5	4000	8000
8	Develop structural framework	10.00	$10,000.00	0.5	4000	8000
9	Line up financing	10.00	$10,000.00	0.25	250	1000
10	Modify design	10.00	$20,000.00	0.25	1500	6000
11	Cut and treat lumber	8.00	$4,480.00	0.1	200	2000
12	Install wiring	7.75	$7,000.00	0.1	300	3000
13	Frame-in shell	8.00	$4,704.00	0.1	400	4000

Ch12 CrashCalculations — Sheet1 / Sheet2 / Sheet3

Figure 12-13:
Project durations include time periods (days, weeks, and so on). If all the units are the same, use Excel's Replace command to remove the units and leave the numbers: Press Ctrl+H and type the unit in the "Find what" box. Leave the "Replace with" box empty, and then click Replace All. If tasks use different time periods, manually convert each duration to the corresponding number of weeks.

5. In the first three blank columns to the right of the copied values, add headings for crash reduction, crash cost, and crash cost per week.

   Fill in each row with the total amount of time you can shorten the task, and how much it costs to do so.

6. In the first blank crash cost per week cell, type the formula to divide the crash duration by the crash cost (for instance, =D2/E2).

   You can then drag the copy handle over all the other crash cost per week cells so Excel can calculate the values.

7. To find the least expensive tasks to crash, sort the rows first by the amount of schedule reduction and then by the crash cost per week.

   In Excel, Choose Data→Sort. In the Sort dialog box, in the "Sort by" drop-down list, choose Crash Reduction or the column name you entered. In the Order drop-down list, choose Largest to Smallest. Click Add Level to add a second sort criterion. In the "Then by" drop-down list, choose Cost Per Week or the column name you entered. This time, in the Order drop-down list, choose Smallest to Largest. Click OK. The tasks appear with the longest reductions in duration first and the smallest cost per week to the largest, as shown in Figure 12-13.

8. Switch to Project and add resources to a task to shorten its duration.

   Review the critical path to see whether the results are what you want. For example, if the task is no longer on the critical path, you may want to scale back on how much you crash it.

   Repeat this step until the project duration is the length you want—or the cost prohibits shortening it any further. At that point, you may need to reduce the project scope. The section "Inactivating Tasks" on page 353 tells you how to handle that in Project.

Playing What-If Games

There's more than one way to skin a cat—or plan a project. The project stakeholders may ask for the moon. Then when they see how much it costs to land on that hunk of rock, they might backpedal and ask for alternative plans. How much less would it cost if we cut this portion of the scope? How much longer will it take if we add these change requests to the plan? And invariably, why can't we do all this extra work in the same timeframe and for the same cost? Project 2010 has two new features to help you evaluate alternatives: inactive tasks and the Compare Project feature. This section shows you how to use both.

Inactivating Tasks

If nothing seems to shorten the schedule or reduce the budget, a reduction in scope may be in order. You don't get to eliminate scope; only the stakeholders can, and even then, only if the project customer approves. Decisions have a way of changing, so making tasks inactive (new in Project 2010) is a great way to cut scope. Should the stakeholders decide to revert to the original plan, you can reactivate the inactive tasks without skipping a beat.

Tip: Inactive tasks also work well if you want to document nice-to-have work. Create tasks, assign resources, and fill in other fields; then make the tasks inactive. Their values are visible (and editable) but don't affect your project schedule. If you find that the project has the time and budget for the work, you can make them active.

Making tasks inactive removes their values from your project's rolled-up schedule and cost. However, the tasks, their resource assignments, and field values remain in the plan, as Figure 12-14 shows, so you have a record of what you cut out. You can edit inactive tasks as you do active tasks. If you reactivate the tasks, you don't have to re-enter any information.

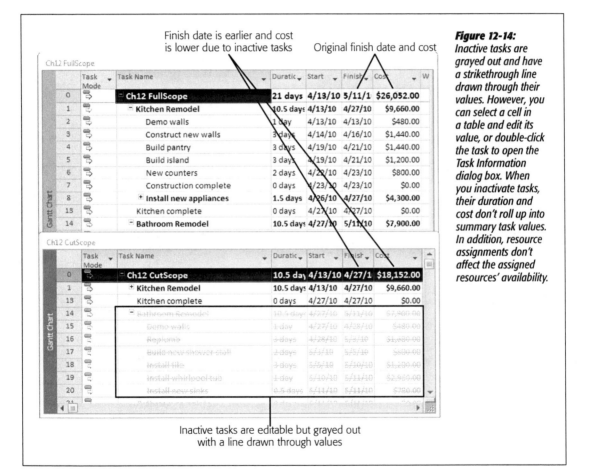

Finish date is earlier and cost is lower due to inactive tasks

Original finish date and cost

Inactive tasks are editable but grayed out with a line drawn through values

Figure 12-14:
Inactive tasks are grayed out and have a strikethrough line drawn through their values. However, you can select a cell in a table and edit its value, or double-click the task to open the Task Information dialog box. When you inactivate tasks, their duration and cost don't roll up into summary task values. In addition, resource assignments don't affect the assigned resources' availability.

Changing tasks to inactive is a snap: Select one or more tasks in a task-oriented view and then choose Task→Schedule→Inactivate. The inactive tasks immediately change to gray with a strikethrough line drawn through their values in the table area. However, you can edit an inactive task's values by double-clicking it to open the Task Information dialog box or by editing directly in the table cells.

To reactivate a task, select it, and then choose Task→Schedule→Inactivate once again.

Comparing Projects

For more involved what-if games, it might be useful to make a second copy of your Project file. With a backup safely in place, you can edit to your heart's content while keeping both the original file and the new one. That way, you can examine both options in detail to see which one is better. For example, you may save copies of a Project file to compare changes in the critical path as you shorten it or at different stages of project execution. No longer must you open files side by side, using your left and right index fingers as you scan through the corresponding fields in each file. In Project 2010, the Compare Projects feature simplifies these types of comparisons.

Say a remodeling contractor prepares a plan for remodeling your condo to set up a home theater. The price is higher than you had hoped, so you ask for an alternative plan that doesn't cost as much. You want to see exactly where the contractor cut costs, though, so you don't end up with the right price and the wrong TV. The Compare Projects feature produces a comparison report that compares values from two files side by side along with a column showing the difference between the two. In addition, the timescale includes two sets of task bars, so you can visually compare when tasks start and finish.

Here's how to compare two versions of the same project:

1. **Open the two project files you want to compare and select the one that's your current version. Then choose Project→Reports→Compare Projects.**

    The Compare Project Versions dialog box opens with the "Compare the current project (<project_name>) to this previous version" label at the top, where <project name> is the name of the active project.

2. **In the drop-down list, choose the name of the previous version you want to compare with your current file.**

    If the other file isn't open, click Browse and then, in the Open dialog box, choose the file you want to compare.

Note: Compare Projects uses *current* to identify the values for the first file you selected and *previous* to identify the values for the file you selected in the Compare Project Versions dialog box. That's why it's easier to keep things straight if you select your current file version first.

---

3. **In the Task Table drop-down list, choose the table that contains the fields you want to compare. In the Resource Table drop-down list, choose the table that contains the resource fields you want to compare.**

    The comparison table that Compare Projects builds can become unwieldy, because it includes three columns for each field in the original table you selected. To focus on the information you care about most, consider creating a custom table (page 611) that contains only the fields you want to compare—for example, for tasks, Task Name, Duration, Finish Date, and Cost.

4. **Click OK.**

A message box tells you it's creating a comparison report, and windows flicker on and off for a few seconds. When things calm down, you see a Comparison Report window at the top and the two versions you're comparing at the bottom, as Figure 12-15 shows.

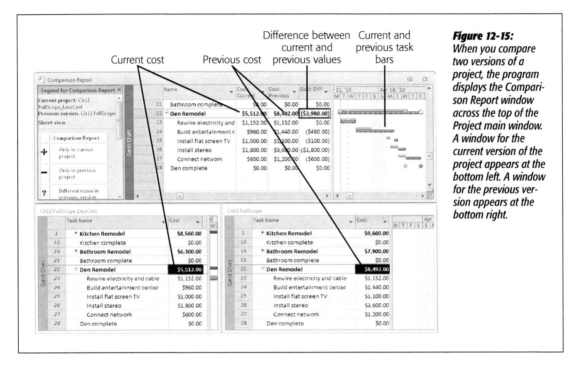

Figure 12-15:
When you compare two versions of a project, the program displays the Comparison Report window across the top of the Project main window. A window for the current version of the project appears at the bottom left. A window for the previous version appears at the bottom right.

A legend on the left side of the Comparison Report window identifies the symbols it uses:

- Tasks that appear only in the current project include a plus sign.

- Tasks that appear only in the previous version include a minus sign to indicate that the task has been removed in the current version.

- The task bars for the current version are green.

- The task bars for the previous version are blue.

- For each column in the table you selected, the Comparison Report displays three columns. For example, Cost: Current shows the cost for the current version. Cost: Previous shows the cost for the previous version. And Cost: Diff shows the difference in the values between the two versions.

The Compare Projects tab appears between the File tab and the Task tab on the ribbon. You can choose Task Comparison or Resource Comparison to switch between the task table and resource table you specified. By choosing Compare Projects→ Show→Filter and then choosing a filter, you can view different aspects of the comparison. For example, in the drop-down list, choose "Changed items" to see only the tasks or resources that changed between the versions. You can also view items that appear only in the current or previous version. If you want to view a task in each version, select the task in the Comparison Report window and then choose Compare Projects→Compare→Go to Item. Project highlights the task in the windows for each version.

CHAPTER 13

Saving the Project Plan

Once you obtain the stakeholders' approval, it's time to save an official, approved version of your project plan. This approved plan wears a lot of hats during the life of your project. It's documentation of the agreed-upon scope, budget, schedule, and so on. If questions arise later, you can turn to the approved plan to help sort them out. The project plan acts as a reference for the project team as they do their work. Finally, the project plan contains the targets you've set for the project. As the team performs the project work, you compare actual performance to the plan to see whether you're on the right track. But first you have a few final planning tasks to complete. A plan is merely a *proposed* plan until the stakeholders accept it and commit their approval in writing.

A project plan covers a lot of ground, and it isn't stored in a single file. Saving a project plan means saving an approved copy of every file that contributes to the plan. This chapter talks about setting up a storage system not only for the planning documents, but also for files generated during the rest of the project's life. You'll learn about different ways to store project files and how to structure project information so it's easy to find and manage.

In some cases, saving a copy is as simple as appending *v1.0* to the end of the filename, but Project files require more attention. This chapter describes how to set a baseline in your Project schedule so you can compare your planned schedule and cost to what you actually achieve. You'll learn how to set baselines at several points during a project to watch for trends over time. Finally, you'll see how to view baselines in Project, either alone or as a comparison to actual performance.

Obtaining Approval for the Plan

With the convenience of email distribution lists, you may be tempted to email a project plan to stakeholders and ask them to email their approvals. Unfortunately, the attached plan is likely to sit unread in all those email inboxes. You may receive approvals, but they may get unapologetically revoked when people realize later that the plan doesn't meet their needs. To obtain approvals that really stick, set up a sign-off meeting to review the plan and snag approvals then and there. The box on page 360 talks about how to handle another approval issue—starting project execution before the plan is approved. Here are some tips for a successful sign-off:

1. Distribute the project plan in advance, and urge the stakeholders to read it beforehand.

2. At the sign-off meeting, don't assume that the stakeholders have read the plan. Your job as project manager is to present the plan at the meeting, covering the key aspects, pointing out potential conflicts, problems, and risks. Encourage questions and discussion—this is your last chance to hash out issues. To jump-start the discussion, ask stakeholders pointed questions about the areas you see as potential problems.

3. A nod or a verbal yes don't constitute approval. Circulate the sign-off page and ask everyone to actually sign it.

REALITY CHECK

Starting Before the Plan Is Approved

Hard deadlines are a fact of life, so some projects start before the project plan is approved—or before the plan is even complete. Beginning work without an approved plan is absurdly risky. The team could work hard for weeks, only to have to backtrack and redo it all when the final plan is approved.

If you can, take a stand and persuade stakeholders and management to delay the execution phase until after the plan is approved.

If your persuasive powers don't work, save the plan as it is, and begin to execute the project with what you have. At the same time, push hard for plan approval. When you get it, save the approved version of the plan and compare performance to the approved version going forward. Don't forget to document any backtracking you have to do, so you can argue against false starts in the future.

Storing Project Documents

Even small projects generate an astounding amount of information. Initially, the project plan is a collection of requirements and specification documents, budget spreadsheets, the schedule in Project, and so on. Don't forget the draft documents you generated before you obtained approval or the emails and memos that flew around as planning progressed. When project execution starts, information expands exponentially with project results like design documents, software that's been written, and blueprints. Meanwhile, managing the project produces status reports, change request forms, and more.

In the good old days, the container for project documentation was called a project *notebook* because it was a three-ring binder (or several) that held paper copies of every project document. These days, a project notebook tends to be electronic, with files stored somewhere on a computer. Either way, you need a filing system so everyone can find and access the information they need.

The best project filing system depends on the project—what sort of information the project produces, who needs access to it, any security issues, and the standards your organization follows. The choice boils down to structure and technology. You need a way to track versions of documents and deliverables—for example, for a construction project, equipment specifications, contracts, architectural design drawings, engineering drawings, construction plans, and as-built drawings. In addition, you may need a system to manage document access and changes. For example, all team members can read the project requirements to see what their tasks are supposed to deliver, but only a few authorized team members can modify the project requirements.

Regardless of the storage technology you use, you need a structure for information so that finding it isn't an Easter egg hunt. Project information typically falls into a few high-level categories that you can use to build the basic storage structure (as illustrated in Figure 13-1):

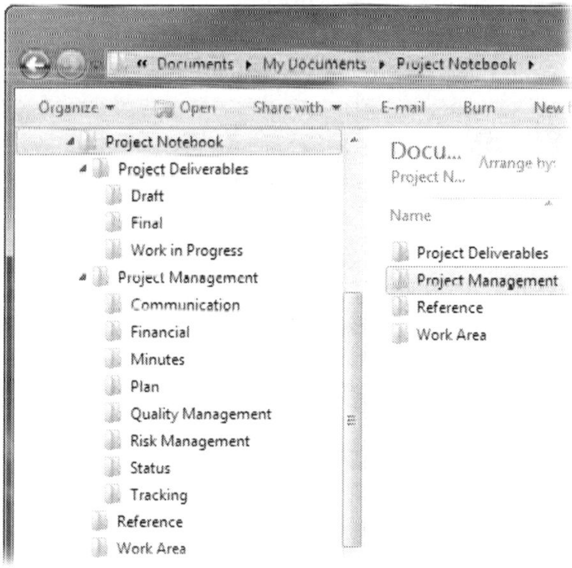

Figure 13-1:
You can design an information hierarchy with different storage tools. For example, you can build a folder structure on a file server, within a Microsoft SharePoint Server, or on an internal FTP site, as the box on page 363 explains.

- **Project deliverables.** As you learned in Chapter 2, deliverables are the tangible results that a project produces. Because payment often hinges on these deliverables becoming reality, you want them to be easy to find and easy to control. Separate subfolders for draft and final versions make it even easier to see whether a deliverable is complete.

- **Project management deliverables.** Managing a project produces all kinds of intermediate deliverables like the project plan, status reports, and change request logs. Separate folders for different types of information can forestall information overload. However, the breakdown of information depends on what makes sense to you. For example, you might organize information by project management phase with folders for planning, execution, control, and closure. On the other hand, you may prefer to organize information by project management activities: planning, communication, finance, risk management, change control, and so on.

- **Reference.** Projects almost always include background information; although not a deliverable, it can be essential. For example, you may need to refer to the building code that construction has to follow, but the local government's building code isn't part of your project.

- **Project work.** All the work products that team members produce have to go somewhere, but that storage may not be your problem. For example, software development projects often store and manage code in source control systems. In other cases, teams may set up their own work areas and organize their files as they see fit, delivering their work to you when it's complete.

Preserving the Original Plan in Project

After stakeholders approve a project plan, they expect the project to follow that plan. If it *doesn't,* the stakeholders expect an explanation of the difference between planned and actual performance (called *variance*). Variance is the foundation to a variety of project performance measures (page 421), like earned value and the schedule performance index. To calculate variance, you must first save the original planned values in your Project schedule.

As you've seen in previous chapters, Project constantly updates fields like dates, duration, work, and cost as you make changes (as long as tasks are set up as automatically scheduled). For example, if you increase the work hours for a task, Project recalculates the duration and the finish date for the task. When you begin to track progress, Project continues these recalculations; for example, as a delayed predecessor task pushes back the start dates for its successors.

TOOLS OF THE TRADE

Document Management Options

How you store project documents depends on the technology available to you. If your organization has a document management system like Documentum, then you can store and manage versions of project documents in high style. Similarly, Microsoft Project Server uses SharePoint to provide document libraries and places for tracking issues and risks.

If you don't have these types of power tools, don't despair. Your far-flung project teams can share documents with plenty of other products and approaches:

- **SharePoint Server.** You don't need Project Server to set up a SharePoint server for sharing documents. A SharePoint website can carry out workflow processes, such as checking documents in and out, storing multiple versions of a document, or requiring approvals before documents proceed to the next step. You can also set up SharePoint with permissions to control who can read or write to different areas. Moreover, Project Professional 2010 lets you export project files

to a SharePoint list (you must have SharePoint 2010 Foundation), so you can share project information with anyone who's interested.

- **Basecamp.** One of many web-based collaboration packages, Basecamp (*www.basecamphq.com*) provides online folders for storing and sharing documents.

- **FTP site.** Team members can upload and download files to an FTP site. Like other tools, you can set up FTP sites with permissions to specify who can access which folders.

- **Directory structure.** Forgoing fancier tools, you can simply set up folders on a shared network disk drive and use file-naming conventions to track versions of documents. For example, track document versions by appending the date saved to filenames. When a file reaches a milestone, such as Approved, you can add that to the filename as well.

Fortunately, Project has no problem keeping track of both your original plan and the current one. Project stores the original plan in a *baseline*, which is a snapshot of schedule and cost information. At the same time, the schedule you see every time you open Project is the *current* plan, which shows the schedule and cost based on any revision you've made, as well as the effects of actual performance. Project uses baseline values and current values to calculate variances and other performance measures, as you'll learn in Chapter 15.

A baseline doesn't save everything in a Project file. From hundreds of Project fields, a baseline gleans key schedule and cost values for each task, resource, and assignment in the Project file. The following fields show the information stored in Project's primary baseline, appropriately named *Baseline*, but the fields in other baselines work the same way:

- **Baseline Start.** Shows the planned start dates for tasks and assignments—that is, the Start field values when you set the baseline. Baseline Start represents the dates Project calculates for automatically scheduled tasks and the dates you specify for manually scheduled tasks.

- **Baseline Estimated Start.** In most cases, when you set a baseline, this field takes on the Scheduled Start dates that Project calculates. For automatically scheduled tasks, Baseline Start and Baseline Estimated Start are *always* identical. If you fill in a manually scheduled task's Start field with a date, Project copies that date to Baseline Estimated Start when you set a baseline. However, if you leave a manually scheduled task's Start field blank or type a note in the field, Project copies the Scheduled Start to Baseline Estimated Start when you set a baseline.

Note: With manually scheduled tasks, you don't look at the scheduled start and finish fields. Baseline Estimated Start and Baseline Estimated Finish are specifically for manually scheduled tasks without specified date values. Project sets these fields to the dates that most closely match where the tasks occur in the project plan. For example, a top-level manually scheduled task without dates or duration has a Baseline Estimated Start equal to the project start date. A manually scheduled subtask without dates has a Baseline Estimated Start equal to the summary task start date.

- **Baseline Finish.** Shows the planned finish dates for tasks and assignments, stored in the Finish field when you set the baseline. Baseline Finish represents the dates Project calculates for automatically scheduled tasks and the dates you specify for manually scheduled tasks.

- **Baseline Estimated Finish.** When you set a baseline, this field is usually copied from the Scheduled Finish dates Project calculates. However, if you fill in a manually scheduled task's Finish field with a date, Project copies that date to Baseline Estimated Finish when you set a baseline. And if you leave a manually scheduled task's Finish field blank or type a note in the field, Project copies the Scheduled Finish to Baseline Estimated Finish when you set a baseline.

- **Baseline Duration.** Represents the planned duration of tasks based on the Baseline Start and Baseline Finish dates.

- **Baseline Estimated Duration.** Shows the duration based on the Baseline Estimated Start and Baseline Estimated Finish dates.

- **Baseline Work.** Contains the planned person-hours for tasks, resources, and assignments. For example, the Gantt Chart view's Baseline Work field shows the total planned work for each task. However, the Resource Sheet's Baseline Work field indicates the hours assigned to each resource. In addition, the Baseline Work field in a time-phased view like Task Usage shows work for each time period.

- **Baseline Cost.** Represents the planned cost for tasks, resources, and assignments. Baseline Cost keeps track of cost over time, so views like Task Usage and Resource Usage show baseline cost for each time period.

- **Baseline Budget Work.** Saves the budgeted person-hours for work resources, and budgeted units for material resources. You can enter values in the budget fields to document the budget targets for the project, as described in detail in Chapter 11. You can compare this field to the Budget Work field to see how actual (or scheduled) budgeted work compares to the baseline budget.

- **Baseline Budget Cost.** Shows the planned budget for project cost resources (page 288).

Note: If you're wondering about the Baseline Deliverable Start and Baseline Deliverable Finish fields, these correspond to the planned start and finish dates for the Deliverable feature in Project Server, which lets you publish project deliverables on which other projects may depend.

Setting a Baseline

Project doesn't set baselines automatically, because it has no way of knowing when your plan is ready to be saved for posterity. When stakeholders approve the project plan, one of your very next steps is to set a baseline in Project to save the targets you've committed to.

To set the first baseline in Project, do the following:

1. **Open the file you want to baseline, and then choose Project→Schedule→Set Baseline→Set Baseline.**

   The Set Baseline dialog box opens, as shown in Figure 13-2.

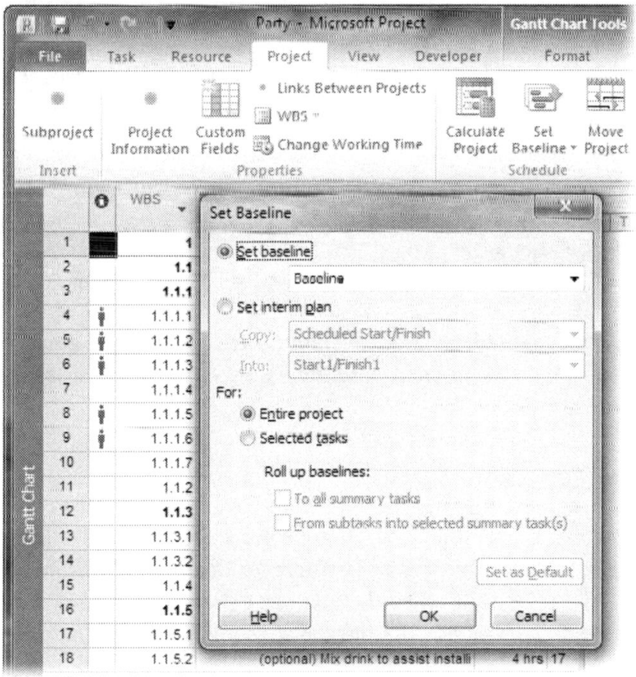

Figure 13-2:
The options that Project selects automatically are exactly what you want for the first baseline you set. In fact, you can set up to 11 different baselines, which is a handy way to track trends in performance over time. The information for the other 10 baselines resides in fields whose names begin with Baseline1, Baseline2, and so on.)

2. **Make sure the "Set baseline" box is set to Baseline, and the "Entire project" option is selected.**

   Whether you plan to set only one baseline or are setting the first of several, save your plan to Baseline this time around, which the box on page 368 explains. When you first set a baseline, you want to save the values for the entire project. Later on, you may want to save values for selected tasks, like when you add tasks to a project.

3. **Click OK.**

   Project stores the current values for start, finish, duration, work, and costs in the corresponding Baseline fields. The next time you open the Set Baseline dialog box, the "Set baseline" box shows the date you set the baseline.

Editing a set baseline

Suppose a stakeholder makes a stink about the project plan *after* you've set the baseline. If the other stakeholders acquiesce, you can modify the project plan to address the issues. If a baseline already has values, you usually don't want to overwrite them because you lose track of any variances between the original baseline and the actual performance.

Here's how to reset the changed tasks in a baseline that already contains values:

1. **In the Set Baseline dialog box, select the name of the baseline you want to reset.**

   If you've saved only one baseline, it appears automatically in the "Set baseline" box.

2. **Select the "Selected tasks" option if the changes affect only a portion of the project.**

   If the changes affect the entire project and you want to replace the baseline completely, select the "Entire project" option.

3. **Click OK.**

   A message box warns that you're about to overwrite a saved baseline. Click Yes, and Project overwrites the current baseline values with the new ones, and changes the "last saved date".

Setting Additional Baselines

Schedule and cost performance can fluctuate when projects continue for months or years. For example, after 3 months, a project is 10 percent behind schedule; at the 6-month mark, it's 20 percent behind schedule; then, at 1 year, your recovery strategy pays off and the project is only 2 percent behind schedule. By setting additional baselines at key points in a project (at the end of each phase or at regular intervals), you can evaluate trends over time.

An additional baseline is also helpful when a project experiences a big change—an interruption to the schedule, a big scope increase, or a spike in the price of materials. Suppose your project is 20 percent complete when a high-priority project intervenes. When you resume your project, the original start and finish dates are too old to produce meaningful variances, and costs may have increased significantly. You need a new baseline that reflects the updated targets when you recommence work on the project. If you don't want to lose the original baseline values, you can save this new baseline to one of the additional 10 that Project provides.

To set another baseline, follow these steps:

1. **Choose Project→Schedule→Set Baseline→Set Baseline.**

   The Set Baseline dialog box opens with the "Set baseline" box set to Baseline, and the "Entire project" option selected.

2. **In the "Set baseline" box, choose the baseline you want to set.**

   Baselines that have already been set include "(last saved on mm/dd/yy)" appended to the end of the baseline name, where mm/dd/yy represents the most recent date you saved the baseline.

3. **Make sure the "Entire project" option is selected.**

   When you save one of the baselines for the first time, you want to save the values for the entire project. Later on, you may want to save values for selected tasks, for instance, when you add tasks to a project, as described on page 142.

4. **Click OK.**

   Project stores the current values for start, finish, duration, work, and costs in the corresponding Baseline fields, such as Baseline1 Start, Baseline1 Finish, Baseline1 Duration, Baseline1 Work, and Baseline1 Cost. The next time you open the Set Baseline dialog box, the "Set baseline" drop-down list shows the last saved date for the baseline.

   If the selected baseline was saved before, Project warns you that the baseline has already been used and asks if you want to overwrite it. Click Yes to overwrite existing values (if, for example, you've used up the 11 baselines and want to reuse an older one). If you don't want to overwrite it, click No, and then select a different baseline back in the Set Baseline dialog box.

Viewing Recent Variances

You can make your life easier by using Baseline to store the most recent baseline, because that's the one Project uses to calculate variances. By saving your most recent baseline to the Project baseline named Baseline, you can see the most recent cost and schedule variances. Project calculates Variance field values by subtracting a baseline field from the current corresponding field value. For example, Cost Variance equals Cost minus Baseline Cost.

Here's how to reserve Baseline for the most recent baseline as you set additional ones:

1. When you save your original plan values, set the baseline name to Baseline.

2. Immediately save the original plan a second time, but this time to Baseline1. Your original baseline values are safely stored in Baseline1. Because the original plan is stored in Baseline, Project variance fields show variances from the original plan.

3. When you set the next baseline, save it to Baseline, so variance fields show variances from the newest baseline.

4. Immediately save the project schedule again to Baseline2. This permanently records the second baseline.

5. For each additional baseline, save the project schedule once to Baseline and once to the next empty baseline.

Adding New Tasks to a Baseline

A baseline starts out representing your original plan, but people ask for changes, which often lead to new tasks in the schedule. For example, a client makes change requests and agrees to the extra cost and time. The new finish dates and cost aren't variances from the plan, so you want the baseline to absorb these additions.

If project execution hasn't started, you can simply reset the entire baseline (page 365). However, when your Project file already includes actual values, overwriting baseline values for existing tasks replaces the original baseline values with current ones, and any variances magically disappear. Instead, you can add tasks to the baseline, setting the baseline values for only those tasks, leaving baseline values for other tasks alone.

To add tasks to a baseline that's already set, follow these steps:

1. **In the Gantt Chart or another task-oriented view, select the tasks you want to add to the baseline.**

   You can select any kind of task, including low-level tasks, milestones, or summary tasks.

2. **Choose Project→Schedule→Set Baseline→Set Baseline.**

   The Set Baseline dialog box opens with Baseline selected, and the "Entire project" option selected.

3. In the "Set baseline" drop-down list, choose the baseline to which you want to add tasks, and then select the "Selected tasks" option.

Suddenly, the checkboxes underneath the "Roll up baselines" label become active, as illustrated in Figure 13-3. These checkboxes tell Project how you want the added baseline values rolled up into summary tasks.

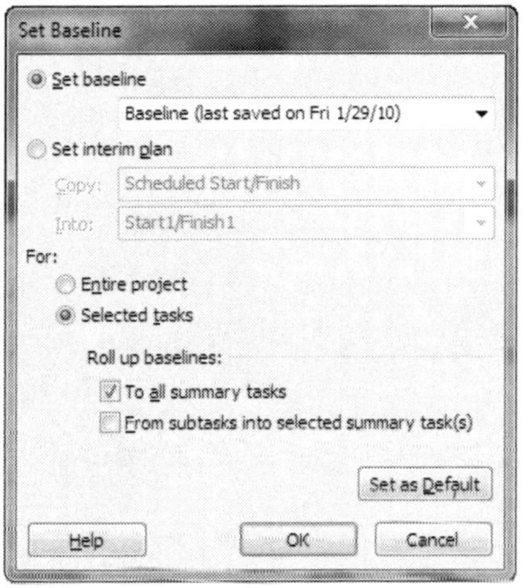

Figure 13-3:
Project doesn't automatically update summary task baseline values when you add tasks to a baseline. It assumes that you want to keep original baseline values for summary tasks so you can see how the added tasks affect performance. In effect, the new tasks immediately produce variances in existing summary tasks because they add to duration, work, and cost.

4. If you want the values for new tasks to update the summary tasks you select, turn on the "From subtasks into selected summary task(s)" checkbox.

This checkbox tells Project to update the baseline values for selected summary tasks with the values from the added tasks. With this option, you can adjust the baseline for the summary task to which the new tasks belong in order to show their effect. At the same time, you can keep higher-level summary tasks as they were, so you can also see the impact of the new tasks on your original schedule and budget.

5. To update all summary tasks with the new task values, turn on the "To all summary tasks" checkbox.

Once you turn on the "To all summary tasks" checkbox, Project updates the baseline values for all summary tasks up to the top level, as illustrated in Figure 13-4.

6. Click OK.

Project updates the tasks you specified. If you want to change the standard roll-up behavior to the checkbox you turn on, click "Set as Default" before you click OK.

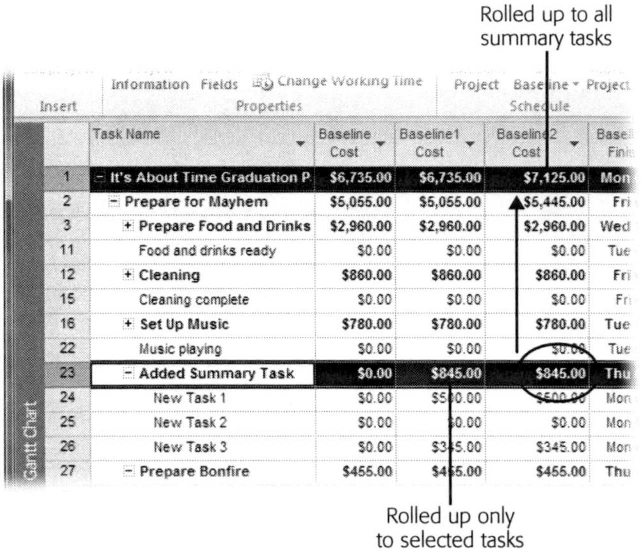

Rolled up to all
summary tasks

Figure 13-4:
*If the "To all summary tasks" checkbox is
turned on, Project rolls up baseline values
to all summary tasks, even if the "From
subtasks into selected summary tasks(s)"
checkbox is turned on.*

	Task Name	Baseline Cost	Baseline1 Cost	Baseline2 Cost	Base Fin
1	It's About Time Graduation P	$6,735.00	$6,735.00	$7,125.00	Mon
2	Prepare for Mayhem	$5,055.00	$5,055.00	$5,445.00	Fri
3	+ Prepare Food and Drinks	$2,960.00	$2,960.00	$2,960.00	Wed
11	Food and drinks ready	$0.00	$0.00	$0.00	Tue
12	+ Cleaning	$860.00	$860.00	$860.00	Fri
15	Cleaning complete	$0.00	$0.00	$0.00	Fri
16	+ Set Up Music	$780.00	$780.00	$780.00	Tue
22	Music playing	$0.00	$0.00	$0.00	Tue
23	Added Summary Task	$0.00	$845.00	$845.00	Thu
24	New Task 1	$0.00	$500.00	$500.00	Mon
25	New Task 2	$0.00	$0.00	$0.00	Mon
26	New Task 3	$0.00	$345.00	$345.00	Mon
27	Prepare Bonfire	$455.00	$455.00	$455.00	Thu

Rolled up only
to selected tasks

Saving Sets of Start and Finish Dates

The second option in the Set Baseline dialog box is "Set interim plan". Unlike Project
baselines, interim plans save only start and finish dates, not duration, cost, and work.
If you don't need a full baseline, which the box on page 371 discusses, you can save
an interim plan instead of a baseline.

To save start and finish dates in an interim plan, follow these steps:

1. **Choose Project→Schedule→Set Baseline→Set Baseline.**

    The Set Baseline dialog box opens.

2. **Select the "Set interim plan" option.**

    The Copy and Into boxes come to life, waiting for you to tell them the start and
    finish fields to copy from and to.

3. **In the Copy drop-down list, choose the set of start and finish dates you want
    to copy.**

    Project automatically fills in the Copy box with Scheduled Start/Finish, which
    copies the current task start and finish dates that Project calculates and is usual-
    ly what you want. However, if you want to copy dates from a baseline or another
    interim plan, choose the name of the baseline or interim plan. Suppose you have
    an old baseline that you want to reuse for more recent information. You can save
    the baseline dates to an interim plan by choosing Baseline1 in the Copy box,
    and then choosing an interim plan in the Into box.

4. In the Into drop-down list, choose the fields into which you want to copy the start and finish dates.

   Project fills in the Into box with Start1/Finish1 to copy dates to the first interim plan. However, if you want to save a new interim plan, choose Start2/Finish2 for the second interim plan, up to Start10/Finish10 for the 10th interim plan.

   The Into drop-down list includes the names of baselines. You might wonder why you would copy interim plan dates into a baseline, particularly if the baseline already has values. It turns out that copying from an interim plan to a baseline is how you bring interim plans saved in earlier versions of Project into your Project 2010 baselines. For example, choose Start3/Finish3 in the Copy drop-down list and Baseline3 in the Into drop-down list. Project copies the interim plan dates into that baseline.

5. Select either the "Entire project" or "Selected task" option, and then click OK.

   Saving values to interim plans works just like saving baselines. You can save the dates for the entire project or save dates for only some tasks, as described on page 365.

FREQUENTLY ASKED QUESTION

Baselines vs. Interim Plans

What should I use interim plans for?

With up to 11 baselines available, you may wonder why Project offers interim plans as well. Interim plans popped up in Project several versions ago, when the program offered only one baseline and project managers clamored for more.

People don't use interim plans very often since Project 2007 came out, but they aren't totally useless. First, if you import a project schedule from Project 2002 and earlier, any additional baseline information resides in interim plan fields (Start1/Finish1 through Start10/Finish10). You can copy that information from interim plan Start and Finish fields (Start2/Finish2, for example) into baseline fields like Baseline2 (page 363).

In addition, if you save additional baselines regularly, 11 baselines may not be enough. As a workaround, you can save interim plans to act as partial baselines in between the full baselines you save. Although interim plans can't track cost and work changes, you can track schedule performance by watching how interim plan task dates change over time.

Clearing a Baseline

When you run out of empty baselines, you can overwrite a previously saved baseline (page 365) with current values. But suppose that you set a baseline by accident or that a set baseline is so obsolete you want to completely eliminate it. Clearing a baseline removes all its values. Here's what you do:

1. Choose Project→Schedule→Set Baseline→Clear Baseline.

   The Clear Baseline dialog box appears.

---

2. **In the Clear Baseline dialog box, make sure the "Clear baseline plan" option is selected.**

   If you want to clear an interim plan instead, select the "Clear interim plan" option, and then, in the "Clear interim plan" drop-down list, choose the plan name.

3. **In the "Clear baseline plan" drop-down list, choose the baseline you want to clear.**

   The "Clear baseline plan" drop-down list automatically chooses Baseline, so you must take care to select the baseline you want to clear.

4. **To clear the entire baseline, select the "Entire project" option.**

   "Entire project" is what you'll choose most often: You don't often clear values for only some tasks. But, for example, if you want to remove tasks from the baseline because the client has agreed to reduce project scope, then you must select the tasks before opening the Clear Baseline dialog box, and then select the "Selected tasks" option.

5. **Click OK.**

   Project clears the values for the baseline. However, higher-level summary tasks don't update to reflect the removal of the task baseline values.

Viewing Baselines

When you initially set a baseline, its values are exactly the same as the current Project-calculated field values. As the project team gets to work, the current values begin to stray from the baseline. Evaluating project performance (page 409) involves a lot of reviewing the variances between current and baseline values. You can see baseline values in several places.

For a 30,000-foot view of baseline and current data, choose Project→Project Information. In the Project Information dialog box, click Statistics to open the Project Statistics dialog box, which shows top-level summary information for the whole project, as shown in Figure 13-5.

Viewing baseline and current values in a Gantt Chart view

When you want to compare the baseline schedule to the current status, the Tracking Gantt view is perfect. It shows gray task bars for the baseline start and finish dates immediately below task bars for the current schedule. To display the Tracking Gantt view, shown in Figure 13-6, choose Task→View→Gantt Chart→Tracking Gantt.

Tip: From the ribbon, you can display any baseline you want in any Gantt Chart view. Display the Gantt Chart view you want and then choose the Format tab. In the Bar Styles section, click the Baseline down arrow, and then choose the baseline you want to display.

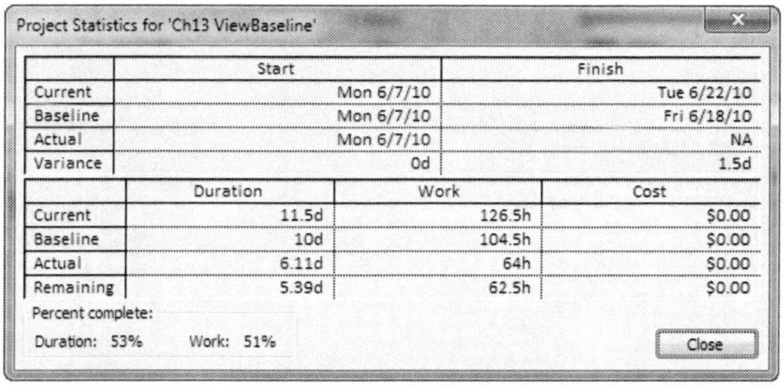

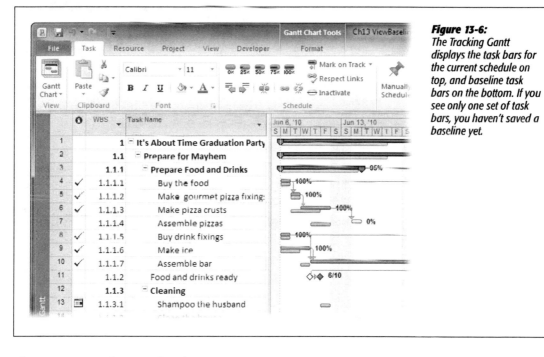

Figure 13-5:
The Project Statistics dialog box contains current, baseline, and actual values as well as the variance for the project start date, finish date, project duration, total project work, and total project cost.

Figure 13-6:
The Tracking Gantt displays the task bars for the current schedule on top, and baseline task bars on the bottom. If you see only one set of task bars, you haven't saved a baseline yet.

If you save more than one baseline, you may want to see them in the same Gantt Chart so you can compare performance from one to the next. The Multiple Baselines Gantt view displays different color task bars for Baseline, Baseline 1, and Baseline 2, as shown in Figure 13-7. To display the Multiple Baselines Gantt, choose View→Other Views→More Views. In the More Views dialog box, double-click Multiple Baselines Gantt.

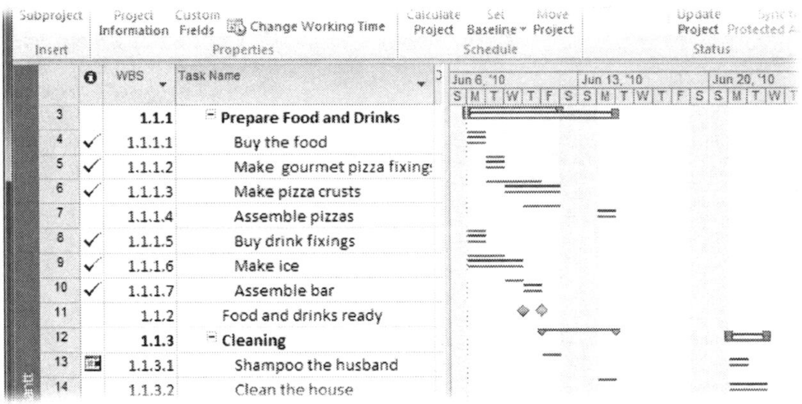

Figure 13-7:
The Multiple Baselines Gantt shows task bars for only the Baseline, Baseline1, and Baseline2 baselines. It doesn't display task bars for the current schedule.

If you want to show more baselines or different baselines in the Multiple Baselines Gantt, you can modify the view to include task bars for other baselines. For example, you may want to see task bars for Baseline1 through Baseline4. The steps for adding more task bars is different from replacing baselines, but both procedures take place in the Bar Styles dialog box.

To change the baselines that the task bars represent, do the following:

1. **Open the Multiple Baselines Gantt view or a copy you've created.**

    Because swapping task bars requires several steps, it's a good idea to copy the view, and then make the changes to the copy (page 582). Then, you can copy the customized view to your global template and use it in other Project files.

2. **On the Format tab, in the Bar Styles section, click Format and then choose Bar Styles from the drop-down menu.**

    The Bar Styles dialog box opens.

3. **Click the cell that contains the first task bar style name you want to replace.**

    For example, click Baseline to edit the normal task bars for Baseline.

4. **Click the same cell a second time to make the name editable, and then type the new baseline number at the end of the name.**

    For example, to change Baseline to Baseline1, make the name editable, and then type *1* at the end. To change Baseline1 to Baseline4, drag over the 1 at the end of the name and then type *4*.

5. In the From cell in the same row, choose the start date field for the new baseline.

   For example, to switch the view to show Baseline4, choose Baseline4 Start. This tells Project to draw the beginning of the task bars based on the Baseline4 Start field values.

6. In the To cell in the same row, choose the finish date field for the new baseline.

   To complete the task bar style that shows Baseline4, choose Baseline4 Finish. These From and To settings tell Project to draw the task bars for Baseline4 from Baseline4 Start to Baseline4 Finish in the timescale.

7. **Repeat steps 3 through 6 to modify the Split, Milestone, and Summary task bars to use the same baseline.**

   Editing the task bar name isn't enough. The fields you choose for the task bar start and finish dates are what really matter.

8. **If you want to replace another baseline in the view, repeat steps 3 through 7.**

   Click OK when you're done.

To include an additional baseline in the view, you must insert task bar rows for the baseline's normal, split, milestone, and summary tasks. To easily define task bars in the Bar Styles dialog box, cut a task bar row, and then paste it back in twice—once for the original task bar, and once for the new baseline task bar. Then you can edit the row to specify the baseline you want to show, as described in the previous section.

Here are the steps for inserting the rows:

1. **Open the Multiple Baselines Gantt view or a copy you've created.**

   Consider copying the Multiple Baselines Gantt view for your new multi-baseline Gantt Chart. If you copy the customized view to your global template, you can use it in other Project files.

2. **On the Format tab, in the Bar Styles section, click Format and then choose Bar Styles from the drop-down menu.**

   The Bar Styles dialog box opens.

3. **Select the row for the task bar you want to duplicate, and then click Cut Row.**

   Project removes the row from the table.

4. **Before you do anything else, click Paste Row.**

   Project inserts the cut row back where it was originally.

5. **Select the row where you want to insert the new row, and then click Paste Row once more.**

   Project inserts another copy of the row immediately above the row you select, as illustrated in Figure 13-8.

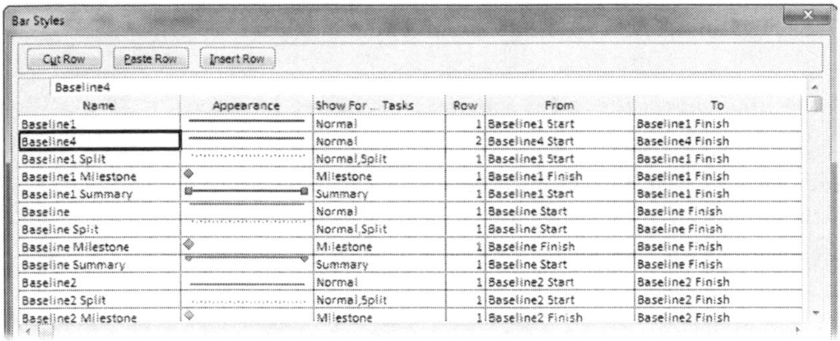

Figure 13-8:
*The Multiple Base-
lines Gantt view in-
cludes task bar styles
for Deliverable fields.
Don't be misled. The
Deliverable feature
is available only
when you use Project
Server.*

6. **Edit the Name, From, and To cells to match the baseline you want to show.**

   To display Baseline4, change the name to include Baseline4, and then, in the From and To cells, choose Baseline4 Start and Baseline4 Finish fields.

7. **On the Bars tab, choose the shape and color you want for the bar.**

   Project uses narrow bars so you can display several baselines on the same row of the Gantt Chart. If you want to display more than three baselines in a view, you must use a second task bar row.

8. **In the Row cell, type *2*.**

   This places the baseline task bar on a second row.

9. **Repeat steps 3 through 8 to create task bars for split, milestone, and summary tasks for the baseline.**

   If you choose the narrow task bars that run at the top, middle, and bottom of a row, you can add three more baselines to the second row of the view, just like the Multiple Baselines Gantt view does in the first row.

Viewing baseline values in a table

Although the Multiple Baselines Gantt timescale shows different task bars for each baseline, you probably want to see baseline costs, duration, and work. The table area of one of the Gantt Chart views is the perfect place to see these values.

Project includes the Baseline table, which displays columns for all the Baseline fields: Baseline Duration, Baseline Start, Baseline Finish, Baseline Work, and Baseline Cost. To display this table, right-click the table and then choose More Tables on the shortcut menu. In the More Tables dialog box, select Baseline, and then click Apply.

When you see values of "0" or "NA" in baseline fields, that's Project's way of telling you that you haven't saved that baseline yet.

If you would rather add baseline fields to another table, you can simply insert columns in the table. To add the Baseline Cost and Baseline Work fields to the Variance table, right-click the table heading area where you want to insert the column. On the shortcut menu, choose Insert Column, and then choose the baseline field to add from the drop-down menu.

Note: The Task Details Form can show baseline start and finish dates. Although the form opens initially with the Current option selected, select the Baseline option to see the baseline start and finish dates.

Part Three:
Projects in Action

III

Tracking Progress

After you finish planning a project and get approval from everyone necessary, you save a baseline of the project and give the signal for work to begin. You may be tempted to sit back at this point and rest on your…ahem…laurels. The hardest part of your job as project manager is done, right?

Wrong. Now that you've stepped over the threshold from planning into execution, plenty of challenges await. The execution phase is when you really earn your salt as a project manager: You monitor progress, evaluate performance, make adjustments as necessary, and manage the changes inevitable in projects.

Before you can see how the project is doing and make corrections, you need to know where the project stands. Tracking progress is all about data gathering: tasks completed, hours worked, and costs incurred. This chapter begins with the first hurdle—collecting progress data from your team—and shows you several ways to do it.

The second step is entering progress data into your Project file. This chapter describes how to enter progress data, depending on the information you collect. You'll also learn how to update progress at the assignment level, whether task by task or for the entire project.

Picking the Best Way to Track Progress

Depending on your project's requirements, just knowing what percentage of a task's work is complete may be enough. For example, Susan says she's 100 percent complete on two tasks and 25 percent complete on a third task, and you have all the information you need to update the schedule. On the other hand, a customer's contract terms may require you to account for every hour worked, and by whom, before you see a payment. In this case, Susan has to tell you how many hours she worked on each task every day of the previous week.

Quick and dirty vs. detailed and time-consuming are the two extremes of project tracking. Whether you choose one of these methods or some happy medium depends on your organization, the type of project, and the level of detail your stakeholders need. From a practical standpoint, it also depends on how much time you have to gather and incorporate progress data into the project plan.

Project doesn't make it easy to decide, because you can enter progress information in any of the following Project fields:

- Percent complete (% Complete)
- Percentage of work complete (% Work Complete)
- Actual duration
- Remaining duration
- Actual start
- Actual finish
- Actual work
- Remaining work
- Actual work by time period

Note: Project extrapolates information you enter into one progress tracking field into other, if not all of, the other progress tracking fields. That is, the values for one field affect the values of others.

If you're going for quick and easy progress reporting, fill in actual start, percent complete, and remaining duration. For more detailed progress reporting, you need to gather actual start, actual work, and remaining work. If you want highly detailed progress reporting, also enter actual and remaining work in the Task Usage or Resource time-phased portion of the Usage view, as illustrated in Figure 14-1.

Note: In projects, progress is primarily measured by milestones met and money spent. Other, less tangible, measures of progress exist, like quality and risk.

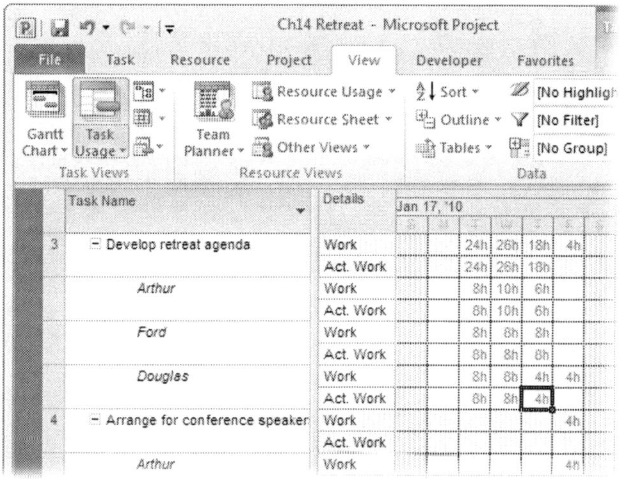

Figure 14-1:
Although you're never locked into one progress tracking method, it's a good idea to pick one that you'll use most of the time. That way, you and your team members don't have to think about what information to collect or what to do with it.

Obtaining Progress and Cost Data

Once you've chosen your preferred progress tracking approach, the battle has only begun. In this section, you'll learn ways to obtain the progress information you need without pulling team members' teeth. You'll also learn about Project views that help you ask the right questions and get the most complete progress information.

Collecting Task Progress from Your Team Members

You can get most progress information from your team members, although it's not always as easy as it sounds. This section describes some of the best methods for extracting reliable and consistent information from resources.

Note: If your organization uses Project Server, then team members can submit their progress information through the Project Web App interface. The data is automatically available for you to review and incorporate into your project plan.

The best place to be to record progress information is at your computer with the Resource Usage view applied in Project. By applying the Should Start/Finish By filter using the start and finish dates of the reporting period, you can see the tasks you need to update. The Resource Usage view groups assignments by resource, so you can enter progress information on all assignments for one resource and then move on to the next resource. If you update work hours, then the Work table has all the work-related fields, as shown in Figure 14-2. The Task Sheet view with the Tracking table is another candidate for a progress reporting view. You can apply the Using Resource filter to create a data collection printout.

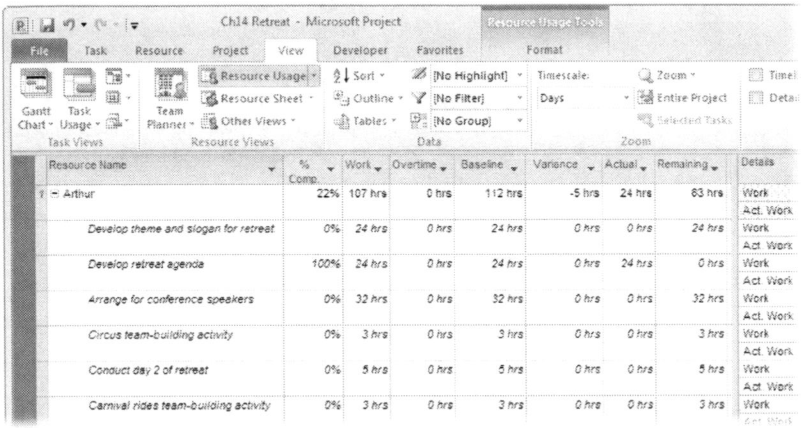

Figure 14-2:
The Resource Usage view groups assignments under the assigned resource. If you want to use a table with the progress tracking fields you use, copy one of the built-in tables, and then modify the fields in the copy to the ones you use (page 611).

You may want to print a report to hand out to resources to request their progress info. Project has several reports that show assignments, which you can use as data-gathering worksheets:

- **Who Does What report.** This report shows all assignments grouped under the assigned resources.

- **Who Does What When report.** This report shows all assignments grouped under the assigned resources with time-phased dates for each assignment.

- **To-Do List.** This report prompts you for the resource whose to-do list you want to print and then displays all assignments for that resource in date order, with the duration, start date, and finish date.

To print any of these reports, choose Project→Reports→Reports. Double-click Assignments, and then double-click the report you want. Click Print.

Receiving progress information via email

Email is an easy way to request and receive regular progress reports about current tasks, as you can see in Figure 14-3. You can copy and paste the progress data you receive in an email into the corresponding Project fields (page 566).

Gathering progress data in person

For small projects, "project management by walking around" can be the answer to data gathering. You actually get up from your desk and meet briefly with each team member, pen in hand, asking for progress information on tasks that are happening right about now. An alternative is to collect progress data during regular status meetings with the entire team or during one-on-one meetings with individual team members. Although they may not be as efficient as email, meetings like these can convey progress as well as updates on issues, risks, accomplishments, and successes.

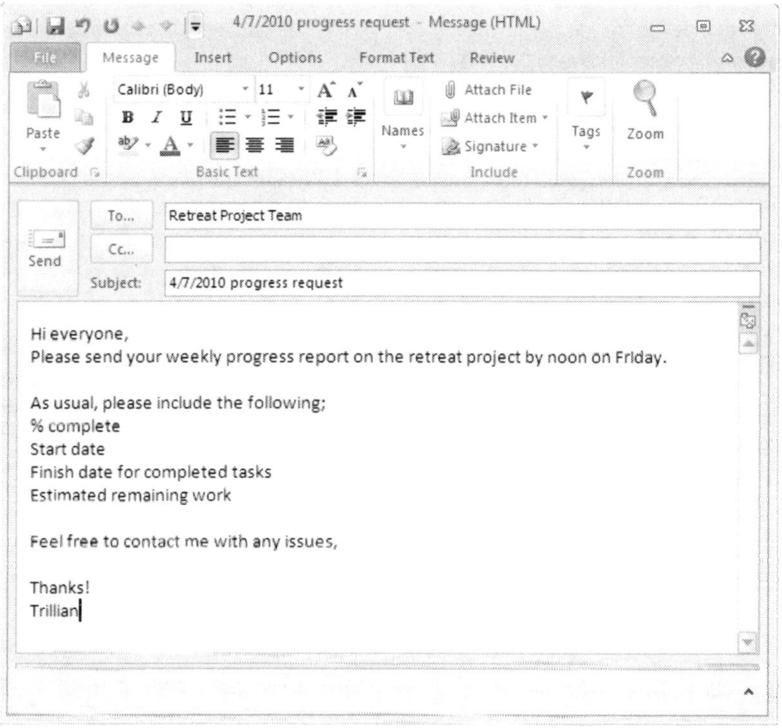

Figure 14-3:
You can automate reminders by using Microsoft Outlook or another similar email and calendar program to create and send a recurring appointment to all team members. A reminder pops up each time progress reports come due.

Tip: Don't underestimate the psychology of competition when going around a table for task progress reports. No one wants to look like a slacker when others are successfully ticking off their tasks one after another. It's counterintuitive, but such status meetings can actually increase your team's productivity.

Importing information from other tracking systems

Many organizations ask people to submit timesheet and cost information into specialized tools like an accounting or time-tracking system. The box on page 386 talks about some of the problems you may face trying to work with other systems.

Getting Team Members to Submit Progress

You may be only too aware that getting team members to provide information is about as easy as herding cats—on a good day. Many team members fork over information when you need it without drama. Others, however, may have concluded that they don't need to do it, they don't want to do it, or it's dumb to do it.

Sometimes, the problem is that people don't want to admit that they dragged their feet getting started. Others may feel they're too busy working on tasks and can't spare the time. Then there's the issue of assigned tasks that don't exactly map to what resources are working on, and they simply don't know *how* to report their time.

The easier and more automated you can make progress reporting, the more consistent results you'll get. Take the time to set up a form for reporting progress. Outlook, Access, and InfoPath all have features for creating data entry forms. If you use a collaboration website like a SharePoint site, you can post the form there for team members to fill in and submit.

Sell the reasons why progress tracking is so important. Let them know that accurate time reporting can help do the following:

- Build reality into task duration estimates for future similar projects.
- Convince the customer and other managing stakeholders of the time required to produce quality work.
- Build a case to obtain additional resources, money, and time to implement tasks that result from approved change requests.
- Identify potential problems with the schedule or budget early enough to take corrective actions so the team doesn't end up pulling as many all-nighters as they did the last time.

If logic doesn't sway your team, maybe bribery will. Promise them that the reward for complete progress reporting throughout the project will be a fabulous party at the local brew pub or an outing up to the nearest ski resort.

If team members are already entering progress information into another system, find out if you can obtain that information so they don't have to report progress data twice. Cajole your good buddy in accounting or IT into creating a periodic report of this information in an Excel spreadsheet or Access database. If the tasks in the other system map to the tasks in your project (see the box on page 387 if they don't), then you can import that data into your project plan, as described on page 516.

If you're bringing information in from another tracking system, designating accounting codes for tasks or resources can help you get data to the right place. For that matter, you may find accounting codes useful if you send information *from* your Project file to another system. If the accounting code is for resources, consider using the Code field, which is just a built-in resource text field to use however you wish. Otherwise, you can create a custom text or number field. Find details about creating an accounting code on page 322.

When Your Project and the Tracking System Don't Jibe

Sometimes the organization's tracking system wants project information in a way that doesn't give you what you need to track progress and cost. Often a timesheet or accounting system asks for information that's too broad. For example, while you might need to know the number of hours a resource spends working on a task each day, the timesheet system may ask only for the hours a resource works on the entire project for the whole week.

In this case, the tracking system data isn't helpful to you. Be prepared to explain discrepancies between the accounting system and your project numbers. Unfortunately,

if your resources are already submitting their time to the timesheet system, they may be resistant to submitting their time *again* to you in the way that you need.

You can prepare management for possible discrepancies ahead of time. Do what you can to persuade resources to report their time two different ways. Then for the next project, move heaven and earth to match up the needs of the organization's tracking system with the needs of accurate progress tracking in the project plan. It'll save *everybody* time and productivity.

Collecting Progress Data About Other Resources

Some key resources may be inanimate objects. No, not like George in the corner cubicle, but rather equipment resources, material resources, and cost resources. Just because you can't chat up these types of resources at the water cooler doesn't mean you can ignore progress information for them. They often represent significant project costs, and their progress is essential to accurately reflecting progress and cost in your Project file.

One way to obtain this information is to have one of the *human* resources report on when equipment resources start working, how many pounds of goop were actually used, or the actual cost of the flight from headquarters to Timbuktu. The people who operate machinery, handle material, or spend money are the logical choices. Even if no one works directly with these resources, you can still assign progress-reporting responsibility to someone or do it yourself. See the box on page 387 for a tip on documenting the owner of this reporting responsibility.

Another idea is to check with the bean counters. The organization's general ledger or accounting system may contain time and costs incurred by equipment, material, and cost resources. If so, you may be able to obtain an Excel or Access file of the data to import into Project (page 516).

Note: If your organization uses the enterprise project management features of Project Professional and Project Server, you can designate a different assignment owner for certain resources that don't have access to Project Server. Not only does this feature provide for people who don't have access to Project Server, but it's also especially handy for making sure that someone reports on progress for equipment, material, and cost resources in that program. (And if you don't have Project Professional or Project Server, see the box on page 387 for a workaround.)

Designating an Assignment Owner

Just as a designated driver gets inebriated partygoers home safely, a designated assignment owner makes sure that inanimate resources get their progress reported properly. Although Project doesn't include the assignment owner feature in its non-enterprise version, you can invent it yourself.

Just create a custom text field (page 641) called something like "assignment owner" or "progress reporter." Add the

new field to a table like Tracking in a task-oriented view, or the Work table in a resource-oriented view.

For the equipment, material, and cost resources that can't speak for themselves, in the custom field cells, type the name of the person who's responsible for reporting that resource's progress.

Entering Actual Progress in Project

Progress information based on what actually happened is usually referred to as project *actuals*. Actuals are made up of data like actual duration, actual start, actual work, and percent complete. (The box on page 389 explains the difference between baseline, scheduled, and actual values in Project.)

In this section, you'll learn how to enter actual progress information into your Project file, including the best dialog boxes, tables, and fields for this purpose. This section covers more popular techniques for tracking progress in Project. Some techniques update from the task's point of view, and other techniques update from the resource assignment's point of view. You'll also learn how to quickly "catch up" to your project if it's gotten stalled for some reason. Finally, you'll learn about the best ways to update cost information in your project.

Note: Although you can also enter remaining information, such as remaining duration or remaining work, those are not considered actuals. That information is a readjustment of the estimate of time needed in the future to complete the task.

Updating Task Progress

You can update progress for entire tasks, whether or not you assign resources to them. This section describes three effective methods for updating task progress: percent complete, actual and remaining duration, and actual start and actual finish. (If you want to update individual assignments, see page 394.)

You can update task progress in several places, each with its pros and cons. Choose from one of the following locations:

- The **Mark on Track command** (choose Task→Schedule→Mark on Track) changes a task to 100% complete and sets the actual start and finish dates to the scheduled task dates. This command is helpful only when a task is complete and finished according to plan.

FREQUENTLY ASKED QUESTION

Baseline, Scheduled, and Actual Values

What's the difference between baseline, scheduled, and actual information?

Now that you're about to enter actuals, you may wonder how baseline, scheduled, and actual fields differ. Here's how they work:

- **Baseline fields.** Also known as *planned* information, baseline fields are a snapshot of the Start, Finish, Duration, Work, Cost, Budget Work, and Budget Cost values when you save a baseline. You save a baseline immediately after the project plan has been approved and just before resources begin working on their first tasks. As you and your team work through the project, you can compare baseline values against scheduled or actual values to analyze variances and predict problems. For manually scheduled tasks without dates, the Baseline Estimated Start and Baseline Estimated Finish dates (page 364) show the dates that most closely match where the tasks occur in the schedule.

- **Scheduled fields.** Also known as *current* information, scheduled information encompasses all the fields throughout Project that have anything to do with the schedule. Unlike baseline information, scheduled information is constantly in flux. Whenever you enter actual progress information, Project recalculates task schedules and costs to accommodate the new reality.

- **Actual fields.** Often abbreviated simply as *actuals*, these fields contain progress information for completed or in-progress tasks. You explicitly enter actuals into the fields you're most concerned about; Project calculates any other actual information based on the formulas defining the relationships between the fields. For example, if you enter dates in the Actual Start and Actual Finish fields, then Project calculates the task Actual Duration as the span between the two dates.

- The **Update Tasks dialog box** (choose Task→Schedule→Mark on Track→Update Tasks) includes all the fields you might use to update progress. If several tasks have the same update values, you can select all the tasks before you open the dialog box. Then you enter the update information, and the program applies the changes to all the tasks. However, if each task has a unique update value, you need to open and close the dialog box for every task you want to update.

- The **Tracking table** (choose View→Data→Tables and then choose Tracking on the drop-down list) in a task-oriented view is the fastest way to enter progress for one task after another. The table also shows how Project updates other progress fields based on the information you enter.

- The **Task Details Form** (choose View→Split View, turn on the Details checkbox, choose More Views, and then double-click Task Details Form) displays the values for the task you selected in the top pane's view. You need to select the Actual option if you want to type actual dates. Right-click the Task Details form and then choose Work if you want to type actual and remaining hours.

Entering percent complete

Percent complete is the easiest type of progress to obtain, but it's the least accurate. If you don't need precise hours and you just want to know the percentage of the task duration that's complete, enter task progress as percent complete, like this:

1. **In a task-oriented view such as the Gantt Chart view, apply the Tracking table, and then select the task whose percent complete you want to update.**

   To update several tasks that have the same percent complete value, select them all at once. If the tasks are adjacent to one another in the table, just drag across the task names to select them all. You can also Shift-click to select adjacent tasks or Ctrl-click to select nonadjacent tasks.

2. **Choose Task→Schedule→Mark on Track→Update Tasks.**

   Project displays the Update Tasks dialog box, shown in Figure 14-4. You can also type a percentage in the Tracking table's % Complete column.

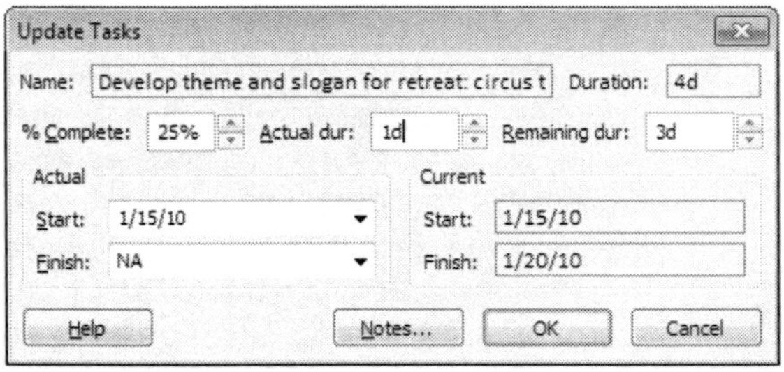

Figure 14-4:
The Update Tasks dialog box includes % Complete, Actual Duration, Remaining Duration, and Actual Start and Finish, so you can report progress any way you want. If you type a value in % Complete and Actual Duration, the program calculates the Remaining Duration and updates the task duration. For example, if you type 25% for % Complete and 1d (a day) for Actual Duration, the Remaining Duration changes to 3d (3 days) and the new scheduled duration is 4d (4 days).

3. **In the % Complete box, type the percent complete for the selected task(s).**

   To keep things simple, you may want to limit the values to a few standard percentages like 25%, 50%, 75%, and 100%. If you do, you can update a task's % Complete field from the task mini-toolbar. Right-click the task and then, on the mini-toolbar, click the 100% down arrow and choose the value you want.

When you enter percent complete for a task, Project calculates other progress-related fields. In the Gantt Chart view, a black line appears in the center of task bars to show how much of the total task is completed, as illustrated in Figure 14-5.

If you don't enter the actual start, then Project sets the actual start to the task's scheduled start date. If you don't enter remaining duration, then Project calculates the remaining duration from the percent complete and actual duration. See the box on page 391 to learn more about the formulas Project uses to calculate the progress fields.

Tip: If many tasks have the same percent complete values, you might find it faster to enter percent complete directly into the table. Right-click the Select All cell at top right of the table, and then choose Tracking to apply the Tracking table to the Gantt Chart view. Enter the percent complete in the "% Comp." field for each applicable task. To copy a value to other cells, select the cell. Then drag the black square in the bottom-right corner of the cell.

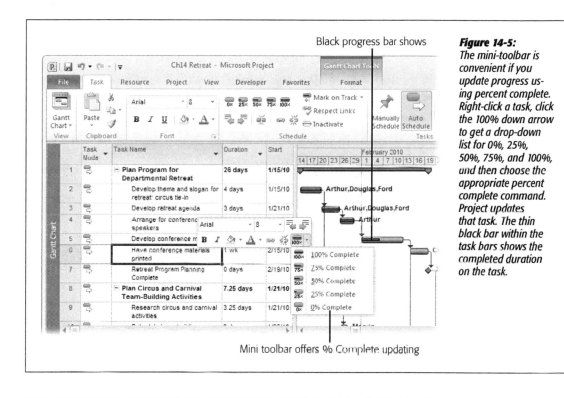

Black progress bar shows

Mini toolbar offers % Complete updating

Figure 14-5:
The mini-toolbar is convenient if you update progress using percent complete. Right-click a task, click the 100% down arrow to get a drop-down list for 0%, 25%, 50%, 75%, and 100%, and then choose the appropriate percent complete command. Project updates that task. The thin black bar within the task bars shows the completed duration on the task.

Project's Progress Calculations for Tasks

Project calculates progress values for any of the progress fields you don't update directly. That is, when you enter information into one progress field, Project calculates the values that belong in any other associated progress fields. The following list gives you an "under the hood" look at the relationship between commonly used task-related tracking fields:

- % Complete = (Actual Duration / Duration) × 100
- Actual Duration = Duration × % Complete

- Remaining Duration = Duration – Actual Duration
- Remaining Duration = Duration – (Duration × % Complete)
- Actual Start = Scheduled Start unless otherwise entered
- Actual Finish = Scheduled Finish unless otherwise entered

Entering actual duration and remaining duration

In this method, you specify the duration that's complete and a forecast for the remaining duration. It's more accurate than the simplistic percent complete method, because it gives you the opportunity to tell Project that you expect the task to take longer than you'd originally planned. (If you enter percent complete and actual duration, Project calculates remaining duration.) To enter task progress using actual and remaining durations, follow these steps:

1. **In a task-oriented view like the Gantt Chart view, select the task whose actual duration and remaining duration you want to update.**

   You can also work in other task-oriented views like the Calendar view or the Network Diagram view.

2. **Choose Task→Schedule→Mark on Track→Update Tasks.**

   Project displays the Update Tasks dialog box, which shows any existing values for actual and remaining duration. The sum of actual and remaining durations is the scheduled duration. If you're comfortable working directly in tables and like to watch the change highlighting feature color the table cells, you can also enter actual and remaining values directly in the Tracking table.

3. **In the "Actual dur" box, enter the actual duration.**

   Use the normal time period abbreviations, like 6h, 2d, or 1w.

4. **In the "Remaining dur" box, enter the remaining duration for the selected task, and then click OK.**

   When you enter an actual duration, the value in the "Remaining dur" box and Duration box doesn't change immediately. Project doesn't recalculate the fields in the dialog box until you click OK.

   On the Tracking table, you can see that Project has updated the Actual Start and % Complete fields based on your duration entries. If resources are assigned, Project also updates the Actual Work field. Likewise, if you had set up these resources with cost rates, then Project automatically updates the Actual Cost field.

Tip: Check the actual start date and make sure it's correct. Change it if necessary to reflect the reality for the task. If you don't enter the actual start, then Project sets it to the task's scheduled start date.

Entering actual start and actual finish

If a task is complete, then the actual start and actual finish dates are the best values to enter. You can set the % Complete field to 100%, but if you do that, then Project assumes that the task started and finished on the scheduled dates. Do the following to enter task progress using actual start and actual finish dates:

1. **In a task-oriented view like the Gantt Chart view, select the task whose actual start and actual finish you want to update.**

   If you have several tasks that share the same actual start and finish dates, you can select them all at once and then update their dates in one fell swoop.

2. **Choose Task→Schedule→Mark on Track→Update Tasks.**

   Project displays the Update Tasks dialog box. If you select just a single task, then the Current section displays the scheduled start and finish dates. If you select multiple tasks, then the Current section boxes are blank.

3. **Under Actual, click the arrow in the Start box, and then choose the actual start date from the calendar drop-down menu, as shown in Figure 14-6. Do the same in the Finish box to set the actual finish date.**

   Looking at the Tracking table, notice that Project updates not only the actual start and finish fields, but also the percent complete, actual duration, and remaining duration fields. If resources are assigned, then the actual work and actual cost fields are updated as well. If you have change highlighting turned on (page 337), then the ripple effect of delayed tasks appears immediately.

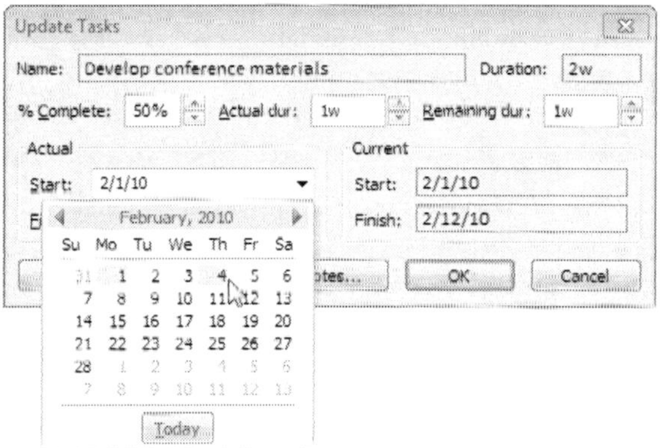

Figure 14-6:
You can choose from the calendar, or type the date in the box if you prefer. The dates in the Actual boxes show "NA" until you enter progress information for the task, whether it's percent complete, actual and remaining duration, or actual start and finish.

Rescheduling incomplete work

Say a task is partially complete and several days have passed since your status date with no additional progress. You can update the task to show the completed work occurring prior to the status date or move the incomplete work to resume as of the status date. Select the task and then choose Task→Tasks→Move. On the Move drop-down menu, choose Completed Parts to Status Date to move the complete work prior to the status date. Or choose Incomplete Parts to Status Date to move the incomplete work into the future.

Tip: To reschedule incomplete work, you have to be able to split tasks that are in progress. Choose File→Options. In the Project Options dialog box, click Schedule. Under "Scheduling options for this project", turn on the "Split in-progress tasks" checkbox.

Updating the Project Using Resource Assignment Progress

When resources are assigned to tasks, you can take progress updates to a more detailed level of tracking. Instead of showing progress on the task as a whole, you can show progress on individual assignments within the task. Admittedly, for tasks that have only one resource assigned, you don't see much of a difference. But for tasks that have multiple resources assigned, entering updates at the assignment level provides more detailed progress information.

You have to enter more data to update resource assignments this way, but it makes your progress information more accurate. Plus, Project uses progress on individual assignments to determine progress statistics for the task as a whole. You don't have to resort to guesswork about a task's overall percent complete when, for example, one resource is 100 percent complete, another is 40 percent complete, and the third is 25 percent complete.

This section describes three effective methods for updating resource assignment progress: percentage of work complete, actual work complete and remaining work, and actual work complete by time period. You'll also learn how to create a specialized tracking view that simplifies entering progress information for resource assignments.

Note: When you enter progress updates for tasks, Project ordinarily rolls down these values to the assignment level, calculating the actual and remaining work and cost for associated assignments. If you prefer to enter these values yourself, choose File→Options, and then choose Schedule. Turn off the "Updating task status updates resource status" checkbox. You can then specify the actual assignment progress when you get it.

Entering percentage of work complete

Percent complete (% Complete field) refers to completion for a task as a whole, based on duration. Percentage of work complete (% Work Complete) refers to completion based on the number of hours worked divided by the baseline work hours. Do the following to enter resource assignment progress as percentage of work complete:

1. Display the Task Usage or Resource Usage view. Choose View→Data→ Tables→Work to apply the Work table to the view and see progress-related fields for assignments.

   In the Task Usage view, the column is titled "% W. Comp." If you don't see the "% W. Comp." column initially, drag the divider between the view's table and timescale to the right until you see the column.

In the Resource Usage view, the column is labeled "% Comp.", but the field behind the scenes is still % Work Complete.

Tip: To see how actuals affect the schedule when you update progress in a usage view, start by displaying the Gantt Chart view in the top pane. Then display the Task Usage view in the bottom pane by choosing View→Split View, turning on the Details checkbox, and then choosing Task Usage in the Details drop-down list. As you enter actuals in the Task Usage view, you see tasks change (including change highlighting) in the Gantt Chart view.

---

2. **Select the assignment whose percentage of work complete you want to update.**

   In the Task Usage view, Project lists the assigned resources under each task. In the Resource Usage view, Project lists the assigned tasks under each resource. Remember that the assignment is the intersection of tasks with resources.

3. **Double-click the assignment.**

   Project opens the Assignment Information dialog box.

4. **Select the Tracking tab.**

   The Tracking tab shows several fields you can use to update progress for the individual assignment, as shown in Figure 14-7.

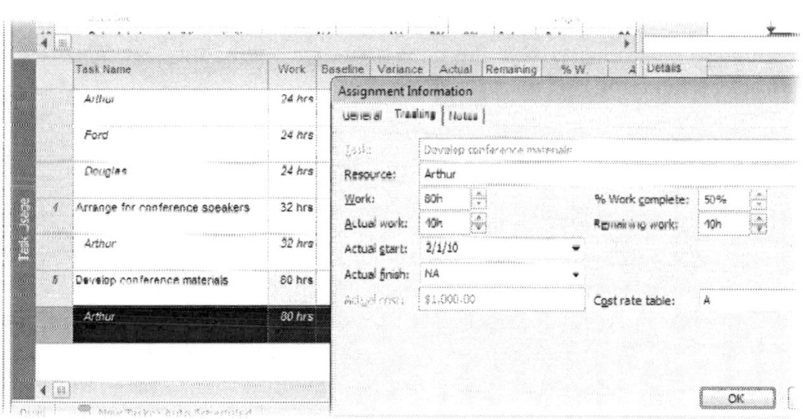

Figure 14-7:
The Tracking tab includes boxes for % Work Complete, Actual Work, Actual Start, Actual Finish, and Actual Cost. To update several assignments with the same data, select them all at once, and then open the Assignment Information dialog box to make the change.

5. **In the "% Work complete" box, enter the percentage that represents the progress the resource has made.**

   Remember, enter the percent complete reflecting the progress on this assignment, not the entire task. Before you click OK, check the assignment's actual start and remaining work. If you don't enter the actual start, Project sets the Actual Start field to the assignment's scheduled start date. If you don't enter remaining work, Project calculates the remaining work from the percentage of work complete.

If you enter only percent work complete without actual start or actual finish, you can enter percent work complete in the "% W. Comp." field in the Task Usage view or the "% Comp." field in the Resource Usage view (these headings both represent the % Work Complete field). Remember to enter the value for the assignment, not for the task or resource.

Note: The percent complete buttons on the mini-toolbar and the Task tab are grayed out when you select an assignment, because they update tasks, not assignments. However, they become active if you select a task in the Task Usage view.

Entering actual work complete and remaining work

While *duration* refers to the span of time from the beginning of a task until the end, *work* on an assignment refers to the person-hours a resource is assigned to work. Project can calculate work from duration and vice versa, but they don't measure the same thing. If you gather hours worked from resources, then entering the actual and remaining work provides the most accurate picture of progress and the corresponding labor costs.

To enter actual work complete and remaining work on an assignment, do this:

1. **In the Task Usage or Resource Usage view, select the assignment whose actual and remaining work you want to update.**

   If multiple assignments have the same actual and remaining work values, you can select them and update their progress at the same time.

2. **Double-click the selected assignment.**

   Project displays the Assignment Information dialog box.

3. **Select the Tracking tab.**

   The Tracking tab includes the "Actual work" and "Remaining work" boxes. Any existing values for actual and remaining work appear in the boxes. The value in the Work box (scheduled work) is the sum of actual work and remaining work. (In Project, the Work field represents scheduled work—the total of actual work performed and the current estimate of remaining work. To learn more about the difference between baseline, scheduled, and actual values, see the box on page 389.)

4. **In the "Actual work" box, enter the actual work amount that has already been done.**

   Use the normal time period abbreviations like 8h, 5d, or 2w.

5. **In the "Remaining work" box, enter the remaining work hours needed to complete the selected assignment. Click OK.**

   When you enter actual work, at first the values in the Work and "Remaining work" boxes don't change. However, after you enter remaining work and click OK, Project recalculates the Work value.

Make sure the actual start date is correct. Change it if necessary. If you don't enter the actual start, then Project sets it to the assignment's scheduled start date.

Entering actual work by time period

For the ultimate in progress detail and accuracy, you can enter actual work by time period. Be forewarned, however, that this is the most time-consuming method for tracking progress, for you and for your resources. You enter actual work in the time-phased portion of a usage view, showing how much work was done on an assignment in each time period (day, week, or whatever).

To enter actual work by time period, follow these steps:

1. **Display the Task Usage or Resource Usage view.**

   Not only do the usage views show assignment information, but they also show time-phased information, like work or cost values over time.

2. **Display Actual Work in the time-phased portion of the view by choosing Format→Details and turning on the Actual Work checkbox.**

   You can also simply right-click in the time-phased portion of the usage view, and then, on the shortcut menu, choose Actual Work.

   With either method, Project adds a row labeled Act. Work to the time-phased portion of the usage view.

3. **In the time-phased portion of the view, drag the right edge of the Details column to the right to show the full text.**

   On the status bar, drag the Zoom slider until the timescale for the usage view shows the level of time detail you want to work with. For example, you can show days, weeks, or months in the timescale.

4. **In the table area, select the assignment whose actual work you want to update.**

   You can actually have one assignment selected in the sheet portion, while another assignment is selected in the time-phased portion of the usage view.

5. **To display the cells for the assignment in the time-phased portion of the view, choose Task→Editing→Scroll to Task.**

   Project scrolls the time-phased portion of the view to show when work is scheduled to begin on the selected assignment.

6. **In the Act. Work field in the assignment row, type the actual work values in the appropriate time periods, as shown in Figure 14-8.**

   If a resource tells you more time is needed, update the Remaining Work cell in the table to the value you received. If you don't explicitly enter a value for remaining work, then Project calculates it by simply subtracting the actual work you just entered from the scheduled work.

Tip: If you want to add a field to the time-phased portion of the view that's not available on the Format tab or shortcut menu, choose Format→Details→Add Details. In the Detail Styles dialog box, select the Usage Details tab. In the "Available fields" box, select the field you want to add, and then click Show. Use the Move arrows to specify the order of fields in the view.

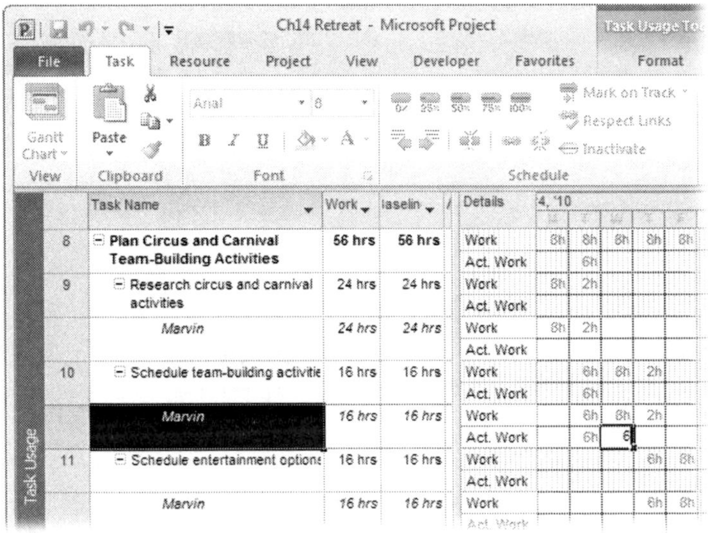

Figure 14-8:
If you've applied the Work table to the view, Project updates the total actual work hours in the table's Actual Work field as you type work hours in cells the time-phased portion of the view.

Globally Updating the Project

Sometimes, a project goes off kilter and you need a quick way to recover. For example, maybe several months of work was complete when you were told to stop work immediately. Then a month later, the project is on again. Unfortunately, in the interim, the dates in your Project file marched forward assuming that people were going to do those tasks when they were scheduled.

Or say you were suddenly drafted to handle customer problems onsite. Upon your return, you're relieved to find tasks completed and milestones met. Except...the Project file doesn't have any actual values for the time you were away. The prospect of gathering and incorporating several weeks' worth of actuals into the file is too overwhelming, especially given the other activities you're behind on.

In this section, you'll learn about two quick-fix recovery methods. One method lets you reschedule unfinished work to move the start or resume dates of all tasks to the present date so you can continue from this point forward. Another method is like the cat that falls off the sofa and lands on its head, then walks away acting as if it meant to do that all along. This is the automatic project update method, which says, essentially, that all tasks in the project have been done exactly according to plan.

Rescheduling unfinished work in the project.

If your project was interrupted midstream and is now resuming, then you have a lot of schedule dates to adjust. Rather than adjust dates manually, it's simpler to have Project reschedule any uncompleted work. To do so, follow these steps:

1. **Display any task-oriented view.**

   The Update Project dialog box is available only for task-oriented views.

2. **To reschedule only certain tasks, select them and then choose Project→ Status→Update Project.**

   The Update Project dialog box appears, as shown in Figure 14-9.

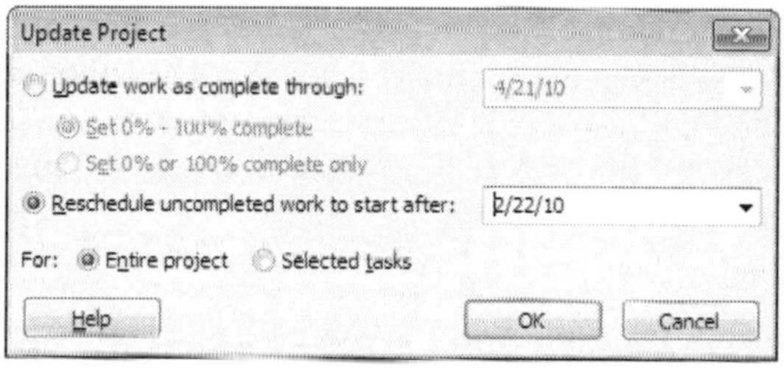

Figure 14-9:
The Update Project dialog box opens with "Update work as complete through" and "Entire project" selected automatically. If you want to update only certain tasks, be sure to select the tasks before you open the dialog box and then select the "Selected tasks" option.

3. **Select the "Reschedule uncompleted work to start after" option, and then type the date when work should resume.**

   Any tasks that were in progress when the project was halted resume on that date. It also means that any unstarted tasks scheduled to start before that date now start on this new date instead. Any successors linked to those tasks reschedule to follow their predecessors as normal.

4. **To reschedule only selected tasks, select the "Selected tasks" option. Click OK.**

   Otherwise, Project reschedules the entire project, as shown in Figure 14-10.

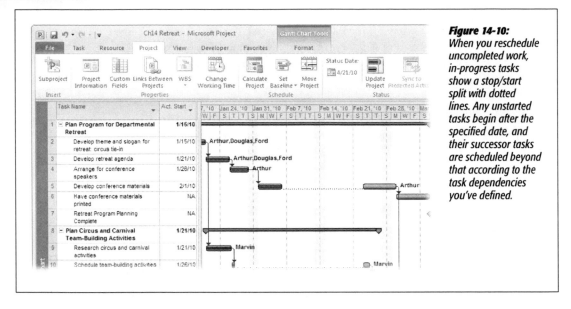

Figure 14-10:
When you reschedule uncompleted work, in-progress tasks show a stop/start split with dotted lines. Any unstarted tasks begin after the specified date, and their successor tasks are scheduled beyond that according to the task dependencies you've defined.

After you reschedule your project, examine it carefully for issues you need to address. If you had set date constraints or created manually scheduled tasks, then reset them as necessary. Check for conflicts between constraints and predecessors (page 251). Also look at milestone dates and the project finish date to see if you should adjust them because of the delay, and look at the project costs to see if anything is now going over budget.

If necessary, submit the new schedule to the managing stakeholders and get their approval again. Once that's done, you may want to save a new baseline. You can either overwrite your original baseline or save a second baseline and work with that as your primary benchmark from now on (page 366).

Updating the project as scheduled

Anyone who says a project has gone exactly as planned is bound to get some suspicious glances. However, suppose your project has been progressing with no major mishaps, and you have also fallen woefully behind in entering progress updates. You can enter a set of automatic updates that says all work is completed or in progress exactly as scheduled through a specified date.

Tip: Keep in mind that updating a project automatically compromises the accuracy of your project data, so you should use it only as a last resort. If you use project actuals for billing or other accounting purposes, then don't use automatic updates. In that case, you simply have to gather the back data and update your file.

To globally update work as completed according to the schedule, follow these steps:

1. **Display any task-oriented view.**

   For example, you can choose the Calendar view or the Detail Gantt view.

2. **If you want to update only certain tasks, select them.**

   Drag across adjacent tasks or Ctrl-click to select nonadjacent tasks.

3. **Choose Project→Status→Update Project.**

   The Update Project dialog box appears.

4. **Make sure the "Update work as complete through" option is selected.**

   Project makes the date box for that option available.

5. **In the date box, enter the cutoff date for updating as scheduled.**

   This means that Project automatically enters progress update information, such as 100 percent complete, for any tasks scheduled to take place before the specified date.

6. **If you want Project to update tasks with partial percent complete, select the "Set 0% - 100% complete" option.**

   This option means that some tasks (the ones that are scheduled to start before and finish after the cutoff date) may update to 50 percent or 75 percent, for example.

   If you want Project to update only tasks that should have been 100 percent complete before the specified date, then select the "Set 0% or 100% complete only" option.

7. **If you want to update only selected tasks, select the "Selected tasks" option, and then click OK.**

   Otherwise, Project updates all applicable tasks throughout the entire project.

Updating Project Costs

Projects can potentially have up to five different sources of costs: human resources, equipment, materials, cost resources, and fixed costs for tasks. Each of these costs needs actual cost information before you can see where you stand against the project budget. In this section, you'll learn how to update each of these five cost sources. The Cost table is a great starting point, with fields for baseline, scheduled, actual, and remaining costs. You can apply the table to a usage view to see costs for individual assignments as well.

You can also insert cost-related fields like Actual Cost into any table. Just remember that these fields represent task costs in a task-oriented table. When you add these fields to a resource-oriented table, their values relate to resources. When you add these fields to a usage view, you can see values for the individual assignments.

Figuring actual costs for human and equipment resources

If you set up resources with standard rates, overtime rates, and costs per use (page 197) and assign the resources to tasks, then Project calculates actual cost as soon as you enter actual work. You never have to update actual labor and equipment costs yourself. See for yourself when you apply the Tracking table to a task-oriented view like the Task Usage view, shown in Figure 14-11.

With equipment resources, the challenge is making sure that actual work time is reported. Designate an assignment owner for equipment resource assignments (page 388).

WORD TO THE WISE

Manually Entering Resource Costs

When you tell Project how much resources cost, assign them to tasks, and enter actual work, Project automatically calculates their actual costs for you. Project lets you update resource costs manually, but that doesn't mean it's a good idea. It's cumbersome, tricky, and the results may not be what you expect. However, if Project's costs are totally out of whack and you want to report costs in Project anyway, then you can type actual costs into the fields that Project usually calculates. Choose File→Options, click Schedule, and then turn off the "Actual costs are always calculated

by Project" checkbox. With this setting in place, you have to enter total actual costs in the Actual Cost field for tasks.

To manually enter time-phased costs for tasks or resource assignments, display the Task Usage view. Choose Format→Details and turn on the Actual Cost checkbox to add the Actual Cost row to the time-phased portion of the view. You can now enter actual costs by time period in the Actual Cost field for the assignment or for the task as a whole.

Calculating actual costs for material resources

With standard rates or costs per use in place for your material resources and the material resources assigned to tasks, Project calculates the actual cost for material resources based on the number of units used or the amount per time period, like 20 boxes of goop at $100 per box or four boxes of goop per day times a 5-day task duration times $100 per box. The actual cost for the material resource is based on the actual duration of the task.

If the actual amount of material used isn't correct, you can change it in the Actual Work field for the material resource assignment. Use the Task Usage view, Resource Usage view, or the Tracking tab on the Assignment Information dialog box.

When you enter actual progress
information for an assignment. . .

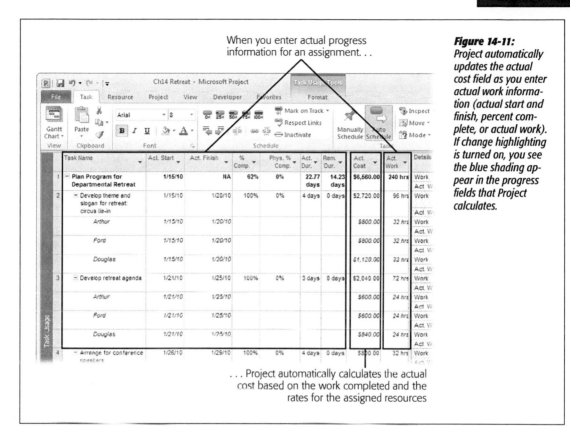

. . . Project automatically calculates the actual
cost based on the work completed and the
rates for the assigned resources

Figure 14-11:
*Project automatically
updates the actual
cost field as you enter
actual work informa-
tion (actual start and
finish, percent com-
plete, or actual work).
If change highlighting
is turned on, you see
the blue shading ap-
pear in the progress
fields that Project
calculates.*

Figuring actual costs for cost resources

When you assign a cost resource to a task, you enter the estimated cost (page 289).
However, when you enter actual progress for task or resource assignments, Project
doesn't include cost resources in its actual cost calculations. Progress information is
based on duration or work completed, and cost resources operate independently of
time spent on a task. This disconnect means that you could set a task to 100 percent
complete, but the cost of the cost resource would still show remaining cost, as illustrated in Figure 14-12.

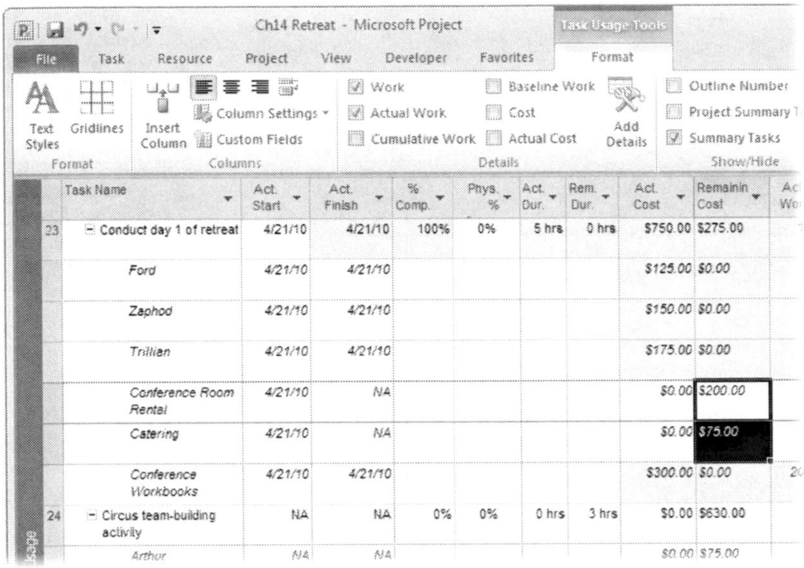

Figure 14-12:
If you assign a cost resource to a task that also has work and material resources, then when you enter actual progress, Project calculates actual work and material costs, but not cost resource costs. If cost resources are the only type of resource assigned to the task, then cost resource costs become actual costs when you enter actual progress.

If a task has work and cost resources assigned, then you have to explicitly update the actual cost for cost resources. To enter cost resource costs as actual costs, follow these steps:

1. **In the Task Usage or Resource Usage view, double-click the cost resource assignment for the task.**

   Project displays the Assignment Information dialog box.

2. **Select the Tracking tab.**

   For cost resources, the only fields available are "% Work complete" and "Actual cost".

3. **Although cost resources are independent of work amount, you can enter a percentage in the "% Work complete" field, and Project calculates an actual cost amount accordingly.**

   For example, suppose you specified $2,420.00 for the Airfare cost resource on this task. If you enter 50% in the "% Work complete" field, then the "Actual cost" field changes to $1,210.00.

   You can also simply enter a value in the "Actual cost" field. If it's not the full amount planned, then the remaining amount goes into the Remaining Cost field for the assignment (the field isn't included in the Assignment Information dialog box).

Updating actual fixed costs on tasks

Although cost resources have mostly replaced fixed costs on tasks, you may have a fixed cost or two lurking in your project (page 293). If you use fixed cost, then when you enter actual progress information on a task, Project calculates the actual cost for the fixed cost along with the work and material costs.

For example, if you had a fixed cost of $300 on a task, and you say that this task is now 50 percent complete, Project moves $150 of the fixed cost to the actual cost side of the equation and leaves the other $150 in the remaining cost side. The actual cost for the task is the total of these fixed cost values and any resource costs on the task.

Unlike most other fields, Project doesn't have a separate field for actual fixed costs. The value in the Fixed Cost field is the total of your estimated fixed costs and actual fixed costs, so be sure to update the Fixed Cost field with the current fixed cost value. The Cost table includes the Fixed Cost field.

15

Evaluating Project Performance

S mall issues can blow up into project wildfires if you don't douse them early. A delay here, a cost overrun there, and suddenly the finish date, cost, and project objectives are at risk. Regular project performance reviews are a must if you want your daily jolt limited to your double espresso. Comparing progress to baseline schedule and cost can give you early warning of trouble brewing.

Schedule, budget, and other project objectives are interdependent, so where you start your evaluation depends on what's most important. If project budget is crucial, you can start by evaluating costs. But in most cases, starting with the schedule makes sense, because delays can affect the finish date *and* the price tag.

This chapter starts by showing you how to evaluate schedule performance, whether you want a quick peek at overall progress or a heads-up about tasks in trouble. You learn how to use Project's views, reports, and filters to see high-level and task-by-task progress, as well as potential problems. You'll learn ways to find overallocated resources and tasks that are exceeding their work budgets. Likewise, you'll learn about reports and filters for comparing project costs to the baseline cost or a budget. And no chapter on project performance would be complete without a section on earned value analysis. You'll learn how earned value and its related measures help you evaluate performance. Then you'll learn how to use them in Project.

Once you know where your project stands, the next step is usually making adjustments to keep the project on time and within budget. Fortunately, most of the techniques you use during project execution are the same ones for fine-tuning a project during planning (see Chapter 12). This chapter reviews those techniques and then describes one more option: assigning overtime.

Note: Evaluating schedule and costs means looking at your project from many directions. This chapter describes some of the ways you may want to customize elements to see performance. ProjectMM_ Customization.mpp at *www.missingmanuals.com/cds* contains many of the customized views, filters, and other elements mentioned. However, Part Five of this book describes customizing Project elements in detail.

Scheduled, Baseline, and Actual Values

During project planning, there's only one set of values to watch—the dates, work, and costs that Project calculates, which are known as *scheduled* or *planned* values. Once a project gets under way, additional types of values suddenly have roles in determining project performance. Before you dive into evaluating performance, it's a good idea to understand the difference between these values and how they contribute to measuring performance. Here are the different types of values and where you find them:

- **Scheduled** values are the forecast values at any point during the project, whether you're putting your plan together or already tracking progress. Scheduled fields like Start, Finish, Work, Cost, and Duration combine actual performance so far with the forecast values for the work that remains. While you're planning, scheduled values are merely forecasts, because no actual values exist. At the end, scheduled values equal actual values, because there's nothing left to forecast. If you've spent $10,000 so far and Project calculates another $35,000 to finish, then the Cost field is the sum of the two: $45,000.

- **Baseline** values are the scheduled dates, work, cost, and duration when you saved your baseline (page 365). In effect, when you set a baseline, Project copies the values from Start, Finish, Work, Cost, and Duration to Baseline Start, Baseline Finish, Baseline Work, Baseline Cost, and Baseline Duration. As you'll learn shortly, the difference between scheduled and baseline values is a huge part of evaluating project performance.

- **Actual** values are what actually happened: when tasks really started and finished, how much work has been done, and how much tasks really cost. The fields for actual values are, unsurprisingly, Actual Start, Actual Finish, Actual Work, Actual Cost, and Actual Duration.

- **Remaining** values are simply the duration, work, and costs that remain. For example, suppose the original work for a task was 120 hours. The assigned resource has completed 60 hours but estimates that it'll take another 80 hours to finish. The amount of actual work doesn't matter; the Remaining Work field is 80 hours.

- **Variances** are the difference between scheduled and baseline values. In Project, variance fields like Cost Variance and Finish Variance are scheduled value minus baseline value, like Cost–Baseline Cost. If the scheduled cost is greater than the baseline cost, the positive variance shows that the task is over budget. Likewise, if the scheduled finish date is later than the baseline finish date, the positive variance indicates that the task is behind schedule. In other words, positive variances are bad; negative variances are good. See page 422 to learn how earned value variances, CV (earned value cost variance) and SV (earned value schedule variance), differ from Project's basic variance fields.

Note: A variance that's equal to zero (0) can mean one of two things: A task is exactly on track—or you forgot to set a baseline. During project execution, tasks that go exactly according to plan produce zero variance. But if *every* task has zero variance, the problem is the absence of a baseline.

Is the Project on Time?

Project dates are usually the first step to evaluating performance, because project duration has a way of affecting the price tag, too. This section reviews ways to review the schedule, whether at the project level, for day-to-day task management, or to calculate schedule performance metrics. The box on page 411 describes another way to evaluate performance that doesn't involve Project.

Because actual progress affects the rest of the project, evaluating performance adds a few techniques to the ones you use to fine-tune a schedule during planning (page 328). You keep tabs on the project schedule at several levels:

- **The project finish date.** The bottom line, of course, is whether the project is going to finish when it should, which is what a quick peek at the overall project finish date shows.

- **Tactical task management.** Keeping the overall schedule on track means keeping individual tasks on time. Most project managers check tasks each week to see if any are in trouble or heading that way. Because delays on the critical path translate immediately into a late project finish date, critical path tasks are the first ones to examine. However, you must still keep an eye on noncritical tasks, because they can become critical if they go on too long.

- **Overall schedule performance.** There's more to schedule performance than the finish date. Schedule performance measures like schedule variance (SV) and schedule performance index (SPI), described on page 424, tell you how well you're managing the project schedule, or whether corrective actions are working. You can compare performance measures from week to week or month to month to look for trends.

Checking Status at the Project Level

Project-wide status for schedule, cost, and work comes as a package deal in several places within Project. Project-level variances are the first hint of problems. Here are three ways to see overall schedule, cost, and work status:

- **Project summary task.** As shown in Figure 15-1, the project summary task is a simple way to see high-level status.

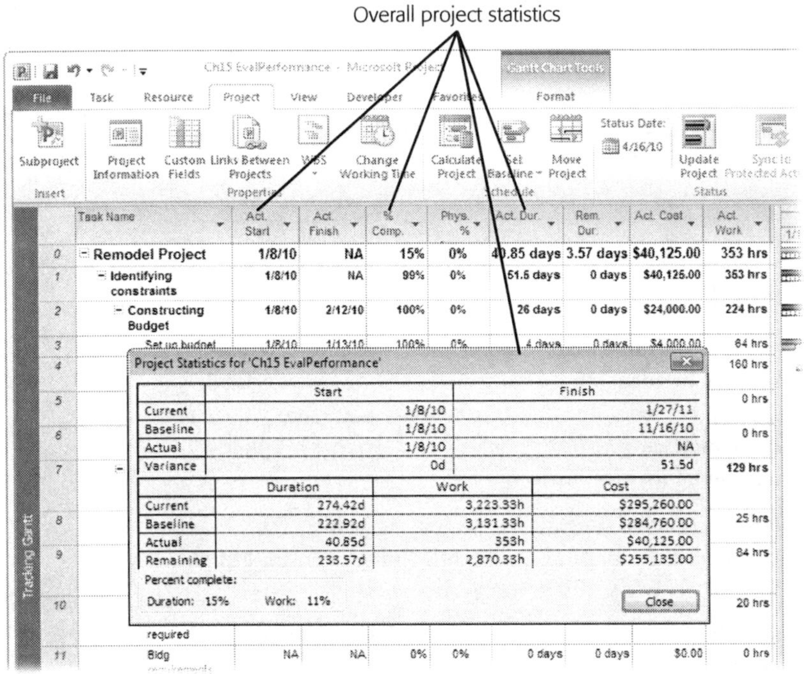

Overall project statistics

Figure 15-1:
*When you apply
different tables to a
view, you can see
different variances in
the project summary
task row. The Tracking
table focuses on
actual values. To see
schedule work, and
cost variances, right-
click the Select All
box, and then choose
Variance, Work, or
Cost, respectively.*

- **Project Summary report.** For a complete report of scheduled, baseline, actual, remaining, and variance values, choose Project→Reports→Reports. In the Reports dialog box, double-click Overview, and then double-click Project Summary. Variance values greater than zero for Start, Finish, Duration, and Work indicate that the project may be behind schedule. Work and Cost variances greater than zero are signs that the project may be over budget.

  % Complete (duration) and % Work Complete fields can be early warning signs. If duration has a higher percent complete than work, then the project may run late because there's more work to finish than duration to finish it in. However, tasks that schedule more work later in the duration exhibit the same characteristic.

- **Project Statistics dialog box.** This dialog box shown in Figure 15-1 is a subset of the Project Summary report; it shows most of the same information except for duration, work, and cost variances. Choose Project→Properties→Project Information. In the Project Information dialog box, click Project Statistics.

Tip: In the Backstage view (the File tab), choose Info to see information about your project. The panel on the right shows the current start and finish date and other basic 411. To see Project Statistics, choose Project Information→Project Statistics.

What Else Could Go Wrong?

When you plan your project, you put together a risk management plan, which identifies potential risks and what you'll do if they become reality. During project execution, you must watch for risks that are threatening or explode suddenly.

Schedule delays and increasing costs can be a sign that a risk has turned into reality, but talking to the team is a more proactive way to track risks. (A risk management plan may identify events that foretell imminent risks, like a subcontractor who doesn't report status when progress is slow.) Ask team members if issues have come up. They may need help but are afraid to ask.

If risks do become reality, it's time to launch the response you laid out during planning. For example, you may replace a subcontractor, dip into project contingency funds, or reduce project scope to maintain the schedule and budget.

Reviewing the Critical Path

The critical path is critical, because its finish date is the project's finish date. The critical path always takes precedence when you have to prioritize work. Otherwise, the schedule may slip.

Exasperatingly, the tasks on the critical path can change if certain tasks take longer than planned. For example, suppose a 2-week task that isn't critical runs into intractable problems that make it take 6 weeks instead. That delay could place the task on the critical path. Because the critical path is dynamic, you must check regularly to see which tasks are currently critical.

Viewing the critical path

Viewing the critical path, baseline, and other schedule information is a lot easier in Project 2010, as you can see in Figure 15-2. Display the task-oriented view you want, such as the Gantt Chart, and then choose Format. Here's how you can use the Format tab to control your view of schedule status:

- **Show critical tasks.** In the Bar Styles section, turn on the Critical Tasks checkbox to show critical tasks in red. If you display late tasks with black task bars, late critical tasks look the same as on-time critical tasks. To see the critical path in red, be sure to turn off the Late Tasks checkbox.

- **Show slack.** To see how much slack (page 329) tasks have, in the Bar Styles section, turn on the Critical Tasks checkbox. A slack bar is a narrow black line extending from the right end of a task bar to show how much the task can delay before it delays its successors.

- **Show late tasks.** To emphasize late tasks with black task bars, in the Bar Styles section, turn on the Late Tasks checkbox.

- **Show the baseline.** To draw task bars for a baseline, in the Bar Styles section, choose the Baseline down arrow and then choose the baseline you want to see.

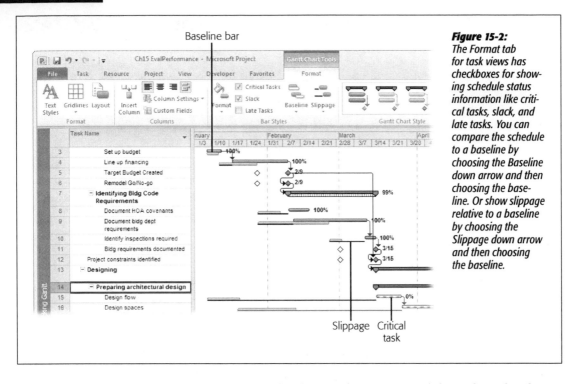

Baseline bar

Figure 15-2:
*The Format tab
for task views has
checkboxes for show-
ing schedule status
information like criti-
cal tasks, slack, and
late tasks. You can
compare the schedule
to a baseline by
choosing the Baseline
down arrow and then
choosing the base-
line. Or show slippage
relative to a baseline
by choosing the
Slippage down arrow
and then choosing
the baseline.*

Slippage Critical
task

- **Show slippage.** Choose the Slippage down arrow and then select a baseline to draw narrow black lines from the baseline start dates to the current scheduled start date. The length of the slippage line shows how far tasks have slipped from the baselined start dates.

The Tracking Gantt view is a natural choice for viewing schedule status, because it draws baseline and scheduled task bars one above the other. The Tracking Gantt also shows critical tasks in red, so you quickly see the tasks that influence the project's finish date. To apply the Tracking Gantt view, select the view's top pane, and then choose Task→View→Gantt Chart→Tracking Gantt. The box on page 413 explains the fields in the Tracking table in more detail.

To see the critical path in a very specific way, you can create a custom view and format its elements. For example, summary tasks on the critical path are simply the summary of all the work packages that belong to them. To correct the critical path, you must correct the work packages. For example, you can hide summary tasks and then filter the task list (page 110) to hide milestones, allowing you to see only work packages on the critical path. Then apply the Variance table so you can see the scheduled and baseline dates. You can obtain a view like this by downloading the Critical Work Pkgs view and CriticalWorkPackages filter from ProjectMM_Customizations. mpp at *www.missingmanuals.com/cds*. Use the Organizer to copy them to a Project file or to your global template.

How Much Is Complete?

The Tracking table includes columns for actual dates, duration, cost, and work, which are self-explanatory. However, the other two columns, % Complete and Physical % Complete, may not be so obvious.

The % Complete field shows the percentage of task duration that's past; it says nothing about how much progress has been made. For example, if 5 days of a 10-day task have passed, the task's % Complete is 50 percent regardless of how much work has been done. On the other hand, the Physical % Complete field lets you specify how much of the task is complete for earned value calculations. You

can type *20%*, *50%*, and so on to tell Project the amount of completion to use. See page 427 to learn more about Physical % Complete and other earned value fields.

% Work Complete is yet another field for percentage completion, although it doesn't appear in the Tracking table; it's the percentage of actual work compared to baseline work. If % Work Complete is less than % Complete, that means the amount of work performed isn't keeping up with the time consumed, meaning the task could be headed for trouble.

Creating a critical task checklist

The Critical Tasks text-based report works well as a hard-copy checklist of critical tasks that haven't started or are in progress, so you still have a chance to correct them. The columns include Duration, Start, Finish, Predecessors, and Resources. To see which tasks may be delaying a critical task, check the Predecessors column. The Critical Tasks report also lists the successors to each critical task. If a critical task is in trouble, its successors may be, too.

Choose Project→Reports→Reports. In the Reports dialog box, double-click Overview, and then double-click Critical Tasks. To learn more about working with Project's text-based reports, see Chapter 17.

Warning: Although Project comes with the Critical Task Status Report, this Visio-based visual report isn't that useful because it shows work and cost values, not the crucial finish dates. However, you can build a customized visual report to show critical task schedule status (page 473).

Looking for Delayed Tasks

Finding tasks whose start dates are delayed can help you correct delays before they get any worse. Delays in noncritical tasks may not affect the project finish date *yet*, but they can if their duration grows. Part of weekly tactical management is looking for delayed tasks (critical and noncritical alike). Then you evaluate each delayed task to try to prevent or at least limit further delays. This section describes several filters and reports that highlight delayed tasks. The box on page 416 describes other ways to spot troubled tasks quickly.

The first step in a task checkup is looking for tasks that should have started but haven't. In many instances, the problem with these late starters is not having entered actual values into Project. Once you've filled in missing actuals, it's time to find out why the remaining tasks are delayed.

The Should Start By filter and the Should Have Started Tasks report both list tasks that should have started by the date you specify (say, your most recent status date) but haven't. This filter and report look for tasks whose start values are earlier than your Should Start By date, but whose Actual Start values are still empty. The Should Start By filter is the more flexible option, because you can switch tables in the view to see different task values. The report, on the other hand, shows values from the Variance table, which is schedule-oriented.

Here's how to filter for delayed tasks:

1. **Choose View→Data, click the Filter down arrow, and then choose More Filters.**

    The More Filters dialog box opens.

2. **Select Should Start By and then click Apply.**

    The Should Start By dialog box opens.

3. **Type your checkup date, and then click OK.**

    The view changes to show only the tasks that should have started but haven't, as shown in Figure 15-3. To run the Should Have Started Tasks report, choose Project→Reports→Reports. In the Reports dialog box, double-click Current Activities, and then double-click Should Have Started Tasks.

Critical tasks don't have slack

Noncritical tasks have slack

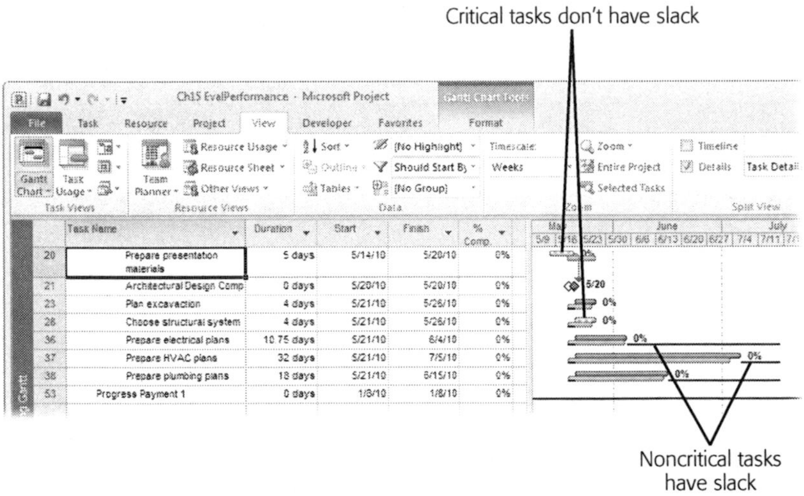

Figure 15-3:
If you apply the Should Start By filter to the Tracking Gantt view, then the red task bars are delayed critical tasks, and blue task bars are delayed noncritical tasks. Alternatively, you can create separate filters (page 620) for delayed critical and noncritical tasks. To see the slack on non-critical tasks, choose Format→Bar Styles, and then turn on the Slack checkbox.

4. To see work packages without the parent summary tasks, choose Format→ Show/Hide, and then turn off the Summary Tasks checkbox.

You see only the lowest-level tasks in your project, as shown in Figure 15-3.

Looking for Tasks Heading for Trouble

The next tactic is looking for tasks whose finish dates are late—later than their base-line finish dates, that is. You can also look for work hours that exceed baseline work, even if they haven't yet delayed the finish date. Here are different ways to look for these at-risk tasks:

- **Tasks that are slipping.** Slipping tasks are those whose finish dates are later than their baseline finish dates. These tasks may be scheduled to start late, have already started late, or are taking longer than planned. By looking for slipping tasks every week, you may have time to recover the slip or prevent it from getting worse.

  The Slipping Tasks filter and the Slipping Tasks report both show slipping tasks. The Slipping Tasks filter is more flexible, because you can apply it to a view and then apply different tables to see dates, variances, work, or cost. The Slipping Tasks report uses the Variance table, so it shows scheduled and baseline dates, along with the start and finish variances.

  Choose View→Data, click the Filter down arrow, and then choose More Filters. In the More Filters dialog box, select Slipping Tasks and then click Apply. To run the report, choose Project→Reports→Reports. In the Reports dialog box, double-click Current Activities, and then double-click Slipping Tasks.

Tip: If you want to see slipping critical tasks, choose Format→Bar Styles, and turn on the Critical Tasks checkbox to show critical tasks in red. Or you can copy the Slipping Tasks filter and add another test for critical tasks (page 621).

- **Tasks that are slipping or falling behind.** The Slipped/Late Progress filter looks for slipping tasks but also checks for tasks whose completed work is less than the amount that should be done. The finish date hasn't changed yet, but it's likely to unless you do something.

Tip: To look for schedule trends, sort the Variance table by finish date. Tasks appear from the earliest finish date to the latest. If the values in the Finish Variance field grow larger as the finish dates progress, the project is falling further behind over time. On the other hand, if the Finish Variance values are growing smaller, it may be a sign that your corrective actions are working.

- **Assignments that are slipping**. It makes sense that an assignment that slips can turn into a task that slips. The Slipping Assignments filter is a resource filter that you can apply to the Resource Usage view to find assignments whose scheduled finish dates are later than their baseline finish dates. One resource with several slipping assignments is a sure sign of someone who could use some help. The problem may be too many tasks at the same time, the wrong skill set, or too many distractions.

Seeing Status

You can spot troubled tasks without filtering task lists and running reports. Scanning for visual status cues is often easier than wading through numbers. Project has a field with built-in graphical indicators for late tasks, but you can customize fields to turn red, yellow, or green based on progress. In addition, progress lines show whether tasks are ahead, behind, or right on schedule in the Gantt Chart timescale. Figure 15-4 includes examples of all of the following status indicators:

- **Status Indicators.** The Status Indicators field shows a clock with a checkmark for tasks that are on time. Tasks that aren't finished but are running late have a clock with an exclamation point inside a red diamond.

- **Custom graphical indicators.** To display graphics based on how late or over budget a task is, you can set up a custom field with graphical indicators like a green happy face if Cost Variance is less than 10

percent of the baseline cost or a red unhappy face if Cost Variance is greater than 25 percent of the baseline cost. The custom field, Number4 (Cost Status), in ProjectMM_Customizations.mpp at *www.missing-manuals.com/cds* does that and more, as long as you've already set a baseline and have some actual values in your schedule. See the box on page 419 for more information about this custom field.

- **Progress lines.** Choose Format→Format→Gridlines→Progress Lines to show progress in the Gantt Chart timescale. A progress line drops vertically from the project status date in the timescale heading, and then points to the progress in each task bar. If the task is on schedule, then the progress line continues its vertical drop. If the task is behind schedule, then the progress line points sharply to the left.

Checking on Work

During planning, you work hard to eliminate resource overallocations, so people receive a relatively steady amount of work while they're assigned to your project. After your project is under way, tasks begin to move—potentially spoiling those balanced resource allocations. Reviewing resource assignments is another regular activity that can show whether task delays are creating new overallocations.

Watching for ballooning work hours is another aspect of project evaluation. Just like time that slips away when attic cleaning turns into reminiscing over old pictures, the time to perform tasks can expand beyond your estimates. These extra hours can produce longer task durations and higher resource costs, so it's especially important to nip these excesses in the bud.

Finding and correcting overallocations works just as effectively while adjusting projects midstream as it does during planning. "Balancing Workloads" on page 259 (Chapter 10) gives the full story on finding and correcting overallocations.

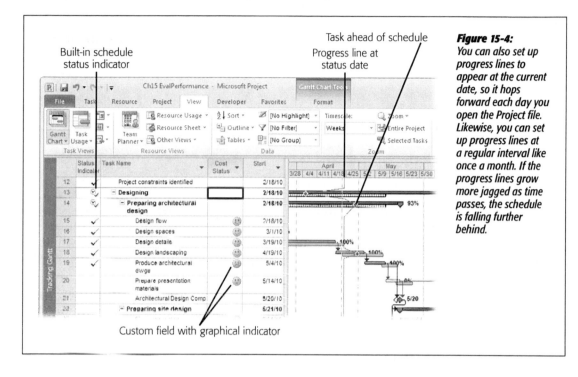

Built-in schedule status indicator

Task ahead of schedule

Progress line at status date

Custom field with graphical indicator

Figure 15-4:
You can also set up progress lines to appear at the current date, so it hops forward each day you open the Project file. Likewise, you can set up progress lines at a regular interval like once a month. If the progress lines grow more jagged as time passes, the schedule is falling further behind.

Checking for Overbudget Work

Work hours that exceed the baseline hours can increase duration and cost. For completed tasks, of course, it's too late to make corrections. Still, it's a good idea to investigate the reason, particularly if the same resources are over budget on task after task. You can also check tasks in progress to see if the amount of work you expect is complete. Use one or more of the following elements:

- **Work table.** The Work table shows several work fields: scheduled, baseline, actual and remaining work, and work variance. It also includes % Work Complete, which is the percentage of the current scheduled work that's done. Positive values in the Variance column show tasks whose scheduled work hours are now greater than the baseline work hours, as shown in Figure 15-5.

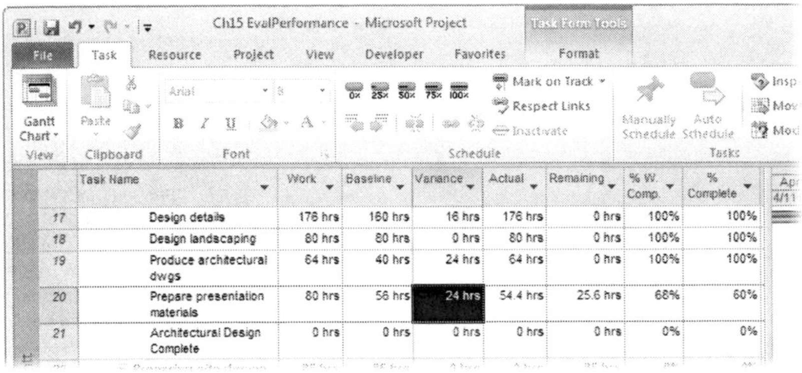

Figure 15-5:
You can look for tasks that may be falling behind by inserting the % Complete field next to the % Work Complete column. If the % Work Complete is less than the % Complete, time is passing faster than work is being completed, which is often a red flag for future delays.

- **Work Overbudget filter.** The Work Overbudget filter shows tasks whose actual work has already exceeded the baseline work, so it's already too late to recover from this overindulgence. However, if several tasks using the same resource are all completed over their work budget, you can try replacing that resource with one who's more productive.

- **Slipped/Late Progress filter.** Although this filter tests for schedule slip, it has a work aspect, too. It looks for tasks in which the completed work is less than what you'd planned at this point.

Is the Project Within Budget?

Checking cost status isn't as simple as seeing whether there's money in your wallet. When budgeted dollars run out in one place, accounting procedures sometimes grab money from another place. With cost and budget resources in Project, you can follow project money without depending on the finance department. In simpler financial environments, cost variance and other earned value measures may be enough. This section describes different ways to compare cost expenditures to the baseline costs you set.

The Project Summary report and the project summary task show the cost variance for an entire project—that is, the difference between scheduled and baseline cost. If the variance is positive, then the project is forecast to be over budget. Unless the project is almost over, you may have time to reduce costs. A negative cost variance means the project may come in under budget, although that outcome isn't assured until the project is complete.

Comparing Costs with Views and Filters

Similar to looking for overbudget work, Project's tables, filters, and reports help find expanding costs. See the box on page 419 for a way to focus on the biggest cost overruns. Here are two of Project's built-in elements that show costs:

- **Cost table.** This table includes the scheduled, baseline, actual, and remaining costs. The Variance column is the Cost Variance field, so you can see whether tasks are forecast to be over or under budget. (Positive variances mean over budget.) The Total Cost column is really the Cost field, which includes labor costs that Project calculates, cost resources you've assigned to tasks, and fixed costs you've set.

- **Cost Overbudget filter.** To display only tasks whose scheduled cost is greater than the baseline cost, apply the Cost Overbudget filter.

POWER USERS' CLINIC

Focusing on Big Money Problems

For large projects, going a few dollars over budget on one task can sometimes distract you from the big budget problems on others. Custom fields can help you focus on serious cost overruns. For example, the Number4 (Cost Status) custom field in ProjectMM_Customizations.mpp (*www.missingmanuals.com/cds*) calculates the percentage of cost variance to baseline cost. It displays graphical indicators based on the value, but you can also filter the task list with a field like this. For example, you could create a custom filter (page 620) that shows tasks whose Number4 (Cost Status) field is greater than 10 percent.

Another approach is to create a filter that displays tasks whose cost variance is greater than a dollar amount like $5,000. Consider a task whose baseline cost is $200 and cost variance $100. That's a 50 percent overrun, but $100 may mean little in a multimillion-dollar project. As long as you're customizing a filter, you can define it to filter by dollar amount *and* percentage! The BigOverrun filter in ProjectMM_Customizations.mpp does just that, although it asks for the cost variance and cost status values you want to use.

Evaluating Costs with Reports

Project has several reports (both text and visual) for studying costs. Chapter 17 describes working with Project's reports in detail. Here's a review of reports for evaluating cost:

- **Baseline Cost.** Choose either the Excel or Visio Baseline Cost visual report. The Excel Baseline Cost report is a bar graph that compares scheduled cost, baseline cost, and actual cost for top-level summary tasks. If the scheduled cost is greater than the baseline, then the summary task is over budget. You can alter the visual report to compare costs by fiscal quarter or drill down to compare costs task by task (or resource by resource). The Visio Baseline Cost visual report adds icons to boxes that are over budget for cost or work.

- **Budget.** The Budget Cost visual report is like the Baseline Cost report with the addition of budget resource costs (page 302). You can compare scheduled costs, baseline costs, and the budget line item value so you can see where expenditures are relative to your allotted budget dollars.

- **Overbudget Tasks.** For a tactical look at overbudget tasks, the Overbudget Tasks report (choose Project→Reports→Reports, double-click Costs, and then double-click Overbudget Tasks) includes tasks whose scheduled costs are greater than their baseline costs. This report sorts tasks by the highest cost variance first, which may give you the most opportunity for cutting costs.

- **Overbudget Resources.** A companion to the Overbudget Tasks report, this report shows resources whose scheduled costs are higher than their baseline costs, from highest to lowest variance.

Note: Earned value analysis is such an effective way to evaluate project costs that it gets its own section (see below on this page). Project's earned value reports are described there.

Comparing Project Costs to a Budget

Budget resources can represent line items in a financial budget. You can allot budget dollars to budget resources in a Project file and then compare your project costs to the budgeted amounts. Setting up budget resources for this type of comparison takes several steps, explained in detail in Chapter 11 (page 302). If you use budget resources, then you can compare budgeted costs to scheduled costs by category, as shown in Figure 11-18 on page 317.

Budget resources are Project resources, so you need a resource view like Resource Usage to compare budget resource costs to scheduled costs. With the Resource Usage view grouped by budget item, Project creates a summary row for each budget category you track. (The BudgetItem group is available in ProjectMM_Customizations. mpp. In the Organizer, select the Groups tab, and then select the Resource option.) The Budget Cost or Budget Work cells in group summary rows show the budgeted values for each budget category, allowing you to see all the work, material, and cost resources associated with that budget item.

Earned Value Analysis

Earned value analysis is like the idea behind that old Smith Barney slogan, "We make money the old fashioned way—we earn it." According to earned value analysis, progress is measured by how much of the project value (its cost) you've earned so far.

Project customers, sponsors, and stakeholders want to know how far along a project is. Earned value alone tells you only how much of the project cost you've earned—it doesn't say anything about the schedule. Other earned value measures provide a picture of schedule status. If a project has spent half the budget, consumed half the project duration, and performed half the work, you're all set. On the other hand, if the budget and duration are half spent, but the work is 25 percent complete, something's wrong. You have only 50 percent of the budget and duration left but 75 percent of the work still to complete.

Earned value analysis requires a baseline in your Project file, so you have a plan to compare to. If you haven't set a baseline yet (page 365), all the earned value fields are zero. You must also enter actual values (page 392) to show what you've accomplished and how much it cost.

Earned value also needs a status date to which you measure progress, like last Friday's date if you evaluate progress at the end of every week. Choose Project→Properties→Project Information. In the Project Information dialog box, in the "Status date" box, choose the date through which you have actual progress values, and then click OK.

Gauging Performance with Earned Value Measures

Earned value analysis uses several calculations to measure schedule and cost status. However, all the earned value measures are based on three basic measurements:

- **Planned cost for scheduled work.** In project management circles, you'll hear *planned value* described as the *budgeted cost of work scheduled* (or BCWS, which is also the name of the corresponding Project field). In English, planned value is the cost you expected to incur for the work scheduled through the status date—that is, the baseline cost for the work that should have been completed as of the status date.

  Suppose you're managing a tiger-taming project that is scheduled to tame 24 tigers over 24 months for a total cost of $240,000—$10,000 per tiger. According to that plan, 10 tigers should be tamed at the end of 10 months at a planned value of $100,000.

- **Planned cost for completed work.** This measure is called *earned value* because it represents the baseline cost you've earned by completing work as of the status date. It's also known as budgeted cost of work performed or BCWP (the name of the corresponding Project field). If you've tamed six tigers as of the status date, then the earned value is $60,000.

- **Actual cost of completed work.** Actual cost is easy: It's how much you actually spent as of the status date. For example, if you've spent $50,000 through the first 10 months, that's your actual cost of completed work. This measure is sometimes called *actual cost of work performed* or ACWP (again, the name of the Project field).

Analyzing an Earned Value Graph

Because planned value, earned value, and actual cost are all monetary values, you can compare them to evaluate schedule and cost performance. The relative positions of the three lines for these measures show whether the project is on schedule and within budget.

Gleaning schedule and cost performance from an earned value graph is easy once you know how to compare planned value, earned value, and actual costs. The new Earned Value Over Time visual report, shown in Figure 15-6, graphs all three measures over time. Here's how you evaluate schedule and cost performance with these three measures:

- **Schedule performance.** Planned value and earned value are the two measures that provide schedule status. Planned value is the baseline cost for the work you *expected* to complete, while earned value is the baseline cost of the work that is actually complete. If earned value is less than planned value (like $60,000 versus $100,000 in the tiger taming project), less work is complete than you expected—thus, the project is behind schedule. If earned value is greater than planned value, then more work is complete than you expected, and the project is ahead of schedule.

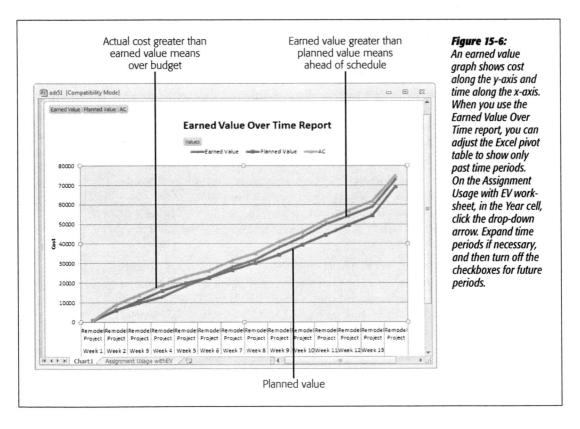

Figure 15-6:
An earned value graph shows cost along the y-axis and time along the x-axis. When you use the Earned Value Over Time report, you can adjust the Excel pivot table to show only past time periods. On the Assignment Usage with EV worksheet, in the Year cell, click the drop-down arrow. Expand time periods if necessary, and then turn off the checkboxes for future periods.

- **Cost performance** Cost performance is the difference between earned value and actual cost. If the earned value is greater than the actual cost, then the work performed cost less than you planned—the project is under budget. For example, the earned value for the tiger taming project is $60,000, while the actual is only $50,000. It's $10,000 under budget. If earned value is less than the actual cost, then the project is over budget.

Using Additional Earned Value Measures

You can combine planned value, earned value, and actual cost to view project performance from different perspectives. Additional measures show the efficiency of the project or forecast final costs based on performance so far. Here are the additional earned value measures, and what they do:

- **Schedule variance** (the SV field in Project) is earned value minus planned value (BCWP – BCWS), the difference between how much work you've completed and how much you planned to complete. If SV is positive, more work is complete than you planned, so you're ahead of schedule. SV for the tiger project is $60,000 minus $100,000 or a negative $40,000, so the project is behind schedule.

- **Cost variance** (the CV field in Project) is earned value minus the actual cost—in other words, the difference between the baseline and actual cost of the work performed (BCWP – ACWP). If CV is positive, then the baseline cost is greater than the actual cost; the project is under budget. CV for the tiger project is $60,000 minus $50,000, or $10,000, so the project is under budget. The box below explains the difference between Project's Cost Variance and CV fields.

GEM IN THE ROUGH

Is Positive Variance Good or Bad?

You don't see the Cost Variance and CV fields side by side in any built-in Project tables, which is good because they seem to contradict one another. For example, if the Cost Variance field shows a variance of $1,000, then the CV field shows a variance of ($1,000)—that is, negative $1,000.

With one variance positive and the other negative, it's hard to figure out whether the cost variance is good or bad. The CV field is earned value minus actual cost, which is the true arbiter of cost performance. As you've already learned, if earned value is greater than the actual cost, then the project or task is under budget. To help you remember, CV is a positive value when the project or task is under budget, a desirable (that is, positive) result.

On the other hand, the Cost Variance field is the Cost field minus the Baseline Cost field, so it's a positive value when the result is undesirable—the project or task is over budget. Keep in mind, CV applies only to completed tasks, because tasks have earned value only when they're complete. Cost Variance, on the other hand, shows variance as long as you have a baseline set. (See page 427 to learn how to change the definition of "complete" in Project.)

- **Schedule performance index** (SPI) is the ratio of earned value divided by the planned value (BCWP / BCWS). For example, when earned value and planned value are equal, the project is on schedule and SPI equals 1.0. An SPI less than 1.0 means earned value is less than planned value, indicating that the project is behind schedule. SPI for the tiger project is $60,000/$100,000 or 0.6.

  Because it's a ratio, SPI tells you how good or bad schedule performance is, regardless of the dollars involved. For example, a small project may have SV equal to $5,000, while a large project SV may be $125,000. However, an SPI of 0.6 shows that both projects have earned value that's 60 percent of the planned value.

- **Cost performance index** (CPI) is the ratio of earned value to actual cost (BCWP/ACWP). If the ratio is greater than 1.0, then earned value is greater than actual cost, which means you spent less to complete the work performed than you'd planned—the project is under budget. For example, CPI of 1.2 means earned value is 20 percent higher than the actual cost. CPI for the tiger project is $60,000/$50,000 or 1.2. The project is under budget, but not by 20 percent! If you remember your algebra, the percentage this sample project is under budget is ($60,000 – $50,000) / $60,000. That's $10,000 / $60,000 or 16.6 percent under budget.

- **Budget at completion** (BAC) is simply the baseline cost. If you look carefully, you'll see that the Baseline Cost and BAC fields are always equal.

- **Estimate at completion** (EAC) is an estimate of how much a task will cost when it's done, based on the performance so far. Here's the formula for EAC:

  ```
  ACWP + ((BAC - BCWP) / CPI)
  ```

  EAC has two components. The first is the actual cost so far (ACWP). The second, (BAC – BCWP) / CPI, is a cost forecast based on the cost performance index. It's the remaining baseline cost (baseline cost minus the earned value) divided by the cost performance index. For example, here's the calculation for the tiger project EAC:

  ```
  Actual cost = $50,000
  BAC - BCWP = $240,000 - $100,000 = $140,000
  (BAC - BCWP) / CPI = $140,000 / 1.2 = $116,666
  EAC = $166,666
  ```

  Because the cost performance index shows the project under budget, EAC assumes that trend will continue. That's why project EAC is only $166,666 compared to project BAC of $240,000.

  The money you need to finish the project is the second component of EAC. For the tiger-taming project, the remaining cost is $116,666.

Note: The Cost and EAC fields are not the same. Cost adds actual costs, remaining labor costs (work multiplied to the resource rates), and overtime. EAC, on the other hand, assumes that the remaining cost will be inflated or decreased by the same amount as the cost so far. It doesn't take remaining work into consideration at all.

- **Variance at completion** (VAC) is the estimated variance when the task or project is done. It's the baseline cost at completion (BAC) minus the estimate at completion (EAC). For example, VAC for the tiger-taming project is $240,000 minus $166,666 or $73,334.

- **To complete performance index** (TCPI) is the ratio of the work that remains (expressed in dollars) to remaining available dollars. Here's the formula:

    (BAC - BCWP) / (BAC - ACWP)

    The numerator of the ratio is the remaining baseline cost for the remaining work. The denominator is the remaining available dollars. If TCPI is greater than 1.0, then the remaining baseline cost is greater than the remaining dollars, which means you don't have enough money left to pay for the remaining work. If the baseline cost for the remaining work is less than the available dollars, then you have a surplus.

    TCPI for the tiger project is $180,000/$190,000 or 0.95, another way of saying the project is under budget.

Tip: For a quick review of these fields and formulas, position the pointer over the column header. When the ScreenTip appears, click the link to the help topic for the column's Project field.

Viewing Earned Value in Project

You can examine earned value measures in several places in Project. To see earned value task by task, nothing beats the earned value tables. Project also has a text-based report that shows earned values by task. The Earned Value Over Time visual report provides a visual status of earned value. Here's where you can find earned value in Project:

- **Earned Value table.** Apply this table, shown in Figure 15-7, to any task-oriented view (choose View→Data→Tables→More Tables, and then double-click Earned Value). The Earned Value table includes all the basic earned value fields: planned value (BCWS), earned value (BCWP), actual cost (ACWP), SV, CV, EAC, BAC, and VAC.

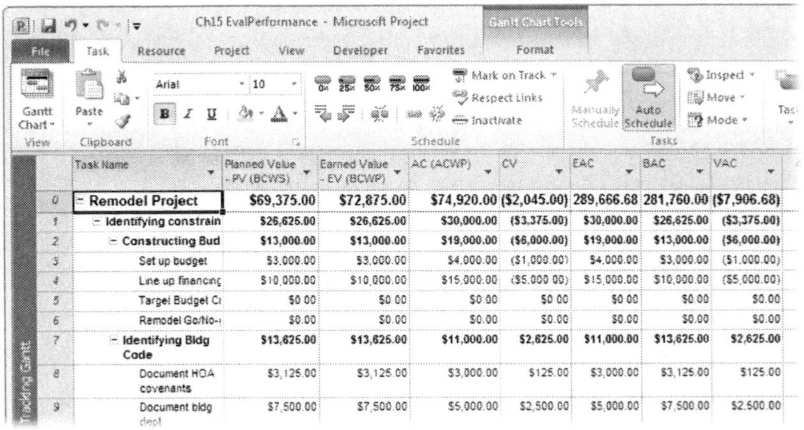

Figure 15-7:
The Earned Value table helps you spot tasks that are behind schedule or over budget. By applying the Incomplete Tasks filter to the list (on the Formatting toolbar, in the filter drop-down list, choose Incomplete Tasks), you can see earned values for tasks that you can still fix.

- **Earned Value Cost Indicators table.** This table focuses on cost performance. It includes basic earned value fields, but adds CV% (CV as a percentage of the planned value), CPI, and TCPI.

- **Earned Value Schedule Indicators table.** This table focuses on schedule performance. It includes planned value (BCWS), earned value (BCWP), SV, CV, SV%, and SPI.

Tip: If you use earned value tables frequently, then you can save time by adding them to the Tables drop-down list. Choose View→Data→Tables→More Tables. In the More Tables dialog box, select the table, and then click Edit. In the Table Definition dialog box, turn on the "Show in menu" checkbox, and then click OK. Now, you can apply the table simply by choosing View→Data→Tables→Earned Value (or the name of another earned value table).

- **Earned Value report.** This report is a hard-copy version of the task list with the Earned Value table applied. Choose Project→Reports→Reports. In the Reports dialog box, double-click Costs, and then double-click Earned Value.

- **Earned Value Over Time visual report.** This report initially shows the graph of earned value over time (see Figure 15-6). As you'll learn in Chapter 17, you can modify this report to show earned value for specific time periods or specific tasks. Choose Project→Report→Visual Reports. In the Visual Reports–Create Report dialog box, select Earned Value Over Time Report, and then click View.

Controlling How Project Calculates Earned Value

Project has a couple of options for calculating earned values. You can specify which saved baseline Project uses as well as which field specifies how complete tasks are. Initially, Project uses values in the Baseline fields. If you want to calculate earned values using Baseline1 through Baseline10, choose File→Options. In the Project Options dialog box, choose Advanced. Under "Calculation options for this project" in the Baseline for Earned Value Calculations drop-down list, choose the baseline you want.

The PMI's Project Management Body of Knowledge (PMBOK) recommends two possible definitions of "complete" for earned value calculations. But you can choose among three ways to define complete:

- **All or nothing.** The conservative approach says a task is complete or it isn't. This means 100 percent complete means complete. Any less and the task is incomplete (and not included in earned value calculations). Project initially takes the all-or-nothing approach. If a task's % Complete field is 100%, then Project calculates its earned value fields. % Complete less than 100% means earned value fields are zero.

- **Unstarted, started, or complete.** If a project has very long tasks, the all-or-nothing approach may be too harsh. Another approach is to leave unstarted tasks as 0% and completed tasks as 100%. However, tasks in progress are set to 50%.

Tip: Another approach is to mimic the values on the task mini-toolbar (right-click a task): 0% for unstarted, 25% for started, 50% for halfway, 75% for almost complete, and 100% for complete.

- **Completed work.** A more accurate approach is to measure completeness by the percentage of work that's complete.

If you want to use the second or third approach, you must tell Project to use the Physical % Complete field to calculate earned value. Unlike % Complete, which Project calculates, Physical % Complete is a value you enter, so you can make it as accurate as you want. For example, you can set Physical % Complete to 0%, 50%, or 100% depending on whether tasks are unstarted, in progress, or complete. Or you can enter the value from the % Work Complete field into Physical % Complete. Although Project lets you select different earned value methods for different tasks, it's best to use the same method for all tasks. If you use % Complete, then you know that Project calculates the values for you. If you use Physical % Complete, then you must type the values.

To use Physical % Complete, choose File→Options. In the Project Options dialog box, choose Advanced. Under "Calculation options for this project" in the "Default task Earned Value method" drop-down list, choose Physical % Complete.

Note: Changing the "Default task Earned Value method" option has no effect on existing tasks, which are usually the ones you want to evaluate. (The option affects tasks added to a Project after the change.) The easiest way to change the setting for existing tasks is to insert the Earned Value Method field into a table. (Right-click the table heading area, and then choose Insert Column. In the "Field name" drop-down list, choose Earned Value Method.) Change the first Earned Value Method cell to Physical % Complete, and then drag that value over all the other cells in the column.

Getting Back on Track

One reason project management can be so, ahem, fulfilling is the plethora of choices you have for addressing problems. When your project isn't meeting the schedule or the budget, you can choose from several tuning techniques—and usually a combination of several—to set the project straight. This section summarizes the fine-tuning methods you learned in Chapter 12, which work as well during execution as they did during planning. Then you'll learn about one additional approach that you turn to only during execution: assigning overtime.

A Review of Project Tuning Techniques

There's no such thing as a free lunch. Techniques that shorten duration may cost more, deliver less, or demand more from resources. Cutting costs may increase duration, decrease scope, reduce quality, or increase risk. Here's a quick review of the ways you can adjust a schedule to correct course:

- **Increasing resource units.** Assigning more of resources' time means more work gets done in a shorter duration (page 341). This approach assumes resources have more time to give, are willing to give it, and remain as productive as they were when they worked a more reasonable schedule.

- **Assigning resources with more availability.** If you have resources who aren't already working around the clock, you can replace busy resources with people who have more available time (page 269). (Don't forget to evaluate the cost of bringing a new person up to speed on the project.)

- **Assigning more resources.** Assigning more resources can shorten duration by providing more work hours every day (page 221). However, the chaos of too many people on one task may actually lengthen duration.

- **Assigning faster or lower-cost resources.** If you're trying to reduce duration, faster resources can help, but often at a higher cost. To save money, you can assign less expensive resources, possibly increasing duration.

- **Juggle assignments to use existing slack time.** If resources working on non-critical tasks can work on critical tasks instead, then you may be able to shorten the critical path (page 329).

- **Shorten lag time.** Reducing lag time (page 162) between tasks can shorten duration. If lag times depend on people's responses, then you must ask whether they can respond more quickly.

- **Fast-track tasks.** You can shorten duration by overlapping tasks that normally run in sequence (page 347). This approach increases the risk of re-work, if earlier tasks affect work that's been done in the successor tasks.

- **Crashing tasks.** Crashing (page 350) means spending more money to obtain shorter duration.

- **Reducing scope.** You can cut duration and cost by reducing the scope of the project, as long as the project customer is OK with that change.

- **Reducing quality.** Cutting quality is another compromise, as long as the customer agrees.

- **Using management reserve.** Management reserve is a pool of money that management can free up to help a project.

Assigning Overtime

Overtime has no place during planning, because it leaves you no room for maneuvering later on. For example, if you plan for resources working 12-hour days 7 days a week, it's unlikely you can shorten a schedule by having resources work 16-hour days. Once a project is under way and the schedule slips, overtime can keep task durations from increasing, in effect by overallocating resources for short periods of time.

Project gives you several ways to represent overtime. You have to resort to the Overtime Work field only when resources cost more for overtime hours. Here are three ways to assign extra hours:

- **Increasing maximum units.** If team members earn a salary or charge the same rate for all hours, you can increase their maximum units (page 195) to represent the longer hours you ask them to work. For example, setting Maximum Units to 125% in the Resource Sheet represents a 10-hour workday (assuming a standard workday of 8 hours). The downfall to this approach is that resources are set up to work these longer hours for the entire project, which is realistic only for workaholics and usually draws irate team members to your office.

- **Increasing work time for a period.** For team members who don't earn higher overtime rates, you can also define longer hours through the resource calendar or the Resource Information dialog box. To change available units for a period of time, in the Resource Sheet, double-click the resource. In the Resource Information dialog box, in the Resource Availability section, specify the start and end date for the extra hours and the units you want to assign during that time.

  To specify work hours for a period of time, define an exception in a resource calendar (page 246). You can set the start and end dates for the period and the start and end times for workdays.

- **Overtime hours paid at an overtime rate.** When resources are paid more for overtime hours, you must assign overtime hours in Project or the labor costs won't be correct. The box below explains how Project tracks overtime and calculates overtime cost. You set a resource's overtime rate in the Resource Sheet's Overtime Rate field.

Overtime Costs

In Project, work hours reside in the Work, Regular Work, and Overtime Work fields. Without overtime, Work and Regular Work are equal; all assigned work hours are regular work hours. If you assign overtime, Project adds the overtime hours you enter in the Overtime Work field and subtracts those hours from the Regular Work field. The Work value stays the same. For example, if a task Work field is 80 hours and you assign 20 hours of overtime, the Overtime Work field changes to 20 hours, while the Regular Work field shrinks to 60 hours.

Project calculates the labor cost for Regular Work hours by multiplying the regular work hours by the standard labor rate (Standard Rate in the Resource Sheet). Overtime labor cost is overtime work hours multiplied by the overtime rate. For example, consider the same 80-hour task. At $50 an hour for regular work, the labor cost is $4,000. If the overtime rate is $60 an hour, then the task cost changes to $4,200 (60 hours × $50 and 20 hours × $60).

A customized usage view simplifies assigning overtime and seeing how Project allocates it. The Resource Usage view with the Overtime Hours field in the table and time-phased area does the trick. The ProjectMM_Customizations.mpp file at *www.missingmanuals.com/cds* contains a view called Overtime Usage, which displays Work and Overtime Work. It initially filters the list for overallocated resources, but you can remove that filter by choosing View→Data and then, in the filter drop-down list, choosing All Resources.

To set up an overtime view of your own, follow these steps:

1. **Create a new view for overtime usage.**

   Choose View→Task Views→Task Usage→More Views. In the More Views dialog box, select Task Usage and click Copy. In the View Definition dialog box in the Name box, type a new view name, like *Overtime Usage*, and then click OK.

2. **To add the Overtime Work field to the table area, right-click the Work column heading, and then choose Insert Column. In the "Field name" drop-down list, choose Overtime Work.**

   The Overtime Work column appears to the left of the Work column.

3. To display Overtime Work in the time-phased area, right-click anywhere in the time-phased grid, and then, on the shortcut menu, choose Detail Styles.

The Detail Styles dialog box opens, showing the fields in the time-phased area. The Resource Usage view includes Work and All Assignment Rows, initially.

4. In the "Available fields" list, select Overtime Work, and then click Show.

Project moves the Overtime Work field into the "Show these fields" list.

5. Click OK.

The Detail Styles dialog box closes, and each assignment in the view includes an additional row for Overtime Work (the label is "Ovt. Work").

6. In the table area, select the Overtime Work cell for the assignment you want to modify, and then type the number of overtime hours.

Project recalculates the task duration due to the extra hours, and allocates the overtime hours over the remaining duration, as shown in Figure 15-8.

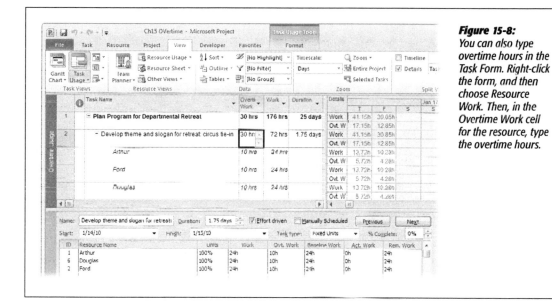

Figure 15-8:
You can also type overtime hours in the Task Form. Right-click the form, and then choose Resource Work. Then, in the Overtime Work cell for the resource, type the overtime hours.

Although the usage timescale shows overtime hours allocated day by day, you can't edit the hours in the individual time periods. You can edit the Work hours.

Managing Change

No matter how flawlessly or exhaustively you plan your project, you can't foresee everything that might bubble up. Project management is a rich gumbo of managing time, resources, and costs. At the same time, you can't forget to add managing risks, issues, and change to the project management pot. In fact, some people say that managing projects is essentially managing change.

Project changes come in all shapes and sizes. A change can be as small as adding a single task you overlooked. Cost-cutting measures that eliminate your contract labor and part-time resources constitute a major change. You can distill all these changes into two main categories: changes you can address without someone else's approval and changes you can't. If a hurricane delays the shipment of essential parts, you can rework the schedule to accommodate that delay. However, if the project customer asks for final delivery one month earlier, you probably need permission before spending the $300,000 required for accelerated delivery.

This chapter introduces the two major aspects to managing project change: setting up a change management system, and incorporating changes into your project plan. A change management system plays two important roles. First, it helps you prevent scope creep by identifying changes to the project and actually deciding whether or not to include them. Second, it provides a consistent process for evaluating change requests and getting them approved (which essentially means getting approval for the effect of those changes on the project schedule). That process may involve a *change review board*—a group of people who have the responsibility and authority to accept or reject change requests. The chapter also describes ways to track change requests.

Equally important, you'll learn ways to incorporate those changes into your project plan, whether the changes are your solution to a delay or a change request from someone else. The chapter describes ways to play what-if games with a Project file, so you can determine the impact of a change request before presenting it to the change review board. These what-if games work equally well for trying different strategies for the schedule adjustments you make every day. Finally, you'll learn how to set a new baseline that includes change requests, and how to track the progress of change requests.

Setting Up a Change Management System

Project managers are continually beset on all sides with demands to change some aspect of their projects. Team members may uncover new information or requirements that seem to be aligned with the project objectives. The powers that be, who are under considerable pressure to deliver faster and with higher profits, can in turn ask you to bring in the schedule date or reduce costs—or both.

A significant part of your project manager role is to handle these change requests and incorporate only the appropriate changes into the project plan. You're like the gatekeeper, the fearsome guardian of project scope, project schedule, and project budget. At the same time, somehow you need to maintain flexibility so you can take advantage of proposed changes, like the one suggested in Figure 16-1.

In this section, you'll learn techniques for controlling project changes like the development of a change request tracking system, and forming a change review board for deciding which changes should go into the project plan.

A tracking system, change review board, and the incorporation of approved change requests into the project plan are three major elements of a change control system. As you learned in Chapter 2, a description of your project's change control processes is part of the project plan. Publish the processes and forms to a central location so stakeholders and team members know what to do when a change request arises.

Managing Change Requests

You could field change requests by scrawling on a yellow sticky note when someone stops by with a suggestion, flagging emails containing requests, or just saying no to all demands, like Dilbert's manager. But project change requests of any sort of volume make these approaches impractical.

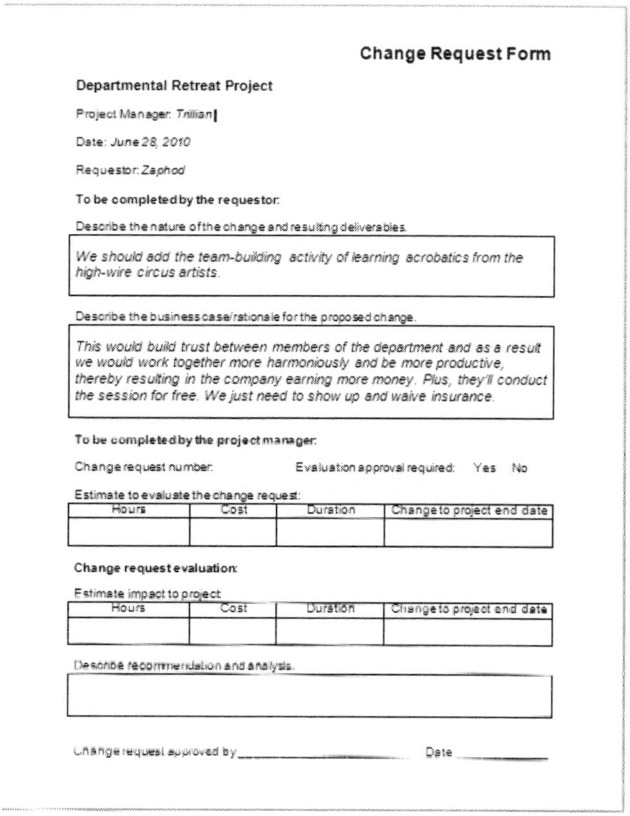

Change Request Form

Departmental Retreat Project

Project Manager: *Trillian*

Date: *June 28, 2010*

Requestor: *Zaphod*

To be completed by the requestor:

Describe the nature of the change and resulting deliverables.

> *We should add the team-building activity of learning acrobatics from the
> high-wire circus artists.*

Describe the business case/rationale for the proposed change.

> *This would build trust between members of the department and as a result
> we would work together more harmoniously and be more productive,
> thereby resulting in the company earning more money. Plus, they'll conduct
> the session for free. We just need to show up and waive insurance.*

To be completed by the project manager:

Change request number: Evaluation approval required: Yes   No

Estimate to evaluate the change request:

Hours	Cost	Duration	Change to project end date

Change request evaluation:

Estimate impact to project:

Hours	Cost	Duration	Change to project end date

Describe recommendation and analysis:

Change request approved by _____   Date _____

Figure 16-1:
*A change request form helps requesters
provide the information you need to evaluate changes. The consistent presentation
makes it easier to compare change requests
if you can't incorporate them all.*

You need a tracking system, which can be as formal or informal as your project or
organization itself. A notebook with a log, in which you or the requester scribbles the
change request, may be sufficient. Or people could submit change requests through
a change request form posted on a collaboration website (like a SharePoint site) that
stores the requests and filters entries depending on their status.

A happy medium between these two approaches may be a simple form in Word like
the one shown in Figure 16-1. Then you can enter and track the status of submitted
change requests with an Excel spreadsheet like the one in Figure 16-2. The box on
page 436 describes some of the features of many change control systems.

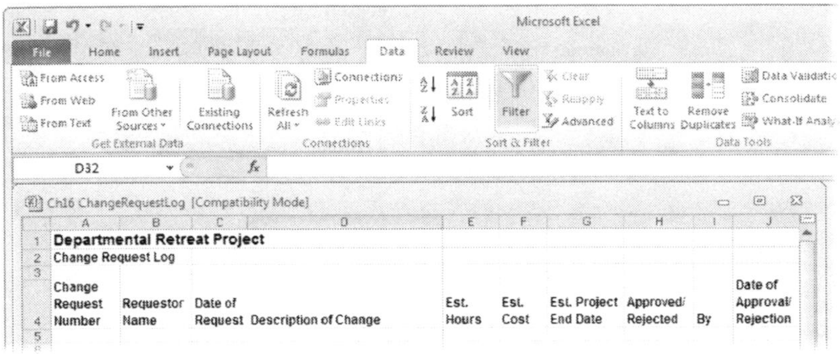

Figure 16-2:
When you use an Excel spreadsheet to track change requests, you can find change requests more easily if you sort rows or apply an AutoFilter, for example, to display only approved change requests. In Excel, Choose Data→Sort & Filter, and then, click either Sort or Filter.

TOOLS OF THE TRADE

Special Change Control Situations

The easiest way to develop a change control system is by using one that already exists, either in your company or the customer's. If the people who sit on the change review board are already familiar with the processes, change control can be up and running in no time.

If you're developing your own change control system, be sure to include procedures to handle the following situations:

- **Automatic change request approval.** You could be overwhelmed by the tsunami of change requests that come in. One way to reduce the load is by defining conditions that trigger automatic change request approval, like changes that have no effect on schedule, cost, or scope. You can set thresholds, like a $500 cost limit, for a change request to be automatic.

- **Emergency change requests.** Sometimes a change request needs to be decided on and put into place before the next change review board meeting. The change control system must have a special process for emergency requests.

- **Documenting changes.** Whether change requests are automatic, emergency, or regular, you need a procedure for documenting the changes and incorporating them into the project plan.

Note: You can download a blank form, Ch16_ChangeRequestForm.docx, from *www.missingmanuals. com/cds*.

The Change Review Board: Deciding on Changes

A change review board evaluates project change requests and gives them a thumbs-up or a thumbs-down. More importantly, a change review board has the authority to do so.

Consider the composition of your change review board carefully. Stakeholders who have the authority to approve changes to the project's schedule, cost, or scope are, of course, essential. But think about including other stakeholders and other team members, like team leaders or resource managers who are familiar with workloads and skill sets. Other candidates are people from departments like accounting, marketing, and procurement. Another approach is to set up a core change review board and invite ad hoc experts to participate as needed.

Of course, you, as project manager, must sit on the change review board. You have the most intimate knowledge of potential impacts to the project, and the power to formulate what-if scenarios (with the help of Project) to help the change review board make informed decisions.

As you build your project plan, you decide how often the change review board should meet, how the meeting should be conducted, and the rules by which changes are approved or denied. For example, you may facilitate the meeting or delegate that responsibility to someone else. All these details become the change management section of your plan. The box below talks about how to handle the time you spend on managing changes.

Now that the project is under way, it's time to use your change request tracking system as the agenda for change review board meetings. The board reviews new change requests, examines information about change requests they're considering, and follows up on the status of approved change requests.

REALITY CHECK

Accounting for Change Management Work

If you foresee spending many hours attending and preparing for change review board meetings, don't forget to add tasks for this work to your Project schedule. You can set up recurring tasks (page 146) for the meetings themselves as well as the time you spend before and after collecting or distributing information.

Preparing for these meetings isn't trivial. You may have to develop what-if scenarios for pending change requests or produce progress reports for approved change requests. Change review board meetings, like status meetings, may not take as long as the preparation for them, but they require far more stamina. It's even more important to reserve time for change management work, especially if you work on other tasks besides your project management activities.

Tracking Change Requests

Whenever you leave a change review board meeting, you probably have several action items to attend to. They fall into these three categories:

- **Update the change tracking system.** You update the change request log with decisions made during the meeting: changes accepted, changes denied, or changes that need more information.

- **Provide project plan information.** If the change review board asks for more information, your job is to collect that information or delegate the task to someone else. The board may want a cost analysis of a change request, a list of who has the necessary skills and availability for a request, or a Gantt chart showing the new dates if a change is accepted, as shown in Figure 16-3.

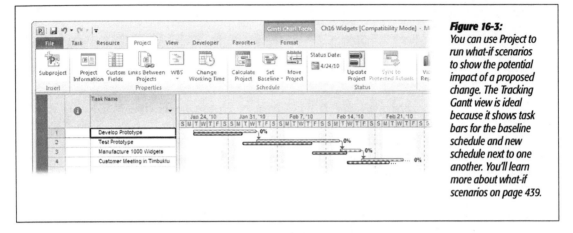

Figure 16-3:
You can use Project to run what-if scenarios to show the potential impact of a proposed change. The Tracking Gantt view is ideal because it shows task bars for the baseline schedule and new schedule next to one another. You'll learn more about what-if scenarios on page 439.

- **Update the project plan.** Update the Project schedule with approved changes, as described in the next section. The change in Project may be as simple as replacing one resource with another, or as complex as developing an entire subproject while still hitting the original project finish date.

Managing Changes in Project

The work of the change review board and your work in Project are closely intertwined, both when the board is evaluating changes and after changes have been approved. The board typically compares the benefits of a proposed change against the costs (in dollars or days) and risk. To make that comparison, the board needs to know how a change request affects the project. After approval, the board wants to know how change requests are progressing. Updating progress on change request tasks is no different from updating original project tasks. But you do need a way to distinguish change request tasks from the original work packages.

In this section, you'll learn how to create simple or extensive what-if scenarios, based on the level of information the change review board needs. You'll get tips about updating your project plan—including the best ways to use baselines in conjunction with change requests, updating and adjusting information, and checking project finish date and budget targets.

Finding the Effects of a Proposed Change

The change review board may want to know how long the finish date would be delayed or how much additional resources would cost if it approves a sizable change request. Project does a great job of number-crunching to come up with the requested information. However, be sure to protect the pre-what-if Project schedule. If the board decides to nix the change, then you want to be able to remove the what-if changes quickly, and you don't want to accidentally leave a remnant of the change request in the project. You can create a copy of your Project file to play what-if games with as much as you want. Another way to add change requests safely is to add the change request tasks to your active Project file and then inactivate them until they're approved. This section describes both strategies.

Creating a what-if copy of a project

One safe way to play what-if games is simply to copy the Project file and then fiddle with the what-if copy to your heart's content. See the box below for reasons why a copy is so important. The only potential catch is that you must name the what-if Project file so you don't accidentally use the what-if copy when you meant to work on the real thing. For example, if your Project filename is "Clown Management Training," don't name the what-if copy "Clown Management Training #2" or "Clown Management Training Copy." Instead, include identifying information like the change request ID, as in "Clown Management Training CR101."

WORD TO THE WISE

Playing What-If with Your Live Project

You may be tempted to play what-if games with your live project, rather than creating a copy of the file. The safe approach is to use your live project only for quick what-if scenarios that are around for maybe an hour, until you either adopt or undo the changes. However, the risk of saving the file without thinking is so likely that the seconds it takes to create a copy can save hours of backtracking.

Change highlighting doesn't tell you everything that's changed: Sometimes, change means "remove," and change highlighting can't show that. When changes are more than additions, you can format a task (choose Task→Font and then choose a Background Color or Text Color) to highlight modified task, resource, or assignment information in a table. However, changes may include new task dependencies or resource assignments that affect parts of tasks.

Setting a change request baseline

If your project is already in progress, you've probably set at least one baseline. If change requests are significant, a new pre-change request baseline makes the effects of the change request scenario stand out. You can compare the schedule, including the change request alterations, to this new baseline you save to find changes to the schedule, budget, and resource workloads. The box on page 441 gives tips on creating a what-if scenario on the fly. Chapter 13 describes saving baselines in detail. Here are the basic steps for saving a change request baseline:

1. **Make sure the what-if change request copy is the active Project file.**

   If you have more than one Project file open, then make sure the what-if copy filename appears in the main Project window's title bar.

2. **Choose Project→Schedule→Set Baseline→Set Baseline.**

   The Set Baseline dialog box opens.

3. **In the "Set baseline" drop-down list, choose the baseline you want to use, and then click OK.**

   Baselines you've already saved include the date they were saved to the right of the baseline name, as shown in Figure 16-4.

Note: If task start and finish dates are your only concern, you can save an interim plan (page 370) instead of a baseline. A baseline saves a snapshot of several scheduling fields like Start, Finish, Duration, Work, Cost, and so on. An interim plan saves only the start and finish dates.

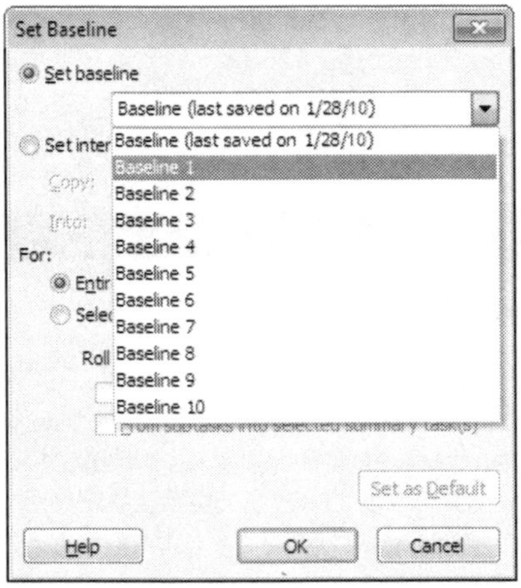

Figure 16-4:
You may think it's OK to save over an old baseline, because you're working in a copy of the Project file. However, if the change request scenario becomes reality, you may turn the copy into your live file. In that case, you'll probably want that old baseline around.

4. **Modify the change request Project file copy with all the alterations the change request entails.**

   Remember, your original Project file is sitting, safe and unsullied, somewhere else on your computer.

5. **Use your favorite techniques for checking the impact of the proposed change.**

   Chapter 12 describes ways to review effects on Project files that don't have baselines. Chapter 15 describes techniques you can use to compare changes to the baselined project. The Tracking Gantt view compares the current schedule to the baseline. The Multiple Baselines Gantt view compares several baselines (page 373).

Be prepared to discuss the effects of the suggested change. If the proposed change has affected the schedule, budget, or other characteristics, come up with suggestions for mitigating these effects. The board needs to know all its options and the possible tradeoffs.

6. **Fast-forward to the change review board accepting the change. If you haven't edited the original Project file in any way since you created the what-if copy, then rename the copy to be your live Project file.**

Rename your original Project file something like "*Corporate Retreat Original. mpp*." Then rename the what-if copy to be the live file. For example, if it was "*Corporate Retreat CR101.mpp*," rename it the original name, "*Corporate Retreat.mpp*."

Quick-and-Dirty What-If Scenarios

Some proposed changes are relatively simple to make. If you can move around Project quickly and, ideally, display your computer's screen up on the wall, you can make proposed changes in Project and show the impact to the change review board in real time. Here are the steps:

1. Save the Project file. Any recent changes are now saved and won't get lumped in with your what-if scenario.

2. Save an additional baseline (for example, Baseline 2 or Baseline 3) for later comparison purposes.

3. Make edits to the schedule. Project highlights cells that are affected by the last edit you make, so you can point out the effects of changes.

4. Switch views to answer questions from the board.

5. If the board approves the change, you can simply save your file, and much of your work is already done. If the board rejects the proposed change and you're certain you saved the project just before you started making the proposed changes, then choose File→Close. When you open the file again, it's back to its original pristine state. To backtrack only a few steps, on the Quick Access toolbar, click the down arrow next to the Undo button to select the edits you want to undo. Remember, you can undo operations only until the last time you saved the file. (See page 339 to learn more about Multilevel Undo.)

Inactivating change request tasks until you need them

In many instances, change requests take the form of one or more new tasks in your Project schedule. In that case, the new Inactive Tasks feature really shines. You can add change request tasks to your Project schedule to determine their effect. Once you produce the reports you need for the change review board, you can inactivate the tasks. You can still see them and even edit their values, but they don't affect your project schedule while they're inactive. If the change review board approves the change request, reactivate the tasks and you're ready to rock and roll.

Here's how to use the inactive tasks feature to work with change requests:

1. **Create the tasks you need for a change request, as you would normally.**

   Make them subtasks below summary tasks if you want. Link them to other tasks in your schedule. Assign resources. In short, work with them like any other tasks you create in your project.

2. **Produce the documentation you need to obtain approval for the change request.**

   For example, if cost is the main concern, a report that shows the cost of the change request tasks may be enough. If schedule is a factor, produce an updated Gantt Chart showing new start and finish dates.

Tip: Use formatting tools to highlight the change request tasks in your documentation. For example, use a custom number field to record the change request number, as described on page 444. Select all the change request tasks, and then right-click one of the selected tasks to display the mini-toolbar. Click Bold, Italic, or the Background Color icon to change the formatting of just those tasks.

---

3. **After your change request documentation is complete, select the tasks in a task-oriented view and then choose Task→Schedule→Inactivate.**

   The inactive tasks immediately change to gray with a strikethrough line drawn through their values in the table area, as shown in Figure 16-5. Despite their appearance, you can edit their values. Double-click an inactive task to open the Task Information dialog box or type a value directly in a table cell.

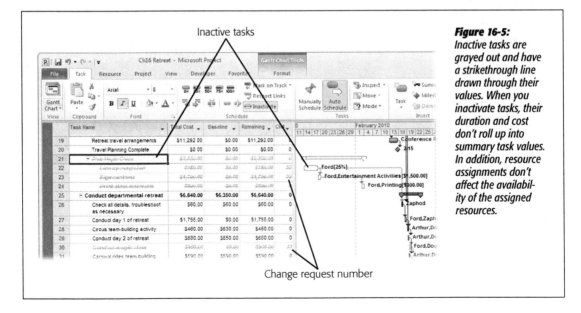

Inactive tasks

Change request number

Figure 16-5:
Inactive tasks are grayed out and have a strikethrough line drawn through their values. When you inactivate tasks, their duration and cost don't roll up into summary task values. In addition, resource assignments don't affect the availability of the assigned resources.

4. If the change request is approved, select the tasks for the change request, and then choose Task→Schedule→Inactivate to reactivate them.

Now the tasks' durations and costs do roll up into summary task values, and resource assignments affect the assigned resources' availability.

Updating Project with Approved Change Requests

You must add approved project changes to your Project file for the same reasons you enter actual progress information (page 392). An up-to-date project lets you report quickly about what has already taken place and, more importantly, lets you accurately forecast what will happen going forward.

If you developed a change request what-if scenario as described in the previous section, most of your work is done. To make the change a permanent part of the project, you may need to add details like accounting codes for added resources or custom fields with more information about new tasks.

How you update the Project file depends on how you want to track the approved change requests you add. Each choice has its pros and cons, so you must choose the one that fits your needs the best. Here are three options you can use:

- **Setting a new baseline.** If you want to track the entire project going forward, you can save a new baseline for the entire project. This approach uses the project state *before* you implemented the change as the line in the sand for comparisons. (Choose Project→Schedule→Set Baseline→Set Baseline.)

  The problem with this approach is that all the original tasks in the Project file have new baseline values. If you compare the current schedule to the baseline, the variances on original tasks represent variances from this more recent baseline. You lose the comparison to your original plan.

- **Adding tasks to a baseline.** If you want to keep track of your original tasks from an older baseline and track new tasks going forward, then you can add tasks to a baseline. Select the tasks you want to add, and then choose Project→Schedule→Set Baseline→Set Baseline. In the Set Baseline dialog box, be sure to select the "Selected tasks" option before you click OK. Project keeps the existing baseline values for existing tasks and adds the current scheduled values for the added tasks to the baseline. You can tell Project whether you want the new values from new tasks to roll up to the summary tasks. See page 368 to learn more.

  This approach works fine for new tasks, like when a change request spawns a whole new section of the project. It falls short for tasks you've modified because of change requests. In that case, you can rebaseline the modified tasks, but future variances will reflect variances from the most recent baselining. You can work around this issue by always creating new tasks for change requests. For example, instead of increasing the work for a task, create a new task with the additional work for the change request.

- **Saving a data cube instead of a baseline.** If you don't want to use up one of Project's 11 available baselines, you can save your Project file as a *data cube* (page 475), an element of Project visual reports. A data cube saves a snapshot of Project data into a special kind of database that you can view in Excel or Visio. You can use these data cubes to retrieve data by different categories, like when you want to compare the progress for your change requests.

After you decide how you want to track change requests, the techniques you use to enter actual values are the same for original, modified, or new tasks (page 392).

Flagging Change Requests in Project

Suppose an approved change request gives birth to an entirely new phase or a set of new tasks scattered throughout the project. With changes that have such a large impact, you need a way to identify the resulting tasks or resources so you can track them separately. Keeping them separate is particularly useful when the project sponsor or customer develops a severe case of amnesia about having approved this significant change. Keeping the change impacts visible during management status meetings can not only be a gentle reminder of "This is what you asked for," but also a subtle and satisfying "I told you so."

Of course, you can use baselines to track approved changes compared with the original plan. This section describes an effective way to identify change request tasks, so you can review them separately from the original plan. The solution is to create a custom field to flag change request tasks and then filter a view to see all the tasks with the change request flag.

Here are the steps:

1. **Create a custom field for tasks, as described on page 640.**

   If you want to flag tasks by their corresponding change request identifiers, use a text or number field. (Then you can type the change request number or name in the field.) To simply track tasks that are related to any change request, you could use a Flag field, which contains Yes if it's an approved change request task rather than an originally planned task. Rename the field something like "Change Request."

2. **Insert the custom field into a table in a task-oriented view like the Gantt Chart view's Entry table.**

   Right-click the table heading, and then choose Insert→Column. In the "Field name" drop-down list, choose the custom field name, which looks something like "Number 11 (CR#)." If you type letters to quickly find the fields you want, then Project conveniently searches by the built-in field name and the alias you create. For example, you can type *N* to jump to the Number fields. Or you can type *C* to find the fields listed as "CR# (Number 11)."

3. **For every task that relates to a change request, type a value in the custom field, as shown in Figure 16-6.**

   The value could be something like "*Jan 2008 CRB*" or "*CRB 080115*" in a text field, "*23*" in a number field, or "*Yes*" in a Yes/No field.

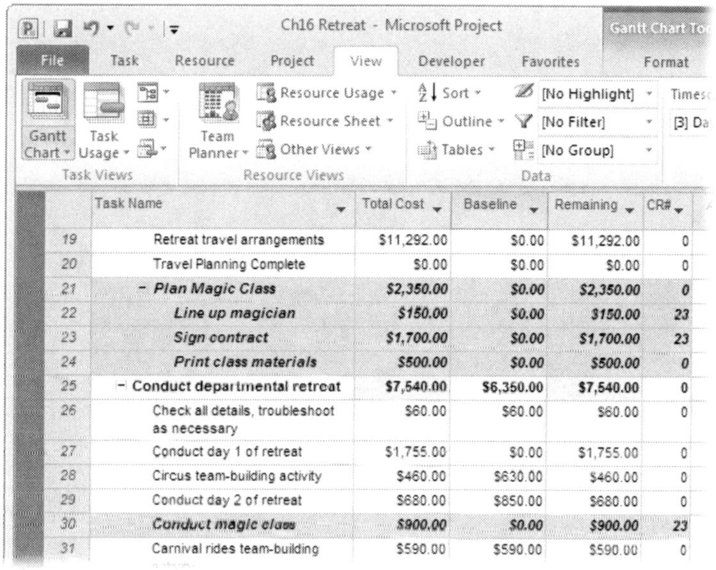

Figure 16-6:
Insert your custom field into a task sheet, and then enter the change request information into the field. If you want to fill multiple adjacent cells with the change request information, you can drag the value from the first custom field cell over adjacent cells, for instance, when a change request creates a summary task with several subtasks. Select the first cell. Position the pointer over the small black square in the cell's lower-left corner. When the pointer changes to a + sign, drag over the other cells.

	Task Name	Total Cost	Baseline	Remaining	CR#
19	Retreat travel arrangements	$11,292.00	$0.00	$11,292.00	0
20	Travel Planning Complete	$0.00	$0.00	$0.00	0
21	− Plan Magic Class	$2,350.00	$0.00	$2,350.00	0
22	Line up magician	$150.00	$0.00	$150.00	23
23	Sign contract	$1,700.00	$0.00	$1,700.00	23
24	Print class materials	$500.00	$0.00	$500.00	0
25	− Conduct departmental retreat	$7,540.00	$6,350.00	$7,540.00	0
26	Check all details, troubleshoot as necessary	$60.00	$60.00	$60.00	0
27	Conduct day 1 of retreat	$1,755.00	$0.00	$1,755.00	0
28	Circus team-building activity	$460.00	$630.00	$460.00	0
29	Conduct day 2 of retreat	$680.00	$850.00	$680.00	0
30	Conduct magic class	$900.00	$0.00	$900.00	23
31	Carnival rides team-building	$590.00	$590.00	$590.00	0

4. **To filter for the custom field, click the down arrow to the right of the custom field heading.**

   A drop-down menu appears.

5. **To filter for an individual change request, turn off the "(Select All)" checkbox and turn on the checkbox for the change request you want.**

   The task list hides all the tasks that don't match the filter. To restore the full list, click the down arrow to the right of the custom field heading, and then turn on the "(Select All)" checkbox.

Reporting on Projects

Because communication is such a large part of project management, you run reports all the time. Along with pictures of schedules, reports are a mainstay for presenting project information to others. They're also handy when *you* want to see what's going on. During planning, reports show you where your schedule needs work to get dates, costs, and resource workloads where they should be. Once the project is under way, you can use high-level reports to see whether the project is on track. If it isn't, more detailed reports help you find the problem spots.

Savvy project managers are proactive and run reports to find tasks that are slipping (not progressing as they should) or are starting or finishing late. These tasks are warning signs of impending project delays. Correcting those problems early can keep the project on track, without the Herculean efforts typically required when time is running out.

Different audiences want different information. For example, teams like to see how much they've accomplished, but they also want to know what still lies ahead. You can use built-in Project reports to build to-do lists or show resources their assignments laid out week by week. Likewise, you can prepare assignment reports to show managers how their folks are doing and when it's time to find them more work. Executives usually don't care about the nitty-gritty. They want a high-level view of progress, and how it compares to the plan. They get concerned if project red flags are flying. Coming prepared with reports that show your plan for course correction can keep status meetings on an even keel.

Project's text-based reports are still around. They aren't fancy, but they're great for day-to-day task and resource management. *Visual reports,* introduced in Project 2007, use Excel pivot tables and Visio pivot diagrams to turn heaps of data into meaningful information. Moreover, visual reports can twist data around to show information from different perspectives. From one angle, you may see tasks that are in trouble. By turning the data on its side, you can see whether specific resources are having problems.

This chapter begins with an overview of the built-in reports that Project offers. You'll learn what each report does, how you might use them, and where to find them. Then you'll learn how to generate and customize text-based reports. You'll also learn other ways to preview text-based reports in Project 2010. This chapter also describes how visual reports work. Because they use Excel and Visio, you'll learn the key features for manipulating visual report data in both of those programs. In addition to changing the appearance of a visual report, you can also customize templates to modify or create your own visual reports.

An Overview of Project's Reports

Although the information in visual reports and text-based reports overlaps a little, you use each type of report for different reasons. Text-based reports spit out information in a specific format, which is fine when you want to see information that way. Visual reports, on the other hand, are ideal when you want to look at project performance from different angles.

Project assigns reports to several categories, which may be different from the way you group them. For example, visual reports are divided into summary and usage reports, and then into reports that cover tasks, resources, and assignments. Because visual reports can look at data in different ways, it's hard to know whether the Baseline Cost report is a task summary visual report or a resource usage report. This section gives some examples of when you might use different built-in text-based (page 454) and visual reports (page 462), and where to find them within Project's report categories.

Overall Status

Several reports provide a high-level view of a project. Visual reports can either summarize results at the project level or drill down to details by task, resource, or time. Here are a few Project reports you can use for a high-level status report:

- **Project Summary.** This text-based report in the Overview category is perfect for a 30,000-foot project view in a no-frills table you can attach to a status report. The box on page 450 talks about other items to include in a project status report. It shows the same high-level information as the Project Statistics dialog box (page 410): baseline, scheduled, and actual values for dates, duration, work, and costs. At the bottom of the report, task status shows the number of unstarted, in-progress, and completed tasks. The resource status shows the number of resources, and how many are overallocated.

- **Task Status.** This Visio-based visual report initially shows work, cost, and the percentage complete for top-level tasks, as shown in Figure 17-1. As you'll learn shortly, you can include other fields like baseline cost or actual work to see how your project is doing at the top level. If you want to examine parts of your project more closely, you can drill down to lower levels in the task list.

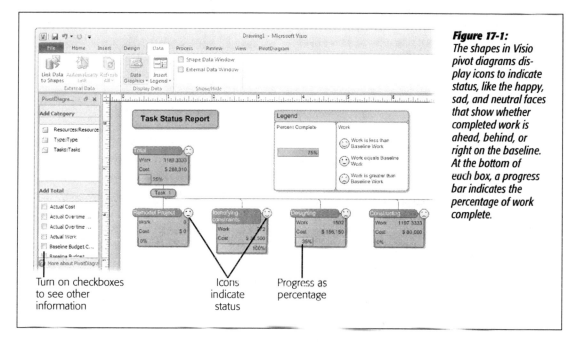

Figure 17-1:
The shapes in Visio pivot diagrams display icons to indicate status, like the happy, sad, and neutral faces that show whether completed work is ahead, behind, or right on the baseline. At the bottom of each box, a progress bar indicates the percentage of work complete.

Turn on checkboxes
to see other
information

Icons
indicate
status

Progress as
percentage

- **Top-Level Tasks.** This text-based report in the Overview category shows tasks at the outline's top level. It shows the planned schedule with information straight from the Summary table: Duration, Start, Finish, % Complete, Cost, and Work.

- **Critical Tasks Status.** This Visio-based visual report shows work and remaining work for critical tasks. You can include more fields, like baseline and actual costs, to see whether the critical path is on track.

- **Critical Tasks.** A text-based report in the Overview category, this report lists all critical tasks along with their successors, so you can see how delayed critical tasks may affect other tasks.

- **Milestones.** This Overview report is a text-based list of the milestones in your project. It shows start and finish dates, so you can see when significant achievements or events occur. Inexplicably, the Milestones report includes a column for Actual Duration and Duration, despite almost all milestones being zero duration. (You can designate a regular task as a milestone by changing its Milestone field to Yes.)

TOOLS OF THE TRADE

Reporting Project Status

Typical departmental project status reports (the ones managers grumble about having to read every week) deal mostly with how much work has gotten done and how much remains to do. But status reports can cover several other topics, including schedule and cost performance, risks, issues, and changes.

How much detail you provide depends on the audience. Small work teams may want to know if other teams have finished what they've been waiting for, or glean handy programming tips from others. Executives prefer a high-level view. Here are typical topics for a management-level status report:

- **Task progress.** This section summarizes completed tasks and provides an update on tasks in progress. The text-based reports described in "Task Management" on page 452 are ideal for gathering this information.

- **Project performance.** Earned values fields like BCWP (budgeted cost of work performed, a.k.a earned value), CV (cost variance), SV (schedule variance), and EAC (estimate at complete) measure performance compared to the baseline. In a status report, you can list the current values and explain any diversions from the baseline. If you present project status to the management team, the Earned Value visual report provides a lovely graph but also lets you alter the report to expose the underlying issues.

- **Corrective action plan.** Provides an update on any corrective actions you're taking to bring the budget or schedule back in line.

- **Change management.** Provides an update on change requests: requests submitted, requests approved or denied, progress on change requests that have been added to the project.

- **Risk management.** Summarizes risks that have become reality, and the success of the risk response you've initiated. Also lists risks you're watching that have mercifully remained hypothetical.

- **Issues.** This section is great for bringing situations to the management team's attention, particularly if you want their help.

- **Items of interest.** Use this section to publicize information, like particularly effective techniques, that may be useful to the team.

You can download StatusReportTemplate.dot, a simple Word template for a project status report, from *www.missingmanuals.com/cds*.

Alas, Project can't produce every portion of a project status report. Project's strengths are task progress and project performance. The other sections of the status report draw upon information you store elsewhere, like Excel spreadsheets, Access databases, or Word documents.

Financial Performance

As you learned in Chapter 15, cost performance is an important part of overall project performance. Several of the new visual reports cover different aspects of financial performance. Some of the text-based reports can help you see which tasks and resources are over budget. Here are the reports that deal primarily with cost:

- **Baseline Cost.** You can use the Excel or Visio Baseline Cost visual reports to compare planned, actual, and baseline costs. With these reports, you can view cost for the entire project, drill down to analyze cost by phase, or switch the report to show cost by fiscal quarter, as shown in Figure 17-2. The Baseline Work visual report is a bar graph of baseline, planned, and actual work.

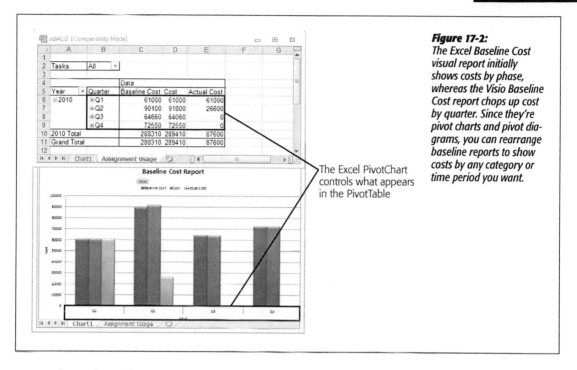

Figure 17-2:
The Excel Baseline Cost visual report initially shows costs by phase, whereas the Visio Baseline Cost report chops up cost by quarter. Since they're pivot charts and pivot diagrams, you can rearrange baseline reports to show costs by any category or time period you want.

The Excel PivotChart controls what appears in the PivotTable

- **Budget.** The Budget Cost and Budget Work visual reports in Excel are graphs of cost or work by quarter. Initially, the bars in the graph show actual, baseline, and budget values, so you can see how actual values compare to the baseline by time period and also compare those values to accounting budget numbers (page 306).

  On the other hand, the text-based Budget report is like a hard copy of the Cost table. It shows total cost, baseline, and actual costs for each task. This report sorts tasks by highest cost first, so the tasks with the biggest price tags are easy to find.

- **Cash Flow.** The Excel Cash Flow report is a graph of cost by quarter with a line for cumulative cost as time passes. You can expand the time periods to show weekly costs—for instance, to make sure your weekly allowance covers the expenses you incur. The Visio Cash Flow report displays orange exclamation points if the actual cost is over budget.

  The Cash Flow text-based report (in the Cost category) shows task cost by week. The last *row* in the report shows the total cost for each time period. The last *column* in the report shows total cost for each task over the entire project duration. The accrual method (page 198) you use determines when costs appear in the report.

- **Earned Value.** The Excel Earned Value Over Time visual report graphs the budgeted cost of work scheduled; the budgeted cost of work performed (if it's less than the cost of work scheduled, then the project is behind schedule); and the actual cost of work performed (if it's less than the budgeted cost of work performed, then the project is under budget). Chapter 15 discusses earned value in more detail (page 421).

  The Earned Value text-based report (in the Cost category) shows earned value fields for each task.

- **Overbudget Tasks.** This text-based report in the Cost category lists tasks whose actual or scheduled costs are higher than their baseline costs, so you can tell which ones you may need to correct. Tasks with the highest cost variance appear first.

- **Overbudget Resources.** This text-based report (another Cost category report) shows resources whose actual or scheduled costs are higher than their baseline costs in order from highest to lowest variance. These variances could mean you've assigned more work to those resources, but overbudget resources may be taking too much time.

- **Resource Cost Summary.** This Excel visual report is a pie chart that shows costs by resource type (work, material, and cost).

Task Management

For checking up on task schedules, the built-in text-based reports win hands down. Several text-based reports pinpoint tasks that may need help. For example, in Chapter 15, you learned how reports like Tasks Starting Soon, Should Have Started Tasks, and Slipping Tasks can help you find tasks that require your attention. The following reports are all text-based reports in the Current category. Here are the reports best suited for keeping tabs on task scheduling:

- **Unstarted Tasks.** This report shows tasks that haven't started, whether they're on time, early, or late. Near the end of a project, you can use this report to see what's left. At the beginning of a project, this report shows most tasks, which isn't particularly helpful.

- **Tasks Starting Soon.** This report's name is a little misleading. The report shows tasks that start or *finish* during the date range you specify, so some tasks may have already started. Nonetheless, this report is great for producing to-do lists of upcoming tasks for project teams.

- **Tasks In Progress.** Tasks in this report aren't necessarily in trouble, but you can see which tasks are in progress and include them in status reports. This report clusters tasks by the month in which they started. If you see a lone task that started several months ago, then it may already be complete, but you haven't recorded that in your Project file.

- **Should Have Started Tasks.** This report asks for a date, and then shows tasks that should have started by then but don't have any actual hours recorded. Tasks in this report may be late in starting or simply missing update values.

- **Slipping Tasks.** The Slipping Tasks report shows tasks that have started, but are due to finish after their baseline finish dates (so it works only when you've set a baseline). Dig deeper into each task to find out what the problems are and to correct them. The report shows current and baseline start and finish dates, and the corresponding variances.

- **Completed Tasks.** This report lists tasks completed each month, which is a great way to boost team morale by showing them how much they've accomplished. At the end of a project, this report summarizes how tasks turned out, which can act as an archive or a foundation for estimating future projects.

Resource Management

Text-based and visual reports both help you manage project resources, whether you're first assigning them or trying to eliminate overallocations. Here are the reports that focus on resources and their assignments:

- **Working Days.** This text-based report in the Overview category is ideal during planning, to see if you've defined project and resource calendars correctly. The report spits out workdays, work hours, and exceptions for each calendar in your project, without marathon sessions in the Change Working Time dialog box (page 240).

- **Who Does What.** This text-based report in the Assignments category shows the tasks assigned to each resource. Use it if you lose a resource, to find the tasks you have to reassign.

- **Who Does What When.** This text-based Assignments report breaks down the information in the Who Does What report period by period. The Who Does What When report includes all resources and all assignments for the entire project duration—which is an overwhelming amount of information and a lot of printed pages. The Resource Work Summary visual report shows similar information but gives you control over the data and timeframe.

- **Resource Work Summary.** This Excel visual report shows everything you want to know about resources in work unit percentages: total capacity, work, remaining availability, and actual work. You can see information for all resources side by side, filter the report to show specific resources, or view work for a specific timeframe.

- **To-Do List.** This text-based Assignments report is like the Who Does What report for a single resource you specify. It's a great way to show each person what she's supposed to work on during each week of the project.

- **Resource Status.** This Visio-based visual report shows work and cost for each resource. It shades bars darker as resources get closer to finishing their assignments.

- **Resource Work Availability.** This Excel-based visual report is like the Resource Graph on steroids. You can see total capacity, work, and remaining availability over time for work resources. Visual report tools let you change the fields, resources, and timeframe you see.

- **Resource Availability.** This Visio-based visual report shows remaining availability, along with a red flag for overallocated resources.

- **Resource Remaining Work.** This Excel-based visual report shows remaining and actual work for each work resource.

- **Overallocated Resources.** Although this text-based Assignments report shows resources who are assigned more work than they can do, it also lists every task assigned to each resource, so you can't tell which tasks are causing the problem. The Resource Usage view (page 263) or the Team Planner view (page 261) are better for finding overallocations.

- **Task Usage.** This text-based report in the Workload category is like a hard copy of the Task Usage view. You can use it to see the work for each task week by week.

- **Resource Usage.** This text-based report in the Workload category is like a hard copy of the Resource Usage view. It shows hours assigned week by week.

Tip: You don't have to stick to Project's text-based and visual reports to share information. For example, you can apply a filter like Overallocated Resources and then print the Resource Usage view to show overallocations (page 476).

Text-Based Reports

Getting Project's text-based reports to show the information you want has always been a challenge. The reports have only the most basic options for choosing, arranging, and formatting data. In Project 2010, you can't preview a report in a separate window to take a closer look before you print. (The box on page 456 tells you how to work around this wrinkle.) Visual reports give you a lot more control, so you may turn to them more often. You can also export Project data (page 524) to Excel or another program to view information the way you want. But text-based reports are still handy in a few situations:

- **Quick results.** A text-based report pulls data directly from Project fields and then lays it out according to the report definition. If the report shows what you want, it's faster than generating a visual report.

- **Day-to-day task management.** Some of the text-based reports, like Tasks Starting Soon and Should Have Started Tasks, provide information that you can't get from visual reports. If you want to hand over upcoming assignments to team leaders, the tabular format of text-based reports is ideal.

Generating a text-based report is easy, whether it's a built-in report or a custom report you created. Because text-based reports don't offer many options, customizing them is relatively easy, too. This section explains how to do both.

Generating Text-Based Reports

Generating a text-based report boils down to three steps: Open the Report dialog box, select the report category, and then select the report. The box on page 457 talks about a way to quickly generate reports you use often. Here's how you generate a text-based report:

1. **Choose Project→Reports→Reports.**

   The Reports dialog box opens with a button for each of the six categories of built-in text-based reports.

2. **Double-click one of the report categories.**

   The dialog box for that category opens. For example, if you double-click Overview, then the Overview Reports dialog box opens.

3. **Double-click the report you want to generate.**

   Project opens the Print page of the Backstage view with a preview of the report. The print options—like the printer, date range, orientation, and paper size—appear on the left side of the Backstage view. Click Page Setup to adjust the margins, page orientation, header, or footer. Frustratingly, the Backstage view's menu and print settings take up so much room that there's little room left for your report preview, as shown in Figure 17-3. The box on page 456 explains ways to preview your report before you commit it to paper.

4. **In the Backstage view, select the number of copies you want (next to the Print button) and, in the Settings section, choose the page range to print.**

   You can also choose a different printer, the paper orientation, and the paper size. To change the page setup, such as margins, headers, and footers, click Page Setup below the Settings section.

5. **To print the report, click Print.**

   If a message box says there's no data to print, several issues may be at work. For instance, a report like Overbudget Tasks doesn't have data if you don't have a baseline set. Other reports that show progress may not have data if tasks don't have actual hours. Resources without rate information or no tasks during the timeframe you specify are other potential causes.

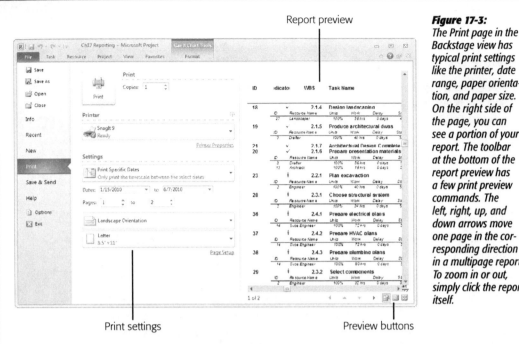

Report preview

Print settings

Preview buttons

Figure 17-3:
The Print page in the Backstage view has typical print settings like the printer, date range, paper orientation, and paper size. On the right side of the page, you can see a portion of your report. The toolbar at the bottom of the report preview has a few print preview commands. The left, right, up, and down arrows move one page in the corresponding direction in a multipage report. To zoom in or out, simply click the report itself.

GEM IN THE ROUGH

Previewing a Text-Based Report

If you've generated a massive report, you don't want to print a hard copy of the entire report unless you're sure it contains the information you want in the format you want. In Project 2010, the Print page in the Backstage view has very little room for the report preview. Although none of them are as convenient as a separate Print Preview window, you do have several options for getting a closer look:

- Zoom in by clicking the report itself or by clicking the Actual Size button (the icon is a page with a magnifying glass) to show the report at full size. Then you have to click the left, right, up, and down arrows to pan around the report.

- In the toolbar at the bottom of the window, click One Page or Multiple Page to show one or more pages of the report. They're too small to read, but you may be able to tell if you're printing too much of the project or too little.

- Send the report to OneNote 2010 (click the Printer down arrow, choose Send To OneNote 2010, and then click Print). After you choose where you want to save the report in OneNote, the program copies the report to that OneNote page. The report fills the One-Note page. You can scroll through the report, zoom in and out, or change the paper size.

- Choose a printer that creates a file, such as Microsoft XPS Document Writer, which creates an XPS file (a file format you can share and read with the Microsoft XPS Viewer). If you have software that includes a PDF printer (for example, Adobe Acrobat Professional), then you can choose Adobe PDF in the Printer dropdown list.

Customizing Text-Based Reports

You may want to change the information in reports, or the way that information appears. For example, the built-in Cash Flow report shows cash flow by week, but you may want to see cash flow by month. The easiest way to customize a text-based report is to copy it and then edit the copy like you do other elements in Project. The original reports are still there if you need them, along with your custom creations. You can also start a new text-based report from scratch. In fact, the options are so simple that creating and copying reports are about the same amount of work. This section describes how to create a customized text-based report, whether you copy an existing one or start one from scratch.

Text-based reports come in four types, each of which offers different customization options. Here are the types and what they do:

- **Task.** A task report creates a list of tasks (all tasks or a filtered list), and then adds columns for the fields you want to include.

- **Resource.** A resource report creates a list of resources (all resources or a filtered list), and then adds columns for the resource fields you want to include.

- **Crosstab.** This report is like a task usage or resource usage view. It can show cost- and work-related values over time.

- **Monthly calendar.** This report is like a hard copy of a Calendar view.

POWER USERS' CLINIC

Easy Access to Your Favorite Reports

You probably generate the same reports for every status period, change control board meeting, or stakeholder meeting. Instead of opening the Reports dialog box, choosing a category, and then choosing a report, you can customize the ribbon (page 658) with entries that generate each of your favorite reports.

Because Project doesn't save reports—it generates one every time you ask for it—you have to create a macro to run a specific report. Recording the macro takes only a few clicks more than running a report, but it saves you several steps from then on. Here are the steps:

1. Start recording a new macro (choose View→ Macros→Macros→Record Macro). Use the report name as part of the macro name, for instance, Prj-SummaryRpt.

2. With the macro recorder running, choose Project→ Reports→Reports, double-click the category, and then double-click the report.

3. Stop recording the macro.

4. If you want to add several reports to a menu, repeat steps 1–3 to record a macro for each report.

5. Add the macros for your reports to a custom group on the ribbon, as described on page 687.

Creating or copying a report

Copying an existing report is usually your best bet. You can keep the settings that still apply and change the rest. Whether you copy a report or start from scratch, the steps are similar:

1. **Choose Project→Reports→Reports.**

   The Reports dialog box opens.

2. **Double-click Custom.**

   The Custom Reports dialog box opens, as shown in Figure 17-4. The Reports list displays all existing reports.

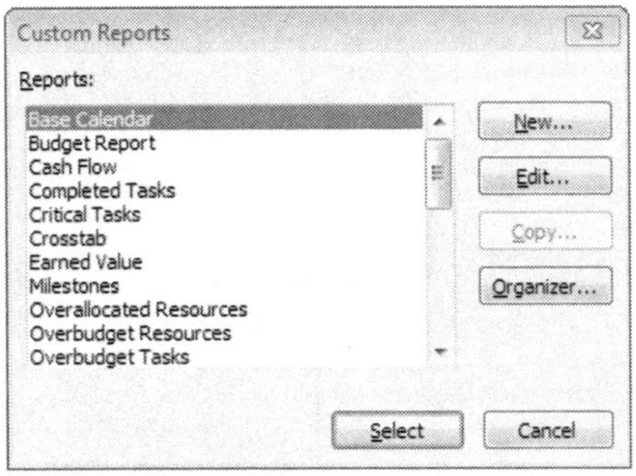

Figure 17-4:
If you aren't sure which report you want to copy, you have no choice but to run it (by clicking Select). Project 2010 has eliminated the Preview button in the Custom Reports dialog box. After you confirm that the report is the one you want, reopen the Custom Reports dialog box, select the report in the Reports list, and then click Copy.

Note: Project 2010 has also eliminated the Page Setup and Print buttons in the Custom Reports dialog box. Click Select to generate the report and view it on the Print page of the Backstage view. From there, you can change the header, footer, and margin settings or print the report.

3. **Select the report you want to copy, and then click Copy.**

   The dialog box that opens depends on the type of report you select (Task, Resource, Crosstab, or Monthly). Each type of report has its own options and settings, as described in the following sections.

   To create your own report from scratch, click New; the Define New Report dialog box opens. Select the type of report you want, and then click OK. The corresponding dialog box (Task Report, Resource Report, Crosstab Report, or Monthly Calendar Report Definition) opens.

4. **In the Name box, type a name for the report.**

   For copied reports, Project fills in the Name box with "Copy of," followed by the report name. If you create a report from scratch, it names it "Report 1."

5. **Modify the report to show the information you want, and then click OK to add the report to the Custom Reports dialog box Report list.**

The following sections explain the options for customizing each type of report.

Tip: To edit an existing report *without* copying it, choose Project→Reports→Reports. In the Reports dialog box, double-click the report category, and then select the report you want to edit. Click Edit. Make the changes you want, and then click OK.

Customizing a task or resource report

Task and resource reports are like tables in a Project view. You choose a Project table to specify the report columns and then choose a filter to control the tasks or resources that appear in the report rows. Depending on the type of report you're customizing, the corresponding dialog box opens. For example, if you copy the Should Have Started Tasks report, then the Task Report dialog box opens, as shown in Figure 17-5.

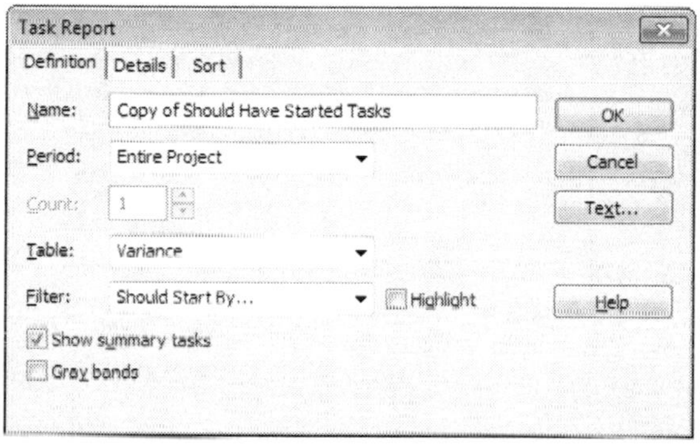

Figure 17-5:
The Task Report dialog box's Definition tab contains the main report settings. The Details tab has checkboxes for including information other than table fields. The Sort tab is identical to the Sort dialog box, so you can tell Project how to sort the tasks or resources.

Here are the settings for a task or resource report:

- **Name.** The name appears in the Reports list and in the heading of the printed report.

- **Period.** The time period you choose creates groups of tasks or resources. For example, you can modify the In Progress task report to see in-progress tasks grouped by the month in which they started. If a task from several months ago shows up, you can check for missing actual values. If you select a time period like days or weeks, then you can change the number in the Count box—for example, type *2* to group every 2 weeks.

- **Table.** Text-based reports display the columns in the table you choose, so pick any table that contains the fields you want to see. The Table drop-down list shows built-in and custom tables. If you want to use a custom table, then you have to create it (page 616) before you begin customizing the report.

- **Filter.** The filter works in the same way as a filter in a view (page 621). It controls the tasks or resources included in the report. Turn on the Highlight checkbox to shade tasks or resources that pass the filter. Otherwise, the filter hides the ones that don't pass.

- **Show summary tasks.** This checkbox is automatically turned on to include summary tasks in a task report. (The checkbox is grayed out for a resource report.) To show only work package tasks, turn this checkbox off.

- **Gray bands.** Turn this checkbox on to draw a gray band between each time period in the report, like when you modify the Critical Tasks report to group tasks by month.

- **Details to include.** On the Details tab, shown in Figure 17-6, you can turn checkboxes on or off to include other types of information. For tasks, you can include task notes, attached objects like documents, predecessors, or successors. For resources, you can include notes, objects, the resource calendar, or the cost rate. For assignments, you can include notes or schedule, cost, or work values.

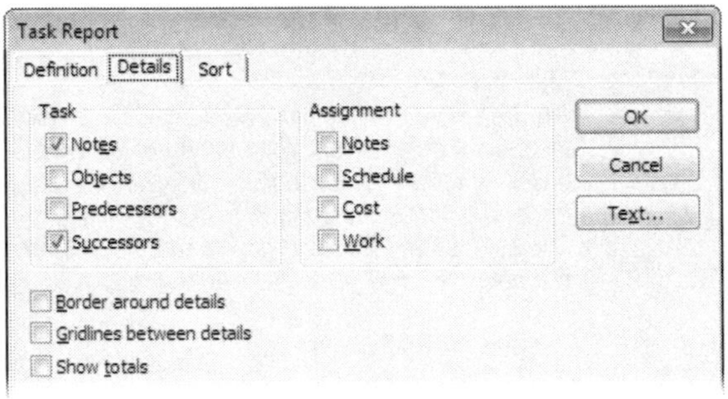

Figure 17-6:
When you include details, the report adds them after every task or resource row. The "Border around details" and "Gridlines between details" checkboxes both draw lines to visually separate the details from the task or resource rows.

- **Sort.** The Sort tab looks just like the Sort dialog box. You can, for example, sort critical tasks by duration and then by cost.

- **Text.** On the Definition and Details tabs, click Text to format different categories of text, like column titles, totals, or critical tasks (page 617).

Customizing a timescaled report

Crosstab reports like the Cash Flow report are like usage views: They include columns for each time period and rows for each task or resource. For crosstab reports, the time period, shown in Figure 17-7, sets the length of time for each column in the timescale. Similar to a usage view, you have to select the field you want to show in the timescale, like Work or Cost. Here are your choices for customizing a crosstab report:

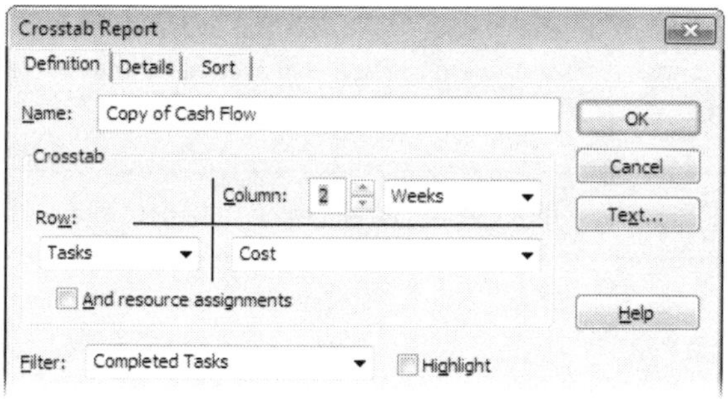

Figure 17-7:
The Definition tab provides visual clues to the report layout. The positions of the Row and Column labels help you visualize what goes into rows and columns. The vertical and horizontal lines are like the gridlines in a usage view. The field drop-down list is below the Column label and to the right of the vertical line to indicate that the field appears in the timescale grid.

- **Name.** The name appears in the Reports list and in the heading of the printed report.

- **Column.** The boxes to the right of Column label set the time period for each column in the timescale. For example, to report every 2 weeks, choose 2 in the first box and Weeks in the second.

- **Row.** A crosstab report can work with tasks or resources. In the Row drop-down list, choose Tasks to create the equivalent of a task usage view. Choose Resources to mimic a resource usage view.

  The second Row drop-down list is the field that appears in the timescale. You can choose different types of cost and work fields, as well as schedule and cost performance fields like SV (schedule variance). For resources, you can also choose fields like Remaining Availability or Percent Allocation.

  To include rows for each assignment, turn on the "And resource assignments" checkbox for a task-oriented report (or "And task assignments" for a resource-oriented report).

- **Filter.** The filter you choose controls the tasks or resources included in the report, just like a filter applied to a table in the Gantt Chart view restricts the tasks that appear in the view. Turn on the Highlight checkbox to shade the rows for tasks or resources that pass the filter (instead of hiding the ones that don't pass).

- **Details.** On the Details tab, the "Summary tasks", "Row totals", and "Column totals" checkboxes are automatically turned on to include summary tasks in the report, totals at the bottom of each time period, and totals at the end of each task or resource row. The "Summary tasks" checkbox is grayed out for resource reports.

  A crosstab report turns on the "Between tasks" checkbox for a task report to draw horizontal lines between each task. If you want horizontal lines between each assignment, turn on the "Between resources" checkbox, too. In a resource report, turn on both checkboxes to see gridlines between every assignment.

The "Show zero values" checkbox is turned off initially, which is usually what you want. The empty boxes for zero values make it easy to see the values that do exist. The "Repeat first column on every page" checkbox is turned on initially so task or resource names are visible on every page as the report. You can also choose the date format for column headings.

Note: The Sort tab and the Text buttons do the same things they do for task and resource reports.

Customizing a calendar report

A monthly calendar report is like a Calendar view with task bars. You can filter the tasks that appear, choose the calendar, and change the task bar appearance. None of Project's built-in text-based reports use the calendar report type. To create a monthly calendar report, choose Project→Reports→Reports. In the Reports dialog box, double-click Custom, and then click New. In the Define New Report dialog box, select Monthly Calendar, and then click OK. Here are the settings you can choose to customize the report:

- **Filter.** Choose a filter to restrict the tasks that appear in the calendar report. Turn on the Highlight checkbox to shade tasks that pass the filter. Otherwise, the report hides tasks that don't pass the filter.

- **Calendar.** Choose the calendar you want to display. For example, you can choose a base calendar or a resource calendar to see the working time for a specific resource.

- **Formatting.** Initially, a calendar shows nonworking days as gray, which is usually what you want. Otherwise, working and nonworking days are white. Turn on "Solid bar breaks" to draw a solid bar when a task continues to the next week to make it easier to see when tasks really end. The "Print gray bands" checkbox comes into play only when a date box can't hold all the tasks that occur during that time. On extra pages, the report prints tasks that occur on each day, with gray bands separating each day.

- **Show tasks as.** In this section, choose an option for the appearance of tasks. The Bars option is selected initially, but you can also show tasks as single lines or as start and finish dates.

- **Label tasks with.** You can include the task ID, name, and duration on task bars.

Working with Visual Reports

The questions that stakeholders ask in status meetings shift like quicksand: "When did costs start exceeding the budget?" "How are employees doing compared with contractors?" "Who's available to help bail out troubled tasks?" Text-based reports have fixed formats, so you're out of luck if your report doesn't answer the question on the table. Project's visual reports use Excel pivot charts and Visio pivot diagrams, so you can change them on the fly, whether to respond to questions or to drill down to unearth problems.

The ability to slice and dice data in different ways sets these reports apart from other reports, whether you use the text-based reports in Project or you generate reports from a high-powered reporting tool. For example, you may start with costs by fiscal quarter, but one quick change and the report can show costs by phase or resource. It's just as easy to change the graph from cost to work, examine a few time periods in detail while summarizing others, or look at specific tasks and resources. The box below explains what makes visual reports tick.

Project gets you started with several built-in visual reports (page 464), whose initial presentation is like the serving suggestions you see on cracker boxes. You can modify the report in real time until it's the way you want.

This section starts with the easy part: generating a visual report. Your options for massaging the report multiply once the report is open in Excel or Visio. The Pivot tools in Excel and Visio are a little different, so this chapter describes how to use both. You'll also learn how to modify or create visual report templates to produce custom visual reports.

Note: Excel-based visual reports show information in bar graphs, pie charts, or line graphs. These reports work best when you want to compare values side by side or look for trends. Visio-based visual reports break information down in a hierarchy, like a work breakdown structure. You can drill down level by level, and use icons to highlight good, bad, and indifferent values.

UP TO SPEED

Changing Your Perspective

Visual reports take advantage of the pivot table concept, so named because you can turn the data in different directions—pivoting it to gain a new perspective. For example, you may want to see your project phase by phase, and then twist it around to see overall performance quarter by quarter.

To make these contortions look easy, a visual report builds a specialized database called an OLAP (online analytical processing) cube on your computer, and then connects it to an Excel pivot table or Visio pivot diagram. A *data cube* (which has a *.cub* file extension) stores data in a format

that makes it easy to retrieve data by different categories. For example, in a marketing department, you may want to find customers by household income, hobbies, or Zip code. Each OLAP cube category is like one dimension of a real-world cube, except that OLAP cubes can go beyond three dimensions. In Project visual reports, tasks, resources, and time are the most common dimensions.

After a visual report creates its data cube, it hooks the cube up to a pivot table or pivot diagram. At that point, it's your turn to use the tools in Excel and Visio to model the data into the presentation you want.

Generating a Visual Report

Generating a visual report is easy: Select the visual report template you want, and off you go. The template takes care of gathering the data for the cube and setting up the initial pivot table or pivot diagram. This section describes the steps for generating a visual report from an existing template:

1. **Choose Project→Reports→Visual Reports.**

   The Visual Reports–Create Report dialog box opens, as shown in Figure 17-8. Although the All tab is selected initially, you can click a tab to see specific types of visual reports. Summary reports show overall results and don't include time-phased data. For example, the Resource Summary visual report totals values for resources, such as actual work or remaining work. Usage visual reports, like their view counterparts, do have time-phased data. The Assignment visual reports are the most useful because they include time-phased data about both tasks and resources, so you can look at your project from every angle.

   When you start developing custom visual report templates, the All tab may fill up. You can look for more specific reports by selecting a tab like Task Summary. For example, the built-in Cash Flow Report is in the Task Usage category, because it focuses on task costs over time. The Critical Tasks Report is in the Task Summary category, because it looks at total results for critical tasks.

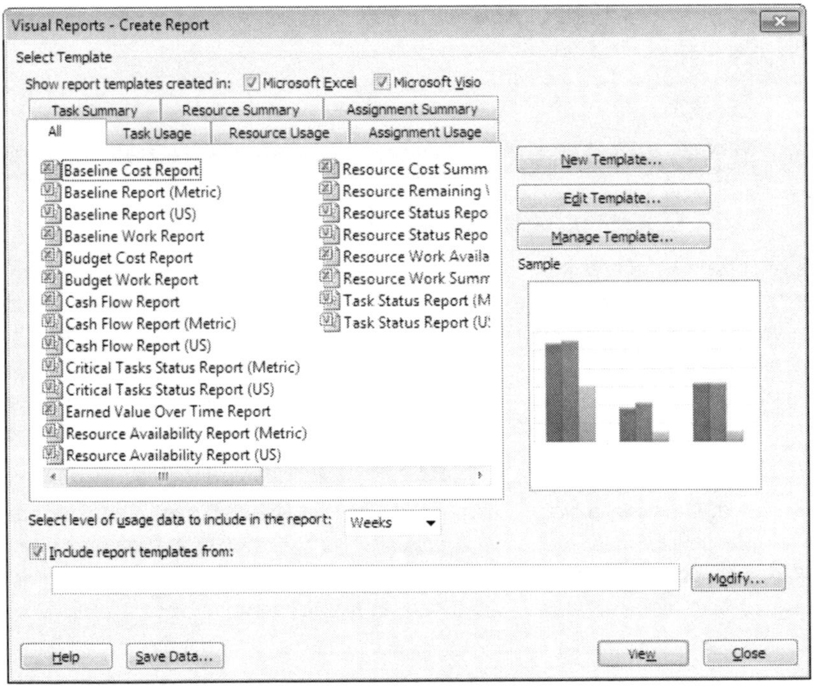

Figure 17-8:
Initially, the All tab is selected, and the checkboxes for both Excel and Visio reports are turned on, so every available visual report appears in the list. Turn either checkbox off to see only Excel or Visio-based visual reports.

2. **Select the visual report you want to use.**

   On the right side of the dialog box, check out the preview of the visual report to see if the general format of the report (bar graph, pie chart, or tree) is what you want. To truly tell whether a visual report is what you want, you need to click View to generate the report.

3. **Choose the time period for usage data.**

   In the "Select level of usage data to include in the report" drop-down list, choose Days, Weeks, Months, Quarters, or Years.

   Days or Weeks are better for shorter projects. For longer projects, choose the shortest period you're likely to evaluate, like Weeks or Months. Collecting too much usage data can slow the visual report performance to a crawl.

4. **Click View.**

   An Excel-based visual report starts Excel and then sets up an Excel file with the data cube attached to it. The Excel spreadsheet has two worksheets. The Chart1 worksheet is a *pivot chart*—a graph that displays the data. The second worksheet is a *pivot table*, which contains the cube data. As you expand, collapse, and re-orient the pivot table, as described on page 469, the pivot chart does the same.

   A Visio-based report starts Visio and creates a pivot diagram. The Visio file usually contains two drawing pages. Page 1 is the diagram itself; if the VBackground-1 page is present, it's simply a Visio background page for adding graphics like your corporate logo.

Rearranging and Formatting an Excel Visual Report

The real fun begins after the visual report is open. Excel's pivot chart tools let you knead the report into the shape you want. This section describes the different ways you can configure an Excel visual report.

When you open a visual report in Excel, you may see only the pivot chart. To display the pivot chart tools and the PivotTable Field List, shown in Figure 17-9, click anywhere in the graph.

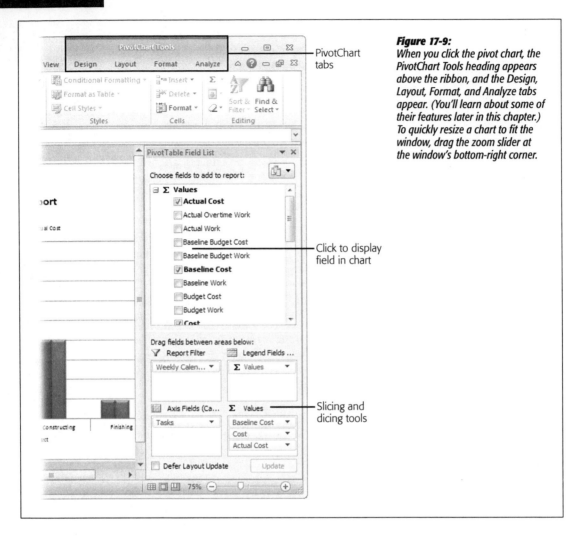

Figure 17-9:
When you click the pivot chart, the PivotChart Tools heading appears above the ribbon, and the Design, Layout, Format, and Analyze tabs appear. (You'll learn about some of their features later in this chapter.) To quickly resize a chart to fit the window, drag the zoom slider at the window's bottom-right corner.

Adding the measures you want to see to the graph

On the pivot chart, the fields you care about (like cost, hours of work, availability, and so on) usually show up as vertical bars in the chart. If you change the type of chart, the values may appear as a series of connected line segments, data points, 3-D bars, and so on. The fields that you select also show up as the columns in the pivot table worksheet.

Although a visual report gathers data into its OLAP cube, the pivot chart doesn't display every field in the cube. When the visual report is open in Excel, you can add, remove, or change the fields that appear in the pivot chart.

The PivotTable Field List is a task pane to the right of the pivot chart, shown in Figure 17-9. A visual report template comes with a few fields turned on, identified by checkmarks in the checkboxes to the left of the names, which are also bolded. Use the following methods to add and rearrange the fields in the pivot chart:

- **Add or remove fields.** To include another field in the pivot chart, simply click its checkbox so the checkmark appears. To remove a field, click the checkbox, and the checkmark disappears. You can also add a field by dragging the field name into the Σ Values box at the bottom of the task pane.

- **Reorder fields.** In the Σ Values box, drag a field to a new location in the list.

- **Change the field calculation.** In the Σ Values box, click the field, and then choose Value Field Settings. In the Value Field Settings dialog box, click the Summarize Values By tab. In the "Summarize value field by" list, select the calculation you want. Depending on the field, you can choose calculations like Sum, Average, Minimum Value, Maximum Value, Count, and so on.

Note: If the PivotTable Field List isn't visible, then under PivotChart Tools, select the Analyze tab and then, in the Show/Hide section, click Field List.

Filtering the data that appears

Like filtering in Project, you can filter the information that appears in a visual report. If costs and delays have cropped up recently, for example, you can filter the report to show data only for the current fiscal quarter. Likewise, you could filter a report to show only specific resources.

To use a field as a report filter, drag the field into the Report Filter box in the task pane. The Baseline Cost report initially uses time (which appears as the Weekly Calendar) as the report filter. To filter by another category, such as tasks, follow these steps:

1. **To switch the report to task filtering, for example, drag Tasks from the Row Labels box into the Report Filter box.**

   The report is set up to filter by tasks but still shows all tasks. When the pivot table is active, the filter label says Row Labels. When the pivot chart is active, the filter label is Axis Fields (Categories).

2. **To select specific tasks to display, in the pivot table, click the Tasks down arrow, as illustrated in Figure 17-10.**

   Initially, the drop-down list shows only the top-level category. For tasks, you see the name of the project. If you filter by time, you see calendar years.

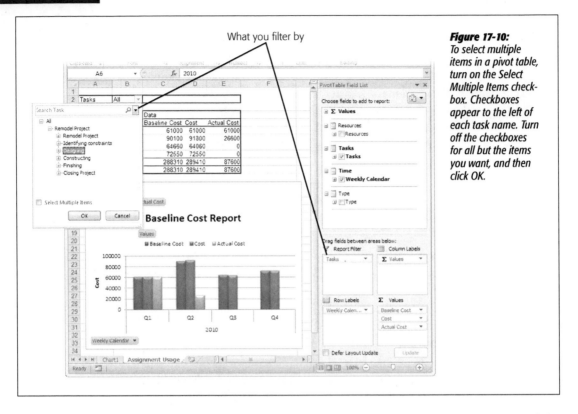

What you filter by

Figure 17-10:
To select multiple items in a pivot table, turn on the Select Multiple Items check-box. Checkboxes appear to the left of each task name. Turn off the checkboxes for all but the items you want, and then click OK.

3. **To select a specific task as the filter, like one phase of the project, expand the tasks until the one you want is visible. Select it, and then click OK.**

   After you select a task to filter by, the name of the task appears in the filter cell to the right of the Tasks cell. When a filter is in place, the down arrow in the filter cell changes to the filter icon, a funnel with a down arrow below it.

Tip: You may notice down arrows to the right of the other fields in the pivot table—for example to the right of the Year cell. You can filter within those categories, too, by clicking the down arrow and then choosing a filter to apply. For example, if you use resources as a category, then select the resources you want to evaluate more closely. If you're looking at the pivot chart, you can apply filters by clicking the buttons at the bottom of the chart. For example, to filter by resources, click the Resources button and then turn checkboxes on or off.

Categorizing information

The rows in a pivot table typically represent tasks, resources, or time. For example, the Baseline Cost report opens a pivot table with a row for the entire project and additional rows for each top-level task (like project phases). Changing the category for rows is how you examine data from different perspectives, for example to show costs over time or by resource. You can also add categories to break down values further, for instance to look at cost per phase broken down to each resource working on a phase.

These categories group information on the pivot chart's x-axis like the top-level tasks in the standard Baseline Cost report. Each top-level task has its own set of field bars. You add or remove categories by adding or removing fields in the task pane's Row Labels box (called Axis Fields if the pivot chart is active). For example, to break down the Baseline Cost report by time periods, drag the Weekly Calendar from the Report Filter box into the Row Labels box.

A pivot chart can slice up your project even further—just add another category to the Row Labels box. For example, to analyze cost by time period and then by resource, as shown in Figure 17-11, drag the Resources field from the Pivot Table Field List into the Row Labels box, and then drop it below the Weekly Calendar. By doing so, each resource who works during a time period has his own set of field bars. For example, the architect has field bars for Q1 and again in Q2.

Tip: In this example, a copy of the pivot chart is pasted onto the pivot table worksheet. That way, you can preview the pivot chart as you tweak settings on the pivot table. When the pivot chart looks good, you can print the one on the Chart1 worksheet, or copy and paste either one into a Word document or a PowerPoint presentation.

Summarizing and drilling down

Drilling down into details or soaring up to summary views is almost effortless in visual reports. Click expand buttons (+) or collapse buttons (–) on the pivot table worksheet. Whatever you can see in the pivot table is what you see in the pivot chart, as Figure 17-11 also illustrates.

For example, the Baseline Cost report in the figure is set up to show costs for different time periods. To expand the year 2010 to show each quarter, click the + sign to the left of 2010.

If you want to expand a quarter to show costs by week, click the + button to the left of the quarter (Q1, for instance). The entire report doesn't have to be expanded or collapsed to the same level. One section of the report can show weeks while the rest of the report stays summarized.

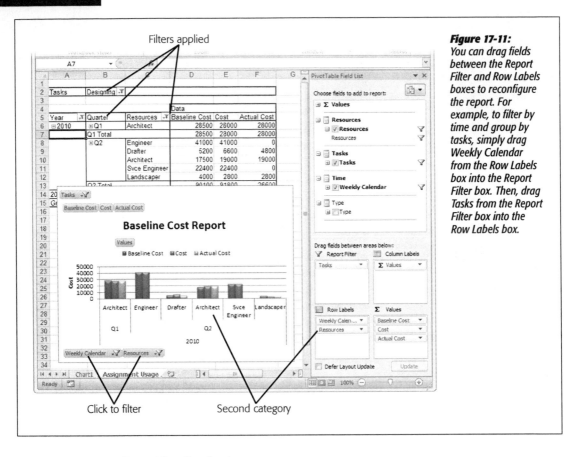

Filters applied

Click to filter

Second category

Figure 17-11:
You can drag fields between the Report Filter and Row Labels boxes to reconfigure the report. For example, to filter by time and group by tasks, simply drag Weekly Calendar from the Row Labels box into the Report Filter box. Then, drag Tasks from the Report Filter box into the Row Labels box.

Formatting the chart

Pivot charts are more muscular than most Excel charts, but you use the same methods for making them look good. For example, you can change the chart type, use a different bar style, and format the labels. Here are a few of the more common formatting tasks:

- **Choose chart type.** Sometimes, a different type of chart shows information more clearly. For instance, cumulative cost is easier to understand when you draw it as a single line. Right-click the pivot chart and then choose Change Chart Type. In the Change Chart Type dialog box, select the type of chart, and then select the appearance of the bars or lines. The other way to open the Change Chart Type dialog box is on the ribbon. Under PivotChart Tools, select the Design tab, and then choose Chart Type to do the same thing.

- **Formatting labels.** To change the appearance of chart labels, select the Layout tab, and then choose Chart Title, Axis Titles, Legend, Data Labels, and so on. You can also format portions of the chart by right-clicking what you want to format and then, on the shortcut menu, choosing a command like Format Chart Title.

- **Rotate text to remove overlaps.** If the pivot chart contains more than a few resources, tasks, or time periods, the labels along the x-axis are likely to overlap. To fix this overlapping, realign the text vertically. Right-click the overlapping labels on the x-axis, and then choose Format Axis. In the Format Axis dialog box, select Alignment. On the Alignment page, in the "Text direction" box, click the down arrow, and then choose "Rotate all text 90°".

Tip: When you right-click the pivot chart, a mini-toolbar appears above the shortcut menu. You can format different parts of the pivot chart by choosing the element in the drop-down list (which initially says Plot Area). Then, on the mini-toolbar, choose the formatting you want to apply, like bold, italic, or a fill color.

Rearranging and Formatting a Visio Visual Report

Visio-based visual reports use a Visio pivot diagram. A pivot diagram opens with a single top node, which represents your entire project. You can break the diagram down to additional levels by adding categories. The nodes in a pivot diagram typically show field values, but a Visio visual report is best when you want to display icons to indicate status.

The tools and settings appear in the PivotDiagram task pane when you open a pivot diagram. Similar to their Excel counterparts, Visio pivot diagrams accept additional fields and several levels of categories. In addition, Data Graphics are the secret behind the status icons you see. The following are several of the more common changes you may make to a pivot diagram:

- **Add a new breakdown.** To break down a node into more detail, you add a category to that node. Right-click the node, and then, from the shortcut menu, choose Add Category. On the submenu, choose Resources:Resources, Type:Type, or Tasks:Tasks, as shown in Figure 17-12. For example, if the first level of the diagram shows project phases, you can add Tasks as the second level to build the equivalent of a work breakdown structure diagram. If you add Resources instead, then you can see how resources contribute to task values.

  To remove a level, right-click the node to which the level is attached, for example, right-click Resources and then, on the shortcut menu, choose Collapse.

- **Change fields in nodes.** Visual report nodes contain some fields, but you can add or remove fields to show what you want. In the PivotDiagram task pane, in the Add Total section, turn on the checkboxes for the fields you want to see. Turn checkboxes off to remove those fields from the nodes.

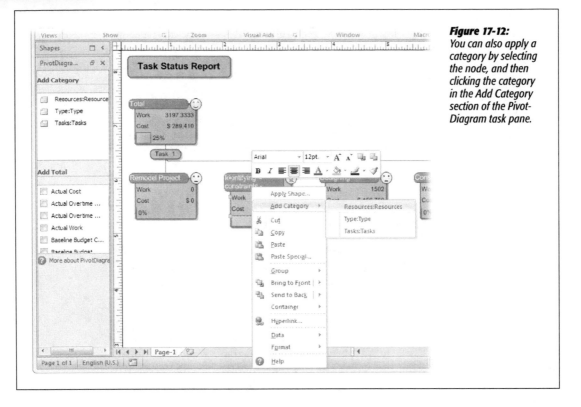

Figure 17-12:
You can also apply a category by selecting the node, and then clicking the category in the Add Category section of the Pivot-Diagram task pane.

- **Filter data.** A level in a pivot diagram initially includes OLAP cube data for your entire project. You can filter a level to show information for part of a project. Right-click the small shape between levels, which contains a category name like Task 1 and then, on the shortcut menu, choose Configure Level. In the Configure Level dialog box, you can define conditions that nodes must meet—for example, a test that requires that Tasks contains "Design" filters the diagram to show only the design tasks in the project.

- **Combine nodes.** You can combine nodes in several ways with the Merge, Promote, and Collapse commands. On the PivotDiagram tab on the ribbon, click the command you want. For example, to combine two summary tasks, select them, and then choose the Merge command. The values in the merged node show the total for both tasks.

- **Change the diagram background.** Background pages are the place to add your corporate logo or a watermark of some kind. Most Visio visual reports include a Vbackground-1 page for just this purpose. If a diagram doesn't include a background page, choose Insert→Pages→Blank Page→Background Page. In the Page Setup dialog box, on the Page Properties tab, select the Background option, and then type a new name for the page. You can drag a background shape from the Visio Backgrounds stencil or insert the graphic file for your corporate logo.

- **Quickly format the diagram.** In Visio, themes are color-coordinated packages of formatting that help you make your diagrams look good (even if you wear plaids with stripes). To change the appearance of your diagram, choose Design→Themes, and then click the theme you want. The diagram changes automatically.

Note: To learn more about Visio pivot diagrams and other types of Visio diagrams, see the *Visio 2007 Bible* by Bonnie Biafore (Wiley).

Customizing Visual Report Templates

Visual reports are so flexible that customizing them may not occur to you. But once you realize that you're frequently making the same field, category, and filter changes, you can eliminate this busywork by saving the modified pivot chart or pivot diagram as a visual report template. A template saves the visual report definition, not the actual data. When you use the new report template, it generates a pivot chart or pivot diagram according to your preferred report settings.

At a lower level, you can also customize the data in a visual report's cube. Cubes come with plenty of fields, but you can add fields you want or remove fields you don't need.

Because visual reports are really Excel pivot charts or Visio pivot diagrams, visual report templates are simply Excel or Visio template files. Whether you copy a built-in template or create one from scratch, you pick the fields to include and the type of cube, and then set up the pivot chart or pivot diagram to look the way you want. Here are the details:

1. Choose Project→Reports→Visual Reports.

   The Visual Report–Create Report dialog box opens.

2. Select the built-in visual report template closest to what you want, and then click Edit Template.

   The Visual Reports–Field Picker dialog box appears. Although you're editing an existing template, later on, when you save the template with a new name, you'll have a brand-new template.

   To create a new template from scratch, click New Template. In the Visual Reports New Template dialog box, select the Excel, Visio (Metric), or Visio (US Units) option to specify the type of visual report. Under Select Data Type, choose the type of cube (Task Summary, Resource Summary, or Assignment Summary for total information; Task Usage, Resource Usage, or Assignment Usage for time-phased data). Click Field Picker, and you're ready for step 3.

3. **In the Available Fields list, select the fields you want, and then click Add.**

The Selected Fields list shows fields already tagged for inclusion in the data cube. When you click Add, the fields you pick jump to the Selected Fields list. To remove fields, select them in the Selected Fields list, and then click Remove. As with other list boxes, Ctrl-clicking and Shift-clicking work for selecting several fields.

Tip: A few fields have "(Dimension)" after their names, which means they're the categories that the cube uses to organize data—the same categories you use to create additional levels in a Visio pivot diagram or to group and filter data in a pivot chart. Most visual reports use up to three dimension fields. For your own reports, keep the dimension fields to less than six, or the report's performance will slow down significantly.

---

4. **In the Visual Reports–Field Picker dialog box, click Edit Template.**

Project builds the OLAP cube with the fields you selected and then starts Excel or Visio (depending on the type of report).

5. **Modify the report so it looks the way you want.**

Use the techniques described in this chapter to customize the arrangement and formatting of the pivot chart. If you're building a brand-new pivot table, the Excel worksheet has some guides to help you add fields in the right place, as illustrated in Figure 17-13.

6. **Save the report as a template.**

For an Excel template, choose File→Save As. In the Save As dialog box, in the "Save as type" drop-down list, choose Excel Template. In the "File name" box, type a new name for the template, and then click Save.

For a Visio template, choose File→Save As. In the Save As dialog box, from the "Save as type" drop-down menu, choose Template. Type a new name for the file, and then click Save.

Note: To see custom templates in the Visual Reports dialog box, make sure the "Include report templates from" checkbox is turned on. Click Modify to set the path to your templates folder.

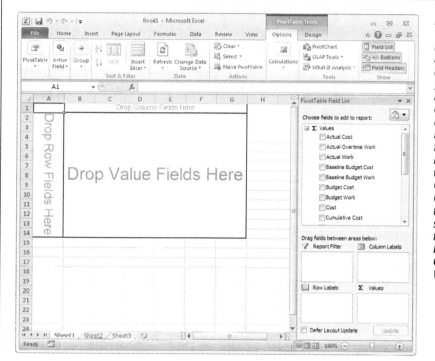

Figure 17-13:
*The PivotTable Field
List task pane in Excel
is exactly the same as
the one you see when
you're working on a
report. You can turn
on field checkboxes to
add them to the table.
Drag fields from the
field area into the
labeled areas on the
worksheet like Drop
Column Fields Here.
Or, if the boxes in the
task pane make more
sense to you, drag
fields into Report
Filter, Row Labels,
Column Labels, and Σ
Values.*

Saving Report Data

When you generate a visual report, Project chugs along for a few seconds (or minutes) as it gathers data into an OLAP cube, like a chipmunk gathering acorns in its
cheeks. That data can work beyond the report you're generating at the moment. For
example, the data cube is a snapshot of project status. And unlike the 11 Project
baselines you can save, the number of data cubes is limited only by your disk space.
You could save a data cube every month and open them to look for trends. You can
open a cube directly in Excel or Visio and then use the built-in pivot chart and pivot
diagram tools to view the information.

Here are the steps for saving project data:

1. **In the Visual Reports–Create Report dialog box, click Save Data.**

   The Visual Reports–Save Reporting Data dialog box opens.

2. **Choose the type of OLAP cube you want to save.**

   Task Summary, Resource Summary, and Assignment Summary cubes contain
   total work and cost data. Task Usage, Resource Usage, and Assignment Usage
   cubes include time-phased data like the data in usage views.

3. To choose fields other than the ones the cube contains, click Field Picker.

   Select fields as described on page 473, and then click OK.

4. **Click Save Cube or Save Database.**

   Saving a cube creates a larger database file but makes data based on the cube dimensions easier to find. Saving a database creates a regular Access database.

5. **In the Save As dialog box, type the name for the file and click Save.**

   Back in the Visual Reports–Save Reporting Data dialog box, click Close.

To open saved data directly in Excel, do the following:

1. **In Excel, choose Insert→PivotTable, and then choose PivotTable or PivotChart.**

   The Create PivotTable or Create PivotChart dialog box opens. Both boxes have the same settings, but the first one creates only a pivot table. A pivot chart creates both the pivot chart and the pivot table that contains the data.

2. **Select the "Use an external data source" option, and then click Choose Connection.**

   In the Existing Connections dialog box, click Browse for More. In the Select Data Source dialog box, navigate to the folder in which you saved the data cube, select the file, and then click Open.

3. **Back in the Create PivotTable or Create PivotChart dialog box, click OK.**

   A new pivot table or pivot chart appears. The PivotTable Field List displays the fields from the cube or database, and you're ready to use the same pivot tools you've already met.

Printing Views to Report Project Information

A picture is worth a thousand words—and more than a thousand numbers in a view table. In Project, you can print views like the Gantt Chart, Task Usage view, or Tracking Gantt to include in the reports you produce for stakeholders, management, and other audiences. (The box on page 478 talks about another way to create a document from a view.) Here's how you set up a view to print the way you want:

1. **Display the view you want and make sure the information is the way you want it when you print.**

   For example, apply the table you want. If necessary, insert, remove, or rearrange the columns in the table. For a view with a table and a timescale, drag the vertical divider so you see the amount of table and timescale you want. Adjust the timescale to the scale you want.

2. Choose File→Print.

   The Print page of the Backstage view appears. Printer settings are on the left side, and a preview of the view appears on the right side of the Print page.

3. **As you would for any other printout, choose the printer, the number of copies, the page range you want to print, the paper orientation, and the paper size.**

   If you change the paper orientation or size, the preview changes to show what the printout looks like.

4. **With views that include a timescale, in the Dates boxes, choose the date range you want to display.**

   Fill in the first box with the earliest date in the date range. Fill in the "to" box with the last date in the range.

5. **To set up the printed page, click Page Setup at the bottom of the Print page.**

   The Page Setup dialog box opens with tabs similar to those in other programs. For example, on the Page tab, you can choose the paper orientation and size, adjust the scale of the view, or specify the number of pages to use to print the view. The Margins tab lets you adjust the margins on the page. The Header and Footer tabs are where you specify information to display in the header and footer of the printout.

6. **To specify whether the printout includes a legend, select the Legend tab, and then select the option you want.**

   Project selects the "Every page" option, as shown in Figure 17-14, which means that a legend that identifies the bars appears on every page. To save some trees and show more of your project on each page, select the "Legend page" option, which includes one page with a legend.

7. **To fine-tune what appears on the printed page, select the View tab. Then turn on the checkboxes for the elements you want.**

   For example, to print all the columns in the table, turn on the "Print all sheet columns" checkbox. To print a specific number of columns on every page of the printout, turn on the "Print first __ columns on all pages" checkbox, and choose the number of columns. You can also choose to print notes, blank pages, or adjust the timescale to fill the page.

8. **When the settings are the way you want, click Print.**

   The view prints.

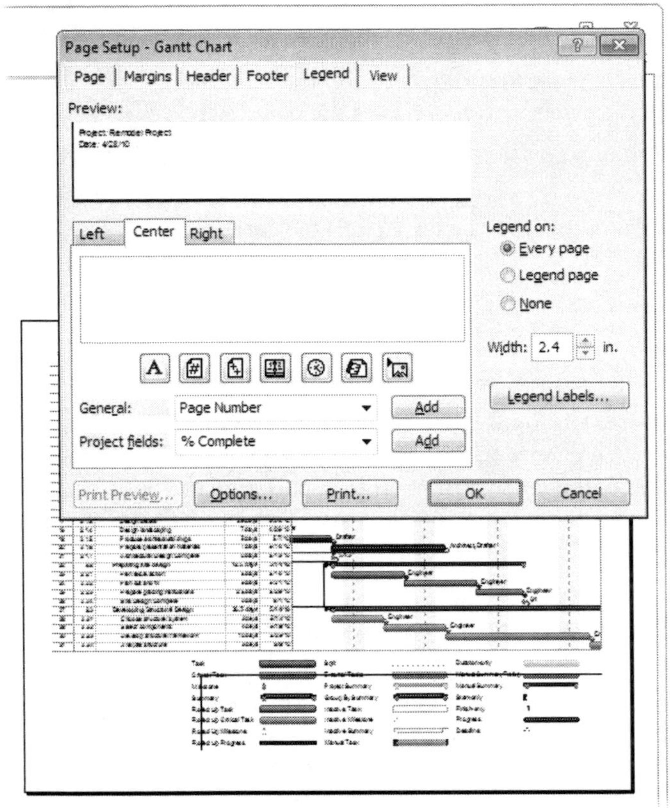

Figure 17-14:
If you know what the elements in the view represent, select the None option. You can also specify the width of the legend by choosing the number of inches in the Width box. If you want to adjust the text formatting for the legend, click Legend Labels.

UP TO SPEED

Creating a PDF or XPS Document

In Project 2010, you can create a copy of your project in PDF or XPS format. These two file formats contain the text data that you save, so you can index the files or copy information out of them. In addition, the file formats keep all the formatting, fonts, and graphics that appear on your screen and spit them out looking the same on almost any computer. Anyone can view these documents using free viewers you can download. To create one of these documents, follow these steps:

1. Choose File→Save & Send.

2. On the Save & Send page of the Backstage view, choose Create PDF/XPS Document, and then click Create PDF/XPS.

3. In the Browse dialog box, navigate to the folder in which you want to save the file.

4. Name the file.

5. In the "Save as type" drop-down list, choose PDF Files or XPS Files.

6. Click OK.

7. If necessary, specify the export options you want, and then click OK.

Closing a Project

If you've ever moved to a new house, you know how additional things to pack seem to appear out of thin air the closer you get to the end. Projects have loose ends to tie up, too. After the project team hands over the last deliverable, the project's scope is complete, but you still have a few project management tasks to finish. Getting formal project acceptance from the customer is first and foremost—because the project isn't done until the customer says it is.

Once the project is done and accepted, it's time to write a final report to wrap up the project and document useful information for the future. A *project closeout report* is like a higher-level version of the status and other project reports you've produced all along. The closeout report summarizes project results, highlighting lessons learned, issues dealt with, and risks that became reality. It should also include a final accounting of schedule and budget—the values and variances of actual dates and costs compared to your baseline.

This chapter describes the information you need to gather for closeout reports, and which Project reports you can use. It also gives tips on identifying lessons learned without ruffling anyone's feathers.

The final step is storing project information for future reference, using information storage strategies introduced in Chapter 13. In this chapter, you'll learn about different destinations for your final project documents.

Obtaining Project Acceptance

You may be waiting for the check to be signed, but project acceptance is the key to closing a project—and keeping it closed. Unless you get formal acceptance from whomever has the final say, someone could come back later claiming a deliverable is missing, or the results aren't quite right after all.

The deliverables and success criteria (page 40) you carefully documented in the project plan guided the project team through project execution. They're even more important at project acceptance, because you and the project customer use them to measure success and finally dub the project complete:

- **Deliverables** tend to be tangible. Either there's a new building at 24 Main Street or there isn't. On the contrary, success criteria can be subjective. The more diligent you are in hashing out clear and quantifiable success criteria, the easier it is to obtain project acceptance.

- If **success criteria** aren't completely clear, acceptance may take some time. When you finally get there, a signature is essential. Signing a document makes it harder for the customer to renege. Face-to-face meetings seem to give a sign-off more weight, but a conference call to deliver acceptance verbally (followed up with a signed hard copy) is the next best thing.

The acceptance form can be straightforward, as illustrated in Figure 18-1. Like other contractual documents, copy the signed document and distribute the copies to the signers and others you need to notify that the project is complete. You can download a sign-off document template, Ch18_Acceptance_Signoff.dot, from *www.missing-manuals.com/cds*.

Tying Up Loose Ends

Transitioning resources is another part of closing a project. What resources do when they finish their work for you may not seem like your problem. However, before they start popping champagne corks and playing Twister, it's in your best interest to make sure that people have completed everything you need for your project, *and* that their managers know when to line up their next assignments. Winning points with resource managers may make it easier for you to get resources on your next project, so managing resource handoffs is a win-win proposition.

Also, any contracts written for your project (with the project customer, vendors, subcontractors, and so on) must be closed. Every contract spells out the steps required to close it. Your job is to perform those steps and get sign-offs on all contracts.

Project financial accounting typically doesn't end right away. It's easier to keep the books open for a while so you can handle project expenses that show up later, like support costs, employee expense reports, and so on. On the other hand, take whatever steps you need to with the accounting department so no one can charge additional hours to the project.

Figure 18-1:
The most important part of the project acceptance document is the John Hancock from whoever has authority to accept the project. You can add other elements like a list of completed deliverables if you want to be very clear about what the customer is accepting.

The figure shows a word processor window with the following content:

<Project Name> Project Acceptance

Project name: [Click here and type project name]

Project manager: [Click here and type project manager name]

Customer name: [Click here and type customer name]

- Deliverables handed off ☐
- Success criteria met ☐
- Project accepted ☐

Approved by: _____

Print name: _____

Title: _____

Date: _____

Project sponsor: _____

Title: _____

Date: _____

Page: 1 of 1   Words: 49

Producing Project Closeout Reports

A project closeout report is like a status report on steroids. It summarizes project results, risks and issues encountered, and lessons learned. It also presents final performance numbers, including schedule and budget performance, and earned value. This section describes what usually goes into a project closeout report, and identifies Project reports you can run to obtain the information you need.

Summarizing a Project

Audiences want to know what's important, and they don't want to spend time digging. A project closeout report summarizes results for quick and easy reading, as the example in Figure 18-2 illustrates. (Folks with a penchant for detail and too much time on their hands can peruse the entire project archive, if they want.)

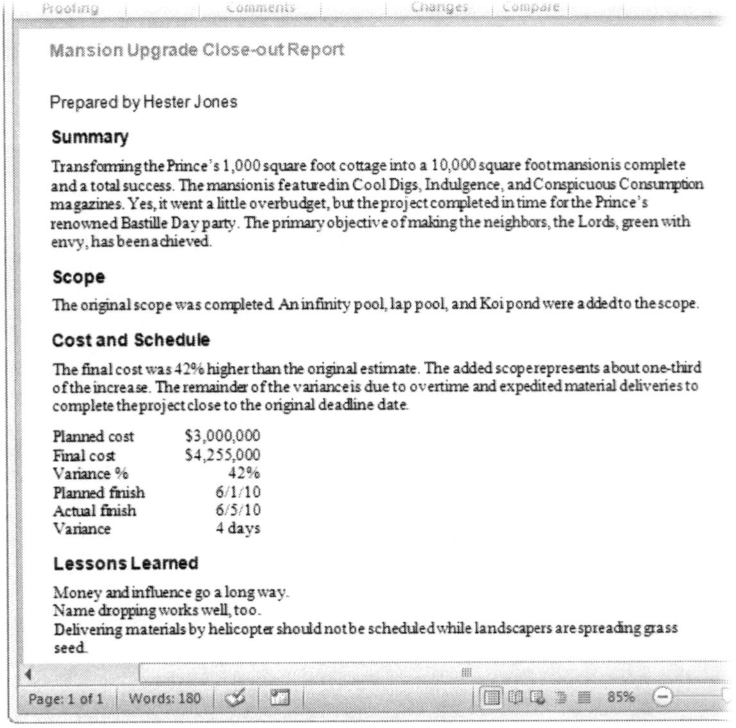

Mansion Upgrade Close-out Report

Prepared by Hester Jones

Summary

Transforming the Prince's 1,000 square foot cottage into a 10,000 square foot mansion is complete and a total success. The mansion is featured in Cool Digs, Indulgence, and Conspicuous Consumption magazines. Yes, it went a little overbudget, but the project completed in time for the Prince's renowned Bastille Day party. The primary objective of making the neighbors, the Lords, green with envy, has been achieved.

Scope

The original scope was completed. An infinity pool, lap pool, and Koi pond were added to the scope.

Cost and Schedule

The final cost was 42% higher than the original estimate. The added scope represents about one-third of the increase. The remainder of the variance is due to overtime and expedited material deliveries to complete the project close to the original deadline date.

Planned cost	$3,000,000
Final cost	$4,255,000
Variance %	42%
Planned finish	6/1/10
Actual finish	6/5/10
Variance	4 days

Lessons Learned

Money and influence go a long way.
Name dropping works well, too.
Delivering materials by helicopter should not be scheduled while landscapers are spreading grass seed.

Figure 18-2: *A closeout report for a small project may require no more than one page. For large projects or those that ran into trouble, you may want to include more detail to answer questions before anyone has a chance to ask.*

In addition to the performance reports described in the next section, the closeout report includes an analysis of what happened and a synopsis of the most significant results. These are the main items in a project closeout summary:

- **Summary.** This section is like the Letter to Shareholders that a CEO writes for a company's annual report; it's a 30,000-foot view of what the project accomplished.
- **Completed scope.** List the completed scope and deliverables. Identify any items from the original scope that weren't completed (and why).
- **Changes.** If the scope changed significantly, summarize what was left out or added. Describe other significant changes, like a major redesign to simplify manufacturing.

- **Explanation of variances.** If the project performance strayed from the baseline, explain why, and include recommendations for improving future performance.

- **Risks and issues.** Document significant issues and risks that arose. Describe what you did in response and the results. Highlight risks that arose that you didn't identify initially in the risk management plan. You may want to include close calls averted by your clever evasive actions and emergency measures.

- **Lessons learned.** Describe the most significant lessons learned (page 484).

Reporting Performance

Closeout reports also include quantitative data like cost and schedule variances or project-specific measures like quality-oriented success criteria. You can produce all kinds of schedule and cost reports in Project using visual reports (page 462) or text-based reports. Here are some of the project performance measures you may include in a closeout report, along with the Project reports that show them:

Cost performance

Closeout reports usually compare actual cost to baseline cost and show the variance between the two. For large projects, you may want to break down costs in other ways, such as labor cost, material cost, and other types of expenses. Here are some of Project's cost-related reports:

- The **Budget Cost** visual report is great for slicing and dicing costs by tasks, resources, and types of cost.

- The **Cash Flow** visual report comes in handy when you want to calculate other financial measures, like return on investment or internal rate of return (page 30).

- The **Earned Value Over Time** visual report charts cost and schedule performance over the life of the project.

- The **Overbudget Tasks** and **Overbudget Resources** text-based reports are great for showing where variances came from.

Schedule performance

A Gantt Chart view that shows the baseline schedule, like Tracking Gantt, for example, may be the most effective way to compare actual dates to the baseline. The timescale shows the variance visually.

You can also use earned value to show schedule performance (page 420). With earned value, schedule variance is shown in terms of dollars—the actual cost minus the planned cost.

Note: Cost gives you some idea how your work estimates compared to reality. The Budget Work visual report can show the hours people worked compared to the baseline.

Quality performance

If quality measures are part of the project success criteria, then include them in your closeout report. The way you present quality performance depends on how you measure quality and where you track that information. For example, if you're measuring the quantity and severity of software defects, you can use your defect-tracking database to produce a graph.

Documenting What You Learned

Most people equate lessons learned with painful or embarrassing experiences. And the alternative term, *postmortem,* is even less appealing. All too many work environments focus on finding a scapegoat rather than identifying and learning from mistakes. Yet improving future project performance requires not only avoiding repetition of past mistakes, but repeating what worked well.

You'd think successes would be easy to find, but they may stay hidden because team members don't realize their significance or don't want to brag. On the other hand, you expect people to shy away from admitting mistakes and failures. It takes a light touch *and* an environment of trust to uncover these touchy subjects.

This section explains why lessons learned are so important to future projects. It also gives some hints on coaxing successes and mistakes out of the project team. After you've identified the lessons, both good and bad, they become part of your project closeout report. In addition, you can publicize this information to help other teams learn from your experience.

Tip: Lessons aren't learned at the end of a project, so why wait until then to identify them? Consider including lessons learned as part of your status meetings, or holding specific lessons-learned sessions upon reaching key milestones.

Don't skip this step!

Sure, everyone's eager to finish the project and get on to something else. Before memory fades, though, get the team together and find out what worked and what didn't. If you need some encouragement to perform this step, here are some ways lessons learned can help:

- **Take advantage of successful techniques.** Continuous improvement is what turned circa-1980 cinder block–sized mobile phones into the tiny, feature-packed cellphones of today. Let everyone build on your team's success, whether you discovered an effective way to obtain approvals quickly, stumbled across a remarkable time-saving technique, or developed reusable documents and checklists.

Tip: Every project may be unique, but you can recycle a lot of your project management work by turning documents and Project schedules into templates (page 676).

- **Defuse unrealistic demands.** Executives are renowned for settings dates and budgets before projects are defined or planned. With past performance and lessons learned, you have ammunition to persuade stakeholders to change the numbers.

- **Don't make the same mistakes.** Mistakes are costly, so you don't want to pay for them more than once. Analyze mistakes and failures so you can prevent them in the future. For example, suppose you used lower-cost resources to save money but ended up spending more because they worked so slowly. On the next project, you can evaluate cost and productivity to decide whom to use. In the business world, cause-and-effect diagrams (also called *fishbone* diagrams, or Ishikawa diagrams after their inventor) and fault-tree analysis are two ways to identify the origins of failure.

- **Build support for project management.** If your organization is new to project management, the opinion may be that it takes too long and costs too much. Lessons learned are real-life examples of why project management is so important, and the results show how project management—or its absence—affected performance. Suppose your project was swamped with changes that blew the schedule and the budget; you can make a case for implementing a change management system.

Gathering what you learned

Without guidance, lessons-learned meetings can alternate between apprehensive silences and finger-pointing melees. Setting up meetings dedicated to lessons learned helps people get in the right mind-set. If you think team members may be hesitant to speak up in front of managers, then set up separate meetings. It's up to you to set a positive tone and run the meetings as effectively as you can. Line up people to perform the following roles, and your meetings will be more productive:

- **Project manager.** OK, you don't have to assign someone to this role, because it's yours. Your job is to plan the meeting beforehand as you would any other type of meeting. Prepare an agenda; set a time limit; schedule the meeting; invite the attendees; and distribute materials like status reports and issues beforehand. At the beginning of the meeting, review the agenda and the materials you distributed. (Don't assume people have read them beforehand.) During the meeting, you can ask questions, take notes, clarify misunderstandings, and so on. Afterward, you help prepare a lessons-learned report and follow up on action items.

Tip: To make these meetings as nonthreatening as possible, set up ground rules in advance. Print the rules on the agenda, have the facilitator review them at the beginning of the meeting, and remind people if they break them.

- **Facilitator.** You may do double-duty as the facilitator, but a dedicated facilitator is a boon if the meeting has a cast of thousands. The facilitator initially spells out the meeting's purpose and ground rules, and then gets the discussion started. During the meeting, the facilitator keeps the discussion focused on the agenda and makes everyone follow the rules. (The box on page 487 provides some tips for getting discussions going.)
- **Scribe.** Taking notes is a full-time job. Assign someone who's familiar with the project, preferably someone with legible handwriting or speedy keyboarding fingers. To be sure the information you want gets captured, give the scribe a template to fill in, like the one shown in Figure 18-3.

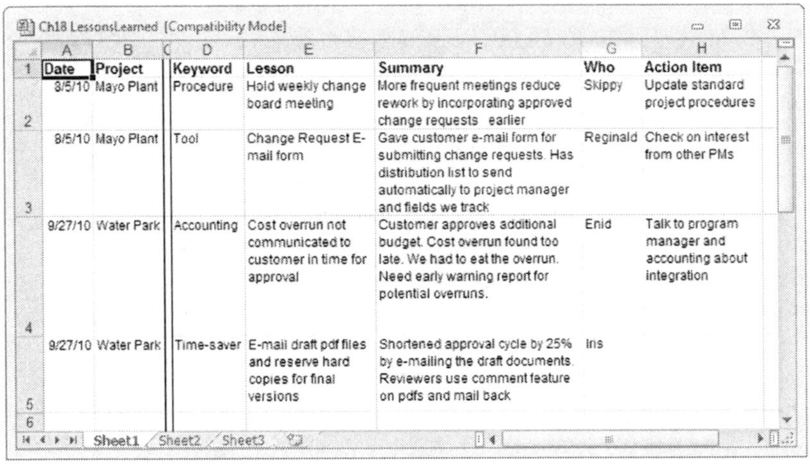

Ch18 LessonsLearned [Compatibility Mode]

Date	Project	Keyword	Lesson	Summary	Who	Action Item
8/5/10	Mayo Plant	Procedure	Hold weekly change board meeting	More frequent meetings reduce rework by incorporating approved change requests earlier	Skippy	Update standard project procedures
8/5/10	Mayo Plant	Tool	Change Request E-mail form	Gave customer e-mail form for submitting change requests. Has distribution list to send automatically to project manager and fields we track	Reginald	Check on interest from other PMs
9/27/10	Water Park	Accounting	Cost overrun not communicated to customer in time for approval	Customer approves additional budget. Cost overrun found too late. We had to eat the overrun. Need early warning report for potential overruns.	Enid	Talk to program manager and accounting about integration
9/27/10	Water Park	Time-saver	E-mail draft pdf files and reserve hard copies for final versions	Shortened approval cycle by 25% by e-mailing the draft documents. Reviewers use comment feature on pdfs and mail back	Iris	

Sheet1 Sheet2 Sheet3

Figure 18-3: *Describe the lesson and include pertinent details. Adding keywords to categorize lessons makes them easier to find later. If action items arise, like updating the project plan template, add them to the lessons learned database and your to-do list.*

Remembering your lessons

The lessons you learn don't do any good if you forget them and no one else finds out about them. Lessons learned are part of the project closeout reports and thus in the project archive, but you need a way to make sure lessons learned get used to improve future projects.

The most effective way to embed lessons learned into the corporate psyche is to add them to existing standard processes and procedures. For example, if a weekly change board meeting improved the turnaround time on change requests, you can update the project plan template or your project management guidelines to recommend that schedule. Publishing a project management newsletter or a company blog are other ways to disseminate significant lessons. A database of lessons learned can come in handy as long as it's easy to search (page 486).

Get Discussions Going

Discussions in lessons-learned meetings can be hard to start. Ask a question like, "Did your assignment go well?" and the answer may be nothing more than "Yes." The trick is to ask open-ended questions—questions that don't invite one-word answers. You might ask, for example, "What helped the most as you worked on your tasks?" "Tell us what you did to deliver your work early," or "What would you do differently next time?"

Ahead of time, review the project and identify tasks that came in early or late, under budget or over budget. Reread the issue and risk logs to see what problems arose. Go through any lessons learned you've collected already. You can use these materials to put together a few questions to jump-start discussion. Ask each attendee about her experiences.

Jotting down notes on a whiteboard or flip chart is another way to prompt discussion. As in brainstorming sessions, these notes may trigger an idea in others.

For mistakes, focus on the problem. Placing blame with a statement like, "You didn't feed the programmers" makes people clam up. Ask questions like, "How can we improve our procedures?" "How did you solve the obstacles you encountered?" or "What would you do differently?"

In poorly managed organizations, you have an added challenge of creating a safe environment for admitting mistakes. You may need a method for providing anonymous feedback.

What to Do with Project Information

After you've prepared final project reports, you stick them in the project notebook (page 361), send them to the stakeholders on the report distribution list, and you're done, right? Well, you *could* stop there, but if you plan to reuse the work you've done or share it with other project managers, you also want to archive project information in a way that's easy for people to find and access. The box on page 488 gives you a few more ways to package and share your project information.

All the ways to store project documents and the different types of technology you can use (discussed in Chapter 13) hold true at the end of a project, too. But now, consider moving your project archive to a location that more people can access. For example, while the project is in progress, you may want only the project team to access files. When the project is done, those files can be helpful to every project manager.

Tip: You may have hundreds, even thousands, of documents by the time a project finishes. At that point, some of them aren't worth the hard disk space they consume. When you archive your project information, take some time to get rid of obsolete documents like individual status reports or the eight draft versions of a document submitted before the client approved the final one.

Handing Off Information

Some projects are like toilet paper stuck to your shoe—you can't shake them off no matter how hard you try. In reality, the project *does* end, but then the ongoing operations kick in. For example, after your project delivers a consumer product, the sales department sells it, and field technicians fix it. In these situations, someone else needs information about what was done (and perhaps what's still left to do).

In addition to storing information in an archive, you may have to hand it off to other groups. Here are some typical documents that operations teams need:

- **Final specs, as-built drawings, product documentation, and so on.** This information gets reused as support teams develop maintenance procedures, marketing produces brochures, and manufacturing retools the assembly line.

- **Test results.** Read-me files for software programs, for example, usually include a list of existing problems and workarounds developed based on tests that didn't completely pass. Product warranty terms are based on the service and replacements a company expects to provide, and test results are one way to forecast these values.

- **Status and unresolved issues.** If customers purchase software maintenance, unfinished features or unresolved issues may be the beginning of the next software release. Similarly, in construction, a "punch list" lists all the tasks that weren't complete at sign-off.

- **Location of archived project documents.** If the next group in line can access the project archive, then it can obtain any document they need.

Part Four:
Project Power Tools

IV

Working on Multiple Projects

I f you're like most project managers, you juggle several projects at the same time. You may have several smaller projects that are part of a larger effort—like the subprojects for building the different parts of a new airplane. Other times, you simply must manage several separate projects at once. In almost every case, you have to share resources with others. For organizations with oodles of projects, Microsoft's enterprise project management software (Project Server) provides tools for managing entire portfolios of projects (page 5). However, both Microsoft Project Standard and Professional have features for managing smaller numbers of projects.

In Project, a *master project* is the easiest way to work with several projects at the same time. You create a new Project file and then insert separate Project files into that one consolidated file. A master project is great for assembling multiple subprojects into one place, but it works equally well if you're just dealing with a bunch of unrelated projects. This chapter describes how to build a master project of related subprojects, and how to consolidate several unrelated projects into one Project file.

Master projects aren't your only alternative, though. Sometimes all you need is a link between one task in one project and one task in another project. Suppose one project in your company has magnanimously funded a new database management system. One of your projects can use the system, but you don't want to start your database work until the stakeholders have approved the other project's database design. You can create what's called an *external task dependency* between the database design milestone and the start of your project's database design. In this chapter, you'll learn how to create external task dependencies.

Whether you fight over resources with yourself or with other project managers, you eventually have to share the resources you use. Project Server has the niftiest tools for finding and sharing resources, but plain-Jane Project can share resources, too. In Project, you can create a Project file called a *resource pool* to hold the information about the resources that are available. In this chapter, you'll learn how to create a resource pool and apply it to your projects. You'll also learn different ways of opening a resource pool and when to use each one.

Managing Multiple Projects

In Project Standard or Professional, inserting subprojects is the key to managing multiple projects, no matter how much or how little the projects have in common. Inserting subprojects usually falls into one of the following situations:

- **A large project with subprojects.** Suppose you're managing a project so large that it requires several project managers to handle different parts. For example, a project to build a new airplane may have subprojects for the fuselage, engines, electronics, wiring, and so on. The separate systems progress individually, but they must come together before the rubber can hit the tarmac. When you set up a master project that contains the separate subprojects, the project managers for the subprojects (whether they're subcontractors or part of your organization) each work on their own Project files. However, you can see the big picture of all the subprojects simply by opening the master project.

Tip: Master projects and subprojects are in way over their heads trying to manage humongous projects with casts of thousands, budgets in the millions, hordes of risks and issues, and project interdependencies galore. For a stable of big projects, Project Server is what you need to stay on top of everything.

- **Several unrelated projects.** If you spend each day juggling several small projects, you'd probably like to juggle those projects within Project as well. By creating a master project and inserting all your Project files into it, you can open all your projects by opening the master Project file. Even better, you can work on the projects without switching Project windows and create links between tasks in different projects. Similarly, you can produce consolidated views or reports for all your projects.

Tip: If you don't require Project's help calculating the schedule for small projects, the new Team Planner view (page 213) is an easy way to assign resources to tasks, move assignments around, and see where things stand.

- **Reporting on overall progress.** You can insert projects into another Project file temporarily to produce consolidated views or reports for several projects.

Although you can insert a Project file into any other Project file, the most common approach is to create a master project—a Project file that contains other projects inserted into it. Here's how a master project works when you insert Project files:

- All the inserted subprojects assemble cheerfully in one Project window, so you can work on and save them all as if they were a single file.

- The inserted projects look like summary tasks, which you can expand to show all the subtasks, or collapse to see the big picture.

- You can work on subproject tasks as if they belong to the master project— modifying, sorting, filtering, and grouping the aggregated tasks.

- Because a master project is a regular Project file, you can add tasks to it—for example, for the work you do supervising the other project managers.

- A master project maintains continuous contact with its inserted projects. If someone modifies information in a subproject, those changes are immediately visible in the master file. Conversely, if you make a change to a project from the master project, those changes are immediately visible to anyone looking at the original Project file for that inserted project.

Creating a Master Project

Setting up a master project is usually just a matter of creating the master Project file and then inserting the subproject Project files into it, as in the aircraft-building example at the beginning of this chapter. (The less-common alternative is to create a master project when you already have a single large project that you want to break into subprojects. The box on page 494 tells you how.)

Here's how you create a master project from several individual projects:

1. **Choose File→New, and then, in the Available Templates screen, double-click "Blank project". (Or click "Blank project" and then click Create.)**

   Project creates a new blank Project file, ready to accept your subprojects.

Creating a Master Project from One Large Project

You've forged ahead on a massive project, putting all the tasks into one Project file. One day, you realize that this big, awkward file is making it harder for you to manage the project and, more importantly, delegate subprojects to other project managers. All is not lost—you can turn your gargantuan project into a master project with subprojects without breaking a sweat. Here's how:

1. Create a Project file for each subproject within your large project. In each new file, be sure to set the project start date to the start date of the original colossal project and pick the same calendar (page 249) as the original project. (In step 7, you'll link the subprojects so they start on the correct dates.)

2. In the original Project file, drag over the ID cells for all the tasks you want to move to the first new subproject file. Then choose Task→Clipboard→Copy to copy all the information about the selected tasks to the Clipboard. (If you drag over the Name cells instead, Project copies only the task names.)

3. Switch to the corresponding Project file for the new subproject, and then choose Task→Clipboard→Paste Special to copy all the tasks from the original Project file. In the Paste Special dialog box, in the As list, choose Project Data, and then click OK.

4. Save the Project file.

5. Repeat steps 2–4 for each new subproject until you've copied all the tasks from the original Project file into subproject files.

6. Create a Project file for the master project, and then insert all the subproject files into it, as described on page 494.

7. Create task dependencies between the subprojects to restore them to the chronological order they had in the original large project.

---

2. **Select the first blank row.**

If you create a master project to track several levels of subprojects, then you can insert projects anywhere in the task hierarchy. For example, if a subproject is large enough to have its own subprojects, then you can insert Project files underneath the higher-level subproject. When you insert the project, it pushes the task you selected down one row and inserts itself at the same level as the task immediately above it.

3. **Choose Project→Insert→Subproject.**

The Insert Project dialog appears. Navigate to the folder that contains the first project you want to insert.

4. **Select the project you want to insert, make sure the "Link to project" checkbox is turned on, and then click Insert.**

Project adds a summary task for the inserted project, as shown in Figure 19-1.

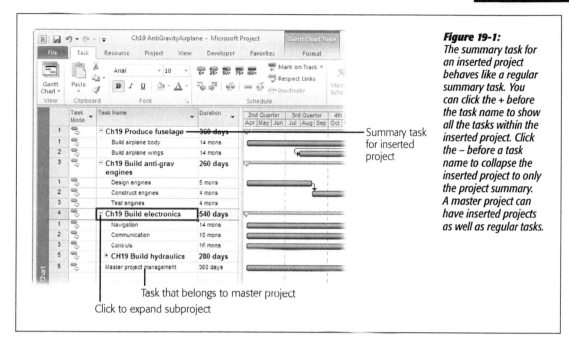

Summary task for inserted project

Task that belongs to master project

Click to expand subproject

Figure 19-1:
The summary task for an inserted project behaves like a regular summary task. You can click the + before the task name to show all the tasks within the inserted project. Click the – before a task name to collapse the inserted project to only the project summary. A master project can have inserted projects as well as regular tasks.

Project automatically turns on the "Link to project" checkbox, which tells Project to update the master project whenever the inserted project changes. You almost always want immediate updates. In some cases, you want subprojects inserted into a master project as read-only entries, as the box on page 497 explains. One time you might turn off the "Link to project" checkbox is when you decide to turn your master project back into one large project. You can unlink all the projects so that their tasks now belong to the master Project file. Of course, when you do this, you should be sure that no one makes changes to the original subproject files.

5. **Repeat steps 2–4 to insert additional projects.**

Remember, you specify where to insert projects by selecting the row below which you want to insert the project. The project in the row you select shifts down, so the inserted projects don't overwrite what's already there. You can also reorder inserted projects by dragging an inserted project summary task to another position in the task table.

Note: When you insert projects into a master project, the ID cells for tasks seem to go crazy, as you can see in Figure 19-1. Project assigns sequential ID numbers to each subproject, beginning with 1. However, the tasks that belong to inserted projects have ID numbers, which also begin with 1. So you're likely to see several tasks with the same ID number. When you work with subprojects, ignore the ID numbers. Instead, refer to the WBS code with a project prefix (page 93) to uniquely identify every task.

---

6. **Work on the inserted projects as you would regular tasks.**

Choose Task→Schedule→Indent Task or Outdent Task (page 152) to move the inserted project to the correct level of the task hierarchy—for example, to include several sub-subprojects underneath a top-level inserted project. You can link tasks within inserted projects to one another, or to regular tasks in the master project, or you can link one inserted project summary task to another.

7. **If you need help identifying tasks and resources from different subprojects, you can insert the Subproject File column into your Gantt Chart table.**

Right-click the Gantt Chart table heading area, and then choose Insert Column. In the drop-down list, choose Subproject File. Figure 19-2 shows the Subproject File cells with the file paths and names for each inserted project.

The Subproject Read Only field shows whether or not an inserted project is read-only. To keep track of subproject editability, insert this column in the Gantt Chart table as well. If an inserted project is read-only, the field value is Yes. Otherwise, it's No.

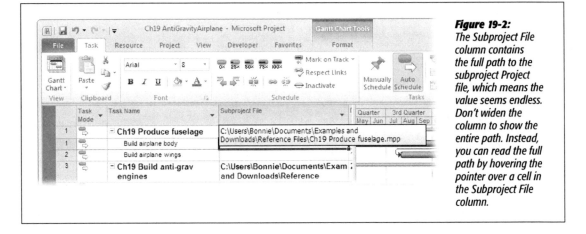

Figure 19-2:
The Subproject File column contains the full path to the subproject Project file, which means the value seems endless. Don't widen the column to show the entire path. Instead, you can read the full path by hovering the pointer over a cell in the Subproject File column.

Tip: If your master project and subprojects contain some of the same resources, the Resource Sheet in the master project also contains duplicate entries for those resources, one for each project Resource Sheet containing that resource. The problem is you have to select the correct resource entry (the one for the subproject) when you assign resources within that subproject. You can tell the resource entries apart by inserting the Project column into the Resource Sheet view. But the best way to solve the duplicate problem is to set up a resource pool for all the projects to share, as described on page 500.

Preventing Changes to Subprojects

Suppose you supervise several newbie project managers, and you want an easy way to review all the projects they manage, but you don't want to change those subprojects by mistake. You can insert projects into a master project as read-only. Then you can view the inserted projects from the master project, but you can modify them only by opening their source Project files. To insert projects as read-only, in the Insert Project dialog box, click the down arrow on the Insert button, and then, from the drop-down list, choose Insert Read-Only.

You can also change an inserted project to read-only *after* it's inserted. Select the inserted project summary task, and

then press Shift+F2 to open the Inserted Project Information dialog box (or choose Task→Properties→Information). Select the Advanced tab, and then turn on the "Read only" checkbox.

One exception to a subproject's read-only status occurs when you open both the master project and the subproject. Then Project changes the read-only subproject file whether you make the change in the master project or the subproject source file.

Removing a Project from a Master Project

If you no longer need an inserted project in your master project, then you can delete the inserted project task while keeping the original subproject file. Suppose another project manager takes over one of your several projects, so you no longer need to see that project. Simply delete it from your master project. The new project manager works on the original Project file. That's it.

To remove an inserted project, do the following:

1. **In the Gantt Chart view, select the ID cell for the inserted project summary task.**

   Project selects the entire task, not just the task name.

2. **Press Delete. Or you can right-click the task and choose Delete Task on the shortcut menu.**

   The Planning Wizard dialog box appears and asks you to confirm that you want to delete a summary task and all its subtasks.

3. **Make sure the Continue option is selected, and then click OK.**

   Project removes the inserted project from the master project but leaves the original subproject file where it is. If you change your mind, click Cancel instead.

Linking Tasks in Different Projects

Maybe only a few tasks in one project link to tasks in another project. For example, your advertising firm has an office move planned, but the partners are adamant that packing won't start until the "Who Needs Pants?" ad campaign is complete. You don't have to insert these two projects into a master project to link their tasks. The easiest way to link tasks in different projects is to open both projects and then create an external task dependency.

To create an external task dependency, follow these steps:

1. **In Project, open the projects that contain the predecessor task and the successor task.**

   Project opens each Project file in its own window, but these windows are initially on top of each other.

2. **To view both projects at the same time so you can see the tasks you want to link, choose View→Window→Arrange All.**

   Project positions the windows for the two projects one above the other, as you can see in Figure 19-3.

3. **Select the task that's the successor in this external task dependency.**

   Because the Task Information dialog box includes a Predecessors tab, you must begin the external link from the successor task.

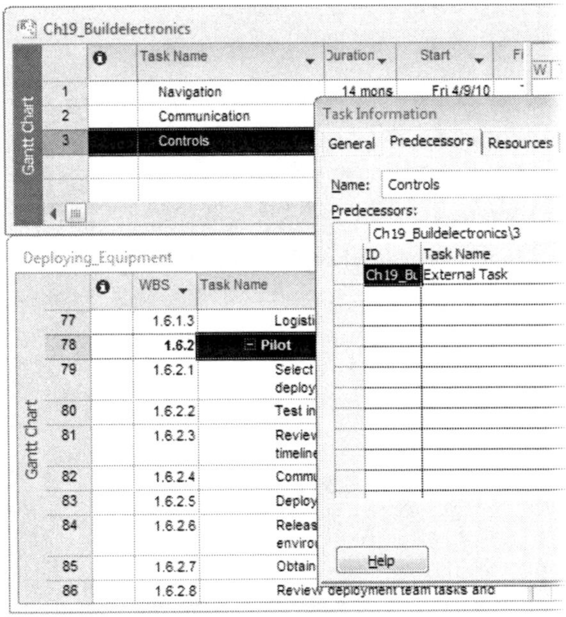

Figure 19-3:
When both projects are open, you don't have to type the entire folder path, file name, and task ID. You just type the name of the project that contains the predecessor, a backslash (\), and then the task ID of the predecessor.

4. To open the Task Information dialog box, press Shift+F2 (or choose Task→Properties→Information), and then select the Predecessors tab.

   The Name box shows the successor task.

5. Click the first blank ID cell, and then type the name of the project that contains the predecessor task, followed by a backslash and the task ID.

   To see the name of the project, look at the title bar of the project's window. In Figure 19-3, the predecessor task's project is *Ch19_Buildelectronics*. The full ID is *Ch19_Buildelectronics\3*, which appears in the text entry box above the Predecessors table.

6. **Press Enter to save the external task dependency.**

   Project fills in the Task Name, Type, and Lag cells with "External Task," and you can't change any of these values. Don't panic. After you click OK to complete the link, you can edit the dependency to change the task dependency type and lag value.

7. **Click OK to complete the link.**

   In the project that contains the successor, the external predecessor appears formatted in gray and immediately above the successor task in the Gantt Chart table area, as shown in Figure 19-4.

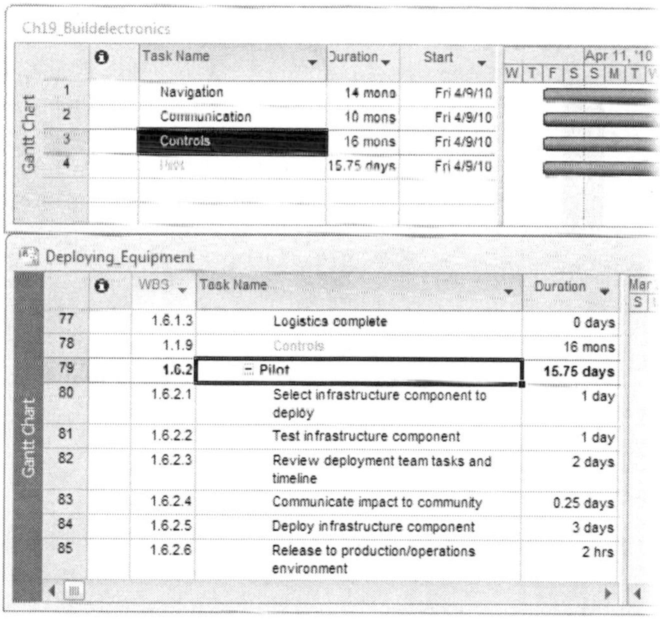

Figure 19-4:
In the predecessor project, the successor task appears formatted in gray, and immediately below the predecessor task.

8. To change the type of task dependency or to set lead or lag time, select the successor task once more, and then press Shift+F2.

The Task Information dialog box opens. This time around, the name of the predecessor task appears. The Type is set to Finish-to-Start and the Lag is set to 0d. To change the type or lag, click the corresponding cell in the row for the external task, and then type the new value. For example, if the predecessor and the successor start at the same time, you can choose Start-to-Start.

Note: When you open a Project file that contains external task dependencies, the Links Between Projects dialog box opens, which shows all the external predecessors and external successors to the file. You can see the effects to your schedule and choose which changes you want to accept. To see the links between projects at any time, choose Project→Properties→Links Between Projects. You can also set options to control the appearance of cross-project links. Choose File→Options. In the Project Options dialog box, choose Advanced. In the "Cross project linking options for this project" section, you can turn off the "Show external successors" and "Show external predecessors" checkboxes (they're on by default) to hide external tasks. If you don't want the Links Between Project dialog box to open automatically, then turn off the "Show 'Links Between Project' dialog box on open" checkbox.

Sharing Resources Among Projects

People usually work on more than one project for more than one project manager. If each project manager creates a resource to represent the same worker in each Project file, then overallocated resources and resource squabbles are soon to follow. The solution in Project Standard and Professional is a *resource pool*, which is a Project file dedicated to resource information—the pool of resources who work on projects, their cost, availability, and most important, how much time they're already allocated to tasks. (A resource pool in Project follows the same idea as the enterprise resource pool in Project Server, although Project Server includes a few more tools for finding the right resources.)

The beauty of a resource pool is that resource information is in one place. Project managers who use those resources simply link their projects to the resource pool. Assigning resources works exactly as it does when resources are contained in the project file. The only difference is that you can see how much of the resources' time is allocated to tasks from all linked projects.

Creating a Resource Pool

The simplest way to set up a resource pool is to create a new Project file, which does nothing but act as a resource pool. Although you can use a Project file with tasks in it as the resource pool, you may run into problems if you want to work on the tasks and someone else wants to work on resource information.

Tip: If an existing project contains all the shared resources in your organization, you don't have to build a resource pool from scratch. Open the existing project, and then choose File→Save As to save a copy of the project. Open the copy, delete all the tasks, and then save the Project file. (To quickly delete all tasks, display the Gantt Chart view. Click the Select All cell immediately above the first ID cell, which selects all tasks. Then press Delete.) Voilà—you have a Project file suitable for a resource pool.

To create a standalone resource pool, do the following:

1. **Choose File→New. Under Available Templates, double-click "Blank project".**

   A blank project opens.

2. **Choose View→Resource Views→Resource Sheet.**

   The Resource Sheet is home to all the data about your resources (page 184).

3. **Fill in information about your shared resources.**

   Typically, you fill in resource names, their standard charge rates or cost, and the maximum availability for work resources. If you want to include other information like work group, overtime rate, or cost per use, fill in those fields, too.

4. **Choose File→Save, and then name the project something meaningful (like "Resource Pool").**

   Be sure to save the resource pool in a location that all project managers can access. Saving the resource pool to your laptop, for example, won't help other project managers who need to link to the file. Save the resource pool to a network drive or shared folder.

Tip: If you have resource information in Microsoft Outlook or a human resources database, then you can import that information into Project, as described on page 185.

Connecting a Project to a Resource Pool

Before you can assign resources from a resource pool to project tasks, you must link the file to the resource pool. Any Project file that uses a resource pool is known as a *sharer file*. With the project–resource pool connection in place, the resource pool resources act as if they're part of your project file.

To connect a project to the resource pool, do the following:

1. **In Project, open the resource pool.**

   Since many project managers may share the resource pool, open the resource pool Project file as read-only so you don't lock anyone out of the file. To do that, when you choose File→Open, select the resource pool filename. On the Open button, click the down arrow, and then choose Open Read-Only.

2. **Open the Project file that you want to access the resource pool.**

   If you have several projects to share with the resource pool, you can open them all at the same time and then cycle through to connect each one to the resource pool.

3. **With the Project file active, choose Resource→Assignments→Resource Pool→Share Resources.**

   The Share Resources dialog box shown in Figure 19-5 opens.

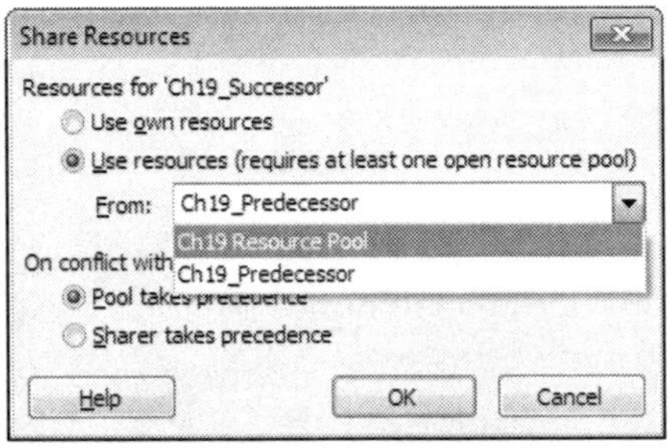

Figure 19-5:
The Share Resources dialog box includes options to tell Project to use resources from the project file itself or from the resource pool. For example, if you want to switch from using the resource pool back to your own file, select the "Use own resources" option.

4. **Select the "Use resources" option and then, in the From drop-down list, choose the resource pool.**

   If you have several projects open, the From drop-down list shows open projects except those that aren't already sharer files.

5. **Under "On conflict with calendar or resource information", select an option to tell Project how you want to resolve resource information discrepancies.**

   The best choice is to let the resource pool take precedence (select "Pool takes precedence"), because the resource pool then has the final say about resource information. When the resource pool takes precedence, changes made in the resource pool overwrite resource information in the sharer file. For example, suppose someone else opens the resource pool and updates everyone's standard and overtime rates. When you open a sharer file, the project automatically uses the new updated rates. In turn, if you change resource information in your project file, the resource pool is immune to those changes.

   If you select "Sharer takes precedence", then resource information you change in your project overwrites information in the resource pool. This approach is fine if you use a resource pool for resources dedicated to only your projects. With this option selected, you can change resource information in a project and update the resource pool when you save the project. If you share the resource pool with several other project managers, though, the "Sharer takes precedence" option usually leads to unwanted resource changes, as each project manager tries to modify resources.

6. Click OK.

The project now obtains its resource information from the resource pool.

Opening and Saving Sharer Projects

When you open a sharer file, Project asks whether you want to open the resource pool (if it's not open), as shown in Figure 19-6. In almost every case, you want to open the resource pool, because you'll see all the resources from the resource pool in your project's Resource Sheet. All resource assignments (from all sharer files) appear in the Resource Usage view, so you can see all the tasks on which a resource works. To open the resource pool, select the "Open resource pool to see assignments across all sharer files" option (see Figure 19-6).

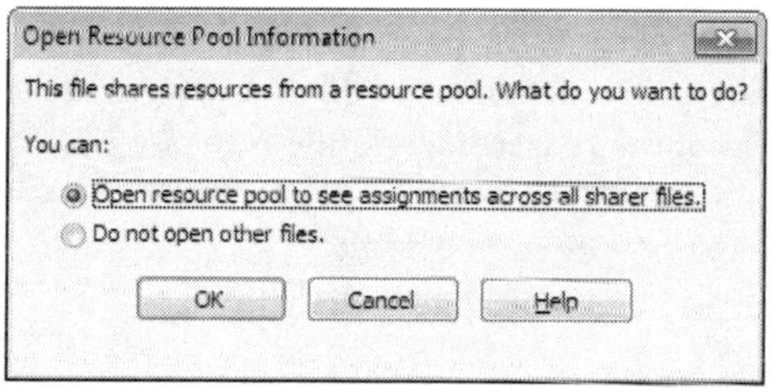

Figure 19-6:
If you level resources to remove overallocations (page 277), be sure to open the resource pool. When you level resources in one sharer file, the resource pool hears about the modified assignments and passes them on to all sharer files.

Tip: Because an open resource pool shows all assignments for a resource, your Resource Usage view is likely to have a lot more tasks than you remember. The problem is you can't tell which assignments are from your project and which come from other projects. To identify the project an assignment belongs to, right-click the heading row in the Resource Usage table area, and then choose Insert Column. In the drop-down list, choose Project. The Project cell for an assignment shows the sharer file that made the resource assignment.

Opening the resource pool also means that the resource assignments you make in your project affect the resource's availability in the resource pool. When you save a sharer file with the resource pool open, Project asks if you want to update the resource pool. To save the resource changes to the resource pool, click OK. (Click Cancel to save the sharer file without saving the resource pool, for example when you're testing what-if scenarios and haven't decided which one you're going to use.)

Note: If other sharer projects are open, updating the resource pool saves the resource changes from all open sharer projects. Before you update the resource pool, be sure to close any sharer files that contain resource changes you don't want in the resource pool just yet. When those sharer files are ready for prime time, open them with the resource pool, and then save the project and update the resource pool.

If you select the "Do not open other files" option, then only the resources already assigned to tasks in your project appear in the Resource Sheet. Likewise, you see only the assignments from your project. When you save the sharer file, the resource pool doesn't receive the resource assignments you make.

Tip: To make sure you're up to date with the most recent changes in the resource pool, choose Resource→Assignments→Resource Pool→Refresh Resource Pool. Project immediately shows the most current information from the resource pool. Similarly, if you've made scads of resource assignments, then you can update the resource pool immediately by choosing Resource→Assignments→Resource Pool→Update Resource Pool.

Detaching a Sharer Project from the Resource Pool

You can disconnect a sharer file from the resource pool, which is perfect if your project gets canned before it gets started. On the other hand, if a project contains a lot of assignment information, keeping the sharer file and the resource pool connected helps you report on all resource assignments at once. For example, if you want to evaluate resource usage for the past year, you want to keep all projects—active, completed, and discontinued—connected to the resource pool.

To remove a project from the resource pool:

1. **Choose Resource→Assignments→Resource Pool→Share Resources.**

   The Share Resources dialog box opens.

2. **Select the "Use own resources" option, and then click OK.**

   Any resources assigned to tasks remain in the project and appear in the Resource Sheet. Other resource pool resources disappear from the Resource Sheet. In addition, the assignments from the detached sharer file (now back to a regular Project file) no longer appear in the resource pool.

Editing Resource Pool Information

When you open a resource pool after it's connected to at least one sharer file, you have three choices for opening the pool. Sometimes you just want to see what's in the resource pool. Sometimes you need full read-write access—for example, when you're updating everyone's cost rates or work calendars.

When you open a resource pool file, the Open Resource Pool dialog box appears with options that win the prize for longest option labels. Here's what your choices are, and when to use each one:

- **Read-only.** The "Open resource pool read-only allowing others to work on projects connected to the pool" option opens the resource pool as read-only. Although the resource pool is opened as read-only, saving your sharer files updates the resource pool with assignments you've made. The benefit of opening a resource pool as read-only is that everyone else who uses the resource pool can continue to work on their projects at the same time.

- **Read-write.** If you must make changes to resources in the resource pool, select the "Open resource pool read-write so that you can makes changes to resource information (like pay rates, etc.), although this will lock others out of updating the pool with new information" option. By selecting this option, you can modify fields like costs and resource calendars. Of course, you want to use read-write mode for as short a time as possible, because no one else can access the resource pool while you're using it. That means other project managers can't see resource assignments and availability across all sharer files. If they open their Project files, they have to do so without opening the resource pool.

- **Create master project.** The "Open resource pool read-write and all other sharer files into a new master project file. You can access this new master project file from the View tab, Switch Windows command" option combines the resource pool and all sharer files into a brand-new master project. If you work on several projects of your own, this is an easy way to build a master project. However, this master project is also useful when you want to produce reports that span all the projects your organization performs. Remember that the resource pool is read-write, so other project managers can't open their sharer files connected to the resource pool while you have it open.

CHAPTER 20

Exchanging Data Between Programs

Managing projects is much more about communicating with people than tweaking Gantt Charts. Project planning is a collaborative effort between you, the stakeholders, and the rest of the project team. For the duration of the project, people communicate continuously as they complete work, identify and resolve problems, and report status.

As you've already seen, Microsoft Project isn't the only program you need for managing projects, especially when it comes to communicating aspects of your projects: Word documents, Excel spreadsheets, PowerPoint presentations, and other types of files often have better tools. For example, tracking issues and risks is easier in a spreadsheet or a database. PowerPoint is ideal for presenting different views of project information at a status meeting.

Information flows in both directions—from other programs to Project and vice versa. For example, after you hammer out costs and estimates in Excel, you can bring them into your Project schedule. Similarly, looking at change request documents or earned value graphs from within Project can save the time it takes to open other files in other programs.

In this chapter, you'll learn how to copy and paste data and pictures between files—the most straightforward way to exchange information. For example, you can copy task names as text from a Project Gantt Chart table into an Excel spreadsheet, or vice versa.

Exporting and importing information from one program to another is yet another way to exchange data. For instance, in Chapter 4, you learned how to import a WBS from a Word document into a Project file. This chapter explains the basics of importing and exporting, no matter which programs you use to create and receive the data.

Project 2010 offers a new way to exchange Project information with your team, although it's helpful only for small and informal projects, as you'll learn on page 535. You can synchronize tasks in a Project file with a SharePoint Tasks list and vice versa (without using Project Server). That way, you can share task information with your team and update your schedule with the progress they report.

An Overview of Information Exchange

With the glut of ways to exchange information, it's hard to know which one to choose. This box is a quick guide to the ways you can exchange information between Project and other programs, and when to use each one.

- **Copy.** For pictures and small amounts of data, copying and pasting is the simplest way to get information from one program to the other. You can copy and edit values like any other data in the file. In fact, you can't tell it came from another program and file. You can copy and paste a picture of a Visio diagram into a Project timescale or copy a picture of your Project schedule into a PowerPoint presentation. Pictures land where you paste them.

- **Import.** Since this book is about Project, importing refers to transferring data from another program into a Project file. For example, you can import cost estimates from an Excel spreadsheet into Project task fields. Once the data is in Project, it acts as if you created it there. Imported data looks and acts like text and numbers you paste in. The advantage is you have more control over the data you import, and where it goes in your Project file.

- **Export.** Exporting data from Project converts the data into a format that other programs can read. For example, as you learned in Chapter 5, you can export task lists from Project to Excel to build a cost-estimating spreadsheet.

- **Synchronize.** Project 2010 and SharePoint 2010 Foundation have a special bond that helps when you manage small, less formal projects. You can synchronize tasks between these two programs to share project tasks with your team or obtain status from them.

The next chapter covers two more ways of sharing information between Project and other programs:

- **Link.** When you want changes in one file to appear automatically in other files, linking is the way to go. It creates a lasting connection between the source data and its destination, so you can update the source data once and see the changes in every linked object. Suppose you use a PowerPoint file to present project status. You can insert a Gantt Chart view as a linked object into a PowerPoint slide to show the current schedule. In the other direction, you might link a risk-tracking spreadsheet to your Project schedule, so you can see where risk responses stand. When you double-click a linked object, the source file opens in the source program, so you always modify the original. The drawback to linking is that the links point to the source file; if those files don't stay where they are, then the links break. In addition, links don't work if they point to a computer or network you can't access.

- **Embed.** This method is a middle ground between copying and linking. When you embed an object from one program into another, you insert a package of data along with its source program into the destination file. The data isn't linked to the source file, so you don't see changes made in the original. When you double-click an embedded object, the commands from the source program appear, but you're editing the *copy.*

Embedding data is ideal for sending the destination file to someone else. The person who receives the file has everything needed: the destination file, the embedded object, and the program commands for editing the embedded data. The downside to embedded data is that it inflates the destination file size, sometimes to gargantuan proportions.

Copying Information

Copying and pasting moves small amounts of data quickly and easily. Copying and pasting is the way to go for reusing boilerplate text in a new proposal, copying a picture into a report, or borrowing from a colleague's invincible resume. You can copy task data from a Project table, and then paste it into Word to create an agenda for a team meeting. Copying numbers from an Excel column into Project table cells works equally well.

Copying Project Data to Other Programs

Copying data from Project tables to another program is blissfully easy; it's like a simple form of exporting. You select the table cells you want in Project, and then paste them into the destination file. Copying and pasting between Project 2010 and other Office 2010 programs brings formatting along with your data, which makes your job easier. For example, if you copy task data from Project to an Outlook email message to show task status, the tasks appear in the email message in a table with the same indenting, highlighting, grouping, and other formatting as the Project table, as shown in Figure 20-1.

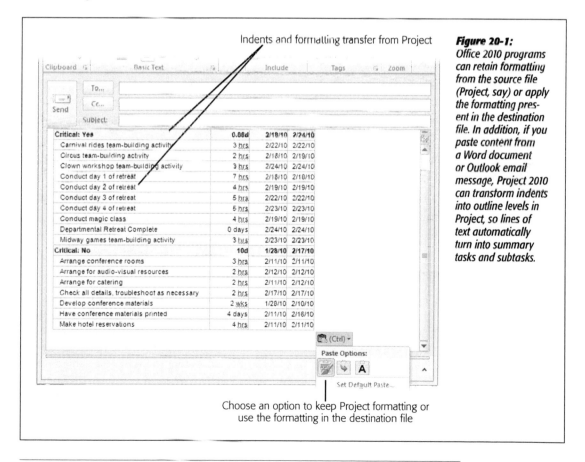

Indents and formatting transfer from Project

Figure 20-1:
Office 2010 programs can retain formatting from the source file (Project, say) or apply the formatting present in the destination file. In addition, if you paste content from a Word document or Outlook email message, Project 2010 can transform indents into outline levels in Project, so lines of text automatically turn into summary tasks and subtasks.

Choose an option to keep Project formatting or use the formatting in the destination file

Here are the steps for copying data from a Project table, using Excel as an example destination program:

1. **In Project, display the view and table that contains the fields you want to copy.**

   To copy tasks and their costs to an Excel spreadsheet (or other table-oriented file), display the Gantt Chart view. Then choose View→Data→Tables→Cost to display columns of cost-related fields. (You can also apply a table by right-clicking the Select All cell above the ID column and then, from the drop-down list, choosing the table.)

Tip: If necessary, choose Insert→Column to add the fields you want to copy to the table. To simplify copying nonadjacent columns, drag the columns in the Project table into the order you want, and then select the cells or columns.

---

2. **In the table, select the data you want to copy.**

   You can select specific cells or entire columns. If the cells are adjacent, drag from the upper-left cell to the bottom-right cell. To select nonadjacent cells, for instance when you don't want all the columns in the table, Ctrl-drag over each set of cells (hold the Ctrl key down as you drag over nonadjacent sets of cells). Select entire columns by dragging across the column headings.

3. **Press Ctrl+C or choose Task→Clipboard→Copy to copy the selected cells to the Clipboard.**

   If you click the Copy down arrow, you can choose Copy to copy data, or Copy Picture to copy an image of the selection.

4. **In the destination spreadsheet, click the top-left cell of the destination cells.**

   The cell you click is the starting point for the data you copy. The data copies from there into cells to the right and below. Even data that's nonadjacent in Project pours into adjacent cells in the destination file.

5. **To paste data in Excel 2010, press Ctrl+V or choose Home→Clipboard→Paste.**

   The data copies into the destination cells. With Office 2010, column headers paste into Excel, even if you don't select them in the Project table.

Copying Data from Other Programs into Project

Copying data into Project requires more finesse because Project is fussy about the type of data that goes into its fields. For example, if you try to copy plain numbers into a Start date cell, Project complains about the mismatch in an error message. To copy data into Project without that kind of drama, take the time to match up the data. For example, you may have to rearrange columns so they're the same in both files. Where you rearrange columns doesn't matter; you can rearrange the columns in the Project table or in the external file. Perhaps the simplest approach is to copy each column individually into its Project cousin.

Copying data between Project files works the same way, as the box on page 512 explains. Otherwise, copying to Project is the same as copying from it:

1. **In the source program (Word, for example), open the file, and then select the data you want to copy.**

   You can copy data from a Word document, an Excel spreadsheet, or a table in an Access database. If necessary, rearrange the columns of data to match the columns in the destination Project table.

2. **Press Ctrl+C or choose Home→Clipboard→Copy.**

   Ctrl+C works whether you use Excel 2003, 2007, or 2010.

3. **In Project, open the Project file, and then apply the view and table you want.**

   If you didn't rearrange the data before you copied it to the Clipboard, then you can insert, hide, or drag columns in the Project table (page 611) to match the source file's column order.

4. **In the Project table area, click the top-left cell where you want to paste the data, and then press Ctrl+V or choose Task→Clipboard→Paste.**

   Pasting data into a Project table doesn't insert new blank rows, so the values you paste overwrite values in the Project cells, starting from the cell you click to the right and down. If you don't want to overwrite data, then insert enough blank rows to hold the data you're pasting—or paste the data in blank rows at the bottom of the table.

   If the data from the source file doesn't match the data type in Project, then you see an error message like the one shown in Figure 20-2.

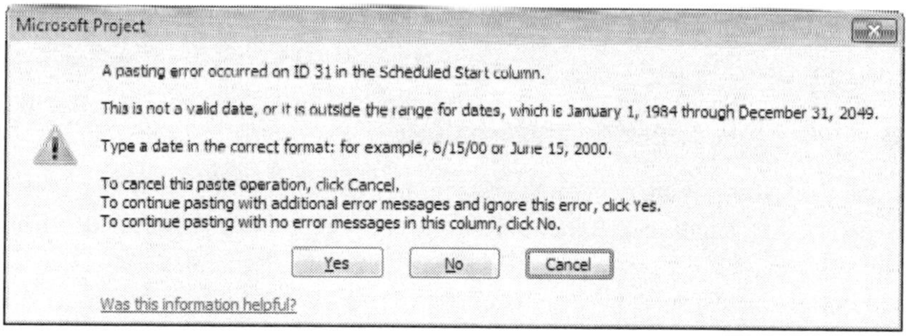

Figure 20-2:
Project displays an error message for every cell with the wrong type of data. The fastest way to resolve the problem is to click Cancel to stop the paste. Correct the mismatch by rearranging either the Project columns or the columns in your source file. Then repeat the copy and paste.

Tip: Project is happy as long as you paste data into a field with the correct data type. For example, you can paste any kind of text into a text-based field like Task Name. However, values you paste into Start cells had better be dates if tasks are auto-scheduled. You can also paste data into custom fields, as long as the data types match. For example, values you copy into a custom Project field like Duration1 must be a length of time like 2d.

Copying Data Between Project Files

Copying data from one Project schedule to another is handy when you want to reuse similar tasks from another project—for example, one you completed last year. Copying is the same whether you're copying within the same Project file, from one Project file to another, or from another program into Project. For example, to copy cells from a table in one Project file to a table in another file, select the cells in the source Project file, and then choose Task→Clipboard→Copy. Then in the destination Project file, select the first cell and then choose Task→Clipboard→Paste. Remember, when you copy cells, the paste starts at the first cell you click and continues to the right and down, overwriting any existing data in those cells.

When you copy data within the same Project file or between two different Project files, you can also copy entire rows in a table. Unlike copying cells, Project inserts new rows when you copy entire rows. Here are the steps:

1. In the table area, select the rows to copy by dragging over the row ID cells. You can select nonadjacent rows by Ctrl-clicking each ID cell.

2. Press Ctrl+C or choose Task→Clipboard→Copy. If you select resource rows in the Resource Sheet, you still choose Task→Clipboard→Copy.

3. To paste the rows in the new location (within the file or in a second Project file), click the ID cell for the row below where you want to copy the data, and then press Ctrl+V (or choose Task→Clipboard→Paste).

Creating Pictures of Project Information

From the time you initiate a project until you put the last tasks to bed, you communicate project information to stakeholders and team members. A *picture* of a project schedule shows where a project stands better than row after row of data. The Copy Picture command captures all or part of the current view and can create an image fine-tuned for displaying on a computer screen, printing, or publishing on the web. For example, you can create an image of the high-level schedule to publish on your Intranet or a Resource Graph to email to a functional manager (that is, the resources' manager outside the project). After you create the image, you can paste it into any destination you want.

To create a picture of a view, follow these steps:

1. **Display the view you want to take a picture of.**

   If you want to see specific rows in the view, then select them before you start the Copy Picture command. Adjust the timescale to show the date range you want in the picture. Partially hidden columns in the view don't appear in the picture; make sure the last column you want in the picture is displayed completely in the view.

2. **Choose Task→Clipboard. Click the Copy down arrow, and then choose Copy Picture.**

   The Copy Picture dialog box opens, as shown in Figure 20-3.

3. **In the "Render image" section, choose the option for how you're going to use the picture.**

   Project automatically selects "For screen", which is perfect for a picture you're copying into a program like Excel. Select "For printer" if you're creating an image for a report most people will read on paper.

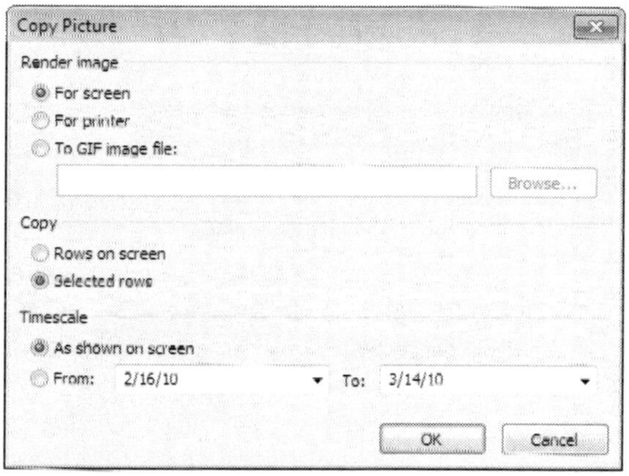

Figure 20-3:
The options you can select depend on the view that's displayed. For example, for Gantt Charts and usage views, you can specify the rows and timescale to include. The Resource Graph doesn't have rows, so the row options are grayed out. The Network Diagram disables the options for rows and timescale.

"For screen" and "For printer" both create an image and place it on the Clipboard. To create an image file, select "To GIF image file", and then enter the path and filename. (Click Browse to navigate to the folder in which you want to save the file.) For example, a GIF file format is what you need for publishing a picture on a web page.

4. **Choose the option for the rows you want to include.**

   If you haven't selected rows in the table, Project automatically selects the "Rows on screen" option, which includes only the visible rows. If you want specific rows or all rows in the project, be sure to select those rows before you start the Copy Picture command. In that case, Project automatically selects the "Selected rows" option.

5. **Choose the option to show the timescale that's visible in the view or a date range you specify.**

"As shown on screen" includes only the dates visible on the screen. To show dates from project start to finish or custom dates, select the From option, and then fill in the From and To boxes with the start and finish dates.

6. **Click OK.**

Project copies the picture to the Clipboard if you selected the "For screen" or "For printer" option. Project creates the file for the "To GIF image file" option.

7. **In the destination file, click the location where you want to paste the picture, and then press Ctrl+V or choose Home→Clipboard→Paste.**

For a GIF file, use the destination program's command for inserting a picture. For example, with Microsoft programs, choose either Insert→Picture or Insert→Object.

Displaying Pictures in Project

You can copy graphics or pictures into Project, for instance to display an Excel graph of bugs reported over time or photos of the customer's employees assigned to the project. Only certain places within Project can host these graphic files:

- A Gantt chart's timescale area.
- The Objects box or the Notes box in the Task Form or Resource Form (right-click the form, and then, on the shortcut menu, choose Objects or Notes).
- The Notes tab in the Task Information, Resource Information, or Assignment Information dialog boxes.

- The header, footer, or legend of a view or report you print.

Copying a picture into Project is similar to copying picture files in other programs. Here are the steps:

1. To copy an Excel graph as a picture, in Excel, select the graph, and then press Ctrl+C.

2. In Project, display the location where you want to copy the graphic file (or Clipboard graphic).

3. Press Ctrl+V. Project pastes the graphic at the selected location, as shown in Figure 20-4.

Importing and Exporting Data

Arranging columns in the right order, selecting data, and copying it to the right place can be tedious and error-prone. A more dependable way to get data from one place to another is importing or exporting, depending on which direction the data is headed. In this book, importing means pulling data into Project from another program, for instance importing data from an Excel spreadsheet or an Access database. Exporting pushes data out of your Project file to another file format like Excel or XML. Unlike linking and embedding (page 544), importing and exporting convert data from one file format to another, so the data is the same as what you enter directly in the destination program.

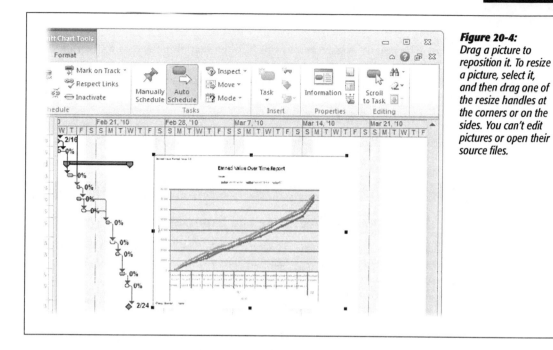

The great thing about importing and exporting is the control you have over the data you transfer and where it goes. Because you map fields in one program to fields in the other, you can make sure the right types of data go where you want.

Project provides wizards for importing and exporting data to and from your Project files. The wizards (as the box on page 516 explains) start automatically when you open a file in another format or save to another format. For example, if you open an Excel spreadsheet in Project, then the Import Wizard starts up. Saving a Project file as a text file launches the Export Wizard.

Maps are sets of settings that match up Project fields with fields or columns in the other program. Project comes with several built-in maps, for example to export cost data, earned value, or basic task information. Because Excel is second only to Project as a project management tool, Excel comes with special templates for transferring data to and from Project. For example, one template places all the information about tasks, resources, and assignments on separate worksheets within an Excel spreadsheet. Visio has special features for exchanging data with Project, as you'll learn on page 528.

Importing Data into Project

Bringing data from other programs into Project is as easy as opening that file in Project. The Import Wizard guides you through mapping the data to the right Project fields, and takes care of transferring the data. Although Project includes a few special tools for importing Excel data, the basic steps for importing any kind of data are the same:

1. **In Project, choose File→Open.**

    The Open dialog box automatically sets the "Files of type" box to Microsoft Project Files, so you have to tell Project which type of file you want to import.

File Formats for Importing and Exporting

Project can take in more file formats than it's willing to spit out. For example, Project can open different types of Project files, Microsoft Access databases, Excel files, text files (tab-delimited), comma-delimited files, and XML files. See Chapter 6 (page 130) for more details about the file formats Project works with.

On the other hand, you can save a Project file to other Project file formats, Excel workbooks, text-delimited files, comma-delimited (CSV) files, and XML. Project doesn't save projects as web pages, because you can use an XML file to generate a web page (as well as for other purposes).

Similarly, you can't save a Project file directly to a database format, although you can use a visual report (page 475) to accomplish that.

The steps you take to open or save these files vary depending on the format. For example, you can open an earlier Project file format simply by choosing File→Open. However, when you choose File→Open with Access databases, Excel file formats, and so on, the Import Wizard starts. Similarly, when you save files to formats other than the standard Project formats, the Export Wizard starts.

---

2. **In the Microsoft Project Files box, click the down arrow, and then choose the file format you want to import, for instance Microsoft Access Databases, Excel Workbook, or "CSV (Comma delimited)".**

    As you navigate to the folder that contains the file to import, the list shows only the files of the type you selected. So if the file you want is conspicuously absent, it might be a different format than you think.

3. **In the file list, double-click the name of the file (or click the filename, and then click Open).**

    The Import Wizard starts. Click Next to bypass the welcome screen, which does nothing but explain the process.

4. **On the Import Wizard—Map page, keep the "New map" option selected. Click Next.**

    If an existing map (either a Project built-in map or one you've saved) matches fields the way you want, then select "Use existing map". This option shortens the import process by several steps, as explained on page 522.

5. **On the Import Wizard—Import Mode page, select an option to tell Project
where you want to import the data. Click Next.**

   Project automatically selects the "As a new project" option, which creates a
   brand new Project file from the data you're importing. The "Append the data
   to the active project" option is ideal when you want to import several files into
   the same project, for instance when you receive WBSs from several team leaders. Appended data appears in the current Project table after the existing rows.

   Selecting the "Merge the data into the active project" option is perfect when
   you want to import values into existing tasks, like importing estimates into your
   Project file (page 113). To import values into existing tasks, Project needs a way
   to match the tasks in each file, as the box on page 517 explains.

FREQUENTLY ASKED QUESTION

Importing Data into Existing Rows

*How do I import data from another program into the cor-
rect tasks or resources in Project?*

If you're importing values and merging them into existing
tasks or resources, like estimates of task work, Project needs
to know how to identify matching tasks or resources. After
you map the fields on the mapping page and then click
Next, a message box might appear asking for a *primary
key* so Project can merge the imported data. This message

means you must tell Project which fields are unique identifiers for tasks (or resources). For example, a WBS code is
an ideal primary key because every task has one, and each
one is different.

On the mapping page, in the table of matched fields, select
the cell in the To column that represents the primary key,
and then click Set Merge Key. Both cells in the row change
to include the words MERGE KEY: in front of the field name.

---

6. **On the Import Wizard—Map Options page, select the types of data you want
to import, as shown in Figure 20-5. Click Next.**

   First, you have to specify the type of data you want to import: tasks, resources, or assignments. The Tasks and Resources options import data specifically
   for tasks or resources. Selecting the Assignments option imports information
   about tasks, and who's assigned to them. (When you exchange data with an Excel spreadsheet, these options turn into checkboxes so you can exchange more
   than one type of data at a time, as you'll learn on page 524.)

   If the first line or row of the source file includes column names, make sure
   the "Import includes headers" checkbox is turned on. The "Include Assignment
   rows in output" checkbox stubbornly remains grayed out no matter what you
   do, because this checkbox only applies to exporting.

7. **On the mapping page, map the import fields to their corresponding Project
fields, as shown in Figure 20-6.**

   The mapping page that appears depends on the data you selected to import:
   Task Mapping, Resource Mapping, or Assignments Mapping page.

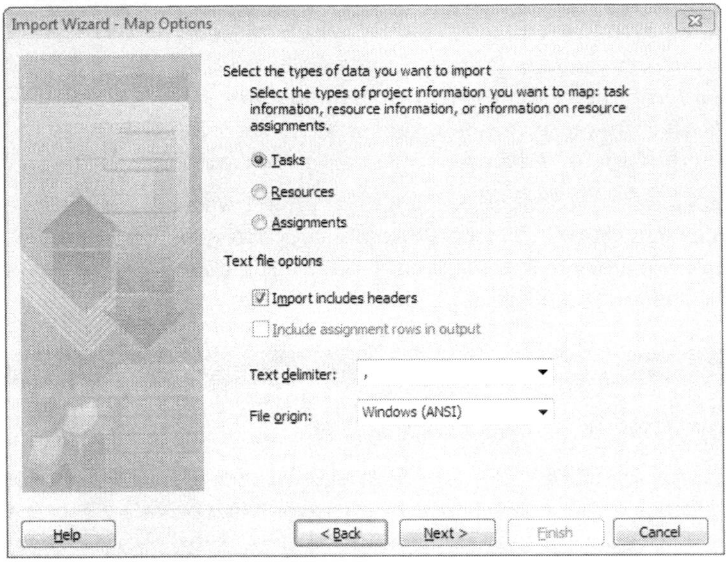

Figure 20-5:
*Project automatically sets the
other options on the Import
Wizard–Map Options screen
depending on the type of file
you're importing. For example,
importing a text file sets the
"Text delimiter" checkbox to
a comma, and "File origin"
to Windows (ANSI). You can
specify a comma, a tab, or a
space as the delimiter.*

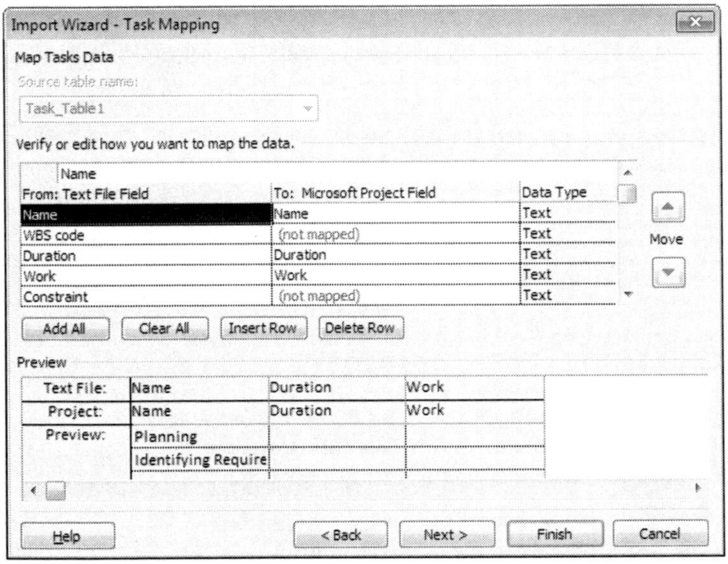

Figure 20-6:
*You don't have to import every
field in an import file. Beneath
the field table, click Delete Row
to remove a mapping pair. Click
Clear All to delete all the rows
and start from scratch. Add All
reads the import file and inserts
rows for each import file field.
Insert Row inserts a blank row.*

The "From: <source> Field" column (where <source> is Text File if you're importing a text file, Excel if you're importing from Excel, and so on) displays column headings from your import file, if they're present. Otherwise, the first cell in the From: Text File Field column displays the number 1.

For each field you want to import, choose the corresponding Project field in the To: Microsoft Project Field cell. Project makes educated guesses about mappings based on the imported column heading name. For example, Project maps a Name field in the import file to the Name field in Project.

The value "(not mapped)" in the To: Microsoft Project Field cell is Project's way of saying that you need to tell it which Project field you want. To choose a field, click the down arrow in the To: Microsoft Project Field cell, and then choose the field. Leaving the value as "(not mapped)" is how you tell Project not to import the field.

The Preview area shows a sample of the import. The first row in the preview shows the names of the selected source fields. The Project row identifies the fields into which the imported data goes. And the Preview rows show several values from that field in the import file, for example, Identifying Requirements as one task name.

8. Optionally, to save the map you've defined, click Next.

   The Import Wizard—End of Map Definition page appears with the Save Map button sitting by itself mid–dialog box. Click Save Map to open the Save Map dialog box. In the "Map name" box, type a short but meaningful name for the map, like *Import WBS Tasks*. Clicking Save adds the map to your global template and closes the dialog box.

9. Click Finish.

   You may see a warning message if you're importing an older file format. Click Yes to continue opening the file. Project imports the tasks into your Project file.

Exporting Data from Project

Most often, you export data from Project so you can work with the data in ways that Project doesn't handle well. For example, financial analysis is Excel's strong suit, not Project's. Exporting data is also useful when colleagues don't have Project, or just want to see the data in another format.

The steps in the Export Wizard bear a strong resemblance to those in the Import Wizard, but there are a few key differences. Here's how you export Project data to another format:

1. **Open the Project file you want to export and choose File→Save As.**

    The Save As dialog box opens.

2. **In the "Save as type" drop-down list, choose the file format you want to use.**

    If you save to one of the Project file formats (Project, Microsoft Project 2007, Microsoft Project 2000-2003, Project Template, or Microsoft Project 2007 Templates), Project opens the Save As dialog box, not the Export Wizard. However, saving to an Excel workbook, a text file, a comma-delimited file, or the XML format all start the Export Wizard.

3. **In the "File name" box, type the name for the file and click Save.**

    Project fills in the "File name" box with the Project file's name, but you can rename the export file to whatever you want. Project sets the file extension based on the file format you choose. If you choose an older file format, such as Excel 97-2003 Workbook or CSV (Comma delimited), when you click Save, a message box tells you that the older file format may be less secure than a new file format. If you want to save the file to that format, simply click Yes. To quit, click No, and then repeat steps 1 and 2 to choose a different format.

    Project starts the Export Wizard. Click Next to bypass the welcome screen.

4. **On the Export Wizard—Map page, select the "New map" option and click Next.**

    To use an existing map to match up fields (page 522), select the "Use existing map" option.

5. **On the Export Wizard—Map Options page, select the types of data you want to import. Click Next.**

    Your choices are the same as the ones on the Import Wizard—Map Options page, with one exception; the "Include Assignment rows in output" checkbox is now active but turned off. If you want to export all the assignment rows for tasks, then turn on this checkbox.

6. **On the mapping page, specify the fields you want to export.**

    You see the mapping page (Map Tasks Data, Map Resources Data, or Map Assignments Data) corresponding to the type of data you're exporting. The Export Wizard mapping pages have a few additional options, as you can see in Figure 20-7.

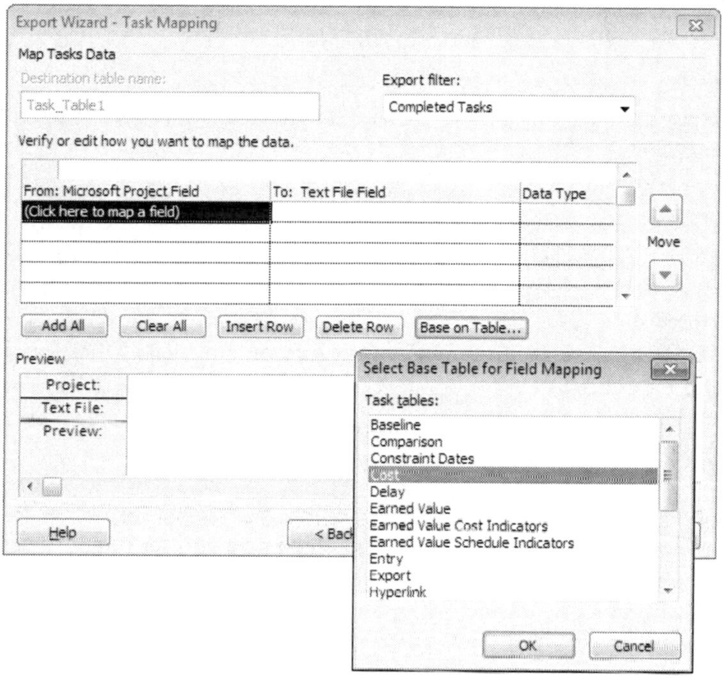

Figure 20-7:
The "Export filter" box lets you choose the items you want to export. For example, you might choose the Completed Tasks filter to export the final costs for tasks that are done. Click "Base on Table" below the mapping grid to jump-start field mappings with a Project table.

Because you're exporting to a blank file, Project doesn't fill in the field table for you. Instead of selecting field after field, you can use a Project table like Entry, Cost, or a custom table you create to fill in the field cells. Underneath the field table, click Base on Table. The Select Base Table for Field Mapping dialog box opens, and you can select any table in your project. The granddaddy of all tables is the Export table, which fills in a whopping 83 fields. (If you're exporting tasks, the dialog box displays all the task tables; it lists resource tables if you're exporting resources.) Remember, you can edit the field names in the To: column to specify the headings you want in the export file.

Tip: To export exactly the fields you want, use the Add All, Clear All, Insert Row, and Delete Row buttons to build a collection of fields.

The Preview area shows values in your Project by field. The Project and <destination> field names (where <destination> is the destination file format you choose) are initially identical. To define the field names in your export file to match the needs of a destination program, change the field name in the To: <destination> Field cells.

---

7. **Optionally, to save the map you've defined, click Next.**

   The Export Wizard—End of Map Definition page presents the Save Map button, which saves a map exactly like the Import Wizard does.

8. **Click Finish.**

   Project exports the data to the file format you selected, but it doesn't open the file for you.

   If clicking Finish displays a message about trying to save a file in an older file format, then Project isn't playing nicely with older Microsoft file formats (as well as other file formats that Project doesn't recognize initially). To correct these poor manners, choose File→Options. In the Project Options dialog box, choose Trust Center, and then click Trust Center Settings. Choose Legacy Formats, select the "Allow loading files with legacy or non default file formats" option, and then click OK.

Using an Existing Map

There's no reason to map the same fields every time you import or export them, for things like monthly reports you produce. Saving a map and reusing it in future imports and exports is a real timesaver. Bear in mind, using an existing map doesn't bypass any of the pages in the Import or Export Wizard, but you don't have to match fields on the mapping page. Moreover, after you apply an existing map, you can tweak the mapping if it isn't quite right.

Here's how to use an existing map:

1. **When you start either the Import or Export Wizard, follow the steps until you get to the Import Wizard—Map page or the Export Wizard—Map page.**

   The wizard pages vary depending on what you're importing or exporting.

2. **On the Import Wizard—Map page or the Export Wizard—Map page, select the "Use existing map" option and then click Next.**

   The Map Selection page appears, as shown in Figure 20-8.

3. **Select the map you want and click Next.**

   If you want to review your settings or make minor adjustments to the map, clicking Next steps you through the remaining wizard pages as described in the previous sections on importing (page 516) and exporting (page 519).

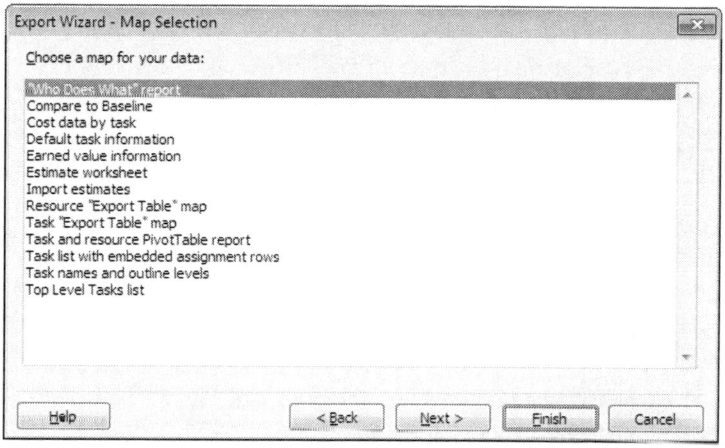

Figure 20-8:
If you're certain the map is exactly what you want, you can click Finish to immediately complete the import or export.

Exchanging Data with Excel

Because Excel spreadsheets can contain more than one worksheet, the settings in the Import and Export Wizards are slightly different from the ones you see when you work with text files. For example, you can import and export tasks, resources, and assignments all at once. Moreover, when you have both Project and Excel installed on your computer, Excel includes two templates to jump-start your data exchange. When you create an Excel file using either of these templates, the column headings are set up to map to Project fields. To export without a hitch, see page 132 to learn how to make Project work with older file formats.

Tip: You can also exchange data between Project and Excel using visual reports. See Chapter 17 for the full scoop on visual reports.

Exporting Project data to Excel

When you want to export specific portions of your Project file to Excel, you can save the Project file as an Excel workbook and use the Export Wizard to specify what's exported. The steps are similar to exporting to other types of files. Here's how exporting to an Excel spreadsheet works:

1. **Open the Project file you want to export to Excel.**

   Display the view that contains the data you want to export, for instance the Gantt Chart view for tasks, the Resource Sheet for resources, or Task Usage for assignments. You can also export specific rows by selecting them. To export all the data in the table, at the top of the ID column, click the Select All cell.

2. **Choose File→Save As. In the "Save as type" drop-down list, choose Excel Workbook. In the "File name" box, type the name for the file, and then click Save.**

   Project launches the Export Wizard. Click Next to get going.

3. **On the Export Wizard—Data page, the wizard automatically selects the Selected Data option, which exports the data you selected in the view. Click Next to continue.**

   The Project Excel Template option takes the reins and exports your entire file, as described on page 525.

4. **On the Export Wizard—Map page, select the "New map" option and click Next.**

   If you already have a map you want to use, select the "Use existing map" option, and then select the map as described on page 522.

5. **On the Export Wizard—Map Options page, turn on the checkboxes for each type of data you want to export and click Next.**

   Because Excel can handle several types of data on separate worksheets, this page includes checkboxes for Tasks, Resources, and Assignments, as you can see in Figure 20-9.

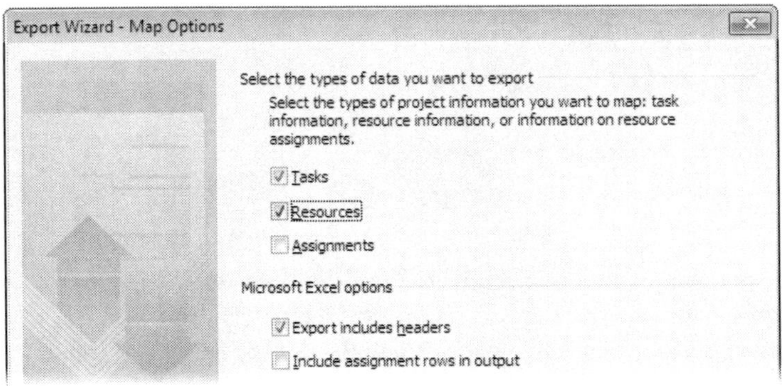

Figure 20-9:
You can turn on any or all of the data checkboxes. Each type of data lands on its own Excel worksheet. If you selected an existing map, then the wizard initially sets the checkboxes to match the map definition. The wizard displays a mapping page for each type of data you export.

The wizard automatically turns on the "Export includes headers" checkbox. This setting exports Project field names to column names in Excel, which is usually what you want. If you want to export all the details about assignments, then turn on the "Include assignment rows in output" checkbox.

6. On the first mapping page that appears, in the "Destination worksheet name" box, type a name for the Excel worksheet.

    The mapping page that appears depends on the checkboxes you selected on the Export Wizard—Map Options page. For example, if you turned on the Tasks checkbox, then the first Mapping page you see is Export Wizard—Task Mapping.

    The "Destination worksheet name" box automatically sets the worksheet name to something like "*Task_Table1*." You can stick with that or change the name to something else.

7. **Set up the field mapping as you would for any other kind of export.**

    You can choose a filter to export specific parts of your Project file. The rest of the mapping page is the same as the one that appears for exporting to a text file or another format (page 520). For instance, you can map fields based on an existing Project table or use the buttons below the table to insert and delete rows.

8. **Repeat steps 6 and 7 for each mapping page that appears.**

    The mapping pages appear in the same order every time: tasks, resources, and then assignments. However, if you aren't exporting a type of data, that mapping page doesn't show up. The wizard creates a separate worksheet in the Excel file for each type of data you export.

9. **Click Finish.**

    Project exports the tasks into a new workbook, but you must start Excel and open the file to see it. After you open the spreadsheet in Excel and try to save it, you may see a message box asking if you want to overwrite the older Excel format (if you exported to Excel 97-2003 format, for example) with the current format. If you click Yes to update the format, Excel saves the spreadsheet to the version of Excel installed on your computer.

Tip: The cells in an Excel export file are set to the General format, which doesn't apply any specific formatting to the values. To display data the way you want or to calculate values, you can change the data types for cells. For example, you can modify cost cells to the Excel Currency format to show dollar signs. To change the data type in Excel, select the column heading. Choose Home→Cells→Format→Format Cells. Choose the category, such as Number or Currency, and then click OK.

Exporting an entire project to Excel

The Export Wizard contains an option for exporting all the task, resource, and assignment data in a Project file with a minimum of effort. Although the resulting export file doesn't include time-phased data, you can create an Excel spreadsheet with separate worksheets for tasks, resources, and assignments. Here are the steps:

1. Open the Project file you want to export to Excel, and then choose File→Save As. In the "Save as type" drop-down list, choose Excel Workbook. In the "File name" box, type the name for the file, and then click Save.

   Project launches the Export Wizard. Click Next to start the wizard.

2. **On the Export Wizard—Data page, select the Project Excel Template option, and click Finish.**

   That's it. Project exports your project data to an Excel file that contains three worksheets: Task_Table, Resource_Table, and Assignment_Table.

Importing data from Excel

Importing data from Excel without a built-in template is almost identical to importing any other kind of data (page 516). In fact, you'll find only two exceptions:

- The Import Wizard—Map Options page has checkboxes for each type of data you want to import, because Excel can create separate worksheets for each type of data.

- On the Mapping pages, Project fills in the Excel worksheet names in the "Source worksheet name" box. If the spreadsheet contains more than one worksheet for a type of data, then choose the name from the drop-down list.

WORKAROUND WORKSHOP

Finding the Excel Templates

The Excel templates actually come with Project, so you won't see the Microsoft Project Task Import Template and the Microsoft Project Plan Import Export Template in the Excel template list unless you have Project installed on your computer. However, you can copy the templates to a folder so anyone can use them.

Using Windows Explorer on a computer running Project and Excel, navigate to Program Files→Microsoft Office→Templates→1033. 1033 is the English language code. If you installed Project in another language, navigate to the folder for that language code. Copy the files Tasklist.xlt and Projplan.xlt to the folder you use to store other custom Excel templates.

Using an Excel template to import data

Suppose you want team leaders and stakeholders to help you build the project task list. Or you want to collect information about tasks, resources, and assignments to load into your Project file. You can use the out-of-the-box importing steps, but Project offers an easier way. If you have both Project and Excel installed on your computer, Excel includes two templates whose worksheets and columns are tailored to work perfectly with Project's Import Wizard:

- The **Microsoft Project Task List Import Template** is an Excel template with columns for basic task fields. It contains a Task_Table worksheet with columns for ID, Name, Duration, Start, Deadline, Resource Names, and Notes.

- The **Microsoft Project Plan Import Export Template** has four worksheets: Task_Table, Resource_Table, Assignment_Table, and Info_Table. The Task_ Table worksheet includes columns for ID, Duration, Start, Finish, Predecessors, Outline Level, and Notes. The Resource_Table worksheet mimics the field you see in the Project Resource Sheet. The Assignment_Table includes columns for Task Name, Resource, Name, % Work Complete, Work, and Units.

First, you create a new Excel file from either of the templates. Give the Excel files to others to fill out. When your colleagues send the filled-in files back, you import them into Project using the Import Wizard. Here are the steps from start to finish:

1. **In Excel, choose File→New.**

   The Backstage view opens to the Available Templates page.

2. **Click Sample Templates.**

   The Available Templates list appears.

3. **Select either Microsoft Project Task List Import Template or Microsoft Project Plan Import Export Template, and then click Create.**

   The Task List template creates a new file called Tasklist1, which contains a worksheet with basic task columns. The Project Plan template creates a file called Projplan1 with four worksheets for tasks, resources, assignments, and information about the template.

   The Info_Table worksheet merely explains what the template can do, not how to fill it in. Tell your team members that they don't have to enter dates despite the presence of the Start and Finish columns. If tasks have critical finish dates, team members can enter them in the Deadlines column.

4. **Choose File→Save. In the Save As dialog box, navigate to the folder where you want to save the file. In the "File name" box, type the file name; in the "Save as type" drop-down list, choose Excel Workbook. Then click Save.**

   Excel saves the file.

5. **Distribute the file to team members, so they can open the file and enter data.**

   The first row in the file displays Project field names, so people know which columns contain which fields. They don't have to fill in every cell. When team members finish entering data, they simply save the file and send it to you to import into Project.

Note: The Excel files based on these templates don't apply specific formatting to the columns, so whoever fills in the files must enter the values correctly. For example, duration is a length of time like 5d or 3w. If the values aren't valid, then the Project Import Wizard displays an error message (page 511).

Now you're ready to import the Excel file into Project. When you import data from an Excel template, the mapping between Excel columns and Project fields is already done. Follow the steps on page 516 to import the Excel data. When you get to the first mapping page, click Finish to import the data.

Working with Project and Visio

Most of the time, your work with Project and Visio revolves around visual reports, which send Project data to Visio pivot diagrams to dynamically display project information. (See Chapter 17 for more on Visio visual reports.) You can also turn to Visio to produce simpler pictures of your project, akin to the weather maps you see on television compared to the ones that meteorologists analyze. Project's Timeline view (page 600) and Gantt Chart formatting options (page 529) go a long way toward creating presentation-quality graphics of your project. However, if you can't get Project's views to look the way you want, try Visio's Schedule template category, which includes templates for Gantt Charts, timelines, PERT Charts, and calendars:

- **Gantt Chart.** A Visio Gantt Chart can make task bars look more interesting, and weed out the details that executive audiences don't want to see. Although most project managers build even the quickest and dirtiest schedules in Project, you can export any information created in Visio Gantt Charts to set up a Project schedule.

- **Timeline.** Project 2010 stole Visio's thunder by introducing its own timeline view. Now you can produce high-level project views of tasks and milestones along a horizontal bar in Project or Visio. However, if you want to produce a vertical timeline of your project, your only choice is Visio's Timeline template.

Tip: Although Visio includes a PERT Chart template, you're better off using the Project Network Diagram view to show PERT boxes. That way, the tasks are available for other views as well. The Visio PERT Chart template doesn't import or export data automatically, so it's difficult to display Project data with this type of drawing.

Because data exchange between Visio and Project takes place in Visio, this section switches the meaning of import and export from previous sections. In Visio, import means bringing Project data into a Visio drawing, whereas export means creating a Project file from Visio data.

Every shape on a Visio Gantt Chart or timeline drawing has its own sets of options, so you can make the drawing look just the way you want. To learn more about working with Visio schedule drawings, refer to the *Visio 2007 Bible* by Bonnie Biafore (Wiley).

Displaying Project data in a Visio Gantt Chart

A Project Gantt Chart can show a project summary, but it often contains too much information for most reports and presentations. Visio Gantt Charts are simpler renditions of their Project cousins, so they may be more suitable for audiences less versed in project management.

Project doesn't include the tools for pushing its data to Visio. Importing Project data into a Visio Gantt Chart takes place within Visio. Here's how to do it:

1. **In Visio, open an existing Gantt Chart drawing or create a new one.**

    To create a Visio Gantt Chart, choose File→New→Schedule and then double-click Gantt Chart. In the Gantt Chart Options dialog box that appears, click OK to accept the settings as they are. You can modify them after you've imported your Project data.

2. **Choose Gantt Chart→Manage→Import Data.**

    The Import Project Data Wizard starts. As a refreshing change, this wizard gets right to business with options on the very first page.

3. **On the first page, select the "Information that's already stored in a file" option, and then click Next.**

    Despite the wizard's name, you can actually import data from Excel spreadsheets and text files, as well as Project .mpp and .mpx (an older exchange format) files.

4. **On the "Select the format of your project data" page, leave Microsoft Project File selected, and then click Next.**

    To import from a different type of file, choose the format in the list.

5. **On the "Select the file containing existing project schedule data" page, open the file you want to import, and then click Next.**

    On the page, click Browse. In the Import Project Data Wizard dialog box that appears, find and select the file you want to import, and then click Open. Back on the wizard page, you see the path and filename filled in.

6. **On the timescale page, choose the major and minor timescale units, as well as the time units you use to enter duration. Click Next.**

    Less robust than the timescale units in Project, Visio timescale units are days, weeks, months, quarters, and years. The duration units come in several variations. For whole numbers, you can choose Weeks, Days, or Hours. To show fractional values, choose Days Hours, Weeks Days, or Weeks Hours.

    Clicking the Advanced button opens a dialog box in which you can specify the shapes for the Gantt Chart. However, changing the shapes once the drawing is complete makes it easier to see whether the results are what you want.

7. **On the "Select tasks to include" page, select the category of tasks you want to import, and then click Next.**

Initially, All is selected, which brings in every task in your Project file. Typically, one of the other selections is more appropriate. "Top level tasks only" shows only the highest-level tasks. "Milestones only" shows milestones without any other tasks. "Summary tasks only" includes all levels of summary tasks so only the work package tasks are eliminated. "Top level tasks and milestones" is a great summary with the highest-level tasks and all milestones.

Note: Project tasks with 0 duration come in as milestones. Visio turns tasks designated as milestones that have a duration other than 0 into milestones with 0 duration.

---

8. **On the last page, review the import properties you've chosen and click Finish.**

Visio creates a new Gantt Chart from the imported data, as shown in Figure 20-10. If you import into an existing drawing, Visio creates a new page and then adds the imported Gantt Chart to it.

To change any import settings, click Back until the appropriate page appears, and then make the changes you want.

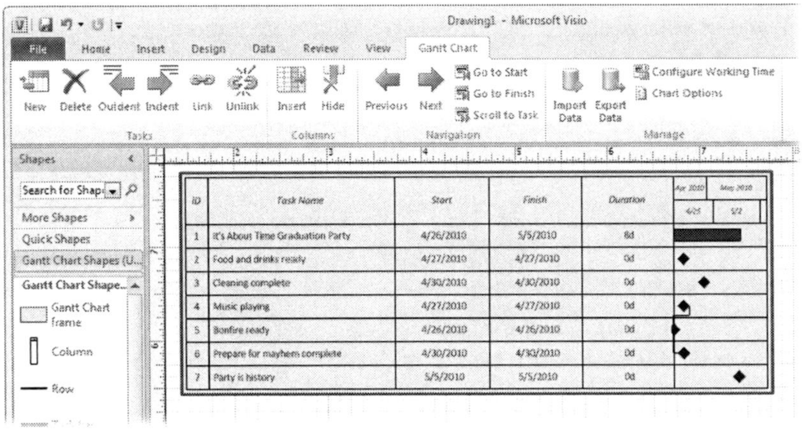

Figure 20-10:
Visio's Gantt Chart tab helps you find task bars and dates. Click "Go to Start" or "Go to Finish" to move the timescale to the beginning or end of the project. Click Previous or Next to move to the previous or next time period. If you select a task, and then click the "Scroll to Task" icon, the timescale moves to display the task bar.

9. **To change the appearance of the Visio Gantt Chart, choose Gantt Chart→Manage→Chart Options.**

The Gantt Chart Options dialog box has the same options the wizard presents when you click the Advanced button. Change the timescale dates, the duration units, and timescale units. The Format tab lets you choose shapes for task bars, summary bars, and milestones, as well as what the bar labels show.

Displaying Project data in a Visio timeline

Timelines are a great way to show when important events occur and how long phases last. Now that Project can produce a timeline, you may not need to import project data into a Visio timeline drawing. However, Visio's timeline tools simplify importing different types of tasks: all tasks in the project or just top-level tasks, summary tasks, and milestones. To import information from Microsoft Project into a Visio timeline, follow these steps:

1. **Make sure the Project file you want to import isn't open in Project.**

   The Import Timeline Wizard can't read a file that's already open.

2. **In Visio, open an existing timeline drawing or create a new one.**

   To create a Visio Gantt Chart, choose File→New→Schedule and double-click Timeline. Visio creates a new drawing and adds the Timeline tab to the Visio ribbon.

3. **Choose Timeline→Timeline→Import Data.**

   The Import Timeline Wizard starts.

   If you don't see Import Data on the Timeline menu, then Microsoft Project isn't installed on your computer. Unlike the wizard for importing data to a Visio Gantt Chart, the Import Timeline Wizard works only with Project files.

4. **On the "Select a Microsoft Project file to import" page, open the file you want to import and then click Next.**

   On the page, click Browse. In the Import Timeline Wizard dialog box that appears, find and select the file you want to import (it must be a Project *.mpp* file), and then click Open. Back on the wizard page, the path and filename appear in the box.

5. **On the "Select task types to include" page, select the category of tasks you want to import, and then click Next.**

   Initially, All is selected, which brings in every task in your Project file. Typically, "Top level tasks and milestones" is best for a summary of the highest-level tasks and all milestones. "Top level tasks only" shows only the highest-level tasks. "Milestones only" shows milestones without any other tasks. "Summary tasks only" includes all levels of summary tasks so only the work package tasks are eliminated. Project tasks with 0 duration import as milestones.

6. **On the "Select shapes for your Visio timeline" page, review the shapes for the timeline, and choose different shapes if you want. Click Next.**

   The timeline shape spans the dates for the full project schedule. Project summary tasks become Interval shapes in Visio, and Project milestones morph into Milestone shapes.

---

7. On the last page, review the import properties you've chosen, and then click Finish.

Visio creates a new timeline from the imported data, as shown in Figure 20-11. If you import into an existing drawing, then Visio creates a new page and then adds the imported timeline to it.

To change any aspect of the import, click Back until you reach the appropriate page, change the settings you want, and then click Finish.

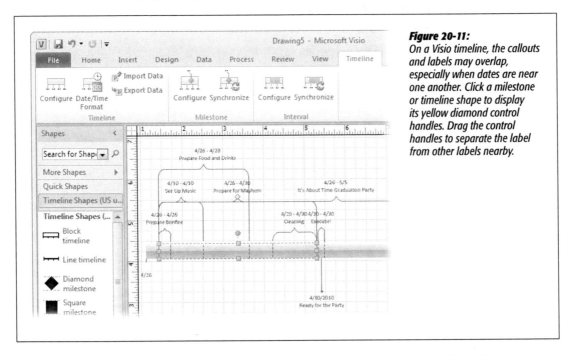

Figure 20-11:
On a Visio timeline, the callouts and labels may overlap, especially when dates are near one another. Click a milestone or timeline shape to display its yellow diamond control handles. Drag the control handles to separate the label from other labels nearby.

8. To change the appearance of the Visio timeline, right-click the shape you want to change and choose one of the commands from the shortcut menu.

To change the time period for the timeline, right-click a timeline shape, and then choose Configure Timeline. You can also choose whether or not to show dates on the timeline. To modify milestones or intervals, right-click the shape and choose Configure Milestone or Configure Interval.

Changing the shape of an element is as simple as right-clicking it, and then, on the shortcut menu, choosing Set Timeline Type, Set Interval Type, or Set Milestone Type.

Exporting Visio Gantt Charts to Project

Suppose you used a Visio Gantt Chart to present a project proposal to the management team for their approval. The information in the Gantt Chart isn't much, but you can export it to Project to jump-start your schedule. The tasks in a Visio Gantt Chart turn into tasks in Project with start dates, finish dates, and durations. Similarly, milestones in a Visio Gantt Chart become milestones in Project.

To export a Visio Gantt Chart to Project, follow these steps:

1. **In Visio, open the Gantt Chart drawing you want to export and select the Gantt Chart frame.**

    Clicking within a Visio Gantt Chart selects individual task bars or task name text boxes, which are subshapes within the Gantt Chart frame. To select the frame, click the very edge of the Gantt Chart. You can tell you've succeeded when selection handles appear at the frame corners and the midpoints along each side.

2. **Choose Gantt Chart→Manage→Export.**

    The Export Project Data Wizard starts.

3. **On the "Export my project data into the following format" page, select Microsoft Project File and click Next.**

    You can also export to Excel files, text files, and Project .mpx files (an older Microsoft exchange format). However, you might as well export directly to Project.

4. **On the "Specify the file to enter project schedule data" page, click Browse and open the folder in which you want to save the exported project file.**

    The Export Project Data Wizard dialog box opens. Navigate on your computer or network to the folder you want. Although this page's title sounds like you're supposed to select ("specify") a file, you actually create a new one. In this step, you simply select the folder in which you want to save the new file. (If you select an existing file, Project asks if you want to replace it.)

5. **In the "File name" box, type the name for the new Project file and click Save.**

    The dialog box closes and returns to the wizard.

6. **Click Next.**

    The last wizard screen shows that you're exporting a Gantt Chart, and it specifies the file you're creating.

7. **Click Finish.**

    A message appears to tell you that the data exported. Click OK.

8. **Open the file in Project.**

    You're ready to build a real schedule starting with the data that you exported from the Visio Gantt Chart. For example, you still must create task dependencies between the tasks and assign resources.

Exporting Visio timelines to Project

You can also export Visio timeline data to Project. Intervals from a Visio timeline turn into tasks in Project with start dates, finish dates, and durations. Milestones in Visio become milestones in Project. The Visio timeline shape also turns into a task with start, finish, and duration.

To export a Visio timeline to Project, follow these steps:

1. **In Visio, open the timeline file and select the timeline shape.**

   Select the timeline shape by clicking anywhere inside it.

2. **Choose Timeline→Timeline→Export Data.**

   The Export Timeline Data dialog box opens. You can navigate on your computer or network to find the folder you want.

3. **In the "File name" box, type a name for the new Project file and click Save.**

   The "Save as type" box is set to Microsoft Project File. When you click Save, a message tells you that the data exported successfully. Click OK.

4. **Open the Project file you created in Project.**

   The timeline data turns into manually scheduled tasks in Project. After you create task dependencies between tasks in Project, you can switch these tasks to auto-scheduled (page 117) so Project can do its job.

Sharing Projects with SharePoint

Many small projects can get by without full-blown project scheduling. For a handful of tasks and a couple of resources, you can probably manually schedule your tasks without breaking a sweat. Even so, as a project manager, you still need to communicate with your team and vice versa. That's where the new "Sync with Tasks List" feature in Project 2010 may be able to help. You can synchronize tasks in a Project 2010 file with a SharePoint 2010 Tasks list to easily exchange project tasks and status with your team. This section explains what you can do with Project and SharePoint, if you don't use Project Server.

Note: If your organization requires enterprise project management (coordinating an entire stable of projects and sharing enterprise resources, for example), this simple synchronization feature won't cut it. You need Project Server and SharePoint for those types of project management activities. In fact, when Project Professional is connected to Project Server, Sync with Tasks List is disabled.

Sharing Tasks with Your Team

Synchronizing tasks between a Project schedule and a SharePoint Tasks list can simplify communication with your project team. Start a task list in Project and publish it to a SharePoint Tasks list for all to see, or brainstorm with your team in SharePoint to create a list of tasks and pull the tasks into Project to build a schedule. Either way, the first step is to create the connection between your Project file and a SharePoint Tasks list. Then, you can push changes from your Project file to SharePoint to keep your team informed or pull the progress updates your team enters in SharePoint tasks into your Project file.

SharePoint doesn't have the scheduling prowess Project does. Before you dive into synchronizing tasks, determine whether Sync with Tasks List satisfies your needs:

- **You must manually set your task start and finish dates.** SharePoint can't calculate project schedules, so tasks you synchronize appear in SharePoint Tasks lists as manually scheduled (page 116). If you synchronize auto-scheduled tasks, SharePoint warns you that it will convert them to Manually Scheduled mode. That means you must specify the start and finish dates for all tasks, manage links between tasks as dates change, and resolve resource overallocations that occur.

- **Resources assigned to tasks must be members of the SharePoint site.** The only resources you can see in a SharePoint Tasks list are people who are members of the SharePoint site. If you assign other resources to tasks, the Resources cells for those tasks are blank.

- **Custom fields that use formulas don't synchronize.** The good news is that custom fields *without* formulas do synchronize to SharePoint. See page 539 for adding fields to the SharePoint Tasks list. The formula limitation is probably not a big hurdle, because you're not likely to customize too many fields with formulas if you're manually scheduling a project.

- **The Notes field doesn't synchronize.** One way to work around this limitation is to add notes to a custom Text field, which does synchronize.

Publishing Project tasks to SharePoint

If you build a task list in Project, here's how to publish it to a SharePoint Tasks list:

1. **Open the Project file you want to synchronize, and then choose File→Save & Send→Sync with Tasks List.**

   The Sync with Tasks List page appears in the Backstage.

2. **In the Site URL box, type the address for the Tasks list site, as shown in Figure 20 12. Click Validate URL.**

   Don't include the name of the Tasks list in the URL. For example, if your SharePoint site is called "ProjectCollaboration," type the URL for the site, something like *http://sharepoint/sites/ProjectCollaboration/*.

3. **In the "Select an existing tasks list, or enter a new name" box, choose the Tasks list you want to use.**

   When you validate the site URL, any existing Tasks lists on that site appear in the drop-down list. To create a new Tasks list, type a name for the new list. (SharePoint creates the Tasks list when you perform step 4.)

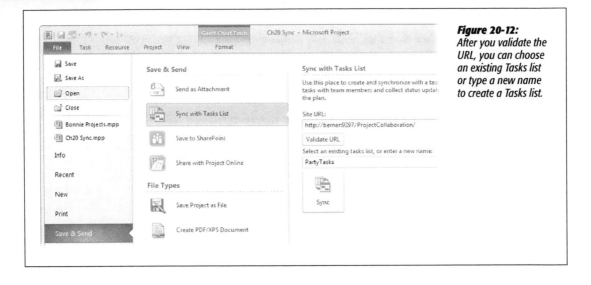

Figure 20-12:
After you validate the URL, you can choose an existing Tasks list or type a new name to create a Tasks list.

4. **Click Sync.**

   A SharePoint Synchronization message box shows progress. If you try to synchronize auto-scheduled tasks, a warning tells you that those tasks will change to manually scheduled. Click OK to continue. Click Cancel to keep the tasks auto-scheduled and cancel the synchronization.

   If any of the resources you've assigned to tasks don't exist within the SharePoint server, a warning tells you that those resources won't be published. Although you won't see the resource names in the SharePoint Tasks list, the assignments remain in your Project file.

5. **To see your tasks in SharePoint navigate to the site in your browser.**

   Tasks lists appear on the site home page under the Lists heading.

6. **Click the name of the Tasks list, for example "Party Tasks," as shown in Figure 20-13.**

   If the project has summary tasks, you initially see only the top-level summary tasks. Summary task names appear in blue text to indicate that you can click them to display their subtasks.

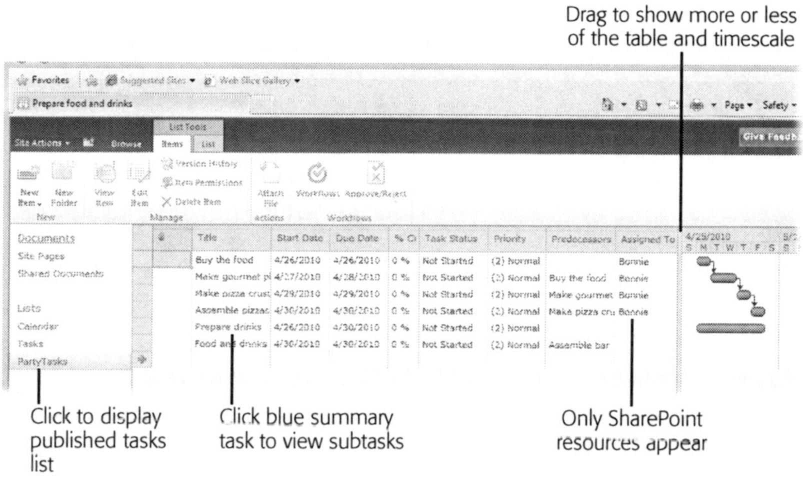

Drag to show more or less
of the table and timescale

Figure 20-13:
*The Tasks list displays
a Gantt Chart–like
view that works like
its counterpart in
Project. You can drag
the vertical divide to
show more or less of
the table or timescale.
Links between tasks
are visible in the
timescale. Summary
task names are blue
to show that you can
click them to display
their subtasks.*

Click to display
published tasks
list

Click blue summary
task to view subtasks

Only SharePoint
resources appear

Saving a SharePoint Tasks list to Project

You can build a list of tasks in SharePoint and then bring those tasks into Project.
When you add tasks to a SharePoint Tasks list, you can specify predecessors, assigned resources, and other task information. Here are the steps:

1. **In SharePoint, create a new Tasks list.**

   Click the Lists heading, and then click Create. On the Create page, under Tracking, click Project Tasks. In the Name box, type the name of the list and then
   Create. SharePoint adds the list to the navigation bar on the left side of the page.

2. **In the navigation bar, click the Tasks list name—for example, Tasks.**

   If any tasks already exist, they appear on the list page.

3. **To add a task to the list, click "Add new item".**

   The Tasks - New Item window appears, as shown in Figure 20-14.

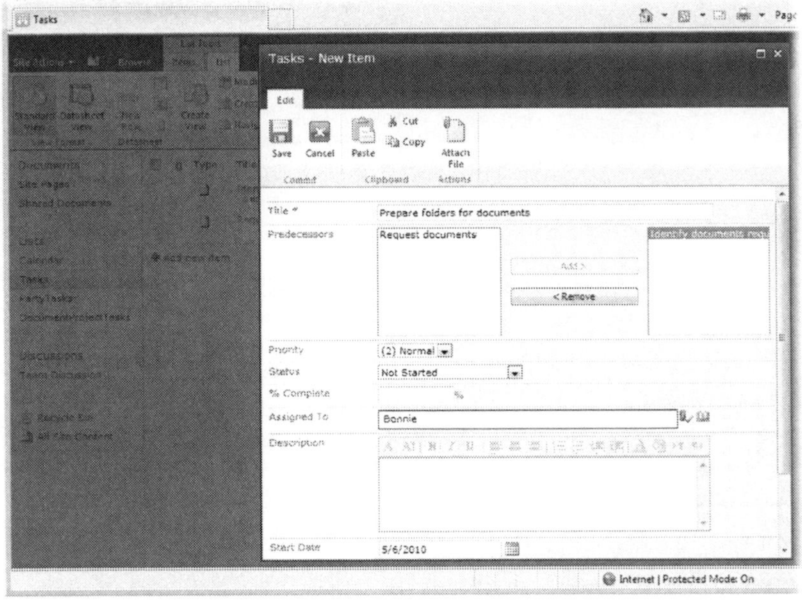

Figure 20-14:
When you create a new task in Share-Point, a form opens so you can name the task, specify prede-cessors, and assign resources to the task. You can also set the priority, status, and start date.

4. **In the Title box, type the name of the task. Specify any other task information you want.**

   To link the task to a predecessor, select the predecessor and click Add. To assign a resource, in the Assigned To box, type the name of the resource. In the Start Date box, type a date.

5. **Click Save.**

   The task appears in the list. Repeat steps 3 and 4 for each task you want to create.

6. **In Project, create a new blank Project file (page 124) and choose File→Save.**

   In the Save As dialog box, name the file and click Save.

7. **To sync the blank Project file to the Tasks list, perform the steps in the section "Publishing Project tasks to SharePoint" on page 535. In the "Select an exist-ing tasks list, or enter a new name" box, choose the Tasks list you created on the SharePoint site.**

   When you validate the site URL, any existing Tasks lists on that site appear in the "Select an existing tasks list, or enter a new name" drop-down list.

8. **Click Sync.**

   The tasks appear in your Project file.

Managing the fields in a SharePoint Tasks list

Once a connection exists between a Project file and a SharePoint Tasks list, you can specify the fields that appear in the SharePoint Tasks list. For example, you can add the WBS field, a cost field, or a custom field to the SharePoint view. The box on page 540 tells you why adding the WBS field can be helpful.

Here's how you specify the fields that sync to a SharePoint Tasks list:

1. **In Project, choose File→Info.**

   Once a Project file is linked to a SharePoint Tasks list, the Info page includes a Sync button. You can also choose File→Save & Send and then choose Sync with Tasks List.

2. **Below Sync with Tasks List, click Manage Fields.**

   The Manage Fields dialog box opens, showing the fields in the Project table and in SharePoint. A checkmark in the Sync column indicates that a field synchronizes between the two programs. In the Manage Fields dialog box, some fields are grayed out, which means you can't change whether they synchronize. For example, the Name, Start, Finish, % Complete, Resources Names, and Predecessors fields are automatically synchronized.

3. **To add a field, click Add Field. In the Add Field dialog box, choose the Project field you want to add, such as WBS (as shown in Figure 20-15), and then click OK. Click OK to close the Manage Fields dialog box.**

   The checkmark in the Sync column is turned on automatically.

4. **Click Sync.**

   You must click Sync to send the WBS information to SharePoint.

5. **In the SharePoint Tasks list, choose List Tools→List. On the List tab, choose Manage Views→Modify View.**

   The Edit View page appears.

6. **To display a field in the view, turn on the field's checkbox. Click OK.**

   To reorder the columns in a view, position the pointer over a column heading. When the pointer turns into a four-headed arrow, drag to the new location.

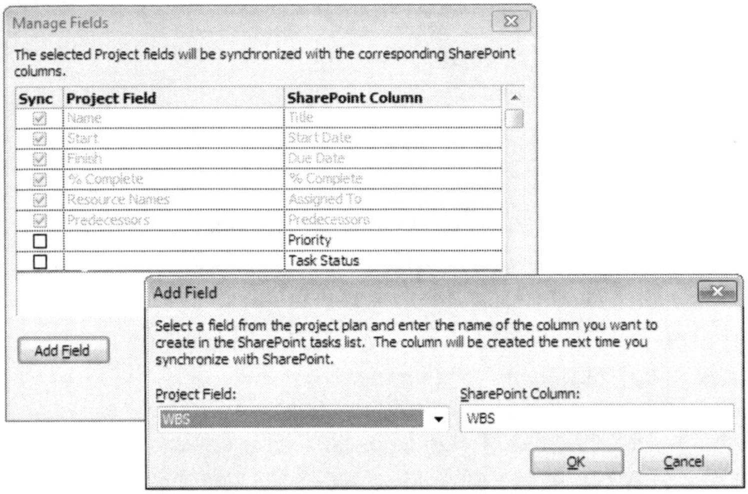

Figure 20-15:
To add a field, in the Project Field box, click the down arrow and choose the field you want to add. Project automatically copies the field name to the SharePoint Column box. If you want the SharePoint column to use a different heading, then type the name in the box before you click OK.

WORKAROUND WORKSHOP

Keeping Tasks in Order

"Sync with Tasks List" has an annoying idiosyncrasy. Sometimes when you synchronize tasks, they come across in seemingly random order. Links to predecessors don't help. In Project, you can easily sort the list (page 349) by ID number, the WBS code, or any other field to order the task list the way you want. You can do the same thing in SharePoint by adding the WBS field to a SharePoint Tasks List view. Then you can sort the Tasks list to match the order in your Project file. Here are the steps:

1. Add the WBS field to the SharePoint view, as described on page 539.

2. Synchronize your Tasks list to transfer the field values to SharePoint (page 540).

3. In the SharePoint Tasks list, choose List Tools→List. On the List tab, choose Manage Views→Modify View.

4. Turn on the WBS field's checkbox and click OK.

5. Click the down arrow to the right of the WBS heading, and then choose Sort A on Top.

Updating the Tasks list

You and your team members can view and edit values in SharePoint. For example, team members can change values in the % Complete field or change a finish date for a task. Then you can synchronize the changes (in Project, choose File→Info→Sync) to bring them back into Project. To edit a value in a SharePoint Tasks list, click the cell and type or choose the new value.

Note: If you and someone on your team both modify the same field—one in Project and the other in SharePoint—when you synchronize, Project displays a Conflict Resolution dialog box. The dialog box has a Project Version column and a SharePoint Version column. The fields that differ between the two are highlighted. To keep the values from Project, click Keep Project Version. To use the values from SharePoint, click Keep SharePoint Version.

Saving a Project File to a SharePoint Site

Storing files on a SharePoint site means you can share your files with others. As long as they have access to the SharePoint site, they can download the files stored there. A SharePoint site comes in handy in other ways. Imagine you travel to another office and your laptop dies en route. You can borrow a computer, go online, download the files you need from the SharePoint site, and continue working with a minimum of interruption. Although Project 2010 provides a command to save a Project file to a SharePoint site, you can choose from three methods:

- **Saving in Project.** Say you just added the finishing touches to a Project schedule and want to store the file on a SharePoint site. You can do that right within Project. Choose File→Save & Send→Save to SharePoint. Below the "Save to SharePoint" heading on the right side of the page, click "Browse for a location", and then choose the SharePoint site you want to use. Click Save As. In the Save As dialog box, click Save, and Project dutifully saves your file on the SharePoint site.

- **Saving on the SharePoint site.** If you're already on the SharePoint site, there's no need to go back to Project. On the SharePoint home page, choose Shared Documents or the name of your document library. Then, on the Shared Documents page, click "Add new document". In the Shared Documents - Upload Document dialog box, click Browse. In the Choose File to Upload dialog box, navigate to the folder with the file you want to save, select the file, and click Open. Back in the Shared Documents - Upload Document dialog box, click OK.

- The **Save As command.** You can also specify the URL for a SharePoint site in Project's Save As dialog box. Choose File→Save As. In the Save As dialog box, copy the URL for the SharePoint site into the folder path box, as shown in Figure 20-16, and click the arrow to navigate to the site. For example, if the Documents Library URL is *http://sharepoint/sites/ProjectCollaboration/Shared%20Documents/Forms/AllItems.aspx*, copy *http://sharepoint/sites/ProjectCollaboration/Shared%20Documents* into the box. When the SharePoint document library appears in the dialog box, click Save.

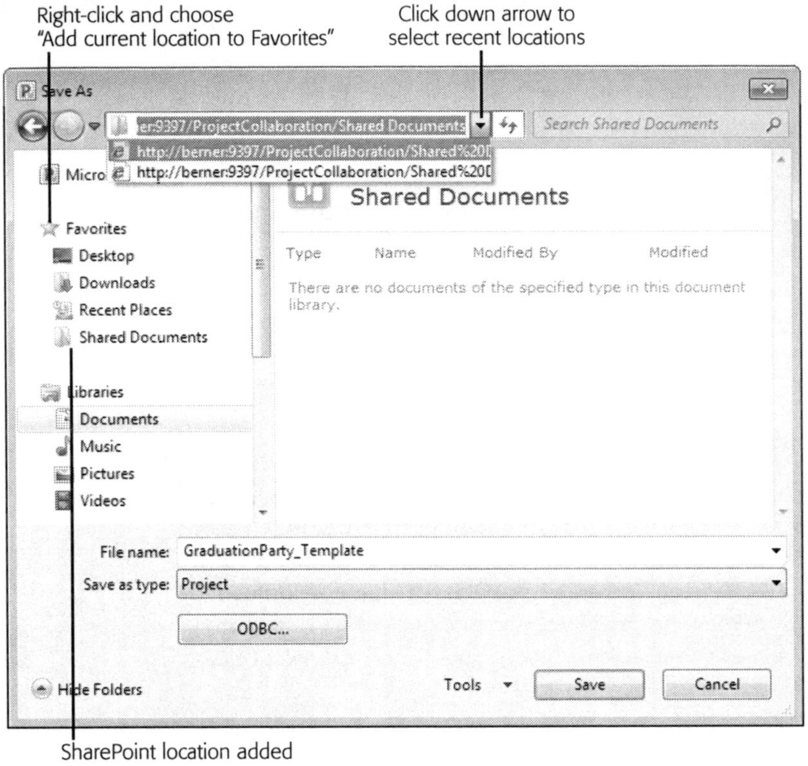

Right-click and choose
"Add current location to Favorites"

Click down arrow to
select recent locations

Figure 20-16:
After you copy a URL into the folder path box, you can choose the URL again by clicking the down arrow on the right side of the box. If you add the SharePoint URL to your Favorites list, you can reach it from any Open, Save, or Save As dialog box. For example, open the Documents Library in the Save As dialog box. Right-click Favorites, and then choose "Add current location to Favorites". The location joins your other favorite locations in the Favorites list as shown here.

SharePoint location added

Linking and Embedding

To manage projects, you usually need several types of information all at the same time. That's why so many project managers have a corkboard plastered with layers of printed pages or a computer screen with a dozen windows open at once. To see information without opening *every* program you own, you take information created in one program and display an editable copy of it in another program. This visual exchange goes in either direction: Project data can appear in other programs like Excel and PowerPoint, or information from other programs can appear in Project.

You have three ways to make this happen: copying, linking, and embedding. You can copy data from one program and paste it into another (see page 509 for copying and pasting). In a way, copying is a lot like embedding, because you create a copy of the data in the destination program, but embedding does more, as you'll learn shortly. *Linking* means connecting directly to information in one program from another program. For instance, a PowerPoint slide can display a high-level schedule from Project. When you update the schedule in Project, that latest, greatest version automatically appears in PowerPoint. On the other hand, *embedding* places a copy of an object (like a spreadsheet or Visio diagram) from one program into another. The embedded object and the original file aren't linked, so you don't automatically see changes made in the original. But embedded objects are ideal when you want to send self-contained files to colleagues.

Here are the differences between linking and embedding:

- **Linking** means the data remains in the source file, and the destination file merely displays the source file data. With linked objects, updating takes care of itself, because the data in the destination file and the source data are one and the same, so the data in the destination file changes when the source data does.

  When you double-click a linked object, the source program starts and you edit the source file. For example, suppose you link your Project schedule to a Power-Point slide, and you spot a schedule change you want to make. Double-click the linked object, and Project opens the source Project file. The changes you make are saved in the source Project file and also appear automatically in the PowerPoint slide.

- **Embedding** means that a separate copy (called an embedded object) of the source file becomes a part of the destination file. The source file still exists, but the embedded object is independent and doesn't change when the source data changes.

  In most cases, when you double-click an embedded object, the source program doesn't start. Instead, you see its menus in place of the destination program menus (page 558). For example, double-clicking an embedded Excel spreadsheet in the Project timescale pane replaces Project's menus with Excel's and you see a hatched border around the object. The menus revert when you deselect the embedded object. Editing the embedded object doesn't affect the source file. In Project, embedded objects can also behave in another way, which page 558 explains.

Tip: Linking and embedding work with any program that supports Object Linking and Embedding (OLE), which Microsoft developed specifically so that files can contain components created in different programs.

Whether linking or embedding is the better choice depends on what you're trying to do. Bottom line, linking is better if the source data is going to change. Embedding is better when you need to widely distribute the destination file, particularly to recipients who can't access your computers. Table 21-1 shows the pros and cons of each approach.

Table 21-1. *Whether you use linking or embedding depends on what you're trying to do.*

Feature	Linking	Embedding
Updating	Linking keeps data up to date in both source and destination files. You can edit the source file from either program and see the updated information in both places.	The destination file doesn't update along with the source. If you want to update an embedded object, then you must either make the same changes to the embedded object or re-embed the object after the changes are made.
Copies of data	Linking means there's only one copy of the data, so you don't have to make the same changes multiple times. The link breaks if you move the source file, but you can repair it (page 556).	An embedded object is a second copy of the data. To show the most recent data in an embedded object, you must edit the embedded object or delete and re-embed it.
Distributing data	When you distribute a file with links, the recipients see the data only if they can access the linked files. If they can't, then the links break, and they see an error message instead.	You can distribute the destination file with the source data in it. The destination file contains everything the recipients need to view and edit the data.
File size	Destination files don't increase in size, because the data remains in the source file.	The size of a destination file increases because it contains the embedded object and all of its data.
Performance	When a file contains multiple links, it takes time to open the links (especially over a network). The file has to examine each source file for updates to the linked objects.	The additional data in embedded objects can make the destination file slower to open and respond.

The procedures for linking and embedding are usually almost identical—except for turning a Link checkbox on or off. However, a few linking and embedding techniques stray further from the typical path, depending on the type of data, and whether you're displaying Project data in other programs, or vice versa. This chapter describes the steps for each approach.

Linking and Embedding Project Data

Project data comes in handy in lots of other programs. For example, a Project schedule shows project status whether it appears in a PowerPoint slide, a Word-based status report, or an Excel spreadsheet. Similarly, you might embed a Resource Graph into a memo requesting resources. This section describes how to link and embed Project data into other programs.

Linking Project Files to Other Programs

Sometimes, pictures of Project views aren't enough. You might want the Gantt Chart in your status report to show the up-to-date project schedule. When you link a Project file to another program, the linked object initially displays the portion of the view that you copied in Project. Once the linked object is in place, you can edit it to change the view, filter the tasks, and so on (as described on page 555).

Note: Office programs can be fussy about linking objects, but the box on page 547 provides a workaround.

Here's how you link a Project file to another program:

1. **Open the Project file and the destination file.**

   You can link to a Project view in any program that supports OLE, including Excel, Word, and PowerPoint.

2. **In Project, set up the view the way you want it.**

   Select the view and the table you want. If necessary, insert or hide columns in the table. Filter the view to show only the tasks, resources, or assignments you want.

3. **Select the data you want to link, and then, on the Task tab, click Copy (or press Ctrl+C).**

   Whether you select cells in a table or entire rows by dragging over their ID numbers, the Copy command places what you've selected on the Clipboard.

4. **In the destination file, click where you want to place the linked view.**

   Unlike pasting table cells, a view comes in as one object with its top-left corner at the location you click.

5. **Choose the Paste Special command.**

   For Office 2010 programs, choose Home→Clipboard→Paste→Paste Special. In Office 2003 (and many non-Microsoft programs), choose Edit→Paste Special.

   The Paste Special dialog box opens.

6. **In the Paste Special dialog box, select the "Paste link" option, as illustrated in Figure 21-1.**

   Be sure to select Paste Link, since the Paste option embeds the object instead of linking it. If the Paste Link option is grayed out, be sure to save the Project file, and then recopy and try Paste Link again.

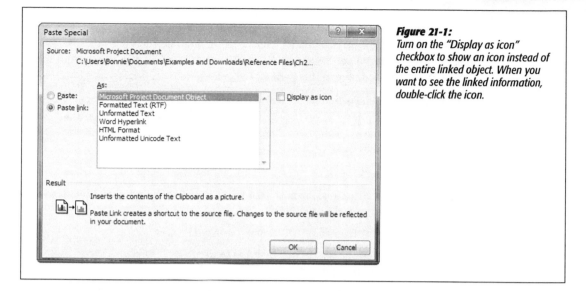

Figure 21-1:
Turn on the "Display as icon" checkbox to show an icon instead of the entire linked object. When you want to see the linked information, double-click the icon.

7. **In the As list, select Microsoft Project Document Object, and then click OK.**

The Project view appears as a single object in the destination file. You can move the linked object around by dragging from the center of the object. To resize the object, select it, and then drag the boxes at the corners and the middle of each side.

TROUBLESHOOTING MOMENT

When Programs Won't Link

If your Office 2010 programs like Excel are reluctant to create links, the problem could be your security settings. For example, you've copied Project data to the Clipboard, but in Excel, the Paste Link command (or the Paste Link option in the Paste Special dialog box) is grayed out. Here's how you tell Excel to play well with others:

1. Choose File→Options.

2. In the Excel Options dialog box, choose Trust Center, and then click Trust Center Settings.

3. In the Trust Center dialog box, choose External Content.

4. Select either the "Enable automatic update for all Workbook links" option or the "Prompt user on automatic update for Workbooks links" option.

Embedding Project Files in Other Programs

Embedding Project data into another program creates a copy of your project in the destination file. Embedding data creates a self-contained file—for example, for the subcontractors who can't access your computer systems. If you send them status reports with linked objects, they would see broken links, not data.

You can create objects to embed as you go, as the box on page 551 describes. However, creating a Project file on the fly is a bad idea, because that file is available only within the destination file. By creating the file in Project, you can embed the file *and* keep the original to work with.

To embed a Project file in another program, follow these steps:

1. **Open the destination file, and then select the location where you want to embed your Project object.**

    Project doesn't have to be running to embed a Project file.

2. **In an Office program, choose Insert→Text→Insert Object (the icon looks like a picture with a cactus).**

    For Office 2003 and many non-Microsoft programs, choose Insert→Object.

    The Object dialog box opens.

3. **Select the "Create from File" tab, and then select the file you want to embed.**

    To locate the file, click Browse. In the Browse window, navigate to the folder that contains your Project file, and then double-click the filename. The path and filename appear in the "File name" box, as shown in Figure 21-2.

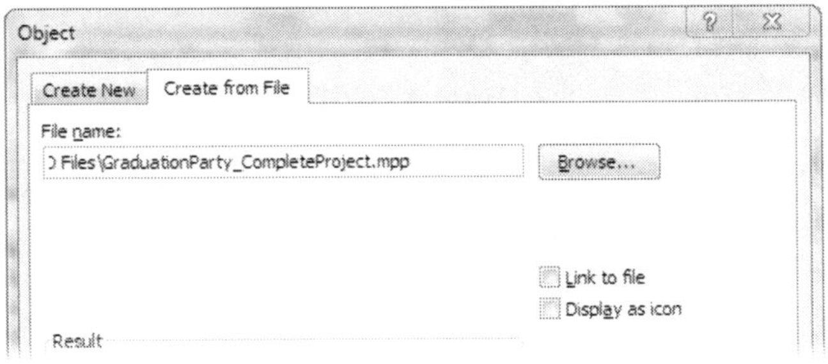

Figure 21-2:
You can turn an embedded file into a linked file in no time flat simply by turning on the "Link to file" checkbox.

4. **To show an icon until you want to see the Project file, turn on the "Display as icon" checkbox.**

    Turning on the "Display as icon" checkbox displays a Change Icon button. In the Change Icon dialog box, you can select the icon you want to show, and the label.

5. Click OK.

The embedded file appears at the selected location in the destination file. If you display an icon for an embedded file, then you can open the file by double-clicking its icon.

Linking Project Table Data to Other Programs

You can create links from selected Project table cells directly to cells in another file, like an Excel spreadsheet. When the Project values change, the linked cells in the other program display the updated values. For example, by linking Project cost cells to Excel, a return on investment spreadsheet could show the rate of return at any time—perfect for surprise executive visits.

Linking and copying both work with Project table cells, but linked cells get their values directly from source Project cells. Copying pastes the text or numbers from the source Project cells into destination cells; copied data is the same as values you enter directly.

Note: You can't embed a portion of a Project table into another file. If you try, the program embeds the entire Project file instead.

To link Project table cells to cells in a program like Excel, follow these steps:

1. **Open both the Project file and the destination file.**

   For example, open an Excel spreadsheet.

2. **In Project, display the table you want to link to Excel.**

   If necessary, display the view you want. To change the table, right-click the Select All cell (the gray cell at the intersection of the column heading row and the ID column), and then choose the table from the drop-down list. If the table doesn't appear on the drop-down list, choose More Tables. In the More Tables dialog box, select the table and click Apply.

3. **Select the data you want to link, and then choose Task→Copy (or right-click and choose Copy Cell).**

   Use any of the usual techniques for selecting data: dragging over column headings to select entire columns, dragging from the top-left to the bottom-right cell of a range, or Ctrl-clicking or Shift-clicking cells.

4. **In the destination file, click the top-left cell for the linked data.**

   The data starts at the cell you click, and then fills in cells to the right and below that cell.

5. **In Excel, choose Home→Clipboard→Paste→Paste Special. In the Paste Special dialog box, select the Paste link option, as shown in Figure 21-3. Select HTML or Text, and then click OK.**

The linked data appears in the selected cells. If you can't see the full values, adjust the column widths in the destination file.

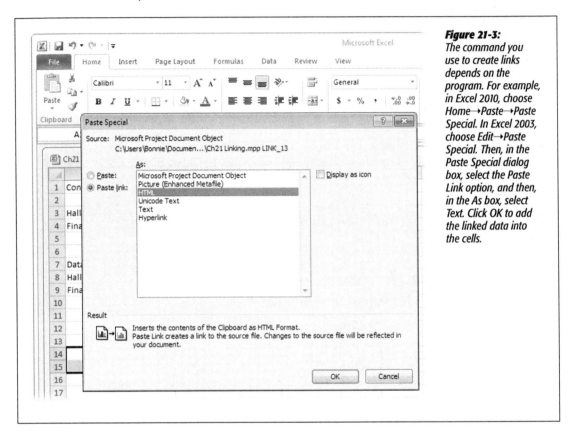

Figure 21-3:
The command you use to create links depends on the program. For example, in Excel 2010, choose Home→Paste→Paste Special. In Excel 2003, choose Edit→Paste Special. Then, in the Paste Special dialog box, select the Paste Link option, and then, in the As box, select Text. Click OK to add the linked data into the cells.

Linking and Embedding Data into Project

Linking and embedding data goes in either direction. Just as a Project schedule can provide information for a status report or presentation, other files can provide background information for the tasks in your Project schedule. For example, you might link information in a risk log spreadsheet to an at-risk task, so the most recent actions and results appear in the Task Information dialog box. Likewise, you could embed a Visio workflow diagram in the Gantt Chart timescale.

You can link or embed entire files into Project, or link cells from an Excel spreadsheet to Project table cells. In addition, you can link or embed portions of other files, like Excel charts or Visio drawing pages. This section explains how to link and embed data into Project.

GEM IN THE ROUGH

Creating Objects from Scratch

When you insert an object in a file, the dialog box (Object or Insert Object depending on the program) offers a two-for-one deal in which you can create an object and, at the same time, embed it in the container file. Although you can edit this embedded object like any other—for example to add formulas to a spreadsheet—the only time this approach makes sense is when the information you create is an inseparable part of the container file. That's because the embedded object you create in this way exists only in that file. If there's any chance you might need the information elsewhere, you should use its source program to create it, and then embed the resulting file.

To create a new embedded object, follow these steps:

1. In the container file (an Excel spreadsheet, for example), select the location where you want the new object.

2. Open the Object or Insert Object dialog box. (In Office 2007 or 2010, click Insert→Text→Object or Insert→Text→Insert Object. For example, in Excel, the Insert Object icon looks like a small landscape.

For Office 2003 and many non-Microsoft programs, choose Insert→Object. If Project is the container, open the Task Information dialog box and select the Notes tab, or display the Notes pane in the Task Form. Then choose the Insert Object icon.

3. If the program you're using opens the Object dialog box (like Word or Excel), then select the Create New tab. If the Insert Object dialog box opens instead (like Project), then select the Create New option.

4. In the Object Type list, select the type of object you want to create. Your choice determines which program menus you see when you double-click the object. For example, to create an Excel workbook, select Microsoft Office Excel Worksheet.

5. Click OK. A blank object appears in the container file.

6. To add content to the object, make sure it's selected, and then use the program menus that appear.

7. To revert to the container file's parent program, simply click outside the boundaries of the embedded object. To edit the object, double-click it.

Linking and Embedding Entire Files into Project

Inserting an entire file into Project is perfect for easy access to additional information—for example, a specifications Word document or a change request tracking database. To see more of the file, simply drag the boundaries of the inserted object. To see a different part of the file, select the object and then edit it, as described on page 555. When you work with entire files, the linking and embedding steps are almost identical:

1. **Open your Project file, and then select the location where you want to insert the other file.**

   Only some areas of a Project file accept inserted objects: the Gantt Chart timescale, the Notes or Objects boxes in the Task Form or Resource Form, and the Notes tab in the Task Information, Resource Information, or Assignment Information dialog box.

2. **On the Notes tab in any of the Information dialog boxes, simply click the Insert Object button immediately above the Notes area.**

   The Insert Object dialog box opens.

   If you want to insert objects in the Gantt Chart timescale, you must customize the ribbon (see Chapter 25) to add the Object command to a custom group (in the "Choose commands from" list, choose All Commands, and scroll until you see the Object command).

3. **Select the "Create from File" option, and then choose the file you want to link or embed.**

   Click Browse to navigate to the folder that contains the file you want. Double-click the filename, and the path and filename appear in the "File name" box.

4. **To link to the file, be sure to turn on the Link checkbox.**

   Initially, the Link checkbox is turned off, which means that Project will embed the file.

5. **To display the file as an icon until you want to see it, turn on the "Display as icon" checkbox.**

   After you insert the link in Project, you will be able to open it by double-clicking it.

6. **Click OK.**

   The object appears at the location you selected in your Project file.

Linking and Embedding Parts of Files in Project

With some programs, you can extract portions of a file to link or embed. A chart from an Excel spreadsheet, a slide from a PowerPoint presentation, or a drawing page from a Visio document are all candidates for inserting into a Project file. The advantage is that the inserted object represents only that portion of the file, so linked objects have less data to update, and embedded objects don't take up as much room.

To link or embed a part of a file into your Project file, follow these steps:

1. **In the source program, open the file and select what you want to show in your Project schedule.**

   For example, in Visio, drag across the shapes you want to link or embed in Project. To select an entire Visio drawing page, make sure no shapes are selected. For an Excel chart, select the chart.

2. **Press Ctrl+C to copy the selection to the Clipboard.**

   In Office 2010 programs, click Home→Clipboard→Copy. For Office 2003 and non-Microsoft programs, choose Edit→Copy or, on the Standard toolbar, click Copy.

3. In your Microsoft Project file, select the location where you want to place the object, and then choose Task→Clipboard→Paste→Paste Special.

   Because you must choose Paste Special from the ribbon, you can't insert these partial objects in the Notes tab of the Information dialog boxes. You can insert them in the Gantt Chart timescale and the Objects box in the Task Form or Resource Form. (To display the Objects box in a form, right-click the top part of the form, and then, in the shortcut menu, choose Objects).

4. In the Paste Special dialog box, select the Paste Link option to create a link to the source data.

   Initially, Project selects the Paste option, which embeds the object. The Paste Link option can be stubborn and appear grayed out. Make sure you've saved the Project file at least once, so the program knows where the file is stored and can define the link. If saving the file doesn't help, try copying and paste-linking the information again.

5. In the As box, select the type of object, as shown in Figure 21-4.

   The choices vary depending on what you copied to the Clipboard.

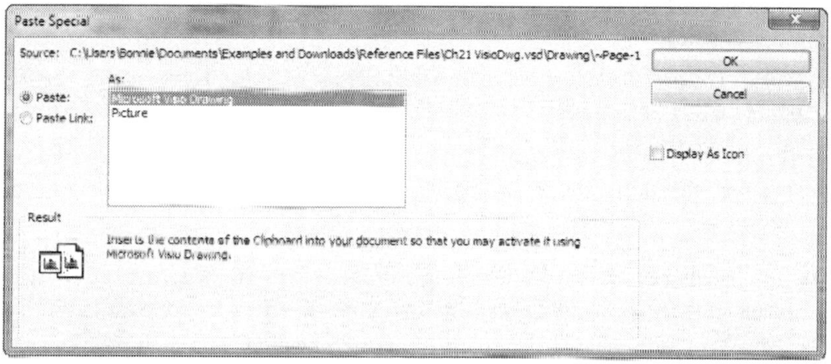

Figure 21-4:
If the object you're linking or embedding is an Excel chart, for example, select Microsoft Office Excel Chart. Select Microsoft Visio Drawing to insert a Visio drawing page.

Note: The Picture type appears in the As list whether you select Paste or Paste Link. If you select the Paste option and the Picture type, then Project inserts a picture as you'd expect. If you select Paste Link and Picture, then Project acts as if you selected a type like Microsoft Visio Drawing. Linking a picture of a Visio drawing actually inserts a linked Microsoft Visio Drawing object. Double-clicking the object opens the Visio file to the drawing page.

---

6. Click OK.

   The object appears in Project at the location you selected.

Linking Tabular Data in Project

Just as you can link Project table cells into other programs, you can bring data from other programs into Project's table cells. When you link data to Project cells, the values look as if you typed them directly into Project, but they're actually linked to the source file, and change when the source data changes. Project demands the right types of data in its fields, so you have to make sure the data types are the same in both places. The easiest way to keep data types in sync is to link column by column:

1. **In Excel or another table-based program, select the first column you want to link (click the column heading), and then press Ctrl+C.**

   Another advantage to linking column by column is that the links don't break if you rearrange the columns. For example, if you link several Excel columns at once, then the Project link expects those columns to stay in the same order. If you move one of the columns in the Excel spreadsheet, then the entire Project link breaks. However, if you link each column separately, then you can move the columns, and the links continue to work.

2. **In Project, display the view and table in which you want to link the data. Then select the first cell for the linked data.**

   Select the top-left cell for the linked data. Project fills in the other cells to the right and below.

3. **Choose Task→Clipboard→Paste→Paste Special, and then select the Paste Link option.**

   If you choose the Paste option, Project simply copies the values into the Project cell as text, numbers, dates, and so on.

4. **In the As box, select Text Data.**

   As you learned on page 552, selecting an object type like Microsoft Office Excel Worksheet inserts a linked object that you double-click to open and edit. By selecting Text Data, Project fills in individual cells with linked values. Each linked cell gets its value from the corresponding cell in the source file.

5. **Click OK.**

   The cells display values from the source file. To link other columns in the source file, repeat steps 1 through 5 for each additional column.

Working with Linked and Embedded Objects

Linking or embedding information into another file is just the beginning. Linked and embedded objects are incredibly versatile, and this section shows you all the things you can do with them. Most of the time, you want the information in linked and embedded objects to be visible at all times, but these objects can just as easily keep a low profile as icons until you want to see what they have to show. Like other elements in files, you can move or resize objects—for instance, to get them out of the way of task bars in a Gantt Chart or graphics on a Visio diagram. And the whole point of inserting a linked or embedded object instead of a picture is to edit it at some point. For linked and embedded objects to work, you need to know how to manage links between files, and this section explains that as well.

Linked and embedded objects work like many other elements in your files. You can select them, move them around, change their size, and delete them. Here's how:

- **Resize an object.** When you select an object by clicking it, resize handles appear at each corner and at the middle of each side. You can drag these handles to change the size of the object. To change the object dimensions while maintaining its proportion, drag a handle at one of the corners. The pointer changes to an angled two-headed arrow. To change the size in only one dimension, drag a handle at the middle of a side. The pointer changes to either a horizontal or vertical two-headed arrow.

- **Move an object.** You can move an object whether or not it's selected by dragging the middle of the object to the new location. The pointer changes to a four-headed arrow to indicate that you're about to move the object. If you drag too close to an edge, then the object resizes instead.

- **Delete an object.** Select the object, and then press Delete.

- **Display the object behind an icon.** When you choose to display an object as an icon, double-click the icon to bring the full object into view. Dragging an icon moves the object, just as dragging the actual object does.

Editing Linked Objects

Whether you're working in the source program or container program when you edit a linked object, you always edit the same source file. Suppose you link an Excel spreadsheet to your Gantt Chart timescale. If you edit the spreadsheet in Excel, then the changes you make show up automatically the next time you open or update your Project file. On the other hand, you can double-click the linked object in Project to start Excel and open the source file for editing.

Editing linked objects works differently from editing embedded objects in that you always do your editing *in the source file*. Here's how it works:

1. **To edit a linked object, double-click it.**

   The source file opens in the source program. For example, double-clicking a linked Excel spreadsheet starts Excel and opens the spreadsheet—as if you'd started Excel yourself and opened the file. You must have read-write privileges for the file in order to edit it, just as you would if you opened the file directly. The box on page 556 explains your options if an error message appears when you try to edit a linked object.

2. **When you see the message box telling you that you're opening an OLE object that could contain viruses and other malicious code, if you're sure it's safe, click Yes to open the file.**

   If you have any doubts about the file, click No.

3. **When you finish editing, save the file as you would normally, and then close the object's program (Excel in this example).**

   Back in the container file, the linked object displays the changes. If the linked object isn't up to date, you can tell the container program to immediately check for updates, as described in the next section.

Opening Reluctant Links

If an error message appears when you try to edit a linked object (or when you open a file with links), a broken link is the most likely suspect. Links are smart enough to change if you rename the file or move it to a new folder on the same drive. However, if the linked file moves to a different file server, you must edit the link to point to the correct file location (page 556).

Alternatively, if the file location is fine, then the problem could be that the file is already open in its source program. Your easiest fix is editing the file there.

The last reason for problems editing links is that the source program isn't installed on your computer. For example, when you edit a linked Visio drawing, Visio starts and opens the file, which means you must have Visio on your computer.

Managing Linked Objects

Linked objects require ongoing care and feeding. For example, you must make sure that links can find the files they represent. If links are broken, then you can redirect them to the correct location for the source file. Conversely, you can intentionally break the link between an object and the source file to transform the object into an embedded object or picture. Finally, you can update a link immediately and tell the container program whether you want it to update links automatically or wait for you to say when.

The Links dialog box, shown in Figure 21-5, is where you begin link management tasks. The Edit Links command isn't on the ribbon, so you must add it to a custom group (page 661) before you can use it.

Here's how to keep links in tip-top condition:

- **Review links.** The Edit Links dialog box lists the links in your file whether they connect to other places in the same file or different files altogether. When you select a link in the list, the Source line shows the path and filename at the bottom of the dialog box. The Type line indicates the type of file.

- **Update a link.** To immediately update a link with changes from the source file, select the link, and then click Update Now.

Note: When you open a file with links, a message box asks whether you want to update the links. Click Yes to display the most recent data from the linked file.

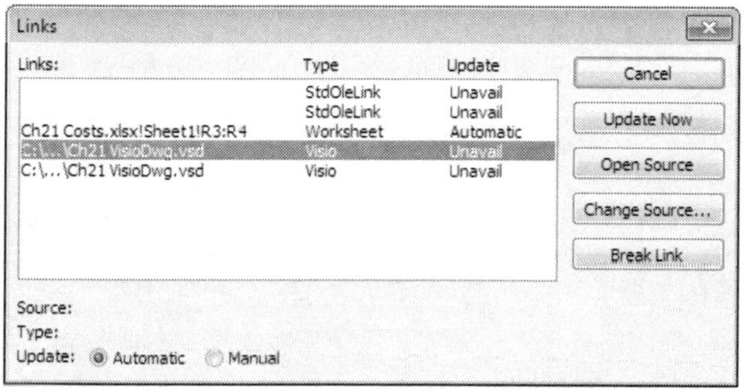

Figure 21-5:
In Project, you can use a keyboard shortcut to open the Links dialog box. Press Alt+E as if you were opening the Edit menu in Project 2007 and then press "." (the period key). Or customize the ribbon to add the Edit Links command to a custom group (page 662). For Office 2010 programs like Excel, open the Edit Links dialog box by selecting the ribbon's Data tab, and then, in the Connections group, choosing Edit Links.

- **Repair a broken link.** You can fix broken links by changing the folder or file that a link looks for. Click Change Source. In the Change Source dialog box, click Browse to find the file. Double-click the filename to update the path and name in the Source box. Click OK to save the link.

- **Change a linked object into an embedded object.** Suppose you linked to a document during its development so you always saw the most recent version. Now that the document is approved, you want to embed it so you can see the document without the baggage of maintaining the link. You can convert a linked object into an embedded object in the Edit Links dialog box by selecting the link and then clicking Break Link. The link disappears from the list in the Links dialog box, but the object remains, and now acts like the embedded object it is.

- **Specify when to update the link.** Initially, Project and other programs create links so they update automatically, which means that the container program checks source files for changes and updates the objects with any changes it finds. All that checking and updating can slow your program to a crawl, especially if the source files change frequently or are located on large or complex networks. In this situation, you can control when updates occur by selecting a link, and then selecting the Manual option.

Editing Embedded Objects

You double-click embedded objects to edit them, just like you do linked objects. The result, in most cases, is that the menus for the container program change to the menus for the embedded object's program. For example, when you double-click an Excel spreadsheet embedded in your Gantt Chart, Excel menus appear where the Project menus just were, as illustrated in Figure 21-6. You can work on the Excel object as if you were working directly in Excel. When you're done, click away from the embedded object, and the Project menus reappear. It's like having two programs at your fingertips.

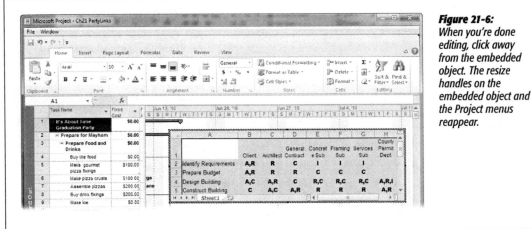

Figure 21-6:
When you're done editing, click away from the embedded object. The resize handles on the embedded object and the Project menus reappear.

If you embed an object in a Project task's note (select the task and choose Task→Properties→Information, click the Notes tab, and then click the Insert Object icon), then double-clicking the embedded object opens the object in the source program. However, if you click the File tab in that program, the heading on the Info screen says "Information about Embedded Object"—which is your clue that you aren't editing a source file.

CHAPTER 22

Project on the Internet

These days, business relies on the Internet as much as cellphones and fax machines. Although Project isn't a web browser or email program, it doesn't leave you stranded offline. Far from it. Just as hyperlinks help you navigate websites, you can access web pages by following hyperlinks in Project files. You can even access other files the same way.

Like any self-respecting Microsoft program, Project also has a strong working relationship with Outlook. For example, you can share tasks and contacts between Project and Outlook (so you can take advantage of Outlook's reminder feature, for example). You can even send email messages and attachments right from Project—ideal for things like circulating reports among project stakeholders.

Hyperlinking to Information

Managing projects means keeping track of information stored in different places and different types of files. As a project manager, your nose is usually buried in a Project file, so why not access the information you need directly from Project? For example, you can add hyperlinks to tasks to access the corresponding work package Word documents, an Excel spreadsheet with financial figures, or the web page with your customer's mission statement. Project hyperlinks can also jump to tasks or resources within the Project file.

Note: You can add only one hyperlink to each task, resource, or assignment.

Creating a Hyperlink to a File or Web Page

Hyperlinks can connect to any kind of file—a Word document, an Excel spreadsheet, a web page, and so on. Although the destination file can reside anywhere (anywhere that's accessible to the people who need it), the file must remain in the same place. If the file moves to another location, the hyperlink can't find the file and becomes what's known as a broken link.

To create a hyperlink in a Project file, do the following:

1. **Display the view that shows the task, resource, or assignment to which you want to add a hyperlink.**

   You can insert hyperlinks in any view.

2. **Right-click the task, resource, or assignment, and then choose Hyperlink. (Or select the task, resource, or assignment, and then press Ctrl+K.)**

   The Insert Hyperlink dialog box opens.

3. **In the "Text to display" box, type a brief description of what you're hyperlinking to.**

   The "Text to display" box is initially empty. If you type a description, as shown in Figure 22-1, Project leaves it in place when you select a destination file.

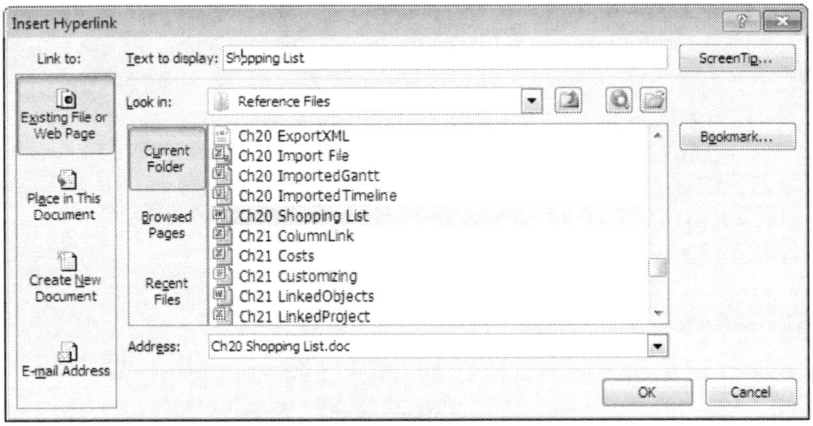

Figure 22-1:
If you don't type a description in the "Text to display" box, Project fills in the path and file name of the destination file or the URL of a Web page. When you position the mouse over a hyperlink indicator, a pop-up box containing the description appears.

The Insert Hyperlink dialog box also has a ScreenTip button. When you position the pointer over a hyperlink indicator without clicking, a ScreenTip appears immediately below the description. If you type a meaningful description in the "Text to display" box, you may not need a ScreenTip, but it's handy if you want to see more information about a hyperlink before you click it.

4. **In the "Link to" section, select the type of destination to which you want to hyperlink, like "Existing File or Web Page".**

   The left side of the Insert Hyperlink dialog box has two navigation bars for choosing what you want to hyperlink to: "Link to" and "Look in". In the "Link to" navigation bar, the aptly named "Existing File or Web Page" and "Place in This Document" are the most popular types of hyperlinks. (The next section describes the steps for linking to a location in your Project file.)

   Although you can create a new document and hyperlink to it at the same time, creating the document outside Project is more expedient. Outside Project, you can create the document based on a template. Moreover, you keep your multitasking to a minimum. You can also create a hyperlink to an email address, so you can easily email the person assigned to a task.

5. **In the "Look in" section, navigate to the folder that contains the destination file, and then select the file name.**

   The "Look in" drop-down list includes all the locations you can reach through the My Computer window: drives on your computer, network drives, and removable drives. To look for the file you want, click the "Browse for File" button (which looks like an open file folder) to the right of the "Look in" box. The "Link to File" dialog box opens.

   The "Look in" area's navigation bar has three choices for finding files or web pages. Current Folder shows the files in the folder you've selected. To hyperlink to files or web pages that you've used recently, select Browsed Pages or Recent Files.

   The "Browse the Web" button to the left of the "Browse for File" button opens an Internet Explorer browser window. Surf to the web page you want. When you click the Address box in the Insert Hyperlink dialog box, Project copies the URL into the box.

6. **Click OK.**

   A hyperlink indicator (which looks like a globe with links of chain) appears in the Indicators column. Double-click the indicator to open the hyperlinked file with its associated program.

   If the Indicators column isn't visible, then you can't tell which elements have hyperlinks. However, if you know a hyperlink exists, you can follow it by right-clicking the task, resource, or assignment, and then, from the shortcut menu, choosing Hyperlink→Open. To insert the Indicators column in the table, right-click the table heading, and then choose Insert Column. In the drop-down menu, choose Indicators, and then click OK.

Modifying Hyperlinks

You can edit or remove hyperlinks. For example, if a destination file moves to a new location or a web page address changes, edit the hyperlink to point to the new location:

- **Modify a hyperlink.** Right-click the task, resource, or assignment, and then, on the shortcut menu, choose Hyperlink→Edit Hyperlink. The Edit Hyperlink dialog box has all the same components as the Insert Hyperlink dialog box. Change the values you want, and then click OK to update the link.

- **Remove a hyperlink.** Right-click the task, resource, or assignment, and then, on the shortcut menu, choose Clear Hyperlinks. Project deletes the hyperlink, and the hyperlink indicator disappears.

Creating a Hyperlink to a Location in the Project File

Hyperlinking from one place in your Project file to another is a great way to find related tasks or resources. A hyperlink can take you from a design task to the corresponding development task or the resource assigned to the task. Although you can add hyperlinks to tasks, resources, or assignments, hyperlinks can point only to tasks or resources in your Project file. Moreover, you must know the task ID or resource ID that you want to link to *before* you open the Insert Hyperlink dialog box.

To create a hyperlink to another location in the same Project file, do the following:

1. **Right-click the task, resource, or assignment to which you want to add a hyperlink, and then choose Hyperlink.**

   The Insert Hyperlink dialog box opens.

2. **In the "Text to display" box, type a brief description of the hyperlink destination.**

   Project keeps your description when you select a destination task or resource. If you don't fill in the "Text to display" box, then Project fills it in with the view name and ID that you select, which isn't particularly informative—for instance, "Gantt Chart!20 for task ID 20 in the Gantt Chart view."

3. **In the "Link to" section, select "Place in This Document".**

   Project replaces the "Look in" area with a box for task or resource ID and a list of views to select, as shown in Figure 22-2.

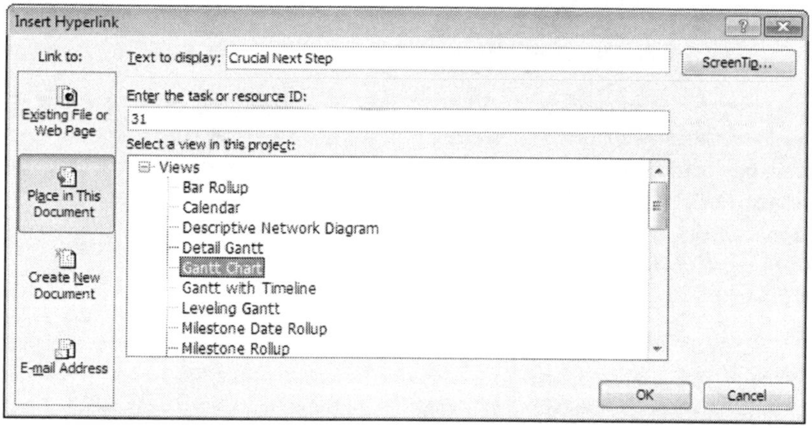

Figure 22-2:
When "Existing File or Web Page" is selected in the "Link to" area, you can still create a hyperlink within the file. Click Bookmark to open the "Select Place in Document" dialog box, which contains an ID box and view list.

4. **In the "Enter the task or resource ID" box, type the number for the task or ID (the number in the first column of the task or resource table).**

   Project determines whether the number is a task ID or resource ID based on the view you select. ID represents a task ID when you select a task-oriented view like the Gantt Chart; selecting the Resource Sheet changes the box to a resource ID.

5. **In the "Select a view in this project" box, select the view you want Project to display when you follow the hyperlink.**

   If you haven't filled in the "Text to display" box, then Project inserts the view name in the box in front of the ID.

6. **Click OK.**

   A hyperlink indicator appears in the Indicators column. Clicking the hyperlink indicator switches to the hyperlinked view and opens the Task Information dialog box (or Resource Information dialog box) for the hyperlinked task or resource.

   If you right-click the task, resource, or assignment and then choose Hyperlink→Open, Project opens the hyperlinked view, and then selects the first cell in the row for the hyperlinked task or resource.

Reviewing Hyperlinks

Checking that hyperlinks are correct is a good idea after time has passed, as files may find homes in new locations. The ScreenTip pop-up box for hyperlink indicators shows the hyperlink description, which typically isn't the file or location you're jumping to. If you right-click an element and then choose Hyperlink→Open, you don't know where the hyperlink goes until Project follows it.

To simplify hyperlink review, display the Hyperlink table, which displays the Task Name, Hyperlink, Address, and SubAddress columns. (Resource views begin with the Resource Name column.) To apply the Hyperlink table, right-click the Select All cell (the cell above the ID column), and then, in the shortcut menu, choose More Tables. In the More Tables dialog box, choose Hyperlink, and then click Apply. This table shows hyperlinks for the tasks or resources; you don't see any values other than task names or resource names if the tasks or resources don't have hyperlinks.

In the Hyperlink table, the Hyperlink column shows the hyperlink description. Address represents the Hyperlink Address field and shows the external files or web pages you hyperlink to. For hyperlinks between locations in the file, the Address cell is empty. Instead, the SubAddress column represents the Hyperlink Subaddress field, which shows the view and ID for internal hyperlinks. All the entries in these cells are "hot," so you can click them to follow the hyperlink.

Integrating Project and Outlook

Outlook is Microsoft's email workhorse, but email is only one of the ways that Outlook and Project work as a team. When you're in Project, you can email Project files without jumping over to Outlook to do so. But because both programs can store lists of tasks and names, you can export Project tasks to Outlook and vice versa. You can even use your Outlook address book to build your resource list in Project. This section explains how to use these features.

Adding Project Tasks to Outlook

If the old saying "out of sight, out of mind" is all too true in your case, you can keep important Project tasks in sight by adding them (one at a time) to your Outlook Task List. By adding a reminder to these Outlook tasks, you can really stay on top of things. All you need is copy and paste. Here are the steps:

1. **In a task-oriented view like the Gantt Chart, select the Task Name cell for the task you want to copy to Outlook and press Ctrl+C. (Or right-click the cell and choose Copy Cell.)**

    You can select only one task at a time. Project copies the task name to the Clipboard.

2. **In Outlook, display the Tasks list.**

    In the navigation bar, click Tasks.

3. Right-click the Tasks list and choose New. (Or choose Home→New Task.)

The Task entry window appears with the heading Untitled–Task.

4. Click the Subject box, and then press Ctrl+V.

In the Subject box, the name of the task appears. If you want Outlook to remind you about the task due date, turn on the Reminder checkbox and then choose the date and time when you want to be reminded.

5. On the ribbon, click Save & Close.

Repeat steps 1 through 4 for other tasks you want to add to Outlook.

Importing Tasks from Outlook

Every once in a while, you quickly create tasks in Outlook that you later realize belong in one of your projects. You can import these tasks into a Project file as a head start. When you import tasks from Outlook, you just create tasks with the task names from Outlook and any notes that you added. Although these imported tasks come in with the standard duration of 1 day? (the question mark indicates estimated duration), they have no task dependencies, resources, or dates. To import Outlook tasks, follow these steps:

1. Open the Project file, display a task-oriented view like the Gantt Chart, and then choose Task→Insert→Task→Import Outlook Tasks.

The Import Outlook Tasks dialog box opens. Outlook doesn't have to be running, but you must have at least one incomplete task in your Outlook Task list. If you have no tasks in Outlook or they're all complete, a message appears telling you there are no tasks to import.

2. Select the checkbox for each task you want to import, as shown in Figure 22-3.

Any notes you typed in the Notes box in Outlook appear in the Notes cell in the table.

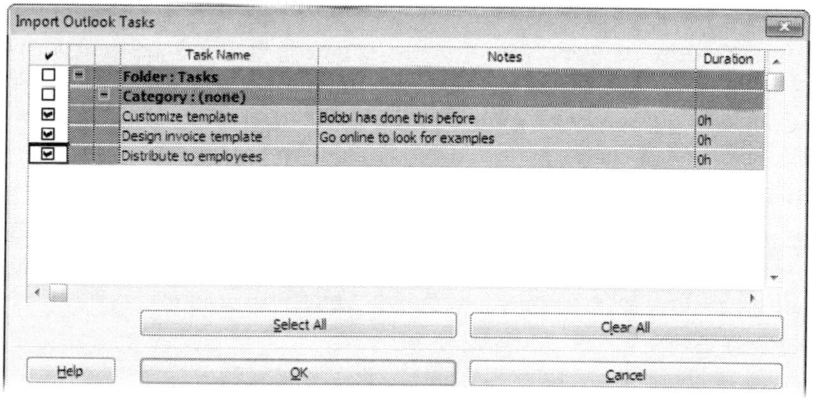

Figure 22-3:
To quickly select all the tasks, click Select All. Click Clear All to turn off all the checkboxes and start over. Don't turn on the checkboxes for folders and categories.

3. **Click OK.**

The tasks appear at the end of the list of tasks in your Project file.

Copying Tasks from an Email

When it comes to copying and pasting, Project 2010 has gotten a lot chummier with its Office 2010 counterparts. If you copy an indented list of tasks from an Outlook email or a Word document, Project 2010 is smart enough to turn them into summary tasks and subtasks in your Project Task list. Figure 22-4 shows the tasks in Outlook and the same tasks after pasting them into Project.

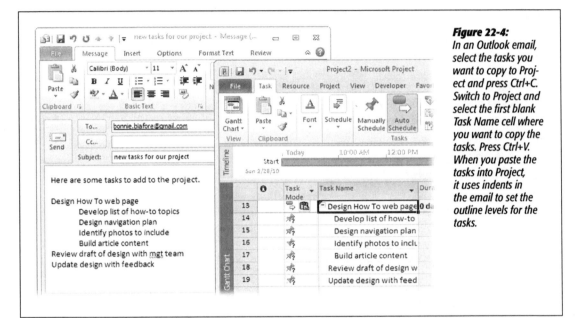

Figure 22-4:
In an Outlook email, select the tasks you want to copy to Project and press Ctrl+C. Switch to Project and select the first blank Task Name cell where you want to copy the tasks. Press Ctrl+V. When you paste the tasks into Project, it uses indents in the email to set the outline levels for the tasks.

Building a Resource List from an Outlook Address Book

If you use Outlook at work, you probably already have information about team members in your Outlook address book or Contacts folder. Rather than retyping all this information in Project, you can import resource names from Outlook into Project. Here are the steps:

1. **In Project, open the file into which you want to import resources.**

    If you use a resource pool (page 500), import the resources into the pool rather than into individual projects. Similarly, if you use Project Server, don't import resources directly into Project but into the enterprise resource pool instead.

2. **Choose Task→View→Resource Sheet.**

    Select the row where you want to insert the new resources.

3. **Choose Resource→Insert→Add Resources→Address Book.**

   The Select Resources dialog box appears.

4. **Select the names of people you want to add to the Resource Sheet.**

   You can select several resources at a time by Shift-clicking the first name in the group and the last name in the group. Select nonadjacent names by Ctrl-clicking each name.

5. **Click Add.**

   The names appear in the Add box.

6. **Click OK.**

   Project adds new rows in the Resource Sheet for the selected resources.

Sending Project Information to Others

You've probably emailed thousands of messages with attachments, so the concept of attaching a Project file to an email is nothing new. However, with Project, you can choose to send the whole project or only a few tasks and resources. If your audience doesn't have Project installed on their computers, you can create a picture of the Project information and mail that instead. Project can send files using any MAPI-compliant (Messaging Application Programming Interface) email program.

Tip: If your organization uses SharePoint, that's a far easier way to share Project information. See page 535 to learn how.

When you need approval for a schedule, the routing mechanism in Outlook can send the file to reviewers in sequence, so you can get their comments and approvals. While sending attachments tends to choke email servers with multiple copies of the same file, publishing a Project file to a Microsoft Exchange folder or to a Microsoft SharePoint site (page 541) lets everyone look at a single copy (which requires that you use Microsoft Exchange or Microsoft SharePoint).

Sending Project files via email

Sending Project files via email is easy, whether you send the message from your email program or directly from Project. In your email program, simply create a new message, and then, in Outlook 2010, choose Insert→Include→Attach File (or your email program's equivalent command) to attach the Project file. If you tend to forget attachments, like most people do, you can create the email message in Project, which automatically attaches the file.

Here are the steps for sending a Project file from within Project:

1. **In Project, open the Project file you want to send, and then choose File→ Share→"Send as Attachment".**

   Your email program starts (if it isn't running already) and opens a new email message form with the current Project file already attached. The Subject line contains the filename.

2. **Click the To: box, and then, in the Select Names dialog box, select the names of the recipients.**

   You can also type email addresses directly in the To: box.

3. **Edit the Subject box to tell your recipients why you're emailing the Project file.**

   In the message area, tell the recipients what you want them to do with the Project file, as shown in Figure 22-5.

4. **Click Send or the equivalent command.**

   The recipients receive an email message with the Project file attached.

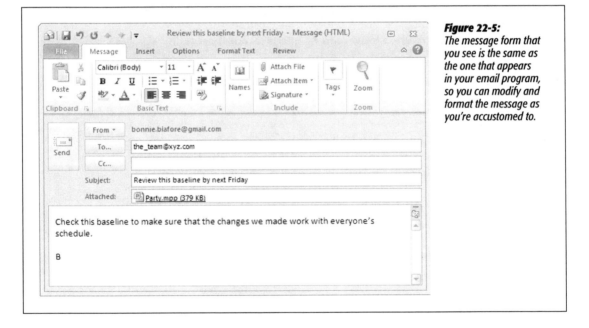

Figure 22-5:
The message form that you see is the same as the one that appears in your email program, so you can modify and format the message as you're accustomed to.

Routing a Project file to several recipients

When several people are in line to contribute to, review, or approve a Project file, routing an email with the file attached to each recipient is easier than trying to remember whom to email next. You can route the drawing to one recipient after another or blast the email to all recipients at once. When the recipients are done, the file comes back to you.

Routing a Project file to several people is similar to sending one to just one recipient. However, the Routing Recipient command is not on the ribbon out of the box, so you have to add it to a custom group that you create (page 661). Then, with the command in a group on the ribbon, do the following:

1. **Open the Project file you want to route, and then choose the ribbon tab to which you added the custom group and choose Routing Recipient.**

   The Routing Slip dialog box appears.

2. **Click Address.**

   Your email program's address book opens.

3. **Select the email addresses for the recipients, click To, and then click OK.**

   The email program adds the names to the To: box.

4. **Modify the Subject line to tell the recipients why you're sending the file. In the "Message text" box, type a message.**

   Remember to begin your email message with what you want people to do. You can add less important information after the opening paragraph.

   Select either the "One after another" or "All at once" option, as shown in Figure 22-6.

   The Routing Slip automatically selects "One after another". Routing a file sequentially takes a lot of time, but each person sees the comments from the person before. Then, each recipient can add his two cents to the routing message. Although the email message shows up in recipients' inboxes, routing the message to the next person on the list occurs in Project. Choose the Routing Recipient command again to pass on the message and its attached file.

   On the other hand, to see what people think without being influenced by others, select the "All at once" option. With this option, recipients email you individually when they're done.

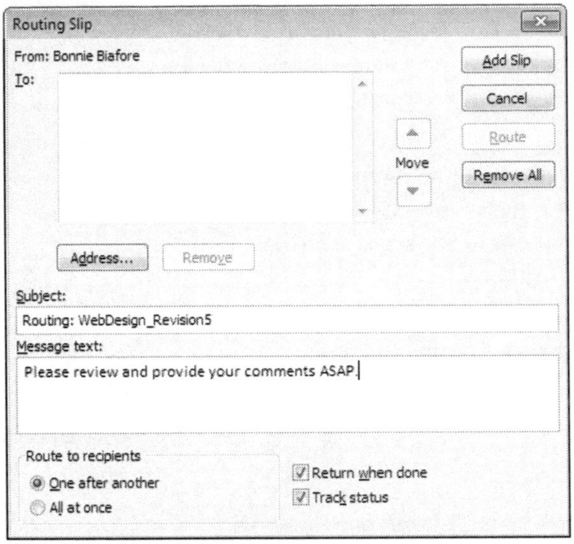

Figure 22-6:
The recipients appear in the order that you select them initially in your address book. If you're routing the file to one person after another, select a name, and then click the up or down arrows to change the order of recipients.

5. **To receive the routing email after every recipient has seen it, turn on the "Return when done" checkbox.**

   If you select the "One after another" option, then the "Track status" checkbox automatically turns on and tells your email program to notify you as the message makes its way through the list.

6. **Click Route.**

   Project sends an email with the file attached to your routing recipients.

Publishing a Project file to an Exchange folder

If your organization uses Microsoft Exchange, you can publish a Project file to an Exchange folder instead of sending the same file to multiple recipients. You must first add the Send To Exchange Folder command to a custom group on the ribbon (page 661). With the Send To Exchange Folder command on the ribbon, publish a file to a Microsoft Exchange folder by following these steps:

1. **In Project, open the file you want to publish to an Exchange folder, choose the tab that contains the custom group, and then choose Exchange Folder.**

   The "Send to Exchange Folder" dialog box appears and lists the available folders.

2. **Select the folder, and then click OK.**

   Project saves the file in the Exchange folder. You can also create a new folder by clicking New Folder, typing a name, and then pressing Enter.

Part Five: Customizing Project

V

Viewing What You Want

Just as the tie-dyed T-shirts you wore in school no longer work in a buttoned-down office, what works for one organization may not be right for another. Even if you stay at the same job or on the same project, what you need to see changes as you go along.

Fortunately, Project gives you lots of control over what you view in its window. You can customize or create views to present the right project information in the right way. For example, you can set up Gantt Chart task bars to emphasize the critical path, progress, or at-risk tasks. Most views include a table of information, and these tables are customizable as well. You can add, remove, or rearrange columns and tweak tables in other ways. Of course, text is omnipresent, and its formatting is at your command—so you can accommodate the reading-glasses crowd or make key information stand out. Project can apply formatting to text that falls into a specific category, like critical tasks, or to individual elements like a crucial task bar.

You can also customize filters and groups. You can modify or create filters and groups to show particular types of information. By filtering tasks and resources, you can display only what meets the conditions you set, such as tasks with duration longer than 2 months. Alternatively, you can use groups to shuffle information into categories. Because groups can roll up the values of the items in the group, it's easy to see how much you're spending on a particular group of contractors. Sorting information also helps you evaluate your project from every angle—for example, to see tasks listed from longest duration to shortest. You can sort any table you display or specify sort order for groups you define.

Note: You'll find other ways you can make Project your own in the next few chapters. You can customize fields (Chapter 24), the ribbon (Chapter 25), and templates (Chapter 26).

Creating Your Own View

When you don't have the full information, making decisions becomes a matter of luck (just ask the contestants on *Deal or No Deal*). Yet too much data can obscure the information you need (as anyone trying to choose an insurance policy can tell you). But the right data shown in the right light exposes flaws, highlights solutions, and generally makes managing projects easier.

Project comes with many views that present project information in different ways, but they boil down to seven basic types. This chapter describes how to customize each of the types. Here are the seven and what they do:

- **Gantt Chart.** The charts project managers spend their days gazing at are called Gantt Charts because Charles Gantt created a winner. This view lists project tasks and information about them in a table on the left side. In the timescale on the right side, task bars visually indicate when tasks occur and how they relate to one another. With additional task bars to show slack time, progress, or delays, a Gantt Chart presents a lot of what a project manager needs to know.

- **Usage.** A Gantt Chart doesn't show specific assignments or values for each time period, which is why you need usage views like Task Usage or Resource Usage. These views have a table on the left like the Gantt Chart does, showing totals for tasks, resources, and their assignments. Instead of task bars on the right, a usage view has another table, where the columns represent time periods. The rows show assignments with summary rows for each task or resource. Each cell in the timescale contains assignment (or summary) values for that period (for instance, work, baseline work, or cost).

- **Timeline.** New in Project 2010, the Timeline view (page 233) distills a project to a simple linear diagram. Out of the box, a bar on the Timeline view indicates the timeframe that's displayed in the timescale of a Gantt Chart or usage view. You can drag that bar to control the dates you see in the timescale (page 233). But you can also add tasks to the timeline—for example, to keep project phases, key milestones, or critical tasks in view at all times.

- **Team Planner.** Another new view in Project 2010, Team Planner (page 213) includes a row for each project resource and the tasks to which it's assigned, like competitive swimmers lined up in a swimming pool. That's why these rows are referred to as *swimlanes*.

- **Resource Graph.** The Resource Graph shows values for work, cost, and so on in a bar graph. Although the Resource Usage view does show resource allocation, the colored bars let you easily see when resources are overallocated.

- **Network Diagram.** Many project managers use a network diagram to define relationships between tasks and to evaluate the critical path. A network diagram draws a box (or node) for each task and lines for the relationships between them. However, because the diagram isn't drawn to a timescale, each task is the same size, which makes it easier for the eye to focus on task dependencies. As long as you use Project, you can build your schedule in the view you prefer, and let Project translate from one diagram to another.

- **Calendar.** Gantt Charts take getting used to, but everyone understands calendars. You can show tasks as bars spanning the days or weeks the way you mark off your much-needed vacation. In Project, the Calendar view is great for showing teams what their upcoming schedule looks like.

Note: Project 2010 still has built-in forms, but you can no longer create your own customized forms.

Depending on the work at hand, you can switch to the view that's most helpful. Within that view, you can change the information you see and how it's displayed. For example, when you're monitoring the critical path, red task bars let you more easily see critical tasks, and variance fields tell you whether progress is good or bad. Creating a view from scratch is an option if none of the existing views are close to what you want. The box on page 576 explains how Project saves the changes you make to views.

Tip: Project is set up initially to display the Gantt Chart view with the timeline above it, which makes it easy to see your project schedule and adjust the date range. However, if you prefer to work with another view—for example, the Task Entry view, which includes the Gantt Chart in the top pane and the Task Form in the bottom—you can change Project's default view. Choose File→Options. In the Project Options dialog box, click General. In the "Default view" drop-down list, choose the view you want Project to apply when you create a new project.

Modifying Basic View Contents

In Project, a view is nothing more than a compilation of many elements: fields, tables, filters, groups, layouts (called *screens*), and forms. To make big, sweeping changes in a view, you change its screens and forms. For example, you may prefer to have the Task Details Form appear in the Gantt Chart view's bottom pane instead of the Task Form.

Modifying views gets a lot easier when you understand the difference between single-pane and combination views. As its name implies, a single-pane view is like a picture window that shows one thing, like the Resource Sheet. A combination view is like a window in which the top and bottom panes slide up and down; it can have one single-pane view on the top and a different single-pane view on the bottom, like the Resource Allocation view, which shows the Resource Usage view on top and the Leveling Gantt on the bottom.

Where Are My View Changes?

Suppose you format task bars and text in your Gantt Chart view. Project stores this modified view in your Project file, so the Gantt Chart view shows your table, formatted task bars, and text each time you open the view. If you want to use your new and improved Gantt Chart view in other files, you must get it into your global template (page 669) or to another Project file.

In Project 2010, you can tell Project to automatically copy your customizations to the global template, which is perfect when you work solo and don't have to worry about other people sharing your global template. However, if you and dozens of other project managers use the same global template, you may want to keep your customizations in your file, to keep them from affecting other Project users. To change this setting, choose File→Options. In the Project Options dialog box, click Advanced. Under Display,

turn off the "Automatically add new views, tables, filters, and groups to the global" checkbox. Then you have to use the Organizer to copy your customized views to the global. mpt file.

If you want to keep Project's original views, you can copy a view before you modify it. Then you can use the original or your customized version. Bear in mind that changes in one view don't spill over into other views, which can be good or bad. The advantage to this barrier between views is that you can make scads of changes to a view without worrying about how those changes affect other views. That's exactly how the built-in Gantt Chart, Tracking Gantt, and Detailed Gantt views can show tasks in different ways. The drawback is that you must repeat formatting in another view if you want to alter it in the same way.

Most of Project's built-in views are single-pane views. The Gantt Chart, Task Usage, and Network Diagram views are all single-pane views; you can display them in the top or bottom pane of a view. You see the Gantt Chart and Task Form together so often because the built-in Task Entry combination view puts them there.

You get to modify different things in single-pane and combination views. Here's what each one contains:

- **Single-pane views.** The *screen* is a basic layout of view elements. For example, all Gantt Chart views use a Gantt Chart screen with a table on the left and a timescale on the right. You can specify the screen to use only when you create a new view. Once a view exists, you can change other settings, but not the screen it uses. A single-pane view also contains a table, group, and filter to apply when the view appears. (It's perfectly OK to set the group to No Group and use a wide-open filter like All Tasks.)

- **Combination views.** A combination view is just a pairing of two single-pane views, so you simply pick the views to show in the top and bottom pane.

Note: Some single-pane views like the Gantt Chart actually have two side-by-side panes: a table on the left and a timescale on the right. These side-by-side panes are features of the screens that the views use, which is why a Gantt Chart is still a single-pane view.

Modifying a single-pane view

The View Definition dialog box shows the settings for the type of view you're working on. For a single-pane view, you can change the table, group, or filter. Here's how to customize an existing single-pane view:

1. **If you plan to use a table, group, or filter that doesn't exist, then create it before you open the View Definitions dialog box.**

    You can't create elements on the fly in the View Definition dialog box. When you modify a view, you tell it the names of the elements to use. The view applies the table, group, and filter you specify, which automatically display any customizations you've made to them—as long as their names haven't changed. See "Creating a New Table" on page 616, "Creating and Editing Filters" on page 620, and "Creating a Group" on page 633 for instructions.

2. **Choose View, click the down arrow next to any view on the ribbon, and then, on the drop-down menu, choose More Views.**

    The More Views dialog box opens.

3. **In the Views list, select the single-pane view you want to modify, and then click Edit.**

    The View Definition dialog box opens with the single-pane settings, as shown in Figure 23-1. The screen for the view appears, but you can't edit it. (Project includes several layouts, which it calls *screens*. For example, the Gantt Chart screen has a table on the left side and a timescale on the right. The Resource Graph screen shows the resource on the left side and a timescale bar graph on the right.) To choose a different screen, you must create a view from scratch (page 582) or start with a view that uses the screen you want.

Tip: If you want to use the existing view as a foundation for a new view, select the single-pane view, and then click Copy. After you save the copy with a new name, make the changes you want to the copy. That way, you can use the original view or the new one.

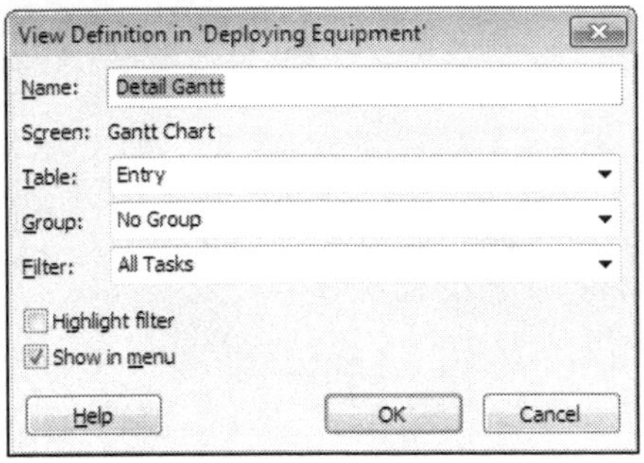

Figure 23-1:
The View Definition title ends with "in 'Project xyz'", which tells you that Project stores the modified view in the project file. You can tell Project to automatically copy views to the global template (page 669), or keep customized views in your Project file unless you explicitly copy them with the Organizer (page 668) to use them in other files.

4. **In the Table drop-down list, choose the table you want the view to display.**

   The tables you see in the drop-down list depend on whether you're editing a task or resource view. For example, if you edit the Gantt Chart or Task Usage view, the drop-down list contains task tables; you see resource tables for views like the Resource Sheet and Resource Usage.

5. **In the Group drop-down list, choose the group you want.**

   To forgo grouping, simply choose No Group. If you want to use a custom group that doesn't exist, then you must close the dialog box and then create the custom group (page 633) first.

6. **In the Filter drop-down list, choose the filter you want to apply.**

   Choose All Tasks or All Resources to leave the view unfiltered. Initially, filters hide items that don't pass the filter tests. You can set up a view that shows all tasks or resources but emphasizes the ones that pass the tests. To do so, turn on the "Highlight filter" checkbox, which uses blue text in rows that make the cut.

7. **To list the view on drop-down menus for faster access, make sure the "Show in menu" checkbox is turned on.**

   You can apply views from the view drop-down menus with a single click, including views you create yourself, as you can see in Figure 23-2. In fact, the "Show in menu" checkbox is turned on automatically, so you must turn it off if you *don't* want the view in the drop-down menus. You can remove built-in views you never use by editing them and then turning off their "Show in menu" checkboxes.

8. **Click OK.**

   The View Definition dialog box closes. To immediately apply the modified view, in the More Views dialog box, click Apply.

Tip: If you make changes to a view as you work—for example, adding a column to a table, applying a group, or filtering the task list—you can quickly save the view as a new view or update the definition of the view. On the ribbon, click a view button's down arrow, and then, on the drop-down menu, choose Save View. In the Save View dialog box, select "Save as a New View" to create a new view in your project. In the Name box, type a name for the view, and then click OK. Project saves the view with the table, fields, filters, and groups you've applied. To update the current view with the changes you've made, select Update Current View, and then click OK.

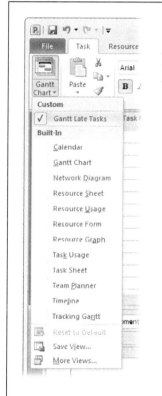

Figure 23-2:
When you click the down arrow next to a view button on the ribbon, a view drop-down menu appears. Customized views that you've created appear at the top of the menu under the Custom heading. Built-in views are listed under the Built-In heading, even if you've customized those views in some way.

Modifying a combination view

Project has only a few built-in combination views, such as Task Entry and Resource Allocation. However, combination views are great because they display the single-pane views you want in both the top and bottom panes. If you create your own combination views (page 577), you can set them up with the single-pane views you want or edit them to change the views they display. The box on page 581 explains how to change the size of each pane or hide the bottom pane. Here are the steps for modifying a combination view:

1. **If you plan to use a single-pane view that doesn't exist, create it first (as described in the next section).**

   You can't create a new single-pane view from within the View Definition dialog box.

2. **Choose View, click the down arrow next to any view on the ribbon, and then, on the drop-down menu, choose More Views.**

   The More Views dialog box opens.

3. **In the Views list, select the view you want to modify, and then click Edit.**

   The View Definition dialog box opens with combination view settings, as shown in Figure 23-3.

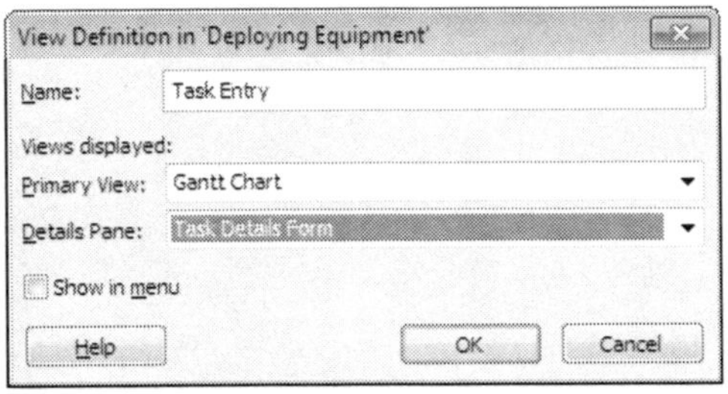

Figure 23-3:
When you modify a combination view, your only choices are the name for the view, which single-pane views appear in the top and bottom panes, and whether the combination view appears on view drop-down menus.

4. **In the Primary View box, choose the view you want in the top pane. In the Details Pane box, choose the view for the bottom pane.**

   Both drop-down lists include all available views, so you can put any view in either pane.

5. **Click OK.**

   The View Definition dialog box closes, and the view is ready to use.

Creating a New View

Most often, you create a new single-pane view to choose the screen you want, because that's the one element you can't change when you edit a view. New combination views come in handy when you prefer a specific combination of views but don't want to touch the ones that Project provides.

Hide and Seek with Panes

Combination views include top and bottom panes that start with an equitable split of the screen height. In many cases, you'd rather see more tasks in the Gantt Chart than rows of assigned resources in the Task Form. Similarly, because a usage view in the bottom pane shows assignments for only the selected task or resource in the top pane, you usually want the top pane to be taller than the bottom one.

You can adjust the height of each pane by dragging the horizontal divider between the panes. If a Gantt Chart or usage view needs the entire screen, then you can temporarily hide the bottom pane. Here's how you make all these adjustments:

- **Adjust the height of the panes.** The horizontal divider is a narrow bar just below the top pane's horizontal scrollbars. Move the pointer over the divider. When the pointer turns into a two-headed arrow, drag up or down until the panes are the height you want.

- **Display the bottom pane.** To bring a hidden bottom pane back, double-click the rectangle where the horizontal and vertical scroll bars meet, shown in Figure 23-4. In Project 2010, you can easily show or hide the bottom pane. With any view visible, choose View→Split View, and then turn on the Details checkbox to display the bottom pane. In the Details drop-down list, choose the view you want in the bottom pane.

- **Hide the bottom pane.** When you're reviewing the overall schedule, you may want the entire screen for your task list. To temporarily hide the bottom pane, double-click the horizontal divider or choose View ‣Split View, and then turn off the Details checkbox.

- **Restore and resize the bottom pane.** Drag the rectangle where the horizontal and vertical scroll bars meet until the bottom pane is the height you want.

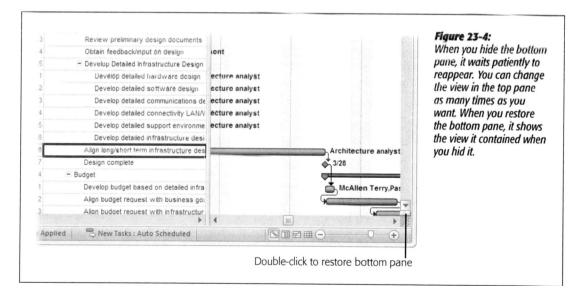

Figure 23-4:
When you hide the bottom pane, it waits patiently to reappear. You can change the view in the top pane as many times as you want. When you restore the bottom pane, it shows the view it contained when you hid it.

Double-click to restore bottom pane

The easiest way to create a new view, whether it's a single-pane or a combination view, is by modifying one that already exists. You can tweak the view until it looks exactly the way you want and then save it with a new name. Here's how:

1. **Display a view that's similar to the new view you want.**

   For example, if you want to create a combination with a Gantt Chart and the Task Details Form, click the down arrow on a view button, and then choose More Views. In the More Views dialog box, select Task Entry, and then click Apply.

2. **Modify the view until it looks the way you want.**

   Apply a different table (page 610), add columns to the table (page 611), apply a group (page 633), or filter the list (page 621).

3. **Click the down arrow on a view button, and then, on the drop-down menu, choose Save View.**

   The Save View dialog box opens.

4. **Select the "Save as a New View" option. In the Name box, type a name for the view, and then, click OK.**

   Project saves the view and adds it to the list of custom views in your project.

Creating a new view from scratch is easy, too, although you won't see what the view looks like until you apply it. If you're creating a combination view and want to include a single-pane view that doesn't exist, create it by following these steps once through first:

1. **Choose View, click the down arrow next to any view on the ribbon, and then, on the drop-down menu, choose More Views. In the More Views dialog box, click New.**

   The Define New View dialog box opens. If you want to create a view from an existing one, select the view, and then click Copy. If you're copying a single-pane view, you can't change the screen, but everything else is up for grabs.

2. **Select the "Single view" or "Combination view" option, and then click OK.**

   The View Definition dialog box opens with the settings for the type of view you selected. The Name box is filled in automatically with a name like "*View 1*."

3. **In the Name box, type a new name.**

   In addition to imbuing a name with meaning, you can add a keyboard shortcut to open the view from the View menu. When entering the name, simply type an ampersand (&) before the letter for the shortcut, in the same way that the built-in Gantt Chart view is set to *&Gantt Chart*. For example, if you create a view named *Gantt Late Tas&ks*, you can apply the view by pressing Alt to display keyboard shortcuts, as shown in Figure 23-5. Then, press W to display the View tab, press G to display the Gantt Chart view drop-down menu, and finally press K (the letter after the ampersand) to display the view. (If another entry uses the same letter for its keyboard shortcut, then you need to press the letter a second time to access your view.)

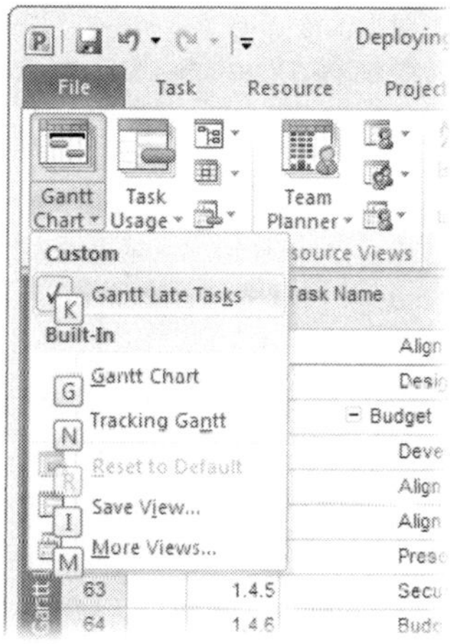

Figure 23-5:
When you first press the Alt key, the keyboard shortcuts for the ribbon tabs appear, for example, H for the Task tab and W for the view tab. Once you press a key to choose a tab, the tab keyboard shortcuts disappear, and the keyboard shortcuts for commands on the tab take their place, such as G for the Gantt Chart view drop-down menu and K for the Task Usage view drop-down menu. If you press a key for a command that displays a drop-down menu, shortcut keys appear on the drop-down menu.

4. **If you're creating a single-pane view, then in the Screen drop-down list, choose the screen you want.**

   The Screen drop-down list includes names that look familiar: Gantt Chart, Task Usage, Calendar, and so on. Each screen represents a particular layout, like the table and task bar timescale of the Gantt Chart and the table and tabular time phased data of Task Usage. You can't create your own screens.

5. **To save the view, click OK.**

   From here on, the steps for creating a view are exactly the same as modifying one, as described on page 577 and page 579. For example, for a single-pane view, you choose the table, filter, and group you want. For a combination view, you select the single-pane views to display in the top and bottom panes.

Changing the Looks of a Gantt Chart View

A Gantt Chart view is a fertile field for formatting. In the table area, you can apply a table, which, in turn, displays columns of Project fields. The timescale displays task bars to show when tasks occur and how they relate to one another.

Every component of a Gantt Chart view has its own formatting features:

- **Table.** The most obvious change is choosing a different table. Within a table, you can add, remove, or rearrange columns; moreover, the column width, title, and alignment are at your command. "Changing Tables" on page 610 is your guide to all these customization features.

- **Timescale.** The timescale chops the project up into time periods, which can be modified to fit the length of your project. Short projects may use days, whereas months may be better for multiyear projects. You can change the timescale units, labels, and how many different units the timescale heading holds. See "Customizing the Timescale" on page 595 for instructions. For more off-the-cuff timescale changes, you can simply drag the bar in the Timeline view to change the date range or timescale units (page 233). Dragging the Zoom slider (page 11) when a timescaled view is active also changes the date range and timescale units.

- **Text.** Text is everywhere. You can modify text appearance to highlight different information, like summary tasks or task bar text. You can also format only selected text. See "Changing the Way Text Looks" on page 616 to learn how.

- **Task bars.** Changing formatting on different types of task bars emphasizes information. For example, you can show critical task bars in red and noncritical task bars in blue. You can also display different types of task bars for each baseline you've set. You can modify the appearance of a category of task bars or only the task bars you select. Link lines and gridlines are customizable, too. The following sections explain how to change the appearance of task bars and other lines in the timescale.

Tip: With the Gantt Chart Style gallery, one click is all it takes to change the colors of tasks set to Auto Scheduled and Manually Scheduled mode. When a Gantt Chart view is active, choose Format→Gantt Chart Style, and then click one of the color combination buttons. The top task bar on the button represents manually scheduled tasks; bottom task bar on the button shows the color for auto-scheduled tasks. The Gantt Chart Style section displays four buttons at a time, but you can scroll to see additional color options.

Changing the way types of task bars look

Task bar color, fill pattern, and shape are all customizable, like the formatting you see in views that highlight critical tasks and progress. Task bars can also have marks at one or both ends, like the diamond for milestone tasks. Project has two categories for task bar formatting. You can apply formatting only to the bars you select, which is perfect for highlighting individual tasks that have special importance, like milestones that trigger a payment. Or you can specify bar styles to format all task bars in a specific category, like external tasks from other projects.

Tip: Displaying critical tasks with red task bars is a lot easier in Project 2010. In any Gantt Chart view, simply choose Format→Bar Styles, and then turn on the Critical Tasks checkbox.

Formatting a category of task bars is efficient, because Project keeps track of which tasks fall into which category and changes formatting if their category status changes. For example, when you're trying to shorten the schedule, you may want critical tasks to appear in a bright red color with stars at the end. If a task falls off the critical path, the stars disappear and the color changes to that of a noncritical task. To change the looks for a category of task bars, do the following:

1. **Display the view with the task bars you want to format.**

   Bar styles apply only to the active view in the active project. (You can use a customized view in other projects if you copy the view to the global template, as described on page 669.) If you want task bars in another view to use the same formatting, then you must repeat these steps for that view.

2. **Choose Format→Bar Styles→Format→Bar Styles or double-click working time in the background of the Gantt Chart timescale.**

   The Bar Styles dialog box opens, as shown in Figure 23-6. (If you double-click nonworking time in the timescale, the Timescale dialog box opens to the "Nonworking time" tab, presumably so you can format the appearance of nonworking time.

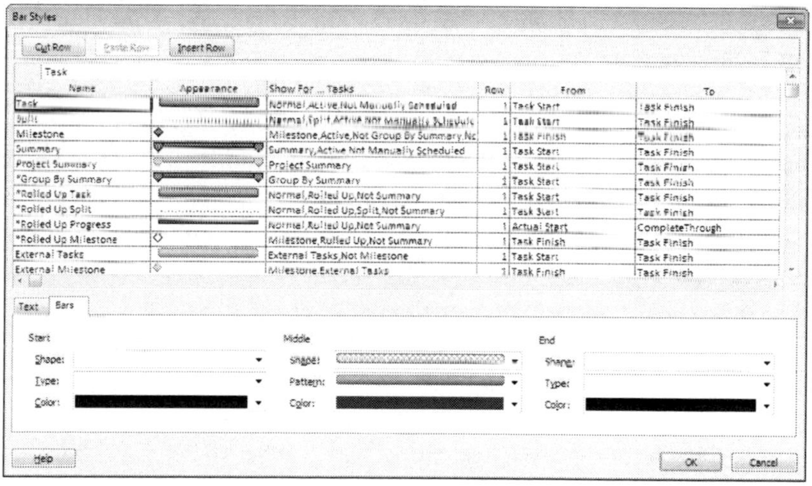

Figure 23-6:
The table in the Bar Styles dialog box includes a row for each type of task bar in the active view. You may be surprised by the number of rows until you see that tasks, critical tasks, progress bars, milestones, summary tasks, and so on each have their own look.

3. **In the table, select the type of task bar, and then select the Bars tab.**

   The Bars tab contains three sections: Start, Middle, and End. The Start and End sections define the marks that appear at the beginning and end of a task bar. You can choose a shape, color, and whether the mark is solid or outlined. The Middle section sets the appearance of the bar itself.

4. **To format a mark at one of the task bar ends, in the Shape drop-down list (in either the Start or End section), select a shape.**

    Your choices are some exciting geometric shapes: the familiar milestone diamond, various arrows, and even a star. In Project 2010, the Shape drop-down list includes shapes for manually scheduled tasks, like the caps that indicate that a task has a start or finish date. Task bars don't have to have a mark at the ends. You can leave the Start and End boxes empty. To remove a mark, at the top of the Shape drop-down list, select the empty entry.

    If you choose a mark, Project initially fills in the Type box with Solid, which is usually the best choice, because it makes small marks more visible. You can also choose Dashed or Framed. If you want a color other than black, you can choose it from the Color drop-down list. Try several colors until you find one that looks good. Darker colors are better, because bright colors like lime and yellow disappear into the white background.

5. **To format the bar, in the Middle section, choose the bar shape you want.**

    Bars can be wide, medium, or narrow, just like men's ties. When bars aren't full height, you can choose a position at the top, middle, or bottom of the task bar row. For example, regular and critical tasks are usually full height. Progress bars are narrow bars in the middle. Slack is a narrow bar at the bottom.

    Because narrow task bars take up less space, you can display more than one in the same task row. That's how the Multiple Baselines Gantt view (page 373) shows three baselines on the same row.

6. **To apply a pattern or color to a bar, in the Middle section, choose the pattern and color you want.**

    Task bars start with a solid pattern. To emphasize task bars or to print a schedule on a black-and-white printer, use crosshatch patterns. Test colors to see how they look in the timescale. In the task bar table, the Appearance cell to the right of the task bar name previews your masterpiece.

7. **To format a different type of task bar, select it in the table, and then repeat steps 4–6. When you're done, click OK.**

    The dialog box closes, and the new formatting appears in the view.

Changing the way selected task bars look

To change the look of individual task bars (for example, to change several deliverable sign-off meetings to purple bars), you format bars, not bar styles. Here's how:

1. **Select the tasks whose bars you want to format, and then choose Format→Bar Styles→Format→Bar. To format a single bar, double-click it in the timescale.**

    The Format Bar dialog box opens to the Bar Shape tab, which has the familiar Start, Middle, and End sections with the same options that are available for bar styles.

2. **Pick the shapes, styles, and colors you want.**

    The preview appears at the bottom of the dialog box. (The background isn't white, though, so you can't judge colors until you see them in the view.)

3. **Click OK.**

    The dialog box closes, and the selected bars sport their new look.

Tip: If all you want to change on a task bar is its color, you can do that from the task bar mini-toolbar (new in Project 2010). Right-click the task bar you want to change. On the mini-toolbar that appears above the task bar, click the Bar Color down arrow, and then choose the color you want. You can find attractive color-coordinated shades under Theme Colors, basic colors under Standard Colors—or click More Colors to pick the exact hue you want.

Changing task bar text

Attaching fields to task bars means you can see key information right in the timescale. For example, displaying the initials of people assigned to tasks lets you see resources without checking the form in the bottom pane. Adding dates to milestones emphasizes key dates.

Working with text on task bars is similar to working with the task bars themselves. You can specify the fields to show for a category, or assign fields to selected task bars. Actually, you can customize the task bar and its text at the same time, because the bar and text formatting are two tabs in the Bar Styles (or Format Bar) dialog box.

To display fields as text for a category of task bars, follow these steps:

1. **Display the view whose task bars you want to format.**

    Bar styles that you customize or create apply only to the active view in the active project. If you want task bars in another view to use the same formatting, then you must repeat these steps.

2. **Choose Format→Bar Styles→Format→Bar Styles or double-click the background of the Gantt Chart timescale.**

    The Bar Styles dialog box opens.

3. **In the Bar Styles table, select the type of task bar, like Critical, and then select the Text tab.**

    The Text tab shows fields already associated with the selected task bar type. Task bars have five places for text, although using them all makes the bars almost unreadable. You can add fields at the left, right, top, bottom, and inside task bars.

4. **Select a position box, like Right for the finish date. Click the down arrow, and then choose the field to display at that position, as shown in Figure 23-7.**

    Repeat this step to add fields at other positions. To remove a field, select the position box, and then press Backspace.

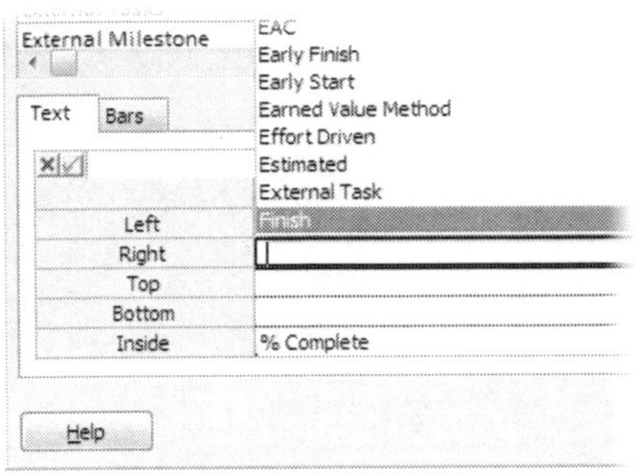

Figure 23-7:
The Start field obviously belongs on the left end of a task bar, and Finish belongs on the right. A field like % Complete or % Work Complete could go on the top, bottom, or inside, because the central position conveys progress.

5. **To add fields to another type of task bar, repeat steps 3 and 4. When you're done, click OK.**

   The Bar Styles dialog box closes and task bars that fall in the categories you changed now show values.

Tip: You may want to add fields to individual task bars, for example to show the finish dates for a few key tasks. Select the tasks you want to format, and then choose Format→Bar Styles→Format→Bar. On the Text tab, choose the fields you want, and then click OK.

Designing your own task bar style

Project views usually have several different task bar styles already defined. For example, the Detail Gantt view includes task bars for regular tasks, critical tasks, progress, milestones, slack, slippage, summary tasks, and more. You may want a new type of task bar, for example to highlight tasks added for change requests and flagged with the Flag6 field.

Designing a new task bar style requires more choices than modifying existing ones. You must tell Project when to use the task bar style and the dates to start and end the bar. To show off your creativity with a custom task bar, follow these steps:

1. **Display the view whose task bars you want to format.**

   Your task bar work of art applies only to the active view in the active project, unless you copy the view to the global template or another file (page 669).

2. **Choose Format→Bar Styles→Format→Bar Styles or double-click the background of the Gantt Chart timescale.**

   The Bar Styles dialog box opens.

3. **Scroll to the end of the table, and then, in the first blank row, select the Name cell.**

   To insert a new task bar style in the middle of the list, select the row below where you want to insert the new row, and then click Insert Row. Project inserts a blank row above the selected row. The box on page 590 explains why you might insert rows in the middle of the table.

   There's no Copy Row button, but you can fake it. Select the task bar style you want to copy, and then click Cut Row. The task bar style disappears from the table, but don't worry. Before you do anything else, click Paste Row to insert the row back into the table. Now select the row below where you want the copy, and then click Paste Row again. The copied row appears above the row you selected, and you can modify it.

4. **In the Name field, type the name for the task bar style.**

   Make the name meaningful. For example, if you're creating a task bar style for change request tasks, you might name it "*ChangeRequestFlag*" or simply "*Change-Request.*"

5. **To tell Project when to use the style, select the style's Show For…Tasks cell.**

   Click the down arrow, and then choose the category of task to which this style applies, as illustrated in Figure 23-8. For example, choose Flag1 if the Flag1 field is your change request indicator. (The style appears when Flag1 equals Yes.) The Show For…Tasks drop-down menu includes useful choices like Critical, Noncritical, In Progress, Not Started, Not Finished, and so on.

   A bar style can also apply when a condition *isn't* true. Suppose you create a task bar style for active change requests. The combination "Active, Flag1" tells Project to use the style for active tasks with Flag1 set to Yes. For inactive change request tasks, choose "Not Active, Flag1". (You must type the *Not* for these combinations.)

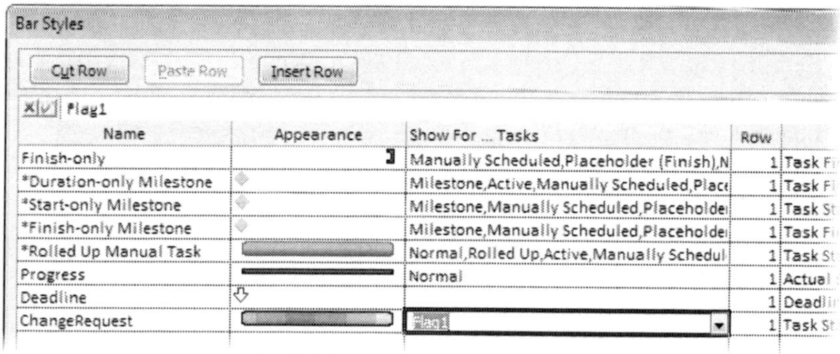

Figure 23-8:
Sometimes, a style applies to more than one condition in the drop-down list, like active tasks with the change request flag turned on. Choose the first condition in the drop-down list. Without closing the list, type a comma, and then choose the second condition. Rinse and repeat for additional conditions.

6. **In the From and To columns, choose the date fields that specify when the task bar starts and ends.**

   For many task bars, the choices are easy: Choose "Start" in the From cell and "Finish" in the To cell to draw the task bar from the start date to the finish date. But other types of task bars use different dates. For example, a progress bar goes from the Start date to the Complete Through date. Slippage runs from the Baseline Start date to the Start date, to show how far the start has slipped.

7. **On the Bars tab and Text tab, select the settings for the bar style and fields you want.**

   See page 584 and page 586 for formatting bars and fields.

8. **If you're done, click OK.**

   Custom bar styles have a way of multiplying. For example, if you create a bar style for flagged tasks, you usually want another style for flagged milestones, and possibly flagged critical tasks. To add more bar styles, repeat steps 3–7.

TROUBLESHOOTING MOMENT

Task Bars Are Missing

In the timescale, Project draws task bars in the order they appear in the Bar Styles dialog box. Full-height task bars obscure narrow task bars drawn earlier. That's why the Progress task bar style follows the Task style. Otherwise, the progress bar is hidden by the task whose progress it reports.

To make sure you can see all your task bars, you must order task bar styles in the Bar Styles table with the same amount of care you use for the seating arrangements at a family reunion. To move a task bar style to another location, do the following:

1. Select the row, and then click Cut Row. The row disappears from the table.

2. Select the row below where you want to place the cut row.

3. Click Paste Row. The new row appears above the selected row.

Stacking more than one task bar in the same space

While defining a new task bar style, you may have noticed the Bar Styles dialog box's Row column, usually containing the number 1. This property is the key to displaying more than one row for each task. For example, the Tracking Gantt view uses narrow bars to show the baseline and current task bars in the same row. If you'd rather use full-height task bars for each, then you can include regular task bars on the first row and baseline task bars on the second row. Here's how it's done:

1. **Open the view that you want to modify, and then choose Format→Bar Styles→Format→Bar Styles.**

   The Bar Styles dialog box opens.

2. **To add another task bar in another row, either insert a new row or copy one of the existing task bar styles.**

   To insert a new row, select the row below the new row, and then click Insert Row.

   To copy an existing task bar style, select the row you want to copy, and then click Cut Row. Click Paste Row twice, once to re-insert the original style, the second time to insert the copy.

3. **In the new or copied row, change the name—for example to "Task Baseline."**

   Use the Bars tab and Text tab to define the bar appearance and text that surrounds it. For example, you might use a full-height task bar with blue diagonal lines for the baseline.

4. **In the Row cell, type 2.**

   Project adds a second row to the timescale for each task, as shown in Figure 23-9.

5. **Repeat steps 2–4 to add other rows, or click OK to close the dialog box.**

   The rows in the table double their height, and the new bars appear for the tasks that meet the task bar style conditions.

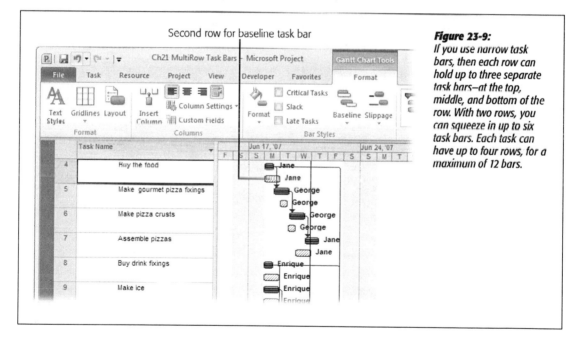

Second row for baseline task bar

Figure 23-9:
If you use narrow task bars, then each row can hold up to three separate task bars—at the top, middle, and bottom of the row. With two rows, you can squeeze in up to six task bars. Each task can have up to four rows, for a maximum of 12 bars.

Changing the layout of task bars

You've probably struggled to follow link lines between predecessor and successor
tasks. Even simple projects can look like a bowl of tangled spaghetti. You can lay
out the timescale to clear up clutter or improve readability. In addition to how link
lines appear, you can change the height of task bars, roll up task bars from subtasks
to summary tasks, or change the date format. To reach the layout options, choose
Format→Format→Layout. Then use any or all of the following settings:

- **Link lines.** The Layout dialog box, shown in Figure 23-10, has three link line
  options: an S, an L, or completely hidden.

- **Task bar date format.** In the Layout dialog box, the "Date format" box sets the
  date format only for task bars. It's best to choose an abbreviated format (like
  1/28), and leave the full dates to table columns.

- **Task bar height.** With bar styles and bar formatting, you can choose task bars
  that are thin, medium, or full-height. "Bar height" defines full-height; 12 is the
  standard. You can vary the height from 6 to 24.

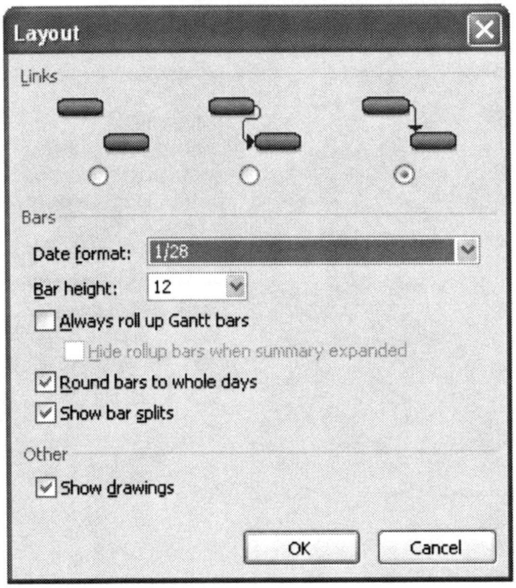

Figure 23-10:
The S shape is better at separating link lines. The L shape
doesn't clutter the diagram as much. For the cleanest look,
hide the links completely.

- **Roll up task bars to summary tasks.** You know that summary tasks roll up field
  values like cost and work. The "Always roll up Gantt bars" checkbox is different;
  turning it on shows subtasks and milestones on summary task bars. These roll-
  ups get messy fast. When the "Always roll up Gantt bars" checkbox is turned on,
  you can also turn on the "Hide rollup bars when summary expanded" checkbox.

This hides the roll-up bars whenever the subtasks are visible, and shows roll-up bars only when subtasks are hidden.

- **Round bars to whole days.** Initially, Project draws task bars to the exact task duration. Very short tasks practically disappear when the timescale is set to weeks or months. Turn on the "Round bars to whole days" checkbox to round out durations in the timescale to whole days. The durations in the table area are still exact.

- **Show splits.** Project chops up task bars into pieces if they contain splits (small delays between working times). Most of the time, you want to see splits. If they become too distracting, then turn off the "Show bar splits" checkbox, and Project draws the task bars as solid lines.

- **Show drawing shapes.** If you use the Drawing toolbar to add shapes or text to the timescale, you can hide those shapes by turning off the "Show drawings" checkbox.

Changing how gridlines look

Even the gridlines that separate table, timescale, and column heading elements are customizable. For example, you can change the line color of the lines that show the project start date and current date. Although the timescale doesn't draw lines between task bar rows initially, you can add them to make it easier to correlate bars to rows in the table. To format gridlines, follow these steps:

1. **Display the view you want to modify, and then choose Format→Format→Gridlines→Gridlines.**

   The Gridlines dialog box opens.

2. **In the "Line to change" list, choose the type of line.**

   The "Line to change" list includes table and timescale categories, like Sheet Rows and Sheet Columns for the table, and Gantt Rows, Current Date, and so on for the timescale.

3. **In the Type drop-down list, choose the line style you want. Choose the color you want.**

   You can draw solid, dotted, small dashed, and long dashed lines. To remove a line, choose the white entry at the top of the list. For example, to show the current date as a bright blue line, in the "Line to change" drop-down list, first select Current Date. In the Type drop-down list, choose the solid line, and then, in the Color drop-down list, choose blue.

4. **To draw lines at intervals, for instance after every fifth row in the table, in the "At interval" section, select the option for the number.**

   If the interval is larger than 4, select the Other option, and then type the number in the box. When you use intervals, select the line style and color for the intervals.

5. If you want to format another gridline, repeat steps 2–4.

When you're done, click OK.

Fast formatting with the Gantt Chart Wizard

When you want to format the Gantt Chart to exacting specifications, you can work through the Bar Styles, Text Styles, and Layout dialog boxes one by one. On the other hand, Project 2010 puts the commands for more common formatting right on the ribbon—like the Critical Tasks checkbox, which automatically changes critical tasks to red. But if you're looking for several types of basic Gantt Chart formatting, the Gantt Chart Wizard could be the answer.

Note: The easiest way to use the Gantt Chart Wizard is to add it to the Quick Access toolbar. Click the down arrow to the right of the Quick Access toolbar, and then choose More Commands. In the Project Options dialog box, in the "Choose commands from" drop-down list, choose All Commands, select Gantt Chart Wizard, and then click Add. Click OK to close the Project Options dialog box.

The Gantt Chart Wizard can show the critical path or baseline information, display text on task bars, and hide or show link lines. Here's how to use the Gantt Chart Wizard:

1. **Display the view you want to format.**

   The Gantt Chart Wizard makes changes to the view definition as if you were doing the work yourself. To keep the current view definition, make a copy of the view before starting the wizard.

2. **In the custom group on the ribbon, choose Gantt Chart Wizard. On the first screen, click Next.**

   The first screen describes what the wizard does.

3. **Select the option corresponding to the task bars you want to see, and then click Next.**

   Standard is selected initially, and it shows blue task bars. "Critical path" changes critical tasks to red. The Baseline option shows the baseline as a narrow gray bar with the current schedule in a narrow blue bar below it. The Other option lets you pick alternative bar styles.

4. **Select the option for the fields you want on the task bars, and then click Next.**

   You can show no text at all, dates, resources, or both. If you select the "Custom task information" option, then the wizard lets you pick the fields you want.

   The Gantt Chart Wizard is a shortcut to removing text on task bars. Select the None option, and the wizard removes all the fields from the task bars that appear in the view.

5. Keep the Yes option selected to show link lines. Click Next or Finish (they both go to the Format It screen).

   Select the No option to hide link lines.

6. On the last page, click Format It, and then click Exit Wizard.

   The box on the left side of the screen is a preview of what your Gantt Chart will look like. If it's not what you want, click Back to the appropriate page, and then select different options.

   When you exit the wizard, the view shows the new formatting.

Customizing the Timescale

Views like Gantt Chart and Task Usage have a timescale on the right side, which shows information over time. Because of this timescale, Gantt Chart task bars lengthen or shorten depending on their duration. In a usage view, each column is a time period, so you can see work or cost per day, per week, and so on.

Note: Timescale modifications apply only to the active view. They appear every time you use the view, but you have to repeat the changes to see them in other views.

Time units are the part of the timescale you change the most. For long projects, units like weeks or months squeeze more onto the screen. Short projects are better with units like days so the task bars don't look scrawny. (To change the time units quickly, drag the Zoom slider on the status bar at the bottom right of the window.) You can customize more of the timescale—for example, choosing the time period labels and their alignment, or shrinking or expanding column width to specific dimensions. A view can show up to three tiers of units in the heading area—for instance, to show the year on the top, then months, and finally weeks; or to show the fiscal year, and then fiscal quarters. To format the timescale, follow these steps:

1. Display a view like a Gantt Chart view, usage view, or the Resource Graph.

   The view displays a timescale on the right side.

2. Double-click the timescale heading or right-click the timescale heading, and then, on the shortcut menu, choose Timescale.

   The Timescale dialog box opens, as shown in Figure 23-11.

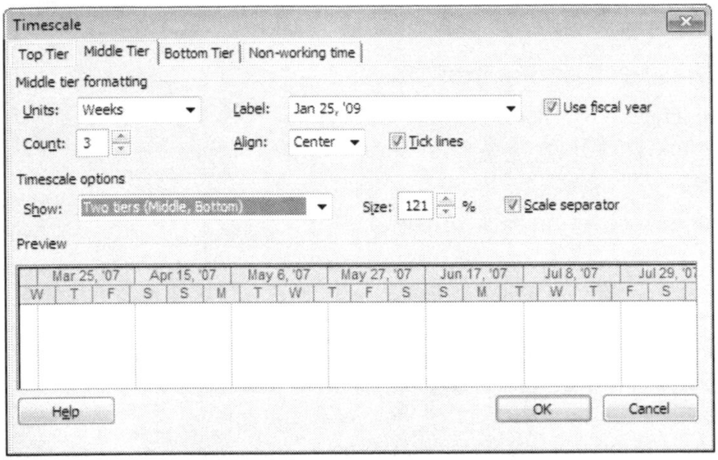

Figure 23-11:
The Timescale dialog box has four tabs: one for each tier of units and the fourth for nonworking time. The Middle Tier tab appears initially. To change the number of tiers, under "Timescale options", choose the number of tiers in the Show dropdown list. When you use less than three, Project drops off the Top Tier first.

3. **Select the tab for the tier you want to format.**

   The top, middle, and bottom tiers have the same settings: units, unit label, alignment, and so on.

   The "Non-working time" tab, on the other hand, controls how nonworking time *looks* on the timescale; it doesn't change the nonworking time itself. See page 243 to learn about setting working and nonworking time in project and resources calendars. Nonworking time starts as gray shading behind task bars. You can change the color and pattern, which calendar the nonworking time comes from, and whether to hide nonworking time or draw it in front of task bars.

4. **In the Units box, choose the time unit you want to use for the selected tier.**

   For the middle tier, typical units are weeks or months. The top tier may be months or years, while the bottom tier may be days or weeks. Choose units that work with the length of your project. Keep in mind that the units for a lower tier must be shorter than the units in the tier above it. If the bottom tier is days, the middle tier must be at least weeks.

   If you track your project by an interval other than one time unit, choose the number in the Count box. For example, a Count equal to 2 and units set to weeks would change the timescale units to 2-week increments.

5. **Change how the tier label looks by choosing one of the formats in the Label box.**

   The formats you see depend on the units you choose. For example, formats for weeks include the robust "Sun January 23, 2011" as well as the most concise "23" (which is the first day of that week). Quarter formats include "1st Quarter", "Q1", and "Q1, Q2, Q3, Q4,...(From Start)", which numbers quarters sequentially from the project start date.

To display the fiscal year instead of the calendar year, turn on the "Use fiscal year" checkbox. You set the fiscal year in the Project Options dialog box (page 319). For example, if the starting month is June, and the calendar year in which the fiscal year starts denotes the fiscal year, then June 2010 is fiscal year 2010. However, if you don't use the starting calendar year, the fiscal year is based on the ending calendar year, so June 2010 represents the beginning of fiscal year 2011.

6. **To position the label within its tier, in the Align drop-down list, choose Left, Center, or Right.**

When the "Tick lines" checkbox is turned on, vertical lines appear between each period in a timescale tier.

7. **If you use more than one tier, repeat steps 3–6 to format the other tiers.**

Although the "Timescale options" section is below the tier formatting section, timescale options apply to all tiers.

8. **If the headings in the Preview section are scrunched up, in the Size box, increase the percentage.**

The Size box is like zooming. Increasing the percentage from 75% to 100% stretches each time unit out, which is helpful when task bars are too skinny. If you see pound symbols (#) instead of values in the view itself, increase the percentage until the values appear. Decreasing the percentage squeezes the periods together to fit more duration on the screen.

Keep the "Scale separator" checkbox turned on to draw horizontal lines between each tier.

9. **When you're finished, click OK.**

The dialog box closes, and the settings appear in the timescale.

Changing a Usage View's Appearance

Usage views like Task Usage and Resource Usage have a table on the left and a timescale on the right, both of which you can customize. The usage timescale is a grid in which each column represents one time unit, and each row represents an assignment or summary row also known as time-phased data. You can choose the fields to display in the timescale. This section describes how to change the fields in a usage timescale and how to format their values. The box on page 599 describes a shortcut for changing column widths in the usage timescale. See other sections in this chapter for customizing the table, text, and timescale.

To choose fields to show in a usage view, follow these steps:

1. **Display a usage view like Task Usage or Resource Usage.**

Remember, the changes you make to the view apply only to the active view in the active project unless you copy the view to your global template (page 669).

2. **In the timescale grid, right-click any cell, and then, on the shortcut menu, choose Detail Styles, as shown in Figure 23-12. In the Details Styles dialog box, select the Usage Details tab.**

The Usage Details tab includes a list of fields you can add to the timescale and lists the different time-phased fields that you can display in the timesheet: work fields, cost fields, allocation, performance measures like CV, and so on.

If you right-click the timescale heading instead, then you don't see Detail Styles on the menu.

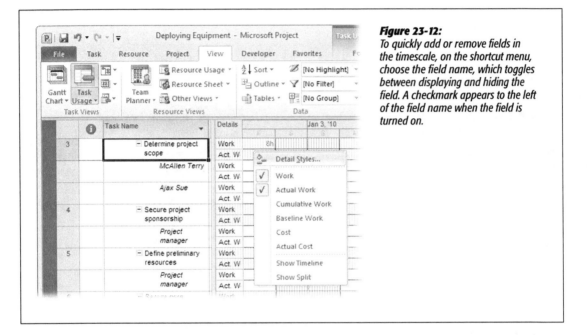

Figure 23-12:
To quickly add or remove fields in the timescale, on the shortcut menu, choose the field name, which toggles between displaying and hiding the field. A checkmark appears to the left of the field name when the field is turned on.

3. **To add a field to the timescale, in the "Available fields" list, select the field, and then click Show.**

The field jumps to the "Show these fields" list, as illustrated in Figure 23-13. Project adds a new row for the field to each assignment.

4. **To format the timescale cells for a field, select the field in the "Show these fields" list, and then change the settings in the dialog box's bottom half.**

The built-in views use a light yellow background for the task or resource rows. The assignment rows have a white background. You can choose a different font, background color, or background pattern. If you want the field listed on the shortcut menu that appears when you right-click the timescale cells, turn on the "Show in menu" checkbox.

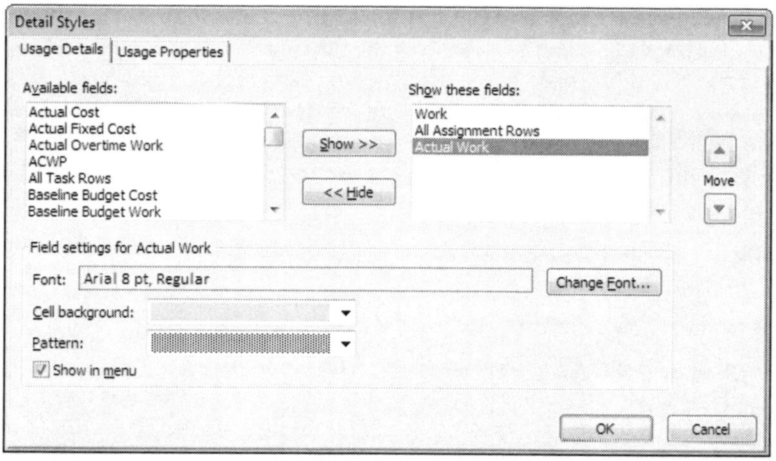

Figure 23-13:
To add more than one field, Ctrl-click each field, and then click Show. Remove a field by selecting it in the "Show these fields" list, and then clicking Hide. You can rearrange the order of the fields by selecting a field, and then clicking the Move up or down arrows.

5. **If you want to format the headers and data, select the Usage Properties tab, and then choose the settings you want.**

    Typically, these settings are fine as they are. The "Align details data" box controls whether values in cells are aligned to the left, center, or right. When "Display details header column" is set to Yes, the timescale starts with a column that shows the field names for each row. Changing this box to No isn't a good idea, because it means you have to remember which row is which when you type or review values. The "Repeat details header on all assignment rows" checkbox is turned on by default so that each row has a header. The "Display short detail header names" checkbox is turned on to abbreviate field names so that the first column is as narrow as possible.

6. **Click OK.**

    The dialog box closes, and the changes you made appear in the timescale.

UP TO SPEED

Quickly Change Column Widths

Because usage values often include decimal numbers, the timescale columns may display pound symbols (#) because the numbers don't fit. You can format the timescale to increase the size of the columns (page 597), but it's faster to drag to make the columns wider. Move the pointer between two column headings in the timescale. When the pointer changes to a two-headed arrow, drag to the left or right until the column is wide enough for values.

If a combination view has timescales in the top and bottom panes, then dragging the column width in one pane changes the column width in the other pane. For example, if you display the Task Usage view in the top pane and the Resource Graph in the bottom, dragging a column edge in either pane adjusts the column width in both so the views stay in sync.

Customizing the Timeline

The new Timeline view (page 233) can control the timeframe shown in the timescale of a Gantt Chart or usage view. You can drag the timeline bar to change the timescale dates and scale. By adding tasks to the timeline, you can emphasize key tasks, such as critical tasks or payment milestones, in a simple linear diagram. Like other Project views, the Timeline view has its own set of customization tools. To customize the timeline, click the timeline pane and then choose the Format tab, shown in Figure 23-14.

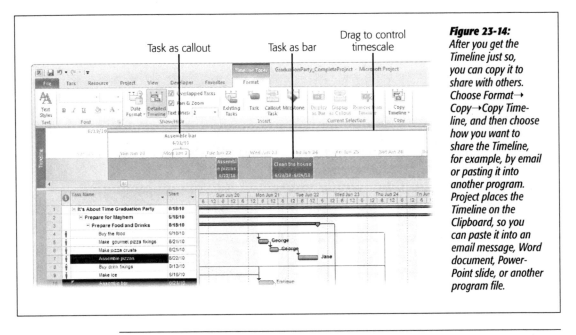

Figure 23-14:
After you get the Timeline just so, you can copy it to share with others. Choose Format→ Copy→Copy Time-line, and then choose how you want to share the Timeline, for example, by email or pasting it into another program. Project places the Timeline on the Clipboard, so you can paste it into an email message, Word document, Power-Point slide, or another program file.

Note: You have to choose between displaying the timeline and the Details pane (the bottom pane of a combination view). To display the timeline, choose View→Split View, and then turn on the Timeline checkbox. If you turn on the Details checkbox, Project automatically turns off the Timeline checkbox, and vice versa.

Here are the ways you can modify the timeline's look:

- **Format text styles.** You can modify the appearance of different categories of timeline text as you can in other views. Choose Format→Text→Text Styles. Page 616 provides the full scoop on formatting text styles.

- **Format text.** Any text in the timeline is fair game for unique formatting. For example, you may want deliverable milestones to stand out with bold green text. Right-click the text you want to format, and then choose formatting commands from the mini-toolbar that appears. Or select the text, choose Format→Font, and then choose the commands you want. Either way, you can change the font, font size, font color, bold, italic, and background color (page 618).

- **Format dates.** Choose Format→Show/Hide→Date Format, and then choose the date format for the timeline. The choices are the same ones you can choose in Project Options (choose File→Options; in the Project Options dialog box, click General, and then click the "Date format" down arrow). When space is at a premium, use abbreviated formats like 1/26. For more detail, choose a format like Wed Jan 26, '11. At the bottom of the Date Format drop-down menu, you can turn the checkmarks on or off to show or hide task dates, today's date, and the timescale dates.

- **Show timeline details.** For tasks you add to the timeline, choose Format→ Show/Hide→Detailed Timeline to toggle between showing only bars and showing bars that contain the task name and dates.

- **Show tasks that overlap.** Turn on the Overlapped Tasks checkbox if you want to see all the tasks added to the timeline, even if they overlap date-wise. With this checkbox turned on, the timeline adds rows to show more tasks on the same dates. If you turn this checkbox off, the timeline shows only the first task for a set of dates.

- **Pan and zoom.** The Pan & Zoom checkbox is turned on initially, so you can drag the timeline scale to change the dates that appear in the timescale. To keep the timeline set to the full project date range, turn this checkbox off.

- **Set the number of text lines in task bars.** In the Text Lines drop-down list, choose the number of lines of text you want to see in tasks you add to the timeline. Initially, only one line of text appears. For longer task names, choose 2 or 3. Although you can choose up to 10 lines of text, larger values mean the timeline takes up more room on the screen.

- **Add tasks to the timeline.** The Insert section of the Format tab has commands for adding existing or new tasks to the timeline. If you choose Existing Tasks, the Add Tasks to Timeline dialog box opens. Turn on the checkboxes for the tasks you want to add to the timeline.

- **Display a task as a bar or callout.** When you select a task in the timeline, the Current Selection section of the Format tab becomes active. The Display as Bar command shows tasks as bars in the timeline. Display as Callout shows the task above the timeline, perfect for project phases. Figure 23-14 shows an example of each. To remove a task from the timeline, choose Remove from Timeline.

Customizing the Team Planner View

Team Planner (page 213) is a new resource-centric view in Project 2010. It contains a row for each resource and shows the tasks to which the resource is assigned in the same row (also known as a swimlane). To change the appearance of the Team Planner view, display the view and then choose the Format tab. Many of the formatting options should be familiar: You can format text styles and change the appearance of different types of tasks. However, the Team Planner view has a few unique formatting options. Here are your choices:

- **Show parent tasks.** The Team Planner view starts out showing all subtasks, which means that each bar in the view shows the name of the actual task. To see a summary of your project, choose Format→Format→Roll-Up, and then choose the outline level you want to see. Instead of the subtask name, bars show the parent task names for the outline level you specify.

- **Format gridlines and text.** Choose Format→Format, and then choose Gridlines, Text Styles, or the number of lines of text to display. See page 617 for text styles and page 593 for formatting gridlines. Choosing a number for text lines determines how many lines of text appear in task bars.

- **Format task bars.** The Styles section of the Format tab has commands for formatting categories of tasks. You can change the border color and fill color for auto-scheduled, manually scheduled, external, and late tasks. You can also specify how to display the actual work that's been done.

- **Prevent Overallocations.** Confusingly, the Prevent Overallocations command appears on the Format tab. When you turn on Prevent Overallocations and assign a task to a resource whose time is already fully allocated for those days, Project automatically moves the task to the resource's next available time. If you turn this command off and assign a task to a resource who's already fully allocated for those days, Project leaves the task where you place it and draws red borders on the top and bottom of the task bars to show the overallocation.

- **Expand resource rows.** This checkbox is turned on initially, which tells Project to expand a resource row if you assign multiple tasks to the resource during the same timeframe. If you turn the checkbox off, you see only the first assigned task for those days.

- **Show unassigned tasks.** This checkbox is turned on initially, which is what you want. That way, the bottom pane shows tasks that aren't assigned to specific resources, so it's easy to see which tasks still require resources.

- **Show unscheduled tasks.** This checkbox is also turned on initially, so that manually scheduled tasks without dates appear in the Unscheduled Tasks column. That makes it easy to see which tasks need additional information.

Customizing the Resource Graph

The Resource Graph is a bar graph of resource data by time period. Although the bars in the Resource Graph are vertical, the right side of the view is still a timescale with values indicated by the height of the bars. Choosing fields to include in the Resource Graph, shown in Figure 23-15, is similar to choosing fields in a usage view. As in a Gantt Chart, you can change the appearance of bars and categories of text.

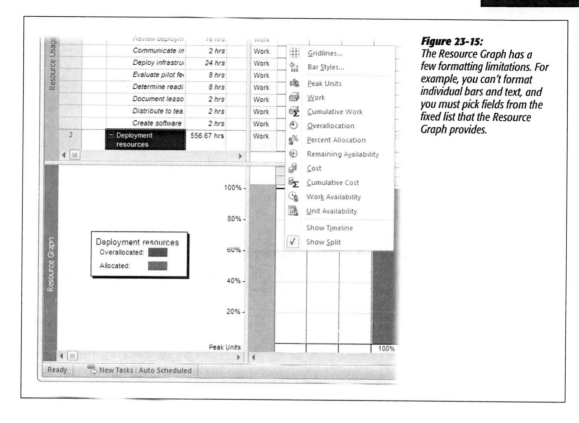

Figure 23-15:
The Resource Graph has a few formatting limitations. For example, you can't format individual bars and text, and you must pick fields from the fixed list that the Resource Graph provides.

Choosing fields to display

To choose fields in the Resource Graph, right-click the background of the time-scale, and then, on the shortcut menu, choose the field name. (You can also choose Format→Data and then choose the fields in the Graph drop-down list.) Here's what each field represents:

- **Peak Units.** The highest percentage of units assigned to a resource during a period. If the peak units are higher than the resource's maximum units, the bar shows overallocation.

- **Work.** The hours assigned to a resource during a period. If the assigned hours are more than the resource's total available hours (based on maximum units and the resource calendar), the over-the-top hours show up as overallocated.

- **Cumulative Work.** The total work assigned to the resource since the beginning of the project.

- **Overallocation.** Only the hours that the resource is overallocated during the period. This field is helpful for finding someone with enough available time to pitch in.

- **Percent Allocation.** The work assigned as a percentage of the resource's available time.

- **Remaining Availability.** The available hours that haven't been assigned.

- **Cost.** The work-hour and per-use cost for the resource during the period.

- **Cumulative Cost.** The total cost for the resource since the beginning of the project.

- **Work Availability.** A resource's total available hours based on maximum units and resource calendar. Unlike Remaining Availability, this field doesn't subtract hours from existing assignments.

- **Unit Availability.** This field is Work Availability as a percentage.

Changing the way Resource Graph bars look

The Resource Graph displays different information depending on whether it's a combination view's top or bottom pane. For example, if you show the Gantt Chart in the top pane, the Resource Graph in the bottom shows data for one resource at a time for the resources assigned to the selected task. You can scroll in the Resource Graph's left pane to see values for other resources. On the other hand, if the Resource Graph is in the top pane, it can also show values for all resources. The Bar Styles dialog box for the Resource Graph contains boxes for formatting each type of bar, but the information that the bars represent changes, depending on the information you choose to display in the Resource Graph itself. For example, if the graph shows a work-related field, then you can format bar styles for overallocated work, allocated work, and proposed bookings. If the Resource Graph displays cost, the bar styles include resource cost and proposed bookings.

To modify bar styles, double-click the background of the Resource Graph, or right-click the background, and then, on the shortcut menu, choose Bar Styles. In the Bar Styles dialog box, the settings on the left side relate to a larger group of tasks or resources (all tasks or filtered resources, for example); the settings on the right side apply to selected tasks or resources. The Resource Graph draws separate bars for the selected resource and the group of filtered resources so you can compare values. To see bars for only selected resources, be sure to choose Don't Show for all the Filtered resources settings on the left side of the dialog box. In the Bar Styles dialog box, choose the bar look you want, the color, and the pattern. You can draw values in different ways by choosing one of the following from the "Show as" drop-down list:

- **Bar.** Displays a separate bar for each time period.

- **Area.** Fills in a triangular or trapezoidal area equal to the value, which can span one or more periods.

- **Step.** Instead of separate bars for each period, all adjacent bars are drawn as one filled-in area.

- **Line.** Draws only the boundary of the area you see if you choose the Area option.
- **Step Line.** Draws the border of the Step filled-in area.
- **Don't Show.** Doesn't show the value on the graph.

Tip: If you look at work or allocation in the Resource Graph, in the Bar Styles dialog box, turn on the "Show availability line" checkbox to see a separate line for resource availability. The availability line compared to the height of bars is a great way to see how much work you can still assign.

Modifying a Network Diagram

A project management network diagram is a latticework of boxes (called nodes) with link lines connecting them. The boxes represent project tasks, and the link lines are the same task dependencies you see in a Gantt Chart view.

Before the dawn of computers and Project software, a network diagram was where you manually calculated the early start, early finish, late start, and late finish dates that, in turn, identify the critical path. You no longer need a network diagram and an abacus to calculate the critical path, because Project does it for you.

A network diagram is perfect for working on task dependencies, because it doesn't show time at all. Whether a task takes 1 day or 6 months, the network diagram box is the same size, and its successor task is right next door. Because a network diagram doesn't have a table area, task fields appear within each network diagram box. Choosing fields to display in boxes is the most common customization, but you can also change the appearance of boxes and how Project lays them out.

Choosing fields and formatting for network diagram boxes

Views in Project are simply different ways to look at the same information. In a network diagram, boxes replace the task bars in a Gantt Chart view. Similar to the fields you can attach to each side of a task bar, network diagram boxes can contain several task fields. Before computers, the fields were the early and late start and finish dates, so you could calculate slack and the critical path. Because Project calculates early and late dates, you can pick the fields you want to see and change what the boxes look like.

Like bar styles for a Gantt Chart view, box styles set the content and appearance of boxes within a category, like Critical, Critical Summary, or Noncritical External. To format a category of boxes, follow these steps:

1. Choose Task→View, click the down arrow on the Gantt Chart button, and then, on the drop-down menu, choose Network Diagram.

   The Network Diagram view appears, showing each task in its own box. Every box is the same size, regardless of the duration of the task.

2. **Choose Format→Format→Box Styles (or double-click the background of the Network Diagram).**

The Box Styles dialog box opens and lists the box styles for the active view, as shown in Figure 23-16.

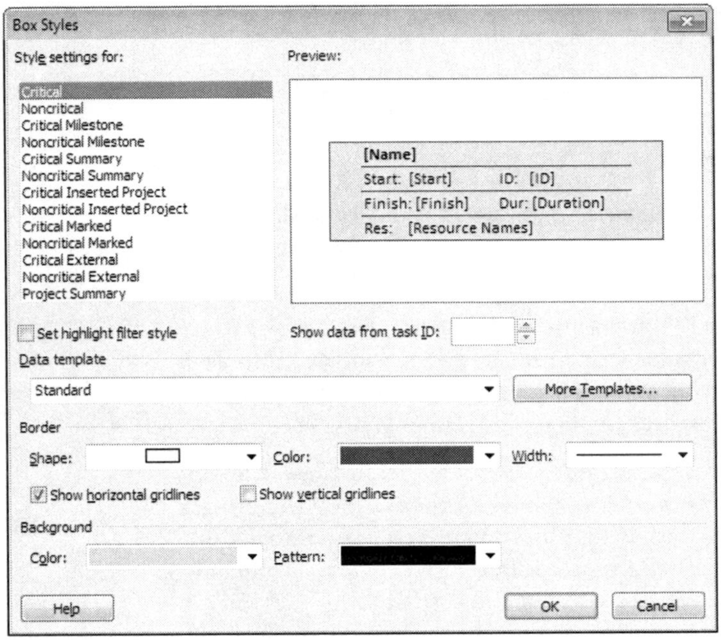

Figure 23-16:
To format individual boxes instead of categories, select the boxes you want to format, and then choose Format→ Format→Box (or double-click the border of a box). The Data Template dialog box includes settings like the ones in the Box Styles dialog box: data template, shape, color, and border.

3. **In the "Style settings for" list, select the category of box you want to format.**

The categories for network diagrams focus on critical and noncritical tasks. Each category combines critical or noncritical with another condition like milestone, summary, marked, or external.

4. **To choose the fields that appear in a box, in the "Data template" drop-down list, choose the template you want to apply.**

Data templates define a set of fields and their position in a box. To see which fields a template includes, select it in the drop-down list and then, in the Preview area, look at the box. To see what a box looks like with real data, in the "Show data from task ID" box, choose a task ID number.

To choose exactly the fields you want—for instance to include a custom field, to create a new data template, or to modify an existing one—click More Templates. In the Data Templates dialog box, choose a template, and then click Edit or Copy. (Or click New to start one from scratch.) The Data Template Definition dialog box opens, as shown in Figure 23-17.

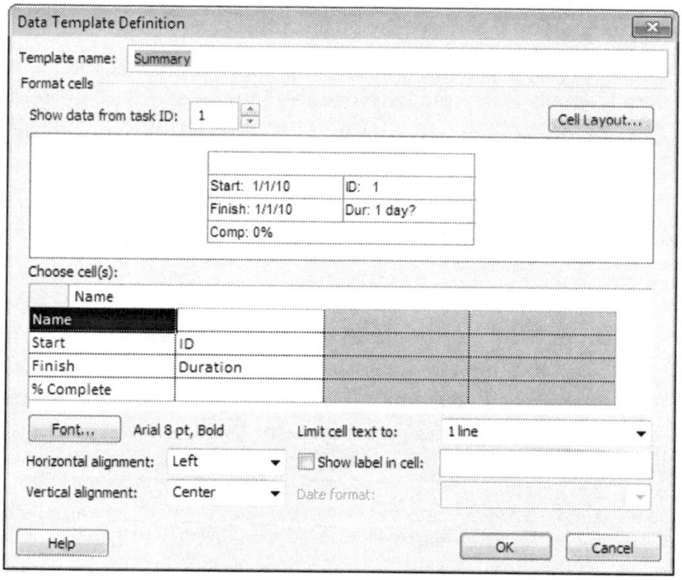

Figure 23-17:
To pick a field in the data template, in the "Choose cell(s)" section, select the cell. Click the down arrow, and then, in the drop-down list, choose the field name. If you want to change the number of rows and columns in a box, click Cell Layout.

5. **In the Border section, select the box shape, color, and width of the box border.**

   Turn on the "Show horizontal gridlines" checkbox or "Show vertical gridlines" checkbox to add horizontal or vertical lines between the fields inside a box. To choose a different background color or pattern for the box, choose the color and pattern in the drop-down lists. Check the preview when you choose colors and patterns to make sure the fields are still legible.

6. **To change the formatting for another category, repeat steps 3–5.**

   When you're done, click OK to close the Box Styles dialog box.

Laying out boxes

A network diagram lays out tasks like a flowchart, with predecessor tasks flowing across link lines to successor tasks. In Project, you can change the arrangement of boxes, including the alignment between rows and columns, the spacing between boxes, row height, and column width. You can also draw link lines straight from one box to the next, or use a combination of horizontal and vertical line segments. Your layout choices also include color selections and a host of other options. Choose Format→Format→Layout, and then use one or more of the following settings:

- **Manual or automatic layout.** In the Layout Mode section, select "Automatically position all boxes" to entrust positioning to Project. The program uses the "Box layout" settings to arrange and space boxes. When Project positions boxes, turn on the "Adjust for page breaks" checkbox so Project doesn't place boxes on top of a page break (which then displays the box on both pages when you print).

If you can't resist fine-tuning box positions, select the "Allow manual box positioning" option. Project initially lays out the boxes based on the settings in the Box Layout section, but you can move the boxes, too.

- **Box layout.** The Box Layout section controls where boxes go, and which boxes you see. The Arrangement drop-down list includes layouts like Top Down From Left and Top Down Critical First. The Row and Column settings include alignment (Left, Center, or Right), spacing (in pixels) between rows and columns, and box width and height.

Unlike the organizing influence of summary tasks in a Gantt Chart, summary tasks tend to muddle a Network Diagram view, which is why turning off the "Show summary tasks" checkbox is a good idea. Without summary tasks, you can see the relationships between work tasks more clearly. On the other hand, if you link summary tasks to other tasks, then keeping the "Show summary tasks" checkbox turned on shows all your links. The "Keep tasks with their summaries" checkbox tells Project to position subtasks near their summary tasks.

Tip: In Project 2010, you can quickly change the display of the network diagram using the ribbon. To turn off summary tasks, choose Format→Show/Hide and then turn off the Summary Tasks checkbox. To display link lines as straight lines, choose Format→Show/Hide and then turn on the Straight Links checkbox.

- **Link line look.** The Link Style section lets you switch link lines from rectilinear (horizontal and vertical segments) to straight from one box to another. The "Show arrows" checkbox is turned on initially, and that's usually what you want. You can also add task dependency text on link lines by turning on the "Show link labels" checkbox.

- **Color.** The Link Color section starts with critical links drawn in red and noncritical links drawn in black. If you use other colors for critical and noncritical, choose them in this section.

- **Other options.** The Diagram Options section is a hodgepodge of settings: background color, background pattern, whether page break lines appear in the diagram, whether to show in-progress and completed tasks, and whether to hide all the fields except the ID (perfect when you're concerned only with task dependencies).

Customizing the Calendar View

The *Calendar view* can't display the entirety of a project, but it's a great view for showing teams what they're doing during a particular period, as Figure 23-18 shows. The bar styles, text styles, and gridlines are all within your aesthetic control. You can also customize the timescale for bars and change the calendar to show 1 week, several weeks, or whole months.

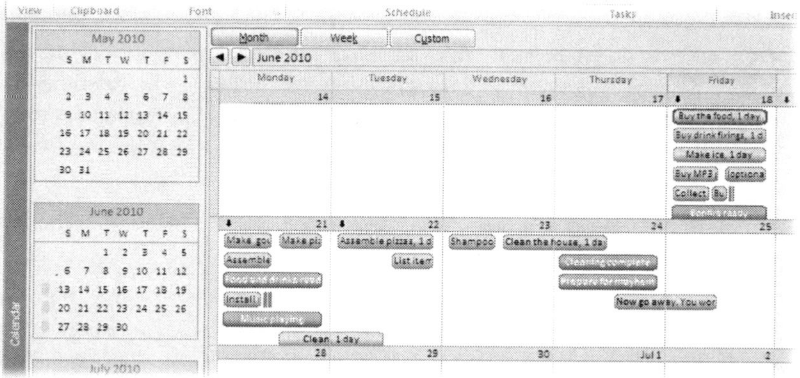

Figure 23-18:
In a calendar view, move to the next or previous period by clicking the left or right arrows just below the Month, Week, and Custom buttons. For example, when the calendar shows an entire month, the left arrow switches to the previous month.

Note: A calendar view is different from a project, resource, or task calendar (page 238). It's like the electronic version of an appointment book filled in with project tasks and assignments. Project, resource, and task calendars are like the shift schedules that workers receive, telling them which days they work or have off, and which shift they work, but not what work they do during that time.

Here's an overview of calendar view settings:

- **Choose a time period.** A calendar view displays 1 month at a time initially, but changing the time period is easy. Above the calendar, click Month, Week, or Custom. If you click Custom, the Zoom dialog box opens, and you can set a number of weeks or the specific dates you want to see. Alternatively, you can drag the Zoom slider to see shorter or longer periods.

- **Add a monthly preview.** To include a preview of the previous and next months like many paper calendars do, right-click the calendar background and then, on the shortcut menu, choose Timescale (or double-click the top of the calendar). In the Timescale dialog box, select the Week Headings tab, and then select the "Display month pane" checkbox.

- **Format the timescale.** Right-click the calendar background, and then choose Timescale (or double-click the timescale header) to open the Timescale dialog box. Select the Week Headings tab to choose the titles for months (for instance, March 2010 or 3/10), weeks (March 25 or M 25), and days (Monday, Mon, or M). To focus on weekdays, select the "5 days" option. For round-the-clock operations, "7 days" shows every day of the week.

The Date Boxes tab determines the information that appears at the top and bottom of each calendar box. For example, the day of the month sits at the top right, and the overflow indicator (which tells you there's more information than you can see), at the top left. You can add text at each corner of the box.

The Date Shading tab controls how working and nonworking time appear. For example, nonworking days on the base calendar are shaded, while working days are white.

- **Layout tasks.** Choose Format→Layout. Click the small arrow at bottom right of the Layout section to open the Layout dialog box. Initially, the calendar shows tasks based on the sort order that's applied (ID, initially). If you select the "Attempt to fit as many tasks as possible" option, then the calendar sorts tasks by Total Slack and then by Duration.

  Turn on the "Automatic layout" checkbox to tell Project to reapply the layout options as you add, remove, or sort tasks.

- **Customize calendar bar styles.** Calendar bars are different from their Gantt Chart siblings, so the bar style options are different, too. To change the way calendar bar styles look, choose Format→Format→Bar Styles. You can use a bar, a line, or simply text, and you can set the pattern and color for each type of bar. In the Field(s) box, choose the field you want to display inside bars. To include more than one field, separate each field with a comma.

Changing Tables

Views like the Gantt Chart and Task Usage come with a table of information—each column is a Project field. Sometimes, the table *is* the view, like in the Resource Sheet. Either way, Project comes with several built-in tables, like Entry and Cost, that contain frequently used collections of fields. Like most elements in Project, you can change tables to suit your needs.

You can easily swap the table you see in a view, for instance to switch from a summary to a table that shows performance compared to the baseline. But you can also change the columns in a table, temporarily adding columns to correct a problem, or permanently adding, removing, and rearranging columns to reflect how you work. Going a step further, the column width, row height, and a few other options are customizable so you can make a table look exactly the way you want.

Switching the Table in a View

Project offers two ways to swap out a table in a view. To choose any existing table, the More Views dialog box is the place to go. For tables on the Table menu, there's a shortcut.

To change the table, use one of these methods:

- **Fast method.** Right-click the Select All box at the intersection of the row and column headings (above the first ID cell), and then, on the shortcut menu, choose the table you want.

- **Never-fails method.** Choose View→Data→Tables→More Tables (or right-click the Select All box, and then, on the shortcut menu, choose More Tables). In the More Tables dialog box, double-click the table name. The More Tables dialog box lists every table that exists in your global template and the current Project file.

Note: Project dutifully records every change you make to a table, so the table shows those changes every time you apply it. Project stores the customized table in your Project file, although it has the same name as the original built-in one. To use both the original and your custom version, make a copy of the built-in table, and then modify it, as described on page 616. For custom tables that you want to use in other files, use the Organizer to copy the custom table from your Project file to the global template or another file (page 668).

Changing Table Contents

You can most easily make table changes by working on the table directly in a view. You can see the results immediately and try again until you get it right. Project records changes in the table's definition, so working in a view changes the table just as working in the Table Definition dialog box (page 613) does. Here are the techniques to use if you like seeing results as you go:

- **Add a column.** Right-click the column heading to the right of the new column, and then choose Insert Column. In the "Field name" drop-down list, choose the field, as shown in Figure 23-19. To quickly scroll to the field you want, start typing the field name. Project selects the first field that matches the letters you've typed. You can also click the Add New Column heading in the last column of the table, and then choose the field you want from the drop-down list.

- **Remove a column.** Right-click the column you want to remove, and then choose Hide Column. Project removes the column from the table definition and view. The box on page 613 provides another way to hide columns.

- **Rearrange columns.** If the table has the right columns in the wrong order, you can drag columns into other positions in the table. Click the column heading for the column you want to move. When the pointer turns into a four-headed arrow, drag the column to the new location. A dark gray vertical line jumps from column edge to edge to show you where the column will appear if you release the mouse button.

- **Edit a column.** Right-click a column and then, on the shortcut menu, choose Field Settings. The Field Settings dialog box opens with the "Field name" box set to the selected field. Then you can change the title, column width, alignment, and text wrapping.

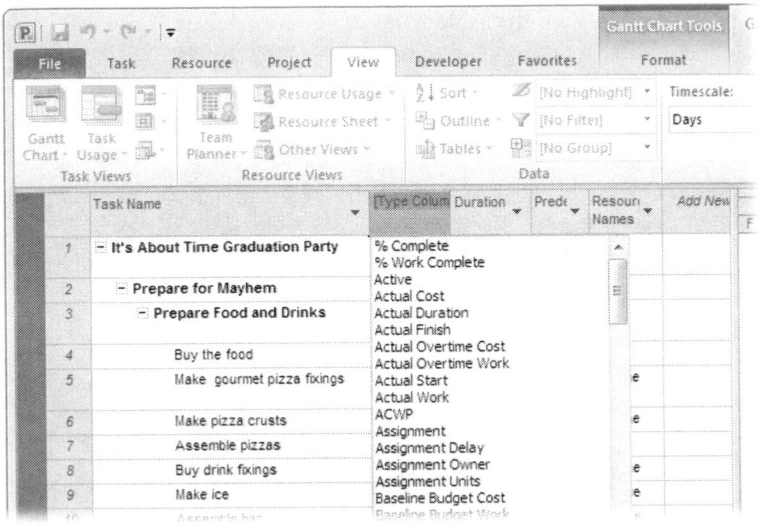

Figure 23-19:
If you start to type values into the Add New Column cells, Project identifies the type of information you're entering and changes the column to an appropriate custom field. For example, if you type a value like 6/17/2010, Project changes the column to a custom Date field like Date1.

- **Change column width.** Move the pointer between two column headings with the column you want to resize on the left. When the pointer changes into a two-headed arrow, drag to the left or right until the left column is the width you want.

Tip: When values don't fit in a column, Project replaces the text with a series of pound symbols (#), which aren't very informative. There's a quick way to resize a column to show all its values. Move the pointer to the right edge of the column heading. When the pointer changes to a two-headed arrow, double-click the edge. In the Field Settings dialog box, click Best Fit to do the same thing.

- **Wrap text.** Project 2010 automatically sets some columns like Task Name to wrap text—for example, to wrap very long task names over several lines as you change the column width. To wrap text in a column, right-click the column, and then, on the shortcut menu, choose Wrap Text.

- **Change row height.** You can change the height of specific rows in a table. Move the pointer to the lower border of the row's ID number, and then drag up or down until the row is the height you want.

- **Fine-tune the column heading.** If you want the column heading to be something besides the field name, in the Field Settings dialog box, in the Title box, type the heading you want. "Align Title" can be Left, Center, or Right. Turn on the "Header Text Wrapping" checkbox to wrap the words in the title over several lines when the column is narrow.

- **Align data.** In the Field Settings dialog box, "Align data" positions values in the column.

GEM IN THE ROUGH

Where's That Column?

You can hide a column without it losing its place in a table, but finding the column again is another matter. To hide a column without removing it from the table, move the pointer to the column heading's right edge. When the pointer changes to a two-headed arrow, drag past the column's *left* border. The column disappears, but a look at the table definition shows the column still there, with a width of zero.

When you're restoring the column to view, your first challenge is remembering where the column is hidden, because Project doesn't give any visual clues. Truth be told, a

column hidden like this may stay hidden forever—you may even insert the column a second time without realizing that it's already there.

Move the pointer between the two column headings where the column is hidden, making sure the pointer is slightly to the right of the border. When the pointer changes into a two-headed arrow, drag to the right until the hidden column stretches into view. You can also open the Table Definition dialog box and type a value greater than zero for the column width.

Modifying a Table Definition

If you prefer to do all your table editing in one dialog box, choose View→Data→ Tables→More Tables. In the More Tables dialog box, select the table you want to work on, and then click Edit. (If the list doesn't contain the table you want, check that you've selected the Task or Resource option to show the correct list of tables.) The Table Definition dialog box opens, with all the customization features available in the view—and a few more besides.

Knowing which keys to press in the Table Definition dialog box is, well, the key to success. To move to the next cell in the grid, press the right arrow. (Pressing Enter doesn't move to the next cell; it closes the dialog box as if you clicked OK.) Tab jumps from group to group. If you're in the grid area and you press Tab, Project fills in the rest of the row with standard choices, and then jumps to the "Date format" box below the grid. To move to the end, press Ctrl+right arrow. To move back again, press Ctrl+left arrow.

The Table Definition dialog box contains a table of its own, so terminology is a challenge. Although Project doesn't have official names for these elements, in this section, the Table Definition table is called the *grid*. A column in the Table Definition grid is a *property*, while a column in the table you're working on is called the *table column*. A row in the Table Definition grid is called a *row* and represents a Project field within the table you're working on. A row in the table is called a *table row* and represents a task, resource, or assignment.

Tip: If you want to go back to the original table definition for the current table, choose View→Data→ Tables→Reset to Default.

Here's how you make changes to a table in the Table Definition dialog box:

- **Add a table column.** You can insert a table column in any row in the Table Definition grid. To insert a table column at the end, click the first blank Field Name cell, and then choose the field you want for the new table column. Keep in mind that the top row in the grid represents the leftmost table column; the bottom row in the grid is the rightmost table column.

  To add a table column in the middle, select the row below the new grid row, and then click Insert Row to insert a blank row, as illustrated in Figure 23-20. In the Field Name cell, choose the field you want to use.

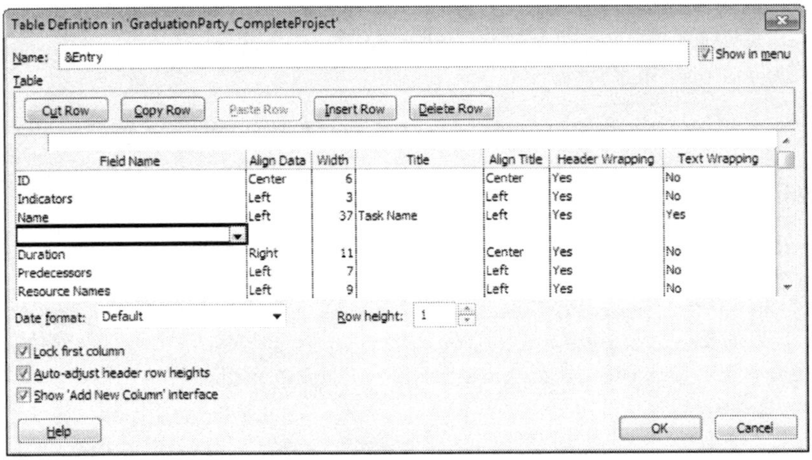

Figure 23-20:
When you're editing a task table, the Field Name drop-down list lists only task fields like Task Name. Similarly, you see resource fields when you work on a resource table, and assignment fields if you edit a table in a usage view.

- **Remove a table column.** In the Table Definition dialog box, select the row containing the field name you want to remove, and then click Delete Row.
- **Rearrange table columns.** Select the field name you want to move, and then click Cut Row. Project places the cut row on the Clipboard. Select the row below where you want to insert the cut field, and then click Paste Row. The cut row slides into its new location.
- **Change table column width.** Select the Width cell, and then type a number.

- **Fine-tune a table column.** The rest of the row cells are the same items you can set in the Field Settings dialog box (page 611): Title, Align Title, Align Data, and Header Wrapping. Change the Text Wrapping property to Yes if you want Project to automatically wrap the text in a column as you change its width.

- **Specify date format.** In the "Date format" drop-down list, choose the date format you want for date fields in the table. Choosing a table date format overrides the project-wide date format (choose File→Options, click General, and then choose a date format in the "Date format" box).

- **Change table row height.** If you want to adjust the height of all the table rows, then in the Row Height box, type or choose a number. The number is a multiple of the standard height; that is, "2" represents row heights that are twice the standard.

- **Keep the first column visible.** Project turns on the "Lock first column" checkbox, which means the ID column remains visible even if you scroll all the way to the right in the table. You can keep task names or resource names in view by making Task Name or Resource Name the first column and then turning on the "Lock first column" checkbox.

  To lock the Task Name column, for example, in the Field Name column, select Name, and then click Cut Row. Select the first row in the grid, and then click Paste Row to insert the Name field in the first row. Make sure the "Lock first column" checkbox is turned on, and then click OK. In the view, the Task Name column is in the first column and shaded to show that it's locked. As you scroll, it remains steadfastly in place.

- **Adjust heading row height.** With header wrapping turned on, Project automatically wraps column headings to fit column width. Project initially turns on the "Auto-adjust header row heights" checkbox, and you should keep it that way. When this setting is turned on, Project adjusts the row height of the column heading to show the entire column title, increasing the height for narrow columns and decreasing the height as the column widens. With the checkbox turned off, the column heading still wraps, but some of the text disappears at the bottom of the cell.

- **Show "Add New Column".** Out of the box, Project turns on the "Show 'Add New Column' interface" checkbox, which means the rightmost column in the table is Add New Column. Page 611 explains how to use this column to add new fields to a table.

Creating a New Table

You can create a new table from scratch or by copying one that's close to what you want. If you've inserted the fields you want into the current table, you can quickly turn it into a new table by choosing View→Data→Tables→Save Fields as a New Table. In the Save Table dialog box, type the name for the table and then click OK.

If you want to start from scratch or choose other settings, the More Tables dialog box is the place to start. To create a new table in this way, follow these steps:

1. **Choose View→Data→Tables→More Tables.**

    The More Tables dialog box opens.

2. **To create a table from scratch, select the Task or Resource option to specify the type of table, and then click New. If you want to copy an existing table, select it in the list, and then click Copy.**

    The Table Definition dialog box opens.

3. **In the Name box, type the name for the table.**

    Project initially fills in names like "Table 1" for a new table or "Copy of" and the table name for a copied table. Replace Project's name with one that describes the table contents, like "Baseline2" or "DateSummary."

4. **To display the table when you choose View→Data→Tables, turn on the "Show in menu" checkbox.**

    The table also appears when you right-click the Select All box at the intersection of the column headings and row IDs.

The table is ready for you to add columns, as described on page 611 and page 612.

Changing the Way Text Looks

Different Gantt Chart views may show the critical path in red or slack time as narrow green lines, but text appears in the same old 8-point Arial font. Project text styles make it easy to format text for different categories of information, like row and column headings, text for critical tasks, or text at the same position on task bars.

Whether you want to emphasize critical tasks with bold red letters or your tired eyes beg for larger text, you can use text styles to change formatting quickly and keep formatting consistent. Choose the type of information to format (headings, milestones, and so on) and the text formatting you want (font, font size, font style, color, and background color). Or you can reformat a single string of text for special emphasis, like the "Manager of the Year" caption under your boss's picture. This section explains how to do both.

Changing Categories of Text

Project text styles are watered-down versions of their Word cousins: Project doesn't let you change as many text characteristics. Just as a heading style in Word changes all the headings in a document, a text style drapes itself over every occurrence of text in its category. Set the text style for milestone tasks to bold green Blackadder ITC font, and the text for every milestone task follows suit. If a task or resource no longer fits the category, then Project takes care of changing the text formatting to that of the task's or resource's new category. Here's how to format text using text styles:

1. **Open the view in which you want to format text.**

   When you modify text styles, the changes appear only in the active view in the active project. Sadly, you can't copy these text styles to other views; you must repeat the text style formatting in each view you want to use them in. On a brighter note, once you modify a view to use attractively formatted text styles, you can use the Organizer (page 668) to copy the view to your global template or another Project file.

2. **Choose Format→Format→Text Styles.**

   The Text Styles dialog box opens.

3. **In the Item to Change drop-down list, choose the category you want to reformat, as shown in Figure 23-21.**

   The categories you can format are built-in, so you can't add your own.

   If you want to format all text in a view, for instance to enlarge text for your aging stakeholders, select All in the Item to Change drop-down list. The formatting applies to all text in the active view, including table headings, table text, and task bar text.

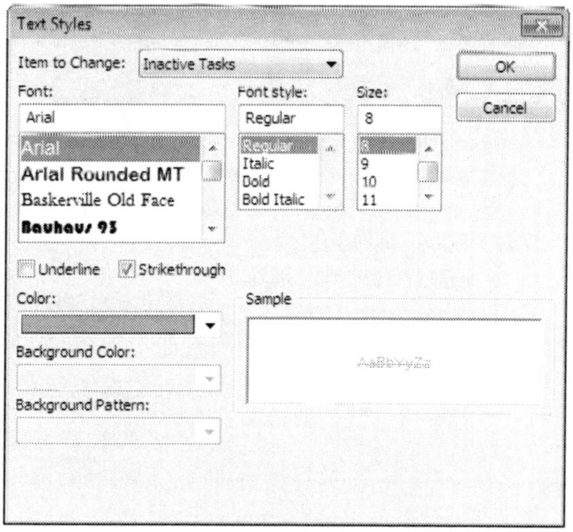

Figure 23-21:
The last two items in the drop-down list are Changed Cells and Inactive Tasks. Changed Cells corresponds to the change highlighting feature. You can change the text and background color for this category to make changed values stand out. The box on page 618 describes change highlighting in more detail. Choosing Inactive Tasks lets you change the appearance of tasks that you set to inactive (page 353).

4. **Choose the font, font style, and font size you want for the category.**

The Font list displays the fonts installed on your computer. Font Style represents formatting like bold and italic. The Size list shows standard font sizes, but you can type a number in the Size box to pick another size. You can also turn on the Underline checkbox to underline text, although underlining gets lost in view tables.

5. **In the Color drop-down list, choose the color you want.**

Colors other than black can be hard to read, although dark colors are better than light shades. Look at the text after you've formatted it, and maybe print samples on both color and black-and-white printers to make sure the colors work.

Tip: If you want Project to take care of choosing text color, background color, and background pattern, then in the Color, Background Color, and Background Pattern drop-down lists, choose Automatic.

---

6. **To highlight cells that use a text style, in the Background Color drop-down list, choose the color you want.**

Similar to the shading that Project applies to changed cells, you can change the background color for critical tasks, summary tasks, and so on. If you tend to print to black-and-white printers, then it's a good idea to choose a background pattern in the Background Pattern drop-down list, because these patterns show up even in black and white. The Sample box shows you what your formatting choices look like.

7. **Click OK.**

The Text Styles dialog box closes. Any text in your selected category displays the new formatting.

UP TO SPEED

Highlighting Cells

If you group tasks and resources (page 632), then you already know how background color can differentiate items. Cell background color says, "Look at me!" Project 2007 added background color and patterns to text styles, so you can highlight cells the way grouping highlights summary rows.

A clever extension of background color makes change highlighting possible. The Item to Change drop-down list in the Text Styles dialog box has the Changed Cells entry.

If you select it, then the Preview area shows the light-blue highlighting that appears when cell values change. If you can't see the light blue due to color blindness, or if you simply prefer a different color, then in the Items to Change drop-down list, select Changed Cells. In the Background Color drop-down list, choose the color you want. When you click OK, cells burst into your favorite color whenever an edit you make changes their values.

Changing Selected Text

Suppose one or two tasks are the CEO's favorites, so you want them to stand out from everything else. You can format text that you select down to an individual cell in a table. In Project 2010, formatting selected text is a snap with the mini-toolbar that appears when you right-click a cell, as shown in Figure 23-22.

You can apply the same kinds of formatting as with text styles, but the basic steps are a little different:

1. **Select all the cells with the text you want to format, and then right-click one of the selected cells.**

   Select a single cell, several cells, a row, or several rows. The formatting commands format whatever text is selected.

2. **On the mini-toolbar that appears above the top selection, click the formatting commands you want.**

   The first line of the toolbar has drop-down lists for fonts and font sizes. The second line has buttons for changing text to bold or italic. Click the down arrows to choose a cell background color or text color. The selected text immediately displays its new formatting. If the CEO becomes enamored with another part of the project, you must select the text again to remove the special formatting you applied.

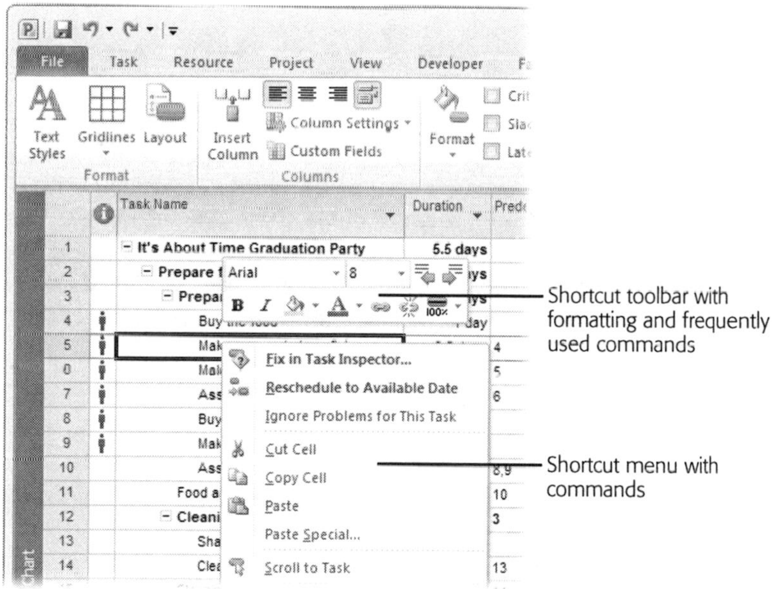

Figure 23-22:
In addition to the shortcut menu that appears when you right-click a cell, a mini-toolbar perches above the cell you right-click. Click a tool to change the font, font size, font color, bold, italic, or cell background color. The mini-toolbar also has frequently used commands, such as Link Tasks, Outdent Task, and Indent Task.

Filtering Through Information

Finding project information can be like sifting for gold—lots of project sediment can obscure the nuggets you're looking for. In Project, filters screen out information you don't care about so you can easily see the information you do want. Project comes with several built-in filters to get you started. For example, the Using Resource filter shows tasks that use specific resources, and the Tasks with Estimated Durations filter shows tasks with question marks in their Duration fields, so you can fill in duration values. You can also create ad hoc filters with AutoFilter. Either way, this section shows you how. The box on page 621 talks about a few commands that act like filters.

Built-in filters can act as a tutorial when you want to create your own filters. They provide examples of combining several tests in one filter, comparing the value of one field to another, or asking for input. You could create a filter to find critical tasks whose dates are slipping by starting with the built-in Slipping Tasks filter and adding a test on the Critical field. Here are some ideas for helpful filters:

- **Critical tasks with overallocated resources.** Filter for tasks whose Critical and Overallocated fields are both equal to Yes, to find tasks that are at risk.

- **Incomplete tasks using a resource.** If a resource gets reassigned to another project, you can find all the tasks that person was assigned to that are in progress or haven't started. Then you can work on finding replacements.

- **Work packages.** Create a filter to turn off the display of both summary tasks and milestones so the task list shows only work packages.

- **Generic resources.** Display only generic resources so you can see which tasks you still need to staff.

Applying Filters

Changes you make to a project can affect what should appear in the filtered list—but you have to update the filter each time. For example, if you shorten a task so that it's no longer on the critical path, you'd expect it to disappear when the Critical filter is in place. It turns out that Project doesn't automatically update the filtered list as you make changes. To make sure you're seeing the right items, quickly reapply the current filter by pressing Ctrl+F3.

Filters are a great way to confirm that you've made all the changes you need. For example, when you apply the "Tasks with Estimated Durations" filter, the task list displays only tasks with estimated durations. After you change durations on those tasks, reapply the filter (by pressing Ctrl+F3). When the filtered list is empty, you know you're done.

Creating and Editing Filters

Filters can be as simple as the Critical filter, which just checks that the Critical field is equal to Yes. AutoFilter (page 629) makes quick work of simple filters like these. But filters can also have several nested tests, like the Slipped/Late Project filter. An existing filter makes a great template, whether you want filter-building guidance or just a shortcut. For example, to set up a group that uses both the Critical and Duration fields, you can copy the built-in Critical group and then modify the copy to add a condition for Duration.

Creating filters from scratch or from copies is almost identical. You create the new filter, change the name Project assigns, and then define the filter conditions. Here are the steps:

1. **Choose View→Data. Click the Filter down arrow and then, on the drop-down menu, choose More Filters.**

   If a task-oriented view is visible, the More Filters dialog box opens with the Task option selected. The Filters list includes all the task-oriented filters, like Completed Tasks and Milestones. If a resource-oriented view like the Resource Sheet is visible, the Resource option is selected automatically. To work on a task or resource filter, select the Task or Resource option.

UP TO SPEED

Summarizing a Project

Most of the time, you want to see summary tasks and their work package tasks. A task list without summary tasks is better when you're working only on work package tasks, for instance to fine-tune your schedule or find tasks without assigned resources. Project 2010 makes it easy to filter out summary tasks:

- **Hide or show summary tasks.** If you want to hide summary tasks to focus on work packages, choose Format→Show/Hide and then turn off the Summary Tasks checkbox. To bring the summary tasks back, turn the checkbox on.

- **Summarize the entire project.** You can add your own top top-level task to summarize an entire project. But it's easier to let Project take care of that. Choose Format→Show/Hide and then turn on the Project Summary Task checkbox. Project adds a row with ID number 0, which rolls up all the values for all tasks in your project. To always show the project summary tasks for new projects, in the Project Options dialog box, choose Advanced, and then, under "Display options for this project" turn on the "Show project summary task" checkbox.

---

2. **To start with an existing filter, in the Filters list, select the filter you want to copy, and then click Copy. To start with a blank slate, click New. To edit an existing filter, select the filter, and then click Edit.**

   You can also start a new filter by choosing View→Data, clicking the Filter down arrow, and then, on the drop-down menu, choosing New Filter.

   The Filter Definition dialog box opens.

3. **In the Name box in the Filter Definition dialog box, type a new name for the filter.**

   Project fills in the Name box with something like "Filter 1" for new filters and "Copy of" followed by the filter name for copied filters, as shown in Figure 23-23. Replace the standard name with one that describes what the filter does, like "Work packages."

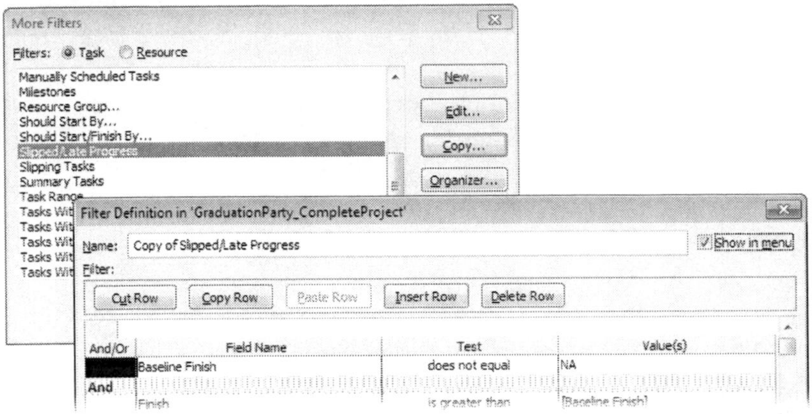

Figure 23-23:
To include a filter on the menu that appears when you choose View→Data and click the Filter down arrow, turn on the "Show in menu" checkbox.

4. **Add or modify the filter tests, and then click OK to save the filter.**

See the next section to learn how to set up filter tests.

Defining Filters

Filters are a gauntlet of tests that tasks, resources, or assignments have to pass in order to appear in the view. For example, the In Progress Tasks filter first tests whether a task has started, and then tests whether it is *not* finished. If a task has started but not finished (that is, it passes both tests), then it appears in the task list. This section describes how to create different types of tests, including the following:

- **Comparing a field to a value.** The simplest tests compare a field to a specific text string, number, or other value, like the Critical filter testing whether the Critical field equals Yes.

- **Comparing two fields.** You can set up a filter to compare the values from two fields like the Cost Overbudget built-in filter, which tests whether Cost is greater than Baseline Cost.

- **Multiple tests.** Filters are often made up of several tests, like the Should Start/Finish By built-in filter. When you combine more than one test, you must tell Project whether items must pass all tests or some combination of them, as you'll learn on page 623.

- **Interactive tests.** In some cases, you want a different filter value each time you apply the filter. For example, you filter tasks by a specific assigned resource depending on whom you're trying to free up. An interactive filter asks for a value and then uses your answer to filter the list.

Comparing a field to a value

Comparing a field to a value is a good introduction to tests. Many basic filters need only one of these tests—like the perennial favorite Critical filter. Here are the steps to create a test that compares a field to a value, using a filter for critical tasks as an example:

1. **In the Filter Definition dialog box, select the Field Name cell, click the down arrow that appears, choose the field you want to test (in this example, Critical), and then press Enter.**

   The field appears in the Field Name cell. When you press Enter, Project selects the Test cell in the same row.

   To quickly select a field in the drop-down list, click the down arrow to open the drop-down list. Then start typing the first few letters of the field name. When Project selects the field you want, press Enter.

2. **Click the Test cell down arrow, and then choose the type of test you want to apply, as illustrated in Figure 23-24. For the critical filter, choose the "equals" test. Press Enter to move to the Value(s) cell in the same row.**

   Table 23-1 describes the tests that Project offers and gives an example of each one. For example, the Work Overbudget filter uses "is greater than" to see whether actual work hours are greater than baseline work hours.

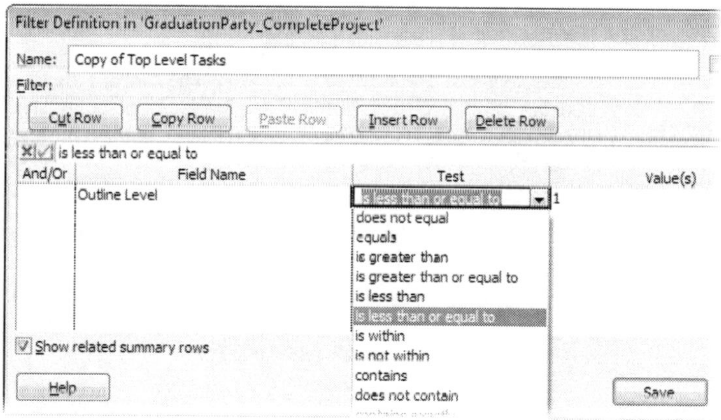

Figure 23-24:
The "Show related summary rows" checkbox tells Project whether to include the summary rows for tasks that pass the tests. If summary rows outnumber the tasks you're looking for, turn off this checkbox to see only the tasks that pass the filter.

3. **In the Value(s) cell, type or choose the value to compare to the field.**

   If the field you're testing is a Yes/No field, you can type *Yes* or *No* or choose the values from the drop-down list. In Figure 23-24, the test checks to see if the outline level is less than or equal to 1.

Table 23-1. *Table 23-1. Project offers several tests for you to use in your filters.*

Test	What it does; example
Equals	The field and test value must be equal. The Critical filter tests whether the Critical field equals Yes.
Does Not Equal	The field does not equal the test value. The Incomplete Tasks filter tests whether % Complete does not equal 100%.
Is Greater Than	The field value must be greater than the test value. The Slipping filter tests whether the Finish field is greater than the Baseline Finish field. Later dates are greater than earlier dates.
Is Greater Than Or Equal To	The field value must be greater than or equal to the test value. The Date Range filter tests whether the start date is greater than or equal to the date you specify.
Is Less Than	The field value must be less than the test value. The Should Start By filter tests whether the Start field is less than (earlier than) the date you specify.
Is Less Than Or Equal To	The field value must be less than or equal to the test value. You can test whether the Schedule Variance field is less than or equal to 0 to find tasks that are on time or early.
Is Within	The field value must be equal to or between two values you specify. The Task Range filter tests whether the ID field is within two task ID numbers. In the Value(s) cell, you type the two numbers separated by a comma, like *50,100*.
Is Not Within	The values must be outside the range you specify. For example, to find the cheapest and most expensive resources, test whether Standard Rate is not within *25,300*.
Contains	This string test checks whether the field value contains the string in the Value(s) cell. For example, you can see whether the Task Name field contains "Payment" to find all the payment milestones.
Does Not Contain	This string test looks for field values that don't contain a string. For example, to eliminate all phase two tasks, you can test whether the Task Name field does *not* contain "Phase 2."
Contains Exactly	This test looks for exact matches between the field and the test value. The Using Resource filter tests whether Resource Name contains the exact resource name you type.

Tip: The "equals" and "does not equal" tests can compare text field values to strings with wildcard characters. "*" is the wildcard for one or more characters; "?" replaces just one character. For example, "* Supervisor" finds all the resources with "Supervisor" at the end of their names. On the other hand, "BigDig ???" finds the BigDig 300 backhoe and the BigDig 500, but not the apartment-cleaning BigDig 50.

Comparing two fields

The most useful filters seem to be ones that compare two fields. For example, if the date in the Finish field is greater than the date in the Baseline Finish field, then a task is running late. Setting up a test to compare two fields is similar to comparing a field to a value. Here are the steps:

1. **In the Filter Definition dialog box, select the Field Name cell, click the down arrow that appears, choose the field you want to test (Finish in this example), and then press Enter.**

   Project jumps to the Test cell in the same row, ready for you to choose a test.

2. **Click the Test cell down arrow, and then choose the test you want to apply—"is greater than" in this example.**

   Press Enter to move to the Value(s) cell in the same row.

3. **In the Value(s) cell, click the down arrow, and then choose the comparison field, Baseline Finish in this example.**

   In the Value(s) column, Project differentiates fields from text by enclosing the field name in square brackets ([ ]), as shown in Figure 23-25.

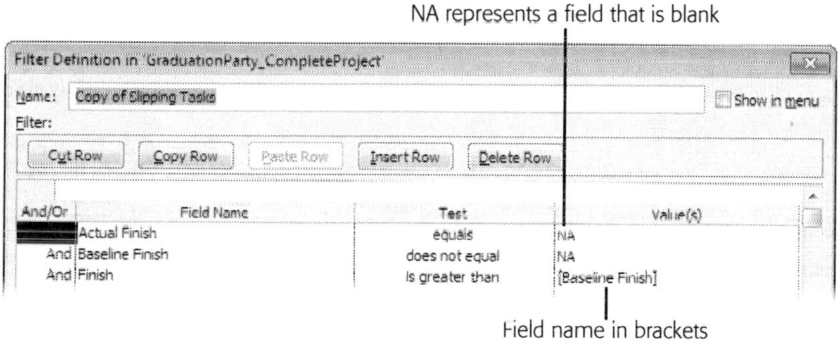

NA represents a field that is blank

Field name in brackets

Figure 23-25:
In the Value(s) column, the drop-down list contains all Project fields, including custom fields like Number 10. However, you see only task fields if you're building a task filter and resource fields for a resource filter.

4. **Repeat steps 1–3 to add more tests to the filter.**

   When you've finished adding tests, click OK to save the filter.

Creating multiple test filters

In many cases, a filter needs more than one test to do what you want. Compound filters mean you have more choices for how you put the tests together. You can set up filters in which items must pass every test or only some of the tests.

Initially, Project evaluates tests in the order they appear in the Filter Definition table, like a worried mother might ask, "Is he single?" "Is he rich?" and only then, "Is he ready to get married?" The items that pass the first test move on to the next test. Project keeps testing until there are no more tests.

And and Or are called Boolean (logic) operators, which you use to specify whether an item has to pass both tests or only one. And and Or work just like they do in real life. If you want items to pass both tests, use And; for instance, "Is he single?" and "Is he ready to get married?" Use Or if the items must pass only one test, like "Is he rich?" or "Is he smart?"

You (or, in this case, your mother) can use additional Ands or Ors to change the order of tests. For example, he has to be smart or rich; only then does it matter whether he's ready to get married.

The following example creates a filter that finds tasks that have overallocated resources *and* are running late. It first finds baselined tasks with overallocated resources. For those tasks, it checks for delayed finish dates or work that's behind schedule. If a task passes both sets of tests, it appears in the task list.

Each multiple test filter is different, but the following steps demonstrate the concept:

1. **In the Filter Definition dialog box, in the Name box, type a filter name.**

   Because multitest filters do so much, build a name from the key features of the filter like "Slipped/LateProgress/Overallocated." If you plan to use the filter frequently, turn on the "Show in menu" checkbox. The filter then appears in the filter list—for example, when you choose View→Data and then click the Filter down arrow, or when you click the down arrow in a table column header and then choose Filters.

2. **In the first table row, define the condition you want (including field, test, and value).**

   In this example, the first condition checks that the task has a baseline (that is, Baseline Finish does not equal NA). The Baseline Finish field contains a date if the task is baselined, NA if it isn't. Type *NA* whenever you want to test for a value that's blank.

3. **In the second row's And/Or cell, choose And, and then add the condition in the other cells. Use Or instead, if a task or resource has to pass only one of the tests.**

   If you add a condition to the row, And appears on the right side of the cell with unbolded text, as shown in Figure 23-26. This And indicates that the condition is one of several that work as a team.

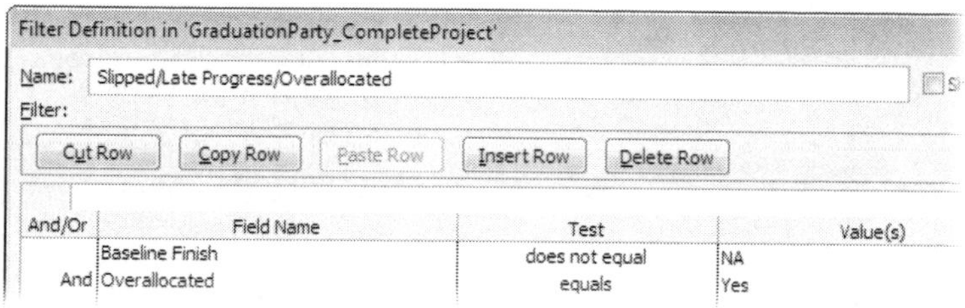

Figure 23-26:
In this example, tasks must pass both tests to move on to the semi-finals. If you add And or Or to adjacent rows that contain tests, the filter runs each test in order.

4. **In the third row's And/Or cell, choose And, and then click another row.**

   As soon as you click any other row, several things happen. The And you just added moves to the left side of the cell, the text is bolded, and the row is shaded. This formatting is Project's way of saying that the row acts like the parentheses in a mathematical equation before and after the empty row. For example, with And in the third row, Project evaluates the first two tests as a set and evaluates the tests after the third row as a set, as the following steps show.

   If you forget to include a test, you don't have to start from the beginning. The box on page 628 explains how to add, remove, and otherwise change condition order after the fact.

5. **In the fourth row, bypass the And/Or cell, and then simply add the test for slipped tasks.**

   You don't have to include an And or an Or, because this test is the first one of the second set. The test for slipped tasks checks whether the Finish field is greater than the Baseline Finish field.

6. **In the fifth row, choose Or in the And/Or cell, and then add the test for late progress.**

   The Or in front of this condition, shown in Figure 23-27, tells Project that a task has to pass either the slipped task test or the late progress test. Either situation means the task is in trouble.

Creating changeable filters

With some filters, you want to use different values each time you apply the filter, which is known as an *interactive filter*. An interactive filter simply means that the filter asks for values to use in tests. For example, when you're trying to find tasks scheduled during people's vacations, you can apply the Using Resource In Date Range filter. Each time you apply this filter, you tell it which resource you're looking for and the beginning and ending dates you're interested in. These values act exactly as though you had placed them in the Filter Definition dialog box, in Value(s) cells.

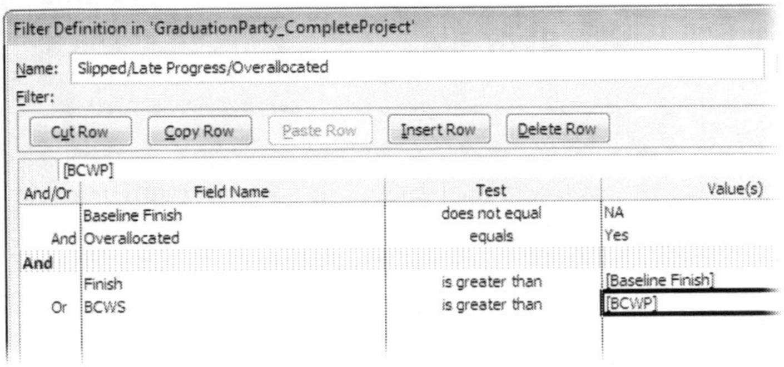

Figure 23-27:
The test for late progress checks for budgeted cost of work scheduled (page 420) greater than the budgeted cost of work completed. What the test means in English is this: For the duration that's passed, was more work scheduled than what has been completed?

UP TO SPEED

Inserting, Deleting, and Rearranging Rows

Without planning ahead, chances are good that you'll forget one of your filter conditions. After testing a filter, you may realize that your logic isn't sound. You'll find the buttons for inserting, deleting, copying, cutting, and pasting rows quite handy. Here's what each button does:

- **Cut Row.** Select a row, and then click Cut Row to place the row on the Clipboard. The Paste Row button becomes active so you can paste the row in another location.

- **Copy Row.** Select a row, and then click Copy Row to place the row on the Clipboard. If one row is almost identical to the one you want to add, then copying

and pasting an existing row may be easier than defining a condition.

- **Paste Row.** Select the row below where you want to paste the row on the Clipboard, and then click Paste Row. Pasting inserts the cut or copied row above the selected row.

- **Insert Row.** Select the row where you want to insert a new blank row, and then click Insert Row. The new row appears above the selected row.

- **Delete Row.** If a condition is wrong or unnecessary, select it and then click Delete Row.

Creating these inquisitive filters is easy once you learn how to define a prompt. Here are the steps:

1. **In the row for the interactive condition, choose the field and the test you want.**

   For example, to find a specific resource, choose the Resource Names field, and the "contains exactly" test.

2. In the Value(s) cell, type the prompt in quotation marks followed by a question mark, as shown in Figure 23-28.

   For example, type a prompt like *"Show tasks assigned to this lucky devil"?*

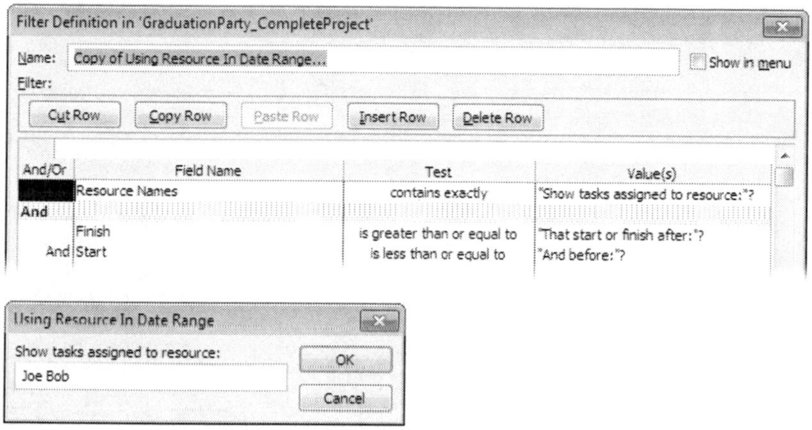

Figure 23-28:
Top: Be sure to place the question mark at the very end of the string outside the quotation marks.

Bottom: When you apply an interactive filter, a dialog box opens with the prompt you typed. Project waits until you enter a value.

Quick and Dirty Filtering with AutoFilter

Interactive filters are great when you frequently filter for different values, like when you filter for just a few resources or different date ranges. But sometimes you just have a quick, one-time question, so saving a filter doesn't make sense. AutoFilter, which is like its relative in Excel, lets you pick filter fields and values as you go. You can change the fields or the values at will, and combine filters on several fields at the same time. The box on page 631 shows you how to whip up a custom AutoFilter test, if the filter you want goes beyond the choices on an AutoFilter drop-down menu.

Here's how to use AutoFilter:

1. **If AutoFilter isn't turned on (down arrows aren't visible to the right of each column heading), then choose View→Data, click the Filter down arrow, and then choose Display AutoFilter.**

   Project comes with AutoFilter turned on. If you want to turn off AutoFilter for new projects for some reason, choose File→Options. In the Project Options dialog box, click Advanced, and then, under the General heading, turn off the "Set AutoFilter on for new projects" checkbox.

2. **Display the view and table you want to filter.**

   A table must be visible, because AutoFilter works on table columns.

3. Click the down arrow in the column you want to filter, for instance, Duration.

   The AutoFilter drop-down menu includes several filter values based on the data in the column, as illustrated in Figure 23-29.

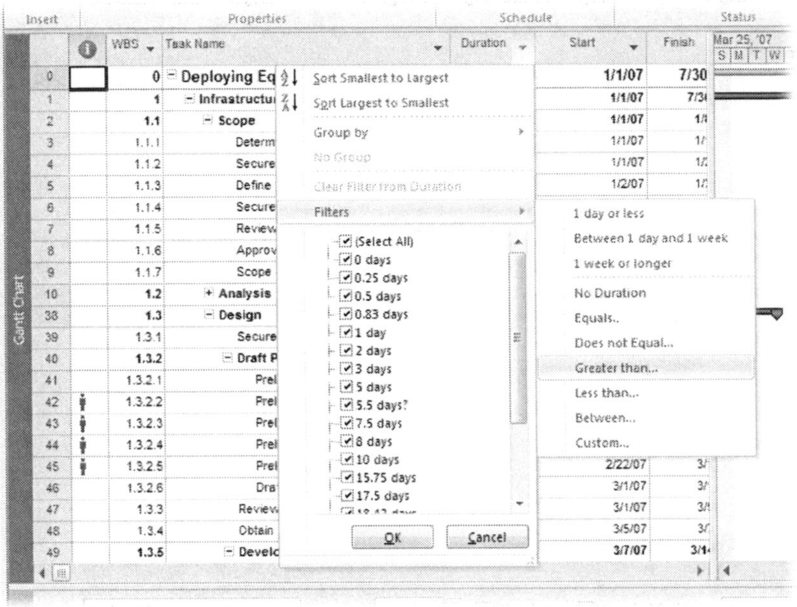

Figure 23-29:
The AutoFilter drop-down menu lists every value found in the column. It also contains likely choices based on the column. For example, the Duration AutoFilter submenu includes "1 day or less", "1 week or longer", Equals, "Greater than", Custom, and so on.

4. To filter by specific values, keep the AutoFilter checkboxes turned on for the values you want to use. Turn off the AutoFilter checkboxes off for values you want to filter out. Click OK to apply the AutoFilter.

   For example, to filter by longer duration, you can turn off the checkboxes for shorter Duration values.

5. To apply a quick AutoFilter test, in the drop-down menu, choose Filters. Then in the submenu, choose the test or condition you want.

   For example, to filter for longer durations, choose "Greater than". The Custom AutoFilter dialog box opens. In the value drop-down list, choose the duration to use, such as "*10 days*", and then click OK. As soon as you apply an AutoFilter to a column, Project filters the list and displays the AutoFilter icon (which looks like a funnel) to the right of the column name.

6. To remove a filter in a column, click the AutoFilter filter icon (which looks like a funnel) in that column, and then choose Clear Filter.

   The filtered list updates to show items that pass the AutoFilters still in place.

7. **To add an AutoFilter to another column, click the down arrow in that column's heading row, and then repeat steps 4–6.**

    AutoFilter doesn't have all the options the Filter Definition dialog box provides. AutoFilter tests act like they're joined with And operators. The results show items that pass all the tests. You can't tell AutoFilter to show items that pass one AutoFilter test or another.

Tip: A funnel icon appears to the right of every column with an AutoFilter applied. In addition, the status bar includes the AutoFilter Applied notification.

Building Custom Filters with AutoFilter

Quite often, the filter you have in mind goes a step or two beyond what the AutoFilter drop-down menu offers, but you don't need the full suite of tools from the Filter Definition dialog box. If that's the case, a custom AutoFilter may be the answer. Custom AutoFilters can have one or two conditions joined with an And or Or. For custom AutoFilters you want to use again, save them and add them to the regular filter list. Here's how to build a custom AutoFilter:

1. Click the down arrow in the column you want to filter, choose Filters, and then, on the AutoFilter submenu, choose Custom.

2. In the Custom AutoFilter dialog box, the field is set to the selected column, as shown in Figure 23-30.

3. For each custom condition, in the drop-down list on the left, choose the test (the same ones you see in the Filter Definition dialog box when you define a filter from scratch, as described on page 621) and then, in the box on the right, choose or type the value.

4. To save the custom AutoFilter, click Save. The Filter Definition dialog box opens with all the tests in the test table. All you have to do is, in the Name box, type a new name and then click OK. If you want to make other changes, for example to add the filter to the menu or to hide summary tasks, modify the settings in the dialog box before clicking OK.

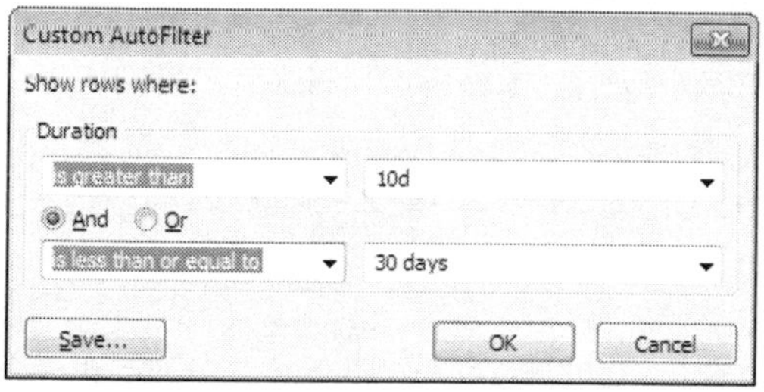

Figure 23-30:
The Custom AutoFilter dialog box is like a simple version of a filter definition. The field is selected for you. You can define two criteria and specify that items meet both or only one of them.

Grouping Project Elements

Grouping tasks, resources, and assignments with similar characteristics makes it easy for you to scan and analyze your project information. For example, if you group tasks by schedule variance, troubled tasks will jump right out at you. You can group resources by hourly rate to find low-cost options. In Project, the Group feature lets you segregate tasks, resources, or assignments by field values. For example, you can group tasks into critical and noncritical (Critical field Yes or No) to find ones to shorten. Grouping resources by overtime rate helps identify the least expensive people for a weekend assignment.

Tip: If you're confused by the different uses of the word "group" in Project, see the box on page 634 for clarification.

Working with Groups

Like filtering and sorting, groups can work with several fields, as Figure 23-31 shows. For example, you can group first by critical and noncritical, and then by task duration, so you can find the longest critical tasks for fast-tracking (page 348).

Here a few methods for applying a group:

- **Choose a popular group.** Choose View→Data. Click the Group down arrow, and then, on the drop-down menu, choose the group you want, like Critical, Milestones, or Complete and Incomplete Tasks.

- **Choose any group.** Choose View→Data. Click the Group down arrow, and then, on the drop-down menu, choose More Groups. In the More Groups dialog box, double-click the group you want.

- **Group by a field.** Click the down arrow to the right of the column heading for the field you want to group by, and then, on the drop-down menu, choose "Group on this field" (for Yes/No fields). For other fields, the drop-down menu may contain the "Group by" command. When you choose "Group by", a submenu of group options appears, for example, if you choose "Group by" in the Duration field, the submenu includes Duration and Weeks.

To remove groupings, choose View→Data. Click the Group down arrow, and then, on the drop-down menu, choose No Group. Or click the down arrow to the right of a column heading and choose No Group on the drop-down menu.

Changes you make to a project can affect the group to which a task, resource, or assignment belongs. For example, if you add resources to shorten task duration, the task should appear in a different Duration subgroup. However, you don't see that happen until you reapply the group.

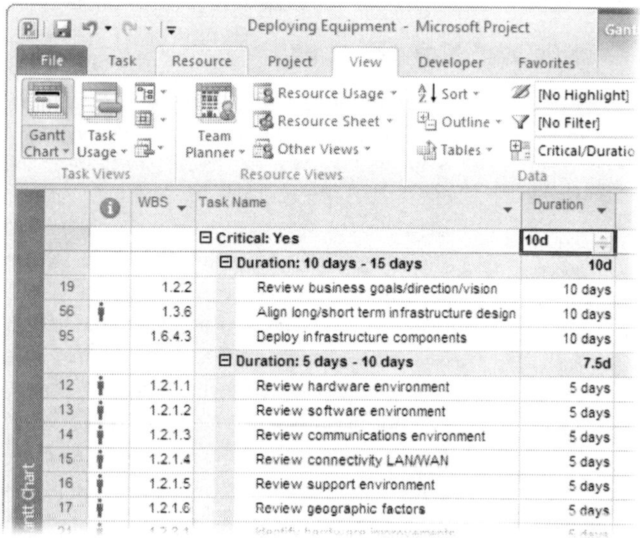

Figure 23-31:
When you group items, the group summary rows calculate the values in the group's numeric fields, as the box on page 636 explains. For example, if you group assignments by employees and contractors, you can see the total hours and cost for each group. Group calculations appear in a Gantt Chart view's table area, the Resource Sheet, as well as the timescale in usage views.

Creating a Group

As with Project tables, the easiest way to create a group is to copy and edit an existing one. That way you get to keep the original group definition, and customize the copy. For example, to set up a group that uses both the Critical and Duration fields, you can copy the built-in Critical group and then add the second condition to the copy. (Basic groups are so simple, though, that there's no problem starting from scratch.)

Project comes with several groups that apply to tasks and resources, but you can expand the list to analyze your projects in many ways. Here are a few examples:

- **Overallocated resources.** Group tasks by the Overallocated field to find tasks with overallocated resources.

- **Overbudget tasks.** Group tasks by Cost Variance to categorize tasks by how much they're over budget.

- **Critical tasks with overallocated resources.** Critical tasks that use overallocated resources are risking a late finish date. Group tasks first by the Critical field, and then by Overallocated, to see the group of critical tasks broken into overallocated and not overallocated resources.

Groups, Groups, and More Groups

The term "group" helps describe several features in Project, each of which does something different. Here are the different kinds of groups Project uses, and advice on keeping them straight:

- **Group By command.** On the View tab, choose Group By to categorize tasks, resources, or assignments by field values. (Or click the down arrow to the right of the column heading for the field you want to group by, and then, on the drop-down menu, choose "Group by".) For example, the built-in Complete and Incomplete Tasks group separates completed tasks from those that aren't finished.

- **Resource group.** In the Resource Sheet, the Group field specifies categories for resources. For example, you could set up group names to associate people with their departments: Sales, Engineering, Espionage, and so on. Then you can use the Group field to find replacement resources from the same department.

- **Group resource.** A group resource represents several interchangeable resources. Suppose you have seven painters who all scrape, power-wash, and paint. You could set up one resource called Painters. The Maximum Units for a group resource is the sum of each individual's maximum units, so the Painters group resource may have maximum units of 700 percent. You can assign the Painters resource to tasks and let the team leader worry about who does what. As long as the assignments don't exceed 700 percent, your work is done.

- **Ribbon group.** If you customize the ribbon, one of the buttons on the Customize the Ribbon page is New Group. This command lets you add a new section to a tab on the ribbon.

- **Internal and external resources**. Group assignments by the Resource Group field to see how much work you've assigned to outside resources.

- **Long critical tasks with little or no work done**. If you're looking for tasks to crash (page 351) to bring a project back on track, critical tasks with longer durations give you the most benefit. If the project is already in progress, tasks that are almost complete won't help. Filter first by Critical, then by % Complete (in ascending order), and finally by Duration (in descending order) so you can see the critical tasks with the least amount of work done and the longest duration.

The steps for creating and copying groups are almost identical. You create the new group (from scratch or by copying), name it, and then define the fields to group by. Here are the steps:

1. Choose View→Data. Click the Group down arrow, and then, on the drop-down menu, choose More Groups.

   If a task-oriented view is active, the More Groups dialog box opens with the Task option selected and task-related groups displayed in the Groups list. To work on a resource-related group (for instance, to group the resources in the Resource sheet by their standard rates), select the Resource option.

2. **In the Groups list, select the group you want to copy, and then click Copy. To start a new group from scratch, simply click New.**

   The Group Definition dialog box opens. Copying a group, and then editing the copy, is usually the better approach. You'll still have the original group definition in addition to the new one.

3. **In the Name box in the Group Definition dialog box, type a new name for the group.**

   New groups start with a name like "*Group 1*," whereas copied groups are named "*Copy of*" followed by the copied group name. Replace Project's name with one that identifies what the group does, like "*Critical/Duration*."

Tip: To list a new group on the group drop-down menu, be sure to turn on the "Show in menu" checkbox.

---

4. **To add a new field to group by, select the first blank Field Name cell, click the down arrow, and then choose the field you want to group by.**

   For example, to add the Duration field to the Critical/Duration group, choose Duration in the first Then By row, as shown in Figure 23-32.

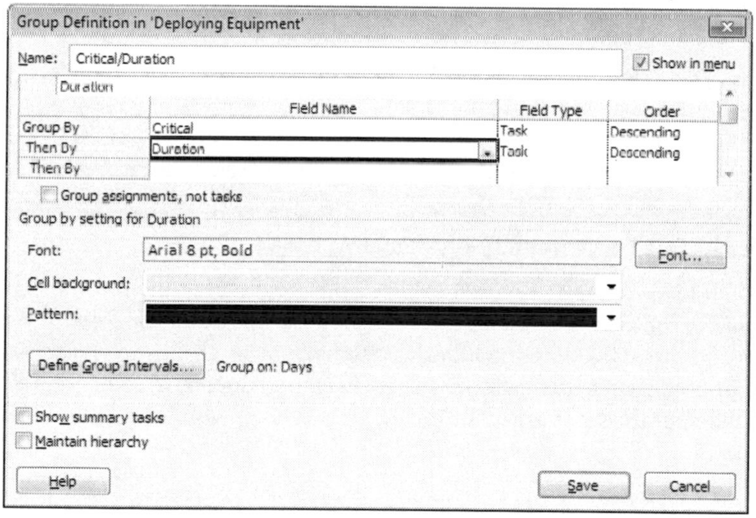

Figure 23-32:
Project fills in the Field Type cell with Task for a task-related group or Resource for a resource-related group. If you want to group by assignments, for instance to see which assignments are taking too long, choose Assignments in the Field Type cell and then turn on the "Group assignments, not tasks" checkbox.

Calculating Rolled-Up Group Values

Rolled-up values for built-in fields like Cost and Work are simply the sum of values in the group. Other calculations like Maximum, Minimum, or Average are available for group summary rows, but only if you use custom fields (page 641), because you can't tell Project how to roll up built-in fields. Set up a custom field like Cost1 to equal Cost, and then set its Rollup value to the calculation you want. Voilà—you can show the average cost of a group of tasks or resources.

On the other hand, rolled-up Duration values may just look wrong. For example, a rolled-up Duration might be 63.5 days, while the four tasks in the group are each only 2 days long. Project calculates the group duration from the start date of the earliest task in the group to the finish date of the last task in the group.

---

5. **In the Order cell, choose Descending or Ascending.**

   For example, to show tasks from the longest duration to the shortest, choose Descending. To show resources from lowest to highest hourly rate, choose Ascending. Ascending shows text fields grouped in alphabetical order. If you group by a Yes/No field like Critical, then choose Descending if you want the fields with Yes to appear first.

6. **To group by assignment instead of by task, turn on the "Group assignments, not tasks" checkbox.**

   In a task usage view, you can group by task or by assignment. For example, group by task to see which tasks have the highest schedule variance. If you want to find out which resources produce those variances, then group by assignments. In a resource usage view, the checkbox label is "Group assignments, not resources".

7. **To change the appearance of the group summary rows, change the values in the "Font", "Cell background", and "Pattern" boxes.**

   When Project subtotals groups, it applies a different font to the summary rows and shades the cells. For example, the primary group rows use 8-point Arial, bolded, with a solid yellow cell background. To print groups to a black-and-white printer, change the Pattern to cross-hatching, or choose colors that show up as different shades of gray. The box on page 636 explains how group calculations work.

Note: If you want to see summary tasks in the groups, turn on the "Show summary tasks" checkbox. On the other hand, turning on the "Maintain hierarchy" checkbox shows all the levels of summary tasks for subtasks within groups. You can also maintain hierarchy from the ribbon by choosing View→Data, clicking the Group down arrow, and then, on the drop-down menu, choosing Maintain Hierarchy in Current Group.

---

8. Click OK.

   The Group Definition dialog box closes. In the More Groups dialog box, click Apply to see the results of your handiwork.

Note: To make changes to an existing group, choose View→Data. Click the Group down arrow, and then, on the drop-down menu, choose More Groups. In the More Groups dialog box, select the group to edit, and then click Edit. The Group Definition dialog box opens, as if you're creating a new group. Make the changes you want, and then click OK.

Changing Group Intervals

Groups often start out with subgroups for each distinct value in the field you're grouping by. This approach is fine for Yes/No fields like Critical or Milestone. When you group by cost, duration, and similar fields, the number of unique values could spawn hundreds of subgroups, for tasks that cost $3,450, $3,455, and so on. Setting group intervals makes subgroups more meaningful. For example, on a short project, the intervals for the Duration group could be days. On a multiyear project, you might modify the Duration group to use 2-week intervals. Here's how you define intervals for a field in a group:

1. **In the Group Definition dialog box, select the field whose interval you want to set, and then click Define Group Intervals.**

   The Define Group Interval dialog box opens, as shown in Figure 23-33. If the selected field doesn't work with intervals like Yes/No fields, then the Define Group Intervals button is grayed out.

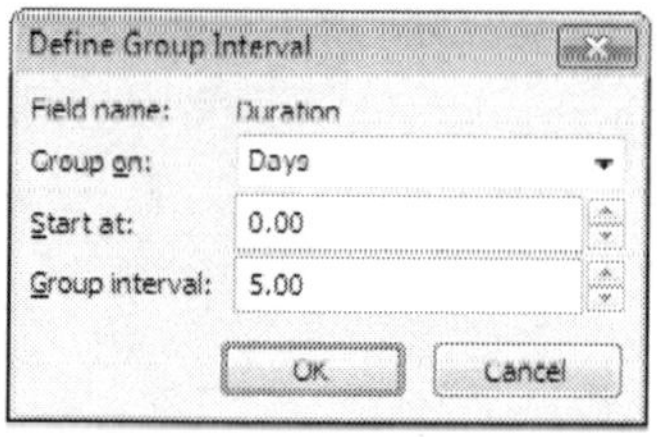

Figure 23-33:
The name of the field you selected appears at the top. The "Group on" field is set initially to Each Value, which creates a separate subgroup for each unique value. To reduce the number of groups, choose an interval value, such as Days or Weeks for the Duration field.

2. **To change the interval, in the "Group on" box, click the down arrow, and then choose the units or type of interval you want.**

   The choices in the "Group on" drop-down list vary based on the field you select. For example, for Duration, the "Group on" choices range from Minutes to Days to Months. % Complete lists typical percentage intervals like "0, 1-99, 100" which groups tasks into unstarted, in progress, and complete. On the other hand, for Cost, choose Interval in the drop-down list to set the interval size ("1000" to group on every $1,000).

---

3. **To start the interval at a specific value, type the number in the "Start at" box.**

   You can group all the rows with tiny values by setting a "Start at" value. For example, if you start with a 1-day duration, then one group contains all tasks that last less than a day.

4. **To define the interval size, type the number in the "Group interval" box.**

   For example, if "Group on" is set to Days and "Group interval" is set to 5-day increments, then tasks are grouped 0 to 5 days, 6 to 10 days, and so on.

5. **Click OK.**

   The Define Group Interval dialog box closes, and you're ready to click OK to save the edited group.

Defining Your Own Fields

I n the previous chapter, you learned all kinds of ways to cajole Project into showing you the information you want to see. In this chapter, you'll go deeper. You
can customize fields to track information that Project's built-in fields don't, and
then add them to tables in Project views (page 610). For example, you can create a
field that holds the number of lines of code written for each development task. With
hours worked and code quantities, you can calculate programming productivity.

You can create custom fields that accept only the values you want by defining lookup
tables. That way, you or anyone else can pick a valid value from a drop-down list.
Custom fields can also contain formulas to calculate results. The usual arithmetic
suspects like addition, subtraction, division, and multiplication show up as buttons
in the Formula dialog box. But Project offers all sorts of fancy functions that you can
combine with any Project field to spit out the answers you're looking for.

Graphical indicators make it easy to see whether a project is on track, going better
than expected, or headed for trouble. By customizing fields, you can tell Project to
display icons instead of numbers or text.

Outline code fields work like the WBS values that project managers know and love.
You can set up outline codes to categorize tasks and resources. Each level of the
outline can have its own rules for values and what those values represent. Outline
codes can be flexible and let people fill in whatever values they desire. Or they can
use lookup tables, if you have a specific set of values you allow.

In this chapter, you'll learn how to create each of these types of customized fields to
show you the information you need to see.

Note: Project 2010 doesn't offer custom forms. No big loss, especially if you're comfortable working in a view table. Dragging over cells to copy values is satisfyingly quick and easy. You can supercharge table editing by arranging the columns you fill in side by side or by creating a custom table with just the columns you want (page 610).

Understanding Custom Fields

The field drop-down list that appears when you insert a column into a Project table is proof of how many fields Project has. For built-in fields, your customization options are limited. You can change the title that appears in a table column heading, the width, and the alignment of text. But the behind-the-scenes calculations and data are set in stone.

Custom fields come in different data types, just like the types Project's built-in fields use. For example, you may set up a custom cost field to track early delivery bonuses, a text field to document that custom cost, or an outline code to categorize tasks based on who's footing the bill. Project has one set of customizable fields for tasks, and a similarly named set for resources. Here are the different types of customizable fields Project provides:

- **Cost.** Cost1 through Cost10 are currency fields for tracking anything that represents money.

- **Date.** Date1 through Date10 are date fields—for instance, to calculate the date halfway between the start and finish date for a task.

- **Duration.** Duration1 through Duration10 contain units of time. For example, you could create a custom duration field to calculate the time to write one page of documentation.

- **Finish.** Finish1 through Finish10 are date fields, although Project does use these fields. It stores finish dates for interim plans in Finish1 through Finish10. If you save interim plans, then leave Finish1 through Finish10 alone, and use Date1 through Date10 for your custom dates.

- **Flag.** Perfect for tagging tasks or resources, Flag1 through Flag20 are fields that contain either Yes or No. What they say yes or no to is up to you.

- **Number.** Because number fields are so versatile—lines of code, lines of code per day, defects reported, and so on—Project provides 20 number fields: Number1 through Number20.

- **Outline Code.** Outline Code1 through Outline Code10 represent a hierarchy of values, which you set up through a code mask (page 323).

- **Start.** Like their finish date counterparts, Start1 through Start10 are date fields, which Project uses to store start dates for interim plans. If you save interim plans, use Date1 through Date10 for your custom dates.

- **Text.** Each of the 30 text fields, Text1 through Text30, can hold up to 255 characters. For short notes, a custom Text field can go right in a table next to another custom field to which it relates—for example, identifying the type of custom cost you've added. Notes (page 267) are another way to annotate tasks and resources, especially when the notes are long or you want to insert pictures or objects.

Customizing a Field

Customizable fields let you decide how they look and behave. You can change the name from, say, Number1 to something more meaningful like LinesOfCode. You can use a formula to calculate the field values or create a lookup list to help others pick valid values. How values roll up to summary rows is customizable, too, whether you want a total like other Project fields or another calculation like minimum, maximum, or average. Initially, fields display values, but you can define graphical indicators instead. For example, you can use stoplight colors to indicate whether a measure is on track, on thin ice, or in need of resuscitation.

This section begins with the basics: choosing a field's data type, whether it applies to tasks or resources, and picking the one you want to work on. From there, you can jump to other sections to learn how to work with lookup tables, formulas, calculations, graphical indicators, and the other available settings. (Because outline codes work a little differently, they warrant their own section, "Coding Tasks and Resources," on page 652.)

No matter which type of custom field you choose, what you can customize remains the same. Here are the basic steps for defining a custom field:

1. **Choose Project→Custom Fields.**

   Project 2010 shortens the path to opening the Custom Fields dialog box by placing the command on the ribbon's Project tab.

2. **Select either the Task option or the Resource option.**

   Project has two sets of custom fields for tasks and resources. The field names are the same, but the fields are different. For example, you can customize a Text1 task field and a Text1 resource field. When you insert a field into a table, the custom field you get depends on the table. For example, in the Resource Sheet, you add the Text1 resource field. In a Gantt Chart view, you add the Text1 task field.

   If you use Project Professional with Project Server, the Project option becomes available so you can define project-level custom fields.

3. **In the Type drop-down list, choose the type of field, as shown in Figure 24-1.**

   The Field list displays the fields for the selected data type. If you've renamed a field, you see the field name and its alias in the list.

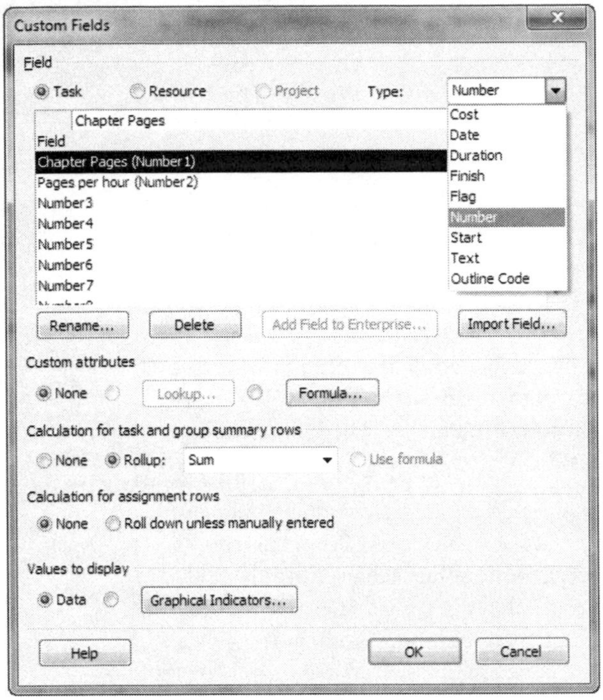

Figure 24-1:
The Custom Fields dialog box in Project 2003 had a separate tab for outline codes. Starting with Project 2007, outline codes are just another type of custom field. To work on a custom outline code, in the Type drop-down list, choose Outline Code, and then go to page 653 for more instructions.

4. **In the Field list, select the field you want to customize, like Number1 or Flag5.**

   You can choose any field in the list that you haven't already customized. If you decide to customize a field you've already used, for example to calculate values with a formula, you may see a warning that the calculated values will overwrite any existing data.

5. **Click Rename.**

   Custom field names start as a combination of the data type and a numeric ID; Cost3 is the third custom cost field. Whenever you customize a field, rename it so it's alias describes what the custom field is for, like "Pages per day" if you're calculating how many pages of documentation the team produces each day.

Tip: Although you can change the title in a column heading cell in a table (page xx), the edited title applies only to the current table. Renaming a custom field displays the alias in drop-down lists and every time you insert the field in a table.

---

6. In the Rename Field dialog box, type a new name for your custom field, and then click OK.

   The alias and the original field name both appear in the field list, as shown in Figure 24-1.

7. If you don't want to do any other kind of customization, then click OK.

   The Custom Field dialog box closes, and then you can insert the renamed field in a table.

At this point, the custom field cheerfully accepts any value you enter as long as it's the right data type. For example, if you use a custom number field in a table, Project complains only if you try to type a date, text, or a value that isn't a number.

Creating Lists of Valid Values

Some custom fields are cut and dried. Flag fields accept Yes or No; those values appear in a drop-down list in a Flag table cell. Similarly, Text fields expect text, but they don't care what that text represents. If you want people to enter correct or at least consistent values, it's a good idea to provide some hints about valid values. For example, if the Text1 field is supposed to contain a room number, then you don't want people typing anything they please. Likewise, you wouldn't want one person to type "Manu" for the Manufacturing group and someone else to type "Mfg." You can control the values that a custom field accepts with a *lookup table*—a list of valid values.

You can set up a lookup table to enforce a list of values or accept additional values not on the list. When a lookup table allows other values, the choices already there act as examples of what's expected. To build a lookup table for a custom field, follow these steps:

1. Choose Project→Custom Fields, and then select the custom field you want to work on.

   You can choose a field you haven't used yet or add a lookup table to a field you've already renamed. If you choose a virgin field, rename it (page 642).

2. Click Lookup.

   The "Edit Lookup Table for <field name>" dialog box opens. Project adds the name of the field or its alias to the title bar. (In Project 2003, the lookup table button was labeled Value List.)

3. **In the Value column, select a blank cell, and then type a value. In the Description cell, type a description of the value.**

    Values that don't match the type of field appear bolded and red. As soon as you correct the discrepancy, the value turns black, and the bolding is turned off. If you include a description, then the value and the description both appear in a table cell drop-down list. For example, "Room 12-105" may not mean anything to people outside the facilities department, but "HQ-phone closet" does. Similarly, the description cell can spell out an abbreviation. That way, people know that "Actg" means Accounting, not Acting.

4. **Repeat step 3 to add more values to the list.**

    Although you can't copy and paste lookup table values from Excel or the rows in the Resource Sheet, the box on page 646 describes a shortcut to building a lookup table.

    The Edit Lookup Table dialog box has buttons for inserting, removing, copying, and rearranging the values in the lookup table, as Figure 24-2 shows.

5. **If you want the custom field to automatically fill in a value, then turn on the "Use a value from the table as the default entry for the field" checkbox. Select the value in the table, and then click Set Default.**

    In the dialog box, the default value changes to blue and bolded. (If you're wondering why the "Display indenting in lookup table" checkbox is grayed out, it's reserved for outline codes.)

6. **To control the order that values appear in a drop-down list, expand the "Display order for lookup table" section. Select either the "Sort ascending" or "Sort descending" option, and then click Sort.**

    Click the + to the left of the section label to expand the section. To display lookup values in a drop-down list in the order they appear in the Edit Lookup Table dialog box, keep the "By row number" option selected. This option is ideal when you want to show the more frequently used values at the top of the drop-down list.

    When you select the "Sort ascending" or "Sort descending" option and then click Sort, Project re-sorts the list.

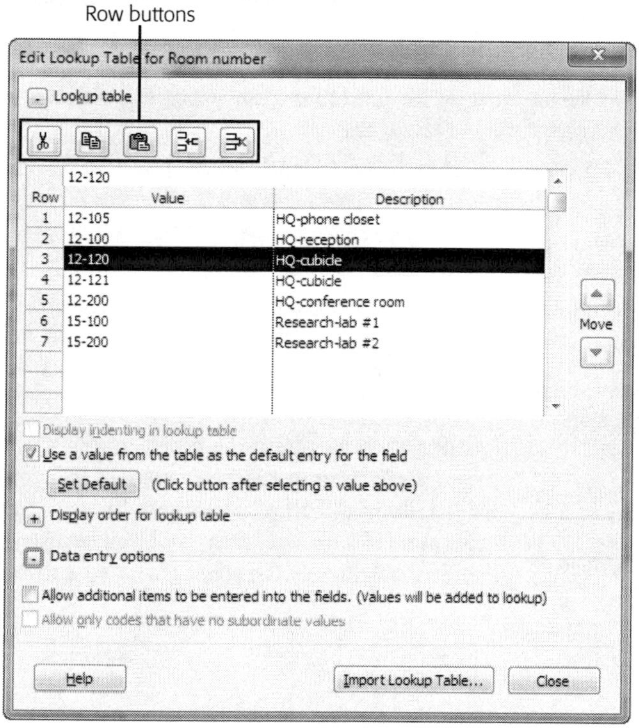

Row buttons

Figure 24-2:
The first two row buttons, Cut Row and Copy Row, both place the row on the Clipboard, so you can relocate it by clicking Paste Row. To insert or remove values, select the value, and then click Insert Row or Delete Row, respectively. Another way to rearrange values is to select a value, and then click the Move up and down arrows to the right of the lookup table.

7. **If it's OK for someone to type a value that's not in the lookup table, expand the "Data entry options" section, and then turn on the "Allow additional items to be entered into the fields" checkbox.**

   Project turns off this checkbox initially so the field accepts only values in the lookup table. By not allowing other values, you can prevent duplicate values or misspellings. If you do allow other values, then Project automatically adds them to the lookup table. The other checkbox in this section, "Allow only codes that have no subordinate values", is grayed out because it applies to outline codes.

8. **Click Close.**

   The Edit Lookup Table dialog box closes, and you're back in the Custom Fields dialog box. If you're finished making customizations, then click OK.

Reusing Lookup Tables

Building lookup tables can take time, especially if the list and descriptions are long. You can bypass this data entry chore if another custom field already has what you want.

If you know that a custom field has *everything* you want—lookup tables, formulas, and so on—in the Custom Fields dialog box, then click Import Field. You choose the Project file, type of field, and field name. Project imports the entire field with all of its customizations, not just the lookup table.

But if you want to import only the lookup table (a list of departments in your company, or a list of vendors, for example) into a custom field, here are the steps:

1. If the lookup table belongs to a custom field in another project, open the Project file first.

2. Return to the Project file that you want to import a lookup table into.

3. Choose Project→Custom Fields, select the field you want to edit, and then click Lookup.

4. In the Edit Lookup Table dialog box, click Import Lookup Table.

5. If the lookup table is in another project, then in the Project drop-down list, select the filename.

6. Select the option for the type of field (Task, Resource, or Project).

7. In the Field drop-down list, choose the custom field with the lookup table, and then click OK. All the lookup table values flow effortlessly into the current custom field.

Importing a lookup table is the perfect solution if you defined a ginormous lookup table for a custom outline code and then realized that you customized a task outline code instead of a resource outline code. You can import the lookup table from the task outline code in the same file.

Calculating Field Values

Another way to fill in custom field values is to calculate them. Don't reach for your calculator; Project can do the calculating as long as you give it the formula. A formula can use every Project field, along with typical numeric and logical functions. For example, a "Pages per hour" custom number field could divide the "Number of pages produced" custom field by the task's Actual Work field.

Tip: If the formula you want already exists in another custom field, then you can import it. First, open the project that contains the custom field with the formula you want. Then, back in the project with the field you're customizing, choose Project→Custom Fields. Select the custom field to which you want to add the formula, and then click Formula. In the Formula dialog box, click Import Formula. In the Import Formula dialog box, fill in the boxes as you do when importing a lookup table (page 646). Unlike most other Project elements, you can't use the Organizer to copy formulas from project to project.

To define a formula to calculate field values, follow these steps:

1. **After selecting the field to edit in the Custom Fields dialog box, click Formula.**

   The "Formula for" dialog box opens with the custom field name or alias in the title bar.

2. **To add a field to the formula, click Field. In the drop-down list, choose the category and then the field you want to add, as shown in Figure 24-3.**

   The categories are similar to different field data types. IDs and outline codes share a spot in the list; and the Project category contains properties related to the Project file, like the date it was created.

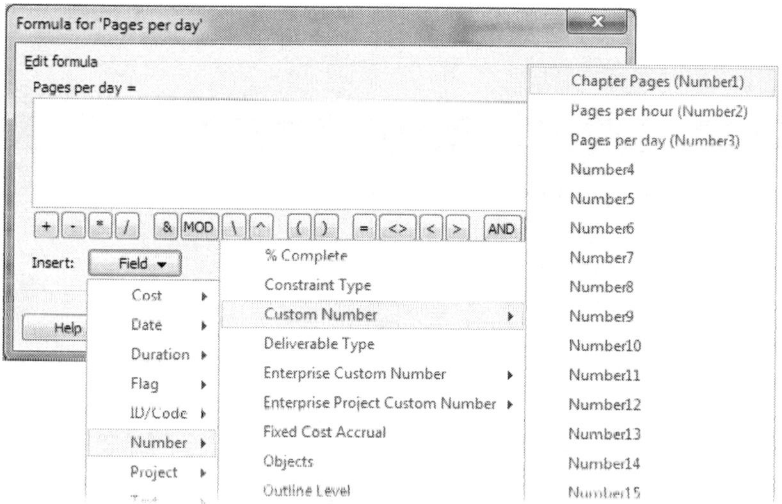

Figure 24-3:
Within a Field category, Project includes both built-in and customized fields. When the list entry represents several fields, for example, Custom Number, a right arrow indicates a submenu waiting. If the function you want doesn't have a button, click Function, choose the function category, and then choose the function.

3. **To insert a function, click where you want the function in the formula, and then click the appropriate function button.**

   The most commonly used functions have their own buttons, including addition, subtraction, multiplication, and division; equals, parentheses, greater than and less than; and logical functions like AND, OR, and NOT. Look at the box on page 648 for a tip on building formulas.

   To find other functions, click Function, choose the category, and then choose the function. Take a few minutes to look at the functions in each category, because you have plenty to choose from. For example, the Weekday function figures out the day of week based on the date and the first day of the work week. The General category has functions for If-statements (IIf), case statements (Switch), and functions that check for null or numeric values (IsNull and IsNumeric). The Text category has a host of string functions, like Len, Left, and Trim, which are familiar to the geeks who've written Visual Basic code.

4. **To insert a value in the formula, click where you want to insert the value, and then type the number or text.**

You can also drag to select part of the formula—if you want to delete a field, for example.

5. **When you've finished the formula, click OK. If you're done customizing the field, click OK in the Custom Fields dialog box.**

If the field already contains values, a message box warns you that any data in the field will be replaced by the formula's calculations. If you want to overwrite existing data, click OK. Otherwise click Cancel, and use a different field.

Tip: When you use a formula, be sure to set up several test cases to make sure the formula does what you want.

Feeding Formulas Values

Suppose you define a formula only to see the custom field cells in a table awash with the dreaded value #ERROR. Dividing by zero is one cause of #ERROR; it's a no-no in Project formulas, as it is in any programming language. To prevent Project from squawking, you can set up formulas to perform calculations only if fields have values, which is where the IIf function comes in.

The IIf function works like an If statement in other programming languages. The function tests a condition, and does one thing if the condition is true and another if the condition is false. For example, the "Pages per day" custom number field may use the basic formula [Number1] / [Actual Duration]. You don't want to calculate the formula unless Actual Duration field has a value other than zero. (Notice that formulas use actual field names, not the aliases you used to rename custom fields.) In this situation, the formula should calculate the result if Actual Duration is not equal to zero, and otherwise, return zero.

Here's what the enhanced formula looks like:

```
IIf([Actual Duration]<>0),[Number1]/
[Actual Duration],0)
```

Unfortunately, this formula still doesn't deliver the result you'd expect. For example, if Number1 equals 5 and Actual Duration equals 1d (one day), the result is 0.01, because of another Project formula idiosyncrasy. Even third-graders know that 5 divided by 1 equals 5. The reason for this discrepancy is that Project converts any time value into minutes. Therefore, the formula is actually dividing Number1 by 480 minutes (8 hours multiplied by 60 minutes). To get the correct answer in days, you must add a conversion to your formula. The final formula looks like this:

```
IIf([Actual Duration]<>0),[Number1]/
([Actual Duration]/480), 0)
```

Calculating Values In Summary Rows

Custom fields don't come with roll-up calculations automatically, but you can control the calculation a custom field uses. The calculation options are in the "Calculation for task and group summary rows" section. The simplest option is "Use formula", which calculates roll-ups using the same formula the field uses. You can also tell the program how to distribute values to assignments, which is described in the box on page 650.

Tip: For built-in fields, Project rolls up values into summary tasks and group summary rows. You don't have a choice in the matter. One way to work around this limitation is to set a custom field equal to the built-in field you want to roll up in a different way. Then simply choose the rollup calculation you want on the custom field.

In the Custom Fields dialog box, when you select the Rollup option, the Rollup drop-down list comes to life with several built-in calculations. Here are your choices:

- **And.** For custom flag fields, this choice sets the summary flag to No if at least one lower-level item is No. The value is Yes only if all lower-level values are Yes.

- **Or.** For custom flag fields, this choice sets the summary flag to No only if all lower-level values are No. The value is Yes if at least one lower-level item is Yes, like the built-in Critical fields does with summary tasks.

- **Average.** For cost, duration, and number fields, this calculation determines the average of all nonsummary values within a group or belonging to a summary task. For example, you could calculate the average productivity for all work tasks assigned to a specific group.

- **Average First Sublevel.** For cost, duration, and number fields, this choice calculates the average of task values one level below the group or summary task (including summary and nonsummary tasks).

- **Count All.** For number fields, Count All counts the number of items below a summary task or group (including summary and nonsummary tasks or resources).

- **Count First Sublevel.** For number fields, this choice counts the number of items one level below the summary task or group.

- **Count Nonsummaries.** For number fields, this calculation counts the number of nonsummary items below the summary task or group, for example, to count the number of resources that are overallocated.

- **Maximum.** For all types of fields except Flag, Text, and Outline Code, Maximum sets the summary value to the largest value underneath the summary or group.

- **Minimum.** For all types of fields except Flag, Text, and Outline Code, this sets the summary value to the smallest value underneath the summary or group.

- **Sum.** For cost, duration, and number fields, this totals the nonsummary values below the summary task or group.

UP TO SPEED

Distributing Task Values to Assignments

In the Custom Fields dialog box, the "Calculation for assignment rows" section is where you tell Project how to distribute the value of a custom field to a task's or resource's assignments. For example, to distribute the pages of documentation written to each assignment, select the "Roll down unless manually entered" option. If you type values into the custom field for each assignment, then you can use those values to calculate individuals' productivity. Otherwise, Project divides the pages written evenly across all assignments.

If you don't want the value distributed to assignments, select None. Project selects this option initially for all custom fields.

Displaying Values Graphically

Displaying pictures instead of values makes it easier to see what's going on, just like an Excel line graph can spotlight the growth rate from a worksheet of numbers. For example, many project managers use traffic light icons to present project performance: a green light means a task is on schedule, a yellow light means a little behind schedule (for example, 2 days), and a red light means an unacceptable delay (perhaps 5 days). You can set up a custom field to display a graphic instead of a number, and specify the conditions under which each graphic should appear.

In the "Values to display" section of the Custom Fields dialog box, Project initially selects the Data option, which simply shows field values. To use graphical indicators instead, follow these steps:

1. **After selecting the field to edit in the Custom Fields dialog box, in the "Values to display" section, click Graphical Indicators.**

    The Graphical Indicators dialog box opens. The custom field name or alias appears in the title bar so you know which field you're working on.

2. **In the "Indicator criteria for" section, select an option to tell Project whether you're defining graphical indicators for summary tasks or nonsummary tasks.**

    Project selects the "Nonsummary rows" option initially. If you define indicators only for nonsummary rows, then summary rows and the project summary row both use the same conditions to choose the indicator to display. In the traffic light example, the summary tasks and project summary task would both show red lights if they were delayed by more than 5 days.

You may want to use different conditions for summary rows, for example to decrease the delay thresholds because you hope that delays and early deliveries will balance each other out (it could happen). In that case, select the "Summary rows" option and then turn off the "Summary rows inherit criteria from non-summary rows" checkbox. Then you can define a separate set of conditions and indicators—for example, to display a red light if summary tasks are delayed by 2 days.

If you want different conditions for the project summary row, select the "Project summary" option, turn off the "Project summary inherits criteria from summary rows" checkbox, and then define the conditions for the project summary row.

3. **To set up a graphical indicator, select the first empty "Test for" cell, click the down arrow, and then choose the test you want.**

   The tests are almost identical to the ones for filters (page 624). The only additional test is "is any value", which displays the indicator as long as the field isn't empty. You can use the "is any value" test for the last condition to ensure that the field always shows a graphical indicator.

4. **In the Values(s) cell in the same row, type the value.**

   Similar to filters, you can type a number or text, or choose a field in the drop-down list to compare the custom field to another field. For example, to define an indicator for the documentation team producing less than five pages per day, in the Test cell, choose "is less than", and then, in the Value(s) cell, type 5.

   Or you could compare a custom Finish field to the Baseline Finish field to display a red light when Finish is greater than Baseline Finish.

5. **Finally, in the Image cell, click the down arrow and then choose the graphical indicator you want to display when the condition is true, as shown in Figure 24-4.**

   If you're testing for less than or greater than, be sure to include at least one test containing "equal to" to make sure you cover every value. For example, if you test for values less than 5 and 10, include a test for values greater than or equal to 10. Otherwise, the test doesn't cover the value 10.

6. **Repeat steps 3 through 5 to define another condition and graphical indicator.**

   When you're done, click OK to close the Graphical Indicators dialog box. Click OK in the Custom Fields dialog box if you're finished customizing fields.

Note: Like other dialog boxes with tables (page 614), Graphical Indicators includes Cut Row, Copy Row, Paste Row, Insert Row, and Delete Row buttons, so you can add, remove, or reorder your tests.

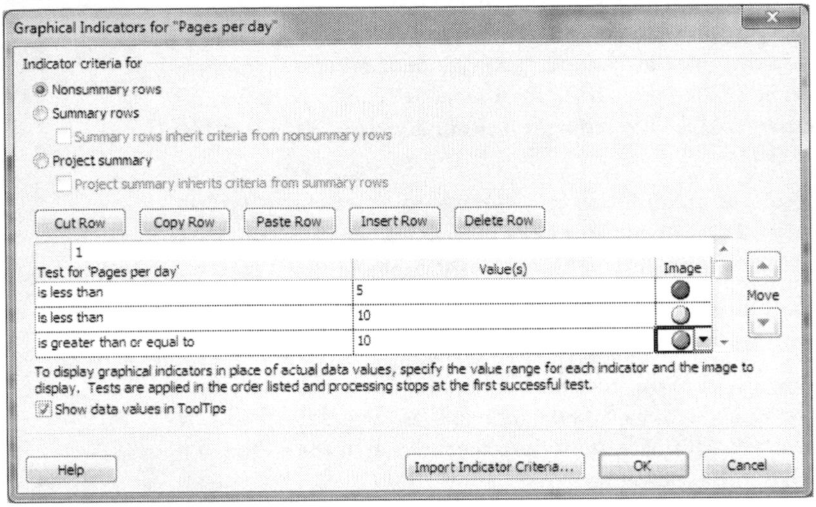

Figure 24-4:
Project steps through the conditions in order until the field value satisfies a condition, thus triggering the appearance of the corresponding graphical indicator. The order of tests is important. For example, for "if less than" tests, test for the smaller value first—less than 5 before less than 10. If you test for less than 10 first, 4 passes that test and displays its indicator instead of the indicator for values less than 5.

Coding Tasks and Resources

In Project, an outline code represents a hierarchy of values. The most obvious example of an outline code is the WBS field (page 93), which includes values that correspond to each level in a work breakdown structure. Sometimes you work with other categorization schemes—for example, a set of expense codes for the accounting department, job codes that define people's skills, or part numbers for material resources.

You can create up to 10 sets of custom outline codes to categorize tasks and another 10 sets to categorize resources. Assigning custom outline codes to tasks and resources is the same as for any other kind of field: You type a value or choose from a drop-down list. Outline codes work for filtering, grouping, or sorting, just like other types of fields.

The difference between an outline code and any other kind of custom field is the multiple levels of values, each separated by a symbol. Each level can be uppercase or lowercase letters, numbers, or characters. Because categorization schemes usually follow rules (similar to the Dewey Decimal System at the library), outline codes typically use a *code mask,* a set of rules that specify the type of characters and the length of each level.

Other than the code mask, customizing an outline code is similar to customizing a text field. For example, you can create a lookup table to help people choose the right values. You can limit values to what's on the list or let folks add new ones. You can sort the values or leave them in the order you placed them in the lookup table.

Setting Up a Template for Outline Code Values

A code mask spells out the characters and length for each level of the outline code, as well as the character that separates each level. The Edit Lookup Table dialog box contains an extra section for the code mask. If you create a lookup table with the complete list of valid values, you may think you can skip the code mask entirely. However, the mask points out lookup table values that don't match the code mask specifications. To set up the code mask, follow these steps:

1. To customize a custom outline code, choose Project→Custom Fields.

   The Custom Fields dialog box opens.

2. Select either the Task option or Resource option, and then, in the Type drop-down list, choose Outline Code. In the Field list, select the outline code you want to work on (Outline Code1 through Outline Code 10).

   As you do for other fields, rename the outline code to indicate what it's for. Now you're ready to set up the guts of the outline code.

3. **Click Lookup.**

   The Edit Lookup Table dialog box opens.

4. Expand the "Code mask" section by clicking the + to the left of the label. Click Edit Mask.

   The Code Mask Definition dialog box opens.

5. In the first Sequence cell, choose the type of characters you want for the top level of the hierarchy, as shown in Figure 24-5.

   Your choices are Numbers, Uppercase Letters, Lowercase Letters, and the no-holds-barred option, Characters, which accepts all three types.

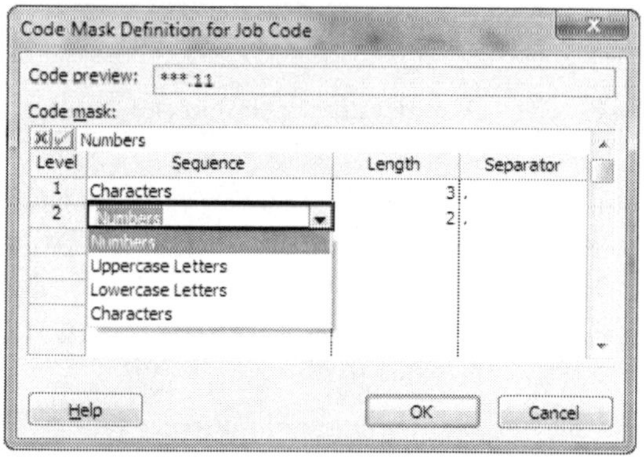

Figure 24-5:
Project automatically fills in the Separator cell with a period (.). The separator in the last row of the code mask never appears. As you define the code mask, the "Code preview" box at the top of the dialog box shows what an outline code value would look like with the code mask you've defined.

6. **In the first Length cell, choose Any or a number from 1 to 10 for the length of the top level.**

   Project initially selects Any, which means any number of characters is valid. For example, with numbers, you could type *5, 50,* or *5000* without Project balking. Choosing a specific number means the value is fixed at that length. For example, if you choose 3, numbers must have three digits.

7. **In the Separator cell, choose the character that separates the top level from the next level.**

   The separator can be a period (.), a hyphen (-), a plus sign (+), or a slash (/).

8. **Repeat steps 5–7 to add additional levels to the mask. Click OK when you're done.**

   The code mask accepts dozens of levels, but outline code values can be no longer than 255 characters. Besides, too many levels make it difficult to choose and read the outline code values.

Now that the code mask is complete, you can start typing values in the "Lookup table" section.

Setting Up an Outline Code Lookup Table

Like other fields, outline codes work best when people know the values that are legit. If you set up a code mask and stop there, then any value that follows the code mask is valid. To provide examples or to restrict values to a predefined list, build an outline code lookup table. The steps are the same as the ones for a regular lookup table, except that you must tell Project how to handle the multiple levels. Here are the steps:

1. **In the Edit Lookup Table dialog box below the lookup table itself, turn on the "Display indenting in lookup table" checkbox.**

   This setting indents values in the lookup table based on their level in the outline, as illustrated in Figure 24-6.

2. **Type a value in the first blank Value cell and a description in the Description cell in the same row.**

   The value must conform to the first level of the code mask. For example, if the first level is supposed to be three numbers, a value of "ab" or "12" shows up in red and bold, whereas "456" is in a regular black font.

3. **In the next Value cell, type a value for the second level of the code mask. Click Indent (a green right arrow) to push the value to the second level.**

   Until you indent the value, it may appear red and bold. Project validates the value at the level you place it.

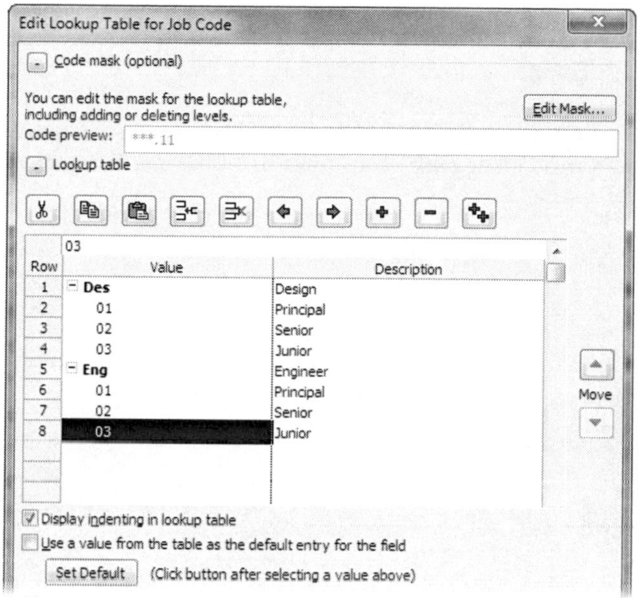

Figure 24-6:
As you work, you can hide or show outline levels by clicking the + and – signs to the left of higher-level values. To indent or outdent values to the correct level, click Indent (green right arrow) or Outdent (green left arrow). Click Show All Subcodes (two + signs) to display every value in the table for your final quality control review.

4. **Repeat step 3 to add more outline code values.**

   You can use the Cut Row, Copy Row, Paste Row, Insert Row, and Delete Row buttons to rearrange values or add values you forgot. For example, in Figure 24-6, you could copy the rows with two-digit numbers from the Des code to the Eng code. Select rows 2, 3, and 4, and then click Copy Row. Then select row 6 and click Paste Rows. To add lookup values at lower levels, simply click Indent until the value is at the level you want.

5. **If an outline code value should include every level of the code, for example, to correctly assign expenses to accounts, turn on the "Allow only codes that have no subordinate values" checkbox.**

   Project initially turns off this checkbox, which means you can enter an outline code with only some of the levels, just like the WBS field works.

6. **When you're done, click Close.**

   If the other settings are the way you want, then in the Custom Fields dialog box, click OK to save the changes.

Note: You can import a custom outline code field or its lookup table as you can with other types of fields (page 646). To import an outline code, in the Custom Fields dialog box, click Import Field. To import only the lookup table from another custom outline code, in the Edit Lookup Table dialog box, click Import Lookup Table.

After the outline code is set up, assigning values should be familiar. You can type values or choose them from a lookup table drop-down list, as shown in Figure 24-7.

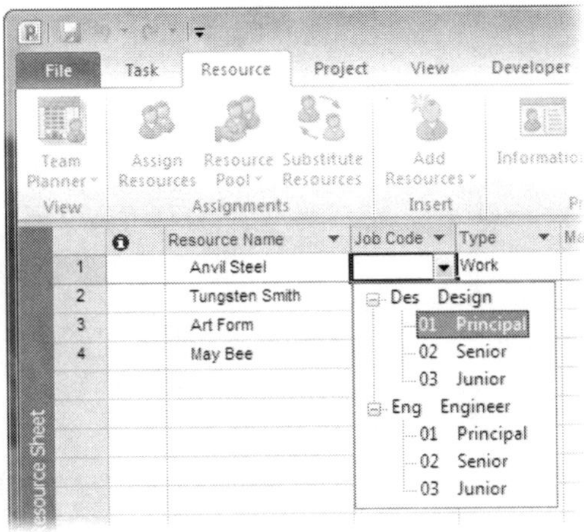

Figure 24-7:
If you didn't create a lookup table, you must type a value and hope for the best. If the value doesn't match the code mask, an error message with the correct format appears. With a lookup table, click the down arrow in the cell, and then choose the value you want.

CHAPTER 25

Customizing the Ribbon and Quick Access Toolbar

When you first start using Project 2010, you pick commands from the ribbon. After using the program for a while, you may discover that some commands get a lot of exercise, that some starve for attention, and that a few you want are nowhere to be found. For example, you may never choose any of the Gantt Chart Style buttons to change the color theme for your task bars. At the same time, you might rather see the Format Painter command on the Format tab. And you need the Edit Links command to update the connections to files you link to your Project schedule.

Fortunately, in Project 2010, you can customize the ribbon to suit your needs. You can turn tabs on or off, create your own tabs and groups, add commands to groups, and rearrange the order of elements (tabs, groups, and commands). This chapter shows you how to do all these things. The Quick Access toolbar sits above the left side of the ribbon. Adding commands to it is even easier than customizing the ribbon. Making changes to the ribbon and the Quick Access toolbar takes only a few minutes, but it might save hours in the long run.

Customizing the Ribbon

As you've seen throughout this book, the ribbon is made up of several tabs, like Task
Resource, Project, View, and Format. Within each tab, groups keep related commands close to one another, like the Split View group on the View tab, which contains commands for working with the Timeline view and Details pane. Commands
reside in a group, even if it's a group of one, like the lonely Subproject command
in the Project tab's Insert group. You can create your own tabs and groups or add
groups you create to the built-in tabs. Either way, the techniques you use to customize the ribbon are refreshingly easy.

Tip: If you want to use your customized ribbon or Quick Access toolbar on other computers, read the box
below.

Customizing the ribbon takes place on the Customize the Ribbon page in the Project
Options dialog box. The fastest way to reach this page is to right-click the ribbon and
then choose Customize the Ribbon. (The long way around is to choose File→Options
and then, in the Project Options dialog box, choose Customize the Ribbon.)

FREQUENTLY ASKED QUESTION

Where Are My Customizations?

*How do I share my ribbon customizations with my
colleagues?*

You may wonder how you can copy your ribbon customization handiwork to other computers, because the ribbon
isn't one of the elements you can copy with the Organizer
(page 668).

To use your ribbon on another computer (or share it with
a fellow project manager), you must export it to a file. Then
you or your compatriot can import that file into Project on
another computer. Here's how:

1. Right-click the ribbon and choose Customize the
   Ribbon.

2. Click Import/Export (at the bottom right of the dialog
   box) and choose "Export all customizations".

3. In the File Save dialog box, navigate to the folder in
   which you want to save the file and type the name

of the file in the "File name" box (something like
"MyPrjRibbon"). The "Save as type" is set automatically to "Exported Office UI file".

4. Click Save.

5. Copy the file to the other computer.

6. Open Project on that computer, right-click the ribbon,
   and choose Customize the Ribbon.

7. Click Import/Export and choose "Import customization file".

8. In the File Open dialog box, navigate to the folder that
   contains the file, and then double-click it.

9. A message box asks if you want to replace all existing Ribbon and Quick Access toolbar customization
   for Project. Click Yes to load the new customizations.
   Click No to cancel.

Turning Tabs On and Off

The ribbon comes with several ready-made tabs, most of which are visible when you first launch Project (page 9). Whether you use the built-in tabs or build your own, you can turn tabs on when you need them and then turn them off to keep the ribbon tidy the rest of the time. For example, if a rousing session of macro development sounds like fun, you can turn on the built-in Developer tab, which is turned off initially. Then when your macros are ready for prime time, you can turn off the Developer tab and run your macros from the Format tab (page 688). Here's how to turn tabs on and off:

1. **Right-click the ribbon, and then choose Customize the Ribbon.**

   The Customize the Ribbon page opens in the Project Options dialog box, as shown in Figure 25-1.

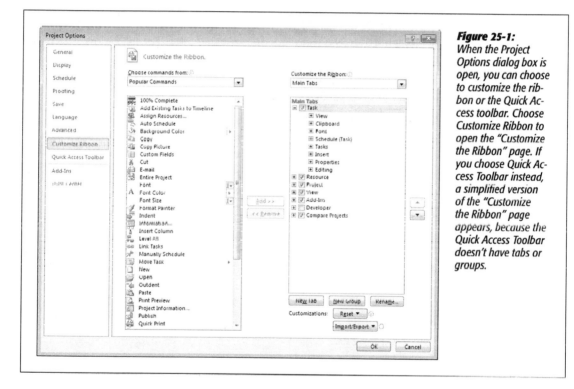

Figure 25-1:
When the Project Options dialog box is open, you can choose to customize the ribbon or the Quick Access toolbar. Choose Customize Ribbon to open the "Customize the Ribbon" page. If you choose Quick Access Toolbar instead, a simplified version of the "Customize the Ribbon" page appears, because the Quick Access Toolbar doesn't have tabs or groups.

2. Below the "Customize the Ribbon" heading on the right side of the page, turn on a tab's checkbox to make it visible on the ribbon (turn it off to hide it). Click OK to close the Project Options dialog box.

The drop-down list below the Customize the Ribbon heading is initially set to Main Tabs, which are the built-in tabs (Task, Resource, Project, View, and so on) and custom tabs you create. If you choose Tool Tabs in the drop-down list, you see the context-sensitive Format tabs for each type of view, such as the Gantt Chart Tools Format tab (page 331) or the Team Planner Tools Format tab (page 600).

Creating Custom Tabs

When existing tabs won't do, you can blaze a new trail by creating a tab from scratch. Completely new tabs are great when you constantly turn to the same set of commands. Once the Customize the Ribbon page is open (page 658), here are the steps:

1. **In the tab list on the right side of the page, select the tab below which you want to add your custom tab.**

If you forget to select a position in the list before you create the tab, you can move the custom tab to another location later (page 662).

2. **Below the tab list, click New Tab.**

Project inserts a new custom tab named New Tab (Custom) containing one custom group named New Group (Custom), as shown in Figure 25-2.

3. **Select the new custom tab and click Rename. In the Rename dialog box, type a short but meaningful name, like "MyFaves," and then click OK.**

The new name appears in the tab list.

4. **Select the new custom group and click Rename. To display an icon for the group, choose the one you want in the Symbol list. In the Rename dialog box, in the "Display name" box, type a short but meaningful name, like "MyViews." Click OK.**

Your custom tab and group are ready for you to add commands (page 662). See page 661 to learn how to add more groups to a tab. Page 664 explains how to rearrange tabs, groups, and commands.

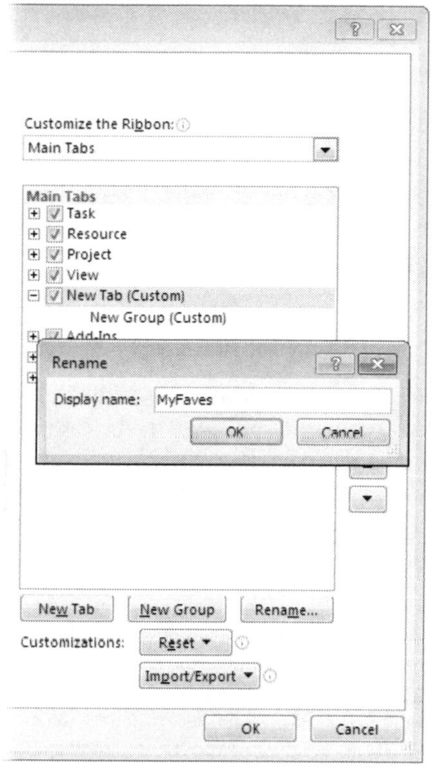

Figure 25-2:
*By automatically adding a custom group, the program saves you a
step. You can add commands only to custom groups, so a custom
tab must have at least one custom group. It's a good idea to immediately rename the custom tab and the custom group to indicate
what they do. Select the tab and then click Rename. Then, select
the group, and click Rename.*

Creating Custom Groups

Visual separators (like the groups on built-in tabs) make it easier to find the commands you want. Project doesn't give you a choice, because you can add commands
only to custom groups. Whether you want to add commands to a built-in tab or a
custom tab, you must first add a custom group. Here are the steps:

1. **In the tab list on the right side of the page, select the tab to which you want to
   add a new group.**

   You can add a custom group to a built-in tab or a custom one.

2. **Select the group below which you want to add the new group.**

   If you forget to select a position before you create the group, you can move the custom tab to another location later (page 664).

3. **Below the tab list, click New Group.**

   Project inserts a new custom group named New Group (Custom).

4. **Select the new custom group and click Rename. To display an icon for the group, choose one in the Symbol list. In the Rename dialog box, in the "Display name" box, type a short but meaningful name, like "Tasks." Click OK.**

   Your custom group takes its place in the tab.

Adding a Command to the Ribbon

All of Project's commands, as well as the macros you develop (page 682), are fair game for the Project ribbon. The "Customize the Ribbon" page in the Project Options dialog box includes categories of commands to help you find the ones you want to add. You can choose a category like Macros to add a macro or Commands Not in the Ribbon to add a command that isn't available on Project's built-in tabs.

Tip: If you can't find the command you want on the ribbon, you may be looking in the wrong place—or the command simply might not be on the ribbon. To see where a command resides on the ribbon, open the Customize the Ribbon page and chose All Commands. Scroll to the command name in the list and hover the pointer over the command. A ToolTip appears to tell you the ribbon tab, group, and name for the command. To see if you can't find a command because it isn't on the ribbon, in the "Choose commands from" drop-down list, choose Commands Not in the Ribbon. If you find the command you're looking for in the list, you must add it to a custom group to use it.

The steps for adding commands to the ribbon are easy:

1. **Right-click the ribbon and choose Customize the Ribbon.**

   The Customize the Ribbon page opens in the Project Options dialog box.

2. **In the "Choose commands from" drop-down list, select one of the command categories.**

   The command categories, shown in Figure 25-3, represent different collections of commands. For example, the "Choose commands from" drop-down list is set initially to Popular Commands, but you can also choose from the commands on all the main tabs or all tabs. When you select a category, the command list shows the choices within that category. If you don't know which category to choose, select All Commands.

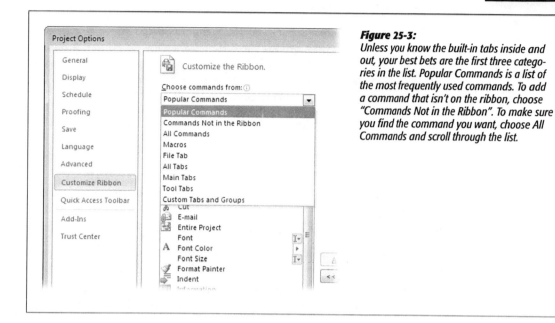

Figure 25-3:
Unless you know the built-in tabs inside and out, your best bets are the first three categories in the list. Popular Commands is a list of the most frequently used commands. To add a command that isn't on the ribbon, choose "Commands Not in the Ribbon". To make sure you find the command you want, choose All Commands and scroll through the list.

3. In the command list on the left side of the page, select the command you want to add to the ribbon.

   When you select a command in the list, the Add button becomes active, indicating that you can add it to the ribbon. But don't click Add just yet.

4. On the right side of the page, expand the tab you want and select the custom group to which you want to add the command. If other commands are in the group already, select the command below which you want to add the new command.

   Although you can *select* a built-in group, you might notice that they're grayed out. If you try to add a command to a built-in group, a message warns you that you can add commands only to custom groups.

5. Click Add.

   The command takes its place in the custom group.

6. Repeat steps 3–5 to add other commands to the group.

   When you're done, click OK to close the Project Options dialog box.

Rearranging Ribbon Elements

Project is fussy about where you put commands. It lets you add, move, or rearrange the commands only in custom groups you create. (You can add custom groups to built-in tabs.) The program is happy to let you rearrange tabs and groups in any way you want, whether the tabs and groups are built-in or custom. For example, if you prefer the View tab to appear before the Task tab, drag it to the top of the Main Tabs list. With the Customize the Ribbon page open, you can drag elements (or click the up and down arrows) to move them to another location. Here's how:

1. **Right-click the ribbon and choose Customize the Ribbon.**

   The Customize the Ribbon page opens in the Project Options dialog box.

2. **On the right side of the page, select the tab, group, or command you want to relocate.**

   You can move only one element at a time.

3. **Drag the element to its new location. Or click the up or down arrows to move the element higher or lower in the list.**

   If you drag the element, position the horizontal bar where you want the element to go, as shown in Figure 25-4, and then release the mouse button.

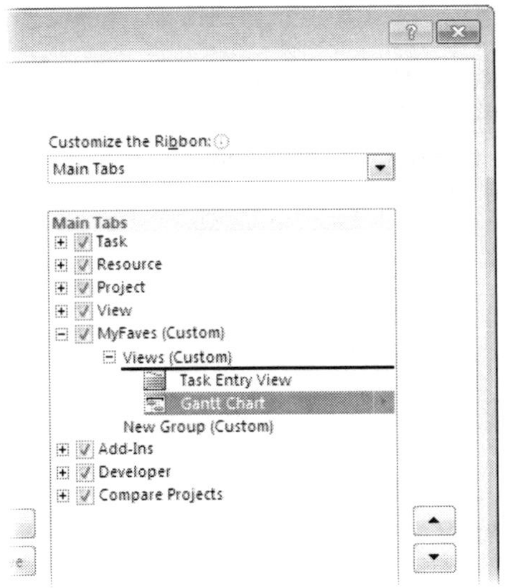

Figure 25-4:
A horizontal bar shows you where the element goes. If you click the up or down arrow, the element moves up or down one position. Because you can add commands only to custom groups, you might see the up or down arrow grayed out or an icon (a circle with a diagonal bar through it) indicating you can't relocate the element to the current location (for example, to a built-in group).

Removing Custom Ribbon Elements

You can't delete the built-in tabs that come with Project. Nor can you remove commands from built-in groups, like Cut, Copy, and Paste in the Clipboard group on the Task tab. However, you can remove custom tabs, custom groups, and commands you add to custom groups. In a surprising twist, the program also lets you remove built-in groups from a built-in tab. For example, you can select the Clipboard group on the Task tab and remove it from the tab. The secret to removing elements is the Remove button on the Customize the Ribbon page. On the Customize the Ribbon page, select the element you want to remove: a custom tab, a custom group, a command in a custom group, or a built-in group. If the Remove button in the middle of the page becomes active, clicking it removes the selection from the ribbon.

Resetting Ribbon Customizations

After you tweak the ribbon, you may decide you want some or all of the tabs back to the way they came off the Project CD. Rather than finding each change you made and changing it back, it's easier to reset them. You can reset the customizations on a single tab or remove all the customizations you've made. Here are the steps:

1. **Right-click the ribbon and choose Customize the Ribbon.**

   The Customize the Ribbon page opens in the Project Options dialog box.

2. **If you want to reset a single tab, on the right side of the page, select the tab.**

   You can reset only built-in tabs. The only way to "reset" a custom tab is to remove it or edit it.

3. **Click Reset and choose either "Reset only selected Ribbon tab" or "Reset all customizations".**

   The "Reset only selected Ribbon tab" is active only if you select a built-in tab in the list or on the ribbon itself. It removes any customizations you made to that built-in tab. If you select "Reset all customizations", Project removes customizations you made to built-tabs and the Quick Access toolbar, and also removes all custom tabs.

Tip: Before you remove all customizations, export your customizations to a file (see page 658). That way, it you want the customizations back, you can import the file.

Customizing the Quick Access Toolbar

The Quick Access toolbar sits above the File and Task tabs. Initially, this toolbar contains Save, Undo, and Redo, but you can add any commands you want to it. The Quick Access toolbar doesn't have tabs or groups, so customizing the toolbar is even easier than customizing the ribbon. Here's what you can do:

- **Add a command to the toolbar.** Click the down arrow to the right of the Quick Access toolbar and then choose the command you want to add, as shown in Figure 25-5. A checkmark appears to the left of the commands on the toolbar. The drop-down menu includes several popular commands, like New, Open, and Print Preview.

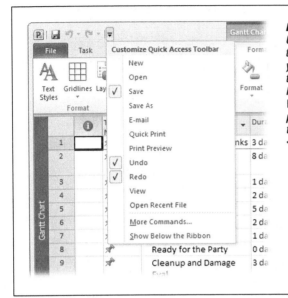

Figure 25-5:
Unlike the ribbon, you can specify whether the customizations you make to the Quick Access toolbar apply to all files you open in Project or just the active one. In the Project Options dialog box, in the Customize Quick Access Toolbar box, Project automatically chooses "For all documents (default)". With that setting, the changes you make to the toolbar appear for every file you open. To customize the Quick Access toolbar for the active file, choose "For <filename>" where <filename> is the name of the active Project file.

- **Add any Project command to the toolbar.** Click the down arrow to the right of the Quick Access toolbar and choose More Commands. The Project Options dialog box opens to the Customize the Quick Access Toolbar page. You can add or remove commands from the toolbar using the same steps as for the ribbon (page 662 and page 665).

- **Show the Quick Access toolbar below the ribbon.** If you put your top commands on the Quick Access Toolbar, you can reduce the distance you have to move your mouse by locating the toolbar below the ribbon. Click the down arrow to the right of the Quick Access toolbar and then choose Show Below the Ribbon. The toolbar appears in between the ribbon and your Project view. To replace it at the top of the Project window, click the down arrow to the right of the Quick Access toolbar and then choose Show Above the Ribbon.

Reusable Project: Templates

I f you go to the trouble of customizing views, tables, and so on, as described in the previous chapters, you probably want to use them in all your projects—or at least show them off to your friends. You can store information you want to reuse in Project files called *templates*. Some customized elements (views, tables, fields, filters, and so on) end up in a special file called the *global template,* while others stay in the Project file in which you created them, which you can turn into a custom template.

Part of the closing process for every project is archiving the work you've done, documenting what you learned, and recording that information so others can benefit from it (page 484). Whether you have tasks that apply to many projects or standard views and reports for communicating status, Project templates can make that information available to anyone who needs it for future projects.

This chapter shows you where Project stores your customized elements and settings—either in the global template or in an individual file. In Project 2010, you can tell Project to save new customized elements in your current Project file or automatically copy them to the global template. Either way, you'll learn to transport and share customized elements using Project's Organizer.

Sharing Custom Elements

The Organizer helps you copy customized elements from the global template to a Project file, from a Project file to the global template, or between two Project files. Here's how the Organizer can help:

- **Using customized elements in new projects.** In many instances, customized elements like views belong to the Project file in which you create them. After you've created customized elements, you can make them available to every new project you create by copying them to the global template (page 669).

- **Sharing customized elements.** Having customized elements in your global template is great when you're working on your computer. But if you're in a colleague's office and fire up Project there, your customized elements aren't available, because they're back in the global template on your computer. Likewise, folks in other offices are out of luck unless you share what you've done. To share customized elements, you can copy them to a Project file and then send that file to someone else. Then they can copy those elements into their global template.

Note: If you use Project Server, there's another file called the Enterprise Global Template, which is like the mother of all global templates—a *global* global template. This template attaches to every Project file that someone checks out, so they get the most up-to-date Project elements.

- **Copying customized elements between Project files.** Sometimes a customized element is important for a specific type of project but not spectacular enough to copy to the global template. In the Organizer, you can copy elements from one Project file to another, as long as both files are open.

- **Creating copies and renaming elements.** You can create copies of elements in the Organizer and rename them without opening them in Project.

- **Removing elements from a Project file or template.** The Organizer simplifies file cleanup. You can select one or more elements and then delete them at one time.

The Organizer bristles with tabs, one for every type of element you can customize. (There's no tab for custom formulas, because they belong to custom fields.) When you select a tab, the Organizer shows the elements available in two different Project files: initially, the global template on the left side, and the active Project file on the right. You can select any Project file that's open on either side, which is how you copy elements between files. To open the Organizer, simply choose File→Info and then click Organizer in the Backstage view.

Tip: Some dialog boxes, like More Views, More Tables, and More Filters, include an Organizer button that opens the Organizer window. These buttons do the same thing as choosing File→Info and then clicking Organizer.

Storing Project Settings and Elements

Project has to keep its settings and built-in elements somewhere, and that somewhere is called the *global template*. It stores settings that tell Project how to behave—like whether you use the Gregorian calendar or want to automatically turn on AutoFilter. If you change a Project-wide setting in the Project Options dialog box, then the global template memorizes it and tells Project about it every time you create a new Project file. (Existing Project files use the settings that were in place in the global template at the time the files were created.) All the built-in elements that Project provides are in this file, too—the standard Gantt Chart view, the Standard calendar, and the Entry table.

Note: The Project Options dialog box also contains settings that apply to specific projects. Those settings reside in the Project file, not the global template.

The global template is so special that the program attaches it to every Project file you create to transfer your program-wide settings and elements. Under the hood, though, the global template is really a regular Project template file called *global.mpt*. If you create a copy of this template file, you can open it in Project like any other file. The box on page 671 tells you where to find your global template file after you install Project. The global template stores the following elements:

- Program-wide settings
- Views
- Tables
- Custom fields
- Calendars
- Filters
- Groups
- Reports
- Import and export maps
- Macros and Visual Basic modules

Note: Project 2010 no longer supports custom forms or toolbars, so you won't find them in the Organizer.

Project stores most elements that you customize, like view, tables, filters, and groups, in the Project file you're working on, so they initially show up only when you open that file. Likewise, Project stores settings that apply to a specific project, shown in Figure 26-1, in the Project file. Other customized elements like maps go directly into the global template, because Project assumes that you want to use them for every project. Fortunately, you can use the Organizer (page 668) to move customized elements to the global template or to a Project file, as described in the next section.

Tip: It's a good idea to make a backup copy of your global template before you add or remove elements in it. If you want to get rid of elements you added, or retrieve elements you deleted, then you can replace the active global template with the backup copy.

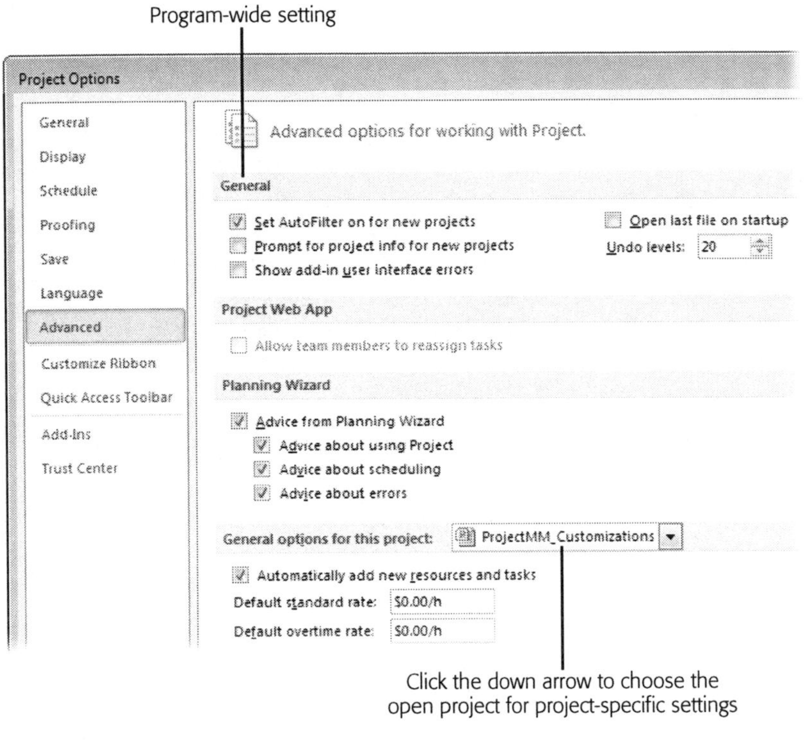

Program-wide setting

Figure 26-1:
In the Options dialog box, the headings for program-wide settings don't have a box for choosing a project, like the General heading shown here. When a heading is something like "General options for this project" and includes a box for choosing a project, you know that the settings are project-specific. For example, if you turn off the "Automatically add new resources and tasks" checkbox in one project, then the next project you create uses the standard setting (the checkbox turned on).

Click the down arrow to choose the open project for project-specific settings

Copying Elements Between Files

The steps for copying elements between files are the same, regardless of which type of element you copy and which two files you use. In the Organizer, you choose the file with the element to copy, and the file you want to copy to, and then copy the element. Although copying in the Organizer eventually becomes second nature, this section describes each type of copying separately for now.

In Project 2010, you can tell Project to automatically copy new views, tables, filters, and groups to the global template, which is a great timesaver if you're the only person who uses your copy of Project. Copying new customized elements to the global template means they're available for every new project you create. To set this behavior, choose File→Options. In the Project Options dialog box, choose Advanced. Under Display, turn on the "Automatically add new views, tables, filters, and groups to the global" checkbox. Then, if you create a new view called AwesomeView, which uses a new table called KitchenSink, Project automatically copies those elements to your global template. On the other hand, if you share a global template with others, you can turn off the checkbox so your new elements remain in your Project files unless you specifically copy them to the global template.

TROUBLESHOOTING MOMENT

Where's My Global Template?

If you want to share your global template with a colleague, you may have trouble tracking it down on your computer. The Organizer isn't any help, because the label on the left side says only "Global.MPT." You have no way of knowing where that file resides.

When you install Project on a computer running Windows 7, Project places a copy of *global.mpt* in *C:\Users\<username>\AppData\Roaming\Microsoft\MS Project\14\1033*, where <username> is the name of the person who installed Project on the computer and 1033 is the language code for English. If you install Project using a different language, the number for the folder is set to the code for the installed language. (On a computer running Windows XP, the folder is *C:\Documents and Settings\<username>*

Application Data\Microsoft\MS Project\14\1033.) If you want to use a global template that someone else sends you, replace the *global.mpt* file in this folder.

You may search for *global.mpt* files on the Start menu by choosing Search and never see the one in the AppData (or Application Data) folder. Windows initially makes these folders hidden, so they don't show up as you browse folders in Windows or use the Windows Search box. To see hidden folders and files in any folder window, choose Tools→Folder Options. In the Folder Options dialog box, select the View tab, and then select the "Show hidden files and folders" option. Then you can see *global.mpt* and replace it with another copy.

Tip: You can make project-specific settings more global by creating a Project template (page 675) with those settings in place. Then, when you create a new project based on that template, the settings you want are already there.

Making customized elements available to new projects

To use a custom element in new projects you create, copy the element from the Project file to the global template. Then, when you create a new Project file, it grabs the built-in and custom elements from your global template. Remember, Project stores import/export maps directly in the global template, so you don't have to copy them to make them available to other files.

Here are the steps for copying elements to the global template:

1. **With the Project file that contains the customized element already open, choose File→Info→Organizer.**

   The Organizer window opens. The Organizer window contains several tabs to cover all the elements it handles, as illustrated in Figure 26-2.

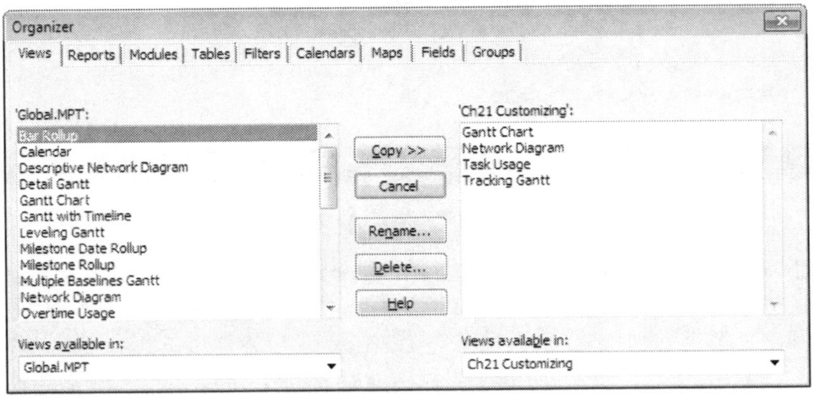

Figure 26-2:
At the bottom of the dialog box, the box on the left shows elements for the global template (indicated by the label "Global.MPT"). The box on the right lists elements in the active project (the one you're currently working on).

Tip: If you forgot to make the project with the customized element active before you opened the Organizer window, don't worry. In the "<element> available in" drop-down list on the right, simply choose the project (it must already be open in Project), where <element> is the name of the tab you've selected. For example, if the Groups tab is selected, then the label is "Groups available in".

---

2. **Select the tab for the type of element you want to copy, like Views.**

   The elements stored in the global template appear in the list on the left. The elements in the active project appear in the list on the right.

3. **Select the element in the list on the right, and then click Copy.**

   If the global template contains the same type of element with the same name, Project asks if you want to replace what's in the global template. Click Yes if you want to overwrite the one in the global template.

   To keep the one in the global template, click No. Then, with the element on the right side selected, click Rename, type a new name, and then click OK. Now you can copy the element without a conflict.

4. **If you don't want to copy anything else, click the Close button.**

   The Organizer window closes.

Sharing a customized element with someone else

For most types of elements, you can share customizations simply by sending someone the Project file in which you created them, because that's where customized
elements are stored. However, maps don't work the same way. Project stores them
directly in the global template; accordingly, you have to copy them to another file
to share them. If you don't want to send a real Project file, you can copy elements
directly from one Project file to another. Here are the steps for both situations:

1. **Open the Project file you plan to use to transfer customized elements. If the
   customized elements are in a Project file rather than the global template, then
   open that file, too.**

   Consider creating a new Project file specifically for transferring elements. Name
   it something like "MyCustomizations" so you and the recipient both know what
   it's for.

2. **Choose File→Info→Organizer, and then select the tab for the type of element
   you want to copy.**

   The list on the right side is either empty or contains a few basic elements, unless
   you've used this transfer project before, as you can see in Figure 26-3.

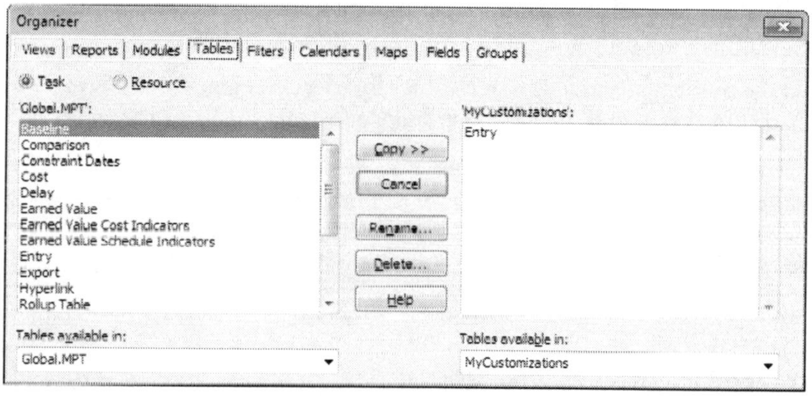

Figure 26-3:
*If you want to copy
from a Project file
instead of the global
template, in the
"Elements available
in" drop-down list on
the left side, select the
Project file. The label
for the list changes
to the name of the
project.*

3. **In the list on the left, select the element, and then click Copy.**

   If you're feeling generous, you can select several elements on the left side (Ctrl-
   click to select individual items or Shift-click to select several adjacent items).
   When you click Copy, Project copies them all to the right at the same time.

4. **If you want to copy other types of elements, select the corresponding tab, and
   then repeat step 3.**

   Click the Close button when you're done.

Removing Customized Elements from Files

Customized elements can be tremendous timesavers, but sometimes you want to get rid of them. For example, after you copy a customized element to the global template, you don't need it in the project in which you created it.

Another reason to delete customized elements is to restore what Project came with. For example, suppose you made a dozen formatting changes to the Gantt Chart view, and now you want the original back. When you modify a built-in element, Project creates a customized version in your Project file. (You can tell because the element shows up in the Organizer, in the box on the right for the active Project file.) To get the original back, in the Organizer, simply delete the customized one.

Deleting customized elements is easy. Just follow these steps:

1. **If you plan to delete a view or a table, first select a different view or table.**

    You can't delete or copy tables and views when they're visible. Switch to another view or right-click the Select All box (the blank cell above the ID numbers). Then, on the shortcut menu, click another table name.

2. **Choose File→Info→Organizer, and then select the tab for the type of element you want to delete.**

    The customized elements appear in the box on the right.

3. **Select the element you want to delete, and then click Delete.**

    In the confirmation dialog box, click Yes to delete the element. Click No if you've had second thoughts. The element disappears from the list when you click Yes.

Warning: Be careful about deleting elements in the global template, because you can delete some built-in elements: views, groups, filters, tables, and so on. If you make a habit of deleting elements in the global template, it's a good idea to keep a backup copy in case you want to get something back.

Renaming Customized Elements

The Organizer also lets you rename customized elements, which is helpful if you're trying to copy elements with the same names between files. For example, if you want to copy a customized Gantt Chart view to the global template without overwriting the original Gantt Chart, you can rename your view before you copy it. Some built-in elements are willing to go by a different name, while others aren't. For example, you can rename built-in groups, except for No Group. On the other hand, you must rename custom fields in the Custom Fields dialog box.

To rename an element, follow these steps:

1. **Open the Project file with the customized elements. Open the Organizer window, and then select the tab for the type of element you want to rename.**

    The customized elements appear in the box on the right.

2. **In the box on the right, select the element you want to rename, and then click Rename.**

   The Rename dialog box is simple, with a "New name" box and an OK button.

3. **In the "New name" box, type the name, and then click OK.**

   The newly renamed element appears in the list.

4. **When you're done working in the Organizer, click the Close button.**

   The Organizer window closes.

Building Templates for Projects

Despite the differences that make every project unique, Project gives you several ways to reuse project work you've done before. Here are just a few examples:

- **Save time.** Past projects make great starting points for new projects. You've already figured out many of the tasks you need, so why not use them to jump-start new projects? A Project template can contain tasks with task dependencies, typical durations, and even resources. Keep anything that stays the same, and change only what's different.

- **Standardize.** Quite often, you learn the hard way what works and what doesn't. You can improve your results by basing new projects on your previous successes, not your past mistakes. In fact, by creating templates that reflect your organization's project management knowledge, everyone can benefit from the lessons learned on each and every project. You can use Project templates to define the standards your organization follows. A template can act like a checklist, with project management tasks that are part of every project. Or it can contain the views, reports, and customized performance measures that your organization uses to evaluate project status.

  In fact, the global template (page 669) stores Project program settings that apply to every project. You can make customized elements available to every new project you create by storing them in the global template.

- **Learn from others.** You don't have to learn everything from the school of hard knocks. Taking advantage of others' expertise can save time and improve your results. Starting with a template built by experts gets a project off on the right foot. You can use templates built by others in your organization or download templates from websites (page 679).

Creating a Project Template

Whether you want to use a completed project as a basis for new projects or build a standard project that shows off your best project management practices, a Project template can help. Project templates can contain tasks, resources, settings, views, calendars, and more. When you create a new Project file from a template, the new file inherits everything the template has to offer.

You can save any Project file as a template. For example, if you completed a project that ran spectacularly well, you can create a template from that Project file including tasks, resources, and all its baseline values. When you save a file as a template, Project knows what you're trying to do; the Save As Template dialog box lets you pick the information you want to throw away (and thus, the information you want to keep). Here's how to save an existing Project file as a template:

1. **Open the existing project, and then choose File→Save As.**

   The Save As dialog box appears as if you're saving a brand-new Project file, because you are.

2. **Before you do anything else, in the "Save as type" drop-down list, choose Project Template.**

   Choosing Project Template creates a file with the .mpt file extension. If you forgot to change the "Save as type" to Project Template, all you'd do is save the file to a regular .mpp Project file with a different filename.

3. **Navigate to the folder in which you want to store the template.**

   If you want the template to show up in the Templates dialog box when you create a file from a template, then save the template in your user templates folder (page 677).

4. **In the "File name" box, type a name for the template, and then click Save.**

   The Save As Template dialog box opens with checkboxes for specifying the data you *don't* want in the template, as you can see in Figure 26-4.

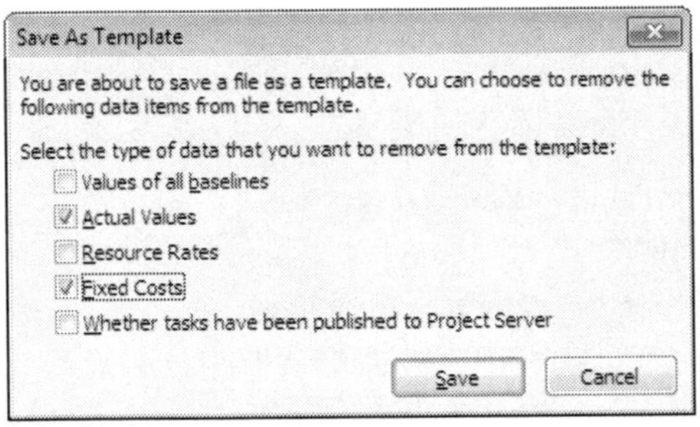

Figure 26-4:
To keep values that worked in the past, make sure to turn off the "Values of all baselines" checkbox. That way, your baseline values stay in the file. If the resources you use still ask for the same amount of money, turn off the Resource Rates checkbox.

5. **Turn on the checkboxes for the items you want to *remove* from the project, not the ones you want to keep.**

   For example, if you want to remove the actual values from the template, turn on the Actual Values checkbox.

6. **Click Save.**

   Project creates a file with an .mpt file extension with only the information you want.

Making Your Templates Easy to Find

After you set up a template with exactly what you want, using it to create a new file should be painless. If you store your templates in the right place, they're waiting for you in the Templates dialog box. All you have to do is tell Project where you store your templates:

1. **Choose File→Options.**

   The Project Options dialog box opens.

2. **Choose Save.**

   In the "Default user template location" box, Project automatically selects "C:\Users\<username>\AppData\Roaming\Microsoft\Templates". If you want to see your templates in the Backstage view, you must use this folder, create a subfolder within it, or set your template folder in another Office program (like Word).

Tip: In Project, if you specify a template folder outside of the default path, your templates don't show up in the "My templates" area of the Backstage view. However, if you specify a template folder anywhere on your computer or network in a program like Word, the templates do appear in "My templates". To specify a template folder in Word, choose File→Options. In the Word Options dialog box, choose Advanced. Below the General heading, click File Locations. In the File Locations dialog box, click "Workgroup templates" and then click Modify. In the Modify Location dialog box, select the folder where you store your templates, and then click OK.

---

3. **Below the "Save templates" heading and to the right of the "Default user template location" box, click Browse.**

   The Modify Location dialog box appears.

4. **Select the folder that holds your templates, and then click OK.**

   When you select the folder in the explorer, the "Folder name" box shows the name of the folder. If you use the default location, your templates appear on the Personal Templates tab in the New dialog box (choose File→New and then click "My templates"). If you create a subfolder, another tab appears in the New dialog box with the folder name as its label.

   When you click OK, the Modify Location dialog box closes, and the path to the template folder appears in the "Default user template location" box, as shown in Figure 26-5.

5. **Click OK to close the Options dialog box.**

   You may have to close and reopen Project to see your user templates in the New dialog box.

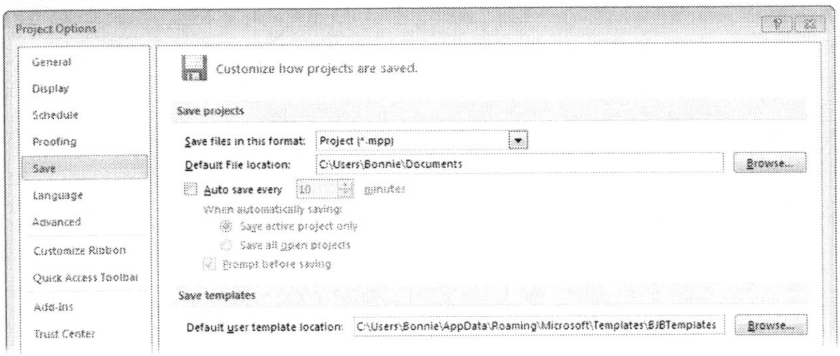

Figure 26-5:
You can copy templates from your colleagues, Web sites, or other sources into your user templates folder, so you can pick them as easily as the templates you create. Be sure to include your custom templates folder in your backup procedure, so you don't lose your hard work to a disk crash.

Editing a Template

When you try to save a template file, Project saves a copy of the file as a regular Project file with an *.mpp* file extension. In other words, Project assumes that you're using the template to start a new Project file and not overwriting the template. To save template changes in the template file, follow these steps:

1. **Choose File→Open.**

   The Open dialog box appears.

2. **In the "Files of type" box, choose Project Template.**

   As you navigate through folders, you see only Project templates.

3. **Double-click the template you want.**

   Project opens the template as it normally would. Make the changes you want.

4. **Choose File→Save as if you were creating a new Project file.**

   The Save As dialog box opens.

5. **In the "Files of type" box, choose Project Template, and then click Save.**

   Because you're trying to save changes to the existing template, a warning appears asking if you want to overwrite the file.

6. **Click OK.**

   The Save As Template dialog box opens. Click Save to overwrite the existing template file with the changes you made.

Creating a Project File from a Template

Creating a project file from a template is easy regardless of where you get your template. Here are the steps:

1. **Choose File→New.**

   The New page appears in the Backstage view.

Note: If you share templates with other project managers, you want the files in a location that everyone can get to, like a shared network drive. You can use templates in any folder to create a new Project file simply by double-clicking the filename in Windows Explorer.

---

2. **To use a template you created and stored in your templates folder, under Available Templates, click "My templates".**

   The New dialog box opens to the Personal Templates tab, shown in Figure 26-6.

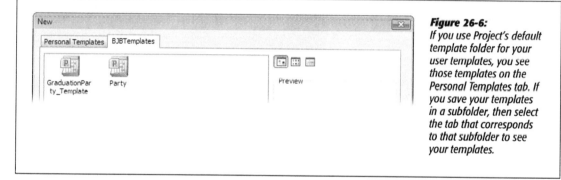

Figure 26-6:
If you use Project's default template folder for your user templates, you see those templates on the Personal Templates tab. If you save your templates in a subfolder, then select the tab that corresponds to that subfolder to see your templates.

To look for more templates online, below the Office.com Templates heading, click a category of templates, like Plans or "More templates". For example, if you click Plans, you'll see subcategories for Business, Community, and Home. The Business category contains templates for launching new products, commercial construction, and so on. To find a particular type of template without browsing through categories, type keywords in the "Search Office.com for templates" box and then click the right arrow.

3. **Double-click the icon for the template you want to use.**

   Project creates a new Project file based on the template. The file looks and acts like a regular file.

4. **Before you save the new file, change the project start date to the date the new project is supposed to start.**

   Choose Project→Properties→Project Information. In the Project Information dialog box, in the "Start date" box, change the date.

5. **After you make the changes you want to the project, choose File→Save.**

   Even though you choose File→Save, Project opens the Save As dialog box and sets the "Save as type" box to Project. These settings automatically save a copy of the template as a regular .mpp file, so you don't overwrite the template file.

CHAPTER 27

Saving Time with Macros

Y ou perform many of the same actions in Project day after day (sometimes, several times each day). Like doing the dishes, vacuuming the carpet, and washing the cat on the delicate cycle, some repetitive tasks are unavoidable— but some timesaving tools sure would help. Instead of hiring a maid or a handyman to take the drudgery out of your Project work, you can write handy mini-programs called *macros*.

You don't have to be a geek to write your own macros. You can create a macro simply by recording the steps you want the macro to perform. Then you can run the macro to replay the steps again and again. The geeky project managers in the audience can build upon recorded macros by editing them in Visual Basic for Applications (VBA).

This chapter explains macro basics: recording them, running them, and adding them to the ribbon or keyboard shortcuts. You can even create full-strength custom solutions if you're up for it. And if you're a programmer wannabe, you'll also find resources for learning more about programming in Project.

What You Can Do with Macros

A macro does one thing really well—it performs a series of steps each time you run it. For example, you can record a macro that hides summary tasks, turns on the critical path, and then sorts tasks by Duration in descending order. Macros are great timesavers because they can perform the equivalent of dozens of mouse-clicks and key presses almost instantaneously. Moreover, macros reduce mistakes because you're not typing and clicking as much.

Any kind of repetitive task is a contender for macrohood. You can create a simple macro that sorts a task list or a humongous one that applies a view, filters and sorts the content, and then produces a picture of the schedule and copies it into a new Word document for your stakeholder status report. Since Project's creators couldn't anticipate every feature that organizations might need, macros let you create your own Project features, calculating project performance and evaluating your project in various ways. For example, a macro can count the number of on-time and slipping tasks to calculate the percentage of tasks that are headed for trouble.

Recording Macros

The best way to get started with macros is to record one. You don't have to write any code or invoke any arcane VBA spells. You start the recorder, click the same menus and press the same keys you always do, and then stop the recorder.

Recording a macro is like working a crossword puzzle in pen; your mistakes are indelibly saved along with what you got right, so you have to re-record the macro until you get it 100 percent right. Before you record a macro, take some time to figure out what you want to record. Then practice the steps a couple of times. Write up a cheat sheet if you're recording more than a few steps.

Make sure you perform any preliminary steps that you *don't* want to record in the macro—like opening a specific project or applying a view. In addition, the Project file must contain values that let you record all the steps you've planned. For example, if you're recording a macro that sorts tasks by their variances, then the Project file must have a baseline set (page 365).

Now you're ready to record:

1. Choose View→Macros→Macros→Record Macro.

   The Record Macro dialog box opens, as shown in Figure 27-1. Before you begin recording, you must name the macro and then tell Project where you want to store it. Also, take time now to describe what the macro does, so you (and project managers to follow) will remember later.

Figure 27-1:
Project automatically fills in the "Macro name" box with a name like Macro1, which you can—and should—change immediately to something more meaningful. The program also fills in the Description box with the name of the macro, the date you record it, and your name.

2. **In the "Macro name" box, type a short name with no spaces, like *Long-CriticalTasks*.**

   You can't include spaces in a macro name. To separate words visually, insert underscores (_) or capitalize the first letter in each word (called camel case).

3. **In the Description box, fill in detailed information about what the macro does.**

   Summarize the macro steps, any conditions that must be in place before you run the macro (like a selected task or a specific view), and what you end up with when the macro ends (views, filters, sort criteria, and so on). Here's an example of an effective description: "Shows best critical tasks to shorten. No setup required. Applies Detail Gantt. Hides summary tasks. Groups tasks by Critical field. Sorts from longest to shortest duration."

4. **To assign a keyboard shortcut to launch the macro, type a letter (numbers aren't an option) in the "Ctrl+" box.**

   The Ctrl key is the only key that works as a prefix for a macro keyboard shortcut in Project. However, as you can tell from Appendix C, lots of keyboard shortcuts that combine Ctrl with letters of the alphabet are already taken (like the ubiquitous Ctrl+S for Save). Project doesn't give hints about which letters are still up for grabs (but it does complain if you try to type numbers or punctuation in the box). A, E, J, L, M, Q, and T are the only letters still available to combine with Ctrl in Project.

Tip: Since you get so few letters to create keyboard shortcuts, save them for the macros you use the most. If you're a prolific macro artiste, create a custom tab or group on the ribbon (page 658) to run your macros.

---

5. **In the "Store macro in" drop-down list, select the file in which you want to store the macro.**

   Project selects Global File, which stores the macro in your global template (*global.mpt*), so you can run the macro in any Project file you open from now on. To save a macro *only* in the Project file you're working in, choose This Project. (The box on page 685 explains how to choose the best place to store macros.)

6. **If the macro includes moving around in the table area, choose options in the "Row references" and "Column references" sections.**

   Project selects the Relative option for row references, which means that Project moves the same number of rows from the selected cell when you run the macro. For example, suppose the first Task Name cell is selected, and you select the fourth Task Name cell during recording. Every time you run the macro, Project jumps down four rows from the cell that's selected. The Absolute (ID) option tells the macro to move to the row with the same ID. In this example, if you select the row with ID 4 while recording, then the macro always selects the row with ID 4.

   The Relative and Absolute options work similarly for columns. The main difference is that the Absolute (Field) option tells the macro to move to the column that contains the same field, as the name implies. For example, if you select the Cost column, the macro always jumps to the Cost column. Project automatically selects the Absolute (Field) option, which is the typical choice, because it gets you to the right field every time.

7. **Click OK to start recording.**

   The Record Macro dialog box disappears, and your Project file looks like it did before you created the macro. But the macro recorder is invisibly poised to record your every move.

8. **Choose the commands and perform the actions you want to automate.**

   For example, the steps for the LongCriticalTasks macro begin with choosing View→Task Views→Gantt Chart→More Views, and then double-clicking Detail Gantt. The next step is choosing Format→Show/Hide, and then turning off the Summary Tasks checkbox. Choose View→Data, click the Group down arrow, and then, in the drop-down list, choose Critical. Next, click the down arrow in the Duration column, and choose Sort Largest to Smallest.

9. **When the steps are complete, choose View→Macros→Macros→Stop Recording.**

   You can't pause recording like you can in Word and some other Microsoft programs.

Tip: Once you've recorded a macro, you can fine-tune it by editing its VBA code. In fact, the macro recorder can be your programming mentor. Record some macro steps in Project, and presto! The macro recorder dutifully logs the corresponding code. You can then study this code to learn about what you might do when writing macros from scratch. See "Learning More About Programming Project" on page 689 when you're ready for more.

Where to Store Macros

Should I store my macros in the global template or in the project I'm working on?

In most cases, storing macros in the global template (Global File in the "Store macro in" box) is the best option, because you can run the macro whenever you're using Project in whatever Project file is open. In fact, anyone who uses the same global template (basically, anyone using your copy of Project) can use the macro.

On the other hand, storing macros in a specific Project file is useful in two instances:

1. If you need to send the Project file to someone who doesn't use your global template. In that case, storing a macro in the Project file lets your recipient run the macro.

2. If your macro works specifically with one Project file, selecting its unique tasks or resources, for example. In that case, the macro runs only when the correct Project file is open, and if you try to use the macro in any other Project file, it won't work.

Running Macros

Project lists all the macros you create in the Macros dialog box (View→Macros→Macro→View Macros). You can run one anytime by selecting it and then clicking Run. But since the whole point of writing macros is to save time on repetitive tasks, clicking several times to run a macro defeats the purpose.

You can run a macro in any of three ways, each with a few pros and cons. In the Macros dialog box, you can select a macro, and then click Run. Adding a macro to the ribbon or the Quick Access toolbar keeps it close at hand, and a click or two runs it. A keyboard shortcut is another way to run a macro, although the limited number of keyboard shortcuts available makes this method best for your most popular macros. (Showoffs who edit code in the Visual Basic Editor: You can run a macro there, too, although this way doesn't count as an everyday method.)

Running Macros in the Macros Dialog Box

The Macros dialog box method requires the most mouse clicks, but it's ideal when you need a refresher course in the macros you have available. Perhaps you've created so many macros that you can't remember them all. Or someone else created the macros, and you want to see what's available. The Macros dialog box lists macros that are available in all open projects. To run a macro from the Macros dialog box, do the following:

1. **Choose View→Macros→Macros→View Macros.**

   The Macros dialog box opens. If you have spare brain cells for memorization, you can also open this dialog box by pressing Alt+F8.

2. **In the macro list, select the macro you want to run, and then click Run.**

When you select a macro, the description appears at the bottom of the dialog box, in the Description area, as shown in Figure 27-2. Make sure the macro does what you want, and that you've performed any setup the macro requires.

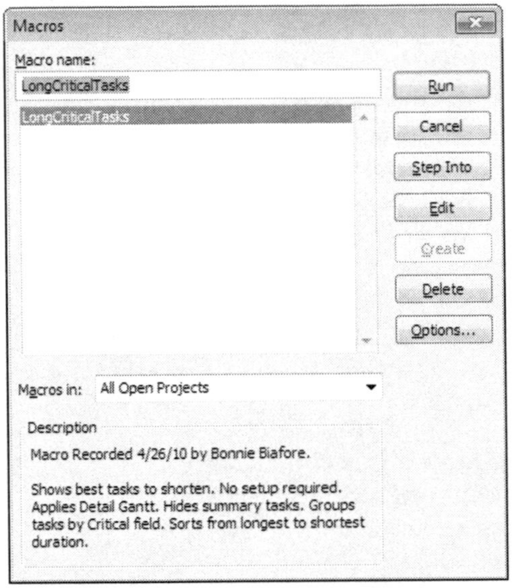

Figure 27-2:
You can do more than select and run macros in the Macros dialog box. Click Delete, for instance, to remove a hopelessly buggy macro you can't fix. Click Edit to open the Visual Basic Editor (page 688) so you can look at or modify the code directly. Click Step Into if you want to run the macro step by step, which helps you find the problem step when a macro isn't working properly.

Initially, the "Macros in" box is set to All Open Projects, which means you can run any macro stored in your global template or in any open projects. To see only the macros in the global template or in a specific Project file, in the "Macros in" drop-down list, choose Global Template, This Project, or the name of the Project file. The box on page 687 explains security features that make sure you run only the macros you want, not malicious ones that hitched a ride in a Project file.

Running a Macro from the Ribbon

Buttons on the ribbon are probably the most popular way to run macros. They're quick. You don't have to remember another keyboard combination. You can show the macro name to jog your memory. And you can add as many macros as you want to an existing tab and group on the ribbon, a custom group on an existing tab, or a custom group on a custom tab (page 658).

Set Security

Project 2010 includes the Trust Center, which makes it harder for viruses and other malware to infiltrate your computer. The Trust Center lets you designate a list of people you trust so that you can open only files that come from those sources. All other files stay unopened, keeping their malicious code to themselves. The security system also includes a way of creating digital *signatures,* so programs like Project can detect who created a given file. Here's how you set the level of security you want:

1. Choose File→Options.

2. In the Project Options dialog box, choose Trust Center, and then click Trust Center Settings.

3. In the Trust Center dialog box, choose Macro Settings.

4. Select the options for the security level you want. Project automatically selects "Disable all macros with notification", which is a good middle ground. It disables all macros, but it tells you what it's doing. To run macros with digital signatures, select the "Disable all macros except digitally signed macros" option.

High security doesn't stop you from running macros *you* write. If you want to run a macro from someone else, the default option works well. It lets you tell Project on an individual basis whether or not to run a macro.

Assigning a macro to the ribbon works almost exactly the same as adding other buttons or commands, as described in Chapter 25. This time, you simply choose the macro to add from the Macros category.

To add a button to the ribbon, follow these steps:

1. **Choose File→Options. In the Project Options dialog box, choose Customize Ribbon.**

   The Customize the Ribbon page appears.

2. **On the right side of the page, select the tab and group to which you want to add the macro.**

   For example, if you create a custom tab called Favorites, click its plus sign (+) to expand the groups it contains. Then select the group you want.

3. **In the "Choose commands from" drop-down list, choose Macros.**

   The available macros appear in the Commands list.

4. **Select the macro and then click Add.**

   The macro appears below the name of the group.

Tip: Initially, the macro name appears on the toolbar or menu (which is one reason to use short macro names). Chapter 25 tells you how to display an icon or different text.

Using Keyboard Shortcuts to Run Macros

If you're not overwhelmed by memorizing Project's built-in keyboard shortcuts, you can assign keyboard shortcuts to run macros, too (see step 4 on page 683). After you rule out the keyboard shortcuts that Project already owns, you have only seven letters of the alphabet left to combine with the Ctrl key (A, E, J, L, M, Q, and T). Yet nothing beats a deft two-key shortcut to run a macro you use all the time. To assign a keyboard shortcut, use one of the following two methods:

- **While creating a macro.** In the Record Macro dialog box, in the "Ctrl+" box, type the letter you want to use.

- **When a macro already exists.** In the Macros dialog box, select the macro, and then click Options. In the Macro Options dialog box, in the "Ctrl+" box, type the letter you want to use, and then click OK.

Note: You can't reuse keyboard shortcuts in the same file. For example, if you assign Ctrl+J to a macro you store in the global template, then no other macro in the global template can use Ctrl+J. However, Ctrl+J is still available in individual Project files. In fact, you can assign Ctrl+J to a different macro in every Project file you create, which is what happens when you assign Ctrl+J to a macro and then store it in the current Project file (page 684). When you press a keyboard shortcut, Project runs the macro assigned to that keyboard shortcut in the file you're working on.

Viewing and Editing Macro Code

Learning a programming language like VBA may be the last thing on your mind, but if you create your own macros, it pays to get familiar with, and even edit, some of your macro VBA code. For example, if you recorded a particularly long macro and made one little mistake, a quick edit in the Visual Basic Editor may be easier than re-recording the whole procedure. Similarly, if a macro references a specific name, which has since changed, then a surgical edit to change the name gets your macro working again. (The box on page 690 provides a quick introduction to what Project's VBA code looks like.)

The Visual Basic Editor is the place to look at and edit your macro code. Here's how you open the Visual Basic Editor and inspect your macro:

1. **Choose View→Macros→Macros→View Macros.**

   The Macros dialog box opens.

2. **Select the macro you want to edit, and then click Edit.**

   The Microsoft Visual Basic window opens, as shown in Figure 27-3. For simple edits, the code window is the only part of the editor you need.

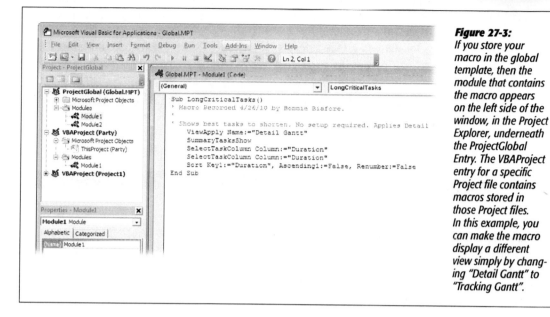

Figure 27-3:
If you store your macro in the global template, then the module that contains the macro appears on the left side of the window, in the Project Explorer, underneath the ProjectGlobal Entry. The VBAProject entry for a specific Project file contains macros stored in those Project files. In this example, you can make the macro display a different view simply by changing "Detail Gantt" to "Tracking Gantt".

3. **When you're done editing, choose File→Save Global.MPT.**

    Visual Basic saves your macro to the global template. If you create the macro in a specific Project file, the File menu entry is "Save <Project filename>.mpp", where <Project filename> is the file prefix.

4. **To close the VBA window, choose File ›Close and Return to Microsoft Project.**

    The Microsoft Visual Basic window closes.

Learning More About Programming Project

Because this chapter barely scratches the surface of macros, you may want to learn how to do more with VBA and Project. As you'll learn in Appendix B, Project Help doesn't provide much of that information. Instead, try these resources and websites to get you going:

- **VBA Help.** In the Microsoft Visual Basic window, press F1 or choose Help→Microsoft Visual Basic for Applications Help. Click the Getting Started link, and then the "Welcome to the Microsoft Project 2010 Developer Reference" link to read about programming Project with Visual Basic. The first page provides some valuable information, like how to access the Project Developer Reference from within Project, from the Microsoft Office website, or from the Microsoft Download Center.

- **Microsoft Developer Network (MSDN).** To reach the Project Developer Center, go to *http://msdn.microsoft.com/office/program/Project/*. This website is awash with information about programming Project, and the articles get pretty geeky pretty fast. On the main page, click the Community link, and then on the Project Community page, click the Blogs link to read blogs written by Project programmers in the trenches.

- **Microsoft Most Valuable Professional website (MVPS.org).** Microsoft MVPs offer a website with great info about many Microsoft programs (page 711). Go to *http://project.mvps.org* to read about all things Project. To jump-start your programming with some examples, click "VBA Sample Code."

POWER USERS' CLINIC

A Quick Look at Macro Code

The code required for a macro may be simpler than you think, particularly when you use macros to apply views, filters, and other settings. The steps that a macro performs belong to what programmers call a *subroutine*, like the one shown here. You can find the beginning and end of a macro by looking for the Sub and End Sub keywords.

```
Sub LongCriticalTasks()
' Macro LongCriticalTasks
' Macro Recorded 4/26/10 by Bonnie Biafore.
'
' Shows best tasks for shortening.
  Displays Detail Gantt with no summary
  tasks. Groups by Critical and then sorts
  from longest to shortest duration.
```

```
ViewApply Name:="Detail Gantt"
    SummaryTasksShow
    SelectTaskColumn Column:="Duration"
    Sort Key1:="Duration", Ascending1:
        =False, Renumber:=False
End Sub
```

The lines that begin with a single quote (') are comments. Use them liberally to explain what the macro does or why you wrote the code you did. Project automatically adds the text from the Description box as comments. The lines that do the actual work are simple, too. For instance, to apply a view, you use the ViewApply command, and then provide the view's name. Changing a setting in VBA code is incredibly easy. For example, to turn summary tasks back on, you simply add another SummaryTasksShow line to the macro.

Part Six: Appendixes

VI

Appendix A: Installing Project

Appendix B: Getting Help for Project

Appendix C: Keyboard Shortcuts

Installing Project

Installing Project 2010 should be comfortingly familiar if you've installed other Microsoft programs. Moreover, the procedure is the same whether your computer runs Windows XP, Windows Vista, or Windows 7. If you're installing from scratch, you barely have to tell the wizard anything.

When an earlier version of Project exists on your computer, you have the option to upgrade the previous version or keep it in addition to installing Project 2010. Installing multiple versions of Project may be the better solution. (If you already have a 32-bit version installed, the other versions you install must also be 32-bit). Not only can you use your old favorite features, but you can also open Project files created with versions prior to Project 1998. Upgrading means that the new version overwrites the earlier one, so you may lose beloved but discontinued features like the Visio WBS Chart Wizard, which disappeared in Project 2007.

In this chapter, you'll learn how to install Project 2010 Standard or Professional from a CD or a hard drive. In the Project 2010 installation, custom options are kept out of the way unless you need them. But you'll learn how to find and use them to choose what you want to install, and where.

After installation, you must activate Project so Microsoft can verify that your copy is legal. Unactivated, Project runs only 25 times and then only with limited features. Activation is quick and doesn't divulge any of your personal information. The truth is, you must activate Project if you want to use it.

Over time, you may want to change what you've installed. And if Project begins to act strangely, repairing the installation often solves that problem. In this chapter, you'll learn how to do both.

Installing Project on Your Computer

The Install Wizard handles a plain-Jane installation, an upgrade to an earlier version, or a custom installation. But before you get started, make sure your computer has what it takes to run the new version.

Tip: The following pages describe how to install Project 2010 on a single PC, but what if your entire team or company is going to use the program? If you need to install Project on many computers at once, see the box on page 699 for suggestions on how to streamline the process.

32-Bit or 64-Bit Project?

Project 2010 comes in both 32-bit and 64-bit versions. However, for the time being, you'll probably want to install the 32-bit software. Here's why:

- If your computer runs a 32-bit operating system, you can install only 32-bit programs.

- You can't run 32-bit and 64-bit Office programs on the same computer, and the 64-bit versions don't play well with tons of 32-bit add-ins, controls, and Visual Basic code you might use. It'll take time for all those add-ins and whatnot to become available in 64-bit.

- Right now, installing 64-bit Office programs makes sense only if you need the horsepower and memory of 64-bit. 64-bit Office programs are great for crunching lots of numbers. For example, to create master projects that contain 500 or more subprojects, you have to use 64-bit Project. Similarly, 64-bit Excel can eat files larger than 2 GB for lunch.

If you download Office 2010, you choose whether to download the 32-bit or 64-bit version. Office DVDs contain both 32-bit and 64-bit versions. Although the folder on the DVD for the 64-bit version is named x64, the folder for 32-bit software is named x86, after the Intel chips that computers used to run.

Before You Install

Microsoft recommends a certain amount of computer horsepower for Project to run properly. If you're managing multiple large projects with resource pools, Microsoft's recommendations are likely to be your minimum requirements. These days, the performance you expect often requires *double* the recommended amounts. Table A-1 lists what Microsoft recommends for running Project 2010 Standard or Professional.

Table A-1. *Your computer needs these resources to run Project 2010.*

System component	Required horsepower
Processor speed	700 megahertz (MHz) minimum
Memory	512 megabytes (MB) minimum
Available hard disk space	2.5 gigabytes (GB) minimum
Media	CD or DVD drive
Operating system (earliest version)	Windows XP Service Pack 3 (SP3), Windows Server 2003 R2 with MSXML 6.0, Windows Vista SP1, or Windows 7
Other software (earliest version)	Outlook 2003 SP2 (for Import Outlook Tasks)
	Excel 2003 SP2 and Visio Professional 2007 SP1 (for visual reports)
	Internet Explorer 7.0 32-bit and Internet connection (for Online Help and other online features)
	SharePoint Foundation 2010 (for task list synchronization)

Note: You initially need the 2.5 gigabytes of disk space to hold the installation files. You can recover some of that space by deleting the installation files after the installation is complete. (However, without the installation files on your hard drive, you must dig out your CD whenever you maintain or repair your installation.)

Installing Project for the First Time

All you do for a typical installation is type your product key, accept the license terms, and then click Install Now. Here's how to install Project 2010 without any bells and whistles on a computer that doesn't contain a previous version:

1. **Close any open programs, including your virus protection software, and then insert the Project 2010 CD into your CD or DVD drive.**

    If AutoRun is turned on, then the CD whirs away, the installation wizard starts, and you're on your way. The Setup program takes a few minutes to extract the files it needs, so refill your coffee and locate your product key, which is usually a bright yellow sticker on the outside of the CD case.

Tip: If Setup doesn't start automatically, the box on page 696 tells you what to do.

2. **On the "Enter your Product Key" page, type the 25-character product key from the label on your CD. Click Continue.**

   When you type in a valid key, your reward is a green checkmark to the right of the box. The product key label shows the product key in capital letters and numbers with every five characters separated by a hyphen. You can type lowercase letters and omit the hyphens without confusing the installation program.

3. **On the "Read the Microsoft Software License Terms" page, turn on the "I accept the terms of this agreement" checkbox, and then click Continue.**

   If you're like most people, you won't bother to read the terms of the agreement. Of course, the legal eagles who read and disagree with the terms must find another project management tool to use.

4. **On the next page, even if you just want to specify your name, initials, and organization, click Customize (and then jump to page 697 to learn how to customize an installation). For a bare-bones installation, click Install Now to install the typical components.**

   A progress bar moves from left to right, which tells you there's time to catch up on email or attain world peace. If you want to install multiple versions of Project or customize the installation in any way, then click Customize instead (described in "Customizing Your Installation" on page 697).

5. **When the installation finishes, click Register for Online Services.**

   In some cases, you may see "Continue Online." Clicking it lets you can take advantage of online help and other Microsoft Office Online features (page 709). If you're champing at the bit to use Project, click Close.

6. **Choose Start→All Programs→Microsoft Office→Microsoft Project 2010.**

   Project 2010 launches and you're ready to go. There are a few more tasks to complete now, as you'll see in the next few steps.

UP TO SPEED

Kick-Starting an Installation

AutoRun is a handy feature that leaps into action as soon as you insert a disc into your CD-ROM or DVD-ROM drive. But the price for convenience can be steep. Because AutoRun starts up immediately, it could run malicious software that's hidden on a disc. AutoRun can also be downright annoying, since it opens an Explorer window every time you insert a photo or music CD in a drive.

If you've turned off AutoRun (in Windows Explorer, right-click the CD or DVD drive, choose Properties, and then select the AutoPlay tab) or it doesn't start for whatever reason, then you must start the Project installation manually:

1. On the Windows task bar, choose Start→Run.

2. In the Run box, type *D:\Setup.exe* (replace "D" with the letter for your CD or DVD drive).

3. Click OK. The Setup Wizard starts.

Customizing Your Installation

When you install Project, you can specify what to install and where to install it. On the same wizard page as the big Install Now button, simply click the smaller Customize button. Then you can choose exactly the features you want to install and when you want to install them. Specifying where to install the software is crucial if your C: drive is packed tighter than a sardine can. Even if you want to specify your name, initials, and organization, you must choose a custom installation.

The beginning steps for a custom installation are the same as for a basic installation. When you click Customize, three tabs of installation options appear, as shown in Figure A-1. Here's what you can do on each one:

- **Installation Options.** To choose the product features you want to install and when to install them, expand the product by clicking the + to the left of its name. Right-click the feature (like Microsoft Project Templates), and then choose one of the options.

  Run From My Computer installs the feature on your computer immediately. **Installed on First Use** may sound like a good idea, but in reality it's more annoying. The first time you try to use the feature, Project prompts you to install it, which means you have to find your Project CD (or get to the installation files, wherever they may be). And you can't do your work until you finish installing the feature. **Not Available** skips the feature during installation (but you can install it later, as described in "Adding and Removing Features" on page 700).

  The icons you see next to products and features tell you which installation options you've chosen. A box containing an icon of a hard drive means the feature will be installed. A white box with a red X means the feature won't be installed. A white box with a drive and the number 1 means the feature will be installed the first time you use it.

- **File Location.** To install Project in a location other than the standard C:\ Program Files\Microsoft Office, select the File Location tab, and then click Browse. Navigate to the folder you want, and then click OK.

- **User Information.** This tab contains boxes for your name, initials, and organization.

When you're done, click Install Now at the bottom right of the wizard page.

Upgrading Project from an Earlier Version

Upgrading Project follows the same steps as a fresh installation, except that you have one more decision to make. When you install Project, it protects its turf by removing previous installations of the program, which may be exactly what you want. However, you may want to keep those earlier versions around. For example, if you sometimes need to open Project files created in versions prior to Project 1998, then you need Project 2002 or earlier. As you've learned throughout this book, each version of Project seems to discontinue a couple of features. You can continue to use these oldies but goodies by keeping previous versions installed.

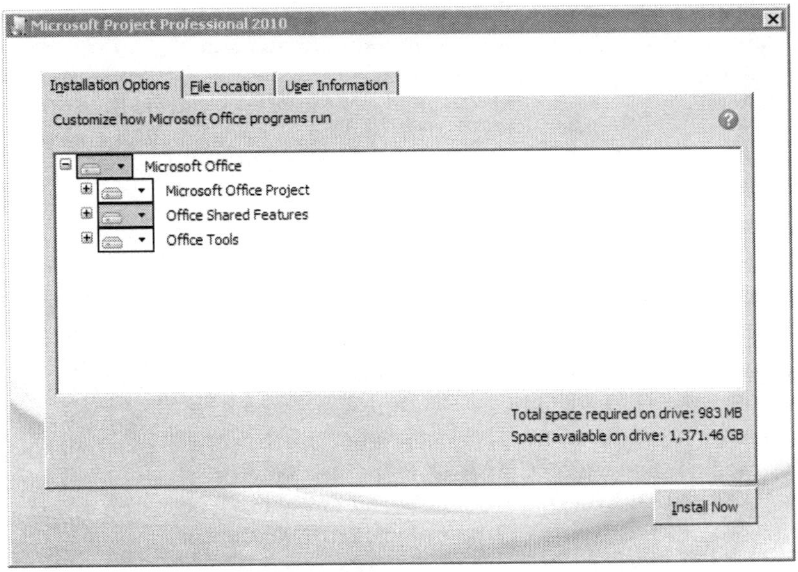

Figure A-1:
On the Installation Options tab, you specify the components you want to install, and whether to install them immediately or the first time you need them. At the bottom of the tab, you can see how much disk space you need to install what you've selected compared to the space that's available on your drive.

When you get to the wizard page with the Install Now and Customize buttons, click Customize. If the wizard finds any earlier versions, you see an Upgrade tab with options for upgrading.

To upgrade Project and remove earlier versions, select the "Remove previous versions of Microsoft Office Project" option. To use multiple versions, select the "Keep all previous versions" option. Then click Install Now to complete the installation as you would normally.

Activating Project

Activation is Microsoft's way of verifying that you're running a legal copy of a Microsoft program. Running Project without activating it turns the program into little more than a viewer and, even so, starts the program only 25 times. When you activate Project, Microsoft doesn't ask for personal information, so there's no harm in doing so.

Other Ways to Install Programs

Installing Project from a CD is fine when you have just your own computer to take care of, but wandering from computer to computer with CD in hand gets old fast. Whether you install on one computer or many, you can speed up the process by installing from other locations. By keeping the installation files on a hard drive, everyone can maintain his programs more easily. Check out the 2010 Office Resource Kit at *http://technet.microsoft.com/en-us/library/cc303401%28office.14%29.aspx* to learn about all kinds of fancy software deployment features.

Here are a few alternatives to installing from a CD:

- **Using a local installation source.** You can keep installation files on your computer or on a network drive to simplify installing and maintaining your software. When you install Microsoft Office 2010 programs, the Setup program copies installation files to your computer, which the Windows Installer then uses to install your programs. These files also let you repair, update, or reinstall programs right from your computer without digging out your software CD.

- **Using an administrative installation point.** As a project manager, you're not likely to set up an *administrative installation point* (a folder containing installation files that sits on the network, so you and

your colleagues simply navigate to that location and then run Setup to install a program). However, your system administrators may use one so everyone can install software from one copy of the installation files. Similarly, updates and program maintenance come from the administrative installation point instead of local installation files. Navigate to the Office 2010 Resource Center and check out the "Plan, Customize, and Deploy" content (*http://technet.microsoft.com/en-us/office/ff519674.aspx*) to get the 411 for IT pros deploying Office 2010.

- **Using a compressed CD image.** A CD image is like a combination of a local installation source and an administrative installation point. This approach is helpful even for managing software on a couple of home-networked computers. You copy the compressed files from the Project CD to a network drive. Then, instead of inserting a CD into a CD drive, you install from the file on a hard disk. Opening a CD image or burning a CD image to a CD or DVD requires special software, which Microsoft doesn't provide. Search the web for "burn ISO image" to find freeware to download.

Note: The Microsoft Office Project Activation Wizard creates a *hardware identifier* for your computer, which means, unfortunately, that you may have to reactivate Project if you rebuild your computer.

The Activation Wizard starts automatically when you run Project for the first time. In the Microsoft Office Activation Wizard page, the "I want to activate the software over the Internet" option is selected automatically, and that's the easiest way to go. Click Next. When your program is activated, click Close, and you're done.

If you have trouble activating Project, check that your Internet connection is working. You can also activate by telephone; when you select the "I want to activate the software by telephone" option, the wizard shows the phone number and instructions.

Maintaining and Repairing Project

After the initial installation, Project requires occasional care and feeding. For example, you may want to add or remove features, or reinstall features that aren't behaving correctly. You can also uninstall the software should you decide to forgo project management and start making origami instead.

If you don't keep installation files on your computer, insert the Project CD in your CD drive, and then run Project Setup. With installation files on your computer, you can use the Add or Remove Programs feature to perform your maintenance tasks. To access the Add or Remove Programs window, do the following:

1. **Choose Start→Control Panel.**

   If you use the Classic menu style in Windows, choose Start→Settings→Control Panel.

2. **If you run Windows Vista or Windows 7, in the Control Panel window, click Programs. Then click Programs and Features. If you run Windows XP, double-click Add or Remove Programs to open the Add or Remove Programs window.**

   The window opens.

3. **To start Project Setup, select Microsoft Project Professional 2010 (or Microsoft Project Standard 2010), and then click Change.**

   The Project Setup Wizard starts, as shown in Figure A-2. The following sections explain how to use each option.

Adding and Removing Features

Adding or removing features is like running a custom installation. You can change which features are installed, or change them to install on first use. In fact, the Installation Options tab you see is identical to the one that appears in a custom installation, shown in Figure A-1.

In the Setup Wizard, select the Add or Remove Features option, and then click Continue. Follow the instructions in "Customizing Your Installation" on page 697. After you've made your changes, click Continue to install or remove the features. When the installation is complete, click Close.

Repairing Your Project Installation

Sometimes Project starts misbehaving. You know this quirky behavior isn't a bug, because the program was working fine a few seconds before. First, try closing and restarting Project. Then try rebooting your computer. If these techniques don't do the trick, then repairing the installation is the next step.

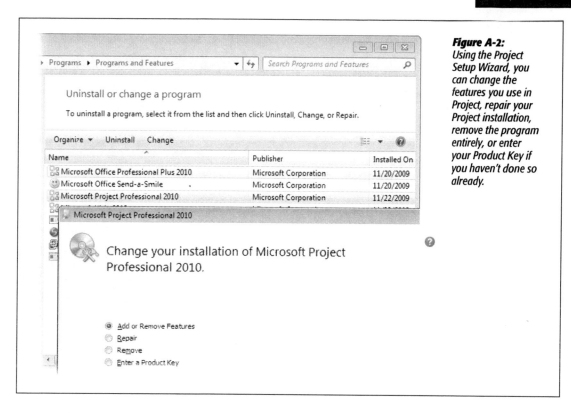

Figure A-2:
Using the Project Setup Wizard, you can change the features you use in Project, repair your Project installation, remove the program entirely, or enter your Product Key if you haven't done so already.

Repairing corrects little problems that crop up, like missing files or registry settings gone awry.

Tip: If repairing the installation still doesn't fix the problem, reinstall Project.

In the Setup Wizard, select the Repair option, and then click Continue. Project analyzes the installation and repairs the problems it finds. As usual, you can tell by the progress bar creeping across the screen that you have time to tackle world hunger—or your own.

Uninstalling Project

In the Project Setup Wizard, select the Remove option. When the message box asks you if you want to remove Project, make sure you really want to, and then click Yes. If you run Windows XP, you can also uninstall Project directly in the Add or Remove Programs window. Simply select the Project item, and then click Remove.

Getting Help for Project

Microsoft Project may be your first introduction to project management concepts like the critical path (page 329) and the work breakdown structure (page 77). For you, Project presents a double challenge: learning what the program's commands and checkboxes *do,* and learning what to do *with them.* Or maybe you're a project management expert and just want the dirt on how to use the features to get your work done: scheduling, budgeting, and reports. For you, learning Project is a technical exercise: which tab to display first, how to get a feature to do what you want, and how to avoid the program's gotchas and limitations.

Project 2010 Help has improved in one important way: Help topics are more likely to tell you why a feature is helpful, the best way to put it to use, and even give examples.

What hasn't changed is that finding the information you need is your biggest challenge. The Project Guide, the one vestige of project management activities linked to Project features, is no longer available in Project 2010. On the other hand, Project 2010 scatters tidbits of assistance throughout the program. For example, if you point to a column heading, a ToolTip tells you what the field represents and may even show the formula Project uses to calculate it, as you can see in Figure B-1. Or if you point to an icon like the Insert Summary Task on the Task tab, you learn that the command inserts a summary task to help you organize the task list and that any selected tasks become subtasks of the new summary task.

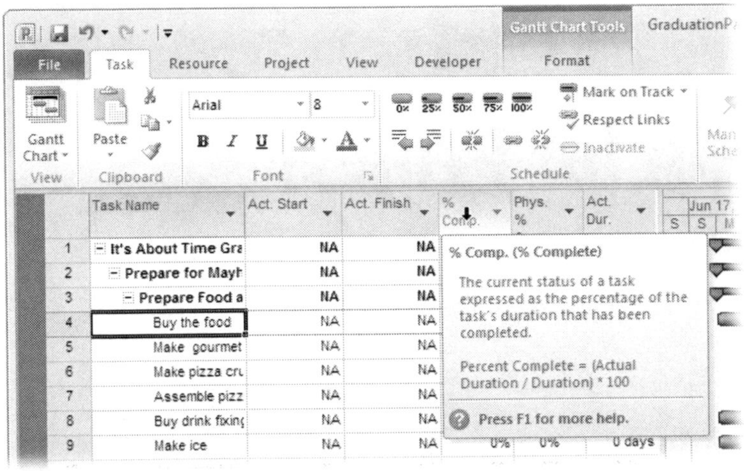

Figure B-1:
The ToolTip for a field provides a brief description of the field and may include the formula Project uses to calculate it. However, the Fields Reference within Project Help provides more information like best uses for the field, examples of how to use it, and so on.

The problem arises when you try to use Project Help to learn the nitty-gritty. For example, if you type *insert summary task* into Project Help's search box, you get bupkus on that command. Project Help is a work in progress, so clicking Help or pressing F1 may take you to a specific help topic—or not. For example, clicking Help in the Task Information dialog box opens the Project Help window to its top-level help headings, as you can see in Figure B-2—not to the help topic about the field you're interested in..

This chapter explains how to make the best of the help that Project offers. These days, searching by keywords is the mainstay, so this chapter explains where to search for answers and how to ask the right questions. If you prefer scanning a table of contents, it's there, too, if you know where to look.

If Project Help leaves you in the dark, the silver lining may be discovering how helpful *other* resources can be. When an enigmatic Project feature is driving you crazy or you want to know how others use Project in the real world, search the Project discussion boards for the answer or post your problem. This chapter also identifies other websites and blogs that provide invaluable Project information.

In Search of Project Help

Naturally, Project Help is the first place you think to look for answers, and yet, finding them can be maddeningly difficult, as the box on page 706 explains. Because Project Help is right there on your screen, you may still want to start there. This section tells you how.

Regardless of how you access Project Help, you end up in the Project Help window, shown in Figure B-2. Project Help works like a web browser, so you can hop from high-level topics to lower-level ones, or follow links within topics to related information. You click links to display topics.

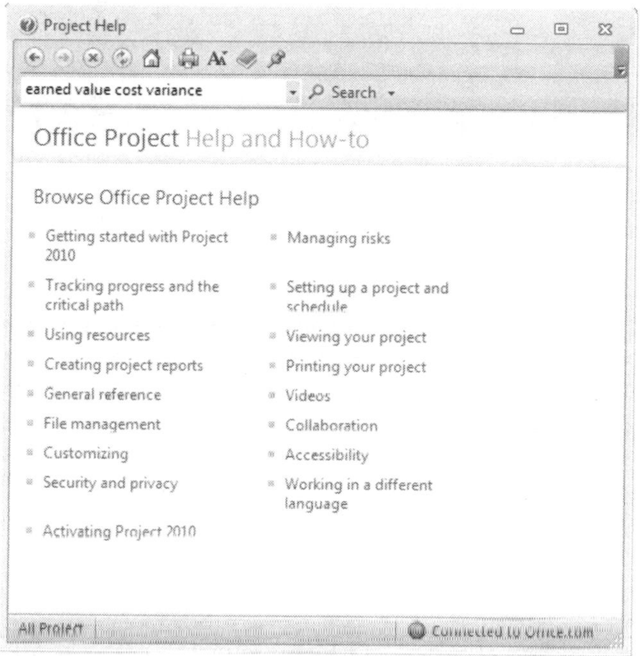

Figure B-2:
Clicking a category link on the Home page displays the Help topics within the category. In turn, Help topic links lead to the nuggets of information the Help topics hold.

The Help window icon bar includes several commands familiar to veteran web surfers: Back, Forward, Stop, Refresh, Home, and Print. Here's what the icon bar commands specific to the Help window do:

- **Change font size.** The initial size is Medium, which may seem small to eyes of a certain age. You can choose from Smallest, Smaller, Medium, Larger, and Largest.

- **Show table of contents.** When you expand the table of contents, this icon looks like an open book, because it opens a separate pane with help categories listed like a table of contents in a book. (If you collapse the table of contents, then the icon changes to a closed book.) The table of contents has several advantages over a pure Browse mode. It lets you expand and collapse categories to see available help topics simply by scrolling in the pane without having to navigate from page to page. Moreover, you can select a help topic in the table of contents pane and immediately see what the selected help topic has to say on the right side of the page. If the topic isn't what you want, just click another topic in the table of contents pane.

- **Keep on top.** The rightmost icon initially looks like a pushed-in pushpin, which means that the Project Help window stays on top of other windows unless you click its Minimize button. Keeping the Help window on top is ideal when you're trying to follow a 20-step procedure and don't want to switch windows after each step. On smaller screens, you may not have room for the Project window and the Help window at the same time. To tell the Help window to back off when you click another window, click the "Keep on top" icon so it changes to "Not on top".

Where's the Help?

Although you can access help on your computer (page 709), Microsoft recommends that you use its online help instead. Especially after a new release, help topics are added and updated frequently, so instructions that are missing initially could show up later. Even up-to-the-minute online Project Help has several issues:

- **Finding the magic keywords or phrases.** Finding the help topic you want means using the right keywords or phrases, just like searching the web. For example, "manual scheduling" retrieves a few topics, but the one closest to helpful is under "What's new in Microsoft Project 2010." However, if you search for "manually scheduled," you see several topics about using manually scheduled tasks and several more for fields related to manual scheduling. See "Searching for Answers" on page 706 for hints on searching help.

- **Missing links.** Sometimes you click Help in a dialog box hoping to learn what turning on a checkbox does, but Project Help merely opens to the main Help window. You're left looking through the hierarchy of help topics or the table of contents (page 705) for the answer you need.

- **Answers for other versions of Project.** Regardless of which Project version you install, help results include topics that apply to both desktop and enterprise project management versions (Project Server and Project Web Access). The topics don't explicitly identify the version they apply to, so you may have to try the steps to see if they work in your version of Project.

Whether you find an answer or not, don't ignore the "Did this article help you?" buttons at the bottom of a help topic, shown in Figure B-3. Microsoft insiders will tell you that the company takes your votes seriously. Microsoft employees are rated by those responses, so content that no one finds helpful is likely to get an overhaul.

Searching for Answers

The most obvious routes to Project Help lead to a search box, although a table of contents is still available, as you learned on page 705. Microsoft instructions tell you to type a question, but, in reality, the help system uses keywords. Finding the right keywords can be as delicate as crafting an apology. If one set of keywords doesn't do the trick, try synonyms or related terms; for instance, instead of "layout links," try "format bars." One keyword usually isn't enough to pinpoint pertinent topics. Too many keywords tend to add results that aren't related. Somewhere between two and seven keywords is usually about right.

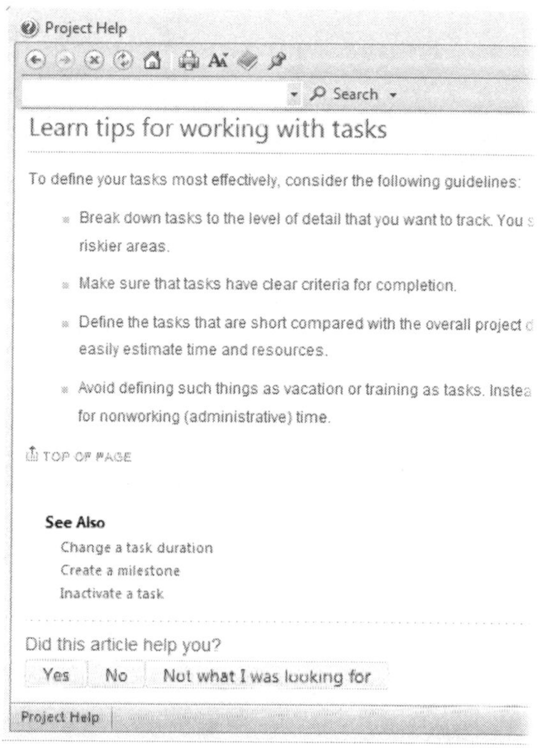

Figure B-3:
If you click No, a text box appears giving you 650 characters to tell Microsoft what you'd like them to change. Clicking Yes opens a text box so you can describe what was helpful. Clicking "Not what I was looking for" opens a text box that asks what you're trying to do—fodder for future Help topics. If the topic you choose isn't quite what you want, some topics include a See Also section at the bottom of the topic, which may have what you're looking for.

You can choose from three ways to access Project Help's search feature, two of which you can see in Figure B-4:

- **F1.** Like many programs, Project's response to pressing F1 is opening the Help window to a list of help categories.

- **The Help icon.** The white question mark in a blue circle at the main Project window's top-right corner also opens the Help window.

- **The Help button.** Some dialog boxes have a Help button at the bottom-left corner, which opens the Project Help window.

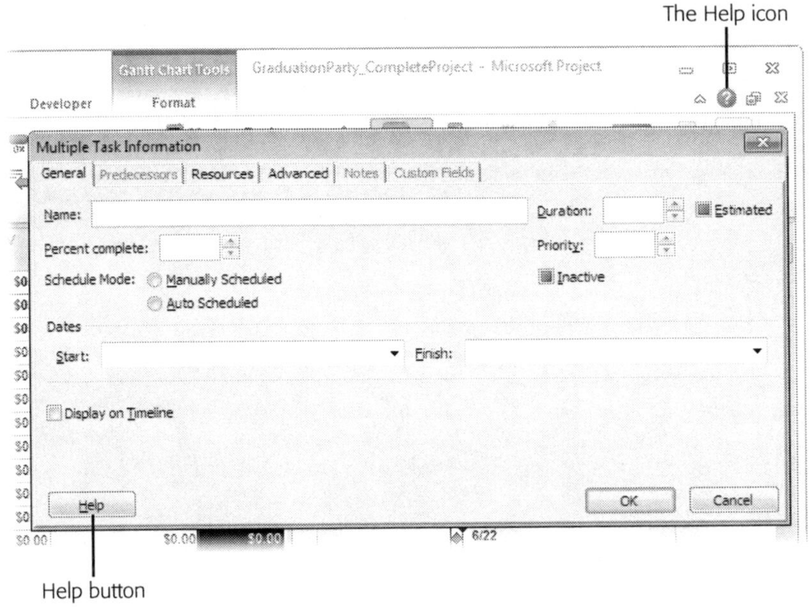

The Help icon

Help button

Once the Project Help window is open, you can type new or revised search terms in its search box, and then click Search. You can tell help which areas to search by clicking the down arrow on the Search button. On the drop-down menu, choose All Project to search all the online areas. To limit results, for example, to eliminate Project templates, choose Project Help or Developer Reference.

Help topics can be quite long, so Project Help uses expand/collapse buttons for each topic section. To display the information within a section, click the plus sign (+) to the left of the heading. To hide that information, click the minus sign (–) next to the heading.

Targeted Help

Many of the more robust dialog boxes, like Task Information, include a Help button in the lower-left corner. In the past, clicking this button opened the Project Help window to a dialog box reference topic that explained what every field, checkbox, and option in the dialog box did. (If you yearn for the old days of goal-oriented help, see page 711.) As of this writing, these Help buttons now simply open the Project Help window to top-level topics with no sign of a dialog box reference topic. Here's hoping that dialog box–specific links reappear someday.

Tip: For folks who'd rather experiment than read, Multilevel Undo (page 339) means you can be adventurous. Try a checkbox or option setting. If you don't like the results, then in the Project window title bar, click Undo, and then backtrack through as many actions as you want.

Project Help has a Reference section that describes Project elements like fields. As this was written, the Fields Reference was the only reference category available. If the Reference section grows to add what it covered in the past, then this section will also describe dialog boxes, how functions (like the ones in custom field formulas) work, and even how many tasks you can have in one Project file. Press F1 to open the Project Help window, and then click General Reference. The General Reference topic may eventually offer four items:

- **Fields Reference.** When you click this link, you see a list of separate help topics for all Project fields.

- **Dialog Box Reference.** This link shows help topics for the more feature-laden Project dialog boxes.

- **Project functions.** When you're building custom formulas, you may want to know how to use a particular function. Click the Project functions link to see a function help topic. Functions are grouped into five categories: Conversion, Date/Time, General, Math, and Text. Quite often, you know what you want to do, but not the function you need. The functions are listed alphabetically by name, so you must research to find the function that does what you want.

- **Project specifications.** Click this link to learn about Project limits like resources or tasks per project. If you're coaxing an old computer into running Project 2010 or if you manage monstrous projects, approaching these limits may affect performance or generate out-of-memory errors. Some limits are so large, like the 400,000 tasks per project or 50,000 predecessors per task, that they usually aren't an issue. Other limits affect day-to-day work, like 10 nonadjacent selections in a table or 255 characters in a text field.

Online and Offline Help

Out of the box, Project Help jumps online to grab help topics from Microsoft Office Online. Online help is the most up-to-date information, feeding you new and revised topics as Microsoft publishes them. Up-to-date online help is no help at all if you're stuck in economy class on an overseas flight or without Internet access at your grandparents' house. In situations like these, you can tell Project Help to use its offline resources.

The source for the help you're getting appears at the bottom right of the Project Help window. Most of the time, you see "Connected to Office.com", which means you're using online help. To go off the grid, click "Connected to Office.com". On the shortcut menu, click "Show content only from this computer". The checkmark switches to this choice, and the status bar says Offline. To go back online, click Offline, and then choose "Show content from Office.com".

Microsoft Office Online

If you look closely at Project Help results, you see more than help topics. Depending on your keywords, specialized templates or online training courses may appear in the list. To go directly to the source for these results, open your browser to Microsoft Office Online and feast on its help, training courses, downloadable templates, discussion groups, and more.

Type *http://office.microsoft.com* in your web browser. At Microsoft Office Online, a set of tabs across the top jump to different areas of the website, like Help and How-to, Downloads, and Templates.

Tip: Microsoft Office Online can display Help and How-to information for only the Office programs installed on your computer. To build a customized list of programs, select the Help and How-to tab. On the left, under Help by Product, click "Select your product". The website can detect the products on your computer, or you can click "manually select your products" to choose the ones you want.

To focus on Project information, select the Products tab. In the left navigation bar, click Project to open the Microsoft Office Project web page. From there, you can search for any type of information, find Project help, download Project templates, or join communities of fellow Project geeks. Here are some of the different types of information the Project web page provides:

- **Search.** The search box label at the top of the page says Microsoft Office Project. As you would in the Help window in Project, type keywords to find what you want. To switch the version of Project you're searching, click the search button down arrow and choose the version—or the extent of Microsoft's online domain.

- **Help and How-to.** In the left navigation bar, under Help and How-to, click the help link for the version of Project you want (as far back as 2000). You get the same help that appears in Project's Help window.

- **Training.** The Project 2003 and 2007 training links aren't worth clicking, because only three courses appear. Perhaps Project 2010 will offer more.

- **Demos.** The Project 2003 Demos and Project 2007 Demos links display a plethora of short videos. Eventually, Office Online should offer Project 2010 demos, too.

- **Templates.** Click "Project Templates" to see categories of templates that are available online. The categories are sparse: Plans, Planners, Schedules, and "More categories". Underneath, there are plenty of templates to choose from. In fact, you can submit a template you created by clicking "Submit a template" under the Community heading in the left navigation bar, or download a template that someone else submitted.

- **Product Support.** In the left navigation bar, under Support and Feedback, click Product Support. On the web page that appears, choose Project 2010. You can read educational or troubleshooting articles in several categories. The next section talks about another great resource for troubleshooting.

Interactive and In-Depth Assistance

Coming up empty-handed in Project Help is depressing. Then again, your problem may not be easily compartmentalized or described in a few keywords. Particularly gnarly problems often need some discussion and brainstorming. Because Project Help focuses on how-to, you may need other resources to learn how to put Project features into practice.

If you're lucky enough to have a Project know-it-all as an officemate, you know how refreshing it is to provide a quick summary and get a quick answer. The online Project discussion groups are that know-it-all for the rest of us. Speaking of know-it-alls, many of them keep blogs (web logs) about Project. Although some of the posts may be over your head, blogs are a great resource for learning how features, old and new, really work. This section tells you where to find all these resources.

Tip: If Project behaves oddly or you see an enigmatic error message, you probably need more assistance than Project Help can give. Sure, you can go to the Microsoft Support website (*http://support.microsoft. com*), but the quickest way to find a solution is to use your favorite search engine: Google, Bing, Yahoo!, and so on. In the search box, type the error message, error number, or keywords that describe your problem. Some of the results will be links to Microsoft's websites, but exactly the answer you need may come from a Microsoft partner's website or someone's blog.

Discuss Among Yourselves

If you like a personal touch, Project discussion groups can be very satisfying. You can search for an answer to your question in previous posts. If you don't find one, you can post a question and get an answer. Some group members are bona fide Project experts, but the answer you need could come from anyone. The two-way communication makes all the difference; you can describe your problem in detail and receive a detailed answer in return.

Discussion groups are part of Microsoft Office Online. Since you have to click through several pages to reach them, create a bookmark in your browser if you plan on visiting often. Here's how to reach the Project discussion groups:

1. **Open the Project page of Microsoft Office Online (*http://office.microsoft. com/project*).**

   You can also select the Products tab, and then, in the left navigation bar, click Project.

2. **In the navigation bar on the left side of the page under Additional Resources, click Discussion Groups.**

   The Office Discussion Groups web page opens to the Microsoft Project General Questions forum, shown in Figure B-5.

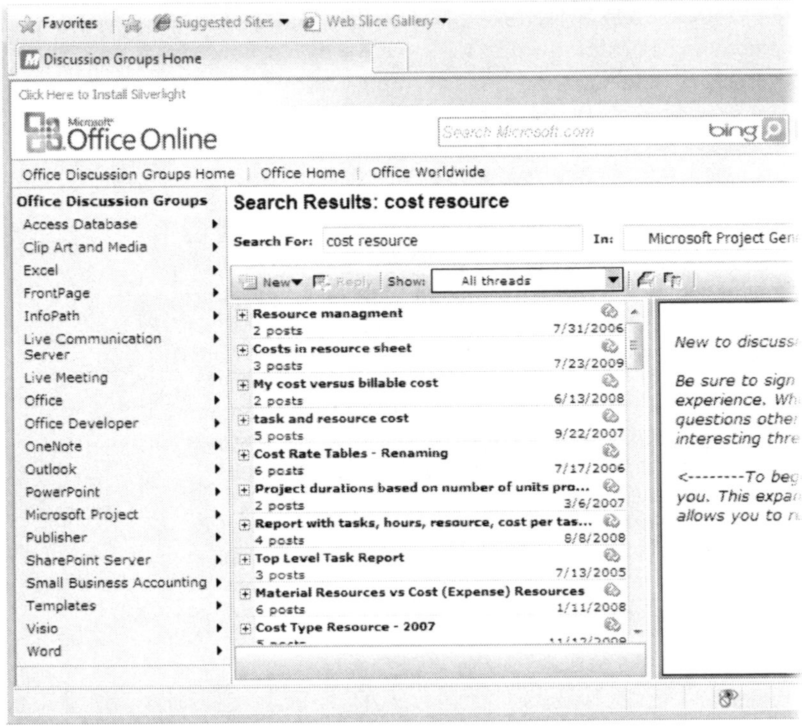

Figure B-5:
To open another Project-related forum, in the Office Discussion Groups list, choose Microsoft Project and the forum you want (General Questions, Server, Developer).

3. **Before you post a new question, search the forum to see if it's been answered before.**

   In the Search For box, type keywords related to your question or problem. Click Go to find matching topics. To see posts and responses, click the plus sign next to the topic title. Click the name for a post or response to display the text in the box on the right.

4. **To post a new topic, choose New immediately below the Search For box, and then choose Question.**

   If you haven't logged in, use your Windows Live ID to log in now. If you haven't signed up for a Windows Live ID, then on the sign-in page, click "Sign up now".

The New Question window opens. Type a subject that briefly describes your problem, like *Can't save global template*. Fill in the Message box with your question and as much background as you can provide. To get an email when someone replies, turn on the "Notify me of replies" checkbox.

5. **Click Post.**

It may take a few minutes before your topic appears in the list.

All the Office Discussion Groups are a volunteer effort. Don't consider them a one-way street. If you see a question you can answer, go for it.

Tip: Some members who answer questions in the discussion groups are called MVPs, which stands for Microsoft Valued Professional. These people voluntarily share their time and expertise to help others. In fact, they run an entire website with more useful info about many Microsoft programs. To reach the Project page, go to *http://www.project.mvps.org*. This site offers answers to frequently asked questions, links to third-party products, sample Visual Basic code, and tons of links to other Project-related websites.

Project Blogs

Blogs tend to be informal and conversational, but don't let that fool you. They can provide a gold mine of in-depth information, in many cases from Microsoft employees. Go to *http://blogs.msdn.com/project*, which is the official Project team blog. To get some real-world examples of using new Project 2010 features, under Tags, click Project 2010.

On the right side of the page, under "project community blogs", click links to check out other Project blogs. Here are some blogs you might want to add to your RSS (Real Simple Syndication) feeds:

- **Jack Dahlgren's Project Blog** (*http://zo-d.com/blog*). This blog covers a lot of ground, much of it not related to Project. However, on the right side of the page, if you click the categories under Project Management, you'll find some clear and amusing explanations of Project and project management.

- **Projectified** (*http://blogs.technet.com/projectified/*). Brian Kennemer's blog is more about Project Server, but his posts on Project are worth finding and digesting.

Keyboard Shortcuts

Keyboard shortcuts are tremendous timesavers, because your fingers can press a key combination in a fraction of a second compared to the seconds it takes to grasp the mouse and move the pointer to the correct location. Those seconds saved add up when you stick to the keyboard for your most frequent tasks—like saving a file regularly to make sure you don't lose any work or adjusting the position of tasks in the outline.

The only apparent disadvantage to keyboard shortcuts is learning their obscure keystroke combinations. If it takes you 10 seconds to remember that Alt+Shift+* displays all tasks in the project, then you really haven't saved any time. Mercifully, Project shares many keyboard shortcuts with other Microsoft programs, so you may not have to memorize as much as you think. On the other hand, a few minutes spent memorizing vital keyboard shortcuts can add up to hours saved down the line.

Now that Project 2010 uses the ribbon, you have two ways to use keyboard shortcuts. You can press tried-and-true keyboard combinations like Ctrl+S to save a file just as you could in previous versions of Project. Or you can display KeyTips and press letters to move around the ribbon and choose the command you want. This chapter tells you how to use both methods.

How to Use Keyboard Shortcuts

Keyboard shortcuts can be a single key, like F3 to show all tasks or resources. But usually you have to press a combination of Ctrl, Shift, or Alt along with other keys.

If you don't know the keyboard shortcut, you can navigate through the ribbon, drop-down menus, and commands with KeyTips (the letters you press to choose a feature). Here's what you do:

1. **To display KeyTips, press Alt.**

   KeyTips appear over each feature in the current tab or menu. For example, on the Task tab, the Gantt Chart command has the letter G next to it, as shown in Figure C-1.

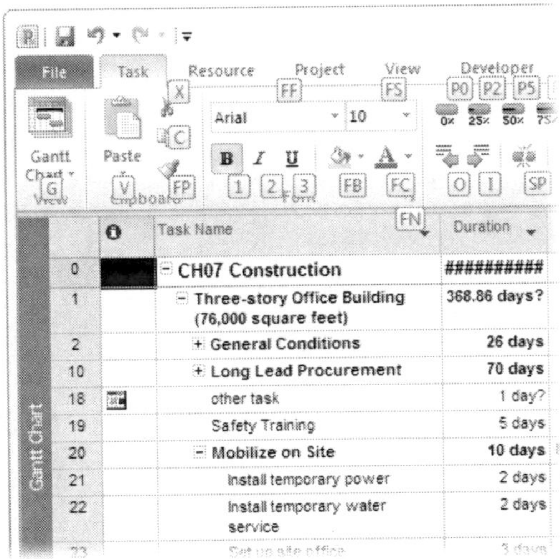

Figure C-1:
If KeyTips are visible, continue to press letters until you press the letter for the specific feature you want to use. For example, after you press Alt to display KeyTips, press R to display the Project tab, then press B to display the Baseline drop-down menu, and finally press S to set a baseline. Pressing KeyTip letters to choose features works only when KeyTips are visible. If you turn KeyTips off, pressing R does not display the Project tab, although it does enter an R if the cursor is in a field that accepts letters.

2. **To choose a feature, press the letter in the feature's KeyTip.**

   As you use KeyTips to switch between tabs and menus, additional KeyTips may show up. For example, if the View tab is visible and you press H, Project switches to the Task tab, which displays the KeyTips shown in Figure C-1.

3. **Repeat step 2 until you press the letter for the command or feature you want.**

   For example, if the Task tab is visible, press G to display the drop-down menu of Project views. Then press M to open the More Views dialog box.

4. **To hide KeyTips, press Alt.**

   When KeyTips are hidden, pressing KeyTip letters doesn't issue commands.

Note: The keyboard shortcuts in Microsoft Help refer specifically to the U.S. keyboard layout. If you use a keyboard layout for another language, your keyboard shortcuts vary depending on how characters map to the keys on your keyboard. For example, Ctrl+Z is the U.S. keyboard shortcut to undo the previous action. However, the French keyboard layout has W located where Z resides on the U.S. keyboard, so the French keyboard shortcut for Undo is Ctrl+W.

Keyboard Shortcuts for Microsoft Project

Some of the keyboard shortcuts in this section apply not only to Project but to every Microsoft Office program, so you can learn them once and then put them to work in all your favorite programs. Project doesn't come with flip cards to help you memorize these esoteric keyboard combinations, but if you memorize the ones for the tasks you perform most, then you can often save time without overtaxing your brain.

Tip: If you memorize the shortcuts in this appendix and are still hungry for more, in Project, choose File→Help→Microsoft Office Help. At the top of the Project Help window, in the search box, type *keyboard shortcuts*, and then click Search. The first help topic link should be "Keyboard shortcuts for Project 2010". Click the link to view a complete list of keyboard shortcuts specific to Project, and many that apply to all Microsoft Office programs.

All-Time Keyboard Shortcut Favorites

These favorites apply to all Microsoft Office programs, and they're commands you use all the time. The keyboard shortcuts in Table C-1 should be at the top of your memorization list.

Table C-1. *Keyboard shortcuts you're sure to use all the time*

Task	Keyboard shortcut
Open a new file (Project file, Word document, and so on).	Ctrl+N
Open an existing file.	Ctrl+O
Save the active file.	Ctrl+S
Print the current view (such as the Gantt Chart).	Ctrl+P
Close the active file.	Ctrl+F4
Undo the last action you performed.	Ctrl+Z
Redo the action you just undid.	Ctrl+Y
Copy a picture of the entire screen to the Clipboard (which you can then paste into a document or file).	Print Screen (might appear as Prnt Scrn or Prt Scr on some keyboards)
Copy a picture of the active window to the Clipboard (for pasting into another file).	Alt+Print Screen

Note: In Project 2003, Ctrl+Z toggled between undoing the one last action you performed and redoing that action; Ctrl+Y wasn't a keyboard shortcut. Project 2007 introduced the ability to undo as many previous actions as you want, either by frenetically pressing Ctrl+Z or, on the Project title bar, using Undo (page 339). Ctrl+Y behaves differently in Project than in any other Office program. In Word, Excel, and so on, Ctrl+Y repeats the previous action. In Project, Ctrl+Y redoes only the last actions you *un*did.

Project Outlining

So much of working with a project schedule is adding tasks and placing them at the proper level in the Project outline. The shortcuts in Table C-2 help you view the outline and indent or outdent tasks.

Table C-2. *Outlining without touching the mouse*

Task	Keyboard shortcut
Insert a new task above the selected task.	Insert
Indent the selected tasks.	Alt+Shift+right arrow
Outdent the selected tasks.	Alt+Shift+left arrow
Hide subtasks of the selected summary task.	Alt+Shift+hyphen (or Alt+Shift+minus sign on the numeric keypad)
Show next level of subtasks. Repeat this keyboard shortcut until you can see all the levels you want.	Alt+Shift+= (or Alt+Shift+plus sign on the numeric keypad)
Show all tasks.	Alt+Shift+* (or Alt+Shift+* on the numeric keypad)

Displaying Project Information

Whether you work on one Project file or several, the shortcuts in Table C-3 make it easy to see the information you want.

Table C-3. *Displaying Project windows and key dialog boxes*

Task	Keyboard shortcut
Make the next Project file window active (when more than one file is open or when you use View→Window→Switch Windows).	Ctrl+F6
Make the previous Project file window active.	Ctrl+Shift+F6
Maximize all Project file windows within the main Project window.	Ctrl+F10
Open the Task Information dialog box with data for the selected task.	Shift+F2
Open the Resource Information dialog box with data for the selected resource.	Shift+F2

Open the Assignment Information dialog box with data for the selected assignment.	Shift+F2
Open the Field Settings dialog box to add or modify a column.	Alt+F3
Reapply the current filter.	Ctrl+Shift+F3
Display all tasks or resources.	F3
Display smaller time units in the timescale, for example, switching from weeks to days.	Ctrl+/ (use / on the numeric keypad)
Display larger time units in the timescale, for example, from weeks to months.	Ctrl+* (use * on the numeric keypad)

Moving Around in a Project View

Whether you're setting up, modifying, or monitoring a schedule in Project, you're likely to move around within the table area or timescale of the Gantt Chart and other Project views. The keyboard shortcuts for moving around in views, shown in Table C-4, are a little easier to remember because they use arrow keys as well as Home and End. For example, to move to the first field in a row, you press Ctrl+left arrow, whereas you press Ctrl+right arrow to move to the last field. The Ctrl key identifies shortcuts for moving within the rows and columns of the table area, and the Alt key applies to the shortcuts for the timescale.

Tip: In Project 2010, the timeline pane is an easy, mouse-driven way to scroll the timescale (page 233)

Table C-4. *Moving within views*

Task	Keyboard shortcut
Move to the first row.	Ctrl+up arrow
Move to the last row.	Ctrl+down arrow
Move to the first field in the current row.	Ctrl+left arrow (or Home)
Move to the last field in the current row.	Ctrl+right row (or End)
Move to the first field in the first row.	Ctrl+Home
Move to the last field in the last row.	Ctrl+End
Scroll the timescale to the left.	Alt+left arrow
Scroll the timescale to the right.	Alt+right arrow
Scroll the timescale to display the task selected in the table area.	Ctrl+Shift+F5

Selecting Elements in a Project View Table

After you display the part of the schedule you want, your next step is often to select a field, task, or resource to perform some editing. Selection shortcuts use the arrow, Home, and End keys in similar ways to the shortcuts for moving within a view. The main difference is that selection shortcuts use the Ctrl+Shift combination. For example, moving to the first row is Ctrl+up arrow. Selecting from the current selection to the first row is Ctrl+Shift+up arrow. Table C-5 lists the keyboard shortcuts for selecting elements in a Project view.

Table C-5. *Selecting within views*

Task	Keyboard shortcut
Expand the current selection to the first row.	Ctrl+Shift+up arrow
Expand the current selection to the last row.	Ctrl+Shift+down arrow
Expand the current selection to the first field in the current row.	Shift+Home
Expand the current selection to the last field in the current row.	Shift+End
Expand the current selection one field to the left.	Shift+left arrow
Expand the current selection one field to the right.	Shift+right arrow
Expand the current selection to the first field in the first row.	Ctrl+Shift+Home
Expand to the last field in the last row.	Ctrl+Shift+End
Expand the selection up one row.	Shift+up arrow
Expand the selection down one row.	Shift+down arrow

Note: These selection shortcuts expand the selection based on the fields or rows that are already selected. For example, if a Task Name cell is selected, then expanding to the first row selects all the Task Name cells up to the first row. If the entire row is selected, then expanding the selection to the first row selects all the tasks up to the first row.

Keyboard Shortcuts for Editing Within a View

You're probably familiar with keyboard shortcuts for editing. Ctrl+X, Ctrl+C, and Ctrl+V still cut, copy, and paste selected elements, as they do in Microsoft Word and other programs. But Project includes a few additional keyboard shortcuts for specialized editing, listed in Table C-6.

Table C-6. *Keyboard shortcuts for Project editing tasks*

Task	Keyboard shortcut
Create a finish-to-start task dependency between the selected tasks.	Ctrl+F2
Remove all task dependencies from the selected tasks.	Ctrl+Shift+F2
Cancel changes without saving.	Esc
Activate a field so you can edit its text.	F2

Navigating Within Dialog Boxes and Forms

Of course, Project has dialog boxes like every other program, and the same keyboard shortcuts for navigating within them. The forms that appear in Project view, such as the Task Entry form, use some additional keyboard shortcuts to navigate within form fields and tables. Table C-7 lists these shortcuts.

Table C-7. *Navigating dialog boxes and forms*

Task	Keyboard shortcut
Display the next tab in a dialog box.	Ctrl+Tab
Display the previous tab in a dialog box.	Ctrl+Shift+Tab
Select an option in a dialog box or toggle between turning a checkbox on and off.	Alt+ the underlined letter in the option or checkbox
Move to a field in a table within a form (such as the Resources and Predecessors tables in the Task Form).	Up arrow, down arrow, left arrow, and right arrow
Switch to the left or right table within a form, like between the Predecessors and Successors table in the Task Form.	Alt+1 for the left table, Alt+2 for the right table

Help Shortcuts

You need just a few keyboard shortcuts, listed in Table C-8, to open the Help window and browse help topics.

Table C-8. *Keyboard shortcuts for viewing Help topics*

Task	Keyboard shortcut
Open the Help window.	F1
Display the previous help topic.	Alt+left arrow
Display the next help topic.	Alt+right arrow

Index

Get even more for your money.

Join the O'Reilly Community, and register the O'Reilly books you own. It's free, and you'll get:

- $4.99 ebook upgrade offer
- 40% upgrade offer on O'Reilly print books
- Membership discounts on books and events
- Free lifetime updates to ebooks and videos
- Multiple ebook formats, DRM FREE
- Participation in the O'Reilly community
- Newsletters
- Account management
- 100% Satisfaction Guarantee

Signing up is easy:

1. **Go to: oreilly.com/go/register**
2. **Create an O'Reilly login.**
3. **Provide your address.**
4. **Register your books.**

Note: English-language books only

To order books online:
oreilly.com/store

For questions about products or an order:
orders@oreilly.com

To sign up to get topic-specific email announcements and/or news about upcoming books, conferences, special offers, and new technologies:
elists@oreilly.com

For technical questions about book content:
booktech@oreilly.com

To submit new book proposals to our editors:
proposals@oreilly.com

O'Reilly books are available in multiple DRM-free ebook formats. For more information:
oreilly.com/ebooks

O'REILLY®

Spreading the knowledge of innovators   oreilly.com

Have it your way.